Legal Research, Analysis, & Writing

FOURTH EDITION

WILLIAM H.
PUTMAN

JENNIFER R.
ALBRIGHT

Options.

We understand that affordable options are important. Visit us at cengage.com to take advantage of our new textbook rental program, which can be bundled with our MindTap products!

Over 300 products in every area of the law: MindTap, textbooks, online courses, reference books, companion websites, and more – Cengage Learning helps you succeed in the classroom and on the job.

Support.

We offer unparalleled course support and customer service: robust instructor and student supplements to ensure the best learning experience, custom publishing to meet your unique needs, and other benefits such as Cengage Learning's Student Achievement Award. And our sales representatives are always ready to provide you with dependable service.

Feedback.

As always, we want to hear from you! Your feedback is our best resource for improving the quality of our products. Contact your sales representative or write us at the address below if you have any comments about our materials or if you have a product proposal.

Accounting and Financials for the Law Office • Administrative Law • Alternative Dispute Resolution • Bankruptcy Business Organizations/Corporations • Careers and Employment • Civil Litigation and Procedure • CP Exam Preparation • Computer Applications in the Law Office • Constitutional Law • Contract Law • Criminal Law and Procedure • Document Preparation • Elder Law • Employment Law • Environmental Law • Ethics • Evidence Law • Family Law • Health Care Law • Immigration Law • Intellectual Property • Internships • Interviewing and Investigation • Introduction to Law • Introduction to Paralegalism • Juvenile Law • Law Office Management • Law Office Procedures • Legal Research, Writing, and Analysis • Legal Terminology • Legal Transcription • Media and Entertainment Law • Medical Malpractice Law • Product Liability • Real Estate Law • Reference Materials • Social Security • Torts and Personal Injury Law • Wills, Trusts, and Estate Administration • Workers' Compensation Law

---

CENGAGE
Learning®

5 Maxwell Drive
Clifton Park, New York 12065-2919

For additional information, find us online at: **cengage.com**

Legal Research, Analysis, & Writing

FOURTH EDITION

WILLIAM H.
PUTMAN

JENNIFER R.
ALBRIGHT

CENGAGE

Australia • Brazil • Mexico • Singapore • United Kingdom • United States

Legal Research, Analysis, And Writing, Fourth Edition
Authors: William H. Putman, Jennifer R. Albright,

SVP, GM Skills & Global Product Management: Jonathan Lau

Product Director: Matthew Seeley

Associate Product Manager: Kelly Lischynsky

Senior Director, Development: Marah Bellegarde

Senior Product Development Manager: Larry Main

Senior Content Developer: Anne Orgren

Product Assistant: Mara Ciacelli

Vice President, Marketing Services: Jennifer Ann Baker

Marketing Manager: Andrew Ouimet

Senior Content Project Manager: Betty Dickson

Managing Art Director: Jack Pendleton

Text Designer: Jay Purcell

Cover Designer: Travis Hoffman

Cover image(s): Library setting - Vereshchagin Dmitry/Shutterstock.com; Business intelligence - VectorForever/ Shutterstock.com; Justice scales - iDesign/ Shutterstock.com; Keyboard icon - WladD/ Shutterstock.com

For product information and technology assistance, contact us at
Cengage Learning Customer & Sales Support, 1-800-354-9706

For permission to use material from this text or product, submit all requests online at **www.cengage.com/permissions**.
Further permissions questions can be e-mailed to
permissionrequest@cengage.com

Library of Congress Control Number: 2017937615

Book Only ISBN: 978-1-3059-4837-2
Loose-leaf ISBN: 978-1-3374-1415-9

Cengage Learning
20 Channel Center Street
Boston, MA 02210
USA

Cengage Learning is a leading provider of customized learning solutions with employees residing in nearly 40 different countries and sales in more than 125 countries around the world. Find your local representative at **www.cengage.com**.

Cengage Learning products are represented in Canada by Nelson Education, Ltd.

To learn more about Cengage Learning, visit **www.cengage.com**
Purchase any of our products at your local college store or at our preferred online store **www.cengagebrain.com**.

Notice to the Reader

Printed in the United States of America

Print Number: 03 Print Year: 2019

Dedication

This book is dedicated to P.Y., whose love,
inspiration, and guidance made this text possible.
Thank you.

This book is dedicated to B.W. for her support,
personal and technical, through this endeavor, and to Bill Putman
for the continued opportunity and belief in me.

Brief Contents

Contents

Chapter 4   Case Law—Research and Briefing   *99*

Chapter 5   Secondary Authority and Other Research Sources—Encyclopedias, Treatises, American Law Reports, Digests, Shepard's   *141*

Chapter 6   Secondary Authority—Periodicals, Restatements, Uniform Laws, Dictionaries, Legislative History, and Other Secondary Authorities   *192*

Chapter 7   Computers and Internet Legal Research   *225*

Chapter 8   Commercial Internet Research   *241*

PART III   THE SPECIFICS OF LEGAL ANALYSIS   *263*

Chapter 9   Legal Analysis—Key Facts   *264*

Chapter 10   Legal Analysis: Issue Identification—Spotting The Issue   *284*

Chapter 11   Legal Analysis: Stating the Issue

Chapter 12   Case Law Analysis—Is a Case on Point?

Chapter 13   Counteranalysis

PART IV   LEGAL WRITING   369

Chapter 14   Fundamentals of Writing   370

Chapter 15   The Writing Process for Effective Legal Writing   421

Chapter 16   Office Legal Memorandum: Issues and Facts   445

Chapter 17   Office Legal Memorandum: Analysis to Conclusion   467

Chapter 18   External Memoranda: Court Briefs   497

Chapter 19   Correspondence   524

Table of Cases

Preface

Paralegals and law clerks are increasingly called upon to perform substantive legal research, analysis, and writing tasks. These tasks range from drafting interoffice legal memoranda summarizing the research and analysis of issues involved in a client's case, to preparing drafts of court documents and legal correspondence. This text provides the student with in-depth knowledge of the fundamentals of legal research, analysis, and writing.

The impetus for this book came from student requests for comprehensive information regarding many of the difficult areas of legal research, analysis, and writing. The desire to provide such comprehensive information has not changed, but there are many things about legal research and writing that have changed. The fundamentals of legal research do not change over time. However, the means of accessing the law and information about the law is changing at a rapid rate. Increasingly in the digital age, legal research is conducted via electronic sources. Many paralegal programs, law schools, and law offices are reducing or eliminating their paper sources in exchange for electronic sources. Although this is understandable in the modern technological era, the methods of electronically searching for law continue to be based on how paper sources are designed and organized. Moreover, if access to electronic sources is lost during a crucial time period, such as when a work or school assignment is due, or when preparing for a hearing, a deposition, or an upcoming deadline to file a document in court, legal researchers must be able to adapt and work with paper sources in their office, school, or local court library. Moreover, *The Bluebook: A Uniform System of Citation* (Columbia Law Review Ass'n et al. eds., 20th ed. 2015), the citation manual most followed by courts and lawyers, "requires the use and citation of traditional printed sources when available, unless there is a digital copy of the source available that is authenticated, official, or an exact copy of the printed source." Thus, this textbook continues to provide students with knowledge of legal research methods based upon paper sources first, and electronic sources second.

Further, the fundamentals of legal writing do not change over time, but the influences over writing ability do change. Increasingly, we are subject to writing in the medium of text messages, informal email, and instant messages. Various written media have drifted away from conventional writing; therefore, many students are more familiar with informal writing than formal writing. I often provide my students with court decisions where the placement of a comma or the meaning of a word is the sole issue to demonstrate how important strong spelling and grammar skills, coupled with strong analytical skills, are in legal writing.

In addition, there is an increasing push, often from state court Access to Justice Programs, to write in a manner easily understood by the average person. Therefore, a balance between the formality of legal writing and the need for nonlegal trained persons to understand court opinions, documents, and legal forms is essential. As such, this edition not only provides in-depth information on the basics of legal analysis and writing, but highlights many techniques and tips for writing about or analyzing and discussing complex legal matters.

This text is designed for use in research and writing classes. It can be useful in schools that have separate research and writing courses, where the first course focuses primarily on research with an introduction to writing, and the second course focuses on writing with research as a secondary component. For the research course, the instructor would use Chapters 1 through 13. For the writing course, instructors would use Chapters 9 through 19. Where both researching and writing are combined in one course, instructors can select the chapters appropriate for such a combined course. Moreover, advanced assignments can be created from the many assignment fact patterns provided throughout the text and requiring students to conduct research for applicable law within the state where the student is located, or in federal law, then drafting the legal document designated by the instructor.

The text is designed to cover the topics of legal research, analysis, and writing in general. It is organized to provide students with comprehensive information about difficult areas of analysis and writing. The text is divided into the following four parts:

Part I: Introduction to Research, Analytical Principles, and the Legal Process. Part I is composed of two introductory chapters. The first chapter presents an overview of the legal system and the legal process, as well as a summary of the basic legal principles involved in the process, such as authority, precedent, stare decisis, and so on. The second chapter introduces legal analysis and the IRAC analytical process.

Part II: Legal Research. Part II consists of six chapters that provide in-depth coverage of legal research and the research process. It begins with two chapters on primary authority; that is, chapters on statutory and case law. Next are two chapters on secondary authority. Two chapters on computers and internet legal research complete Part II. All of these chapters contain brief overviews of legal citation format.

Part III: The Specifics of Legal Analysis. Part III covers matters essential to the analysis of a legal problem. It begins with a chapter on a principal component of a legal question (legal issue), the key facts, which are facts critical to the outcome of the case. Next are chapters on identifying and writing legal issues:

- Identifying the issue—The identification of the legal issue presented by a fact situation
- Stating the issue—How to present the issue

Part III concludes with two chapters on topics fundamental to legal analysis:

- Case law application—The analytical process used to determine if a court opinion applies to a legal question
- Counteranalysis—The process of discovering and considering the counterargument to a legal position or argument.

Part IV: Legal Writing. The focus of Part IV is on legal writing and the legal writing process. It covers the application of the principles presented in the previous chapters to the drafting of legal research memoranda, court briefs, and legal correspondence, with chapters on the following topics:

- Fundamentals of writing
- The legal writing process in general
- Office legal memoranda (two chapters)
- Court briefs
- Correspondence

Chapter Features

Each chapter is designed to help students completely understand and apply the concepts presented in the chapter. Chapters include the following features:

Hypothetical

Each chapter begins with a hypothetical that raises a question or questions involving the subject matter of the chapter. Following the hypothetical is a presentation of the principles, concepts, guidelines, and information concerning the subject matter. After the discussion of the subject matter, the principles and information discussed in the chapter are applied to answer the question or questions raised in the hypothetical.

The use of the hypothetical at the beginning of the chapter creates student interest in the subject matter of the chapter. The answer to the hypothetical toward the end of the chapter allows the student to see how the subject matter ties together and is applied.

Key Points Checklist

Each chapter has a list of key points that may be used as a quick reference and checklist when applying the concepts presented in the chapter. This checklist allows both the instructor and the student to make sure nothing is missed when reviewing or applying the principles presented in the chapter.

In-Depth Coverage of Topics

The greatest advantage of this text, for both teachers and students, is its comprehensive and in-depth coverage of topics not thoroughly covered in most texts. These topics include:

- Issue stating
- Issue identification (issue spotting)
- Case law analysis (whether a case is "on point")
- Counteranalysis
- Statutory analysis
- Office legal memoranda preparation

Examples

A major advantage of the text is that every principle, concept, and so on is followed by an example that illustrates it. One of my students requested that there be "plenty of examples." This text has plenty of examples. These examples help the instructor teach principles and concepts and help the student understand them.

Internet Resources

Each chapter contains a list of websites related to the chapter topic. This allows access to additional information on chapter topics from the Internet.

Assignments

There are assignments at the end of each chapter that range in difficulty. The assignments require students to apply the principles and techniques presented in the text. For example, there are numerous cases provided in Appendix A that instructors can assign to students for briefing. Chapter 13 contains five office legal memoranda assignments (based on the facts and law presented in the assignment and the court opinions in Appendix A). The answers to all the assignments are presented in the Instructor's Manual. Chapters 13, 16, and 19 also provide fact patterns for use in drafting various other legal writing assignment associated with the content of those chapters.

Appendices

The text has two appendices and a glossary of terms. Appendix A consists of court opinions that are necessary for the chapter assignments. Appendix B presents the brief of an appellant in a case filed in the Court of Appeals of the State of New Mexico, a legal memorandum and sample legal correspondence. The legal research, legal analysis, and initial drafts of the appellate brief and the legal memorandum were performed by a paralegal who, at the time, worked for one of the authors.

Readability

The text is written in a manner that a layperson can understand. The text avoids legalese, illustrates concepts with examples, and presents the subject matter simply and clearly.

New Features in This Edition

The major changes in this edition are to the legal research chapters of the text—Chapters 3 through 8. Chapters 3 through 6 are updated in regard to the increased use of online and electronic sources in legal research. They also include updated exhibits and examples that reflect changes in recent editions of the most referenced print sources. Chapter 5 (on secondary and other research sources) is updated to reflect the use of *Shepard's* online and Westlaw's *KeyCite* to update and validate research. Chapter 7 covers the ethics of and basic research techniques for conducting legal research on noncommercial legal websites. Chapter 8, on the other hand, focuses on WestlawNext and LexisAdvance along with other significant commercial legal research sources. Because these commercial sources change their user interface often (Westlaw and LexisNexis changed the look and several basic features of their products more than once just in the time this text was being updated) the author chose to remove screenshots and step-by-step research instructions. Chapter 8 instead focuses on basic principles of searching all commercial databases to allow the content to be relevant across a variety of databases. In addition, new assignments are added to Chapters 3 through 8.

Unlike other areas of the law, such as criminal and constitutional, where there are continuous changes in the case and statutory law, the process of legal analysis and writing remains essentially the same over time. Therefore, there are few substantive changes in the legal analysis and legal writing sections of this text.

However, there are new assignments and updated assignments throughout Chapters 14, 18, and 19. In response to requests for additional material on basic writing skills, there are additions to Chapter 14 (on the fundamentals of writing). In addition, Chapter 8 (on legal citation) was deleted and the content on legal citation was moved into the end of Chapters 3 through 8 using the latest editions of *The Blue-book: A Uniform System of Citation*, and the *ALWD Citation Manual: A Professional System of Citation*.

Support Material

The text is accompanied by the following support materials designed to assist students in learning and instructors in teaching.

Paralegal MindTap

Paralegal MindTap is available for *Legal Research, Analysis and Writing*, Fourth Edition.

MindTap: Empower Your Students MindTap is a platform that propels students from memorization to mastery. It gives you complete control of your course, so you can provide engaging content, challenge every learner, and build student confidence. Customize interactive syllabi to emphasize priority topics, then add your own material or notes to the eBook as desired. This outcomes-driven application gives you the tools needed to empower students and boost both understanding and performance.

Access Everything You Need in One Place Cut down on prep with the preloaded and organized MindTap course materials. Teach more efficiently with case studies, chapter objectives, quizzes, and more. Give your students the power to read, listen, and study on their phones, so they can learn on their terms.

Empower Students to Reach their Potential Twelve distinct metrics give you actionable insights into student engagement. Identify topics troubling your entire class and instantly communicate with those struggling. Students can track their scores to stay motivated towards their goals. Together, you can be unstoppable.

Control Your Course—and Your Content Get the flexibility to reorder textbook chapters, add your own notes, and embed a variety of content including Open Educational Resources (OER). Personalize course content to your students' needs. They can even read your notes, add their own, and highlight key text to aid their learning.

Get a Dedicated Team, Whenever You Need Them MindTap isn't just a tool, it's backed by a personalized team eager to support you. We can help set up your course and tailor it to your specific objectives, so you'll be ready to make an impact from day one. Know we'll be standing by to help you and your students until the final day of the term.

Instructor's Manual

Each chapter has several exercises ranging in difficulty. The Instructor's Manual provides complete answers to each exercise, general guides for instructors, and suggested additional assignments. Among other things, the manual includes examples of briefs of court opinions office legal research memoranda, and appellate briefs. The manual also provides a test bank of true/false and multiple-choice questions for each chapter. A test bank answer key is also included.

Instructor Companion Website

Spend less time planning and more time teaching. This instructor companion website to accompany *Legal Research, Analysis, and Writing* allows you "anywhere, anytime" access to all of your resources.

- The **Instructor's Manual** contains various resources for each chapter of the book.
- The **Testbank** in Cognero, Word, and several LMS-friendly formats makes generating tests and quizzes a snap. With many questions and different styles to choose from, you can create customized assessments for your students with the click of a button. Add your own unique questions and print rationales for easy class preparation.
- Customizable **PowerPoint® Presentations** focus on key points for each chapter. (PowerPoint® is a registered trademark of the Microsoft Corporation.)

To access additional course materials (including MindTap), please go to login.cengage.com, then use your SSO (single sign on) login to access the materials.

Supplements At-A-Glance

SUPPLEMENT:	WHAT IT IS	WHAT'S IN IT:
Paralegal MindTap MINDTAP From Cengage	Customizable online interactive teaching and learning platform that provides everything you need in one place. Go to login.cengage.com to access.	Interactive teaching and learning tools, including: • MindTap Reader (interactive e-book) • Quizzing • Case studies • Chapter Objectives • Assignments • Flashcards • Weblinks • PowerPoint® presentations
Online Instructor Companion Site	Resources for the instructor accessible via Cengage Single Sign On	• Instructors Manual with answers to text questions, assignments, and test bank and answer key • Testbank in Cognero, Word, and LMS-friendly formats, with many questions to choose from to create customized assessments for your students • PowerPoint® presentations

Please note that all Internet resources are of a time-sensitive nature; URL addresses may often change or be deleted.

Acknowledgments

I wish to gratefully acknowledge and express my deep appreciation to a number of individuals who took time and effort to assist in the development of this book. Without their expertise, suggestions, and support, this text would not have been remotely possible. I am particularly indebted to the following individuals:

Pamela A. Lambert, Esquire, who reviewed the text for intellectual and legal content and consistency. Her legal expertise, analytical skills, and input were invaluable. Pam's encouragement and positive attitude helped me through the rough spots.

Kate Arsenault, who reviewed the text for general readability. Kate's patient support and encouragement helped ensure that the text would be completed.

Beck Weber for technical assistance with various computer programs and input on web-related terminology and technology. Beck's overall support and input helped ensure the updates to the fourth edition were reasoned and completed.

Beth DiFelice, David Gay, and Tara Mospan, of Arizona State University's Sandra Day O'Connor School of Law library for their assistance, support, feedback, and advice on technical and conceptual aspects of legal research as it is today and its rapid evolution. All three are exceptional librarians who have provided invaluable insight into the changing face of legal research.

Jennifer Van Weil for permission to reproduce the Interoffice Memorandum provided in Appendix B. Jennifer is currently working as a paralegal and she is a former paralegal student. The Interoffice Memorandum provided was used to create a brief in chief and reply brief before the New Mexico Court of Appeals.

A former student, working as a paralegal, for permission to reproduce the Client Advisory letter and Interoffice Memorandum 2 in Appendix B.

The individuals at Cengage who helped with the development of the fourth edition. Their encouragement, suggestions, patience, and support were essential to its completion.

Thomson Reuters, for permission to publish most of the cases in this text.

Finally, I would like to thank the reviewers who provided very valuable comments and suggestions for the text:

Regina Graziani,
University of Hartford, Hartford, CT

Lisa Matich,
Northwestern College, Chicago, IL

About the Authors

William H. Putman received his Juris Doctor degree from the University of New Mexico School of Law and has been a member of the New Mexico Bar since 1975. For ten years, he was an instructor in the Paralegal Studies Program at Central New Mexico Community College in Albuquerque, New Mexico, and in the Paralegal Studies Program at Santa Fe Community College, in Santa Fe, New Mexico.

He is the author of the *Pocket Guide to Legal Writing*, the *Pocket Guide to Legal Research*, and the textbooks *Legal Research, Analysis and Writing; Legal Analysis and Writing*; and *Legal Research*. He also authored the legal writing column in *Legal Assistant Today* (James Publishing Co.) for two years, and published several articles on legal analysis and writing in the magazine.

Jennifer R. Albright is a senior policy analyst for the Arizona Supreme Court, Administrative Office of Courts. She was the Director of the Paralegal Studies and Judicial Studies programs at Central New Mexico Community College for six years and a full-time instructor in both programs for nine years. She currently teaches as an adjunct faculty member in Legal Assistant Studies at Phoenix College. Jennifer received her Juris Doctor degree from the Southern Illinois University School of Law and her Masters of Law (LL.M.) from Arizona State University. She is the co-author of *Legal Research* with William H. Putman.

Part 1

Introduction to Research, Analytical Principles, and the Legal Process

Overview

Part I presents two introductory chapters designed to provide a review of basic information fundamental to legal research, analysis, and writing. Chapter 1 is an overview of the legal system and the legal process, including a summary of basic legal principles and authorities involved in the process. Chapter 2 introduces legal research, analysis, and the research and analytical process.

Chapter 1

Introduction to Legal Principles and Authorities

Learning Objectives

After completing this chapter, you should understand:

- The main sources and types of law
- The basic structure of the state and federal court systems
- The hierarchy of the various sources of law
- The types of legal authority
- When and how legal authority applies

Renee works in a clerical position at the Addison law firm. Last fall she entered the paralegal program offered by the local community college. Renee is an excellent employee. The firm, in support of her continued education, pays her tuition and allows her to leave work early so that she can attend a late afternoon class. The firm recently reassigned Renee to work in the paralegal division and directed that she be assigned some substantive legal research and analysis tasks.

Two weeks ago, Renee started working on a gender discrimination case. In that case, the client, Mary Stone, worked for a company for 11 years. She always received excellent job performance evaluations. Her coworker, Tom, asked her on several occasions to go out with him. Ms. Stone always refused his invitations. The last time he asked her out was about a year ago. After she refused, he told her, "I'll get even with you." Nine months ago, Tom was promoted to the position of department supervisor. After his promotion, he did not ask Ms. Stone out again. On her evaluation three months ago, he rated her job performance as "poor" and stated that she was uncooperative and abrasive. He recommended that she be demoted or fired. Ms. Stone feels that she has been discriminated against, and she wants the "poor" evaluation removed from her file.

Renee's assignment is to locate the pertinent state and federal law governing gender discrimination and any other relevant information on the subject and prepare a memo summarizing her research and how it applies to the case. Renee located a federal and a state statute prohibiting discrimination in employment on the basis of gender, a federal and a state court case with facts similar to those in Ms. Stone's case, and two law review articles discussing the type of gender discrimination encountered by Ms. Stone.

While analyzing the law and preparing her memo, Renee realizes that she must determine what part of her research applies and how. She asks herself, "In which court should the claim be filed, federal or state? If a complaint is filed in state court, which statutes and court opinions must the state court follow? Why?" This chapter presents general guidelines that assist in determining when and how legal authorities apply. The Application section at the end of this chapter presents guidelines to answer Renee's questions.

I. INTRODUCTION

As attorneys become more aware of the capabilities of paralegals and legal researchers, they increasingly assign them substantive legal research, analysis, and writing tasks. **Legal research** is the process of finding the law that applies to a client's problem. **Legal analysis** is the process of determining how the law applies to the problem. The **legal writing process** is the systematic approach to legal writing. The goal of this text is to provide comprehensive coverage of the legal research, analysis, and writing process. Emphasis is on in-depth coverage of many difficult areas of legal research, analysis, and writing, such as:

- Issue and key fact identification
- Issue statement (how to write the issue)
- Location of statutory and case law
- Location of secondary authority
- Statutory and case law analysis
- Counteranalysis
- How to effectively conduct legal research and analysis
- How to present the results of legal research and analysis in writing

Before considering these areas in subsequent chapters of the text, it is necessary to have a general understanding of the law, the legal system, and some of the basic doctrines and principles that apply to legal analysis. This is essential because legal analysis involves determining how the law applies to a client's facts, which in turn requires knowledge of what the law is, how to find it, and the general principles that govern its application. This chapter presents an overview of the legal system and fundamental principles that guide its operation. The definitions, concepts, doctrines, and principles addressed are referred to and applied in the subsequent chapters and familiarity with them is essential when studying those chapters.

The term *law* has various definitions, depending on the philosophy and point of view of the individual defining it. For the purposes of this text, **law** is defined as the body of enforceable rules that govern individual and group conduct in a society. The law establishes standards of conduct, the procedures governing the conduct, and the remedies available when the rules of conduct are not followed. The purpose of the law is to establish standards that allow individuals to interact with the greatest efficiency and the least amount of conflict. When conflicts or disputes occur, law provides a mechanism for a resolution that is predictable and peaceful.

The following sections focus on the various sources of law and the principles and concepts that affect the analysis of these sources.

II. SOURCES OF LAW

The legal system of the United States, like the legal systems of most countries, is based upon history and has evolved over time. When America was settled, English law governed most of the colonies. As a result, the foundation of the American legal system is the English model, with influences from other European countries.

In England, after the Norman Conquest under William the Conqueror in 1066, a body of law called the *common law* developed. The common law consisted of the law created by the courts established by the king. When colonization of America took place, the law of England consisted primarily of the common law and the laws enacted by Parliament. At the time of the Revolutionary War, the English model was adopted and firmly established in the colonies.

After the Revolutionary War, the legal system of the colonies remained largely intact and remains so to the present time. It consists of two main categories of law:

1. Enacted law
2. Common law/case law

A. Enacted Law

As used in this text, the term **enacted law** means the body of law adopted by the people or legislative bodies. It includes:

- Constitutions—adopted by the people
- Statutes, ordinances—laws passed by legislative bodies
- Regulations—actions of administrative and regulatory bodies that have the force of law

Laws are established by two governing authorities in the United States: the federal government and the state governments. Local governments are a component of state governments and have the authority to govern local affairs. Each governing authority has the power to enact legislation affecting the rights and duties of members of society. It is necessary to keep this in mind when analyzing a problem, because the problem may be governed by more than one law. The categories of enacted law are addressed in the following subsections.

1. Constitutions

A **constitution** is a governing document adopted by the people. It establishes the framework for the operation of government, defines the powers of government, and guarantees the fundamental rights of the people. Both the federal and state governments have constitutions.

United States Constitution. The United States Constitution:

- Establishes and defines the powers of the three branches of federal government: executive (president), legislative (Congress), and judicial (courts)
- Establishes the broad powers of the federal and state governments and defines the relation between the federal and state governments
- Defines in broad terms the rights of the members of society

State Constitutions. Each state has adopted a constitution that establishes the structure of the state government. In addition, each state constitution defines the powers and limits of the authority of the state government and the fundamental rights of the citizens of the state.

2. Statutes

Laws passed by legislative bodies are called **statutes**. Statutes declare rights and duties, or command or prohibit certain conduct. As used here, *statute* includes any law passed by any legislative body: federal, state, or local. Such laws are referred to by various terms, such as *acts, codes, statutes*, or *ordinances*. The term *ordinance* usually refers to a law passed by a local government. Statutory law has assumed an increasing role in the United States, as many matters once governed by the common law are now governed by statutory law.

For Example

Criminal law was once governed almost exclusively by the common law. Now statutory law governs the majority of the criminal law, such as the definition of crimes.

Statutes are usually designed to cover a broad range of present and future situations; therefore, they are written in general terms.

For Example

Section 335-1-4 of a state's Uniform Owner Resident Relations Act provides, "If a court, as a matter of law, finds that any provision of a rental agreement was inequitable when made, the court may limit the application of such inequitable provision to avoid an inequitable result." The statute is written in general terms so that it covers a broad range of landlord–tenant rental situations and provisions. It is designed to cover all provisions of all rental agreements that may prove to be inequitable. The general terms of the statute allow a court a great deal of flexibility when addressing an issue involving an alleged inequitable lease provision. The court "may limit the application . . . to avoid an equitable result." How and to what degree the court limits the application of the lease provision is left to the court to decide.

3. Administrative Law

A third type of enacted law is **administrative law**. Legislative bodies are involved in determining what the law should be and enacting the appropriate legislation. They do not have the time and are not equipped to oversee the day-to-day running of the government and implementation of the laws. Legislatures delegate the task of administering the laws to administrative and regulatory agencies. The agencies are usually under the supervision of the executive branch of the government.

When a law is passed, the legislature includes enabling legislation that establishes and authorizes administrative and regulatory agencies to carry out the intent of the legislature. This enabling legislation usually includes a grant of authority allowing the agency to create rules and regulations necessary to carry out the law. These rules and regulations have the authority of law. The body of law that results is called *administrative law*. It is composed of the rules, regulations, orders, and decisions promulgated by the administrative agencies when carrying out their duties.

Administrative law is usually more specific than statutory law because it deals with the details of implementing the law.

For Example

The federal Environmental Protection Agency, in order to implement the Clean Air Act, adopted various regulations setting air quality standards. Many of these regulations establish specific numerical standards for the amount of pollutants that may be emitted by manufacturing plants. The Clean Air Act is written in broad terms, but the regulations enforcing it are specific. For example, the regulations define the exact amount of pollutants a new automobile may emit.

Enacted law covers a broad spectrum of the law. The process of analyzing enacted law is covered in detail in Chapter 3.

B. Common Law or Case Law

In a narrow sense, **common law** is law created by courts in the absence of enacted law. Technically, the term includes only the body of law created by courts when the legislative authority has not acted.

For Example

The courts have created most of the law of torts. Tort law allows a victim to obtain compensation from the perpetrator for harm suffered as a result of the perpetrator's wrongful conduct. From the days of early England to the present, legislative bodies have not passed legislation establishing or defining most torts. In the absence of legislation, the courts have created and defined most torts and the rules and principles governing tort law.

Case law encompasses a broader range of law than common law. Case law includes not only the law created by courts in the absence of enacted law, but also the law created when courts *interpret* or *apply* enacted law.

Often the term *common law* is used in a broad sense to encompass all law other than enacted law (i.e., law enacted by legislatures or adopted by the people). This text uses the term *common law* in the broadest sense to include case law (often called judge-made law). Throughout the remainder of this text, the term *case law* is primarily used and should be interpreted to include all law other than enacted law.

As mentioned, the case law system in the United States is based on the English common law, and much of the English common law has been adopted by the states. William the Conqueror established a king's court (Curia Regia) to unify the country through the establishment of a uniform set of rules and principles to govern social conduct throughout the country. The courts, in dealing with specific disputes, developed legal principles that could apply to all similar disputes.

With the passage of time, these legal principles came to embody the case law. The case law process continues to the present day in both England and the United States, with new rules, doctrines, and principles continually being developed by the courts.

For Example

There was no remedy in tort law for strict products liability (liability of manufacturers and sellers for harmful or dangerous defective products) 150 years ago. The tort was developed by the courts in the 20th century to address the needs of a modern industrial society.

The ability to research and analyze case law is an essential skill for a legal researcher. The researcher usually needs court opinions to determine how a law has been interpreted and how it might apply to specific fact situations and problems such as those of the client's case.

1. Role of the Courts

Disputes in our society arise from specific fact situations. The courts are designed to resolve these disputes. When a dispute is before a court, it is called a *case*. The role of the court is to resolve the dispute in a peaceful manner through the application of the law to the facts of the case. To accomplish this resolution, the court must identify the law that controls the resolution of the dispute and apply that law to the facts of the case.

When there is no enacted or case law governing a dispute, the court may be called upon to create new law. If the meaning or application of an existing law is unclear or ambiguous, it may be necessary for the court to interpret the law. In interpreting and applying existing law, courts often announce new legal rules and principles. The creation of new law and the interpretation and application of existing law become law itself.

The result reached by a court is usually called a *decision*. The court's written decision, which includes how it ruled in a case and the reasons for that ruling, is called an **opinion**. The case law is composed of the general legal rules, doctrines, and principles contained in court opinions.

2. Court Systems

A basic understanding of court systems is necessary for anyone analyzing a legal problem. The approach to a problem and the direction of research may depend upon whether relief is available in federal or state court or both. This section presents a brief overview of the court systems.

There are two parallel court systems, the federal court system and the state court system. A concept common to both systems is that of jurisdiction. An understanding of this concept is essential to understanding the operation of both systems.

a. Jurisdiction

The types of cases that can come before a particular court in either system are determined by the jurisdiction of the court. **Jurisdiction** is the extent of a court's authority to hear and resolve specific disputes. A court's jurisdiction is usually limited to two main areas:

1. Over persons by geographic area—personal jurisdiction
2. Over subject matter by types of cases—subject matter jurisdiction

(1) Personal Jurisdiction **Personal jurisdiction** is the authority of the court over the parties to a legal dispute. The jurisdiction of state courts is limited to the geographic boundaries of the state or to matters that have some connection with the state.

For Example

New York state courts do not have authority to decide matters that take place in the state of Ohio. Their authority is limited to the geographic boundaries of the state of New York. State courts in New York have jurisdiction over an Ohio resident if the resident is involved in an automobile accident in New York.

In addition, personal jurisdiction requires that both the plaintiff and the defendant be properly before the court. Assuming the correct court is chosen, a plaintiff properly comes before the court by filing the pleading that starts the lawsuit (the complaint in a civil case or an indictment, information, or complaint in a criminal case). A defendant is properly before the court when the defendant is notified of the lawsuit, that is, correctly served with a copy of the complaint (service of process).

(2) Subject Matter Jurisdiction **Subject matter jurisdiction** is the court's authority over the types and kinds of cases it may hear and decide. Regarding subject matter jurisdiction, there are basically two types of courts in both the federal and state court systems:

1. Courts of general jurisdiction
2. Courts of limited jurisdiction

Courts of general jurisdiction have the authority to hear and decide any matter brought before them, with some limitations. The United States District Courts are the courts of general jurisdiction in the federal system. They have the authority to hear and decide all matters involving the United States Constitution or federal law (*federal question jurisdiction*) or cases where the parties are citizens of different states and the amount in controversy exceeds $75,000 (*diversity jurisdiction*). All states have state courts of general jurisdiction that have authority over state matters. The courts of general jurisdiction are the main trial courts in both systems.

Courts of limited jurisdiction are restricted in the types of cases they can hear and decide. There are courts of limited jurisdiction in both the federal and state court systems.

For Example

1. The authority of the United States Tax Court is limited to matters involving federal tax law.

2. Most state court systems have courts whose authority is limited by dollar amount. Such courts are limited to hearing and deciding matters where the amount in controversy does not exceed a certain amount, such as $10,000. These courts are called by various names: small claims, magistrate, and so on. Some state courts are limited to hearing specific types of cases, such as matters involving domestic relations or probate.

(3) Concurrent Jurisdiction **Concurrent jurisdiction** exists when more than one court has the authority to deal with the same subject matter. In such cases, the plaintiff may choose the court in which to file the case.

For Example

1. In diversity jurisdiction (disputes between citizens of different states) in which the amount in controversy exceeds $75,000, the matter may be tried in either federal court or the state court of general jurisdiction. Both the federal and state courts have authority to try the case; they have concurrent jurisdiction. The party initiating the case must choose the court in which to file the case.

2. A state court of limited jurisdiction, such as a county court, may have authority to try cases where the amount in controversy does not exceed $10,000. Such cases may also be tried in the state's court of general jurisdiction, such as a district court, which has authority to try a claim of any dollar amount. These courts have concurrent jurisdiction over claims that do not exceed $10,000; that is, the matters may be tried in either court.

Jurisdiction is a complex subject. An exhaustive and detailed treatment of jurisdiction is the subject of many texts and is properly addressed in a separate course of study. The brief discussion here is designed to acquaint the student with the fundamentals.

b. Federal Court System

The federal court system is composed of three basic levels of courts.

(1) Trial Courts The **trial court** is where the matter is heard and decided. The testimony is taken, other evidence is presented, and the decision is reached. The role of the trial court is to determine what the facts are and how the law applies to those facts. A trial is presided over by a judge and may include a jury. If the trial is conducted before a judge and a jury, the judge decides **questions of law** such as what the law is or how it applies. The jury decides **questions of fact** such as whether a person performed a certain act. If the trial is conducted without a jury, the judge decides both questions of law and fact.

The United States **District Court** is the main trial court in the federal system. This court has jurisdiction over cases involving federal questions. This includes matters involving the United States Constitution, federal laws, United States treaties, and so on. The United States District Court also has the authority to try diversity cases. Each state has at least one United States District Court (see Exhibit 1-1).

In addition to the United States District Court are other federal courts whose authority is limited to specific matters, such as the United States Tax Court, the United States Court of International Trade, the United States Court of Federal Claims, and the United States Bankruptcy Court.

(2) Court of Appeals A party aggrieved by the decision of a trial court has a right to appeal the decision to a **court of appeals** (also referred to as an appellate court). The primary function of a court of appeals is to review the decision of a trial court to determine and correct any error that may have been made. A court of appeals only reviews what took place in the trial court. It does not hear new testimony, retry the case, or reconsider the evidence. A court of appeals reviews the record of the lower court and takes appropriate action to correct any errors made, such as ordering a new trial or reversing a decision of the trial court. The court of appeals in the federal system is called the United States Court of Appeals. These courts are also called *circuit courts*. There are 13 federal courts of appeals (see Exhibit 1-1).

(3) United States Supreme Court The United States Supreme Court is the final court of appeals in the federal system. It is the highest court in the land. With few exceptions, an individual does not have an absolute right to have a matter reviewed by the **Supreme Court**. A party who disagrees with the decision of a court of appeals

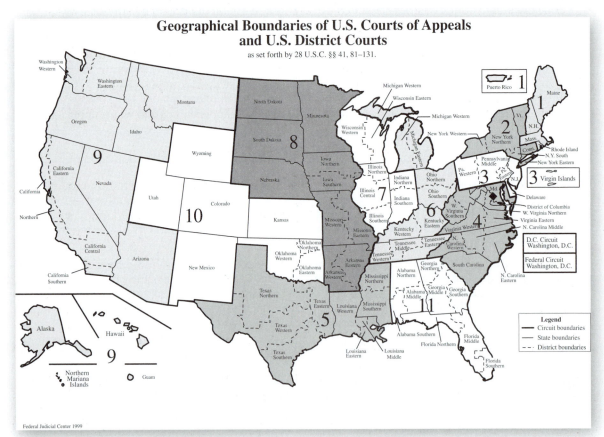

Exhibit 1-1   United States Circuit Courts of Appeals and United States District Courts *http://www.uscourts.gov/sites/default/files/u.s._federal_courts_circuit_map_1.pdf*

must request (petition) the Supreme Court to review it. The request is called a **petition for writ of certiorari**. The Supreme Court has discretion to review or not review a decision of a court of appeals. If the Court denies the petition, the decision of the court of appeals stands. If the Court believes that the matter involves important constitutional issues, if the challenged decision conflicts with other federal court decisions, or if there is a conflict between the opinions of the courts of appeals, then the Supreme Court may grant the petition and review the decision of the lower court.

The organization of the federal court system and the various federal courts is presented in Exhibit 1-2.

c. State Court System

Every state has its own state court system each with unique features and variations. The names of the courts vary from state to state.

For Example

The highest court in many states is called the supreme court. In New York, however, the highest court is called the court of appeals.

Because of the unique features of each state system, it is essential that you become familiar with the court system in your state. Like the federal court system, most state court systems are composed of three basic levels of courts.

(1) Trial Courts All states have trial courts where the evidence is presented, testimony taken, and a decision reached. Usually there are trial courts of general jurisdiction and trial courts of limited jurisdiction. The court of general jurisdiction is often called a *district court* or **superior court**. There are various courts of limited jurisdiction, such as probate courts, small claims courts, domestic relations courts, magistrate courts, and county courts.

(2) Courts of Appeals Many states have intermediate courts of appeals that function in the same manner and play the same role in the state court system as the federal court of appeals does in the federal system.

(3) State Supreme Court Every state has a highest appellate court, usually called the supreme court. This court is the highest court in the state, and its decisions are final on all questions involving state law. In states that have intermediate courts of appeals, the state supreme court often operates like the United States Supreme Court in that

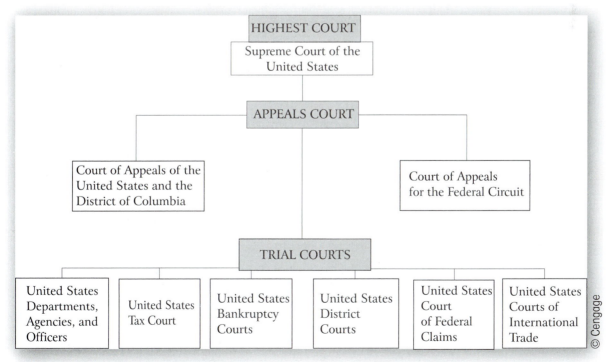

Exhibit 1-2 Organization of the Federal Court System.

there is no automatic right of appeal. Like the federal Supreme Court, the state supreme court grants leave to appeal only in cases presenting important questions of state law. In those states where there is no intermediate court of appeals, a party who disagrees with a trial court's decision has a right to appeal to the highest court. In either system, state or federal, all individuals have at least one opportunity to appeal the decision of a trial court to a higher court.

3. Precedent and Stare Decisis

It is apparent, when you consider the number of courts in the state and federal court systems, that the courts address an immense number of legal questions and problems. Often, similar legal questions and fact situations arise in the same court system or in different court systems. If a court in an earlier case has developed a legal doctrine, principle, or rule that helps resolve a legal question, then later courts addressing the same or a substantially similar question should be able to look to the earlier decision for guidance. The efficiency of the court system is greatly enhanced because courts do not have to "reinvent the wheel" in every case—they may rely on legal doctrines, principles, or rules developed over time in previous cases.

Reliance on doctrines, principles, or rules to guide the resolution of similar disputes in the future also makes the legal system more stable, predictable, and consistent. If the law governing a specific subject or legal question is established in an earlier case, then individuals can rely on a court addressing the same or a similar question to base its decision on the principles established in the earlier case. Outcomes can be predicted to some extent, and stability and consistency can become part of the court system.

Two complementary doctrines have developed to provide stability, predictability, and consistency to the case law. These doctrines are precedent and stare decisis.

a. Precedent

Precedent is an earlier court decision on an issue that applies to govern or guide a subsequent court in its determination of an identical or similar issue based upon identical or similar facts.

For Example

> The state's highest court, in the case of *State v. Ahrens*, held that bail must be set in all criminal cases except when a court determines that the defendant poses a clear and present threat to the public at large or to an individual member or members of the public. If a case before a subsequent court involves a situation in which the defendant has made threats against the life of a witness, *Ahrens* applies as precedent and can serve as a guide for the court's determination of the question of whether bail must be set.

A case that is precedent is often called "on point." Chapter 12 discusses the process and steps to follow when determining if a court opinion may apply or be relied on as precedent.

b. Stare Decisis

The doctrine of **stare decisis** is a basic principle of the case law system that requires a court to follow a previous decision of that court or a higher court when the current decision involves issues and facts similar to those involved in the previous decision. In other words, similar cases will be decided in similar ways. Under the doctrine, when the court has established a principle that governs a particular set of facts or a specific legal question, the court will follow that principle and apply it in all future cases with similar facts and legal questions. In essence, stare decisis is the doctrine providing that precedent should be followed.

For Example

> A statute of state X prohibits employment discrimination on the basis of gender. In the case of *Ellen v. Employer, Inc.*, an employee was fired because the employee was homosexual. The supreme court of state X interpreted "discrimination on the basis of gender" as used in the statute to include discrimination based on an individual's sexual preference. The doctrine of stare decisis requires that in subsequent cases, the supreme court of state X and all the lower courts of state X follow the interpretation of the statute given in *Ellen v. Employer, Inc.* In other words, the lower courts must follow the precedent set in *Ellen v. Employer, Inc.*

The doctrine of stare decisis, however, does not require rigid adherence to the rules or principles established in prior decisions. The doctrine does not apply if there is a good reason not to follow it. These reasons include:

1. The earlier decision has become outdated because of changed conditions or policies.

For Example

In *Plessy v. Ferguson*, 163 U.S. 537 (1896), the court adopted the "separate but equal doctrine" that allowed segregation on the basis of race. In *Brown v. Board of Education of Topeka*, 347 U.S. 483 (1954), the Supreme Court refused to follow *Plessy* and overruled it, holding that separate educational facilities were inherently unequal and denied equal protection of the law.

2. The legislature has enacted legislation that has, in effect, overruled the decision of an earlier court.

For Example

In *Stevens v. Soro, Inc.*, a state supreme court ruled the phrase "on the job" in the Workers' Compensation Act means that an employee is "on the job" from the moment the employee leaves for work until he or she arrives home. After the decision, the state legislature amended the act, defining "on the job" to include only the time the employee is on the premises of the employer. The amendment in effect overrules the prior court decision, so courts are not required to follow that decision in subsequent cases.

3. The earlier decision was poorly reasoned or has produced undesirable results.

For Example

Review the gender discrimination example presented in the beginning of this subsection. Suppose the supreme court of state X, in a later case, decides that the reasoning in the court's decision in *Ellen v. Employer, Inc.*, was incorrect and the term *gender discrimination* should not be interpreted to include discrimination on the basis of sexual preference. The court can overrule *Ellen* and courts are not bound to follow it thereafter.

When a court follows the doctrines of precedent and stare decisis, the court can be relied on to reach the same decision on an issue as an earlier court when the cases are sufficiently similar. Without these doctrines, a similar case could be decided in an entirely different manner based upon the unique beliefs of the individual judge and jury. The result would be little or no consistency in the case law, and chaos would reign. Later in this chapter, we discuss when a decision of an earlier court may or must be relied on by a subsequent court (see section IV. Authority).

III. HIERARCHY OF THE LAW

A hierarchy of authority exists between the two primary sources of law: enacted law and case law. When a question arises concerning which source applies in a case or there is a conflict between sources, a hierarchy governs which source will apply.

In general, within each jurisdiction, the constitution is the highest authority, followed by the other enacted law (legislative and administrative law), and then case law. This means that legislative acts and court decisions must not conflict with the provisions of the constitution. A court decision may interpret a legislative act, but it cannot overrule an act unless it is determined that the act violates the constitution.

The United States Constitution separates the powers to govern between the federal and state governments. This separation of powers is called **federalism**. The **supremacy clause** of the Constitution (Article VI) provides that between federal and state law, federal law is supreme. If an enacted law or court decision of a state conflicts with a federal law or court decision, then the state law or decision is invalid to the extent it conflicts with the federal law or decision. It is important to note not all differences between state law and federal law equal a conflict.

For Example

A state passes a law declaring that it is illegal to burn the American flag. The state supreme court upholds the statute. Both the state statute and the state supreme court decisions are invalid because they conflict with the United States Constitution. The United States Supreme Court has ruled that the freedom of speech provisions of the Constitution include the right to burn the flag. The federal law is supreme, and the state law is invalid to the extent it conflicts with federal law.

IV. AUTHORITY

To analyze the law, in addition to knowing the sources of law, you must become familiar with the concept of authority, principles relating to authority, and the various types of authority. **Authority** may be defined as anything a court may rely on when deciding an issue. It includes not only the law, but also any other nonlaw source that a court may look to in reaching a decision.

This section discusses the two types of authority and the two roles that authority plays in the decision-making process. The two types of authority are:

1. Primary authority—the law itself; constitutions, statutes, administrative law, and case law
2. Secondary authority—nonlaw sources on which a court may rely; treatises, *Restatements of the Law*, model codes, or legal encyclopedias

The two possible roles that authority may play are:

1. Mandatory authority—the authority a court must rely on and follow when deciding an issue
2. Persuasive authority—the authority a court may rely on and follow, but is not bound to rely on or follow

The following subsections first address the two types of authority (primary and secondary), then discuss the role of authority, that is, the value or weight a court must or may give to authority (mandatory and persuasive authority). (See Exhibit 1-3.)

A. Types of Authority

1. Primary Authority

Primary authority is the law itself. It is composed of the two main categories of law, enacted law and common law.

Courts refer to and rely on primary authority first when resolving legal problems.

2. Secondary Authority

Secondary authority is any source a court may rely on that is not the law, that is, not primary authority. Secondary authority consists of legal resources that summarize, compile, explain, comment on, interpret, or in some other way address the law.

Secondary authority can be used in several ways:

- To obtain a background or overall understanding of a specific area of the law. Legal encyclopedias, treatises, and periodicals are useful for this purpose.

Types of Authority	
Primary Authority	The law itself, such as constitutions, statutes, ordinances, administrative agency rules and regulations, and court opinions
Secondary Authority	A source a court may rely on that is not the law, such as legal encyclopedias, *American Law Reports (ALR)*, *Restatements of the Law*, treatises, and law review articles
Role of Authority	
Mandatory Authority	A source of law a court must rely on when reaching a decision, such as an enacted law (statute, ordinance, etc.) that governs the legal question being addressed, or an opinion of a higher court in the jurisdiction that addressed the same or a similar legal question and facts
Persuasive Authority	Any authority a court is not bound to consider or follow but may consider or follow when reaching a decision, such as an opinion of a court in another state on the same or a similar issue, or a secondary authority source (encyclopedia article, legal dictionary definition, etc.)

© Cengage

Exhibit 1-3 Types and Role of Authority.

For Example

If the researcher is unfamiliar with a specific area of law, such as defamation, then a treatise on tort law will provide an overview of the area. The treatise will also include references to key court cases and enacted law (primary authority) concerning defamation.

- To locate primary authority (the law) on a question being researched. *American Law Reports (ALR)*, legal encyclopedias, and treatises can be used for this purpose. See Chapter 5. All secondary authority sources include references to primary authority.
- To be relied on by the court when reaching a decision, but only when there is no primary authority governing a legal question or it is unclear how the primary authority applies to the question. Treatises, law reviews, and *Restatements of the Law* are relied on for this purpose.

There are literally hundreds of secondary sources. An in-depth discussion of all of them is beyond the scope of this text; therefore, only some of the major secondary sources are summarized here.

a. Annotations

Annotations are notes and comments on the law. A well-known annotation is the *American Law Reports (ALR)*. The *ALR* is a series of books that contain the complete text of selected court opinions, along with scholarly commentaries explaining and discussing issues raised in the case. The commentaries also include an overview of how the issues are treated nationally, focusing on the majority and minority views, and a list of cases from other jurisdictions dealing with the same issues. The *ALR* is useful for obtaining an in-depth overview of the courts' treatment of specific questions and issues. These annotations are also useful as an aid in locating court decisions dealing with specific issues.

b. Law Dictionaries

Legal dictionaries include definitions of legal terms and guides to pronunciation. The two major legal dictionaries are *Black's Law Dictionary* (West, a Thomson Reuters business) and *Oran's Dictionary of the Law* (Delmar Cengage Learning).

c. Law Reviews

Law reviews are scholarly publications usually published by law schools. They contain articles written by professors, judges, and practitioners and include commentaries written by law students. The articles usually discuss specific topics and legal questions in great depth and include references to key cases on the subjects. These reviews are useful as a source of comprehensive information on specific topics.

d. Legal Encyclopedias

A *legal encyclopedia* is a multivolume set of books that provides a summary of the law. The topics are arranged in alphabetical order, and the set includes an index and cross-references. The two major legal encyclopedias are *Corpus Juris Secundum (CJS)* and *American Jurisprudence* (now *American Jurisprudence Second*) (*Am. Jur.* or *Am. Jur. 2d*), both published by West, a Thomson Reuters business. An encyclopedia is a valuable source when seeking an overview of a legal topic.

e. Restatements of the Law

Published by the American Law Institute, the *Restatements of the Law* present a variety of topics and discuss what the law is on each topic, or what it should be. Following a presentation of the law is a "Comment" that explains the rule of law presented, discusses why the rule was adopted, and gives examples of how the rule applies. The *Restatements* are drafted by authorities and experts in specific areas and are often relied on and adopted by legislatures and courts.

f. Treatises

A *treatise* is a single- or multi-volume work written by an expert in an area that covers that entire area of law. A treatise is a valuable resource because it provides a comprehensive treatment of a specific area of law, reference to statutes and key cases in the area, and commentaries on the law.

B. Role of Authority

After the types of authority have been identified, it is important to understand the role these sources play in the decision-making process. Not all authority referred to or relied on by a court when deciding an issue is given equal weight. Authority is divided into two categories—mandatory authority and persuasive authority—for the purpose of determining its authoritative value, or the extent to which it must be relied on or followed by a court (see Exhibit 1-3).

1. Mandatory Authority

Mandatory authority is any source that a court must rely on or follow when reaching a decision (e.g., a decision of a higher court in the jurisdiction on the same or a similar issue). Primary authority can be mandatory authority because courts are required to follow the law itself. As discussed earlier, primary authority is composed of enacted law and case law. Secondary authority can never be mandatory authority. A court is never bound to follow secondary authority because it is not the law.

Not all primary authority, however, is mandatory authority. Primary authority becomes mandatory authority only when it governs the legal question or issue being decided by the court.

The factors involved in deciding when enacted law and case law are mandatory authority are briefly discussed here.

a. Enacted Law

Chapter 3 details the process for determining whether an enacted law applies to govern a legal question or issue before a court. The three-step process presented in that chapter is summarized here.

STEP 1:   *Identify all the laws that may govern the question.* This requires locating all statutes or laws that might possibly govern the legal question.

For Example

Some legal questions and fact situations, such as gender discrimination, are governed by both state and federal law, and occasionally by more than one state or federal law.

Once you identify the laws that may govern the question, determine which of these laws applies to the specific legal area involved in the dispute. This requires an analysis of the law.

For Example

In the preceding example, an analysis of the law may reveal that even though both federal and state law govern the question of gender discrimination, the federal law requires that the matter be tried in state court before being pursued in federal court. The federal law, therefore, does not apply until the remedies available under state law have been pursued in the state courts.

STEP 2:   *Identify the elements of the law or statute.* Once you determine the specific law or laws that govern the question, identify the elements of the law or statute, that is, the specific requirements that must be met for the law or statute to apply. It is necessary to identify the elements before moving on to step 3, which is determining whether the requirements of the law or statute are met by the facts of the case.

For Example

Mary bought a toaster at a local store. It did not work when she plugged it in. The store owner refused to replace the toaster or give her a refund when she returned it. The legal question is whether Mary can get a new toaster or her money back. Assume that, after performing the first step of the analysis, you determine that article 2 of the state's commercial code is mandatory authority because article 2 applies to the sale of goods and a toaster is considered goods. Article 2 provides that a warranty is created if:

1. The transaction involves the sale of goods, and

2. The seller of the goods is a merchant.

These are the elements of the statute. These elements must be identified to determine what the section requires for the warranty to exist. It is necessary to identify these requirements before it can be determined how the section applies to the client's facts. The statute further provides that the seller must replace the item or refund the purchase price if the item does not work.

STEP 3:   *Apply the facts of the case to the elements.* The final step is to apply the facts of the client's case to the elements to determine how the law or statute applies. If the elements match the facts raised by the legal issue, then the law applies and governs the outcome. Even if some of the elements are not met, the law still applies, but the outcome may be different.

For Example

Referring to the previous example, the warranty exists if the two elements are met. In this case, the first element is met because a toaster is considered goods. The second element is met because the store owner is considered a merchant because he routinely sells toasters. The elements are met and Mary is entitled to a new toaster or a refund.

If the transaction does not involve the sale of goods, such as the sale of land, or the seller is not a merchant (the toaster was purchased at a yard sale), the elements of article 2 are not met, there is no warranty, and Mary is not entitled to a new toaster or a refund.

After you determine that an enacted law governs a legal question, the law is mandatory authority, and a court must apply the law unless the court rules that the law is unconstitutional.

b. Case Law

For a court opinion to be mandatory authority (often referred to as *mandatory precedent*) that binds another court to follow the rule or principle of law established in the opinion, three conditions must be met:

1. The court opinion must be on point.
2. The court opinion must have been issued by a higher court in that jurisdiction.
3. The court opinion must be "published" or a "precedential" opinion.

For Example

If the highest court in state A defines malice as used in the state's murder statute, then all the lower courts in state A (intermediate appellate and trial courts) are bound to follow the highest court and apply the highest court's interpretation of the term in cases involving the statute.

Regarding this example, is the highest court in state A, in later cases, bound to follow its own earlier definition of malice? No. The highest court is always free to overturn the opinion and change the definition. The court will follow its earlier decision unless it overturns it or in some way amends it. The lower courts do not have this option.

What if the decision of the highest state court is different from the decision of a federal court? If a state court decision conflicts with the Constitution or federal law, then the state court must follow the dictates of the federal law. State courts usually have the final say over interpretations of state law. If a federal court is addressing an issue involving state law, then the federal court usually follows the interpretation of the state law rendered by the state's highest court.

Chapter 12 presents an in-depth discussion of case law analysis and the process involved in determining whether a case is on point.

2. Persuasive Authority

Persuasive authority is any authority a court is not bound to consider or follow but may consider or follow when reaching a decision. When mandatory authority exists, persuasive authority is not necessary, although its use is not prohibited. Persuasive authority consists of both primary authority and secondary authority.

a. Primary Authority as Persuasive Authority

On occasion, courts look to enacted law as persuasive authority.

For Example

A court, when interpreting a term not defined in an act, may apply the definition of the term that is given in another act. Suppose the term *gender discrimination* is not defined in the state's fair housing act but is defined in the state's fair loan act. The fair loan act is not mandatory authority for questions involving the fair housing act because it does not govern housing. It can, however, be persuasive authority. The court may follow or be persuaded to apply the definition given in the fair loan act.

Primary authority represented by case law is often used as persuasive authority (often referred to as *persuasive precedent*). Even though case law is primary authority, it may not be mandatory authority in a specific situation if it does not apply to govern the situation. The court is not required to follow such authority. A court may, however, be guided by and persuaded to adopt the rule or principle established in another court opinion.

For Example

1. The courts in state A have not addressed a legal issue. Therefore, there is no mandatory authority that state A courts must follow. State A courts may consider and adopt the rules and reasoning of federal or other state courts that have addressed the issue. It is not mandatory that state A follow the primary authority of the other federal or state courts, but state A may be persuaded to adopt the primary authority of these courts.

2. Neither the legislature nor the courts of state A have adopted strict liability as a cause of action in tort. State A's highest court can look to and adopt the case law of another state that has adopted this tort.

3. A trial court in state A has written an opinion on a legal issue. A higher court in state A is not bound by the lower court opinion (it is not mandatory authority), but it may consider and adopt the rule and reasoning of the lower court.

When no mandatory authority exists that a court is bound to follow, as in the preceding examples, the court may look to and rely on other primary authority as persuasive authority.

b. Secondary Authority as Persuasive Authority

As discussed earlier, secondary authority is not the law and, therefore, can never be mandatory authority. When mandatory authority on an issue exists, it is not necessary to support it with secondary authority, although it is permissible to do so. Secondary authority should not be relied upon when there is mandatory authority. In such situations, the mandatory authority governs. If there is no mandatory authority but there is persuasive primary authority, the secondary authority may be used in support of the primary authority.

For Example

The courts in state A have never addressed a certain issue. The courts in state B have addressed the issue. The rule of law established by the state B courts can be persuasive primary authority for state A courts. Secondary sources, such as *ALR* commentaries and law review articles, may be submitted to a state A court in support of the persuasive primary authority from state B. Secondary authority also may be submitted to the court for the purpose of opposing the adoption of the persuasive authority from state B.

Secondary authority is most valuable when there is no primary authority, either mandatory or persuasive. However, this situation is rare. Few matters have never been addressed by either some legislature or some court. As noted earlier, secondary authority is also valuable because it is useful in locating primary authority. Some secondary authority is given greater weight or considered to have greater authoritative value than other secondary authority.

For Example

A court will more likely rely on and give greater weight to a *Restatements of the Law* drafted by experts in the field than to a law review article written by a local practitioner in the field.

Always locate the available primary authority and exhaust all avenues of research in this direction before turning to the location of secondary authority. There are two reasons for this:

1. Courts must look to and consider primary authority before considering secondary authority.
2. Primary authority will often lead to key secondary authority sources.

V. INTRODUCTION TO LEGAL CITATION

At the conclusion of your legal research, you often are required to present the results in writing, as discussed in the chapters of this text explaining the legal writing process. In doing so, you must include citations to the legal authorities you have identified. Legal citation is akin to citation in other forms of writing in that it serves to alert the reader that the content is from another source and not the author's own thoughts. However, legal citation has the added task of demonstrating to the reader the strength of the law and whether a court is bound by the source cited (primary, mandatory authority versus persuasive authority).

It is important that the person reading the written document, whether it is an internal office memorandum or a legal document filed in court, be able to easily identify the source cited and quickly locate the source itself. As such there must be a uniform method of citation. There are two manuals that provide the rules and format of legal citation: *The Bluebook: A Uniform System of Citation*, 20th ed. (2015) and the *ALWD Guide to Legal Citation*, 5th ed. (2014). It is also important to know the local standard or rule regarding which manual to use. There are some differences between the two manuals although the differences are generally related to how words are abbreviated in citations, rather that the citation format itself.

The next sections will provide general information on citation in *Bluebook* and *ALWD Guide* format on specific sources covered in this text. Below is a brief overview of both citation manuals, with information on citing specific resources provided in later chapters. More specific references to citation format for various legal sources is included in the chapters on those specific sources. However, it is not the place of this text to provide the detailed rules of legal citation. Always be sure you consult with the latest edition of either citation manual, and any local rules governing citation of state sources to determine the exact citation format required for the particular sources you are citing and the specific venue for which you are writing.

A. *The Bluebook: A Uniform System of Citation* (*The Bluebook*)

The *Bluebook* is organized into four main parts: Introduction, Bluepages, Rules, and Tables. The Introduction explains how the *Bluebook* is organized and it is essential to understanding how to navigate the manual. Although the *Bluebook* contains instructions for citing legal resources in legal practice ("basic" citation rules) and citing resources in academic documents such as law journals, it is primarily designed for use in the latter. For this reason many lawyers and students find the *Bluebook* difficult to use. However, some courts require the *Bluebook* format be followed and even where there is no requirement to follow a specific format, most lawyers are taught the *Bluebook* format in law school and require their paralegals to follow that format unless a local rule dictates otherwise. As such, students must understand the organization and interplay between the different parts of the *Bluebook* to ensure they are citing resources properly for a document drafted for use in legal practice.

One major improvement in the *Bluebook* has been that its content is available online for a fee. Many students and legal practitioners now subscribe, for a fee, to the *Bluebook* online rather than in print. Advantages of online access to the *Bluebook* include keyword and phrase searching, as well as the ability of the subscriber to annotate or make notes which are searchable. In addition, the *Bluebook* is now available via the Rulebook app for all Apple iOS devices.

Citing legal resources in *Bluebook* format requires students to become familiar with three essential components, described next.

1. The Bluepages and Bluepage Tables

The Bluepages summarize the rules for citing legal resources in documents prepared for filing in court or for use in a law office. This part of the *Bluebook* contains specific information on citing statutes, case law, secondary authority, and other legal resources in a format and typeface commonly used by the legal profession. Bluepages rule B2 provides detail regarding typeface for court documents. Bluepages Table BT.1 contains abbreviations commonly used in titles of court documents. Bluepages Table BT.2 contains references to sources for local citation rules. Remember both local citation rules and the applicable citation manual must be consulted to determine the required citation format for a given jurisdiction.

2. Citation Rules

There are rules of citation for each type of legal source, which are explained in the white pages section of the *Bluebook*. This section is referred to as the Rules section. The rules in the Bluepages and the Rules section have some overlap. If the citation is covered in the Bluepages, you may not need to consult the Rules section. It is important to note the explanations in Rules 1 through 9 use general standards of citation used in all forms of legal writing. Rules 10 through 21 present rules for specific types of authority and the examples are printed in a typeface standard used for law journals, not court documents.

3. Tables

Tables are on pages with blue borders. They list necessary abbreviations for use in citations. The Tables section is extensive, covering not only federal and state sources, but also international sources. It is important to use the proper abbreviation and the proper table for the type of citation being drafted.

B. The *ALWD Guide to Legal Citation* (*ALWD Guide*)

The *ALWD Guide* is used in many colleges and law schools, even when the Bluebook is the citation manual deemed the official citation manual for a particular jurisdiction. The *ALWD Guide* is often preferred by instructors over the *Bluebook* because of its ease of use and in-depth explanations of the various citation rules. The fifth edition expanded its appendices to include abbreviations of more legal sources. Unlike the *Bluebook, the ALWD Guide* is focused on citation format for legal documents instead of legal periodicals and law reviews. However, the fifth edition does include explanations and examples of how to modify citation formats from those used for legal documents to those used for scholarly writing side-by-side with the format used in legal documents. The *ALWD Guide* also has an online companion that is designed to allow students to address the most common challenges and errors in legal citation through extensive exercises.

The *ALWD Guide* is organized into seven parts. The following components of the *ALWD Guide* are essential to its effective use.

1. Part 1: Introductory Material

Part 1 explains several key aspects of effective citation. In particular, it explains how to use the manual, how word processor settings affect citation format, and the overall organization of the manual. Importantly, Part 1 explains that the *ALWD Guide* focuses on citation format of United States federal and state legal sources and does not address foreign or international sources as the *Bluebook* does.

2. Text of Citation Rules

Parts 2 and 3 provide detailed explanations of the citation rules. Part 2, Citation Basics, emphasizes key concepts for all citation formats. Part 3, Citing Specific Sources, contains numerous examples and templates that diagram the citation format for specific legal sources, such as court opinions, statutes, constitutions, and many secondary sources. These specific formats cover both print and internet sources. In addition, Part 3 contains fast-format pages and side bar pages that act as quick references, contain tips, information on common errors, and cross-references to other rules that may affect citation format. The rules are divided according to the type of authority. Use the Table of Contents and Index to locate particular rules.

3. How to Use Citations

Part 5, Incorporating Citations into Documents, explains and provides examples of the placement of citations in text. This part covers both legal documents used in court and scholarly legal text. In addition, this section provides guidance on how to choose which source to cite when there is more than one source and how to organize citations when citing multiple sources in a single citation.

4. The Appendices

There are eight appendices in the *ALWD Guide*. Most of them provide abbreviations for use in various citation formats, much like the Tables in the *Bluebook*. There are two other appendices that are very helpful. One is the Table of Primary Authority, which details which legal sources are official and unofficial sources, and the abbreviation for those sources. Official sources are those published by or published at the direction of the government. Unofficial sources are published by a commercial publisher. The content of the law in official and unofficial sources is the same. The difference is that unofficial sources often contain extra content, such as cross-references to other sources, annotations, and historical information not usually included in official sources. There is also an appendix containing each state's local citation rule. Many states have adopted local rules dictating the citation format required when citing that state's primary law, such as statutes, administrative regulations, and court opinions.

VI. KEY POINTS CHECKLIST: Legal Principles and Authorities

✓ When analyzing a legal question or issue, always identify the primary authority (the law) that governs the question. First consider primary authority, then look to secondary authority. As a general rule, courts will rely on primary authority before considering secondary authority.

✓ When you are searching for the law that governs a topic, always consider all the possible sources of law:
  1. Enacted law—constitutions, statutes, ordinances, administrative and regulatory law, and so on
  2. Case law—law created by courts in the absence of enacted law or in the process of interpreting enacted law

✓ Remember that there are two court systems operating in every jurisdiction: state and federal. A legal problem may be governed by either federal or state law or both. Both sources of law and both court systems must be considered when analyzing a problem.

✓ Keep in mind the hierarchy of primary authority. Constitutions are the highest authority, followed by other enacted law, then by case law. When there is a conflict between federal and state law, federal law governs.

✓ The doctrines of stare decisis and precedent provide that doctrines, rules, or principles established in earlier court decisions should be followed by later courts in the same court system when addressing similar issues and facts. Therefore, when researching a question, always look for and consider earlier cases that are on point.

✓ Courts are required to follow mandatory authority; therefore, always attempt to locate mandatory authority before searching for persuasive authority.

✓ Do not rely on persuasive authority if there is mandatory authority. No matter how strong the persuasive authority, the court will apply mandatory authority before persuasive authority. Secondary authority is never mandatory authority.

VII. APPLICATION

The following example illustrates principles discussed in this chapter. The example addresses the questions raised in the hypothetical presented at the beginning of the chapter.

Renee's research on the subject of gender discrimination identified the following authority that might apply to the issues raised in the client's case:

1. Title VII of the Civil Rights Act of 1964, which prohibits employment discrimination on the basis of gender
2. Section 59-9-4 of the state statutes, which prohibits employment discrimination on the basis of gender
3. *Erik v. Coll, Inc.*, a federal court case with facts almost identical to Ms. Stone's, which held that the conduct of the employer constituted gender discrimination in violation of Title VII
4. *Albert v. Conrad Supplies*, a state supreme court case with facts almost identical to those presented in Ms. Stone's case, which held that the employer's conduct violated the state statute
5. Two law review articles addressing gender discrimination, which concluded the type of conduct encountered by Ms. Stone constituted gender discrimination. One article addressed the question in the context of Title VII, and one article focused on the question in the context of the state statute.

Renee's assignment is to prepare a memo that includes a summary of her research and an analysis of how the law applies to the client's case. She realizes that she must organize and analyze her research before she can draft the memo. After reviewing the principles and concepts presented in this chapter, she proceeds with the following steps.

STEP 1: *Identify and separate primary authority and secondary authority.* This step is important because the court will rely on and consider primary authority before referring to secondary authority.

1. Primary authority:
   - Enacted law—Title VII and Section 59-9-4 of the state statutes
   - Case law—*Erik v. Coll, Inc.* and *Albert v. Conrad Supplies*

2. Secondary authority: the two law review articles

STEP 2: *Organize the presentation of the primary authority.* The highest authority in the hierarchy of primary authority is the enacted law, followed by the case law; therefore, Renee organizes her summary of the law with a presentation of the enacted law first. (She did not locate applicable constitutional law.)

1. *Enacted Law.* Regarding the enacted law, Renee determines which law applies to govern the situation. It is possible that both the state and federal laws apply and that a potential cause of action exists in both federal and state court. It is also possible that the federal law requires that the state remedies be exhausted before a claim in federal court can be pursued. This means that the federal law requires that any remedy available under state law be completely pursued before a claim can be brought under federal law. It is possible that the federal act does not apply to the specific legal question raised by the facts of the dispute, or the federal act may apply exclusively and there may be no possible cause of action under the state law. All of these possibilities must be considered when she analyzes the enacted law.

   Once Renee concludes this part of the analysis, she must identify the elements or requirements of the law or laws that do apply. She then applies the elements to the facts of the client's case to determine how the laws apply and what remedies are available. In her memo, she will include a summary of the law and her analysis. Chapter 3 provides guidelines to follow when analyzing enacted law.

2. *Case Law.* Renee next addresses the relevant case law. She first determines whether the cases are on point. A case is on point if there is a sufficient similarity between the key facts and legal issue addressed in the court opinion and the client's case for the court opinion to apply as precedent. If a case is on point, it provides the present court with guidance in resolving a legal question or issue.

If the enacted law is clear and there is no question about how the enacted law applies to the facts of the client's case, then there is usually no need to refer to case law.

For Example

A client is ticketed for driving 90 mph in a 60-mph zone. The statute establishing the speed limit at 60 mph is clear, and there is no need for case law to interpret the statute. A speed of 90 mph is clearly in violation of the statute.

Even if there appears to be no question about how the statute applies, always be sure to check the case law for possible interpretations of the statute.

If Renee concludes that federal law exclusively governs the area, then the state case, *Albert v. Conrad Supplies*, does not apply. If she concludes that only state law applies, then the federal case does not apply.

Once Renee has analyzed the case law, she includes in the memo a summary of her case analysis, discussing whether each case applies and how.

STEP 3: *Organize the presentation of the secondary authority.* The secondary authority is summarized last in the memo because it has the least authoritative value. In the client's case, there is primary authority, so the secondary authority will be used, if at all, in support of or opposition to arguments based on the primary authority. Renee includes a summary of each law review article, emphasizing those aspects of the articles that focus on questions and issues similar to those in the client's case. Even if the articles will not be used in court as secondary authority, a summary is included in the memo because it may provide Renee's supervising attorney with information that proves helpful in the case.

Renee's understanding of the primary and secondary sources of law, and the hierarchy of the sources, is an essential aid in her organization of the research, analysis of the issues, and preparation of the memo. Chapter 15 through Chapter 17 provide useful information concerning the actual preparation of legal memoranda.

Summary

The process of legal analysis and legal writing requires a determination of what law applies to a legal question and how it applies. To engage in the process, you must have an understanding of the law and the basic doctrines and principles that govern and guide the analysis of the law.

The two primary sources of law in the United States are:

1. Enacted law
2. Case law

Enacted law, as used in this text, consists of constitutions, laws passed by legislative bodies, and administrative law adopted by administrative and regulatory bodies to aid in the enforcement and application of legislative mandates. Case law is composed of the law created by the courts in two situations:

1. When there is no law governing a topic
2. Through interpretation of enacted law where the meaning or application of the enacted law is unclear

There are two court systems in the United States: the federal court system and the state court system. Although there are differences in each system, they have basic similarities. Both systems have trial courts where matters are initially heard, trials held, and judgments rendered, and both have courts of appeals where the judgments of trial courts are reviewed and possible errors corrected.

To provide consistency and stability to the case law, two doctrines have evolved:

1. Precedent
2. Stare decisis

Precedent is an earlier court decision on an issue that applies to govern or guide a subsequent court in its determination of identical or similar issues based on identical or similar facts. The doctrine of stare decisis provides that a court must follow a previous decision of a higher court in the jurisdiction when the current decision involves issues and facts similar to those involved in the previous decision.

The two sources of law, enacted and case law, are called primary authority. Primary authority is the law itself. Any other authoritative source a court may rely on in reaching a decision is called secondary authority. Secondary authority is not the law but consists of authoritative sources that interpret, analyze, or compile the law, such as legal encyclopedias and treatises. Courts always rely on and look to primary authority first when resolving legal issues.

If primary authority governs the resolution of a legal question, it must be followed by the court. This type of primary authority is called mandatory authority. Secondary authority can never be mandatory authority. Any authority the court is not bound to follow, but that it may follow or consider when reaching a decision, is called persuasive authority. Both primary authority and secondary authority can be persuasive authority.

The remaining chapters of this text address the application of the basic concepts and principles presented in this chapter. Each concept and principle plays a critical role in legal analysis and writing.

Quick References

Administrative law	5	Opinion	6
Authority	12	Personal jurisdiction	6
Case law	5	Persuasive authority	16
Common law	5	Petition for writ of certiorari	9
Concurrent jurisdiction	7	Precedent	10
Constitution	4	Primary authority	12
Court of appeals	8	Question of fact	8
District court	8	Question of law	8
Enacted law	3	Secondary authority	12
Federalism	11	Stare decisis	10
Jurisdiction	6	Statutes	4
Law	3	Subject matter jurisdiction	7
Legal analysis	3	Superior Court	9
Legal research	3	Supreme Court	8
Legal writing process	3	Supremacy clause	11
Mandatory authority	14	Trial court	8

Internet Resources

http://www.findlaw.com
Considered one of the best sites for finding legal resources in general.

http://www.uscourts.gov
Information about federal court justices, statutes, court procedures; access to forms, court opinions, and links to other sites.

http://www.law.cornell.edu
Cornell University Law School Library; links to primary law and U.S. and international legal reference websites

https://web.law.asu.edu
Arizona State University, Ross Blakley Law Library; go to the law library page and the materials for visitors include research guides, forms, state court information, how to research specific areas of law, and information about Arizona laws.

http://www.gpo.gov/
This is the official site for the Government Printing Office; access to FDsys (Federal Digital System) which includes searchable databases of federal law and federal legislative history.

https://www.justia.com/
Links to federal and state law, legal forms, legal blogs and news.

Exercises

ASSIGNMENT 1

Answer the following questions regarding the courts in your state:

1. Are there limited jurisdiction courts in your state?
   a. Name those courts.
   b. What types of cases can each of those courts preside over?

2. What is the general jurisdiction court in your state?
   a. How are those courts organized—by county, district, etc.?
   b. Does that court have appellate jurisdiction over cases from any limited jurisdiction courts?

3. What are the appellate jurisdiction courts in your state?
   a. Is there an intermediate appellate court? What is it called and is it a single court or are there multiple divisions?
   b. What is the highest appellate court?

ASSIGNMENT 2

Describe the differences between a trial court and a court of appeals.

ASSIGNMENT 3

When is a court opinion considered precedent?

ASSIGNMENT 4

Facts

The researcher is analyzing a problem involving the sale of goods on credit in state A.

Authority

The following authority has been located concerning the problem:

1. State A's Uniform Commercial Code Act

2. State A's Consumer Credit Act

3. State B's Uniform Commercial Code Act

4. A federal statute—Consumer Credit Act

5. *Iron v. Supply Co.*—a decision of the highest court in state A

6. *Milk v. Best Buy, Inc.*—a decision of the highest court in state B

7. *Control Co. v. Martin*—a decision of an intermediary court of appeals in state A

8. *Lesley v. Karl Co.*—a decision of a trial court in state A

9. *Irene v. City Co.*—a federal case involving the federal Consumer Credit Act

10. Regulations adopted by state A's Corporation Commission that apply to consumer credit and the sale of goods

11. *Restatements of the Law* defining sales, consumer credit, and other terms related to the problem

12. An *ALR* reference that directly addresses the issues in the case

Assume that all the cases are on point, that is, they are sufficiently similar to the facts and issues involved in the problem to apply as precedent.

Questions

a. Which authority is primary authority, and which is secondary authority?

b. Which authority can be mandatory authority? Why? What would be required for any of the sources to be mandatory authority?

c. Which authority can be persuasive authority? Why?

d. Assuming that all the primary authority applies to the issues raised by the facts of the client's case, list the authority in the hierarchical order of its value as precedent;

that is, authority with greatest authoritative value will be listed first, followed by other authority in the order it will be looked to by the court.

ASSIGNMENT 5

Facts

Your client is the plaintiff in a workers' compensation case. She was injured in 2008 in state A. In 2010, her employer destroyed all the business records relating to the client. The destruction of the records was apparently accidental, not intentional. They were destroyed, however, while the client's workers' compensation claim was pending.

Authority

You have located the following authority, all of which is directly related to the issues raised by the facts of the client's case:

1. *Idle v. City Co.*—a 1995 decision by the highest court of state A in which the court created a cause of action in tort for the wrongful destruction of business records. The court ruled that a cause of action exists if the records were destroyed in anticipation of or while a workers' compensation claim was pending. The court also held that a cause of action exists if the destruction was intentional or negligent.

2. A 2004 state A statute—a law passed by the legislature of state A that created a cause of action in tort for the intentional destruction of business records. The statute provides that a cause of action exists if the destruction occurs in anticipation of or while a workers' compensation claim is pending.

3. *Merrick v. Taylor*—a 2005 decision of the court of appeals of state A. The court of appeals is a lower court than the state's highest court. The court held that the term *intentional*, within the meaning of the 2004 statute, includes either the intentional destruction

of records or the destruction of records as a result of gross negligence.

4. *Davees v. Contractor*—a decision of the highest court of state B interpreting a state B statute identical to the 2004 state A statute. The court held that the term *intentional*, as used in the statute, includes gross negligence only when the gross negligence is accompanied by a "reckless and wanton" disregard for the preservation of the business records.

5. A 2006 federal statute—the statute is identical to the 2004 state statute but applies only to contractors with federal contracts.

6. An *ALR* reference—addresses specific questions similar to those raised in the client's case.

Questions

a. Which authority is primary authority, and which is secondary authority? Why?

b. Which authority can be mandatory authority? Why? What would be required for any of the sources to be mandatory authority?

c. Which authority can be persuasive authority? Why?

d. Can *Idle v. City Co.* be authority at all? Why or why not?

e. If *Idle v. City Co.* is authority, to what extent?

f. Discuss the impact of *Merrick v. Taylor* in regard to the 2004 state A statute.

g. Discuss the authoritative value of *Davees v. Contractor*.

h. Assuming that all the primary authority applies to the issues raised by the facts of the client's case, list the authority in the hierarchical order of its value as precedent; that is, authority with greatest authoritative value will be listed first, followed by other authority in the order it will be looked to and relied on by the court.

Chapter 2

Introduction to Legal Research and Analysis

Learning Objectives

After completing this chapter, you should understand:

- The definition of legal analysis
- Legal research and the elements of legal analysis
- How the elements of legal analysis apply in specific situations
- The importance of focus and intellectual honesty
- When and how legal authority applies

Marian has worked as Robert Walker's paralegal for the past four years. She conducts initial client interviews, manages the case files, and performs basic research. Robert, a solo practitioner, always determines the merits of a case and performs the substantive research. Marian started law school last fall and now works only part-time at the law firm.

Robert called Marian into his office one morning. "Marian," he said, "I'm going to hire another paralegal to do your assignments." Robert continued, "Now that you are in law school, I want you to take over some of the more substantive legal work. I want you to start performing the legal analysis of some of the new cases and determine what, if any, possible causes of action exist. Your new responsibilities will be to study the cases and provide me with memoranda of law identifying the legal issues and analyzing how the law applies to the issues. This will free me to concentrate more on trial work. Start with Mr. Lietel's case."

Marian remembered the initial interview with Mr. Lietel. Jerry Lietel has a hot temper. He got into an argument with his neighbor, Tom Spear. Mr. Lietel's temper got the best of him. He punched Tom and a fight ensued. Steve Spear, the father of Tom and a retired deputy sheriff, came out of the house and announced that he was placing Mr. Lietel under citizen's arrest. After a short struggle, Steve Spear subdued and handcuffed Mr. Lietel. After Mr. Lietel was handcuffed and had ceased resisting, Steve Spear kicked him about six times, cracking one of his ribs. Mr. Lietel incurred medical bills and lost two days of work. Since the incident, Mr. Lietel has had a lot of trouble sleeping, and he is taking sleeping pills on his doctor's advice. He is fearful of Steve Spear whenever he sees him.

Jerry admits that he punched Tom without provocation and that the citizen's arrest was probably justified, but he wants to sue for his medical bills and the loss of work.

Marian realizes that this, her first analysis assignment, is very important: the quality of her product will determine whether she continues to be assigned this type of substantive legal work. She asks herself, "What's the best way to approach a legal problem? What is a systematic way to analyze a client's problem that will produce the best result in the least amount of time?" The Application section at the end of this chapter presents an analysis of Mr. Lietel's case and the answers to Marian's questions.

I. INTRODUCTION

As discussed in the preface, the focus of this text is on the process of analyzing legal questions raised by the facts of a client's case, legal research, and the process of communicating research and analysis in written form. This chapter presents an overview of the process of legal analysis and some concepts and considerations involved in that process.

Most cases begin like the Lietel case. A client relates a set of factual events that the client perceives entitle him or her to legal relief. The client seeks a solution to what he or she believes is a legal problem. The problem may be as simple as the need for a power of attorney or as complex as a question involving multiple parties and several legal issues. The problem may be one for which there is no legal remedy, or it may not be a legal problem at all.

For Example

> An individual is fired in retaliation for disclosing a defect in the employer's product. The state where this occurs does not have a statute prohibiting retaliatory discharge, nor have the state courts adopted a cause of action in tort for retaliatory discharge. Therefore, it may be that no legal remedy for this type of discharge is available under state law. It is possible that the client's only recourse is political; that is, the client may have to attempt to get legislation passed prohibiting retaliatory discharge, or to exert social pressure through the media.

The purpose of legal analysis and legal research is to analyze the factual event presented by the client and determine:

1. The legal issue (question) or issues raised by the factual event
2. The law that governs the legal issue
3. How the law that governs the legal issue applies to the factual event, including what, if any, legal remedy is available

Once this is accomplished, the client can be advised of the various rights, duties, and options available.

II. LEGAL ANALYSIS DEFINED

Before addressing the steps involved in the legal analysis process, it is necessary to understand what is meant by legal analysis. The term has different meanings, depending on the context of its usage (the type of legal analysis being performed).

For Example

> The term *legal analysis* can refer to, among others, statutory analysis (discussed in Chapter 3), case law analysis (Chapter 12), and counteranalysis (Chapter 13).

In this chapter, **legal analysis** is used in a broad sense to refer to the process of identifying the issue or issues presented by a client's facts and determining what law applies and how it applies. Simply put, legal analysis is the process of applying the law to the facts of the client's case. It is an exploration of how and why a specific law does or does not apply. Legal research is the part of the legal analysis process that involves finding the law that applies to the legal question raised by the facts of a client's case.

III. LEGAL RESEARCH AND THE ANALYSIS PROCESS

A **legal analysis process** is a systematic approach to legal research and analysis. It is an organized approach that helps you develop research skills. It makes legal research easier, saves time, and helps develop research skills.

The most common approach to legal analysis involves a four-step process:

STEP 1:   *Issue.* The identification of the issue(s) (legal question) raised by the facts of the client's case

STEP 2:   *Rule.* The identification of the law that governs the issue(s)

STEP 3:   *Analysis/Application.* A determination of how the rule of law applies to the issue(s)

STEP 4:   *Conclusion.* A summary of the results of the legal analysis

An acronym commonly used in reference to the analytical process is **IRAC**. It is composed of the first letter of the descriptive term for each step of the legal analysis process. The use of the acronym is an easy way to remember the four-step legal analysis process—*i*ssue, *r*ule, *a*nalysis/*a*pplication, and *c*onclusion.

The research component of this process involves steps 1 and 2. Steps 3 and 4 of the process involve the analysis of the research results once the research is complete. The subsequent sections of this chapter address steps 1 and 2 in detail. Steps 3 and 4 are summarized in this chapter and then discussed in detail in Chapter 15 in the legal writing section of the text.

Before the legal analysis of a case can properly begin, however, the following preliminary preparation must take place:

1. All the facts and information relevant to the case should be gathered.
2. Preliminary legal research should be conducted to gain a basic familiarity with the area of law involved in the case.

A. Facts and Key Terms

1. Facts

It is important to keep in mind the crucial role the **facts** play in the analytical process. The four steps of the analysis process involve the facts of the client's case, and the facts play a major role in each step:

1. *Issue.* The key facts are included in the issue. The issue is the precise question raised by the *specific facts* of the client's case. A properly stated issue requires inclusion of the key facts. This is discussed in detail in Chapters 10 and 11.

For Example

Under the provisions of the state battery law, is a battery committed by an individual, *present at the scene of a battery, who encourages others to commit the battery but does not actively participate in the actual battering of the victim?* The key facts of this issue are italicized.

2. *Rule.* The determination of which law governs the issue is based on the applicability of the law to the facts of the client's case.

For Example

If the issue involves oppressive acts by a majority shareholder against the interests of minority shareholders in a closely held corporation, then the facts govern the determination of which corporation statutes apply. Only those statutes that address acts by majority shareholders can apply. In most states, this is limited to a few statutes.

3. *Analysis/Application.* The **analysis/application** step is the process of *applying the rule of law to the facts.* It obviously cannot take place without the facts. Without the facts, the law stands in a vacuum.

For Example

The client was ticketed for driving 65 mph in a 55-mph zone. The client believes that the speed limit was actually 65 mph and that the officer made a mistake. A determination of whether the client violated the law requires the application of the rule of law to the facts of the client's case. Was the speed limit where the ticket was given 65 mph or 55 mph? The *facts are essential* to the process. Without the facts, one cannot make a determination of how the law applies.

4. ***Conclusion***. The **conclusion** is a summation of how the law applies to the facts, a recap of the first three steps. It too requires the facts.

In every case, the analytical process involves a determination of how the law applies to the facts. In court opinions, courts determine how the law applies to the facts presented to the court. Very often students pay too little attention to the facts, focusing on what the law is and what it requires. They ignore the crucially important role the facts play.

In a sense, cases are fact driven—the facts determine the outcome of the case. Often, if a single fact is changed, the outcome is different. The application of the law results in a different conclusion.

For Example

In a murder case, the degree of the offense can depend on a single fact. First-degree murder requires specific intent. It requires not only that the defendant intended to shoot the victim but also that the defendant intended the shooting to kill the victim. If the facts of the case show that the defendant intended to shoot but not kill the victim, the offense is not first-degree murder. The defendant's intent is a fact, and changing this single fact changes the outcome of the case. The application of the law results in a different conclusion. The offense is not first-degree murder but a lesser offense.

With this in mind, the analysis process should begin with a consideration of the facts of the client's case. *Identify and review the facts at the outset.* This preliminary step should include the following:

1. Be sure you have all the facts. Ask yourself if you have all the interviews, files, statements, and other pieces of information that have been gathered concerning the case. Are the files complete? Are facts or information missing? As discussed in the murder case example, a single fact can determine the outcome of a case. If key facts are missing, your analysis may result in an erroneous legal conclusion.
2. Study the available facts to see if additional information should be gathered before legal analysis can properly begin.
3. Organize the facts. Group all related facts. Place the facts in a logical order, such as in the sequence in which they occurred (chronological order) or according to topic (topical).
4. Weigh the facts. The value of some factual information, such as hearsay, may be questionable.
5. Identify the key facts. Determine which facts appear to be critical to the outcome of the case. Chapter 9 discusses the importance of key facts and the process for identifying key facts.

2. Key Terms

All legal resources, print or electronic, primary or secondary authority, are indexed according to key terms. Many sources, such as statutory codes, legal encyclopedias, legal treatises, and digests, contain one or more indexes. These and other sources also may contain a table of contents, or a table of contents may be the only method of indexing. To use indexes and tables of contents effectively, in print or electronically, you must identify the relevant terms in the client's case. These are the **key terms,** or **search terms,** that help guide the researcher in the area being researched. Regardless of whether you are researching in print or electronically, searches are conducted using key terms.

Key terms are identified by reviewing the case file and listing all the terms relevant to the legal questions raised by the facts of the case. When preparing this list, keep in mind the following:

- Parties involved (e.g., private citizen, corporation, public official)
- Places and things (e.g., public or private property [places]; cars or computers [things])
- Actions or omissions that form the basis of the case. These are often referred to as potential claims (e.g., negligence, intentional acts)
- Defenses available (e.g., self-defense)
- Relief sought (e.g., money, injunction)

Key terms may be broad terms you use as a guide to perform preliminary research to gain a familiarity with the area of law governing the client's case, or narrow terms if you are already familiar with the area of law and want to focus your research on a specific aspect.

For Example

The client's case involves a question about child custody and the researcher is unfamiliar with this area of law. The researcher decides to read about the topic in a legal encyclopedia. The first step is to list all the terms that the subject "child custody" might be indexed under, such as *divorce, marriage, custody, parent and child, child custody, children,* and *domestic relations.* By listing the terms, you focus the search in the index and avoid having to scan the entire index. The topic will be under at least one of the search terms.

Because the key term may not be indexed in the way you think it should be, it is important to think of all the terms or categories that may apply. One role of legal education is to teach key terms and the categories where they fit.

Key terms may include key facts from the client's case. This often occurs when the researcher is familiar with the general area of law and is seeking the specific law that governs the client's fact situation.

For Example

The assignment is to locate the federal law the client may be charged with breaking. The client placed a bomb made of nitroglycerin under a bridge. Assume these are the key facts. The researcher, based on her legal education and previous experience, knows that the general research topic is "federal criminal law" and the subtopic is "explosives." By identifying the key search terms *nitroglycerin* and *bridges,* the researcher is guided to the specific law within the general area of "federal criminal law" and "explosives."

Develop a list of key terms while you are reviewing the client's case and identifying the key facts. If you are unfamiliar with the area of law, use a list of terms related to the general topic of the case to perform general research and become familiar with the area of law (see the preceding child custody example). Once you are familiar with the area of law, identify the key facts and the legal issue before conducting research.

B. Preliminary Research

Before conducting any research, check the office research files for previous memos or research that may have addressed the issue(s) you are researching. This may obviate the need for further research, or provide a basis for narrower research specific to the client's case.

It may, however, be necessary to conduct some basic research in the area(s) of law that govern the issue or issues in the case. You may be unfamiliar with the area of law in general or with the specific aspect of the area that

STEP 1: Issue	Identify the issue (legal question) or issues raised by the facts of the client's case.
STEP 2: Rule	Identify the law that governs the issue.
STEP 3: Analysis/ Application	Determine how the rule of law applies to the issue.
STEP 4: Conclusion	Summarize the results of the legal analysis.

Exhibit 2-1   Steps in the IRAC Legal Analysis Process. *Source: http://www.uscourts.gov*

applies in the client's case. You may obtain a general overview of the law by referencing a legal encyclopedia or a single-volume treatise. If the specific question or area is known at the outset, use of the *American Law Reports* or a multivolume treatise may be appropriate.

C. IRAC Analysis

Once the facts have been gathered and reviewed, follow the four steps of the IRAC legal analysis process in Exhibit 2-1 and outlined below.

STEP 1:   **Issue.** Identify the issue(s) (legal question) raised by the facts of the client's case. The **issue** is the precise legal question raised by the facts of the dispute. The first and most important step in the analytical process is to identify the issue. You must identify the problem before you can solve it. The issue is the starting point. If it is misidentified, each subsequent step in the process is a step in the wrong direction. Time is wasted, and malpractice may result.

For Example

A client complains the individual who sold and installed the tile in his bathroom installed it in a defective manner. After a few months, the tile began to fall off the wall. The person who installed the tile gave no oral or written warranty covering the quality of the installation or the quality of the tile.

The researcher assumes, without conducting research, the entire transaction is a sale of goods covered by state statutes governing the sale of goods. The researcher makes this assumption because the transaction involved the sale of goods—the tiles. Under the sale of goods statutes is a section creating an implied warranty that goods are merchantable when sold, which in this case means the tiles will not fall apart.

The statute as interpreted by the state courts, however, does not apply to the service portion of such transactions, which, in the client's case, is the installation of the tile. Based on an incorrect assumption, the researcher identifies the issue as a question of whether the implied warranty of merchantability was breached. The identification of the issue is incorrect because of the erroneous assumption. The question is not about the quality of the tile but about the quality of the installation. Research on the existence of an implied warranty of merchantability is misdirected.

The case may be lost because the issue is incorrectly identified. The laws governing the sale of a service are different from those governing the sale of goods. A lawsuit claiming breach of an implied warranty of merchantability will probably not prevail because the implied warranty of merchantability statute does not apply.

The client does not pay to have the wrong question answered. The subjects of issue identification and presentation are of such importance that Chapters 10 and 11 are devoted to them. Some important considerations involving issues are discussed briefly here.

a. Multiple Issues

The client's fact situation may raise multiple legal issues and involve many avenues of relief. The implied warranty example involves one issue, but there may be several issues in a case. You should be aware of and keep in mind that one set of facts may raise multiple issues and include multiple causes of action.

For Example

Mr. Elvan rear-ended the client's car at a stoplight. After the impact, Mr. Elvan exited his car, approached the client's car, and started yelling at the client, threatening to hit the client. He grabbed the client's arm but never struck him. As a result of the incident, the client's car was damaged. The client suffered whiplash from the collision and a bruise on his arm from being grabbed, and since the wreck, he has been upset and has had trouble sleeping.

The client may have several causes of action against Mr. Elvan: a claim of negligence arising from the rear-end collision, civil assault for his conduct of approaching the client in a threatening manner, battery for grabbing the client, and intentional infliction of emotional distress for his conduct after the collision. Each of these potential causes of action may raise legal issues or questions that must be addressed. This example is referred to in this chapter as the rear-end collision example.

b. Separate the Issues

Analyze and research each issue separately and thoroughly. If you try to research and analyze several issues at once, it is easy to get confused and frustrated. If you find information relevant to another issue, make a reference note and place it in a separate research file.

c. Focus on the Issues of the Case

Keep your focus on the issues raised by the facts of the client's case or on those issues that you have been assigned to research.

For Example

In the rear-end collision example, assume there was a passenger in the vehicle with the client and the passenger is represented by another law firm. Although there may be many interesting issues involving potential legal claims available to the passenger, the passenger is not the client. The focus should be on the issues in the client's case. The issues involving the passenger are outside the scope of the problem and should not be allowed to become a distraction.

Avoid getting sidetracked and wasting time on interesting aspects or issues of a case you were not assigned to address.

STEP 2:   **Rule.** Identify the law that governs the issue (legal research). The second step in the IRAC analytical process is to identify the **rule of law** that applies to the issue; that is, to solve the client's problem you must find the law that applies to the problem. This is the legal research component of legal analysis. The three-part process presented in Exhibit 2-2 is recommended for conducting legal research.

The first part is locating the general law, such as a statute, that governs the question. The second part is locating the law, such as a court opinion, that interprets how the general law applies to the specific fact situation of the issue. The third part is to update the research sources.

PART 1	Locate the general law that governs the issue—usually statutory or case law.
PART 2	Locate the law that interprets how the general law applies to the specific fact situation of the issue—usually case law. Reference to secondary authority is necessary if there is no primary authority that applies or if additional authority is needed to help interpret the primary authority.
PART 3	Update research to ensure that the source you are reading has not been amended, repealed, revoked, overruled, modified, or otherwise changed.

© Cengage

Exhibit 2-2 Three Parts of Step 2: Rule.

For Example

The client is a divorced parent who does not have custody of her child. The father, the custodial parent, was recently convicted of possession of a small amount of cocaine. The client wants to obtain custody of the child due to the father's drug conviction. The issue is: "Under the state's child custody law, may a change of custody be obtained due to a custodial parent's conviction for possession of cocaine?"

The first step of the legal research component of the legal analysis process requires locating the state statute that governs the modification of child custody. Assume that the statute provides that custody will not be changed unless there has been a substantial change in circumstances that affects the welfare of the child. The statute does not define or give examples of a "substantial change in circumstances." The second step requires locating a court opinion (case law) that answers the question of whether a custodial parent's conviction of possession of drugs is a "substantial change in circumstances" within the meaning of the statute. The third step is to update the research sources to ensure that the source is current law.

Chapters 3 through Chapter 8 present detailed instructions on how to research specific types of primary and secondary authorities, such as statutory law, case law, and treatises. A summary of the three-part research process follows.

a. Part 1: Locate the General Law That Governs the Issue

This requires the identification of terms that you will use to search for the law that governs the issue. Ask yourself, "What type of law applies to the question raised by the facts of the case?" This may be enacted law or case law.

(1) *Enacted Law* The legal issue may be governed by enacted law, such as a constitutional provision, statute, ordinance, or regulation. Ask yourself, "What terms will I use to search a statutory index or computer database to locate the law that applies to this issue?" List all the possible terms that might encompass the relevant law. Search the enacted law index or database using the search terms you have identified.

Review the annotations to the statute or administrative law for cases that interpret the statute in fact situations similar to your case. Also, check the annotations for secondary sources such as encyclopedias, *ALR* annotations, and law review articles that discuss the statute. To avoid having to look up the law more than once, save the relevant research concerning the rule of law as you go along. This should include the proper statutory citation, a copy of the relevant portions of law, case citations (if any), and references to secondary sources.

For Example

In the child custody example, think of all the terms for the laws governing child custody. Laws involving child custody could be indexed under "family law," "domestic relations," "divorce," "marriage," "child custody," "custody," or "parent and child." The laws governing changes in custody should be indexed under one of these terms.

(2) *Case Law* Rules or principles established by the courts may govern the issue. In such cases, there may be no statutory law that applies. As with searching for enacted law, ask yourself, "What terms will I use to search a case law digest or computer database to locate the law that applies to this issue?" List all the possible terms under which the court opinions governing the issue may be categorized.

For Example

An individual, while not paying attention, runs a stop sign and hits the client's vehicle. The client is suing for the damage caused to her vehicle. Lawsuits between individuals arising out of accidents are governed by tort law. Most tort claims are based on case law, that is, the law defined by the courts in court opinions. Think of all the terms under which the court opinions governing automobile collisions may be categorized. The opinions may be listed under "negligence," "automobile collisions," and other topics.

Search the case law digests or computer databases using the search terms you have identified. Chapter 4 addresses the research of issues governed by case law. Chapters 7 and 8 present techniques for conducting electronic legal research.

b. Part 2: Locate the Law That Interprets How the General Law Applies to the Specific Fact Situation of the Issue

The rule of law that governs the issue may be written in such broad terms that it is necessary to look to another source, such as case law or secondary authority, to determine how the law applies to the specific fact situation of the issue. Ask yourself, "What terms will I use to search a case law digest or computer database to locate the court opinion that interprets how the general law applies to the specific fact situation raised by the issue?"

For Example

In the child custody example presented at the beginning of this subsection, it is necessary to find case law that addresses the question of whether a drug conviction is a "substantial change in circumstances" within the meaning of the statute. Think of all the terms or phrases that may help locate cases that interpret the statute in this fact situation. These terms may be *child custody, custodial parent and drug convictions, change of custody and drug convictions*, or *change of custody and parental misconduct*.

Chapter 12 addresses how to determine when a court opinion applies to a specific fact situation.

When looking for primary authority, be sure to conduct counteranalysis; that is, always look for authority that may present a counterargument in response to your analysis of an issue. If you find a case on point in support of your position, look for other cases that have a different holding.

Role of Secondary Authority Although it is essential to locate the primary authority that governs an issue, be sure to note important secondary authority as well. The court may rely on secondary authority if there is no primary authority or if it is unclear how the primary authority applies. Sources such as *ALR* annotations, legal encyclopedias, and treatises often discuss and list the statutes and cases related to a topic. Reference to such sources ensures that you have found all the law related to the issue being researched. Also, secondary authority sources such as *ALR* annotations are helpful in locating counterarguments when performing counteranalysis.

c. Part 3: Update Research

Update all research to ensure that sources are current. Statutes must be checked to determine if they have been repealed or amended, cases checked to ensure they have not been reversed or modified by later cases, and secondary sources checked for additions and amendments.

When conducting research, follow a **research sequence.** First, locate the primary authority that governs the issue. As mentioned in Chapter 1, the courts refer to and rely on primary authority first when resolving legal problems.

When researching primary authority, look first for the enacted law, that is, the constitutional provisions, statutes, and so forth that govern the issue. There are two reasons for this. One, the constitutional or statutory provision may answer the question, so that reference to case law is not required.

Two, the annotations (summary of court opinions and other references that interpret the law) that follow the constitutional or statutory provision may include an opinion or a secondary authority source that interprets the law in a fact situation similar to the facts of your issue. Therefore, you will not need to spend time researching other sources for relevant case law.

For Example

The issue is, "Does a majority shareholder of a corporation engage in oppressive conduct when he or she refuses to issue dividends?" The corporation statute prohibits oppressive conduct but does not define what constitutes oppressive conduct. The annotations that follow the statute make reference to a court opinion in which the court held that the refusal to issue dividends was oppressive conduct. The researcher does not have to research other sources for a case that interprets the statute.

The second part in the research sequence is looking to secondary authority, if there is no primary authority that applies or if additional authority is needed to help interpret the primary authority (see Exhibit 2-3).

See Chapter 15 for an additional summary of the research process.

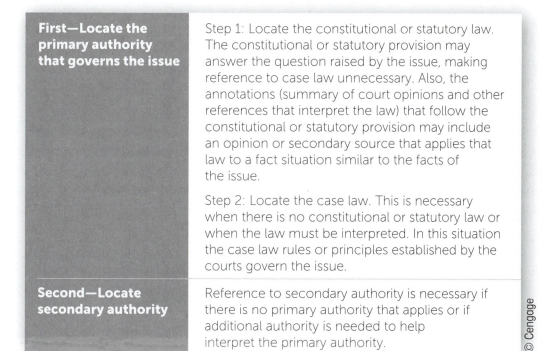

First—Locate the primary authority that governs the issue	Step 1: Locate the constitutional or statutory law. The constitutional or statutory provision may answer the question raised by the issue, making reference to case law unnecessary. Also, the annotations (summary of court opinions and other references that interpret the law) that follow the constitutional or statutory provision may include an opinion or secondary source that applies that law to a fact situation similar to the facts of the issue.
	Step 2: Locate the case law. This is necessary when there is no constitutional or statutory law or when the law must be interpreted. In this situation the case law rules or principles established by the courts govern the issue.
Second—Locate secondary authority	Reference to secondary authority is necessary if there is no primary authority that applies or if additional authority is needed to help interpret the primary authority.

© Cengage

Exhibit 2-3 Sequence for Conducting Research.

PART 1	Identify the component parts (elements) of the rule of law.
PART 2	Apply the elements (the component parts) of the law to the facts of the client's case.
PART 3	Consider the possible counterarguments to the analysis of the issue (i.e., conduct a counteranalysis of the analysis).

© Cengage

Exhibit 2-4   Three Parts of Step 3—Analysis/Application.

STEP 3:   **Analysis/Application.** *Determine how the rule of law applies to the issue.* Once you have located the rule of law, you must analyze the law to determine how it applies to the facts of the client's case. In other words, you apply the law to the legal issue. This is a three-part process (see Exhibit 2-4).

An in-depth discussion of this step regarding statutory law and case law is presented in Chapter 3 and Chapter 12, respectively. The role of the key facts is addressed in Chapter 9. Counteranalysis is discussed in Chapter 13. Therefore, only a brief summary of this step is included here.

a. Part 1: Identify the Component Parts (Elements) of the Rule of Law

For the rule of law to apply to a fact situation, certain conditions established by the rule must be met. These conditions or component parts are called the *elements*. You must identify the requirements (elements) of the rule of law before you can apply the rule to the issue raised by the facts of the client's case.

For Example

Section 93-85A of the state statute governing the execution of a will provides: "The execution of a will must be by the signature of the testator and of at least two witnesses as follows:

1. The testator, in the presence of two or more witnesses:

    a. signifies to the witnesses that the instrument is the testator's will, and

    b. signs the will or has someone else sign the testator's name at the testator's specific direction.

2. The attesting witnesses must sign in the presence of the testator and each other."

    To determine how the statute applies to a client's facts, first identify the elements of the statute. The elements of the statute follow:

1. The testator must indicate to two or more witnesses that the instrument is the testator's will.

2. The testator must sign the will or have someone sign it at the testator's specific direction.

3. The witnesses must sign.

4. Steps 1 through 3 must be done in the presence of the witnesses and the testator.

This example is referred to in this chapter as the wills example.

b. Part 2: Apply the Facts of the Client's Case to the Component Parts (Elements)

Once you have identified the elements of the rule of law, match or apply the facts of the client's case to the elements and determine how the rule applies.

For Example

If the client's case involves a question of whether a will was validly executed in accordance with the statute presented in the wills example, match the facts of the client's case with the elements of the statute to determine if the execution was valid. Assume the will was signed by someone other than the testator, and not at his specific direction. The testator never specifically directed the person to sign the will, but was aware of what was happening and did not object. When this fact is matched to the element of the statute requiring that a will be signed by the testator or someone at the testator's specific direction, the requirement of the element may not be met.

Once the facts of the client's case have been matched to the elements of the rule of law, you may determine how the rule applies in the client's case.

For Example

In the preceding example, one could reach a conclusion that the element allowing a signature by "someone else" at the testator's specific direction was not met. Although the testator was present, he did not specifically direct the other person to sign the will. One could also conclude that additional research is necessary to determine how the courts have interpreted "specific direction" as used in the statute.

In some cases, the way the rule applies is clear from the face of the rule, and there is no question how the rule applies. All that is required is the application of the elements of the rule of law to the facts to determine how the law applies in the case.

For Example

An 18-year-old client wants to know if she is eligible to run for the position of probate judge. Section 34-214 of the election code provides that the minimum age for candidates for the position of probate judge is 21 years. It is clear from Section 34-214 that the client is not eligible to run.

In many cases, it is not clear from the rule of law how an element applies in a specific fact situation. In such instances, it may be necessary to refer to court opinion where the court, in a similar fact situation, interpreted how the law applies.

For Example

The rule of law defines *slander* as the "publication of a false statement of fact concerning the plaintiff that causes damages." In the client's case, the client's neighbor orally communicated to another neighbor a false statement of fact concerning the client. While visiting her neighbor's house, she falsely stated that the client was a thief. The statement damaged the client.

The answer to the question of whether an oral communication to one person constitutes "publication" within the meaning of the statute is not clear from a mere reading of the statute. You must refer to case law to determine how the courts have interpreted the term *publication.* You must then apply the courts' interpretation of the term to the client's case. If the courts have defined *publication* as "communication to any third person," then the communication to the neighbor is slander.

This example is referred to in this chapter as the slander example.

c. Part 3: Consider the Possible Counterarguments to the Analysis of the Issue (Conduct a Counteranalysis of the Analysis)

Once you complete the analysis and application of the rule of law, consider any potential counterarguments to the analysis or application. This involves the anticipation and consideration of any argument an opponent is likely to raise in response to the analysis. (Chapter 13 addresses counteranalysis.)

For Example

Refer to the wills example in which the testator did not specifically direct a third party to sign the will, but was aware of the signing and did not object. It can be concluded that the element of the statute allowing a third party to sign the will at the testator's specific direction was not met. Although the testator was present, he did not specifically direct the other person to sign the will.

The counterargument is that this element of the statute is met because the equivalent of "specific direction" took place. The testator was aware that the third person was signing on his behalf and did not object. The failure to object is evidence that the signing took place at his specific direction.

Undertake research to determine if this counterargument has support in the case law. You should consider and address the counterargument in this step of the analysis process.

STEP 4:   **Conclusion.** *Summarize the results of the legal analysis.* The final step in the analytical process is the conclusion, the result of the analysis. As discussed in step 3, part of the analysis/application process is a determination of how the rule of law applies to the client's facts. This determination is, in effect, a conclusion. Therefore, the conclusion step in the analytical process is a summing-up and commentary that may include:

a. A recap of the determination reached in the analysis/application step.
b. A consideration or weighing, based on the analysis, of what action a court may take or how a court may rule upon the issue.
c. The identification of additional facts or other information that may be necessary because of questions raised during analysis of the problem.
d. The identification of further research that may be necessary regarding the issue. Further research may be required because the necessary research sources are not readily available, the analysis is preliminary owing to time constraints, or the factual investigation of the case has not been completed.
e. The identification of related issues or concerns that became apparent as a result of the research and analysis.

IV. GENERAL CONSIDERATIONS

The process of analyzing a legal problem can at times be difficult, especially for a beginner. In addition to the steps addressed in the previous section, the following general considerations and guidelines will prove helpful when researching and analyzing a legal issue.

A. Focus

Focus is critical when performing the steps of the analytical process. Focus has several meanings, depending on what part of the process is being performed. At the broadest level, it means to concentrate on the specific task assigned, to analyze only the issue or issues assigned.

For Example

Referring to the rear-end collision example, if the assignment is to analyze the question of whether a cause of action for civil assault is present, stay focused on that issue. Answer only that question. If you come across information relevant to another issue, note it, but do not pursue it. Valuable time may be lost and work may be duplicated, if you research and analyze the other issue.

When identifying the issue, focus on the facts of the client's case. Ask yourself, "What must be decided about which of the facts of the client's case?"

When identifying the rule of law, focus on the facts of the case and the elements of the rule of law. This will help you quickly eliminate rules of law that do not apply.

For Example

The fact situation involves a credit purchase by the client. There may be several rules of law that govern the transaction, such as the state's usury laws, the state sale of goods statutes, and the federal truth-in-lending laws.

The interest charged in the transaction in question was 1 percent and the usury statute provides that interest rates in excess of 20 percent are void. If you keep this fact in mind when locating the laws that might possibly apply to the transaction, you can immediately eliminate the usury statute from consideration. The interest charged does not violate the usury statute, so that statute clearly does not apply. It does not have to be considered when analyzing the problem in step 3.

When analyzing and applying the rule of law in step 3, focus on the client's facts and the issue or question being analyzed. It is easy to get sidetracked, especially when reading case law. Interesting issues may be addressed in a court opinion that are close but not directly related to the issues in the client's case. Stay focused. Ask yourself, "Is the issue being addressed in this opinion really related to the issue in my case? Is it on point?" The guidelines and principles addressed in Chapter 12 are helpful in this regard.

If you do not stay focused, after you have completed your research, you may have several cases in front of you that are only marginally related to the specific issue you are analyzing. A lot of time can be wasted reading cases that are not really on point.

Focus on the work. Avoidance and procrastination are deadly. When you are stuck or having a difficult time analyzing or researching an issue, it is sometimes easy to procrastinate, to avoid working on the problem. You may find excuses for not working on the problem, such as working on an easier project. The way to overcome this is to *start*. Do not put it off. If you are at the research stage, *start researching*. If you are at the writing stage, *start writing*. Do not be discouraged if the results seem poor at first. Focus on the problem and begin. Often the barrier is beginning.

B. Ethics—Intellectual Honesty

Rule 1.1 of the American Bar Association's Model Rules of Professional Conduct requires that a client be represented competently. This means that it is your ethical duty to possess and exercise that degree of knowledge and skill ordinarily possessed by others in the profession. One aspect of competence requires that a legal problem be researched with intellectual honesty. **Intellectual honesty** includes researching and analyzing a problem objectively. Do not let emotions, preconceived notions, personal views, or stubbornness interfere with an objective analysis of the client's case. Do not assume you know the law. Check your resources. Just because you "feel" a certain outcome should occur, do not let that feeling prevent you from objectively researching and analyzing the issue.

For Example

The person who interviews clients in a law office has a personal history of domestic violence. When he was a child, there was domestic violence in the home. He thus has a strong aversion to domestic violence and harbors a prejudice against perpetrators of domestic violence. He interviews a client who complains, the night before the interview, her husband hit her in the face with his fist. She states he has beaten her frequently and savagely throughout their 10-year marriage. The client appears to have been severely beaten. She has two black eyes, and her face is swollen around the eyes.

The interviewer is outraged and upset by what happened to the client. As a result of his outrage, he fails to conduct a thorough and objective interview. He does not ask questions to elicit the details of the events of the previous night. He assumes the battery was unprovoked and does not ask questions concerning the reasons the client's husband hit her. His emotions and personal feelings cause him to focus on punishing the husband.

The interviewer knows that in addition to the remedies available under the criminal law, a civil cause of action for domestic battery is available under the state's recently passed domestic violence statute. He recommends that the supervising attorney file a civil complaint for domestic battery under the domestic violence statute. Relying on the paralegal's record for thoroughness, the supervising attorney directs that a complaint be drafted and filed.

A few weeks later, the husband's counsel, a friend of the supervising attorney, calls concerning the case. "Why did you file this complaint?" she asks. "My client was acting in self-defense. He hit his wife after she stabbed him." As it turns out, the client decided to kill her husband rather than face a future of continued beatings. She took a kitchen knife and stabbed him in the chest. In self-defense, he hit her once, and the blow caught her between the eyes, causing the two black eyes and facial swelling.

Had the interviewer not lost his objectivity, he would have conducted a thorough interview. Probing questions concerning the events of the night in question would have revealed all the facts, and the lawsuit might not have been filed.

This is an extreme example, but loss of objectivity occurs in varying degrees. Personal prejudices, personal beliefs, or sympathy for the client can combine to affect objectivity, which may lead to a failure to conduct an objective, critical analysis of the case, to not vigorously pursue potential opposing arguments, or to discount opposing authority.

Remember, the client may not be telling the whole truth. This may not be intentional. It may be the result of forgetfulness or a personal tendency to discount or downplay the importance of adverse facts. In this example, the client may have been so focused upon the years of abuse, and the desire to escape from further abuse, that she truly considered the stabbing insignificant when weighed against her past experiences.

Pursue the analysis of all legal issues with intellectual honesty. Identify all facts affecting the case. Locate all legal authority concerning the issues, including any authority that may negatively affect the client's position. Ignoring adverse authority will not make it go away. Most state and federal courts either have a rule or have issued a court opinion directing that adverse law be presented and addressed. The importance of counterargument and counteranalysis is detailed in Chapter 13.

For additional rules of ethics, refer to the National Association of Legal Assistants (NALA) Code of Ethics and Professional Responsibility and the Model Standards and Guidelines for Utilization of Paralegals, available at http://www.nala.org; and the National Federation of Paralegal Associations (NFPA) Model Code of Ethics and Professional Responsibility and Guidelines for Enforcement, available at http://www.paralegals.org.

C. When to Stop Researching

Many students new to legal research ask, "When do I know to stop researching?" This question arises in two situations. The first is when to quit researching a specific source if you find nothing. The second, and more common, situation is when to stop researching after finding several legal sources that address the research topic. In other words, when is your research complete? Both of these situations are discussed in this section.

1. When to Stop Researching If You Find Nothing

One of the more difficult problems is when to stop looking if your research fails to produce any results.

There are several different approaches to take in this situation.

a. Look to Another Source of Law

In the previous example, there may simply be no statutory law that governs the question. Then, once you have conducted research using all the possible terms the statute may be categorized under, it is time to look to another source, such as case law. It may be that the subject is covered by federal rather than state law. If you have exhausted all possible avenues of research under a specific source, look to another source.

b. Reconsider the Issue and Key/Search Terms

It may be that your issue or search terms are stated so broadly or narrowly that your search turns up nothing.

For Example

The issue is stated as: "Is a will valid when the testator wrote 'invalid' on the title page of the will?" The researcher finds nothing when looking in the statutory index under *wills, testator,* and *validity.* A simple rephrasing of the issue to "Is a will validly revoked when the testator wrote 'invalid' on the title page of the will?" might improve the research results. Expanding the search terms to include *revoked* or *revocation* may lead to the answer.

In this regard, it may be necessary to consult the person who gave you the assignment for guidance or to make sure the assignment is clear. In addition, reference to a secondary source such as a treatise may help you reframe the issue or identify additional key/search terms.

c. Reconsider the Legal Theory

It may be that you have incorrectly analyzed the question and are searching in the wrong area of law. Review the question to see if another area of law may be involved. It may be necessary to consult a secondary source such as a legal encyclopedia for an overview of the law that compiles all the ways a topic may be addressed.

For Example

The client runs a small business and a competitor induced a customer of the client to breach a contract with the client. Because the matter involves breach of contract, the researcher looks to state contract law for remedies that may be available against the competitor and finds nothing. The matter, however, is governed by the state's tort law: the tort of interference with contractual relations. Reference to contract law in a legal encyclopedia will reveal that third-party interference with a contract is often governed by tort law.

d. Matters of First Impression

It may be that the issue you are researching has not been addressed in your state; that is, it is a matter of first impression with no law on the subject in your jurisdiction. If this is so, refer to a secondary source such as a legal encyclopedia, treatise, or *ALR* annotation to identify how other jurisdictions have answered the question. The results of your research should not simply inform the supervising attorney that the state has not decided the matter. It should include the various ways in which other states have addressed the question.

2. When to Stop Researching after Finding Several Legal Sources

A more difficult problem is to know when to stop researching after finding several sources. There may be an endless variety of sources that address a specific question you are researching. There may be a statute, case law, encyclopedia references, *ALR* annotations, law review articles, and so on. There is no simple answer to the question of when to stop. Learning when to stop becomes intuitive with experience. The following considerations may help you determine when to stop.

a. Stop When You Have Found the Answer

The first research step is to find the primary authority that answers the question. If the primary authority clearly answers the question, then stop researching.

There may be case law directly on point that answers the question being researched. If this is the situation, then you must Shepardize or KeyCite the case to determine if it is good law and identify any cases that may criticize or affect its application. In addition, check the appropriate digest for other cases that may analyze the issue differently. Also, check a secondary source such as an *ALR* annotation on the topic for authority that may provide a different analysis. Include any cases that are on point in the research.

b. When You Find Several Authorities on the Research Topic

Keep the following factors in mind if you locate several authorities that address the research issue.

(1) Primary Authority (Constitutions, Statutes, Cases) Always try to find a mandatory primary authority source(s) for each issue. If you have several cases that address the topic, use the mandatory authority cases. If you have case law that is mandatory authority, you do not need persuasive authority such as cases from other jurisdictions.

If you have several mandatory authority cases, select the case that is most on point, that most clearly analyzes the law, and is most recent. Courts, or the person reading your research, do not have time to read through numerous cases addressing the same legal arguments. Select only the lead case or cases.

(2) Secondary Authority You do not need to include secondary sources in your research if the primary authority clearly provides the answer to the issue. However, you may wish to include secondary authority sources to support your research if they specifically address the research topic. A reference to an *ALR* annotation or law review article on the issue allows the reader to review a comprehensive analysis of the topic if additional reference is desired.

If there is no primary authority on a topic, then reference to secondary authority is necessary. The more specific the secondary authority source, the better.

For Example

If you have a legal encyclopedia citation that generally addresses the question being researched and an *ALR* annotation that specifically addresses the question, the *ALR* annotation is preferable.

Courts often refer to *Restatements of the Law, ALR* annotations, law review articles, and treatises when relying on secondary authority.

c. Other Factors Governing When to Stop

Time and economic factors may govern how thorough your research should be and when you should stop. The assignment may be governed by a short time constraint, or you may be informed to not spend too much time on the project because the potential claim is small. The assignment may be to draft a three-page legal memorandum. Each of these situations limits the amount of research to be performed.

When this occurs, first locate the primary authority that answers or addresses the question, that is, the enacted law (statute, etc.) that applies and the case law that is on point. Follow the research sequence presented earlier in this chapter until you run out of time.

Discuss the amount of research time you should spend on the project when it is assigned. If you find that you are running out of time or the project is more complex than you anticipated, consult your supervisor.

V. KEY POINTS CHECKLIST: Legal Research and Analysis

✓ Always pay attention to the facts. Keep them in mind when performing each step of the analytical process. The analysis process involves determining how the law applies to the facts. Make sure you have all the *facts* at the outset.

✓ Before beginning the IRAC process, perform preliminary research to become familiar with the area of law involved in the case.

✓ Remember IRAC. An easy way to remember the legal analysis process and what to look for when reading a court opinion is to use the acronym IRAC: *i*ssue, *r*ule, *a*nalysis/*a*pplication, and *c*onclusion.

✓ When conducting research, locate the primary authority that governs the issue first. If there is no primary authority that applies or additional authority is needed to help interpret the primary authority, then look to secondary authority.

✓ When conducting legal analysis, address one issue at a time. If the assignment involves several issues, consider each issue separately. Complete the analysis of one issue before proceeding to the next issue. By doing so, you will be more efficient and avoid confusion.

✓ Remember counteranalysis. Always look for authority or arguments counter to your position.

✓ Stay focused. Concentrate on the specific issue you are assigned to analyze and the facts of the client's case. Keep asking yourself, "What must be decided about the facts of this case?"

✓ Maintain intellectual honesty. Do not lose your objectivity. Do not let personal beliefs or feelings interfere with a thorough legal analysis.

VI. APPLICATION

The steps of the analytical process are illustrated here through their application to the hypothetical presented at the beginning of the chapter.

Marian's new assignment requires her to analyze the Lietel case, identify the issues, and determine if Mr. Lietel has any cause of action against Steve Spear. Marian realizes that she must first familiarize herself with all the information concerning the facts of the case. She reviews the case file and all interviews that have been conducted. Next, she reviews the notes from the legal research and analysis course she took when she was studying for her paralegal degree. She notes a four-step approach for analyzing a case:

STEP 1:   *Issue.* Identify the issue (legal question) or issues raised by the facts of the client's case.

STEP 2:   *Rule.* Identify the law that governs the issue.

STEP 3:   *Analysis/Application.* Determine how the rule of law applies to the issue.

STEP 4:   *Conclusion.* Summarize the results of the legal analysis.

A. Battery Issue

STEP 1: Identify the Issue(s)

Assume for the purposes of this problem that there is no question concerning the lawfulness of the citizen's arrest by Steve Spear. He had authority to make a citizen's arrest.

Marian, based upon her education and experience as a paralegal, quickly identifies two possible civil causes of action that Mr. Lietel may have against Mr. Spear:

1. Battery
2. Intentional infliction of emotional distress

From her training, Marian knows that the best approach to legal analysis is to address and completely analyze one issue before proceeding to the next one. She decides to begin with the battery issue.

Marian knows that the issue is the legal question raised by the facts of the client's case; therefore, the statement of the issue must include reference to the law and the facts. She identifies the issue as follows: Under the state's tort law, does a civil battery occur when an individual encounters resistance while making a lawful arrest, uses force to overcome the resistance, and kicks the person being arrested several times after the resistance ceases?

STEP 2: Identify the Rule of Law

The second step is to identify the rule of law governing battery. Marian first looks for any state statute that defines civil battery. Based upon her familiarity with tort law, she is fairly certain that civil battery is defined in the case law, and there is no applicable statutory law. She researches the statutes, however, to be sure that the state legislature has not enacted any legislation concerning civil battery. Her research reveals that there is no statute. She finds that the case law definition of *battery* adopted by the state's highest court is: "A civil battery is the unprivileged, intentional, and harmful or offensive contact with the person of another."

STEP 3: Analysis/Application

The third step is a determination of how the rule of law applies to the facts of the client's case. This is a three-part process:

- Part 1: Identify the component parts (elements) of the rule of law.
- Part 2: Apply the facts of the client's case to the component parts.
- Part 3: Consider the possible counterarguments to the analysis of an issue (i.e., conduct a counteranalysis of the analysis).

a. Part 1: Identify the Components (Elements) of the Rule of Law

After reviewing the definition of battery, Marian identifies the following elements that are required to be present for a battery to occur:

1. Unprivileged
2. Intentional
3. Harmful or offensive
4. Contact

b. Part 2: Apply the Facts of the Client's Case to the Component Parts (Elements)

If the elements of the case law are met or established by the facts of the case, then a cause of action exists. Elements 2, 3, and 4 appear to be clearly established by the facts of the case. Mr. Spear's actions of kicking Mr. Lietel were clearly intentional and harmful and did contact Mr. Lietel's body. Admittedly, Mr. Spear was making a lawful citizen's arrest, and he did encounter resistance. Did the continued use of force after resistance ceased constitute a battery? Was the continued use of force unprivileged?

The case law definition of battery does not provide sufficient guidance for a determination of whether the conduct was unprivileged. Marian must, therefore, refer to additional case law to determine what constitutes "unprivileged" contact. She looks for a court opinion that is on point—an opinion with facts similar to the client's facts in which the court addressed the question of the use of force in making a lawful arrest.

Assume that she finds the case of *Art v. Kelly*. In this case, an off-duty police officer, while making a citizen's arrest, continued to use force after the arrest had occurred and resistance had ceased. The court held that whenever a lawful arrest is made, either by a citizen or a law enforcement officer, the privilege to use force in conducting the arrest ceases when resistance ceases. Any continued use of force is a civil battery.

Applying the rule from *Art v. Kelly* to the facts of the case, Marian concludes that the requirements of the first element are met. Although Mr. Spear may have been privileged to use force to overcome resistance when making the citizen's arrest, the continued use of force after resistance ceased constituted a battery under the rule announced in *Art v. Kelly*. Marian concludes that a cause of action exists for civil battery. Mr. Spear's actions of kicking Mr. Lietel after Mr. Lietel had ceased resisting constituted unprivileged, intentional, harmful contact with Mr. Lietel.

c. Part 3: Conduct a Counteranalysis

Before proceeding, Marian should conduct a counteranalysis, identifying and addressing any counterarguments to the analysis.

For Example

Suppose Marian found a court decision involving an arrest by law enforcement officers holding that some continued use of force after resistance ceases is permissible if the situation is extremely heated. The court reasoned that law enforcement officers are not perfect, and if the situation is extremely heated, the brief continued use of force is privileged. In Marian's analysis, she would have to include the case in her memorandum and discuss how it does or does not apply to the facts of the client's case.

STEP 4: Conclusion

The final step in the analysis of the battery issue is a conclusion. When applying the rule of law to the facts of the case in step 3, Marian reaches a conclusion that there is a cause of action for civil battery in Mr. Lietel's case. Law firms vary with regard to what should be included in the conclusion. Marian's conclusion could include, among other things, any or all of the following:

- A summary of the analysis

For Example

"The case law defines battery as the nonprivileged, intentional, harmful, or offensive contact with the person of another. In the court opinion of *Art v. Kelly*, the court stated that when a lawful arrest is being made, the continued use of force after resistance ceases is unprivileged. Mr. Spear's actions of kicking Mr. Lietel after Mr. Lietel had ceased resisting constituted unprivileged, intentional, harmful contact with Mr. Lietel. Therefore, a cause of action for civil battery is available in this case."

- A weighing or consideration, based on the analysis, of the merits of the cause of action.

For Example

"There is strong support for a battery claim in this case. The testimony of the witnesses supports Mr. Lietel's statements that Mr. Spear kicked him after he was subdued. All the elements of the cause of action are established by the facts of the case. Under the rule of *Art v. Kelly*, Mr. Spear's continued use of force was clearly unprivileged."

- An identification of additional facts or information that may be necessary. In this case, the statements of additional witnesses or other information may be required.
- The identification of further research that may be required. Further research may be necessary because part of the research could not be performed due to time constraints (the memo was due) or the research sources were not readily available.
- The identification of other issues or causes of action that became apparent during the analysis of the case, which is not necessary in this example because Marian's assignment is to identify all possible causes of action and issues. Suppose Marian's supervisory attorney believed that only a battery claim was present in this case and Marian's assignment was to address that issue. If her analysis of the battery issue revealed other possible causes of action, she should mention those possibilities in her conclusion.

B. Intentional Infliction of Emotional Distress Issue

When performing step 1, Marian identified intentional infliction of emotional distress as a possible cause of action. After concluding her analysis of the battery claim, she follows the same steps in analyzing the possibility of an intentional infliction of emotional distress claim.

STEP 1: Identify the Issue.

As with the battery issue, Marian knows that this issue is the legal question raised by the facts of the client's case; therefore, the statement of the issue must include reference to the law and the facts. She identifies the issue as follows: Under the state's tort law, does intentional infliction of emotional distress occur when an individual, who encounters resistance while making a lawful arrest, kicks the party being arrested six times after the resistance has ceased, causing the party to have trouble sleeping and be fearful whenever he sees the individual?

STEP 2: Rule of Law

Marian's research reveals that there is no statutory cause of action for intentional infliction of emotional distress. The state case law does establish a cause of action for intentional infliction of emotional distress. There is no cause of action for negligent infliction of emotional distress. Intentional infliction of emotional distress is defined in the case law as intentionally causing severe emotional distress by an act of extreme or outrageous conduct.

STEP 3: Analysis/Application

a. Part 1: Identify the Components (Elements) of the Rule of Law

Marian's review of the case law reveals four elements:

1. Extreme or outrageous conduct
2. Intent to cause severe emotional distress
3. Severe emotional distress is suffered
4. The conduct causes the distress

b. Part 2: Apply the Facts of the Client's Case to the Elements

Marian's application of the elements to the facts of Mr. Lietel's raises several questions about whether the requirements of intentional infliction of emotional distress are met in this case

1. Was Mr. Spear's conduct "extreme or outrageous"?
2. Mr. Spear obviously intended to kick Mr. Lietel, but did he intend to cause severe emotional distress?
3. Was the harm suffered by Mr. Lietel "severe emotional distress"?

The answers to these questions are not apparent from a reading of the definition of intentional infliction of emotional distress. Marian turns to additional case law for guidance and locates the case of *Addik v. Garay*, which appears to answer her questions. In the case, Mr. Garay and Mr. Addik got into a fight at a party. Garay knocked Addik down and, while Addik was down, kicked him multiple times yelling, "I'm not gonna kill you, but you'll remember me in your dreams. You'll never forget this." Addik was so affected by the incident that he had a nervous breakdown and was out of work for two months.

The court, addressing Addik's claim for intentional infliction of emotional distress, ruled that public humiliation, such as that suffered by Addik, constitutes "extreme and outrageous conduct." Ruling that the requisite intent was present, the court held that there must be some *specific conduct* indicating an intent to cause emotional distress. The mere intentional act of kicking was not sufficient to evidence an intent to cause emotional distress, but Mr. Garay's statements while kicking Mr. Addik were specific conduct indicating an intent to cause emotional distress. The court went on to rule that the emotional distress suffered must be severe: The mere loss of sleep is not sufficient. Instead, severe harm, such as loss of work or medical expenses, must result.

Applying the guidelines presented in *Addik v. Garay*, Marian concludes that there is probably not a cause of action for intentional infliction of emotional distress in Mr. Lietel's case. Mr. Spear's conduct of kicking Mr. Lietel in public is sufficiently extreme and outrageous. It is questionable, however, whether the requirements of elements 2 and 3, intent and severe emotional distress, are met by the facts of the case. There was no conduct by Mr. Spear evidencing a specific intent to cause emotional distress. According to *Addik v. Garay*, the act of kicking alone was not sufficient evidence of such intent. If Mr. Lietel's loss of work and medical expenses resulted from the battery and were not related to the emotional distress, then there is no evidence that Mr. Lietel suffered severe harm as required by *Addik v. Garay*. Fearfulness and loss of sleep are probably not sufficiently severe to meet the *Garay* standards.

c. Part 3: Counteranalysis

In this part, Marian would identify and address any authority or counterarguments to her analysis. We will assume that she did not identify any counterargument to her analysis of the emotional distress issue.

STEP 4: Conclusion

As with the battery issue, Marian begins her conclusion with a summary of the analysis.

For Example

The case law definition of *intentional infliction of emotional distress* is the intentional causing of severe emotional distress by an act of extreme or outrageous conduct. In the case of *Addik v. Garay*, the court ruled that:

1. Public humiliation by kicking constitutes outrageous conduct.

2. The act of kicking alone is not sufficient evidence of intent—there must be additional conduct evidencing an intent to cause severe emotional distress.

3. Severe harm must result from the severe emotional distress.

In Mr. Lietel's case, there is no evidence of the required intent, and it is questionable whether there was severe harm. Therefore, a cause of action for intentional infliction of emotional distress does not appear to be present.

Marian may include some other items in her conclusion similar to those presented in the conclusion to the battery issue.

For Example

Marian may identify additional information that is needed. She may note that the client and witnesses should be reinterviewed to determine whether Mr. Spear said anything while he was kicking Mr. Lietel.

Summary

Most clients enter the law office with a problem that must be analyzed and solved. Legal analysis of the problem involves the identification of the legal issues in the client's case and a determination of what law applies and how it applies. The commonly used legal analysis format involves four steps:

1. Identification of the legal issue or issues
2. Identification of the rule of law that governs the issue
3. Analysis and application of the rule of law to the facts of the case. This step is composed of three parts:
   a. A determination of the elements or requirements of the rule of law
   b. A matching of the facts of the client's case to the elements and a determination of how the rule of law applies to the facts
   c. A counteranalysis that addresses any counterarguments to the analysis
4. A conclusion that summarizes the previous steps. The conclusion may also include a weighing of the merits of the case and an identification of other information or avenues of research that should be pursued.

The four steps of the analysis process can be easily referred to and remembered by the acronym IRAC: *i*ssue, *r*ule, *a*nalysis/*a*pplication, and *c*onclusion.

It is important to keep three general considerations in mind when engaging in legal research and analysis:

1. Focus
2. Intellectual honesty
3. When to stop researching

Stay focused on the task. Focus on the facts of the client's case, and analyze only the issue or issues raised by those facts. Avoid being distracted by interesting or related issues that need not be addressed.

Perform analysis with intellectual honesty. Always look for the correct answer, even though that answer may not be in the client's favor or in accordance with your beliefs. Do not let preferences, prejudices, or politics interfere with your duty to objectively and honestly analyze the legal question. Base the conclusion on an objective analysis of all the facts and law and include both the supporting and opposing positions.

Quick References

Internet Resources

The following sites may provide useful support information to paralegals engaged in legal analysis.

http://www.nala.org

This is the site for the National Association for Legal Assistants (NALA). The NALA site provides a wealth of information, ranging from articles on the profession to education and certification programs for paralegals. It includes information on court decisions affecting paralegals and links to other related sites.

http://www.paralegals.org

This is the web page for the National Federation of Paralegal Associations (NFPA), another national paralegal organization. The web page provides links to a wide range of sites of interest to paralegals: research sources, publications, products, and so forth.

http://www.paralegaltoday.com

Paralegal Today is a magazine geared toward the needs of paralegals. It often includes helpful articles on legal analysis and writing.

Using http://www.google.com as a search engine and "IRAC legal analysis" as a topic can identify several hundred websites (too many to list here) related to the topic "legal analysis and the IRAC process."

Exercises

ASSIGNMENT 1

Describe in detail the steps of the IRAC legal analysis process.

ASSIGNMENT 2

Client's Facts

The client found a check written out to cash in the amount of $750. The check was completely made out when he found it. He took it to the bank, signed it on the back as instructed by the teller, and cashed it. He was subsequently arrested and charged with forgery.

Rule of Law

Section 30-236 of the state penal code defines *forgery* as "falsely making or altering any signature to, or any part of, any writing purporting to have any legal efficacy with intent to injure or defraud."

Section 45-3-109d of the state commercial code provides that when a negotiable instrument is made out to cash it is a "bearer instrument." The section goes on to provide: "A bearer instrument refers to an instrument that is payable to anyone possessing the instrument and is negotiable by transfer alone, it is the same as cash." Note: A check is a negotiable instrument.

Assignment: Based on the information presented in the problem, prepare a complete and detailed analysis of the question of whether there is sufficient evidence to support a charge of forgery.

ASSIGNMENT 3

Client's Facts

The client is charged with burglary. He broke a window, entered his neighbor's garage, and took three cases of beer. The garage is a separate building located about six feet from the neighbor's house.

Rule of Law

Section 2397 of the state penal code defines *burglary* as the breaking and entering of the dwelling house of another with the intent to commit a crime.

Case Law

In the case of *State v. Nelson*, the court ruled that "a dwelling includes outbuildings close to but not physically connected with a dwelling house, if such buildings are capable of being fenced in."

Assignment: Based on the information presented in the problem, prepare a complete and detailed analysis of the question of whether there is sufficient evidence to support a charge of burglary.

ASSIGNMENT 4

Client's Facts

The client is a local public library that has recently decided to allow an anonymous Internet browsing network called Sepositus to use its servers. Sepositus allows people to communicate anonymously. It relies on layers of computers all over the world to hide the identity of its users. It is essentially a web browser.

Because the library is a local public library, the city council approves the budget of the library. The city council warned the library that if it allowed Sepositus to use its servers, the city would revoke the portion of the library's budget that went to its computer network system, which includes the servers that house the library catalog, patron records (like checkout records and overdue fine records), and allow access to e-books, as well as the computers used by patrons to search the library catalog, and use the Internet at computers housed at the library. After the library's Sepositus node went live the city council held a special session and revoked the portion of the budget that went to the library's computer network system. The library claims the action violates its rights to intellectual freedom, freedom to read, and privacy rights. The library believes intellectual freedom and freedom of communication is essential to maintaining a democracy.

The law firm handles cases involving the violation of constitutional and privacy rights.

Assignment: The researcher is assigned the task of identifying and analyzing the possible causes of action that the client may have against the city council.

   a. Discuss and describe in detail the steps you should follow when conducting the legal analysis.

   b. Assume there are possible causes of action based on freedom of speech under the First Amendment and equal protection under the Fourteenth Amendment. For each issue, describe in detail each step of the analytical process.

   c. Discuss factors that may possibly affect a researcher's objectivity and how those factors could affect the legal analysis of the problem.

ASSIGNMENT 5

Client's Facts

The client was cited for passing in a no-passing zone. Frustrated by a slow-moving vehicle on a two-lane highway, the client admits that he passed the vehicle entirely in a no-passing zone—that he began and ended the passing maneuver in an area where the center of the road was marked with two solid stripes. There was no oncoming traffic, and he made the maneuver safely.

Rule of Law

The state's motor vehicle code, Section 293–301, provides that it is a violation of state law to pass a vehicle in a no-passing zone. In the statute, a no-passing zone is defined as that portion of the road marked by two solid lines painted in the center of the road. Passing zones are indicated by single, eight-foot stripes down the center of the road.

Case Law

The only relevant case on the subject is *State v. Roth*. In that case, Mr. Roth was cited for improper passing. He began the passing maneuver in the last 30 feet of a no-passing zone and completed it in a passing zone. There were no oncoming vehicles. Evidence presented to the trial court established that the last 30 feet of the no-passing zone should have been marked as part of the passing zone. Mr. Roth appealed his conviction in the trial court. On appeal, the state's highest court held that the purpose of the state motor vehicle code is to ensure safety on the public highways. The court ruled that Mr. Roth's passing maneuver was clearly made safely, and in light of the evidence that the no-passing zone was improperly marked, a strict reading of the statute was not appropriate. Mr. Roth's conviction was set aside.

Assignment: The researcher is assigned the task of analyzing the likelihood that the client's ticket can be set aside.

a. Based upon the information presented in the problem, conduct an analysis of the client's case and prepare a complete and detailed analysis of the problem.

b. Repeat assignment a, assuming the following facts: The client began the passing maneuver approximately 20 feet from the end of the no-passing zone and completed it in a passing zone. There was no oncoming traffic, and the client completed the maneuver safely.

c. Repeat assignment a, assuming the following facts: The client began the passing maneuver in a passing zone, but completed it in a no-passing zone.

d. What additional information, if any, may be necessary for a complete analysis of the preceding problems?

ASSIGNMENT 6

What should you do when you do not find anything while researching a specific source? After finding several legal sources that address the research topic, what considerations should you keep in mind concerning when to stop researching?

Part 2

Legal Research

Overview

Legal research is the process of locating the law that applies to the question raised by the facts of the case. Legal research and analysis are interrelated, and performing legal research usually involves the use of analysis principles. It is helpful, however, to have an understanding of legal research sources and the legal research process before studying the legal analysis process.

Part II covers legal research and the research process. It begins with two chapters on primary authority, specifically enacted law (statutory and administrative) and case law, followed by two chapters on secondary authority. It concludes with a chapter on computers and legal research.

Chapter 3

Constitutions, Statutes, Administrative Law, and Court Rules—Research and Analysis

Learning Objectives

After completing this chapter, you should understand:

- The meaning of statutory law
- The components of a statute
- How to find constitutional, statutory, and administrative law and court rules
- How to analyze a statute and apply it to specific problems
- The role of legislative history and canons of construction

Alan attended one year of paralegal classes before being admitted to law school. After his first year, he obtained a part-time job with a law firm. Initially, Alan's assignments had involved the preparation of deposition digests. He is good at preparing deposition digests but wants to be involved in projects in the early stages of the litigation process. At his request, he was assigned to work exclusively with Ms. Tilton, who is a litigation attorney specializing in corporation and contract law.

His first assignment from Ms. Tilton is to determine if Mr. Jackson has a cause of action against Outdoor Extreme Sports for breach of warranty under the sales provisions of the state's commercial code. Mr. Jackson went to Outdoor Extreme Sports to get their "premium beginner safety climbing kit." Outdoor Extreme Sports made no warranties about the climbing gear in the kit. It did not provide Mr. Jackson, either orally or in writing, any statements concerning the quality of the climbing gear.

Three days after Mr. Jackson bought the beginner climbers kit, he went climbing at Mt. Crag. Mr. Jackson was 10 feet off the ground when he lost his grip and fell from the rock wall. The climbing rope would have kept him from falling more than 4 or 5 feet, but the climbing harness severed at the seams as the rope was pulled tight. Consequently, Mr. Jackson fell the entire distance to the ground. He was very lucky and only suffered a broken arm and a great deal of bruising.

Alan's assignment is to determine if there is a possible breach of warranty claim under the state's commercial code.

Alan has not worked with statutes since he took a paralegal research course. Several questions occur to him: "How do I find the commercial code statutes? Does the Commercial Code Sales Act apply? Is this a sale of goods within the meaning of the act? If this is a sale of goods, which warranty applies? How do you analyze a statute?"

I. INTRODUCTION

This chapter focuses on how to research and analyze enacted law and court rules. As discussed in Chapter 1, enacted law includes constitutions (governing documents adopted by the people), laws passed by legislative bodies, and the rules and regulations adopted by administrative agencies.

Laws passed by Congress or state legislatures are generally called *acts* or *statutes*. This body of law is commonly referred to as **statutory law**. **Ordinances** are laws usually passed by local governing bodies, such as city councils and county commissions, and thus are statutory law. Administrative agencies, under the authority granted by legislative bodies, adopt rules and regulations that have the force of law. Courts adopt rules that regulate the conduct of matters brought before the court.

Statutory law is a major source of law that a researcher must become familiar with when researching and analyzing the law. Statutory law has assumed an ever-increasing role in the United States, as has administrative law. With the passage of time, the body of statutory and administrative law has expanded greatly. Many matters once governed by case law are now governed by these two forms of enacted law.

Consequently, with the growth of statutory law, more and more legal problems and issues are governed by it. Because an ever-increasing number of legal problems and issues require the interpretation and application of statutory law, researchers are more frequently called upon to engage in statutory analysis. **Statutory analysis** is the process of determining if a statute applies, how it applies, and the effect of that application. That same process is used regarding administrative law.

Due to the increase in statutory and administrative law governing legal issues, many researchers begin by identifying the applicable statutory or administrative law, reading it, and engaging in statutory analysis to determine whether and how a statute or regulation applies in a specific fact situation. This is often followed by reviewing court opinions (case law) and other sources that interpret the law.

The focus of this chapter is the process of statutory research and analysis. It begins with a presentation of the anatomy of a statute, follows with a discussion of the process of statutory research and analysis, and ends with general considerations involving statutory construction and analysis. For the sake of clarity, throughout this chapter the discussion and examples focus upon laws passed by legislative bodies, that is, statutory law. Note, however, that the principles presented in the chapter also apply to the analysis of constitutions, administrative law, and court rules.

II. ANATOMY OF A STATUTE

Before you can analyze a statute, you must be familiar with the basic structure of statutory law. Assume, for the purposes of illustration, you are interested in whether a contract for the sale of goods must be in writing, and the governing law is the Arizona Revised Statutes. Exhibits 3-1 through 3-4 show selected portions of the Arizona Revised Statutes concerning commercial law, specifically the chapter on sales. Exhibit 3-5 presents the section of the *United States Code Annotated* (U.S.C.A.) concerning ransom money. To the left of sections of the codes (in the margins) are terms that describe the components of the codes. The following text discusses those components. Not all of the statutory components discussed are included in every statute. For example, some statutes may not have a definitions section. It is important, however, to discuss the components so you will be familiar with them if you encounter them in other statutes.

Understanding the structure of statutory law is essential to conducting effective statutory analysis. A researcher must be able to identify whether the **statutory scheme** (the organizational structure of the statutory law) assists in determining if a particular statute is applicable to a set of facts or whether other sources, such as legislative history or case law, need to be consulted to determine the applicability of the law.

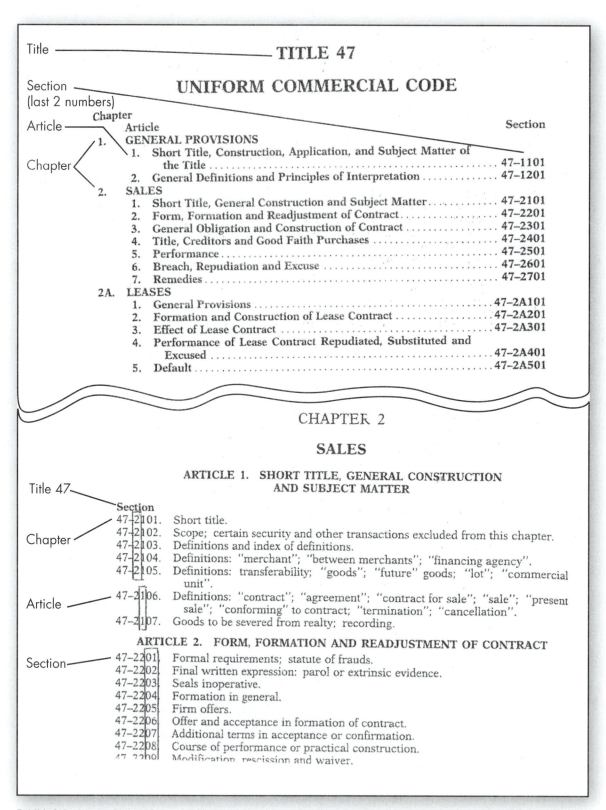

Exhibit 3-1 Arizona Revised Statutes, Title 47—Uniform Commercial Code, Table of Contents excerpt and Chapter 2—Sales, excerpt of Table of Contents for Articles I and II. Reprinted from Arizona Revised Statutes Annotated with the permission of Thomson Reuters.

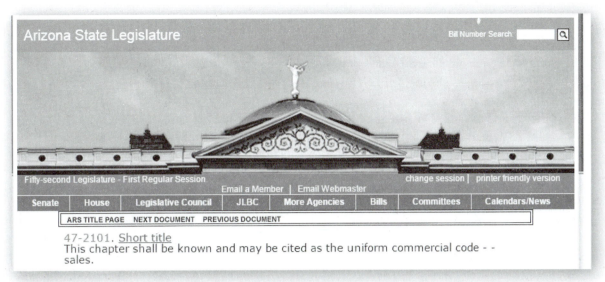

Exhibit 3-2   A.R.S. § 47-2101. Arizona Revised Statutes from Arizona Legislature webpage (2016). *Source: http://www.azleg.gov/ FormatDocument.asp?inDoc=/ars/47/02101.htm&Title=47&DocType=ARS*

A. Numbers

Each statute has numbers assigned for each part of the statute. These numbers represent the organizational structure, or statutory scheme, of the particular statutory code. Every legislative authority— local, state, and federal—follows a different numbering system. It is not practical to discuss separately the numbering system for every statutory code; however, there are some general similarities that can be addressed.

Most laws are usually divided into broad categories, each of which is assigned a number. Those broad categories are divided into topics or smaller categories that are also assigned a number. The topics are further divided into subtopics and assigned a number, and so on. The number of categories and divisions depends on the statutory scheme of the particular legislative authority. A researcher must be able to identify and understand the particular numbering system in order to effectively conduct statutory research and analysis.

For Example

The Arizona Revised Statutes are divided into broad categories called *titles*. The Uniform Commercial Code is assigned number 47. (See "Number of Title" on top of Exhibits 3-1 and 3-2.) Each title is divided into topics called *chapters*. Chapter 2 governs sales of goods. (See "Number of Chapter" in Exhibit 3-1.) Each chapter is further divided into *articles* which contain *sections* and each section of each article is assigned a number. (See "Article" and "Section" in Exhibit 3-1.) Each article contains sections that make up the text of the statute governing a specific subject. The article of Chapter 2 that contains statutes on the form and formation of contracts is Article 2 (see Exhibit 3-1) and within that article is the specific section establishing when a contract must be in writing, section 201, called *Formal Requirements; Statute of Frauds*. (See § 47-2201 in Exhibit 3-1 and Exhibit 3-4.) Notice that the chapter number, article number, and section number are combined. Therefore, if you want to read the law in the Arizona Revised Statutes governing when a contract must be written, you refer to Title 47 (Uniform Commercial Code), Chapter 2 (Sales), article 2, section 01 (Statute of Frauds). This is known numerically as § 47-2201.

B. Short Title

The **short title** is the name by which the statute is known. It is a name that is easy to use when referring to the statute, rather than referring to it by its numbering only. Example 3-2 is an example of a short title statute from the Arizona Revised Statutes, Article 47, Chapter 2, section 101, Uniform Commercial Code— Sales (§ 47-2101).

C. Purpose Clause

The **purpose clause** includes the purpose the legislative body intended to accomplish when drafting the statute. It is helpful in determining the legislative intent, which is important in conducting statutory analysis.

D. Scope

Some statutes have sections that state specifically what is covered and not covered by the statute. These are called **scope** sections. A researcher should first review this section when analyzing a statute, because a review of this section may allow a determination at the outset whether the statute applies. Exhibit 3-3 is an example of a "scope" section from the Arizona Revised Statutes, Article 47, Chapter 2, section 102, Uniform Commercial Code—Sales (§ 47-2102).

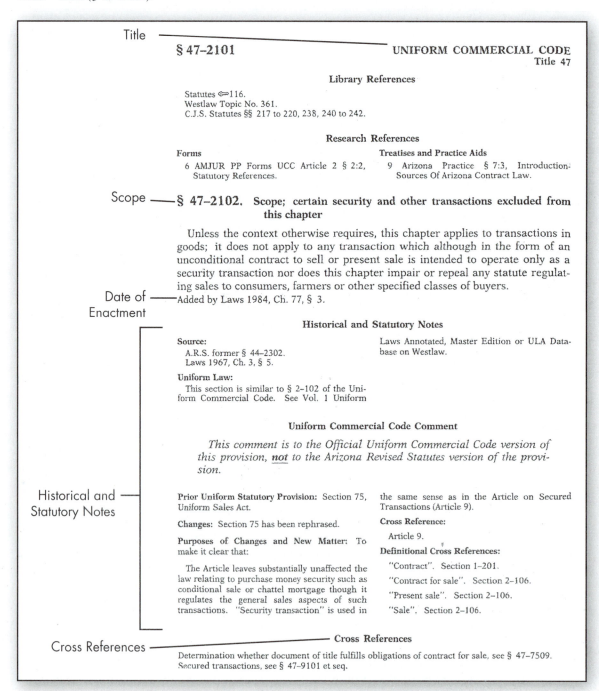

Exhibit 3-3 A.R.S. § 47-2102 and § 47-2103 with annotations. Reprinted from Arizona Revised Statutes, Title 47, with the permission of Thomson Reuters.

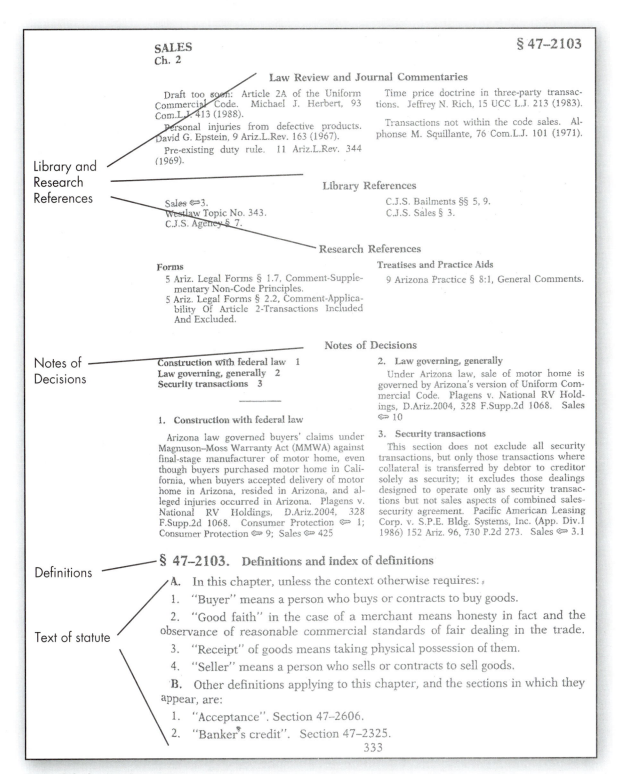

Library and Research References

Law Review and Journal Commentaries

Draft too soon: Article 2A of the Uniform Commercial Code. Michael J. Herbert, 93 Com.L.J. 413 (1988).

Personal injuries from defective products. David G. Epstein, 9 Ariz.L.Rev. 163 (1967).

Pre-existing duty rule. 11 Ariz.L.Rev. 344 (1969).

Time price doctrine in three-party transactions. Jeffrey N. Rich, 15 UCC L.J. 213 (1983).

Transactions not within the code sales. Alphonse M. Squillante, 76 Com.L.J. 101 (1971).

Library References

Sales ⟜3.
Westlaw Topic No. 343.
C.J.S. Agency § 7.

C.J.S. Bailments §§ 5, 9.
C.J.S. Sales § 3.

Research References

Forms

5 Ariz. Legal Forms § 1.7, Comment-Supplementary Non-Code Principles.
5 Ariz. Legal Forms § 2.2, Comment-Applicability Of Article 2-Transactions Included And Excluded.

Treatises and Practice Aids

9 Arizona Practice § 8:1, General Comments.

Notes of Decisions

Construction with federal law   1
Law governing, generally   2
Security transactions   3

1. Construction with federal law

Arizona law governed buyers' claims under Magnuson–Moss Warranty Act (MMWA) against final-stage manufacturer of motor home, even though buyers purchased motor home in California, when buyers accepted delivery of motor home in Arizona, resided in Arizona, and alleged injuries occurred in Arizona. Plagens v. National RV Holdings, D.Ariz.2004, 328 F.Supp.2d 1068. Consumer Protection ⟜ 1; Consumer Protection ⟜ 9; Sales ⟜ 425

2. Law governing, generally

Under Arizona law, sale of motor home is governed by Arizona's version of Uniform Commercial Code. Plagens v. National RV Holdings, D.Ariz.2004, 328 F.Supp.2d 1068. Sales ⟜ 10

3. Security transactions

This section does not exclude all security transactions, but only those transactions where collateral is transferred by debtor to creditor solely as security; it excludes those dealings designed to operate only as security transactions but not sales aspects of combined sales-security agreement. Pacific American Leasing Corp. v. S.P.E. Bldg. Systems, Inc. (App. Div.1 1986) 152 Ariz. 96, 730 P.2d 273. Sales ⟜ 3.1

Definitions / Text of statute

§ 47–2103.   Definitions and index of definitions

A.   In this chapter, unless the context otherwise requires:

1.   "Buyer" means a person who buys or contracts to buy goods.

2.   "Good faith" in the case of a merchant means honesty in fact and the observance of reasonable commercial standards of fair dealing in the trade.

3.   "Receipt" of goods means taking physical possession of them.

4.   "Seller" means a person who sells or contracts to sell goods.

B.   Other definitions applying to this chapter, and the sections in which they appear, are:

1.   "Acceptance". Section 47–2606.

2.   "Banker's credit". Section 47–2325.

333

Exhibit 3-3 *(Continued)*

For Example

You are researching a question under Arizona law involving a contract that grants a security interest in goods that are being sold. The scope section of the Uniform Commercial Code—Sales (§ 47-2102) provides that the section does not apply to such transactions. You know at the outset that the state Uniform Commercial Code does not apply and need not be considered further.

E. Definitions

Some statutes have **definitions** sections defining terms used in the statute. Those definitions sections may provide specific definitions or refer to other statutory sections within the code. (See Exhibit 3-3, § 47-2103, showing both specific definitions and references to other sections.) The definitions are helpful in determining the parties and situations covered by the provisions of the statute. Definitions also help in determining if the legislature gave specific meaning to terms within statutes. The presence or absence of a definitions section impacts the statutory analysis process. If a definition section exists, the definition of certain terms has been pre-determined by the legislative body that enacted the statutes. If there is no definition section, then other sources, such as legislative history or case law, may be needed to determine the meaning, and therefore the applicability, of a statute to a particular set of facts.

F. Substantive Provisions

The substantive sections set forth the substance of the law—the text of the law. (See Exhibits 3-4 and 3-5.) They establish the rights and duties of those governed by the statute: that which is required, prohibited, or allowed. A substantive section of the Arizona Revised Statutes addresses the question posed at the beginning of this section, "When must a contract for the sale of goods be in writing?" (See § 47-2201 in Exhibit 3-4.)

The substantive sections may include sections that provide remedies, such as fines or imprisonment in criminal cases. There may be sections governing procedure, such as which court has jurisdiction over the matters

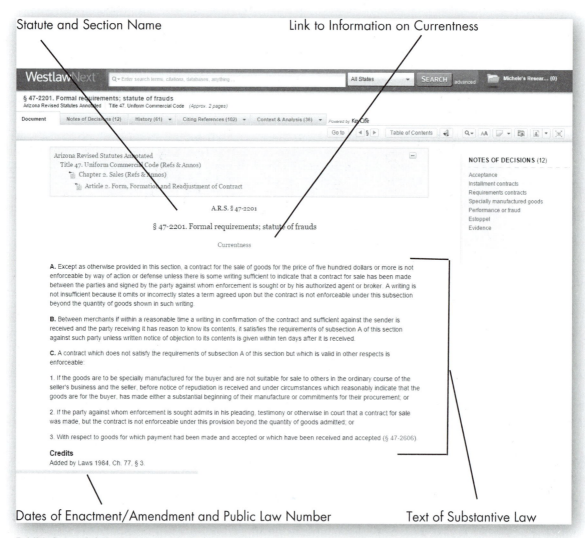

Exhibit 3-4   A.R.S. § 47-2201. Screenshot, reprinted from West Publishing, Arizona Revised Statutes Annotated, from A.R.S. § 47-2201 with permission of Thomson Reuters.

Title

Notes of. Decisions

Asylum 1

_____

1. Asylum

Native and citizen of Ethiopia had objectively reasonable fear of being subjected to female genital mutilation (FGM), as required for asylum, where state department report indicated that approximately 90% of all females in Ethiopia were subjected to some form of practice of FGM, threat of FGM came from alien's own relatives and also any future husband and his relatives, and alien was only nine-years-old at time of hearing. Abay v. Ashcroft, C.A.6 2004, 368 F.3d 634. Aliens, Immigration, And Citizenship 533

Section Number

§ 117. Domestic assault by an habitual offender [1]

(a) In generaL-Any person who commits a domestic assault within the special maritime and territorial jurisdiction of the United States or Indian country and who has a final conviction on at least 2 separate prior occasions in Federal, State, or Indian tribal court proceedings for offenses that would be, .if subject to Federal jurisdiction-

(1) any assault, sexual abuse, or serious violent felony against a spouse or intimate partner, or against a child of or in the care of the person committing the domestic assault; or

(2) an offense under chapter llOA,

shall be fined under this title, imprisoned for a term of not more than 5 years, or both, except that if substantial bodily injury result from violation under this section, the offender shall be imprisoned. for a term of not more than 10 years.

(b) Domestic assault defined.-In this section, the term "domestic assault" means an assault committed by a current or former spouse, parent, child, or guardian of the victim, by a person with whom the victim shares a child in common, by a person who is cohabitating with or has cohabitated with the victim as a spouse, parent, child, or guardian, or by a person similarly situated to a spouse, parent, child, or guardian of the victim.

(Added Pub.L. 109-162, Title IX, § 909, Jan. 5, 2006, 119 Stat. 3084; amended Pub.L. 113-104, § 3, May 20, 2014, 128 Stat. 1156.)

[1] Section was enacted without corresponding amendment to analysis.

HISTORICAL AND STATUTORY NOTES

Historical and Statutory Notes

Revision Notes and Legislative Reports
  2006 Acts. House Report No. 109-233, see 2005 U.S. Code Cong. and Adm. News, p. 1636.

References in Text
  Chapter 11OA, referred to in subsec. (a)(2), is Domestic Violence and Stalking, I'!i U.S.C.A. § 2261 et seq.

Amendments
  2014 Amendments. Subsec. (a)(l). Pub.L. 113-104, § 3, inserted ", or against a child of or in the care of the person committing the domestic assault" following "intimate partner".

Exhibit 3-5 United States Code Annotated, 18 U.S.C.A. §§ 117 & 118 with annotations. Reprinted from pages 488-489 18 U.S.C.A. §117 with permission of Thomson Reuters.

Library references
and Research References

Ch. 7   ASSAULT   18 § 119

LIBRARY REFERENCES

Corpus Juris Secundum

CJS Criminal Law§ 2321, Counsel in Prior Proceeding.

Research References

Encyclopedias

Am. Jur. 2dAssault and Battery§ 14, Federal Law.
Am. Jur. 2d Habitual Criminals & Subsequent Offenders § 16, Assistance of
    Counsel in Proceeding Resulting in Prior Conviction.
27 Am. Jur. Trials 1, Representing the Mentally Disabled Criminal Deferidant.

Notes of Decisions

Notes of Decisions

Assistan e of counsel   1

1. Assistance of counsel

Sixth Amendment prohibited admission of defendant's uncounseled convictions in tribal court for domestic violence as evidence to establish element of offense under domestic abuse by habitual offender statute, which attached federal penalty to commission of domestic assault.in Indian country, where prosecution was unable to prove that defendant had validly waived his right to counsel under the United States Constitution in the prior tribal proceedings. U.S. v.· Kirkaldie, D.Mont. 2014, 21 F.Supp.3d 1100. Criminal Law 662.40; Indians *311*

§ 118. Interference with certain protective functions

Any person who knowingly and willfully obstructs, resists, or interferes with a Federal law enforcement agent engaged, within the United. States or the special maritime territorial jurisdiction of the United States, in the performance of the protective functions authorized under section 37 of the State Department Basic Authorities Act of 1956 (22 U.S.C. 2709) or section 103 of the Diplomatic Security Act (22 U.S.C. 4802) shall be fined under this title, imprisoned not more than 1 year, or both..

Dates of Enactment

(Added Pub.L. 109-472, § 4(a), Jan. 11,2007, 120 Stat. 3555.)

LIBRARY REFERENCES

Corpus JUris Secundum

CJS Obstructing Justice or Governmental Admin. *§* 35, Generally; Statutory
    Provisions.
CJS Obstructing Justice or Governmental Admin. § 94, Federal Sentencing and
    Punishment for Obstruction.

§ 119. Protection of individuals perfor!"ing certain official duties

(a) In generaL-Whoever knowingly makes restricted personal information about a covered person, or a member of the immediate family of that covered person, publicly available-

(1) with the intent to threaten, intimidate, or incite the commission of a crime of violence against that covered person, or a member of the immediate family of that covered person; or

Exhibit 3-5 (Continued)

covered by the statute. The substantive provisions are the law the researcher refers to when addressing the client's legal problem.

G. Annotations/Reference Information

Immediately following the text of each statutory section, may be references to various sources of information related to the section. This **reference information**, usually referred to as *annotations*, includes:

- *Dates of enactment or amendment.* This information follows the text of a statutory section along with citation to the law(s) that enacted or amended the section. In print sources and commercial Internet research sources, such as Westlaw and Lexis, these immediately follow the last line of the statutory section. (See "Date of Enactment" following the text of the statutes in Exhibits 3-3 and 3-5; "Credits" in Exhibit 3-4.) Free public websites, such as state legislature websites, often do not have dates of enactment or amendment. (See Example 3-2.)
- *Historical and Statutory Notes.* This information may also refer to dates of amendment and the public law that enacted or amended the section. It often includes summaries of any amendments and previous statutory numbers if the section number has changed due to a recodification. (See the first page of Exhibit 3-3 and Exhibit 3-5 "Historical and Statutory Notes.") In many commercial Internet research sources, such as Westlaw and Lexis, historical and statutory notes may be found in hyperlinks following the text of the section, tabs above the text, hyperlinks to the side of the text, tabs on the screen where the text is displayed, or a combination of these. Free public websites, such as state legislature websites, often do not have historical and statutory notes.
- *Official comments on the section.* (See the first page of Exhibit 3-3, "Uniform Commercial Code Comment".)
- *Cross References.* This information provides cross-references to other related statutes. (See first page of Exhibit 3-3.)
- *Library References and Research References.* These provide references to other sources that may be useful when analyzing the statute, such as books, digest key numbers (see Chapter 5), law review and journal articles (see top of page 2, Exhibit 3-3), *American Law Review* (*ALR*) cites, and legal encyclopedia cites (*CJS, Am. Jur. 2d,* etc.) that discuss the section (see the last page of Exhibit 3-3 and the first page of Exhibit 3-5). The location of these types of annotations in print sources follow the text of the statutory section (see Exhibits 3-3 and 3-4), but like Historical and Statutory Notes, these annotations may be located in varying hyperlinks or tabs in commercial Internet research sources.
- *Notes of Decisions.* This particular type of annotation is helpful in many ways. These notes provide the name, citation, and summaries of key court decisions that have discussed, analyzed, or interpreted the statute. When a statute has been interpreted or referred to in a large number of cases, the cases are indexed according to subject and each category assigned a number. If you have a question concerning the interpretation of a statute, by scanning the notes you may immediately locate a case on point. This often saves time in locating a case through other means. (See the last pages of Exhibit 3-3 and Exhibit 3-5.)

Annotations are sources of information and are not part of the statute. They are not the law and do not have legal authority; therefore they themselves may not be relied upon or cited. Rather, the researcher must go to the actual court opinion and read and analyze it to determine if it is useful in answering the legal question in the client's case. (See Chapters 4 and 12.)

It is important to note not all statutory sources are annotated. If the statutory source you are working with is not annotated you would need to conduct additional research, such as case law research, secondary source research, and legislative history research to obtain the same types of information located in the annotations of an annotated source.

III. STATUTORY RESEARCH—LOCATING STATUTES

Statutory research is the process of finding the statutory law that applies to a problem. The first two parts of this section discuss statutory research sources, that is, where statutory law can be found. The third part presents research strategies or techniques, that is, how to conduct statutory research. Locating uniform laws and model acts is covered in Chapter 5. Note that the United States Constitution is included with the *United States Code Annotated* (U.S.C.A.) and the *United States Code Service* (U.S.C.S.), the main research sources for federal law, and most state constitutions are included with their state statutes. Constitutions, however, are not statutory law. The research techniques and strategies that apply to statutory research also apply to constitutional research.

A. Federal Law

1. Publication

Each law passed by Congress is assigned a public law number. The number reflects the order in which the law was passed and the session of Congress. For example, Public Law No. 107-35 was the 35th law passed by the 107th session of Congress. The full text of each law is published separately by the United States Government Printing Office (GPO) and is referred to as a **slip law.** Slip laws are available at law libraries and at public libraries that are designated as United States Government Depository Libraries. Slip laws are also available electronically through the GPO's Federal Digital System (FDsys) website (www.gpo.gov).

The *United States Code Congressional and Administrative News (USCCAN)*, published by West Publishing, is a monthly softbound pamphlet that contains all of the public laws passed in the prior month. Each softbound monthly publication also contains a cumulative index for the session and tables to locate by popular name the *United States Code* section affected. It is available in print and electronically by subscription. At the end of each Congressional session the *USCCAN* pamphlets are compiled into hardbound volumes. Note that each session of Congress lasts one year. Because there is a new Congress every two years with the election of the House of Representatives, there are two sessions for each Congress.

At the end of each session of Congress, the slip laws are placed in chronological order (according to the date the law was passed) and published in volumes titled the *United States Statutes at Large*. The *Statutes at Large* is the official compilation of the laws of each session of Congress. Because the laws are placed in chronological order, it is difficult, if not impossible, to conduct research using the *Statutes at Large*. For example, if you were assigned the task of locating the laws relating to the distribution of drugs, you would have to search every volume of the more than 120 volumes. A further impediment to research is that each volume has a separate index. There is no single index that would inform you which volumes contain laws relating to the distribution of drugs. The *Statutes at Large* are also available electronically from commercial Internet research sources such as Westlaw and LexisNexis and non-commercial sources such as the Library of Congress (www.loc.gov) and the GPO FDsys website (www.gpo.gov).

First published in 1926, the *United States Code* (U.S.C.) organizes all of the laws contained in the *Statutes at Large* by subject into 52 categories called titles, with each title covering a different area of law. (Note the titles range from 1-54, with Title 34 having been removed and Title 53 reserved.) Each title is further divided into chapters and sections. A citation to a U.S.C. statute refers to the title number, the name of the code, the section, and the year. Note that the year is the copyright date and not the year the statute was enacted.

For Example

18	U.S.C.	§	1115	(2000)
Title	Code	Section Symbol	Section No.	Year

A new edition is published every six years, and cumulative supplements called *pocket parts* are published for each volume during intervening years. The U.S.C. is the "official" code of the laws of the United States. A publication of a code of laws is considered official when the government itself publishes the code or arranges for or directs a commercial publisher to publish the code.

A drawback of the U.S.C. is that it is unannotated; it merely recites the federal statutes. It does not provide the researcher with the valuable information included in the annotations, such as library references and notes to court decisions that have interpreted the statutes. Another drawback is the six-year time period between publications of the U.S.C. Although the GPO strives to maintain an updated electronic version on its FDsys website, researchers should verify their search results through another source before relying on them. The Office of the Law Revision Council has an excellent website with the text of the U.S.C., tables, information, and links on the currency of the Code (see www.uscode.house.gov).

The two privately published annotated codes are the *United States Code Annotated* (U.S.C.A.), published by West Publishing and also available on Westlaw; and the *United States Code Service* (U.S.C.S.), published by

LexisNexis, a division of Reed Elsevier, PLC (referred to in the remainder of this text as LexisNexis). These codes are considered "unofficial" codes; that is, they are not published at the direction of the government. A discussion of these annotated codes follows.

2. United States Code Annotated

The U.S.C.A. consists of approximately 200 volumes and includes the General Index. In the front of each volume is a list of the 52 titles of the U.S.C. (see Exhibit 3-6). Each volume has a table of contents listing the chapters and features in the volume and a cite page listing the citation to use for the volume. The first volumes contain the United States Constitution with annotations. The subsequent volumes include the entire text of the titles of the U.S.C. Most titles include a title index, as well as appendix material, and each volume is periodically supplemented with pocket parts that update the main text. The appendix material may include previous sections of the *Code of Federal Regulations* and other materials such as international conventions. (See Exhibit 3-5 for an example of a U.S.C.A. section.)

a. General Index

The General Index is a softbound, multivolume set that is updated annually. It consists of descriptive words or phrases, arranged alphabetically, with headings and subheadings. Following each subheading are the title and section number(s) of the relevant statutory provision. When the reference to a section number is followed by the abbreviation *et seq.*, it means that the reference is to a group of sections beginning with that section. (See Exhibit 3-7 for an example of an index page.)

b. Pocket Parts and Supplementary Pamphlets

The hardcover volumes of the U.S.C.A. are updated with pocket parts that are placed in a pocket at the back of each volume. The pocket parts include any revisions to a statute and additional annotations, such as recent cases interpreting

TITLES OF THE UNITED STATES CODE

Title 1 General Provisions	Title 27 Intoxicating Liquors
Title 2 The Congress	Title 28 Judiciary and Judicial Procedure
Title 3 The President	Title 29 Labor
Title 4 Flag and Seal, Seat of Government, and the States	Title 30 Mineral Land and Mining
Title 5 Government Organization and Employees	Title 31 Money and Finance
Title 6 Domestic Security	Title 32 National Guard
Title 7 Agriculture	Title 33 Navigation and Navigable waters
Title 8 Aliens and Nationality	Title 35 Patents
Title 9 Arbitration	Title 36 Patriotic and National Observances, Ceremonies, and Organizations
Title 10 Armed Forces	Title 37 Pay and Allowances of the Uniformed Services
Title 11 Bankruptcy	Title 38 Veterans' Benefits
Title 12 Banks and Banking	Title 39 Postal Service
Title 13 Census	Title 40 Public Buildings, Property and Works
Title 14 Coast Guard	Title 41 Public Contracts
Title 15 Commerce and Trade	Title 42 The Public Health and Welfare
Title 16 Conservation	Title 43 Public Lands
Title 17 Copyrights	Title 44 Public Printing and Documents
Title 18 Criminal and Criminal Procedure	Title 45 Railroads
Title 19 Customs Duties	Title 46 Shipping
Title 20 Education	Title 47 Telecommunications
Title 21 Food and Drugs	Title 48 Territories and Insular Possessions
Title 22 Foreign Relations and Intercourse	Title 49 Transportation
Title 23 Highways	Title 50 War and National Defense
Title 24 Hospitals and Asylums	Title 51 National and Commercial Space Programs
Title 25 Indians	Title 52 Voting and Elections
Title 26 Internal Revenue Code	Title 54 National park Service and Related Programs

© Cengage

Exhibit 3-6 List of United States Code Titles.

the statute. If a statutory section is not included in the pocket part, the section has not been amended and there are no new annotations. The pocket parts are cumulative—they update the volume from the date of the volume's publication. For example, if the hardbound volume was published in 2009, then the 2014 pocket part will include all the changes, updates, and new cases construing the statutes contained in the volume during 2010, 2011, 2012, and 2013.

If the pocket part is too large to fit in the back of a volume, the publisher will produce a softbound supplement that sits next to the volume. Occasionally, a new hardbound volume is printed that includes the information contained in the pocket part or supplements. When this occurs, the publisher places in the pocket the notice "This

---

KEROSENE

Reference to Title 7 Section 515 and the Sections that follow —

KEROSENE—Cont'd
Summer Fill and Fuel Budgeting Programs,
    42 § 6283
KERR-MILLS ACT
Medical Assistance, generally, this index
KERR-SMITH TOBACOO CONRTOL ACT
Generally, 7 § 515 et seq.
    —KETOBEMIDONE
Controlled Substance, generally, this index
KETTLE RIVER
Wild and scenic rivers, 16 § 1276
KETTLEHOLES
Ice Age National Scientific Reserve, generally,
    this index
KEWEENAW NATIONAL HISTORICAL PARK
Generally, 16 § 410yy et seq.
KEY LARGO CORAL REEF PRESERVE
Generally, 16 § 461, nt, PN 3339
KEY LARGO NATIONAL MARINE
    SANCTUARY
Designation, 16 § 1433 nt
KEYS

Reference to Title and Section —

Defense Department, Security, theft,
    forgery, fines, penalties and forfeitures,
    18 § 1386
Internal Revenue Service, proprietors of distilled
    spirits plants to furnish to Secretary,
    26 § 5203
KHMER REPUBLIC
Kampuchca, generally, this index
KIAVAH WILDERNESS
Generally, 16 § 1132 nt
KICK-BACK RACKET ACT
Generally, 40 § 276c
Public Building, Property, and Works, generally,
    this index
KICK-BACKS
Anti-Kickback, generally, this index Health insur-
    ance for aged and disabled,
    42 § 1320a-7b
Income tax, deductions, 26 § 162
Medical assistance programs, grants to States for,
    criminal penalty, 42 § 1320a-7b
Presidential Election Campaign Fund,
    26 § 9012
Presidential primary matching payment account,
    26 § 9042
Public works, 18 § 874
Real Estate Settlement Procedures,
    this index Sentence and punishment,
    18 USSG §2B4.1
KICKAPOO INDIANS
Indians, this index
KIDNAPPING
Generally, 18 § 1201 et seq.
Aircraft, jurisdiction, 18 § 1201
Attempts, 18 § 1201
Attorney General, this index

KIDNAPPING—Cont'd
Banks and banking, robbery, 18 § 2113
Cabinet departments, heads and deputies,
    Interception of wire, oral, or electronic
    communications, 18 § 2516
    Kidnapping, attempts, conspiracy, penalties
    and forfeitures, 18 § 351
Chief Justice of Supreme Court, kidnapping,
    attempts, conspiracy, fines, penalties and
    forfeitures, 18 § 351
Children and Minors, this index
CIA, director, deputy director, fines, penalties and
    forfeitures, 18 § 351
Congress, this index
Conspiracy,
    Against right of inhabitants, fines, penalties
    and forfeitures, 18 § 241
    Fines, penalties and forfeitures, 18 § 1201
    Foreign countries, 18 § 956
Deprivation of rights under color of law, fines,
    penalties and forfeitures, 18 § 242
Domestic violence, parental kidnapping, reports,
    28 § 1738A nt
Employee Retirement Income Security Program,
    protection of employee benefit rights,
    fiduciary responsibility, 29 § 1111
Evidence, congress, cabinet department heads,
    knowledge, 18 § 351
Fair housing, sale or rental, intimidation,
    interference, penalties, 42 § 3631
FBI database, crimes against children,
    registration, 42 § 14072
Federal officials, fines, penalties and forfeitures,
    18 § 1201
Federally protected activities, intimidation, inter-
    ference, fines, penalties and forfeitures,
    18 § 245
Fines, penalties and forfeitures, 18 §1201
    Indian lands and reservations, 18 § 1153
    Ransom money, 18 § 1202
    Transportation, interstate commerce, 18 § 1201
Foreign countries.
    Children and minors, 42 § 11608a
    Conspiracy, 18 § 956
    U.S. citizens, 22 § 2715a
Foreign Diplomatic and Consular Officers, this
    index
Forfeitures. Fines, penalties and forfeitures,
    generally, ante
Indians, this index
Interception of wire, oral, or electronic
    communications, President, congress,
    18 § 2516
International Child Abduction Remedies,
    generally, this index
Interstate and Foreign Commerce, this index
Involuntary servitude, intent to sell, 18 § 1583
Jurisdiction,
    Indian Lands and reservations, 18 § 3242
    Internationally protected persons, victims,
    18 § 1201

Exhibit 3-7   Excerpt from the U.S.C.A. General Index. Reprinted from West Group, United States Code Annotated, General Index (2000), p. 787.

Amendment to law _____

§511. Liability of States, instrumentalities of States, and State official for infringement of copyright

(a) In General.—Any State, any instrumentality of a States, and any officer for employee of a States or instrumentality of a State acting in his or her official capacity, shall not be immune, under the Eleventh Amendment of the Constitution of the United States or under any other doctrine of sovereign immunity, from suit in Federal court by any person, including any governmental or nongovernmental entity, for a violation of any of the exclusive rights of a copyright owner provided by section 106 through 121, for importing copies of phonorecords in violation of section 602, or for any other violation under this title.

[See main volume for text of (b)]

(As amended Pub L. 106-14, § 1(g)(6), Aug. 5, 1999, 113 Stat. 222.)

HISTORICAL AND STATUORY NOTES

Amendments

   1999 Amendments. Subsec. (a). Pub.L. 106-44, § 1(g)(6), substituted "121" for "119."

LIBRARY REFERENCES

Text and Treatises
   Business and Commercial Litigation in Federal Courts §§ 65.2, 65.3, 65.4, 65.10, 65.15 (Robert L. Haig ed.) (West Group & ABA 1998)

7A Fed Proc L Ed, Copyrights § 18:187

NOTES OF DECISIONS

New annotations

Constitutionality 1/2
Immunity 2
Waiver 3

_____

1/2. Constitutionality
   Statute purporting to abrogate states' sovereign immunity in copyright infringement suits was not enacted pursuant to a valid exercise of congressional power to enforce the guarantees of the Fourteenth Amendment's due process clause and thus did not validly waive states' immunity. Rodriguez v. Texas Com'n on the Arts, C.A.5 (Tex.) 2000, 199 F.3d 279, 53 U.S.P.Q.2d 1383.

2. Immunity
   Provisions of Copyright Art and Lanham Act that purported to require states to submit to suit in federal court for violation of those statutes exceeded Congress's constitutional powers. Chavez v. Arte Publico Press, C.A.5

(Tex) 1998.157 F.3d 282, rehearing granted, vacated 178 F.3d 601, 53 U.S.P.Q.2d 2009.
   University employee who allegedly authorized printing of copies of author's book in violation of Copyright Act was entitled to qualified immunity, where contractual provision relating to duration of university's publishing license was ambiguous and was susceptible of interpretation that permitted employee's actions. Chavez v. Arte Publico Press, C A.5 (Tex.) 1995, 59 F.3d 539, 35 U.S.P.Q.2d 1609, vacated 116 S.Ct. 1667, 517 U.S. 1184, 134 L.Ed.3d 772, on remand 139 F.3d 504, 46 U.S.P.Q.2d 1541, on remand 157 F.3d 282, certiorari denied 116 S.Ct. 1672, 517, U.S. 1187, 134 L.E.d.2d 776.

3.Waiver
   University waived its Eleventh Amendment immunity from suit for copyright infringement . . .

Exhibit 3-8 Pocket Part Update for 17 U.S.C.A § 511. Reprinted from West Group, United States Code Annotated, 2001 Cumulative Annual Pocket, Title 17 § 511, p. 27, with permission of Thomson Reuters.

Volume Contains No Pocket Part." If there is no pocket part and no notice that the volume does not contain a pocket part, assume that the pocket part is missing and check with the librarian. (See Exhibit 3-8 for an example of a portion of a pocket part.)

   Pocket parts are published only once a year. To ensure that the information contained in the U.S.C.A. is current, supplemental pamphlets, titled "Statutory Supplements," are published every three to four months following the publication of the pocket part. Like pocket parts, they include any revisions to a statute and additional annotations. These pamphlets are not cumulative; each one covers a specific time period. This means that you must check each supplement when updating your research. These supplemental pamphlets are usually located at the end of the U.S.C.A. set. *You must always check the pocket parts and supplemental pamphlets to ensure that your research is current and that there have not been changes in the law subsequent to the publication of the main volume.*

If you are conducting electronic research you must check the currentness of the statute. Most commercial Internet research sources have a tab or hyperlink that will lead the researcher to a statement regarding the currentness of the law (see Exhibit 3-4) and if there is a pending amendment or change to the law, there will be a link to the public law that will enact the change or amendment. If the Internet source does not provide information about the currentness of the law, the researcher must use another source to verify they have the most current law before using it.

c. Popular Name Table

Statutes are often referred to by a popular name, such as the Americans with Disabilities Act or the Freedom of Information Act. If you know a statute's popular name but do not know the citation, a quick way to locate the statute is through the popular name table found in the last volume of the General Index. The table provides you with the public law number, the *Statutes at Large* citation, and the title and section numbers. (See Exhibit 3-9 for a page from the table.) When conducting electronic research, many commercial Internet research sources have tabs or links to the popular name table.

d. Conversion Tables

If you know the *Statutes at Large* citation, the public law number, or the year and chapter of a law, you can use the conversion tables to find where the law is classified in the U.S.C.A. The conversion tables are located in the "Tables" volume. They are published annually, and updates are located at the end of each noncumulative supplement.

3. United States Code Service

LexisNexis publishes the *United States Code Service* (U.S.C.S). It consists of approximately 150 volumes and contains the wording of the federal statutes published in the *Statutes at Large*. The U.S.C.S. and U.S.C.A. are competitive sets, published by different publishers to accomplish the same basic task: to publish the federal laws and provide the information necessary for researchers to interpret and answer questions concerning federal law. Sample pages from the U.S.C.S. are presented in Exhibit 3-10.

The sets are similar in most respects; therefore, most researchers do not use both sets. Which set you use is often based on availability or personal preference. The similarities and differences between the sets are presented here.

Similarities between the two sets are:

1. They are organized in the same way. The organization is based on the titles of the U.S.C. For example, Title 42 Section 1983 will be found at 42 U.S.C.A. § 1983 and 42 U.S.C.S. § 1983.
2. They have general indexes, popular name tables, and conversion tables.
3. They are annotated. In both sets, the annotations provide information on the history of the statute, direct you to other research sources, and briefly summarize cases that have construed the statute.
4. They are similarly updated. Both sets are updated annually with pocket parts for each volume and supplemental pamphlets.

Differences between the two sets are:

1. The *U.S.C.A.* includes more court decisions in the "Notes of Decisions" section of the annotations. The *U.S.C.S.* tends to be more selective and reference only the more significant cases.
2. The "Research Guide" section of the *U.S.C.S.* annotations is more comprehensive than the "Library Reference" section of the *U.S.C.A.*, in that it includes more references to research sources.
3. The supplements to the U.S.C.S., called the *Cumulative Later Case and Statutory Service*, are cumulative. Therefore, you need check only the latest supplement. The U.S.C.S. also publishes a monthly pamphlet called *U.S.C.S. Advance*, which includes new public laws, presidential proclamations, and executive orders.
4. In the U.S.C.A., the topics covered in the "Notes to the Decisions" are arranged alphabetically; in the U.S.C.S., the "Interpretive Notes and Decisions" are arranged according to topic.

B. State Statutory Law and Codes

The enactment and publication of state legislation varies in detail from state to state, but they are similar in many respects to the federal system. Most states initially publish their laws in pamphlets similar to the federal slip laws. When the legislative session is over, the laws are published in books often referred to as *session laws*. These are similar to the *Statutes at Large* in that the laws are presented in the order in which they were passed.

POPULAR NAME TABLE

Freedom of Information Act (FOIA)
  Pub.L. 89-487, July 4, 1966, 80 Stat. 250 (See 5 § 552)
  Pub.L. 90-23, § 1, June 5, 1967, 81 Stat. 54 (5 § 552)
  Pub.L. 93-502, §§ 1 to 3, Nov. 21, 1974, 88 Stat. 1561 (5 § 552)
Freedom of Information Reform Act of 1986
  Pub.L. 99-570, Title I, Subtitle N, Oct. 27, 1986, 100 Stat. 3204-48 (5 §§ 552, 552 notes)
FREEDOM Support Act
  See Freedom for Russia and Emerging Eurasian Democracies and Open Markets
    Support Act of 1992
Freedom to E-File Actw
  Pub.L. 106-222, June 20, 2000, 114 Stat. 353 (7 §§ 6901 note, 7031 to 7035)
Freedom to Farm Law
  See Emergency Farm Financial Relief Act
French Spoliation Claims Act
  Jan. 20, 1885, ch. 25, 23 Stat 283
Fresh Cut Flowers and Fresh Cut Greens Promotion and Information Act of 1993
  Pub.L. 103-190, Dec. 14, 1993, 107 Stat. 2266 (7 §§ 6801, 6801 note, 6802 to 6814)
FRIENDSHIP Act
  See Act For Reform In Emerging New Democracies and Support and Help for
    Improved Partnership with Russia, Ukraine, and other New Independent States
FRLA
  See Federal Regulation of Lobbying Act
FRRAPA
  See Forest and Rangeland Renewable Resources Planning Act of 1974
FRRRRA
  See Forest and Rangeland Renewable Resource Research Act of 1978
FRSA
  See Federal Railroad Safety Act of 1970
Frye Acts
  See Shipping Acts
FSC Repeal and Extraterritorial Income Exclusion Act of 200 (Foreign Sales Corporation
  Repeal and Extraterritorial Income Exclusion Act of 2000)
  Pub l. 106-519, Nov. 15, 2000. 114 Stat, 2423 (see Tables for classification)
FSIA
  See Foreign Sovereign Immunities Act of 1976
FSLMRA
  See Federal Service Labour-Management Relations Act
FSPA
  See Uniformed Services Former Spouses Protection Act
FTCA
  See Federal Tort Claims Act
FTCPMA
  See Federal Timber Contract Payment Modification Act
Fuel Distribution Act
  Sept. 22, 1922, ch. 413, 42 Stat. 1025
Fugitive Felon Act
  June 22, 1932, ch. 271, § 1, 47 Stat. 326
  May 18, 1934, ch. 301, 48 Stat. 301 (See 18 § 1073)
Fugitive Slave Laws
  Sept. 18, 1850, ch. 60, 9 Stat. 462
  June 28, 1864, ch. 166, 13 Stat. 200

Annotations (handwritten labels): Public law number — U.S.C.A. Citation — Statutes at Large citation

Exhibit 3-9 U.S.C.A. Popular Name Table Page. Reprinted from West Group, United States Code Annotated, Popular Name Table (2000), p. 787, with permission of Thomson Reuters.

State laws are then organized according to topic (codified) and published with annotations similar to those in the U.S.C.A. and U.S.C.S. Most state codes are similar to the U.S.C.A. and U.S.C.S. in the following ways:

- Each set has a general index, and some sets have a separate index following each title.
- Some statutes have popular name tables and conversion tables that allow you to locate statutes that have been renumbered or repealed.

18 USCS § 1201, N 64

CRIMES & CRIMINAL PROCEDURE

64. Appellate review

In prosecution under predecessor to 18 USCS § 1201, objection that letter which codefendant had taken from kidnapped victim and which was later found by police in defendant's apartment was obtained by illegal search could not be raised for first time on appeal from conviction. *Eaker v United States* (1935, CA.10 Colo) 76 F2d 267.

Defendant who had been convicted of interstate transportation of person who had been unlawfully kidnapped could not by writ of habeas corpus applied for in United States District Court for Western District of Oklahoma affect his sentence for such unlawful interstate transportation rendered in United States District Court for Northern District of Texas, nor cause his trial for kidnapping offense in Western District of Oklahoma, wherein no charge for such offense was pending against him. Trafford v Yellow Cab Co. (1961, CA3 Pa) 293 F2d 43.

65. Habeas corpus proceedings

Whether defendant was member of conspiracy and did conspire in violation of law raised issue of fact, and where that issue was resolved against him in trial court, it could not be relitigated in habeas corpus proceeding. Hudspeth v McDonald (1941, CA10 Kan) 120 F2d 962, cert den (1941) 314 US 617, 86 L Ed 496, 62 S Ct 110, reh den (1945) 325 US 892, 89 L Ed 2004, 65 S Ct 1181.

Motion to vacate sentence for kidnapping conviction of 30 years will be denied when petitioner was adequately made aware of charge against him and where his plea of guilty was voluntarily entered into without fear of death penalty. Wilson v United States (1969, WD Va) 303 F Supp 1139.

§ 1202. Ransom money

Whoever receives, possesses, or disposes of any money or other property, or any portion thereof, which has at any time been delivered as ransom or reward in connection with a violation of section 1201 of this title, knowing the same to be money or property which has been at any time delivered as such ransom or reward, shall be fined not more than $10,000 or imprisoned not more than ten years, or both.

(June 25, 1948, ch 645, § 1, 62 Stat. 760.)

HISTORY; ANCILLARY LAWS AND DIRECTIVES

Prior law and revision:

This section is based on Act June 22, 1932, ch 271, § 4, as added Jan. 24, 1936, ch 29, 49 Stat. 1099 (former 18 U.S.C. § 408c-1).

The words "in the penitentiary" after "imprisoned" were omitted in view of 18 USCS § 4082 committing prisoners to the custody of the Attorney General.

Minor charges in phraseology were made.

CROSS REFERENCES

Sentencing guidelines, Statutory Index, Sentencing Guidelines for U.S. Courts, 18 USCS Appendix.

RESEARCH GUIDE

Annotations:

What constitutes violation of 18 USCS 1202, Prohibiting receipt, possession, or disposition of ransom money. 31 ALR Fed 916.

INTERPRETIVE NOTES AND DECISIONS

1. Generally
2. Relationship with other laws
3. Delivery of ransom
4. Conspiracy
5. Jurisdiction
6. Indictment

Exhibit 3-10 Title 18 U.S.C.S 1202. Lawyers Cooperative Publishing, United States Code Service, Title 18 Crimes & Criminal Procedure § 1202 (1994), p. 2000. Reprinted with permission of LexisNexis.

CRIMES   18 USCS § 1203

1. Generally

18 USCS § 1202 was intended to extend federal jurisdiction to persons having only indirect connection with actual kidnapping and to discourage any co-operation with those primarily responsible. United States v Ortega (1975, CA3 NJ) 517 F2d 1006, 31 ALR Fed 909.

2. Relationship with other laws

18 USCS § 1202 is not separate, detached violation with regard to primary federal kidnapping statute (18 USCS § 1201) and § 1202 is directed to only portion of larger offense which includes number of components. United States v Ortega (1975, CA3 NJ) 517 F2d 1006, 31 ALR Fed 909.

Establishing violation of 18 USCS § 1202 requires proof of money or property which was delivered as ransom or reward, elements that are clearly not identical to any of elements of USCS § 1201 kidnapping offense, and therefore trial court was correct in refusing to instruct that § 1201. Durns v United States (1977, CA8 Mo) 562 F2d 542, 2 Fed Rules Evid Serv 462, cert den (1977) 434 US 959, 54 L Ed 2d 319, 98 S Ct 490.

3. Delivery of ransom

For ransom to have been "delivered" within meaning of § 1202 does not require transfer of possession to kidnappers; all that is needed is for transferor to have placed ransom at place specified by kidnappers, and fact that transferor may have mistak-enly placed ransom at wrong location does not vitiate "delivery" for purposes of § 1202; thus, violation thereof occurred where defendant found and appropriated ransom mistakenly delivered and concealed fact after learning that it was ransom United States v Ortega (1975, CA3 NJ) 517 F2d 1006, 31 ALR Fed 909.

4. Conspiracy

Conspiracy to violate predecessor to 18 USCS § 1202 began with plan to abduct and ended when ransom money was changed into unmarked money. Laska v United States (1936, CA10 Okla) 82 F2d 672, cert den (1936) 298 US 689, 80 L Ed 1407, 56 S Ct 957.

5. Jurisdiction

18 USCS § 1202 being prohibition of integral part of kidnapping scheme which concededly is within federal jurisdiction, violation of prohibition is within federal jurisdiction even if interstate commerce is not directly involved. United States v Ortega (1975, CA3 NJ) 517 F2d 1006, 31 ALR Fed 909.

6. Indictment

Indictment charging defendant with three separate offenses of transmitting communications in interstate commerce demanding ransom money under 18 USCS § 875(a) and with receiving, possessing and disposing of ransom money in violation of 18 USCS § 1202, is not duplicative as each count charges separate offense. Amsler v United States (1967, CA9 Cal) 381 F2d 37.

Exhibit 3-10 *(Continued)*

- The statutes are organized by subject, with each subject title being subdivided into chapters and so on. (See Exhibit 3-1.)
- The state constitution with annotations is included in the code.
- State codes are usually updated annually by some form of supplement. These may be pocket parts inserted in the statutory volume or separate pamphlets.
- State statutes are annotated. The annotations include the history of the section, cross-references to other statutes, research guides, and notes to court decisions (see Exhibit 3-3.)

C. The Research Process—Techniques and Strategies

1. Step 1: Locate the Statute

Inasmuch as federal and state codifications share similar features, the process for locating and researching federal and state constitutional and statutory law is essentially the same, and thus are discussed together here.

The beginning step of all research, including statutory research, is to identify what you are looking for as precisely and narrowly as possible. Define your research question as specifically, and in as concise terms, as possible. Time spent narrowing the focus of your search will save a great deal of research time later. A tightly focused identification of the research question saves time because the researcher is immediately directed to the specific area of the law in question and does not waste time searching multiple statutes.

For Example

The question involves the issue of whether a shareholder of a corporation must attend a meeting in person to vote on an issue. If a researcher thinks, "Oh, this is a corporation question" and immediately looks at corporations in the index to the statutes, the researcher will waste time looking through the entire corporation section. If the research is conducted electronically and the search term is simply *corporations*, all the corporation statutes will come up. If, however, the research is focused to *corporations, shareholders, meetings of corporations, shareholders*, and *voting*, the search is narrowed at the outset and the statute is located more quickly, whether the research is manual or electronic.

After you have defined your search as specifically and concisely as possible, you have three main ways to approach locating a statute, as discussed here.

a. General Index

The most common approach to locating statutes is to use the General Index. When using this approach, identify as specifically as possible the words that describe the problem. If the term you initially use is not the term used in the index, the index often will refer you to the correct term. For example, if you are looking for statutes concerning trailers, the index under *trailers* may read, "See Manufactured Homes." (See Exhibit 3-7 for an example of an index page.) Note: most Internet research sources do not have a General Index. These sources may have an index, but it is not usually as comprehensive as the print index. This means the index does not refer the researcher to other related terms or sections. Researchers have to be more familiar with terms when conducting electronic research.

After you have found the correct index entry, the index will list the appropriate title and section. With that information, you can locate statutes in the appropriate statutory volume. Most statutes are arranged by title and the titles covered in each volume are indicated on the spine. For example, the spine may read "Titles 5–7," thus indicating that Titles 5 through 7 of the code are included in that volume. Be sure to check the index pocket part if you cannot find a term in the main index volume. It may be that the term has been recently added to the index.

b. Title Table of Contents

Most statutory codifications include a table of contents at the beginning of each title that lists the name and number of the chapters within the title. At the beginning of each chapter, a table of contents typically lists the statutory section number and name of each section. If you know the number of the title you are looking for, you can go directly to the volume and scan the table to quickly locate a statute. It is not necessary to consult the General Index. Most Internet research sources have tables of contents that allows the researcher to click through the table and link directly to statutes. In addition, most commercial Internet research sources have the added benefit of allowing the researcher to search for specific terms within the table of contents, allowing the researcher to find other title and sections of statutes that contain specific terms. This offsets the lack of comprehensive indexes in these Internet research sources.

For Example

You want to locate the statutory definition of a term in the Arizona Commercial Code and you know from experience that the commercial code is Title 47. You can go directly to Title 47 and scan the table of contents to Article 1 and immediately locate the appropriate sections, 2104, 2105, 2106. (See the first page of Exhibit 3-1, for 47-2104, 47-2105, 47-2106.)

Beginning researchers should be aware that some subjects are covered by more than one set of laws. Therefore, referring to a specific title requires that the researcher be sufficiently familiar with the law to know that the search topic is covered only by that title.

For Example

The question being researched involves identifying the statutes that govern a loan. Several statutes may cover loans: the commercial paper chapter of the commercial law title of the code, the state's small loan act, and the federal truth-in-lending statutes.

c. Popular Name

Many laws are commonly known by their popular name, such as the Good Samaritan Act or the Truth in Lending Act. Many state statutes and the U.S.C.A. and U.S.C.S. have popular name tables listing in alphabetical order the popular names and citation. The tables are usually located with the table of contents volume(s) or as a separate volume. When conducting electronic research, many Internet sources have a link to the popular name table that lists the popular names alphabetically. *Shepard's Acts and Cases by Popular Name: Federal and State* also lists the popular names and citations of federal and state laws. If you know the popular name of the act you are looking for, consult the popular name table, and you will be directed to the appropriate section of the statutes.

2. Step 2: Update Your Research

After you locate a statute, check the pocket parts and supplementary pamphlets to ensure the statute published in the main volume has not been amended or repealed. Also check the annotations to locate new case law that may affect the interpretation of the statute. *Shepard's Citations* provides updates to state and federal statutes. The process of updating research through the use of *Shepard's Citations* is called "Shepardizing." Westlaw has its own system of updating state and federal statutes called KeyCite. *Shepard's* and KeyCite are discussed in Chapter 5. Many Internet research sources of statutory law have links to the currentness of statutes. Because many non-commercial Internet research sources are not current, researchers need to be familiar with the methods of updating statutes to be sure the most current law has been located.

D. Ethics—Competence and Diligence

There are considerations of **ethics** to keep in mind when conducting any type of research, whether it be on enacted law, case law, or secondary authority. Rule 1.1 of the American Bar Association's Model Rules of Professional Conduct requires that a client be provided competent representation. Rule 1.3 provides that a client be represented with diligence and promptness. These rules mean that a researcher must possess sufficient knowledge of the law and legal research to research completely the issues raised by the facts of the client's case. They also mean that all avenues of research must be pursued promptly and explored thoroughly.

IV. ADMINISTRATIVE LAW

As discussed in Chapter 1, federal and state legislatures delegate the task of administering laws to administrative agencies. The legislatures pass enabling legislation authorizing administrative agencies to carry out the intent of the legislature. This enabling legislation usually includes a grant of authority to create the rules and regulations necessary to carry out the law. These rules and regulations have the authority of law; they are primary authority. The body of law that results from the rules and regulations and the court opinions interpreting them is called **administrative law.** The terms *rules* and *regulations* are often used interchangeably when discussing administrative law. To avoid repetition, the term *regulation*, when used in this section, includes both administrative rules and regulations.

Administrative agencies exist on state and federal levels of government. As noted at the beginning of this chapter, like statutory law, administrative law has an ever-increasing role; therefore, you may be called upon to research issues involving the interpretation or application of an administrative agency regulation.

STEP 1	Determine if the statute applies. ■ Part 1: Locate all possible applicable statutes. ■ Part 2: Determine which statutes apply.
STEP 2	Analyze the statute. ■ Part 1: Read the statute. ■ Part 2: Identify the statutory elements—What does the statute specifically declare, require, or prohibit?
STEP 3	Apply the statute to the legal problem or issue. ■ Chart format ■ Narrative format

© Cengage

Exhibit 3-14 *Statutory Analysis Three-Step Approach.*

might govern the problem and have located all potential applicable statutes. Some matters are covered by more than one statute.

2. Determine Which Statutes Apply

Determine whether each statute applies by asking yourself, "Does the general area of law covered by this statute apply to the issue or question raised by the facts of my client's case?" You can usually answer this question by referring to the scope of the statute, the definitions section, or case law.

Reference to the scope section of the statute often answers the question of whether the statute applies.

For Example

The problem involves the validity of a contract for the sale of a security interest in a car. The scope section of the Commercial Code—Sales statute provides, "This chapter applies to the sale of goods, it does not apply to any transaction which . . . is a sale of a security interest or intended to operate only as a security transaction. . . ." Reference to this section clearly indicates that this statute does not cover such transactions. If the facts involved the sale of the car, rather than the sale of a security interest in the car, the statute might apply.

In some instances, reference to the definitions section of a statute will help you determine whether a statute applies.

For Example

The legal problem involves the sale of a farm. The question of whether this sale is governed by the provisions of the Commercial Code—Sales statute is answered by reference to the definitions section of the statute. In that section, goods are defined as "all things that are movable at the time of the contract for sale. . . ." The statute clearly does not apply to the sale of a farm.

In some instances, reference to case law may be necessary to determine if a statute governs a situation.

For Example

The client's case involves the lease of goods, and neither the scope nor the definitions sections of the Commercial Code—Sales statute indicates whether the term *sale* includes a lease of goods. Reference to case law may be necessary. Court decisions often define terms not defined in a statute.

For Example

Rule 60B of the Federal Rules of Civil and Criminal Procedure provides that a judgment may be set aside on the grounds of "excusable neglect." It may be necessary to research the case law to determine how the courts have defined "excusable neglect."

The Federal Rules of Civil and Criminal Procedure are included in the *United States Code*. By consulting the U.S.C.A. or U.S.C.S., you will find annotations that direct you to summaries of cases and secondary sources, such as legal encyclopedia sections and *ALR* annotations, which have interpreted the rules. Like the federal rules, state court rules are usually published with the state statutes. Locating the rules in the annotated statutes is usually the starting point when researching court rules.

The state and federal rules are available electronically on Westlaw and LexisNexis, through http://www .findlaw.com, and on state or individual court websites. In addition, multivolume treatises, such as *West's Federal Practice and Procedure*, provide exhaustive analysis of the federal rules.

There are also many publications that compile rules according to areas of practice. These compilations are found in law offices and law libraries. Some of these compilations are annotated, others merely contained the text of the rules. Most of these compilations are published yearly and updated mid-year through pocket parts.

In addition to the rules governing civil and criminal procedure, federal courts and many state courts have so-called **local rules.** Consult these rules before filing any pleading or other document with the court. These rules are specific to the court and generally govern administrative matters such as the size of papers accepted, the number of copies of pleadings that must be filed with the original, and how to file electronically (e-file) if e-filing is available. If the court has a website, the local rules may be available there. If not, local rules are available through the clerk of the court.

VI. ANALYSIS—THE PROCESS

The analysis of enacted law and court rules is the process of determining if a law applies, how it applies, and the effect of that application to a specific fact situation. When analyzing a legal problem or addressing an issue governed by constitutional, statutory, or administrative regulation, or a court rule, it is helpful to have an approach—an **analysis process.** This process should allow you to approach the matter in a way that efficiently solves the problem in the least amount of time with the least confusion and greatest accuracy. For the sake of clarity, throughout this section the discussion and examples focus upon laws passed by legislative bodies, or statutory law. Note, however, that the principles presented here apply to the analysis of constitutions, statutes, administrative law, and court rules.

It is recommended that you follow the three-step approach presented in Exhibit 3-14 when addressing a legal problem or issue governed by statutory law. These steps are a helpful approach to statutory analysis, although in some instances a step may be unnecessary (for example, step 1 is unnecessary if you already know that the statute applies) and in other instances, a different approach may be required. Each step in this recommended approach is discussed separately in the following sections. These steps also apply to analyzing administrative regulations, constitutions, and court rules.

A. Step 1: Determine if the Statute Applies

The first step in the process is to determine which law, if any, covers the legal issue raised by the client's fact situation. The first task, then, is to determine which statute or statutes govern the question.

This step involves two parts:

1. Locate all possible applicable statutes.
2. Determine which statutes apply.

1. Locate All Possible Applicable Statutes

Before you can determine if a particular statute applies, you first must locate all statutes that possibly apply. The location of one applicable statute does not mean you should stop your search. Make sure your research is thorough and complete. Continue researching until you are confident that you have explored all areas of law that

STEP 1	Determine if the statute applies. ■ Part 1: Locate all possible applicable statutes. ■ Part 2: Determine which statutes apply.
STEP 2	Analyze the statute. ■ Part 1: Read the statute. ■ Part 2: Identify the statutory elements—What does the statute specifically declare, require, or prohibit?
STEP 3	Apply the statute to the legal problem or issue. ■ Chart format ■ Narrative format

© Cengage

Exhibit 3-14   Statutory Analysis Three-Step Approach.

might govern the problem and have located all potential applicable statutes. Some matters are covered by more than one statute.

2. Determine Which Statutes Apply

Determine whether each statute applies by asking yourself, "Does the general area of law covered by this statute apply to the issue or question raised by the facts of my client's case?" You can usually answer this question by referring to the scope of the statute, the definitions section, or case law.

Reference to the scope section of the statute often answers the question of whether the statute applies.

For Example

The problem involves the validity of a contract for the sale of a security interest in a car. The scope section of the Commercial Code—Sales statute provides, "This chapter applies to the sale of goods, it does not apply to any transaction which . . . is a sale of a security interest or intended to operate only as a security transaction. . . ." Reference to this section clearly indicates that this statute does not cover such transactions. If the facts involved the sale of the car, rather than the sale of a security interest in the car, the statute might apply.

In some instances, reference to the definitions section of a statute will help you determine whether a statute applies.

For Example

The legal problem involves the sale of a farm. The question of whether this sale is governed by the provisions of the Commercial Code—Sales statute is answered by reference to the definitions section of the statute. In that section, goods are defined as "all things that are movable at the time of the contract for sale. . . ." The statute clearly does not apply to the sale of a farm.

In some instances, reference to case law may be necessary to determine if a statute governs a situation.

For Example

The client's case involves the lease of goods, and neither the scope nor the definitions sections of the Commercial Code—Sales statute indicates whether the term *sale* includes a lease of goods. Reference to case law may be necessary. Court decisions often define terms not defined in a statute.

OCTOBER 2011

5

CHANGES JANUARY 3, 2011 THROUGH OCTOBER 31, 2011

TITLE 1—GENERAL PROVISIONS

Chapter I—Administrative Committee of the Federal Register (Parts 1—49)

9 Revised	6312
11.4 Revised	6313
12.3 Removed	6313

Chapter III—Administrative Conference of the United States (Parts 300—399)

304 Added	18636

Proposed Rules:

304	1542

TITLE 2—GRANTS AND AGREEMENTS

Chapter VII—Agency for International Development (Parts 700—799)

Chapter VII Established	34144
780 Added	34144
782 Added	34574

Chapter XXIV—Department of Housing and Urban Development (Parts 2400—2499)

2429 Added	45166

Chapter XXX—Department of Homeland Security (Parts 3000—3099)

3001 Added	10207

Proposed Rules:

300—399 (Ch. III)	20568
400—499 (Ch. IV)	22058
600—699 (Ch. VI)	26651
1100—1199 (Ch. XI)	16700, 32330
1400—1499 (Ch. XIV)	10526, 40645
1800—1899 (Ch. XVIII)	31884
2400—2499 (Ch. XXIV)	11395, 31884
2800—2899 (Ch. XXVIII)	11163, 34003
3000—3099 (Ch. XXX)	20568

TITLE 3—THE PRESIDENT
Presidential Documents

Proclamations

6641 *See* Proc. 8682	30499
6867 *See* Notice of Feb. 24, 2011	11073
7463 *See* Notice of Sep. 9, 2011	56633
7747 *See* Proc. 8682	30499
7757 *See* Notice of Feb. 24, 2011	11073
8097 *See* Proc. 8682	30499
8214 *See* Proc. 8682	30499
8271 *See* Notice of Jun. 23, 2011	37237
8405 *See* Proc. 8682	30499
8522 Superseded by Proc. 8681	30497
8536 *See* Proc. 8682	30499
8622	2241
8623	3817
8624	3819
8625	6305
8626	6307
8627	6521
8628	11927
8629	11929
8630	11931
8631	11933
8632	11935
8633	12265
8634	12817
8635	12919
8636	12921
8637	15209
8638	16523
8639	17327
8640	17329
8641	18629
8642	18631
8643	18633
8644	19259
8645	19261
8646	19263
8647	19265
8648	19899
8649	20215
8650	20829
8651	20831
8652	20833
8653	21221
8654	21223
8655	21999
8656	22001
8657	23685
8658	24785

Exhibit 3-13 Page from Electronic List of CFR Sections Affected (LSA). Source: *http://www .gpo.gov/fdsys/pkg/LSA-2011-10/pdf/LSA-2011-10.pdf*

and regulations is the same when searching electronically as searching in print. Of utmost importance is knowing the currentness of the Internet research source you are using and taking the steps to ensure you have located the regulation in its current form.

e. Court and Administrative Decisions

Your research may require you to consult administrative agency or court decisions for an interpretation of a rule or regulation. Agency decisions may be available through the Government Printing Office (GPO) and commercial publishers such as Commerce Clearing House (CCH) and the Bureau of National Affairs (BNA). Agency websites are often one of the best sources for locating decisions issued from administrative law judges. Administrative and court decisions can also be accessed through Westlaw and LexisNexis.

Shepard's *United States Administrative Citations* and Shepard's *Code of Federal Regulations Citations* include citations to administrative agency and court decisions. *West's Federal Practice Digest* will direct you to federal cases and secondary sources that have interpreted federal regulations.

f. Updating Administrative Law Research

The *Code of Federal Regulations* is updated by consulting the *List of CFR Sections Affected (LSA)* (see Exhibit 3-13). This softcover monthly publication lists changes to any C.F.R. regulation. It is cumulative; therefore, you need only check the most recent issue. The cover indicates the time period addressed in the pamphlet. The *LSA* is organized by title and part; indicates the nature of the change, such as "revised" or "removed"; and includes a reference to the page number in the *Federal Register* where the revised section is published.

To locate changes that have occurred since the last *LSA* publication, check the "Reader Aids" at the end of the most recent *Federal Register*. The "Reader Aids" includes a table of "CFR Parts Affected" that lists parts and sections of the *Code of Federal Regulations* affected. The *CFR* can be updated to the current date through reference to the *LSA* and "Reader Aids."

When researching the e-CFR on the GPO's website, determine what the latest revision date is for the title you are researching. There will be large bold type stating the date the data in the e-CFR was last updated on each page as you navigate through the e-CFR. Once you know the date of the latest revision, check the electronic *List of CFR Sections Affected* for proposed, new and amended regulations that have been published in the *Federal Register* since the most recent revision date. There is a link on the page for the C.F.R. on the GPO website for the *List of CFR Sections Affected*. The C.F.R. can also be updated through Westlaw and LexisNexis. Administrative agency and court decisions can be updated through Shepard's *United States Administrative Citations* and Shepard's *Code of Federal Regulations Citations*.

B. State Administrative Law

The publication of state rules and regulations varies from state to state, and it would require a separate text to cover each state. The publication and research of state administrative law, however, often follows in varying degrees that of federal administrative law. Therefore, an understanding of the federal administrative law discussed in the previous two subsections will help you when researching state administrative law. Some states publish agency rules and regulations in a single code like the *CFR*. In some states the regulations are published by the separate agency. Probably the quickest way to locate where an agency's regulations and administrative decisions are published is to contact the individual agency. Often individual agencies have websites, and the information may be available through the agency or state government website.

V. COURT RULES

Court rules regulate the conduct of matters brought before the court. They range in the subjects they cover from the technical, such as the format of pleadings, to the substantive, such as grounds for dismissal or when an appeal must be filed. Each jurisdiction has the authority to promulgate its own set of rules, although many states' rules follow in substantial part the Federal Rules of Civil and Criminal Procedure.

On occasion you may need to research matters involving the rules to determine what a rule requires or how a rule has been interpreted.

Subchapter ————————— **SUBCHAPTER A—GENERAL**

Part ————————— **PART 1000—COMMISSION ORGANIZATION AND FUNCTIONS**

Section

Sec.
1000.1   The Commission.
1000.2   Laws administered.
1000.3   Hotline.
1000.4   Commission address.
1000.5   Petitions.
1000.6   Commission decisions and records.
1000.7   Advisory opinions and interpretations of regulations.
1000.8   Meetings and hearings; public notice.
1000.9   Quorum.
1000.10   The Chairman and Vice Chairman.
1000.11   Delegation of functions.
1000.12   Organizational structure.
1000.13   Directives system.
1000.14   Office of the General Counsel.
1000.15   Office of Congressional Relations.
1000.16   Office of the Secretary.
1000.17   Office of the Inspector General.
1000.18   Office of Equal Employment Opportunity and Minority Enterprise.
1000.19   Office of the Executive Director.
1000.20   Office of the Budget.
1000.21   Office of Hazard Identification and Reduction.
1000.22   Office of Planning and Evaluation.
1000.23   Office of Information and Public Affairs.
1000.24   Office of Compliance.
1000.25   Office of Human Resources Management.
1000.26   Office of Information Services.
1000.27   Directorate for Epidemiology.
1000.28   Directorate for Health Sciences.
1000.29   Directorate for Economic Analysis
1000.30   Directorate for Engineering Sciences.
1000.31   Directorate for Laboratory Sciences.
1000.32   Directorate for Administration.
1000.33   Directorate for Field Operations.

Authority : 5 U.S.C. 552(a).

Source : 56 FR 30496, July 3, 1991, unless otherwise noted.

§1000.1 The Commission.

(a) The Consumer Product Safety Commission is an independent regulatory agency which was formed on May 14, 1973, under the provisions of the Consumer Product Safety Act (Pub. L. 92-573, 86 Stat. 1207, as amended (1.5 U.S.C. 2051, et seq.)). The purposes of the Commission under the CPSA are:

(1) To protect the public against unreasonable risks of injury associated with consumer products;

(2) To assist consumers in evaluating the comparative safety of consumer products;

(3) To develop uniform safety standards for consumer products and to minimize conflicting State and local regulations; and

(4) To promote research and investigation into the causes and prevention of product-related deaths, illnesses, and injuries.

(b) The Commission is composed of five members appointed by the President, by and with the advice and consent of the Senate, for terms of seven years.

§ 1000.2 Laws administered.

The Commission administers five acts:

(a) The Consumer Product Safety Act (Pub. L. 92-573, 86 Stat. 1207, as amended (15 U.S.C. 2051, et seq.)).

(b) The Flammable Fabrics Act (Pub. L. 90-189, 67 Stat. 111, as amended (15 U.S.C. 1191, et seq.)).

(c) The Federal Hazardous Substances Act (15 U.S.C. 1261, et seq.).

(d) The Poison Prevention Packaging Act of 1970 (Pub. L. 91-601, 84 Stat. 1670, as amended (15 U.S.C. 1471, et seq.)).

(e) The Refrigerator Safety Act of 1956 (Pub. L. 84-930, 70 Stat. 953, (15 U.S.C. 1211, et seq.)).

§ 1000.3 Hotline.

(a) The Commission operates a toll-free telephone Hotline by which the public can communicate with the Commission. The number for use in all 50 states is 1-800-638-CPSC (1-800-638-2772).

(b) The Commission also operates a toll-free Hotline by which hearing or speech-impaired persons can communicate by teletypewriter with the Commission. The teletypewriter number for use in all states is 1-800-638-8270.

(c) The Commission also makes information available to the public product recall information, its public calendar, and other information through its

Exhibit 3-12 Page from the Code of Federal Regulations (C.F.R.). Code of Federal Regulations, Title 16, Part 1000 to End, Commercial Practices (2001), p. 7, National Archives and Records Administration, Washington, DC.

d. Computer-Aided Research

As noted above, the C.F.R. and *Federal Register* are available through the GPOs website. The C.F.R. and the *Federal Register* are also available electronically on Westlaw and LexisNexis. You also may obtain information from individual agency websites. Searching the C.F.R. and the *Federal Register* on each of these Internet research sources is different. However, the concepts of first checking for an index and then using other sources for locating rules

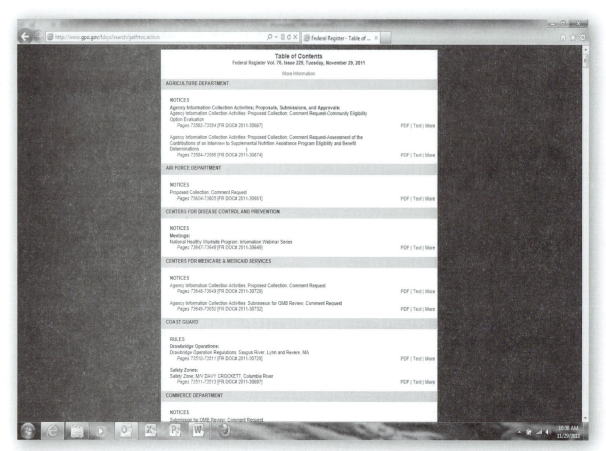

Exhibit 3-11   Screenshot of Electronic Table of Contents of Federal Register. *Source: http://www.gpo.gov/fdsys/search /getfrtoc.action*

a. Indexes and Table of Contents

You may locate regulations in the C.F.R. by subject matter or agency by consulting the *CFR Index and Finding Aids* volume. If you know the number of the U.S.C. enabling statute, you may locate the code title in the *Parallel Table of Authorities and Rules* in the index volume or the electronic version of the parallel table. If you already know the code title or section, you may go directly to the code volume and scan the table of contents for the title to locate the appropriate section. You may also consult the index following the title.

You may also locate regulations through the *Index to the Code of Federal Regulations*. This commercial publication by the Congressional Information Service indexes the C.F.R. by subject and geographic information. Another print index is *West's Code of Federal Regulations, General Index*. This index provides access to the C.F.R. by subject matter or geographic location. Both are usually available at a law library.

b. Other Sources for Locating Rules and Regulations

You may be directed to specific C.F.R. sections by other publications. If you know the statute that established the administrative agency, the annotations following the statute in the U.S.C.A. or U.S.C.S. may include cross-references to specific C.F.R. sections. Other secondary sources, such as law review articles and *ALR* annotations, may reference specific C.F.R. sections.

c. Federal Register

Inasmuch as the C.F.R. is updated annually and issued in parts, it will be necessary to refer to the *Federal Register* to locate rules and regulations published since the last time the C.F.R. volumes were issued. Consult the latest *Federal Register Index*, issued monthly, to locate rules and regulations promulgated after the issuance of the latest C.F.R. volumes. Entries in the *Federal Register Index* are alphabetical by agency. There is also a section called "Reader Aids" at the end of each daily *Federal Register* that lists sections of the C.F.R. affected, reminders of effective dates, and other helpful information.

Beginning researchers should be aware that some subjects are covered by more than one set of laws. Therefore, referring to a specific title requires that the researcher be sufficiently familiar with the law to know that the search topic is covered only by that title.

For Example

The question being researched involves identifying the statutes that govern a loan. Several statutes may cover loans: the commercial paper chapter of the commercial law title of the code, the state's small loan act, and the federal truth-in-lending statutes.

c. Popular Name

Many laws are commonly known by their popular name, such as the Good Samaritan Act or the Truth in Lending Act. Many state statutes and the U.S.C.A. and U.S.C.S. have popular name tables listing in alphabetical order the popular names and citation. The tables are usually located with the table of contents volume(s) or as a separate volume. When conducting electronic research, many Internet sources have a link to the popular name table that lists the popular names alphabetically. *Shepard's Acts and Cases by Popular Name: Federal and State* also lists the popular names and citations of federal and state laws. If you know the popular name of the act you are looking for, consult the popular name table, and you will be directed to the appropriate section of the statutes.

2. Step 2: Update Your Research

After you locate a statute, check the pocket parts and supplementary pamphlets to ensure the statute published in the main volume has not been amended or repealed. Also check the annotations to locate new case law that may affect the interpretation of the statute. *Shepard's Citations* provides updates to state and federal statutes. The process of updating research through the use of *Shepard's Citations* is called "Sheparding." Westlaw has its own system of updating state and federal statutes called KeyCite. *Shepard's* and KeyCite are discussed in Chapter 5. Many Internet research sources of statutory law have links to the currentness of statutes. Because many noncommercial Internet research sources are not current, researchers need to be familiar with the methods of updating statutes to be sure the most current law has been located.

D. Ethics—Competence and Diligence

There are considerations of **ethics** to keep in mind when conducting any type of research, whether it be on enacted law, case law, or secondary authority. Rule 1.1 of the American Bar Association's Model Rules of Professional Conduct requires that a client be provided competent representation. Rule 1.3 provides that a client be represented with diligence and promptness. These rules mean that a researcher must possess sufficient knowledge of the law and legal research to research completely the issues raised by the facts of the client's case. They also mean that all avenues of research must be pursued promptly and explored thoroughly.

IV. ADMINISTRATIVE LAW

As discussed in Chapter 1, federal and state legislatures delegate the task of administering laws to administrative agencies. The legislatures pass enabling legislation authorizing administrative agencies to carry out the intent of the legislature. This enabling legislation usually includes a grant of authority to create the rules and regulations necessary to carry out the law. These rules and regulations have the authority of law; they are primary authority. The body of law that results from the rules and regulations and the court opinions interpreting them is called **administrative law.** The terms *rules* and *regulations* are often used interchangeably when discussing administrative law. To avoid repetition, the term *regulation*, when used in this section, includes both administrative rules and regulations.

Administrative agencies exist on state and federal levels of government. As noted at the beginning of this chapter, like statutory law, administrative law has an ever-increasing role; therefore, you may be called upon to research issues involving the interpretation or application of an administrative agency regulation.

For Example

The client's business is fined by the Occupational Safety and Health Administration (OSHA) for failure to have fire extinguishers located in the proper places in the business. The client challenges OSHA's interpretation of the agency's regulation governing fire extinguishers. Research would be necessary to locate the regulation and the court opinions that have addressed the regulation.

A. Federal Administrative Law

This section discusses research involving the location and interpretation of federal administrative regulations.

1. Publication

Administrative regulations are published in two sources, the *Federal Register* and the *Code of Federal Regulations* (C.F.R.).

a. Federal Register

The *Federal Register* is published daily by the United States Government Printing Office (GPO). All proposed new regulations, amended regulations, interim and final regulations are published in the *Federal Register*. It also contains summaries of regulations, effective dates, notices of hearings on proposed regulations, and persons to contact for further information. Presidential documents, such as executive orders, are included in the *Federal Register*.

The components of the *Federal Register* are the same in print and electronic format. The *Federal Register* includes a table of contents in the front of each issue, arranged by agency (see Exhibit 3-11). At the end of each issue is a section called "Reader Aids" that includes valuable information such as a list of telephone numbers to obtain information, and a table of "CFR Parts Affected" listing parts and sections of the *Code of Federal Regulations* affected. The pagination of the *Federal Register* is continuous, beginning with the first issue of a year and ending with the last. The issues are not cumulative; thus, using the *Federal Register* as a research source is difficult.

However, a cumulative *Federal Register Index* is published at the end of each month. This index, which is arranged by agency, references all the information published in the previous months of the year.

b. Code of Federal Regulations

It is much easier to conduct regulatory research using the *Code of Federal Regulations* (C.F.R.) for regulations that were published a year or more ago. The regulations of administrative agencies are codified in this multivolume, softbound set of books. The regulations are published in 50 titles, each of which represents a different subject area. The title numbers often, but not always, correspond to the titles assigned in the *United States Code*. The titles are subdivided into chapters, and each chapter usually covers the regulations of an individual agency. The chapters are divided into parts that consist of regulations governing a specific topic. The parts are divided into sections that are the specific regulations (see Exhibit 3-12). The C.F.R. is reprinted annually on a quarterly basis; that is, one-fourth of the code is reprinted each quarter. Titles 1–16 are issued each January; Titles 17–27 are issued each April 1; Titles 28–41 are issued each July 1; and Tiles 42–50 are issued each October 1.

There is a table of contents for each title, chapter, and part. At the end of each title is an index. In addition, there is an index volume called the *CFR Index and Finding Aids* through which regulations may be located by subject matter or agency. The index includes a parallel table that allows you to locate the C.F.R. title if you know the citation of the U.S.C. statute that established the agency. The index also includes a list of the agencies and 50 titles, chapters, and parts.

2. Researching Federal Administrative Law

Due to its organization, it is easier to locate federal rules and regulations through the *Code of Federal Regulations* than the *Federal Register*; therefore, the following guides focus on researching the C.F.R. in print and electronically (e-CFR). The e-CFR is available through the GPO's FDsys website (www.gpo.gov) and is a regularly updated unofficial compilation of C.F.R. material and Federal Register amendments. The C.F.R. can also be searched on Westlaw or LexisNexis.

Note that you may often locate the relevant case law by looking to the reference information following the section of the statute. It may be that two laws apply and govern a legal question. In this event, two causes of action may be available.

For Example

A small loan may violate provisions of both the federal Truth in Lending Act and the state usury law. In this case, there may be a cause of action under the federal law and a cause of action under the state law. If this occurs, steps 2 and 3 would be followed in regard to each statute.

When determining if a statute applies, always check the effective date of the statute to be sure that the statute is in effect. This is usually found in the statute itself or in the historical notes or comments in the reference sections following the statute. Also, *always* check the supplements to the statute to make sure the statute you are researching is the latest version. In print sources, supplementary material published after the publication of the main text is often located immediately following the statute or in a separate section or pamphlet. The supplements include any changes in the statute or reference material that have occurred since the publication of the book containing the statute.

When conducting electronic research, be sure to check for a link to the currentness of the statutes (discussed above in the section on updating statutory law). If the Internet research source does not provide information about currentness, consult another source to be sure you have the latest version of the statute.

B. Step 2: Analyze the Statute

After you determine that a statute applies, you must carefully read and analyze it to determine how it applies. Some statutes are lengthy and difficult to understand. You may need to check the library references to locate other library sources that explain and interpret the statute. It may be necessary to make a chart to assist you in understanding the specific provisions and operation of a statute.

Step 2 involves two parts:

1. Read the statute.
2. Identify the statutory elements: What does the statute specifically declare, require, or prohibit?

1. Read the Statute

Keep the following points in mind when reading statutory law:

1. Read the statute carefully several times.
2. Does the statute set a standard, or merely provide factors that must be considered?
3. Does the statute set out more than one rule or test? Are other rules or tests available? Are there exceptions to the rule or test?
4. All the words and punctuation have meaning. Always check the definitions section for the meaning of a term. If there is no definitions section, consult case law, a legal dictionary, or *Words and Phrases*. Do not assume you know what a term means. Your assumption may be wrong. A legal term may have several meanings, some of which may be unknown to you.

For Example

The word *publication* in tort law means more than presentation in the print or visual media. It means communication to a third party by any means. Under this definition, two neighbors gossiping over a backyard fence can constitute publication.

All punctuation counts. If you cannot understand how to read a statute, consult a secondary source, such as a treatise or legal encyclopedia.

5. Review the entire statute (all sections) to determine if other sections in some way affect or relate to the section you are researching.

For Example

Section 611-9 of the statute provides:

a. A will that does not comply with Section 611-8 is valid as a holographic will if the signature and the material provisions are in the handwriting of the testator.

b. If a holographic will does not contain a statement as to the date of its execution and it is established that the testator lacked testamentary capacity at any time during which the will might have been executed, the will is invalid unless it is established that it was executed at a time when the testator had testamentary capacity.

c. Any statement of testamentary intent contained in a holographic will may be set forth either in the testator's own handwriting or as part of a commercially printed form will.

Note that a *holographic will* is a will written entirely by the testator in his or her own handwriting and not witnessed. Subsection (a) sets the standard for when a holographic will is valid. Subsection (b), however, addresses a situation that affects the validity of a holographic will even if the requirements of subsection (a) are met. Subsection (c) establishes how testamentary intent may be set forth.

The preceding example illustrates a point that cannot be overemphasized: *Read and consider all parts of a statute.* Suppose the legal question is, "What is required for a holographic will to be valid?" If you stopped reading the statute at subsection (a) because it appeared to answer your question, you would miss the other provisions that also affect the answer to the question. Always read the entire statute. Also, if the statute refers to another section, read that other section to determine how it affects the statute.

6. Certain common terminology must be understood. Be aware of the meaning of the commonly used terms, such as *shall*, *may*, *and*, and *or*.

The term **shall** makes the duty imposed mandatory—it must be done. The term **may** leaves the duty optional. If **and** is used, all the conditions or listed items are required. If the term **or** is used, only one of the conditions or listed items is required.

For Example

Section 24-6-7-9 provides "A person is concerned in the commission of a crime if he:

a. directly commits the crime;

b. intentionally causes some other person to commit the crime; or

c. intentionally aids or abets in the commission of the crime."

The use of *or* means that a person is covered by the statute if he or she does *any* one of the listed acts.

For Example

Section 50-9-1 provides that holographic wills are valid if they are:

a. Entirely in the handwriting of the testator, and

b. Signed by the testator

The use of *and* means that both conditions must be met for the will to be valid.

7. Keep in mind the canons of construction when reading. These are presented in the General Consideration section of this chapter.

2. Identify the Statutory Elements

After you carefully read the statute, the next part of step 2 is to analyze the section of the statute in question. What does the statute specifically declare, require, or prohibit? How does the statute apply? Ask yourself, "What specific requirements must be met for the statute to apply? What are the elements?" For a statute to apply, certain conditions established by the statute must be met. These conditions or components of the statute are called **statutory elements.** After the elements are identified, you can determine how the statute applies.

After you have a sufficient understanding of the statute, begin this part of step 2 by breaking the statute down into its elements. Identify and list the elements that must be met for the statute to apply. This is necessary because you must know what the statutory elements are before you can proceed to step 3 and apply them to the legal problem or issue raised by the client's facts.

Identify the elements by reading the entire statute, analyzing each sentence word by word, and listing everything required. This includes listing all the various conditions and exceptions contained in the subsections of the statute in question and the conditions and exceptions included in other statutes that may affect the statute in question.

For Example

Consider Section 2-2-315 of the Commercial Code—Sales Act of state X:

Where the seller at the time of contracting has reason to know any particular purpose for which the goods are required and that the buyer is relying on the seller's skill or judgment to select or furnish suitable goods, there is an implied warranty that the goods shall be fit for such purpose.

Read the statute in the preceding example and determine the elements. For the implied warranty of § 2-2-315 to apply, the following requirements must be met:

1. *The person must be a seller of goods.* How do you know "of goods" is required? Section 2-2-315 quoted previously does not read "seller of goods"; it only states "the seller." You know "of goods" is required because in step 1, in order to determine if the statute applied to the issue in the client's case, you reviewed the scope section of the act. It provides that the act applies only to the sale of goods.

   How is the term *goods* defined? Assume the term is defined in the definitions section of the Commercial Code—Sales Act as: "All things movable at the time of sale." The statute also requires the individual to be a seller. How is *seller* defined in the definitions section of the act? Assume the term is defined as anyone who sells goods.

2. *The seller has reason to know the purpose for which the goods are required.* For the act to apply, the seller must have reason to know the purpose for which the buyer wants the goods. The statute does not require actual knowledge on the part of the seller. It uses the phrase, "has reason to know." You may need to refer to case law to determine what "reason to know" means or requires.

3. *The seller has reason to know the buyer is relying on the seller's skill or judgment.* This is usually established by the words or actions of the buyer that indicate to the seller the buyer's reliance on the seller's skill or judgment.

4. *The buyer must actually rely on the seller's skill or judgment in furnishing suitable goods.* This is required because the statute provides that "the seller … has reason to know … that the buyer is relying."

5. *The seller must have known of the purpose for which the goods were required and the buyer's reliance on the seller's skill or judgment in furnishing the goods at the time the sale was taking place, not later.* This is required because the statute provides, "the seller at the time of contracting. …"

Be sure to complete both parts of step 2 before proceeding to step 3.

C. Step 3: Apply the Statute to the Legal Problem or Issue

After you have identified the elements, which are the conditions necessary for the statute to apply, then apply the elements to the legal problem or issue raised by the client's fact situation. This entails applying or matching the facts of the client's case to the elements of the statute, which may be accomplished in several ways. One way is to chart the elements of the statute. Next to the elements, list the facts from the client's case that match or establish each of the elements or requirements of the statute. Another way is to prepare a narrative summary of the elements and how the facts of the case apply to match or establish the elements. The following examples illustrate the performance of step 3 in both chart and narrative summary format.

1. Chart Format

In the following example, a **chart format** is used.

For Example

Tom goes to the local hardware store and informs the salesperson that he needs to grind metal with a power metal grinder. He tells the salesperson that he needs goggles to protect his eyes. The salesperson, after looking through his stock, hands Tom a pair of goggles and tells him, "These are what you need." Tom purchases the goggles, and when he uses them, a piece of metal pierces the lens of the goggles and damages Tom's eye.

Can Tom state a claim under the provisions of the implied warranty statute, § 2-2-315, presented in the previous example? How does the statute apply?

STATUTORY ELEMENTS	FACTS OF CLIENT'S CASE
1. Seller of goods	The seller was a salesperson at the local hardware store, a seller within the meaning of the statute. The item sold, goggles, meets the definition of goods (the goggles are "things movable at the time of sale").
2. Has reason to know the buyer's purpose in purchasing the goods	Tom explicitly told the seller the purpose for buying the goggles.
3. Has reason to know of buyer's reliance on seller's judgment	This is implied from Tom's conduct of allowing the seller to select the goods without any input from Tom.
4. Reliance by buyer on seller's skill or judgment	Tom relied on the salesperson's judgment. He indicated the purpose and accepted, without independent judgment or act, what the seller selected.
5. At the time of contracting	The seller knew at the time of the sale, not later, of Tom's purpose and reliance.

After the elements of the statute have been identified and the facts of the client's case compared and matched with the required elements of the statute, you can determine how the statute applies. In this example, you can conclude that the statute covers the conduct of the salesperson and that an implied warranty was created. All the required elements of the statute are established by the facts in Tom's case:

1. The salesperson was a seller within the meaning of the statute, and the item sold meets the definition of goods.
2. At the time of the sale, the buyer informed the seller of the specific purpose for which the goods were being purchased.
3. The seller knew of the buyer's reliance on his skill and judgment.
4. The buyer relied on the expertise and judgment of the seller.
5. The seller knew at the time of sale, not later.

2. Narrative Summary

In the following example, a **narrative summary** is used rather than a chart format.

For Example

Section 56-6-1 of the Open Meetings Act provides that "all meetings of two or more members of any board ... at which any public business is discussed or at which any action may be taken or is taken are declared to be public meetings open to the public." The section further provides:

a. Such meetings shall be held only after full and timely public notice.

b. This section does not apply to chance meetings or social gatherings at which discussion of public business is not the central purpose.

Ida and Dan are members of a three-person state board. They run into each other at a Christmas party and discuss board business.

Is this meeting an open meeting governed by § 56-6-1? The application of step 2 reveals the statute requires an open meeting when the following elements are present:

1. Two or more board members
2. Meet at other than a chance or social gathering where discussion of public business is not the central purpose, and
3. Public business is discussed or action may be or is taken.

A narrative summary of the elements and the application of the statute to the facts illustrates step 3:

1. *Two or more board members.* This element is met. Both Dan and Ida are board members.
2. *Meet at other than a chance or social gathering where discussion of public business is not the central purpose.* It appears that this element is not met by the facts. This was a social gathering and also possibly a chance meeting. The gathering was a Christmas party. It does not appear that the discussion of public business was the central purpose. If it is discovered that the sole reason they went to the party was to discuss public business, the exclusion in subsection (b) of the statute probably does not apply and the meeting may be covered by the act.
3. *Public business is discussed or action may be or is taken.* This element is met. Public business was discussed.

After performing step 3, it appears that this was not a public meeting within the meaning of the act. Although the requirements of the first and third elements are met (two or more board members met and discussed public business), the requirements of the second element are not met.

When performing step 3, remember to match the client's facts with the required elements of a statute. When this is accomplished, you can determine how the statute applies. In the example concerning the purchase of goggles, all the required statutory elements were met by the facts of the client's case and an implied warranty was created. In the public meetings example, the facts did not meet the requirements of the second element of the statute; therefore, the meeting was not a public meeting within the meaning of the statute.

D. Summary of the Statutory Analysis Process

The three steps presented in this section are a useful approach to statutory analysis. These steps may be summarized as follows:

- Step 1: Determine if the statute applies in any way to the legal problem or issue.
- Step 2: Carefully read the statute and identify the required elements.
- Step 3: Compare or match the required elements to the facts of the problem and determine how the statute applies.

In addition to this three-step approach, there are other general considerations to keep in mind when analyzing statutory law. These considerations are presented in the following section.

VII. GENERAL CONSIDERATIONS

Always keep in mind two major considerations and guidelines when engaged in statutory analysis:

1. Legislative history
2. Canons of construction

These considerations come into play, and are of the greatest importance, when the meaning of the statute is unclear and the meaning has not been determined by a court.

When required to interpret a statute, a court will first look to the plain meaning of the language of the statute. This is called the **plain meaning rule**. The rule mandates that a statute be interpreted according to its plain meaning; that is, words will be interpreted according to their common meanings. The court will render an interpretation that reflects the plain meaning of the language and is consistent with the meaning of all other sections of the act. If the meaning is clear on its face, then no additional inquiries concerning the meaning of a statute are allowed. If there is still an ambiguity in the meaning of a statutory section, the court will then look to the legislative history of the statute and apply canons of construction.

When engaging in statutory analysis, be mindful of the considerations that the court applies when interpreting the meaning of a statute. The reason for this is obvious: You want your interpretation of the meaning of a statute and how it will be applied to coincide with that of the court. Each of these considerations is addressed in this section.

A. Legislative History

To determine the meaning of a statute, a court may look to the legislative history of the statute to discover what the legislature intended it to mean. **Legislative history** is the record of the legislation during the enactment process before it became law. It consists of committee reports, transcripts of hearings, statements of legislators concerning the legislation, and any other material published for legislative use in regard to the legislation.

Legislative history may be of assistance in several ways when interpreting a statute. The history may identify why an ambiguous term was used and what meaning the legislature intended, what the legislature intended the statute to accomplish, the general purpose of the legislation, and so on. Researching legislative history is discussed in Chapter 6.

B. Canons of Construction

Canons of construction are rules and guidelines the courts use when interpreting statutes. A fundamental rule of construction that determines when canons of construction are applied by a court is the plain meaning rule, which governs when the canons of construction apply. If the meaning is clear on its face, there is no room for interpretation and a court will not apply the canons of construction.

The canons of construction are too numerous to be addressed individually in this text. Some well-known canons are presented here.

1. Expressio Unius

The entire Latin phrase is *expressio unius est exclusio alterius*, which translates as "the expression of one excludes all others." If the statute contains a list of what is covered, everything else is excluded.

For Example

If a statute governing artists lists potters, glass blowers, painters, poets, writers, and sculptors, but does not include weavers, weavers are not covered by the statute. Only the occupations listed are covered, all other occupations are not covered.

Note, however, that a statute often is written to state that a list is not exclusive. When so written, this canon of construction does not apply, and the statute is not limited to the items listed.

For Example

"A 'Building' as used in this statute means a structure on private or commercial property and includes *but is not limited to* a dwelling, an office of fixed location. ..."

2. Ejusdem Generis

The Latin term *ejusdem generis* means "of the same genus or class." As a canon of construction, it means that whenever a statute contains a specific list followed by a general term, the general term is interpreted to be limited to other things of the same class or kind as those in the list.

For Example

A statute regulating self-propelled vehicles lists "bicycles, tricycles, unicycles, and other devices." Here "other devices" is limited to mean devices of the same class or kind as bicycles, tricycles, and unicycles. Motorized vehicles are not "other devices" within the meaning of the statute.

3. Pari Materia

The Latin term *pari materia* translates as "on the same subject matter." This canon means that statutes dealing with the same subject should be interpreted consistently.

For Example

A state's Fair Housing Act prohibits discrimination against an individual on the basis of "gender preference." The state's Fair Employment Act also uses the term *gender preference*. The term should be interpreted consistently in both statutes unless each statute has a definitions section that gives a clearly different meaning.

4. Last Antecedent Rule

The last antecedent rule states: Qualifying words and phrases apply to the words or phrase immediately preceding and do not extend to other more remote words or phrases.

For Example

A DWI statute provides that "driver means every person who drives or is in actual physical control of a motor vehicle upon a highway. ..." The phrase "upon a highway" modifies the term *motor vehicle*. It does not modify the term *drives*.

5. Intended Remedy

Intended remedy means that statutes are to be interpreted in a manner that furthers the intended legislative remedy.

6. Entire Context

The words, phrases, and subsections of a statute are to be interpreted in the context of the entire statute.

7. Constitutionality

Statutes are assumed to be constitutional and should be construed in a manner that preserves their constitutionality, if possible.

8. Criminal Statutes

Criminal statutes are to be narrowly interpreted.

It is important to remember that, as with all matters involving case law, when a court interprets a statute, the principle of stare decisis applies. A court will follow the interpretation previously adopted unless the previous interpretation is overruled and a new interpretation is adopted.

VIII. CITING CONSTITUTIONS, STATUTES, ADMINISTATIVE LAW, AND COURT RULES
A. Citing Constitutions

The citation format for constitutions can be found in Bluepages B11 and Rule 11 of the *Bluebook* and Rule 13 of the *ALWD Guide*. The citation format for state constitutions is shown on the inside back cover of the *Bluebook*. Despite descriptive differences in the rules of each citation manual, the citation format is the same for both. The *Bluebook* states that constitutional subdivisions, such as articles and clauses, should be abbreviated according to Table T.16 (T16), and the *ALWD Guide* refers to its Appendix 3(C) for such abbreviations. Note that for state and the United States Constitution you do not include a date unless the provision being cited has been repealed, amended, or superseded.

The only short-form citation appropriate for use with constitutional citations is *Id*. If the use of *Id*. is not appropriate, the full citation must be given. The *Bluebook* dictates that when citing a constitutional provision from an electronic database, you must indicate in a parenthetical the publisher, editor, or compiler, unless the electronic source is a government source. You must also indicate the name of the database and the currentcy of the database as provided by the database itself.

Many states have adopted a state procedural rule addressing citation format. Those local rules may dictate citation format of the state's primary law in documents filed in state courts or may dictate which citation manual must be followed. Be sure to check your state's local procedural rules for a local rule and follow that rule. If no local rule exists controlling citation format, then either the *Bluebook* or *ALWD Guide* may be followed.

Each example is presented with a ^ symbol, indicating where spaces are placed, followed by the example without the space symbol.

For Example

U.S.^Const.^art.^IV,^§^3
U.S. Const. art. IV, § 3
Conn.^Const.^art.^XII^§^1
Conn. Const. art. XII § 1
U.S.^Const.^amend.^V^(West,^Westlaw^through^P.L.^114–51)
U.S. Const. amend. V (West, Westlaw through P.L. 114-51)

According to the *Bluebook*, Rule 8 parts of the United States Constitution are capitalized when discussed in textual sentences.

For Example

Fourth Amendment
Equal Protection Clause
Article 1, Section 1

B. Citing Statutes

The citation format for statutes can be found in Bluepages B12 and Rule 12 of the *Bluebook* and Rule 14 of the *ALWD Guide*. Statutes can be found in both official and unofficial codes as well as in print and online. The source you obtain the statute from dictates the citation format. Table T1 in the *Bluebook* and Appendix 1 in the *ALWD Guide* indicate which code is official and which is unofficial, as well as the detailed cite for each. *Bluebook* Rule 12.2 and 12.3 and *ALWD Guide* Appendix 1 also explain which code to cite when more than one publisher prints the code, how to abbreviate each code, and what if any information should be included in a parenthetical.

1. General Rules When Citing Statutes

The following rules apply when citing both federal and state statutes. Note, this is a summary of the general rules. Researchers should carefully consult the appropriate citation manual for all of the details regarding proper citation form for a particular statutory code.

a. Official versus Unofficial Codes

The *Bluebook* dictates that the official code should be cited when a statute is found therein. However, citing to unofficial codes is permissible, but requires that the name of the publisher, editor, or compiler be included in the parenthetical with the year of the code.

For Example

Official: 42^U.S.C.^§^1983^(2012)
         42 U.S.C. § 1983 (2012)
Unofficial: 12^U.S.C.A.^§^300a-7^(West^2001)
         12 U.S.C.A. § 300a-7 (West 2001)
State unofficial: Ariz.^Rev.^Stat.^§^47-1201^(LexisNexis^2014)
         Ariz. Rev. Stat. § 47-1201 (LexisNexis 2014)

b. Print versus Electronic Databases

When citing a print source be mindful of whether material is taken from main volumes of supplemental volumes. When the citation is to material from supplemental volumes, the *Bluebook* Rules 3.1 and 12.3 require the supplement and its date be identified in the parenthetical.

For Example

Print official: 18 U.S.C. § 510(b) (Supp. I 1983)
Print unofficial: 12 U.S.C.S. § 1710 (LexisNexis 1993 & Supp. 2004)

When citing a statute obtained from a code in an electronic database, the *Bluebook* Rule 12.5 requires that the name of the database and the currency of the database be provided parenthetically. The name of the publisher, editor, or compiler must also be provided in the parenthetical unless the publisher, editor, or compiler is the government or is acting at the direction of the government.

For Example

Electronic from nongovernmental source: 18 U.S.C.A. § 1956 (Westlaw through P.L. 114-51)

c. Section Symbol (§) and Multiple Sections

The section symbol (§) is used to indicate a section of a statute. Note, however, that you may not use the symbol to start a sentence. In such cases the word *section* is used.

For Example

Correct: "Section 2253 of the Act provides. ..."
Incorrect: "§ 2253 of the Act provides. ..."

Refer to "Sections and Paragraphs" later in this chapter for rules on citing multiple sections.

d. Short Citation Format

Once citation to a statute has been presented in a document in the full format, subsequent cites may be in short citation format. If the use of *Id.* is appropriate, it is the preferred short form. Otherwise the short-form citation involves use of the numbers associated with the statutory scheme—in other words, the abbreviation for the statutory code and the parenthetical information is left off of the citation. The exception to this is when the statutory code cited is from an electronic database; then the name of the database must be provided in a parenthetical.

For Example

Full Citation: 15 U.S.C. § 7 (1988 & Supp. 2002)
Short Citation(s): 15 U.S.C. § 7 or *Id.*
Full Citation: Minn. Stat. § 519 (1990)
Short Citation(s): § 519 or *Id.*

2. Session Laws and Slip Laws

If a citation is not available in the official or unofficial codes, then it is appropriate to cite the session law. Citation format for session laws can be found in Rule 12.4 of the *Bluebook* and Rules 14.7 to 14.13 in the *ALWD Guide*. Citation to session or slip laws may be necessary when a recently passed law has not been published in the official or unofficial codes. As with state statutes, the form for session laws varies from state to state. The abbreviations and formats for session laws are presented in Table TI of the *Bluebook* and Appendix 1 of the *ALWD Guide*.

C. Citing Administrative Law

The citation format for administrative law can be found in Bluepages B14 and Rule 14 of the *Bluebook* and Rule 19 of the *ALDW Guide*. The citation form for citation to the *Code of Federal Regulations* and *Federal Register* are the same in both manuals. Generally citations to the *Code of Federal Regulations* are to title, section, part and year, citing the most recent edition. Be aware that certain titles of the C.F.R. have specific and peculiar citations. Citations to the *Federal Register* should include the commonly used name of the rule or regulation, the volume and page in which the regulation begins, and the date of the rule or regulation. If the *Federal Register* indicates the title and section in the C.F.R. where the rule or regulation will appear, provide that information parenthetically.

For Example

C.F.R.:   27 C.F.R. § 20.235 (1988)
       FCC Broadcast Radio Services 47 C.F.R. § 73.609 (2014)
Federal Register: Approval and Promulgation of Air Quality Implementation Plans; New Mexico; Albuquerque/Bernalillo County, 80 Fed. Reg. 63,431 (Oct. 20, 2015)
       Importation of Fruits and Vegetables, 60 Fed. Reg. 50,379 (Sept. 29, 1995) (to be codified at 7 C.F.R. pt. 300)

D. Citing Court Rules

The citation format for court rules can be found in Bluepages B12 and Rule 12 of the *Bluebook* and Rule 17 of the *ALWD Guide*. The citation format is the same in both guides. When citing rules no longer in force, indicate the repeal parenthetically.

For Example

Federal Rules of Civil Procedure (govt. publication): Fed. R. Civ. P. 4 (2015)
Federal Rules of Evidence (nongovt. publication): Fed. R. Evid. 407 (West 2015)
State Rule of Criminal Procedure: Ariz. R. Crim. P. 45 (2015)

E. Sections and Paragraphs

The following is a summary of citation rules when enacted laws are organized by sections or paragraphs:

1. Insert a space before and after the section (§) or paragraph (¶) symbol.
2. Do not use "at" when referring to a paragraph or section.

For Example

Correct: *Id.* § 2111
Incorrect: *Id.* at § 2111

If the authority is divided into subsections or paragraphs, use the punctuation of the original source to separate sections and subsections. If the source does not have any punctuation, place the subdivisions in parentheses—18 U.S.C. 842(a)(1). Note how there is no space between the main section "842" and the subsections "(a)(1)."

A section may include a letter as part of the designation. In this case, the letter does not refer to a subsection; therefore, do not separate it with punctuation: for example, 42 U.S.C. 2000e(1)(a) (1994). The "e" is part of the section designation and does not refer to a subsection.

When citing consecutive sections or paragraphs, include the first and last sections and separate with a hyphen, a long dash, or "to." Retain all digits on both sides of the span. Use consecutive section or paragraph symbols to indicate multiple sections or paragraphs.

For Example

Correct:	¶¶ 115–121
Incorrect:	¶¶ 115–21
Correct:	§§ 107–110
Incorrect:	§§ 107–10

When citing multiple sections or paragraphs that are not consecutive, place a comma between the sections or paragraphs and do not place "and" or an ampersand (&) before the final section or paragraph.

For Example

Correct:	¶¶ 115, 123, 129
Incorrect:	¶¶ 115, 123, and 129
Correct:	§§15, 17–19, 21
Incorrect:	§§ 15, 17–19, and 21

IX. KEY POINTS CHECKLIST: *Working with Statutes*

Keep the following key points in mind when working with statutes:

- ✓ When conducting research, identify the question or research terms as narrowly and concisely as possible.

- ✓ *Always* update your research—check the pocket parts and supplements to print sources or find the information on currency when using Internet research sources to make sure that the statute has not been changed or repealed.

- ✓ When researching federal regulatory law, it is easier to use the *Code of Federal Regulations* than the *Federal Register*.

- ✓ When reviewing a statute, do not limit your focus to a specific section. Remember, a section is one part of an entire act that usually contains several statutory sections. Read a section in the context of the entire act. Be sure you are familiar with all the sections of the act; there may be another section, such as a definitions section, that affects the interpretation of the statute you are reading.

- ✓ When you find a statute that appears to apply, do not stop your research. In many instances, more than one statute or legislative act applies to a specific question or fact situation.

- ✓ Read statutes carefully and slowly. Several readings may be necessary. You may have to make a chart or diagram of the various sections and subsections of a statute to gain an understanding of the operation of the statute.

- ✓ All the words of a statute have meaning. If a word does not seem necessary or appears repetitive, you may have misread the statute. Read it again. Consult a secondary source that contains a discussion or interpretation of the statute.

- ✓ Do not assume you know the meaning of a word. Many statutory words are terms of art, loaded with meaning. Check the definitions section of the statute, case law, or a legal dictionary to ensure you give the correct meaning to a term.

✓ The plain meaning of a statute governs its statutory interpretation. If the meaning is clear, the statute is not subject to interpretation.

✓ If the statute is unclear or ambiguous, look to other sources for guidance, such as legislative history or applicable canons of construction. Are there court opinions that interpret the statute? Are there secondary sources, such as law review articles or encyclopedia sections that discuss the statute?

X. APPLICATION

The application of the principles of statutory analysis is illustrated in the following examples.

A. Chapter Hypothetical

In the hypothetical situation presented at the beginning of the chapter, Alan's assignment is to determine if Mr. Jackson has a cause of action against Outdoor Extreme Sports for breach of warranty under the sales provisions of the state's commercial code. The scope of his research has been narrowed greatly by the assignment. He needs to locate the sales provisions of the commercial code, then identify the statutes that address warranties. Alan can look for various terms in the index of the statutes, such as *sales, commercial code, warranties,* and *contracts.* He may look to the popular name table for commercial code, or sales of goods. If he is conducting research electronically, he may begin with the terms *contracts, sales,* and *warranties.*

His research turns up five sections of the state's Commercial Code Sales Act that may apply:

- Section 47-2102 provides that the act applies to the sale of goods only; services are specifically excluded by the act.
- Section 47-2105 defines *goods* as "all things which are movable at the time of the contract for sale."
- Section 47-2313 provides that an express warranty is created by a seller's affirmation of fact or promise that relates to the quality of the goods.
- Section 47-2314 states that "a warranty that the goods shall be merchantable is implied in a contract for their sale if the seller is a merchant with respect to goods of that kind."
- Section 47-2315 provides: "Where the seller at the time of contracting has reason to know any particular purpose for which the goods are required and that the buyer is relying on the seller's skill or judgment to select or furnish suitable goods, there is a warranty that the goods shall be fit for such purpose."

After conducting research on how to analyze statutory law, Alan applies the steps recommended in this chapter.

STEP 1.   *Determine If the Statute Applies*
When reviewing the statutes, Alan notes that § 47-2102 provides that the Commercial Code Sales Act only applies to the sale of goods. If this transaction is not a sale of goods, then neither the statute nor the warranty provisions of the act apply.

Section 47-2105 defines goods as "all things which are movable. …" This definition is applicable. The climbing gear in the beginner's kit was clearly movable. In this case, only goods are involved.

Alan's conclusion is based on his interpretation of the law. Because he is new at statutory analysis, however, Alan knows his analysis could be wrong. To be on the safe side, he continues his analysis in order to provide his supervisory attorney a complete review of the law. Alan proceeds to steps 2 and 3.

STEP 2.   *Analyze the Statute*
Since the act does apply—that is, if the conclusion is that the transaction is a sale of goods—which of the warranty remedies, if any, would be available to Mr. Jackson? Alan carefully reads the statute and determines that the three warranties included in § 47-2313, § 47-2314, and § 47-2315 are the only possible warranties available in the act. Which of these would apply?

Clearly § 47-2313 and § 47-2315 would not apply. Section 47-2313 requires some affirmation or promise by the seller relating to the quality of the goods. In Mr. Jackson's case, there was no statement by a salesperson, either oral or written, concerning the quality of the climbing gear. Section 47-2315 also would not apply, as Mr. Jackson did not communicate any particular purpose for which the goods were required. Also, there are no facts to indicate that he in any way relied on a salesperson's expertise in selecting the climbing gear. To be on the safe side, Alan reviews the courts' interpretation of the term *particular purpose.* The case law indicates that the term refers to a unique and specific purpose for which the goods are required that is clearly and specifically communicated by the buyer to the seller. The facts in Mr. Jackson's case show there was no specific communication.

Alan's last hope is § 47-2314. He reads the statute and identifies the following as the elements of an implied warranty of merchantability:

1. The transaction must be a contract for the sale of goods.

2. The seller must be a merchant of those goods.

On the face of it, it appears that this statute would apply. Alan proceeds to step 3.

STEP 3.   *Apply the Statute to the Legal Problem or Issue*

Alan applies the statute to the problem through the use of a chart.

STATUTORY ELEMENTS	FACTS OF CLIENT'S CASE
1. Contract for sale of goods.	Assuming that the predominant factor test led to the conclusion that this transaction is a sale of goods, not services, then this is a sale-of-goods transaction.
2. Seller is a merchant of those goods.	The act defines *merchant* as a person who deals in goods of the kind sold. If Outdoor Extreme Sports routinely sells climbing gear, then the seller is a "merchant." In Mr. Jackson's case, the store routinely sells climbing gear. Therefore, the seller is a "merchant."

After performing this step, Alan can reach a conclusion as to whether the statute applies and whether Mr. Jackson has a cause of action for breach of warranty under § 47-2314. Assuming that the transaction is a sale of goods, it appears that the statute would apply: There was a contract for the sale of goods by a merchant of those goods.

Under § 47-2314, the seller warrants that the goods are merchantable, which is defined in case law as meaning "fit for the ordinary purposes for which such goods are used." In Mr. Jackson's case, the goods obviously were not fit for their ordinary purpose. The climbing harness severed at the seams during the first climb and an average distance fall. Mr. Jackson was properly roped to the mountain and the rope caught him at the proper distance. Had the harness stayed intact he would not have fallen the entire distance to the ground and suffered the broken arm and multiple bruises. If § 47-2314 applies, Mr. Jackson clearly has a claim for breach of warranty.

B. Will Revocation Statute

Section 50-5 of the state statutes is the applicable statute in this example. It provides as follows:
No will in writing, nor any part thereof, shall be revoked unless, with the intent to revoke, the testator:

a. executes a subsequent will or codicil,
b. prepares a writing declaring an intention to revoke the same which is executed in a manner in which a will is required to be executed, or
c. the testator or some person in the testator's presence and by the testator's direction … cancels, or destroys the same with the intent to revoke.

The following facts apply in this example. Before Mary Glenn died, she directed her brother, Tom Glenn, to cancel her will. Because she was too weak to write, she directed her brother to cancel the will by writing across the first page, "I hereby revoke this will. It is my intent that this will be no longer valid. I direct my brother to do this because I can no longer write." Tom took the will to Mary's kitchen, a room adjacent to her bedroom, and wrote what Mary had requested on the first page of the will and added, "This was done at the request of Mary Glenn by me, Tom Glenn."

Was the will validly revoked under the terms of the statute?

STEP 1.   *Determine If the Statute Applies*

The statute appears on its face to apply to this fact situation. The statute governs will revocations, and this is an attempted revocation.

STEP 2. *Read and Analyze the Statute*

After a careful reading, the statute can be analyzed and the required elements identified. The statute provides three ways in which a written will can be revoked:

1. By a subsequent will or codicil executed by the testator, with the intent to revoke the prior will

2. By a writing intended to revoke the will, executed in the same manner as a will is required to be executed

3. By the testator or some person in the testator's presence and by the testator's direction canceling or destroying the will with the intent to revoke

STEP 3. *Apply the Statute to the Legal Problem or Issue*

When the statute is applied to the fact situation, it appears that subsections (a) and (b) clearly do not apply. Subsection (a) requires a subsequent will or codicil, neither of which is present in Mary Glenn's case. Subsection (b) requires a writing revoking the will, executed in a manner in which a will must be executed. Assume that research reveals that the state statutes require a will to be witnessed by two witnesses. There were no witnesses in this case. The requirements of this subsection are not met because the writing by Tom was not executed in the required manner.

If there is a valid revocation under the statute, it can have occurred only under the cancellation provisions of subsection (c). For a revocation to occur under subsection (c), the following elements must be met:

1. The testator or some person
   a. In the presence of the testator, and
   b. By the testator's direction
2. Cancels or destroys the will
3. With the intent to revoke

In this example, the required elements of the statute will be applied to the facts of the case in a different way than in the previous example. In the previous example, a chart was used; here a narrative summary is used:

1. *Testator or some person.* The requirements of this element are met. The testator did not cancel the will but "some person," her brother, did.
   a. *In the presence of the testator.* It is questionable whether this element is met. Does "in the testator's presence" mean actual physical presence in the same room? If the person canceling the will is in an adjacent room, is that "in the testator's presence"? If the statute does not define the term *presence*, case law must be consulted. If the courts have not interpreted the term, the legislative history of the act may shed some light.
   b. *By the direction of the testator.* This element is met. Mary Glenn directed her brother to revoke the will.

2. *Cancels or destroys the will.* This element appears to be met. The language clearly revokes the will and appears on the will itself. The statute does not require that the revocation language appear on a specific page of the will such as the signature page. Case law should be consulted to see if the courts have established where the revocation language must be placed.

3. With the intent to revoke. This element is met. The intent to revoke is clearly indicated in the language Mary Glenn chose.

The conclusion is that the statute applies, and the will has been revoked if the presence requirement is met and if cancellation language is effective when placed on the first page of a will. By following the three steps recommended, subsections (a) and (b) of the statute were eliminated from consideration, and subsection (c), which could possibly apply, was identified. The application analysis helps focus the attention on what research is needed to reach a final conclusion. Note that the final conclusion cannot be reached in step 3 until research is conducted to determine what "in the testator's presence" requires under the statute. The research should begin with a review of the case annotations following the statute to determine if a court has interpreted "in the testator's presence."

Summary

This chapter focuses on how to research and analyze enacted law and court rules. The principles presented in the chapter apply to the research and analysis of constitutions, statutory law, administrative law, and court rules.

An increasingly expanding source of law in the United States is statutory law. This body of law assumes a greater role because many matters once covered by the case law are now addressed by state and federal legislative bodies. As a result of this growth, researchers are more frequently engaged in analyzing legal problems and issues governed by statutory law.

Statutory research is the process of finding the statutory law that applies to a problem. Most federal and state laws are organized according to topic (codified) and published with annotations. The beginning step of all research, including statutory research, is to identify what you are looking for as precisely and narrowly as possible. Most statutes are located through use of the general index, although they also may be found through use of the table of contents or the popular name table.

Administrative law is the body of law consisting of the rules and regulations of administrative agencies and the court opinions interpreting them. The main research source for locating federal administrative law is the *Code of Federal Regulations*. Court rules regulate the conduct of matters brought before the court.

The analysis of enacted law and court rules is the process of determining if a law applies, how it applies, and the effect of that application. For the sake of clarity, the chapter discussion and examples focus upon the analysis of laws passed by legislative bodies, called statutory law. A prerequisite to analyzing a law is a familiarity with the parts or components of the law.

The most efficient way to address a problem involving a statute is to have a process for or an approach to statutory analysis. This chapter presents a three-step approach.

The first step is to determine whether the statute governs the situation in any way. This step involves locating all the possible statutes that may apply, then deciding which apply to the facts raised by the legal problem.

The second step is to carefully read the statute and identify what is required for the statute to apply. These requirements are usually referred to as the elements of the statute. A careful analysis may require several readings of the statute and reference to interpretative sources such as court opinions or secondary sources such as treatises and law review articles.

The third step is to apply the elements to the facts of the legal problem. This involves matching the elements of the statute to the facts of the case and determining how the statute applies.

When engaging in statutory analysis, it is important to be mindful of certain guidelines. Most of these come into play when the meaning of a statute is unclear or ambiguous. In addition to court opinions, which give guidance to the interpretation of a statute, legislative history and canons of construction may be consulted. Legislative history is composed of all the legislative material and records concerning a statute before it became law. Canons of construction are guidelines developed by courts for use in interpreting ambiguous statutes. These sources should not be used if the meaning of the statute is clear on its face.

The ease with which you are able to locate and analyze statutes increases with practice. The more you read and analyze statutes, the easier it becomes. The exercises at the end of this chapter may prove helpful in this regard.

Quick References

Internet Resources

http://www.law.cornell.edu
The Legal Information Institute (LII) housed at Cornell Law School provides free, open access to the United States Constitution, the United States Code, the Code of Federal Regulations, and the federal Rules of Criminal, Civil, Appellate, and Bankruptcy Procedure, the federal Rules of Evidence, as well as links to many state laws.

http://www.findlaw.com
FindLaw is an excellent source for locating federal and state statutes. Simply type in the name of the state you are researching. Court rules and some state administrative regulations may also be found at this site. Although the laws are not current, the website provides information on how to update laws.

http://www.gpo.gov
This Government Printing Office's FDsys website provides access to the United States Code, the Code of Federal Regulations, the Federal Register, United States Constitution, and numerous other laws. The GPO's website includes information on currentness of the C.F.R. and indicates the U.S.C. is not current and researchers should use another source to ensure that the latest most updated version of a law is obtained.

http://www.house.gov
This site is the home page for the United States House of Representatives, and it provides information on the legislative process and links to the current activities and calendar of the House.

http://www.senate.gov
This site is the home page for the United States Senate and provides information on the legislative process, how to find bill numbers, copies of bills, access to active legislation and a virtual reference desk with links and contacts for many legislative and administrative related agencies.

http://congress.gov
This is the official website for United States federal legislative information. The website is presented by the Library of Congress and provides accurate information and access to federal legislation including current bills, public laws, and the congregational record.

http://www.regulations.gov
This is an online source for U.S. government regulations from nearly 300 federal agencies. The website provides a quick tutorial on how to use the site.

Exercises

ASSIGNMENT 1

Your state's paralegal association has a yearly two-day conference that provides both continuing education credits and booths where vendors of various types of law office software can share information and demonstrations of their product. This year the paralegal association also wants to have a formal gala to raise money for scholarships for students at local colleges who are working toward their paralegal degree. The association wants to sell alcohol at the gala. Does your state have a law requiring a special license in order for alcoholic beverages to be sold?

ASSIGNMENT 2

Monique has good credit and a good job. She is moving with her wife to a new town for a new job. Monique and her wife rented their last apartment for five years. They believe that a landlord in the new town refused to rent them an apartment because they are gay. Refer to either the U.S.C.A. or the U.S.C.S., and identify the federal law that governs this. Does your state have a law that governs this issue?

ASSIGNMENT 3

Refer to the U.S.C.A. What is the definition of a "digital audio recording device" under the copyright law? If you used the U.S.C.A. in print, when was the section last amended? If you used an Internet source, what source did you use? Did it allow you to check the currentness of the section? If so, what was the public law number and date that the section was current through?

ASSIGNMENT 4

Refer to the U.S.C.S. Cite the title and section of the code that addresses equal opportunity in contract solicitation, housing, and community development by the Federal Home Loan Mortgage Corporation. If you used the U.S.C.S. in print, when was the section last amended? If you used an Internet source, what source did you use? Did it allow you to check the currentness of the section? If so, what was the public law number and date that the section was current through?

ASSIGNMENT 5

What is the authorized term of imprisonment for possession of biological weapons by a restricted person under Title 18 of the *United States Code?* Cite the title and section. If you used the U.S.C. in print, when was the section last amended? If you used an Internet source, what source did you use? Did it allow you to check the currentness of the section? If so, what was the public law number and date that the section was current through?

ASSIGNMENT 6

Refer to the Fifth Amendment to the United States Constitution in the U.S.C.A. or U.S.C.S. Cite the 1967 United States Supreme Court decision addressing the applicability of the privilege against self-incrimination in the case of juveniles.

ASSIGNMENT 7

Look up a statute of your choosing in your state. You may find it in a print source, a commercial Internet source, or a noncommercial source, such as your state legislature's website.

1. What source did you use?
2. When was the statute originally enacted?
3. When was the statute last amended (date and public law number)?

4. Did the source you used allow you to update the statute to ensure you had the most current version of the statute?
5. If the answer to number 4 was yes, how were you able to check for updates to the statute?

The following exercises present a statute followed by questions concerning the statute.

ASSIGNMENT 8

Statute: Criminal Code Section 20-4-102, Arson

A person who knowingly sets fire to, burns, causes to be burned, or by use of any explosive, damages or destroys, or causes to be damaged or destroyed, any property of another without his consent commits arson.

Questions

a. What are the required elements of arson?

b. Tom breaks into a neighbor's barn, sets off 20 sticks of dynamite, and blows up the barn. The barn does not catch fire, but it is blown to small bits and completely destroyed. Has Tom committed arson? Why?

c. Lois breaks into a house intending to steal cash and jewelry. She lights a match to locate a safe. She drops the match, it falls in a trash can, and the house catches fire. Has Lois committed arson? Why?

d. Dai's Diner is losing money and about to go out of business. Dai and Steve own the building where the diner is located. One evening Dai sets the building on fire in order to collect the insurance on the building. Has Dai committed arson? Why?

ASSIGNMENT 9

Answer the questions in assignment 8 using your state law governing arson.

ASSIGNMENT 10

Access the *Code of Federal Regulations*. What, if any, federal regulation applies to environmental impact statements for activities in Antarctica?

ASSIGNMENT 11

Refer to the *Federal Register* for October 19, 2015. On what page(s) of the *Federal Register* is the final rule of the Parole Commission on the topic of paroling, recommitting, and supervising federal prisoners; prisoners serving sentences under the United States and District of Columbia Codes? On what date is the final rule effective?

ASSIGNMENT 12

Statute: Section 30-1-6, Nuncupative Wills

a. A nuncupative will may be made only by a person in imminent peril of death and shall be valid only if the testator died as a result of the impending peril, and must be:

1. Declared to be his last will by the testator before two disinterested witnesses;

2. Reduced to writing by or under the direction of one of the witnesses within 30 days after such declaration; and

3. Submitted for probate within six months after the death of the testator.

b. The nuncupative will may dispose of personal property only and to an aggregate value not exceeding $1,000.

c. A nuncupative will does not revoke an existing written will. Such written will is changed only to the extent necessary to give effect to the nuncupative will.

   Note: A nuncupative is an oral will, a will that is not written.

Questions

a. To what type of will does this statute apply?

b. What requirements must be met for a nuncupative will to be valid; that is, what are the elements?

c. Mr. Lang, on his deathbed, writes his will on a piece of notepaper, signs it, and delivers it to his sister for safekeeping. Does the statute govern the validity of this will?

d. Larry, on his deathbed, declares that it is his will and that all his property should go to his girlfriend, Beth. Three witnesses are present: Beth, Larry's sister Mary, and the next-door neighbor, Tom. Tom is in an adjoining room. The door to the adjoining room is open. Tom hears what Larry is saying. Assume for the purposes of this example that the will is reduced to writing within 30 days and is submitted for probate within six months.

1. Is this a valid will under this statute? What additional information may be necessary?

2. Assume this is a valid will, and also that Larry had a previous valid written will. What impact does the nuncupative will have on the written will? What is disposed of by the nuncupative will?

ASSIGNMENT 13

Statute: Section 2-201, Statute of Frauds

The following statute is a section of the Commercial Code Sales Act adopted by the state legislature.

A contract for the sale of goods for the price of $500 or more is not enforceable by way of action or defense unless there is some writing sufficient to indicate that a contract for sale has been made between the parties and signed by the party against whom enforcement is sought or by the party's authorized agent or broker. A writing is not insufficient because it omits or incorrectly states a term agreed upon, but the contract is not enforceable under this paragraph beyond the quantity of goods shown in such writing.

Assume that the act applies to the sales of goods. *Goods* are defined in § 2–100 as "those things movable" and do not include real property.

Questions

a. Does the statute apply to the lease of goods?

b. What are the required elements of the statute? In other words, for a contract for the sale of goods of $500 or more to be enforceable, what is required?

c. Mary orally contracts to buy 10 car tires at $70 each. The seller prepares a contract and gives it to Mary. Neither party signs the contract.

1. Who can enforce the contract under the provisions of the statute?

2. Assume that only Mary signs the contract. Who can enforce the contract?

3. Assume that both parties sign the contract and the written contract incorrectly provides for 9 tires at $70 each. Is the contract enforceable under the statute? If so, to what extent is it enforceable?

4. Assume both parties sign the contract and it reads 15 tires at $70 each. Is the contract enforceable under the statute? If so, to what extent is it enforceable?

5. Assume there is no written contract. The seller hands Mary a slip of paper upon which he has written, "This is to confirm our oral agreement." He and Mary both sign the paper. Is there an enforceable contract under the provisions of the statute? If so, to what extent is it enforceable?

ASSIGNMENT 14

Statute: Section 35-1-4, Privileged Communications—Husband and Wife

In all actions, husband and wife may testify for or against each other, provided that neither may testify as to any communication or admission made by either of them to the other during the marriage, except in actions:

1. between such husband and wife, and,

2. where the custody, support, health or welfare of their children or children in either spouse's custody or control is directly in issue.

Questions

a. Prepare an outline of the statutory elements.

b. When can a husband or wife testify against each other? When are they prohibited from testifying against each other?

c. Husband, while driving under the influence of alcohol, ran a stop sign, and his vehicle collided with a vehicle driven by Mr. Smith. Husband's spouse (Wife) and two children were passengers in the car. The day after the wreck, Husband told Wife that he knew he ran the stop sign because he was drunk. Mr. Smith sues Husband for negligence. When answering the following questions, identify any additional information that may be necessary to fully answer the question.

1. Can Wife be compelled to testify concerning her conversation with Husband? Why or why not?

2. Can Wife voluntarily testify concerning the conversation? Why or why not?

3. If Husband and Wife are legally separated, can Wife voluntarily testify concerning the conversation? Why or why not?

4. Is the conversation admissible if they are divorced at the time of the lawsuit? Why or why not?

5. Husband and Wife have lived together as husband and wife for the past 20 years. They have never been formally married. Can Wife testify against Husband concerning the conversation? Why or why not?

6. Is the conversation admissible in a divorce action between Husband and Wife? Why or why not?

ASSIGNMENT 15

Go to www.gpo.gov/fdsys/ and link to the United States Code. Select the year 2013 and locate the statute regarding the crime of domestic assault by a habitual offender.

Questions

a. What is the citation for the statute?

b. What is the term of imprisonment for this offense?

c. How is "domestic assault" defined in this statute?

ASSIGNMENT 16

Using www.gpo.gov/fdsys, link to the *Code of Federal Regulations*. Select the title "Parks, Forests, and Public Property," select the chapter for "Forest Service, Department of Agriculture," select the part for "Travel Management," and then the subpart for "Designation of Roads, Trails and Areas for Motor Vehicle Use."

Questions

a. What section covers public involvement in decisions?

b. What does that section say about the right of the public to be involved in determining the use of trails and roads?

c. When is absence of public involvement authorized?

Chapter 4

Case Law—Research and Briefing

Learning Objectives

After completing this chapter, you should understand:

- The role and importance of court opinions
- The elements of a court opinion
- How to find court opinions
- The role and importance of a case brief
- The elements of a case brief
- How to brief a case

Amelia has just earned her associate's degree in paralegal studies. She was able to obtain a full-time position at the law firm she interned at for her program. The firm specializes in personal injury and torts. After a week of being introduced to the law office procedures, software, and how various matters are handled in the firm, Amelia received her first assignment.

The client is the father of 16-year-old Jackson. Jackson was the passenger in the car of his best friend Josh when another car pulled alongside Josh's car at a stoplight and began yelling at the boys. Jackson and Josh were on their high school football team. The other car was driven by an older boy and there were two passengers, both who were on a rival high school's football team. The recent game between the two schools had seen some rough play, hard hits, and a star player for the rival team was injured—which is what prompted the boys in the other car to start yelling at Jackson and Josh.

Jackson jumped out of Josh's car at the stoplight and went up to the other car. According to Josh, Jackson yelled back at the other boys to "grow up" and to "let it go" and said, "Bad hits happen; no one means to hurt anyone—but it happens." The backseat passenger of the second car pulled out a small caliber handgun and shot Jackson several times; then the car sped off. Jackson survived, but he will not walk unassisted ever again. The other car was not insured. Josh had full coverage insurance, including uninsured motorist coverage.

Amelia's first assignment was to locate and brief a court opinion (case) that could be used to advise Jackson's dad, who is the personal representative for Jackson, on whether Jackson could recover from Josh's uninsured motorist insurance.

Amelia was nervous about the assignment. She realized she needed to refresh her memory on how to locate and brief a court opinion. It had been a while since she did case law research or briefed a case. She asked herself, "How do I find a case that addresses our client's question? How do I brief the case once I find one?" The case Amelia located is presented as Exhibit 4-1 and this chapter refers to the case throughout, including discussion of how Amelia found the case and how she briefed the case.

I. INTRODUCTION

The focus of this chapter is on court opinions—their elements, where they are published, how to find them, and how to read and brief them. The chapter addresses the same questions Amelia faced when undertaking her assignment; that is, what are the elements of court opinions, where opinions are published, how to find them, and how to brief them. Throughout this chapter, a court opinion will be referred to as a *court case* and a brief of a court opinion will be referred to as a *case brief*. Chapter 12 discusses case law analysis. Case law analysis is the process you engage in to determine if a court opinion governs or applies to a client's case, that is, if a case is on point.

II. COURT OPINIONS—IN GENERAL

As discussed in Chapter 1, the two major sources of law are enacted law (e.g., constitutions, laws enacted by legislative bodies, administrative regulations) and case law. **Case law** is the body of law on a particular subject created by court opinions and is commonly referred to as **common law** or judge-made law. Case law is the most commonly used term and will be used throughout this chapter. Case law is found in the written opinions of the courts.

Case law consists of the law made by courts when they interpret existing law or create new law. It is composed of the legal rules, doctrines, and principles adopted by the courts. Courts often announce rules of law when interpreting statutory or constitutional provisions or create new law when there is no statutory or constitutional law governing a legal dispute.

For Example

Statutory Interpretation:

A statute uses the term *publication* but fails to define it. The court, addressing the issue of what constitutes publication, announces a rule of law that the term *publication* as used in the statute means "communication to a third party."

For Example

Creating Law:

A state has not enacted legislation recognizing strict liability as a cause of action in tort. The highest court in the state, in a case before it, announces a rule of law adopting strict liability as a cause of action in the state.

A **court opinion** is the court's written statement explaining its decision in a case. It is the court's resolution of the legal dispute before the court and the reasons in support of its resolution. It usually includes a statement of facts, points or rules of law, and rationale.

Often the terms *court opinion*, *case*, and *decision* are used interchangeably to refer to a court's resolution of an issue or a decision in a dispute. In this chapter, the terms *court opinion* and *case* are used to refer to the written opinion of a court.

For Example

"The case stands for the principle that . . . ."
   The court upheld the juvenile court's adjudication of the minor stating that the jury had the sole authority to determine if a knife met the statutory definition of "deadly weapon."

III. COURT OPINIONS—IMPORTANCE

Of the two major sources of law, enacted law and case (common) law, case law constitutes the largest body of law, far larger in volume than constitutional or statutory law. It is essential to acquire a general familiarity with this body of law, as it represents such a large portion of the law. Also, you must study case law because so many areas of law are governed by it.

There are numerous additional reasons why reading and analyzing court opinions and studying case law are important. Overall, the major reasons are as follows:

1. *To learn the case law.* Much of the law is court made. To determine the elements of a cause of action for a court-made law, you must refer to case law. Case law may govern your client's fact situation, and to determine what law applies and the probable outcome, you must analyze case law.

For Example

In most states, the cause of action for civil battery is a creation of case law, not statutory law. To identify the elements necessary to state a battery claim, the case law must be researched.

2. *To interpret constitutional or statutory law.* Court opinions often announce rules of law that govern how a statutory or constitutional term or provision is interpreted or applied. Therefore, you must consult case law to understand how to interpret and apply statutes and constitutional provisions.

For Example

The United States Supreme Court has issued many opinions on the types of speech protected by the First Amendment. To determine if an individual who burns a state flag in front of the state capital is protected by the First Amendment's freedom of speech provisions, Supreme Court opinions interpreting freedom of speech must be consulted.

3. *To understand the litigation process.* Court opinions often address legal questions that arise in the context of the litigation process—either before, during, or after trial. Court opinions give insight into the process by explaining what conduct is appropriate, which arguments are successful, where errors are made, how procedural rules apply, how trials and motion hearings should proceed, and so on.

For Example

Appellate courts review questions of law de novo and questions of fact for an abuse of discretion. To determine if a particular issue has been treated as a question of law or a questions of fact, case law can be researched for other court opinions that address the same or similar issue and how the court treated that issue.

4. *To gain insight into legal analysis.* In a court opinion, the court often analyzes the law. The court discusses what law applies, how it applies, the reasons for its application, and how the reasons operate to govern the application of the law to the facts of the case. By studying court opinions, you learn how to assemble a legal argument, how to determine if a law applies, and how to support a legal argument.

5. *To develop legal writing skills.* Judges are usually experienced in legal writing, and most opinions are well written. You may read opinions with an eye to how sentences and paragraphs are structured, how case law and statutory law are referred to and incorporated into legal writing, and how transitions are accomplished. If you have a problem putting some aspect of your research into writing, look at an opinion to see how a court handled a similar matter.

For Example

You are preparing a research memorandum. There is no case law in your jurisdiction governing the issue; however, there is strong persuasive precedent from another jurisdiction. You are unsure about how to introduce the persuasive precedent in your memorandum. By reading a court opinion in which the court relied on persuasive precedent, you can study the language the court used to introduce the persuasive precedent and use the court's language as a guide after which to model your introduction.

For Example

In *Smith v. Jones*, the court stated, "There is no case law in this jurisdiction interpreting the term 'publication' as used in § 55-5-67A. The state of Texas, however, has an identical statute, and the Supreme Court of Texas, in the case of *Frank v. Inex*, interpreted 'publication' to mean communication to a third party." You can use this language as a guide in your introduction of persuasive precedent.

For these reasons and many others, the study of case law is important. The skill of being able to correctly locate, analyze, and apply case law is essential to legal analysis.

IV. COURT OPINIONS—ELEMENTS

A. In General

The first requirement for proper analysis of a court opinion is to be familiar with the elements of an opinion. A court opinion usually includes some or all of the following components:

1. The facts that gave rise to the legal dispute before the court
2. The procedural history and posture of the case—that is, what happened in the lower court or courts, who appealed the decision, and why
3. The issue or issues addressed and resolved by the court
4. The rule of law that governs the dispute
5. The application of the rule of law to the facts—in other words, the holding
6. The reason or reasons supporting the court's application of the rule of law to the facts, that is, why the court decided as it did
7. The relief granted or denied (e.g., "The judgment of the trial court is up-held.")

B. Annotated versus Unannotated Court Opinions

Prior to the advent and popularity of electronic research, published or reported court opinions were only accessible in print in books called *reporters*. West Publishing Company (West), a Thomson Reuters business, produces the majority of reporters, including the regional reporters and federal reporters. (The National Reporter System is discussed later in this chapter.) West, therefore, set a standard for the format of published opinions. One of those standards was the addition of editorial material, such as key numbers, headnotes, and a syllabus. LexisNexis adopted a similar format for its *Supreme Court Reports: Lawyers Edition*. Published court opinions with any of these editorial additions are referred to as annotated opinions.

It is important to note not all reporters and not all published court opinions will be in the annotated format. Moreover, it is important to understand that any editorial material added to court opinions is not part of the opinion itself and, therefore, cannot be relied upon or cited. However, editorial materials are excellent tools to aid in the research process and the navigation of a court opinion.

Because of the prevalence of West's National Reporter System and because West and Lexis online research websites are heavily used by researchers, examples in this chapter will be of an annotated court opinion.

C. Elements of a Reported Case

Because the majority of court opinions are published by West, an example of an opinion published by West is presented in Exhibit 4-1. The case, *Miera v. State Farm Mutual Automobile Ins. Co.*, is published in the *New Mexico Reports* and the *Pacific Reporter*. Note that the components of the case are identified in the left margin next to each section of the opinion. These components are summarized in the following text.

1. Citation

The **citation** refers to the volume number, page number, and the name of the reporter where the case may be found. The citation for *Miera v. State Farm Mutual Automobile Ins. Co.*, is 2004-NMCA-059, 135 N.M. 574, 92 P.3d 20. That means the printed opinion of this case is published and may be found in two reporters: volume 135 of the *New Mexico Reports* at page 574, and volume 92 of the *Pacific Reporter*, third series, at page 20. The opinion also has the public domain or vendor neutral citation of 2004-NMCA-059, which does not correlate to a set of reporters, but represents information regarding the court that issued the opinion. Here, *Miera* was decided in 2004 by the New Mexico Court of Appeals (NMCA) and was the 59th opinion of that court that year. Public domain citations are assigned by the court who issued the opinion, not the publisher of a reporter. (See "Citation" in Exhibit 4-1.) When an opinion may be found in more than one set of books, or contains a public domain citation in addition to a citation to a reporter, the additional citations are referred to as **parallel citations**.

Note that court opinion citations vary from state to state and jurisdiction to jurisdiction and are dependent on the rules of citation which take into account the many factors that influence citation format. Be sure to consult the appropriate citation manual to determine the proper citation format for specific cases.

In the section "Court Opinions—Researching" below, you will learn the difference between published and unpublished cases. An unpublished case lacks the elements that make up citation format. As such, an unpublished court opinion will not have a citation, but it may have a unique numeric identifier located in the same area a citation would be found on a published court opinion.

2. Caption

The **caption** includes the names of the **parties** to the lawsuit and their court status. Robert J. Miera Sr. was the plaintiff at the trial court level, and he is the appellant on appeal. (The *appellant* is the person who lost at the trial court level and who filed the appeal.) State Farm Insurance Company and Safeco National Insurance Company were the defendants at the trial court level and are the appellees on appeal. (The *appellee* is the person against whom the appeal is filed, the person who won at the trial court level.) The caption of the case used on appeal is usually the same as the caption used in the trial court. Note that the plaintiff's last name is printed in all capitals. (See "Caption" in Exhibit 4-1.) Often when referring to or citing the case, only the names in all capitals are used. Also note that only the first defendant listed has their name in all caps. Usually when there is more than one plaintiff or defendant, only the name of the first one is used when referring to or citing the case. However, you should always consult the appropriate citation manual to determine which names to present in a citation.

For Example

When citing this case, the citation should read: *Meira v. State Farm Mutual Automobile Ins. Co.*, 2004-NMCA-059, 135 N.M. 574, 92 P.3d 20.

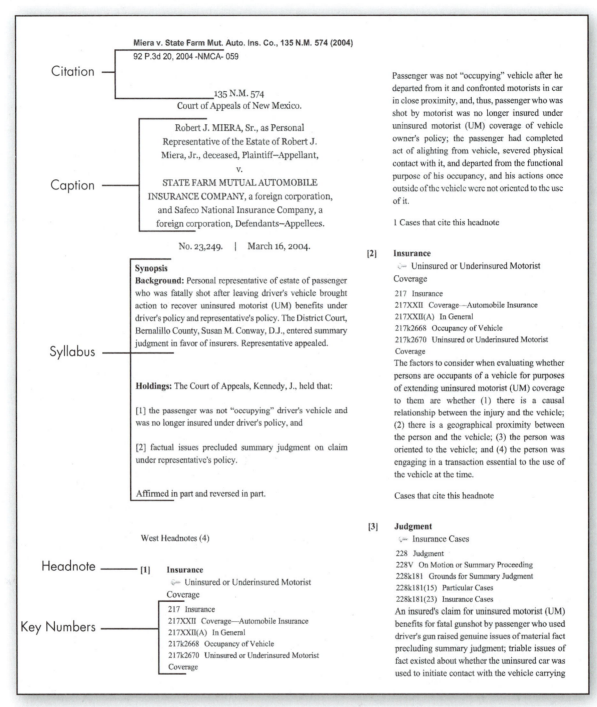

Citation

Miera v. State Farm Mut. Auto. Ins. Co., 135 N.M. 574 (2004)
92 P.3d 20, 2004 -NMCA- 059

135 N.M. 574
Court of Appeals of New Mexico.

Caption

Robert J. MIERA, Sr., as Personal
Representative of the Estate of Robert J.
Miera, Jr., deceased, Plaintiff–Appellant,
v.
STATE FARM MUTUAL AUTOMOBILE
INSURANCE COMPANY, a foreign corporation,
and Safeco National Insurance Company, a
foreign corporation, Defendants–Appellees.

No. 23,249. | March 16, 2004.

Syllabus

Synopsis
Background: Personal representative of estate of passenger
who was fatally shot after leaving driver's vehicle brought
action to recover uninsured motorist (UM) benefits under
driver's policy and representative's policy. The District Court,
Bernalillo County, Susan M. Conway, D.J., entered summary
judgment in favor of insurers. Representative appealed.

Holdings: The Court of Appeals, Kennedy, J., held that:

[1] the passenger was not "occupying" driver's vehicle and
was no longer insured under driver's policy, and

[2] factual issues precluded summary judgment on claim
under representative's policy.

Affirmed in part and reversed in part.

West Headnotes (4)

Headnote

[1]   **Insurance**
        Uninsured or Underinsured Motorist
Coverage

Key Numbers

217 Insurance
217XXII Coverage—Automobile Insurance
217XXII(A) In General
217k2668 Occupancy of Vehicle
217k2670 Uninsured or Underinsured Motorist
Coverage

Passenger was not "occupying" vehicle after he
departed from it and confronted motorists in car
in close proximity, and, thus, passenger who was
shot by motorist was no longer insured under
uninsured motorist (UM) coverage of vehicle
owner's policy; the passenger had completed
act of alighting from vehicle, severed physical
contact with it, and departed from the functional
purpose of his occupancy, and his actions once
outside of the vehicle were not oriented to the use
of it.

1 Cases that cite this headnote

[2]   **Insurance**
        Uninsured or Underinsured Motorist
Coverage

217 Insurance
217XXII Coverage—Automobile Insurance
217XXII(A) In General
217k2668 Occupancy of Vehicle
217k2670 Uninsured or Underinsured Motorist
Coverage
The factors to consider when evaluating whether
persons are occupants of a vehicle for purposes
of extending uninsured motorist (UM) coverage
to them are whether (1) there is a causal
relationship between the injury and the vehicle;
(2) there is a geographical proximity between
the person and the vehicle; (3) the person was
oriented to the vehicle; and (4) the person was
engaging in a transaction essential to the use of
the vehicle at the time.

Cases that cite this headnote

[3]   **Judgment**
        Insurance Cases

228 Judgment
228V On Motion or Summary Proceeding
228k181 Grounds for Summary Judgment
228k181(15) Particular Cases
228k181(23) Insurance Cases
An insured's claim for uninsured motorist (UM)
benefits for fatal gunshot by passenger who used
driver's gun raised genuine issues of material fact
precluding summary judgment; triable issues of
fact existed about whether the uninsured car was
used to initiate contact with the vehicle carrying

Exhibit 4-1 Court Opinion—Miera v. State Farm Automobile Insurance Co. Reprinted from Arizona Revised Statutes
Annotated with the permission of Thomson Reuters.

Miera v. State Farm Mut. Auto. Ins. Co., 135 N.M. 574 (2004)
92 P.3d 20, 2004 -NMCA- 059

Judge

Body of opinion begins

KENNEDY, Judge.

{1} This appeal invites us to reverse the district court's summary judgment granted to Defendants State Farm Mutual Automobile Insurance Company (State Farm) and Safeco National Insurance Company (Safeco), thus extending uninsured motorist (UM) coverage to Robert Miera Jr. when he was shot and killed by an occupant of an uninsured vehicle after Miera got out of the car in which he was riding and was in a confrontation with the occupants of the uninsured vehicle.

{2} We first hold that when Miera severed both his physical contact with the insured vehicle in which he rode and departed from the functional purpose of his occupancy in it, he ceased to be "occupying" that car. Consequently, he was no longer an "insured" under the vehicle's State Farm UM policy. Summary judgment for State Farm was therefore appropriate, and we affirm the district court's judgment on that issue.

{3} Second, we hold that summary judgment was improper as to Safeco because material issues of fact exist as to the elements allowing recovery under UM coverage. We accordingly reverse the district court's granting of summary judgment in favor of Safeco.

FACTUAL AND PROCEDURAL BACKGROUND
{4} On April 22, 1998, Miera, Ruben Baros, Tara Hardern, and two other friends were in Hardern's Chevy Tahoe going to a party. As the Tahoe approached a stop sign, its occupants noticed a Ford Mustang approaching the intersection. The Mustang was driven by its owner Andreas Yates and Robbie McGrew was his passenger. The Mustang made a U-turn and stopped approximately twenty feet behind the Tahoe. The purpose of the U-turn and stop is disputed. There is evidence that Yates thought he saw some gesturing from the Tahoe and that he might know its occupants; he maneuvered so as to check his impression. There is also evidence that Yates thought the occupants of the Tahoe "were flipping [him] off" and that he looked menacingly at them as he passed and pulled up behind them. A few moments later, Miera and Baros demanded to be let out of the Tahoe and approached the Mustang. An argument and confrontation ensued between Miera and Baros and the occupants of the Mustang. Miera spat and threw beer cans at the Mustang and poked Yates. Within minutes, McGrew took Yates' .40–caliber Glock pistol from the middle console of the Mustang and shot Miera to death.

---

the insured, and whether using the car to carry the accessible weapon resulted in the car being used to facilitate passenger's intentional tort, and thus whether the incident was shown to arise out of the ownership or use of the uninsured motor vehicle.

Cases that cite this headnote

[4]   Insurance
      Uninsured or Underinsured Motorist Coverage

217 Insurance
217XXII Coverage—Automobile Insurance
217XXII(A) In General
217k2676 Ownership, Maintenance, Operation, or Use
217k2679 Uninsured or Underinsured Motorist Coverage

An insured's right to uninsured motorist (UM) benefits for fatal gunshot by passenger who used driver's gun depended on whether there was a sufficient causal nexus between the use of the uninsured car and the resulting injury, whether an act of independent significance broke the causal link between the use of the car and the shooting, and whether the vehicle was put to its normal use.

Cases that cite this headnote

Attorneys and Law Firms

Attorneys

**21 *575 Rosemary L. Dillon, Robert C. Gutierrez, Will Ferguson & Associates, Floyd Wilson, McCary, Wilson & Pryor, P.C., Albuquerque, NM, for Appellant.

Joe A. Sturges, Kenneth J. Tager, Sturges & Houston, P.C., Albuquerque, NM, for Appellee, Safeco National Insurance Company.

Rudolph A. Lucero, Ruth Fuess, Miller Stratvert, P.A., Albuquerque, NM, for Appellee, State Farm Mutual Automobile Insurance Company.

OPINION

Exhibit 4-1 *(Continued)*

Miera v. State Farm Mut. Auto. Ins. Co., 135 N.M. 574 (2004)

92 P.3d 20, 2004 -NMCA- 059

{5} Hardern's Tahoe was insured by State Farm; her policy included UM coverage. Miera, who lived at home, had UM coverage under his father's Safeco policy. Yates' Mustang was uninsured. Both Safeco and State **22 *576 Farm moved for and were granted summary judgment in the district court. Both alleged that under their policies Miera was not covered by their UM insurance.

DISCUSSION

Standard of Review

{6} The question of whether application of the law to undisputed facts supports summary judgment in a case seeking to benefit from UM coverage is a question we review de novo. *Cuevas v. State Farm Mut. Auto. Ins. Co.*, 2001–NMCA–038, ¶ 6, 130 N.M. 539, 28 P.3d 527. On appeal from summary judgment, we consider the facts in the light most favorable to support a trial on the issues. *Maralex Res., Inc. v. Gilbreath*, 2003–NMSC–023, ¶ 8, 134 N.M. 308, 76 P.3d 626.

State Farm's Insurance Policy Does Not Provide UM Coverage for Miera's Death Because Miera Was Not "Occupying" the Tahoe When He Was Shot

[1]   {7} As a passenger in Hardern's Tahoe, Miera was a class-two insured for purposes of UM coverage under her State Farm policy. According to the terms of the State Farm policy, UM coverage applies only if Miera could be considered to have been "occupying" the Tahoe when he was shot and killed. Under State Farm's policy, "occupying" means "in, on, entering or alighting from." In consideration of New Mexico case law on this issue, we hold that Miera was not "occupying" the Tahoe.

{8} It is true that Miera was in close proximity to the Tahoe at the time of the shooting; however, contrary to Plaintiff's contention, this does not mean that Miera was "occupying" the Tahoe. In this case, Miera got out of the Tahoe to pursue an altercation on the road. "Alighting" is an action that Miera had completed before he reached the Mustang. There was no causal connection between Miera's being shot and his occupation of the Tahoe. The altercation occurred after Miera got out of the Tahoe, and his actions once out of the vehicle were not oriented to the use of the Tahoe. *See Allstate Ins. Co. v. Graham*, 106 N.M. 779, 780, 750 P.2d 1105, 1106 (1988) (holding claimant was not an occupant because she was "not engaged in a transaction oriented to the use of the [insured vehicle]," when engaged in changing the tire on

another vehicle); *see also State Farm Mut. Auto. Ins. Co. v. Baldonado*, 2003–NMCA–096, ¶¶ 17, 18, 134 N.M. 197, 75 P.3d 413 (holding that the passenger "was not injured while occupying [the insured vehicle]," but rather was in retreat from the other car when shot). *But see Cuevas*, 2001–NMCA–038, ¶¶ 12,13, 130 N.M. 539, 28 P.3d 527 (holding that the plaintiff was occupying the insured car at the time of the accident because he was engaged in repairing the insured car at the time of the accident, was within close proximity of the insured car, and there was a causal connection between the plaintiff and the insured car at the time of the accident).

[2]   {9} In *Cuevas*, we applied *Graham* and other factors presented by case law in evaluating whether persons are occupants of a vehicle for purposes of extending UM coverage to them. *Id.* The factors that we considered there, as we will consider here are whether: "(1) there is a causal relationship between the injury and the vehicle; (2) there is a geographical proximity between the person and the vehicle; (3) the person was oriented to the vehicle; and (4) the person was engaging 'in a transaction essential to the use of the vehicle at the time.' " *Id.* ¶ 8. Considering the factors that our courts have used to construe the meaning of "occupying" for the purpose of UM coverage, *id.* ¶¶ 8–11, we hold that Miera is not covered under State Farm's policy. It is not enough that Miera was within close proximity of the Tahoe or that he in all likelihood would have returned to the Tahoe after the altercation and resumed on the way to his destination. The facts show that Miera engaged himself in a confrontation that he participated in away from the Tahoe. Demanding to be let out to pursue a confrontation with occupants of another car in this case was a transaction unrelated to the use of the Tahoe for purposes of UM coverage. Miera therefore severed any casual connection to the use or occupancy of the Tahoe. By doing so, he ceased to be the Tahoe's occupant, and the district court did not err in granting summary judgment to State Farm.

23 *577 A Question of Fact Exists Whether Safeco's Insurance Policy Provides UM Coverage for Miera's Death

[3]   {10} Plaintiff argues that he is entitled to collect damages under Safeco's policy because Yates' Mustang was uninsured at the time of the shooting. Miera was living with his father at the time of the incident and is therefore a household member covered under his father's Safeco policy. Plaintiff contends that the shooting was an accident as defined by the policy and Miera's death arose out of the operation, maintenance, or use of the Mustang. Under the Safeco policy, it will pay damages, caused by an "accident,"

Exhibit 4-1 (Continued)

Miera v. State Farm Mut. Auto. Ins. Co., 135 N.M. 574 (2004)
92 P.3d 20, 2004 -NMCA- 059

which an insured is legally entitled to recover from the owner or operator of an uninsured motor vehicle, but the owner's or operator's liability for damages "must arise out of the ownership, maintenance or use of the uninsured motor vehicle[.]" We hold that whether Yates bears any legal responsibility for the shooting, and whether his actions give rise to Safeco's liability involve a dispute over facts that are sufficiently material as to defeat summary judgment.

[4] {11} The Safeco policy extends coverage only when the owner or driver of the uninsured vehicle is legally liable to the injured person. Thus, in this case, because Yates, the owner and operator of the Mustang, did not shoot Miera, we must determine whether Yates can be held responsible when his passenger, McGrew, shot Miera using Yates' gun. *See Britt v. Phoenix Indem. Ins. Co.,* 120 N.M. 813, 814–15, 907 P.2d 994, 995–96 (1995). We determine whether there was a sufficient causal nexus between the use of the Mustang and the resulting injury to Miera, whether an act of independent significance broke the causal link between the use of the Mustang and the shooting, and whether the vehicle was put to its normal use. Under the analysis set forth by *Britt* and its progeny, *see, e.g., Barncastle v. Am. Nat'l Prop. & Cas. Co.'s,* 2000–NMCA–095, 129 N.M. 672, 11 P.3d 1234; *Farmers Ins. Co. of Arizona v. Sedillo,* 2000–NMCA–094, 129 N.M. 674, 11 P.3d 1236, there are issues of material fact about whether Miera's shooting death arose out of the use of Yate's Mustang.

{12} Though Safeco argues a different interpretation of the facts, other surrounding facts support a view of Yates' conduct that night that could support a jury's finding him legally culpable. Yates and McGrew had been drinking that afternoon, and Yates regarded McGrew as a "crack-head" with a "reputation for violence" who "doesn't think straight." Neither party disputes that Yates had his pistol in the car, in a location accessible to McGrew, and that Yates' pistol was the one with which McGrew fatally shot Miera. Yates kept the gun in the car because he had been shot at in the past. Twenty-eight cartridges and casings from different calibers of ammunition were taken from his car by the police. Because Yates believed that McGrew's collection of guns was mostly stolen, Yates told McGrew that he would bring his gun so McGrew would not need to bring one of his own. Yates stated that he did not want to be stopped by the police with a stolen

gun in his car. At the same time, he made a U-turn to come up behind the Tahoe, thinking that its occupants were either "flipping us off" or "flagging us down," either one of which had potential for a confrontation of some sort.

{13} These facts, though disputed, could fairly establish Yates' culpability and connection to McGrew's use of the gun. The next step is to evaluate the connection between Yates' behavior and the use or operation of the car.

{14} To avoid summary judgment the incident must be shown to "arise out of the ownership ... or use of the uninsured motor vehicle[.]" As Yates and McGrew drove around that night, Yates' car amounted to little more than a holster on wheels. It held both a person and an instrumentality Yates knew to be dangerous—McGrew and a large-caliber handgun. Plaintiff can fairly argue that Yates used the car to maneuver to a point that accelerated the confrontation with Miera and Baros. This passes *Britt's* test requiring Yates' "active participation in or facilitation of the passenger's commission of the harmful act." *Britt,* 120 N.M. at 818, 907 P.2d at 999.

{15} There are triable issues of fact about whether the Mustang was used to initiate ****24 *578** contact with the Tahoe; whether using the Mustang to carry the accessible weapon resulted in the Mustang being used to facilitate McGrew's intentional tort; and thus whether the incident was shown to "arise out of the ownership ... or use of the uninsured motor vehicle." Therefore, the district court erred in granting summary judgment in favor of Safeco.

CONCLUSION
{16} We affirm the summary judgment entered in favor of State Farm and reverse the summary judgment in favor of Safeco.

{17} **IT IS SO ORDERED.**

WE CONCUR: LYNN PICKARD and MICHAEL E. VIGIL, Judges.

All Citations

135 N.M. 574, 92 P.3d 20, 2004 -NMCA- 059

End of Document

Exhibit 4-1 (Continued)

Note that below the caption is "No. 23,239." This is the docket number of the case assigned by the court of appeals. Above the names of the parties is the name of the court that decided the case. Next to the docket number is the date of the decision. This is indicated in the citation as: (2004-NMCA in the public domain citation). When there is no public domain citation the court and year is provided in parentheses at the end of the citation. If the citation does not include a state reporter citation, a reference to the state is included in the parentheses along with the court and year. Again, you should always consult the appropriate citation manual to determine all the components to present in a citation.

For Example

Smith v. Jones, 292 S.W.2d 425 (Tex. 1980).

3. Syllabus

The **syllabus** is a brief summary of the opinion. It is an editorial enhancement written by the publisher, not the court, and cannot be relied upon as the holding of the court. It is presented as a useful aid in providing the reader with a brief overview of the opinion. (See "Syllabus" in Exhibit 4-1.)

4. Headnotes

The **headnotes** are summaries of the points of law discussed in the case. Headnotes follow, in sequential order, the relevant paragraphs of the opinion. The number to the left of the headnote corresponds to the bracketed number in the body of the opinion.

Headnotes can be used in several ways. One way is to review the headnotes when you first locate a court opinion to see if it covers the area of law relevant to your research. Another way to use headnotes is as a table of contents, using the number of the headnote to locate particular content in an opinion. (See "Headnotes" in Exhibit 4-1.)

For Example

In *Meira v. State Farm Mutual Automobile Ins. Co.*, Headnote [1] contains a summary of the point of law discussed in the body of the opinion between [1] and [2].

If a researcher was looking specifically for the portion of the opinion discussing the factors to be considered in evaluating whether a person is an occupant under uninsured coverage, Headnote [2] addresses that topic and so the researcher could go directly to where Headnote [2] is signaled in the opinion (third page of Exhibit 4-1).

Note that headnotes are prepared by West and are not part of the case. They are prepared for the convenience of individuals researching the case and are useful in providing a quick overview of the law and legal principles addressed in the opinion. They are not the opinion of the court and have no authority of law. Any reference to or quote from an opinion must be taken from the opinion itself, not from the headnotes.

5. Key Numbers

In bold print next to the headnote number are a few words indicating the area of law addressed in the headnote. Below this bold-print description of the area of law is a series of numbers. (See "Key Numbers" in Exhibit 4-1.) West has divided all areas of American law into various topics and subtopics. Each area is identified by a topic name (the bold print), and each specific topic or subtopic is assigned a **key number**. West publishes separate volumes called *digests* that contain summaries of court opinions organized by topic and subtopic.

For Example

Next to headnote 2 in *Meira v. State Farm Mutual Automobile Ins. Co.* is "Insurance," followed by a key symbol and the number 217. The key symbol and the number 217 refer to the topic of Insurance. Below this key number are additional key numbers and specific subtopics of Insurance. If the researcher wanted to read additional court opinions regarding Insurance, Occupancy of Vehicle, they would go to topic 217 Insurance and subtopic 2668 in the digests. If researching electronically you may be able to click on the entry "217k2668" and link directly to a list of other cases, depending on what Internet research source you are using.

Through this system, you have easy access to all court opinions dealing with the question you are considering. The key number system is an invaluable research tool.

6. Attorneys

This section provides the names and cities of the attorneys in the case at the appellate level and the parties they represent. (See "Attorneys" in Exhibit 4-1.)

7. Judge

At the beginning of the opinion is the name of the judge who wrote it. (See "Judge" in Exhibit 4-1.) Cases at the appellate level are reviewed and heard by a panel of judges. The number of judge's varies from state to state. However, it is usually an odd number and is at least three judges. It takes a simple majority of the panel to reach a decision as to how the issue(s) should be decided in a case (majority opinion). One of the judges in that majority is then assigned to author the opinion.

8. Body of the Opinion

The **body of the opinion** usually includes the facts of the case, the prior proceedings, the issue or issues addressed by the court, the rule or rules of law governing the dispute, the holding, the reasoning in support of the holding, and the relief granted. (See "Body of the Opinion" in Exhibit 4-1.) There are no hard-and-fast rules dictating what must be contained in a court opinion, and often one or more of the components listed here may be missing. Each of the components of the body are discussed separately here.

a. Facts

Opinions usually include the facts that gave rise to the legal dispute. Often the opinion may include some background facts and the facts relevant to the decision reached by the court, but sometimes very few facts are included in the opinion.

b. Prior Proceedings

In this part of the opinion, the court presents a summary of what happened in the lower court and who appealed. This may be a lengthy summary, as in *Meira v. State Farm Mutual Automobile Ins. Co.*, or it may be far more brief. The more levels of appeal sought in the case, then longer the summary of prior proceedings can be.

For Example

A case was tried in the magistrate court (lower trial court) and the defendant appealed to the District Court (trial court of general jurisdiction and next highest court). The District Court affirmed the magistrate court, so the defendant appealed to the state Court of Appeals which overturned the lower court's decisions. The plaintiff then appealed to the state Supreme Court, which granted review and issued the decision.

c. Issue or Issues

The *issue* is the legal question addressed by the court in the opinion. The court may present the issue narrowly in the context of the facts.

For Example

Did Josh's insurance policy provide uninsured motorist coverage for Jackson's injuries when Jackson was outside the car when shot?

The court may state the issue broadly, merely phrasing the issue in the context of the area of law.

For Example

When is someone "occupying" a vehicle?

In many instances, a case addresses more than one legal issue. Also, the court may not present a statement of the issue or issues at all, and it may be difficult to determine what they are.

Identifying and understanding the issue make up the most important task of reading an opinion. If the issue is not understood, then the rule of law applied by the court may not be understood, and the opinion consequently may be misanalyzed and misapplied.

d. Rule of Law

The rule of law is the law that governs the issue. It may be a statutory or constitutional provision or a case law doctrine, rule, principle, and so on. In *Miera v. State Farm Mutual Automobile Ins. Co.*, case law governs both issues.

e. Holding

The holding is the court's application of the rule of law to the facts of the case. It is the court's answer to the issue(s) in the case. The holding is usually presented immediately after the rule of law in the opinion or after the reasoning at the end of the opinion. It is the direct answer to the issue. Be careful not to confuse the holding with the court's reasoning.

f. Reasoning

The **reasoning** is the court's explanation of how or why the rule of law applies to the dispute. It can also explain how the court reached its decision. On occasion, the reasoning is difficult to follow. Often, it is helpful to read the holding first and determine how the court ruled, then read the reasoning. By first understanding what decision was reached, you may be better able to understand the reasoning in support of the decision. Also, if the court opinion contains a detailed reasoning, it can often be useful in learning how to analyze a particular issue.

g. Disposition/Relief Granted

The relief granted is usually a one-sentence statement by the court that includes the order of the court as a result of the holding.

For Example

In *Miera v. State Farm Mutual Automobile Ins. Co.*, under the heading CONCLUSION, "We affirm the summary judgment entered in favor of State Farm and reverse the summary judgment in favor of Safeco."

A court has several options when granting relief:

- It may agree with the trial court and *affirm* the trial court's decision.
- It may disagree with the trial court and *reverse* the trial court's decision. If it reverses the decision, it will *remand*, that is, send the case back to the trial court. When a case is remanded, the appellate court may order the trial court to:

  1. Enter a judgment or order in accordance with the appellate court decision
  2. Retry the case (conduct a new trial)
  3. Conduct further proceedings in accordance with the appellate court decision

- If there are several issues, it may affirm the trial court on some of the issues and reverse the trial court on other issues.

h. Concurring Opinion

In some instances, a judge may agree with the majority holding but for different or additional reasons than those presented by the majority. The judge may then set out his or her reasons in support of the majority in what is called a *concurring opinion*. There may be more than one concurring opinion if other judges also agree with the majority conclusion but for different or additional reasons. This can lead to a *plurality opinion* where a sufficient number of judges agree with the outcome, but all for different reasons.

i. Dissenting Opinion

If a judge disagrees with the majority decision, the judge may present his or her reasons in what is called a *dissenting opinion*. Because a dissenting opinion does not agree with the majority view, it does not have the force of law. It is valuable, however, because it may help a reader understand the majority opinion.

For Example

The dissent may summarize what the court stated in the majority opinion. Note, however, that because the dissent disagrees with the majority view, it may mischaracterize the majority opinion.

The dissenting opinion is also important because it may become the majority view in the future when the composition of the court changes or there is a shift in the court's position. The dissent may provide the basis for future arguments in support of overruling outdated precedent. Remember, at one time the United States Supreme Court ruled that segregation on the basis of race was legal, *Plessey v. Ferguson*, 163 U.S. 537, 16 S. Ct. 1138, 41 L. Ed. 256 (1896). Now, segregation on the basis of race is illegal, *Brown v. Board of Education of Topeka*, 347 U.S. 483, 74 S. Ct. 686, 98 L. Ed. 873 (1954).

V. COURT OPINIONS—RESEARCHING

Researching case law is the process of finding a court opinion that answers a question being researched. Usually the search is for case law that governs or guides the resolution of an issue in a client's case. Such a court opinion is often referred to as being *on point*. Chapter 12 discusses how to determine whether a case is on point. This section focuses on how to find court opinions. The first part of this section discusses case law research sources, that is, where federal and state court opinions are published. The second part presents research strategies or techniques, that is, how to conduct case law research.

A. Publication of Court Opinions

1. In General

Not every decision by a court is published. To begin, except for federal district courts, trial courts generally do not write court opinions. If a trial court, such as a federal district court, writes an opinion and that opinion is published, it will not be mandatory precedent. Rather, trial court opinions are merely persuasive authority.

The court opinions that are referred to as the body of case law, or court-made law—those that make up primary authority and become precedent—are published court opinions from appellate courts. This chapter focuses on researching published appellate court opinions. However, for the few trial courts that publish opinions, the research strategies are the same.

Court opinions that are chosen for publication generally are those that establish a new rule of law, effect change to an existing rule of law, interpret existing law, clarify or define existing law, address matters of significant public interest or resolve conflicts of authority. Intermediate appellate courts do not publish all of their decisions; rather those that advance the law in some manner are chosen for publication. Generally, all opinions of the courts of last resort, such as state supreme courts or the United States Supreme Court, are published.

Just as there are so-called official and unofficial publications of statutory law, there are official and unofficial publications of case law as well. The official publications of case law are those published at the direction of the government. Court opinions that are not published at the direction of the government are considered unofficial publications. Both official and unofficial publications include, at a minimum, the full text of court opinions.

2. Unpublished Opinions

Do not assume that because a decision is not published that it is not available. Today, due to the prevalence of Internet research sources such as Westlaw, LexisNexis, Fastcase, state and federal court websites, and law school hosted websites such as Cornell Law School's Legal Information Institute, both published and unpublished opinions are easily accessible. In fact, in recent years there has been an increase in readily accessible unpublished opinions, which has caused controversy as to the use of those unpublished opinions in legal research and in legal documents. Further, in 2001 West Publishing created the *Federal Appendix*, which is a reporter containing the unpublished opinions of the federal courts of appeals. The increased availability of unpublished opinions is not only due to the increase in Internet research sources, but also due to laws such as the federal E-Government Act of 2002, requiring federal appellate courts to make all opinions accessible via the Internet, regardless of whether the opinion is published or not.

Often, unpublished opinions appear fully annotated just as a published opinion appears. This is particularly true of unpublished opinions located on commercial websites such as Westlaw and in those located in the *Federal Appendix*. However, there often is a notation on unpublished opinions indicating they are not published and not for use as primary authority.

There continues to be controversy as to whether unpublished opinions may be cited in legal documents. Early on, most courts had "no citation" rules barring use of opinions not designated as published opinions. In addition, unpublished cases lacked any reporter to cite to. However, the advent of vendor neutral citations cured the lack of citation in many jurisdictions, as did the assignment of numeric identifiers to unpublished opinions by commercial Internet research sources such as Westlaw and LexisNexis. Courts are now increasingly replacing "no citation" rules with rules dictating how and when unpublished cases can be cited, as well as dictating the value or effect of unpublished opinions. As such, it is extremely important that you know the rules and limits on use of and citation to unpublished opinions before you begin case law research, so that you know whether to invest time reviewing unpublished opinions that are part of your research results.

3. Forms of Publication

Most court opinions are published three times in three formats: slip opinions, advance sheets, and bound volumes called reports or reporters.

a. Slip Opinion

Most court decisions are first published by the court in the form of a slip opinion. Where there is a court website, the slip opinions may also be published and quickly available on that site. The **slip opinion** is usually in the form of a pamphlet that contains the full text of the court's opinion in a single case. It includes any concurring or dissenting opinion in the case. It also includes the case name, date of the decision, and attorneys' names. If a state has adopted public domain or vendor-neutral citation, that citation may also be included. However, the opinion will not yet have a full reporter citation.

Slip opinions do not usually include a syllabus (synopsis or summary of the facts, issues, and holding of a case), nor do they include headnotes. They are not organized by legal topic. All slip opinions are distributed to the parties involved in the lawsuit. In some jurisdictions they are also available by subscription.

Increasingly, both published and unpublished court opinions are issued in slip opinion form. Therefore, be careful to check for a notation on all slip opinions indicating whether the opinion is designated for publication before determining if and how the opinion might be used.

b. Advance Sheets

The permanent hardbound volumes of court decisions are published when there are a large number of court decisions sufficient to fill an entire volume. Therefore, many opinions may not appear in a bound volume until up to a year or more after the decision is rendered. **Advance sheets** are temporary pamphlets (often softcover books) that contain the full text of a number of recent court decisions. They are designed to provide quick access to recent court decisions. The publishers of the permanent volumes publish advance sheets frequently, often weekly. They are placed next to the last hardbound volume and are discarded when a permanent volume is published that contains the opinions printed in the advance sheets.

The decisions are presented chronologically and are sequentially paginated; that is, the volume and page number in the advance sheet will be the same as the page and volume number of the bound volume when the bound volume is published.

For Example

An opinion that appears in volume 525, page 756 of the advance sheet will appear in volume 525, page 756 of the permanent bound volume.

The advance sheets usually contain a case synopsis and headnotes for each case and an index and tables that appear in the permanent volume. They include a Key Number Digest section that arranges the cases by digest topic and subtopic.

c. Reporter

Court opinions are permanently published in hardbound volumes usually referred to as a **reporter**. A reporter volume is published when there are a sufficient number of advance sheets to fill a bound volume. The cases are presented chronologically, and as mentioned previously, paginated with the same page numbers as the advance sheets. Each bound volume usually includes a subject index and an alphabetical list of the opinions reported in the volume. The volumes are numbered consecutively so that the highest numbered volume will contain the most recent cases. Often, when there are a large number of volumes in a series, a second or even third series will be started. Each new series will begin at volume 1.

For Example

West's *Pacific Reporter* publishes the state court opinions for the western states. When the number of volumes of the *Pacific Reporter* (cited as P.) reached 300, a second series, *Pacific Reporter, Second Series* (cited as P.2d), beginning at volume 1, was started. When the second series reached 999 volumes, the *Pacific Reporter, Third Series* (cited as P.3d), beginning at volume 1, was started. The series number is indicated in the citation. The P.3d in the citation "100 P.3d 646" indicates that the decision is found in *Pacific Reporter, Third Series*. The volume number is 100, and the page number is 646.

4. National Reporter System

Most court decisions, both federal and state, are published by West Publishing in multivolume sets called *reporters*. These sets are available from the publisher in hardbound volumes. West's collection of reporters is referred to as the **National Reporter System**. West publishes reporters for almost every jurisdiction, as well as some specialty reporters. These reporters all have several common features, presented here rather than repeated in the discussion of each reporter:

For Example

The decisions of the United States Supreme Court are published in the *Supreme Court Reporter*, the decisions of the United States Courts of Appeals are published in the *Federal Reporters*, and the decisions of the various state appellate courts are published in regional or state-specific reporters.

* A table of cases, which lists in alphabetical order the opinions presented in the volume. Most sets have an additional table of cases in which the cases are arranged by state or by circuit.

For Example

Each volume of the *Federal Reporter* has a table of cases listing all the cases alphabetically and a table that arranges the cases alphabetically by circuit. All the cases from the First Circuit, Second Circuit, and so on are arranged alphabetically by circuit. The *South Western Reporter* includes a table of cases that lists the cases alphabetically and a table that arranges the cases alphabetically by state so that all the cases from each state are listed separately.

* A table of statutes listing the various statutes, constitutional provisions, and often rules interpreted or reviewed, and relevant court opinions.

For Example

If you are researching cases that have interpreted the First Amendment to the United States Constitution, the table will direct you to all the cases in the volume that have interpreted the amendment.

* A table of words and phrases listing alphabetically words and phrases judicially defined and indicating the page number in the volume where they are defined.
* A Key Number Digest in the back of each volume, which provides a summary of each case in the volume arranged by topic and key number.
* A case syllabus (a synopsis case summary), headnotes, and key numbers, which are located at the beginning of each case presented in the volume. This allows a researcher quick access to all related cases through West's Digest System. (See the first page of Exhibit 4-1.)

5. Publication of Federal Court Decisions

a. United States Supreme Court

Three different sets publish the decisions of the United States Supreme Court: *United States Reports*, *Supreme Court Reporter*, and *United States Supreme Court Reports, Lawyers' Edition*. The decisions of the United States Supreme Court are also available on the court's own website and through other Internet research sources.

(1) United States Reports The *United States Reports* (cited as U.S.) is the official reporter for the Supreme Court of the United States. It is published by the United States Government Printing Office (GPO) and contains the full text of all the decisions of the Supreme Court. The decisions are initially published as slip opinions,

followed by advance sheets and then, finally, hardbound volumes. The reports are indexed but do not include headnotes or key numbers.

(2) Supreme Court Reporter The *Supreme Court Reporter* (cited as S.Ct.) is an unofficial publication of the decisions of the United States Supreme Court published by West and is part of West's National Reporter System. It includes the decisions of the Supreme Court since 1882. It is published much more quickly than the *United States Reports*. Advance sheets are published at least twice a month.

The headnotes with links to the key numbers make the *Supreme Court Reporter* a valuable research tool. The key numbers, through their link to West's Digest System, allow a researcher to research a point of law discussed in a Supreme Court opinion in all reported decisions—both federal and state.

(3) United States Supreme Court Reports, Lawyers' Edition The *United States Supreme Court Reports, Lawyers' Edition* (cited as L. Ed. or L. Ed. 2d for volumes since 1956) is an unofficial publication of the decisions of the United States Supreme Court published by LexisNexis. It includes all the decisions of the Supreme Court since 1789. Advance sheets are published at least twice a month.

Like the *Supreme Court Reporter*, a summary of the case and headnotes precedes each opinion. Each headnote is assigned a topic and section number (see Exhibit 4-2). The topics are printed in *United States Supreme Court Digest, Lawyers' Edition*. This allows researchers to locate other cases addressing the same topic. In addition, there are summaries of the briefs of counsel and, for some cases, annotations that analyze important points of law covered in the cases are presented.

Researchers need to remember that the publisher prepares the case summaries, headnotes, and so on presented in both the *Supreme Court Reporter* and the *United States Supreme Court Reports, Lawyers' Edition*; they are not part of the actual court opinion. They are valuable research tools, but they are not the law. Any reference or quote in research should be to the court opinion itself and not to the material prepared by the publisher.

(4) Loose-Leaf Services and Newspapers There are various sources to obtain quick access to the decisions of the Supreme Court of the United States. The *United States Law Week* (U.S.L.W.), published by the Bureau of National Affairs (BNA), is a loose-leaf service that publishes weekly decisions of the Supreme Court. The service includes additional information, such as summaries of cases pending before the court and reports on oral arguments. Often, law firms and law libraries subscribe to legal newspapers that print the decisions of the United States Supreme Court and other federal courts.

(5) Computer and Internet Resources Access to most federal court opinions, especially United States Supreme Court opinions, is available through Westlaw and LexisNexis. In addition, court opinions are often available through the official court website and other Internet resources (see Internet Resources at the end of this chapter). The United States Supreme Court website provides access to the slip opinions by term, the bound volumes of the fourth and final generation (volume 502 and forward) of the *United States Reports*, in-chambers opinions, and opinions related to orders. Moreover, the Supreme Court's website provides a way to search the Court's docket, a link to merits briefs, orders of the court, and other materials related to the various other functions of the Court.

b. United States Courts of Appeals

The *Federal Reporter* (cited as F.), the *Federal Reporter, Second Series* (cited as F.2d), and the *Federal Reporter, Third Series* (cited as F.3d), by West Publishing, contain the decisions of the United States Courts of Appeals that are designated for publication. Like the *Supreme Court Reporter*, the *Federal Reporter* series is part of West's National Reporter System. The cases are initially published in advance sheets, which are later compiled in hardbound volumes. The *Federal Reporter* is an unofficial reporter, but it is the only reporter that publishes the "published" decisions of the United States Circuit Courts of Appeals. Therefore, there are no parallel citations for these decisions.

Over the years, the *Federal Reporter* has included decisions of courts other than the United States Circuit Courts of Appeals, such as decisions of the United States District Courts up to 1932 and the United States Court of Claims from 1960 to 1982. As mentioned at the beginning of this section, due to the large number of cases, not all decisions are published.

The *Federal Appendix*, also by West Publishing, contains many of the opinions of the United States Court of Appeals from 2001 to date that are not selected for publication. These are the "unpublished" opinions discussed earlier in this chapter. The *Federal Appendix* is also part of West's National Reporter System. Like all opinions in West's National Reporter System, the decisions in the *Federal Appendix* include case summaries, headnotes, and

GEISSAL V MOORE MEDICAL CORP.
(1998) 524 US 74,141 L Ed 2d 64,118 S Ct 1869

defendants (1) had violated COBRA by renouncing an obligation to provide continuing coverage, and (2) were estopped to deny him COBRA continuation coverage. The parties agreed to have a magistrate judge conduct all proceedings. The individual (1) moved for partial summary judgment on the first two counts, and (2) included an argument that the defendants' reliance upon § 1162(2)(D)(i) to deny him continuation coverage was misplaced, as he had first been covered under his wife's plan before he had elected continuation coverage. While the motion was pending, the individual died and his wife, who was also the personal representative of his estate, replaced him as plaintiff. The magistrate judge granted partial summary judgment in favor of the defendants on the two counts, as the magistrate judge expressed the view that under § 1162(2)(D)(I), an employee with coverage under another group health plan as of the date on which the employee elected COBRA continuation coverage was ineligible for such coverage (927 F Supp 352, 1996 US Dist LEXIS 7145). On appeal, the United States Court of Appeals for the Eighth Circuit, in affirming, expressed the view that (1) under § 1162(2)(D)(i), it was within the defendants' rights to cancel the individual's COBRA benefits unless there was a "significant gap" between the coverage afforded under the corporation's plan and that afforded under his wife's plan; and (2) the wife had failed to carry her burden of showing that such a significant gap existed (114 F3d 1458, 1997 US App LEXIS 13589).

On certiorari, the United States Supreme Court vacated the Court of Appeals' judgment and remanded the case for further proceedings. In an opinion by SOUTER, J., expressing the unanimous view of the court, it was held that § 1162(2)(D)(i) did not allow an employer to deny COBRA continuation coverage to a qualified beneficiary who was covered under another group health plan at the time that the beneficiary made a COBRA election, as (1) under the plain meaning of § 1162(2)(D)(i) as it read at the time pertinent to the case at hand, the medical corporation could not cut off the individual's COBRA continuation coverage, where the individual (a) was covered under his wife's plan before he made his COBRA election, and (b) so did not first become covered under his wife's plan after the date of election; and (2) there was no justification for disparaging the clarity of § 1162(2)(D)(i).

HEADNOTE

Classified to United States Supreme Court Digest, Lawyers' Edition

Pensions and Retirement Funds § 1—Employee Retirement Income Security Act—group health plan—continuation coverage

For purposes of some provisions (29 USCS §§ 1161 et seq.) of the Employee Retirement Income Security Act of 1974 as amended by the Consolidated Omnibus Budget Reconciliation Act of 1985 (COBRA)-which provisions authorize a qualified beneficiary of an employer's group health plan to obtain continued coverage under the plan when the beneficiary might otherwise lose that benefit for certain reasons, such as the termination of employment-29 USCS § 1162(2)(D)(i) (later amended) does not allow an employer to deny COBRA continuation coverage to qualified beneficiary who is covered

Exhibit 4-2   Page Showing Headnote from Opinion Published in United States Supreme Court Reports, Lawyers' Edition. *Geissal v. Moore Medical Corp.*, 524 U.S. 74, 118 S.Ct. 1869, 141 L.Ed.2d 64 (1998), page 65. Reprinted with the permission of LexisNexis.

key numbers. Each volume contains a table of cases, words and phrase, and a key number digest just as the rest of the reporters in the West National Reporter Series.

c. United States District Courts

West publishes selected decisions of the United States District Courts from 1932 to 1997 in the *Federal Supplement* (cited as F. Supp.) and from 1998 to present in the *Federal Supplement, Second Series* (cites as F. Supp. 2d). This reporter set includes the decisions of the United States Court of International Trade since 1956 and the Judicial Panel on Multidistrict Litigation since 1932. Like the *Federal Reporter*, it is an unofficial reporter, but it is the only reporter that publishes the decisions of the United States District Courts. Therefore, there are no parallel citations for these decisions. It is part of the National Reporter System. Like the other reporters, the cases are initially published in advance sheets, which are later compiled in hardbound volumes.

West's Other Federal Reporters

West publishes the following specialized federal reporter sets.

(1) Federal Rules Decisions (cited as F.R.D.) This set includes selected opinions of the United States District Courts concerning the Federal Rules of Civil and Criminal Procedure. Some cases involving court rules will appear in the *Federal Supplement*. However, if a decision is published in one set, such as the *Federal Rules Decisions*, it generally will not be published in the other set.

(2) West's Bankruptcy Reporter This reporter publishes selected decisions of the United States Bankruptcy Courts and District Courts involving bankruptcy. It includes bankruptcy opinions from the United States Supreme Court and the Courts of Appeals.

(3) United States Claims Court Reporter This set publishes selected trial court decisions of the Claims Court and relevant opinions from the Supreme Court and the Courts of Appeals.

(4) West's Military Justice Reporter This set includes the decisions from the United States Court of Military Appeals and Courts of Military Review.

(5) West's Veterans Appeals Reporter This reporter publishes decisions of the United States Court of Veterans Appeals.

6. Publication of State Court Decisions

a. Regional Reporters

In addition to the reporters that publish the federal court decisions (discussed in the previous subsection), West's National Reporter System includes sets of reports and reporters that publish selected decisions of the state appellate courts. Each reporter volume includes the features discussed above in subsection "National Reporter System," such as a table of cases reported and words and phrases defined. The National Reporter System publishes state court decisions by geographic region in reporters called **regional reporters**. These reporters are: *Pacific Reporter*, *North Western Reporter*, *South Western Reporter*, *North Eastern Reporter*, *Atlantic Reporter*, *South Eastern Reporter*, and *Southern Reporter*. West created the geographic grouping of regions, and there is no particular significance to the organization of the regions. The map in Exhibit 4-3 shows the reporter regions and the states in each region.

Due to the large number of cases from California, New York, and Illinois, West created separate reporters for these states. The *California Reporter* publishes the decisions of the California Supreme Court and appellate courts. The California Supreme Court decisions are published in both the *Pacific Reporter* and the *California Reporter*; the appellate court decisions are published in the *California Reporter* only. The *New York Supplement* publishes the decisions of the New York Court of Appeals and the intermediate appellate decisions. The New York Court of Appeals decisions are also printed in the *North Eastern Reporter*; the intermediate appellate decisions are not printed in the *North Eastern Reporter*. The *Illinois Decisions* publishes decisions of the Illinois Supreme Court and appellate courts.

West also publishes individual reporters for many states that are limited to the supreme and appellate court decisions of the state. These reporters are designed for attorneys who are mostly interested in the decisions of the state in which they practice. These decisions are also published in the regional reporter.

For Example

A practitioner in Arizona may need ready access to Arizona case law for the vast majority of their work. It may be worthwhile to purchase a set of the *Arizona Reports*, which consists of fewer volumes than the *Pacific Reporter* and consequently will be less costly to obtain and keep current.

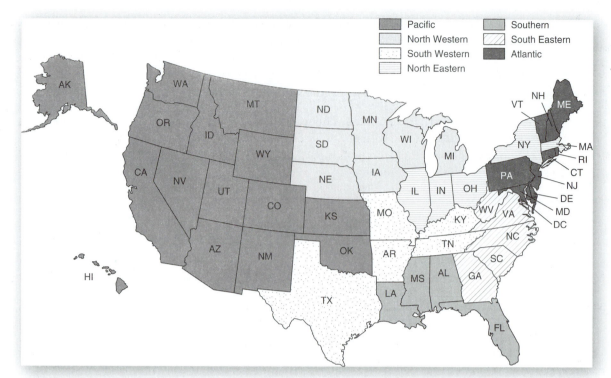

Exhibit 4-3   West's National Reporter System Map. Reprinted from West Group, copyright 2002. Reprinted with permission of Thomson Reuters.

Advance sheets are published for each regional reporter and the advance sheets include the features discussed previously in this chapter.

Many states have discontinued the official publication of state appellate court decisions. In those states, the court decisions are published only in the regional reporter, and the only citation is to the regional reporter.

For Example

Colorado discontinued its official publication of cases in 1980. The only citation to Colorado decisions is to the *Pacific Reporter* cite, for example, *People v. J.D.*, 989 P.2d 762 (Colo. 1999).

Some states have an official publication as well as a public domain citation (also referred to as *medium-neutral citations* or *vendor-neutral citations*). When this is the case multiple citations will be required. In some states the official publication is an authenticated PDF bearing a public domain citation. Those authenticated PDFs may or may not be compiled into print volumes, but the authenticated PDF is the official publication in whatever form(s) published, and all other publications are unofficial.

For Example

State v. Dickert, 2012-NMCA-004, 268 P.3d 515. The official publication, the *New Mexico Appellate Reports*, uses the public domain or vendor-neutral citation (2004-NMCA-004). The unofficial *Pacific Reporter* citation is 268 P.3d 515.

b. Computer and Internet Resources

Access to most state court opinions is available through Westlaw and LexisNexis. In addition, court opinions are increasingly available through the official court websites and other Internet sites (see Internet Resources at the end of this chapter).

At least one state has ceased to publish its official state reporter and moved to a purely electronic archive of its appellate court opinions. In 2012 New Mexico broke with 160 years of publishing tradition and ceased publication of the print *New Mexico Reports* and moved to a digital archive maintained electronically by the New Mexico Compilation Commission, known as the *New Mexico Appellate Reports*. Arkansas and Illinois have designated their judicial opinions in electronic format as their official decisions as well.

7. Attorney General Opinions

The chief attorney for the federal or state government is usually referred to as the attorney general. Upon the request of legislators or other government officials, an attorney general may issue a written opinion interpreting how the law applies. This usually occurs when there is no court opinion interpreting how a specific law applies or there are conflicting court opinions. These opinions are **secondary authority**; they are not enacted law or the opinion of a court. They are not primary authority and do not have to be followed by a court. Nevertheless, because they are written by the attorney general, they are often relied on in the absence of a law or court opinion addressing a specific question.

Attorney general opinions are available through Westlaw and LexisNexis. In addition, they are often available through federal or state government websites and other Internet resources. The opinions are also individually available, in slip form, through the attorney general's office. Bound volumes of all the opinions can be available at law libraries.

B. Researching Court Opinions—Locating Case Law

After you know where the various court opinions are published, the next step is to become familiar with the many research sources and techniques for locating cases (see Exhibit 4-4). Whenever you conduct case law research, *remember to check the advance sheets, pocket parts, or whatever is used to update the source you are researching to ensure that you locate the most recent court decision that answers your question.* Where and how you conduct research depend on the amount and type of information you have at the outset. The main ways to locate case law are discussed here.

1. Statutory Annotations

If your research involves a situation that requires the interpretation of a statute, the *first step is to read the statute and look to the case annotations following the statute.* Often the annotations to the key court decisions following the statute will include a case that is on point. This saves time spent using another research source such as a digest.

Statutory Annotations	If your research involves a situation that requires the interpretation of a statute, read the statute and look to the case annotations following the statute.
Digest	If the question being researched does not involve a statute or the annotations do not direct you to a relevant case, look to a digest.
Other Case Law Research Sources	If you need to locate additional court opinions, then use other research sources such as legal encyclopedias, treatises, *ALR*s, and law review articles.
Shepard's Citations; West's *KeyCite* and Updating Research	If you know the citation of a case and you are looking for other cases that have referred to the case or if you Want to know whether the case has been reversed or modified, refer to the appropriate *Shepard's* citator.
Computer-Aided Research	Research sources and court opinions may be located through Westlaw and LexisNexis.

© Cengage

Exhibit 4-4 Research Sources and Techniques for Locating Cases.

For Example

The client robbed a bank with a toy handgun that looked exactly like a real handgun. The client is charged with bank robbery with a dangerous weapon under 18 U.S.C. § 2113(a) & (d). The question is whether a toy handgun is a dangerous weapon under the statute. Referring to the annotations to the statute in the *United States Code Annotated* or the *United States Code Service*, you will find cases that address the question of whether a toy gun is considered a dangerous weapon. Other than checking to determine if the case has been reversed or modified or to verify there are no recent cases also on point, no further search may be necessary. A digest does not need to be consulted.

If the case located is not exactly the case you are looking for, that is, it is not quite on point, the opinion may reference other cases that are on point or provide you with a key number that will lead you to the proper case. Always read the statute first, because the answer may be in the statute itself or in the annotations.

2. Digest

If the question being researched does not involve a statute or the annotations do not direct you to a relevant case, the next step is to look to a digest. West publishes sets of volumes called *digests* for the various reporters. There is a digest for each regional and state reporter, such as the *Pacific Digest* for the *Pacific Reporter*, and a *Federal Practice Digest* for federal reporters. As discussed earlier in this chapter, West has divided the areas of law into various topics and subtopics. Each area is identified by a topic name, such as "Insurance," and each topic is divided into subtopics and assigned a key number. The digests contain summaries of all the court opinions under each key number subtopic.

If you know a case name, you can quickly locate it in a digest's table of cases. If you don't have a particular case in mind but are looking for a case that addresses the question you are researching, scan the topic area, locate the relevant key number, and scan the case summaries to locate the case on point. If there is no case under a particular key number, the digest will refer you to other research sources, such as to a legal encyclopedia.

3. Computer-Aided Research

Court opinions may be located through Westlaw and LexisNexis. Also, court opinions are often found through other Internet sources, including many court's official websites. Chapters 7 and 8 discuss searching court opinions on the Internet in more detail as well as the differences and limitations between free and fee-based Internet research sources. Generally, the techniques of searching for case law in print are applicable to searching for case law electronically with the only difference being in the structure and limitations of a given website. When using Westlaw and LexisNexis, the techniques are nearly identical.

4. Other Case Law Research Sources

You may also locate court opinions through other research sources, such as legal encyclopedias, treatises, *American Law Reports* (*ALRs*), and law review articles. These and other secondary authority research sources for locating case law are discussed in Chapters 5 and 6. Usually, however, there are quicker ways of locating cases than through these sources.

For Example

The question you are researching is similar to the question raised in *Miera v. State Farm Mutual Automobile Ins. Co.*, (presented in Exhibit 4-1): When is a passenger "occupying" a driver's vehicle for purposes of being covered under driver's uninsured motorist coverage? You can look under "insurance" in an encyclopedia and eventually find a section that addresses this question and be directed to specific cases. You may, however, spend a lot of time reading before you locate the specific topic you are looking for and spend even more time checking the numerous cases listed before you find the case on point. Through the use of a digest or Westlaw or LexisNexis, your search is more focused and you will usually find cases quicker.

If there is an *ALR* annotation on the question you are researching, it will provide an in-depth analysis of a specific question and reference to key cases addressing the question. First, however, follow the steps mentioned earlier in the "Statutory Annotations" section, because if you find a case on point you may not need the in-depth analysis, or the case you find may mention a relevant *ALR* annotation and save you the time locating it.

5. Updating Research

If you know the citation of a case and you are looking for other cases that have referred to the case, or if you want to know whether the case has been reversed or modified, refer to the appropriate **Shepard's** citator in print, *Shepard's Online*, or if you are using Westlaw, West's **KeyCite**. The use of *Shepard's* and Westlaw's *KeyCite* is discussed in Chapter 5.

You must always check to determine if the case you have located is good law, that is, whether the court opinion or part of the opinion you are relying on has been reversed or modified by a subsequent court decision. Increasingly, public and school law libraries are discontinuing their subscription to *Shepard's* citator in print due to cost and instead providing at least one computer with public access to *Shepard's Online*. Often this access is through LexisAcademic. If you have a subscription to Westlaw, then *KeyCite* updates can be directly referenced from a tab associated with the case, or the citation to the case you are updating can be directly input into the West Search box to determine if any subsequent cases have overruled or overturned the case you are updating.

Updating case law using *Shepard's* and *KeyCite* and the use of both of these resources as a means of conducting legal research are discussed in more detail in Chapter 5.

VI. COURT OPINIONS—BRIEFING (CASE BRIEF)

A. Introduction

As a researcher, you may be assigned the task of reading and briefing court opinions. A court opinion is usually called a *case*, and a brief of a court opinion is usually called a *case brief*. A **case brief** is a written summary identifying the essential components of a court opinion.

B. Importance of Briefing

The process of briefing a case serves the following purposes and functions:

1. *Analysis/learning*. Writing a summary of the essential elements of an opinion in an organized format leads to better understanding of the case and the reasoning of the court. Opinions are often complex, and the reasoning is hard to identify, difficult to follow, or spread throughout the opinion. The preparation of a case brief requires study of the opinion, identifying the essentials, and elimination of the nonessentials. This process of studying a case and analyzing it helps the reader gain a better understanding of it. The analytical process of focusing on the structure of the case helps you gain an understanding of the reasoning, thereby assisting your analysis of the law.

2. *Research/reference*. A case brief is a timesaving research tool. It provides a summary of the essentials of a case that can be quickly referred to when reviewing the case. This saves the time that would be spent rereading and reanalyzing the entire case in order to remember what the court decided and why. When working on a complex legal problem involving several court opinions, or when time has passed since a case was read, the availability of case briefs can result in a considerable saving of time, because it is often difficult to remember which opinion said what.

    A case brief is a valuable tool for the attorney assigned to the case. The attorney may not need to read all the cases related to an issue. The attorney can read the case briefs prepared by the researcher and quickly weed out those cases that are not key and identify and focus on the cases that should be read.

3. *Writing*. The process of briefing a case is a valuable writing tool. It provides you with an exercise in which you learn to sift through a court opinion, identify the essential elements, and assemble your analysis into a concise written summary.

C. How to Read a Case

Before you can brief a case, you must first read it carefully. Sometimes it is necessary to read the entire opinion or parts of it several times to gain an understanding of the decision and the court's reasoning. You cannot expect to skim or quickly read an opinion and hope to understand it. It cannot be read like a newspaper or novel for several reasons:

1. Judges write opinions with the assumption that the reader has an understanding of the law, legal terminology, and the legal system. If you are a beginner, you are slowed by having to look up the meaning of legal terms and become familiar with the style of legal writing.

For Example

In the first sentence of an opinion, the court uses the phrase "jointly and severally liable." Without a legal background, a novice would have to stop reading and look up these terms before continuing to read the case.

Do not get discouraged if at first it takes a long time to read and understand case law. It is normal to "crawl through" court opinions when you are a novice at reading them. As you become familiar with the terminology and style of legal opinions, you will read them faster and with greater understanding. The process, however, is gradual and usually takes months rather than days to learn. No matter your skill level, you must read cases carefully to acquire a full understanding.

2. Some opinions are difficult to read and take time because they involve complex, abstract, or unfamiliar subjects with multiple issues. In such instances, you may have to read the entire case or portions of it several times. You may have to prepare outlines or charts as you read to help you follow and understand the court's reasoning. You may have to refer to a treatise, encyclopedia, or other research tool to obtain an understanding of the area of law involved in the case.
3. Some opinions are difficult to read because they are poorly written. Not all judges are great writers. The reasoning may be scattered throughout the case or not completely presented.
4. Some opinions are difficult to read and understand because the court may have incorrectly interpreted or applied the law. You may be surprised when you read the holding that the court reached a conclusion that is the opposite of the outcome you expected. Remember that some decisions are overruled because a higher or subsequent court determined that the earlier opinion was incorrect. Therefore, *it is important to read each case with a critical eye.*

The purpose of reading a court opinion is to obtain an understanding of the law or principle addressed by the court. To gain this understanding, cases *must* be read and analyzed with *close scrutiny*. The ability to read cases with greater understanding and speed comes with experience.

Several chapters in this text present specific guidelines to assist the reader in reading, interpreting, and analyzing court opinions:

1. Identification of the key facts of a court opinion is discussed in Chapter 9.
2. Identification of the issue in a court opinion is addressed in Chapter 10.
3. How to determine if a court opinion is on point and may be used as precedent is covered in Chapter 12.
4. Counteranalysis in case law is discussed in Chapter 13.

D. Case Brief—Elements

There is no standard form for a brief of a court opinion, nor are there any hard-and-fast rules governing format. Some texts recommend that case briefs contain as few as five parts, some as many as sixteen. The style of a case brief may vary from individual to individual and office to office. Be prepared to adapt to different styles, even within the same office.

The goal of a good case brief is a concise summary of the essentials of the court opinion that may be used as a quick reference in the future. Therefore, the brief should be concise. It certainly should not be as long as or longer than the case. Do not fill the brief with excessive quotes from the case or long summaries. Spend more time thinking than writing. Reduce the opinion to its essence.

A recommended outline for a case-brief format is presented in Exhibit 4-5. This format should be viewed as a basic outline of the essential parts of a case brief. It can be adapted as necessary to meet your needs. A discussion of each section of the outline follows.

1. Citation

The citation includes the name of the parties, where the case can be found, the court that issued the opinion, and the year of the opinion. Remember citation format is governed by the rules of citation found in citation manuals such as the *Bluebook* and local rules. Be sure to consult the citation manual or rules that govern the particular jurisdiction you are in to determine proper cite format. Citations are covered generally in the Citing Case Law section of this chapter.

For Example

In *Miera v. State Farm Automobile Ins. Co.* the citation is *Miera v. State Farm Automobile Ins. Co.*, 2004-NMCA-059, 135 N.M. 574, 92 P.3d 20.

- *Miera v. State Farm Automobile Ins. Co.*—name of the case

- 2004-NMCA-059—the public domain citation

- 135 N.M. 574, 92 P.3d 20—the volume and page numbers of the books where the case can be found. This case can be found in volume 135 of the *New Mexico Reports* at page 574 and in volume 92 of the *Pacific Reporter*, second series, at page 20.

- The court that rendered the opinion and the year of the opinion is contained within the public domain citation (2004-NMCA)—the year the case was decided is 2004 and the court deciding the case was the New Mexico Court of Appeals (NMCA). When there is no public domain citation that includes the yead court of decision, the information is provided in parentheses at the end of the citation.

Citation:	Name of case and where it can be found
Parties:	Names and legal status of the parties
Facts:	A summary of those facts that describe the history of events that caused the parties to be in court (background facts) and those facts to which the law applies and are essential to the decision reached by the court (key facts)
Procedural History:	What happened in the lower court or courts and disposition in the court issuing the opinion
Issue:	The specific question(s) addressed and answered by the court (State the issue as narrowly and concretely as possible in the context of the case facts. The issue statement should include the rule of law and the key facts.)
Holding:	The court's answer to the issue
Comments:	Observations concerning the opinion

© Cengage

Exhibit 4-5 Case-Brief Format.

2. Parties

The caption at the beginning of the opinion gives the full name and legal status of each party.

For Example

- Robert J. Miera Sr.—Plaintiff-Appellant
- State Farm Mutual Automobile Insurance Company—Defendant-Appellee
- Safeco National Insurance Company—Defendant-Appellee

The legal status refers to the litigation status of the parties. This includes the status at the trial and appellate court levels. The status is usually indicated in the caption. The *plaintiff* is the person who brought the lawsuit, and the *defendant* is the party against whom the suit is brought. Often terminology other than plaintiff and defendant is used.

For Example

Petitioner and *respondent* are often used in divorce cases. The petitioner is the party who filed the divorce petition, and the respondent is the person against whom the divorce petition is filed.

The appeal status of the parties immediately follows the trial court status in the caption.

For Example

In *Miera v. State Farm Automobile Ins. Co.*, Robert J. Miera Sr. was the plaintiff at trial (he filed the lawsuit), and he is the party who filed the appeal (he lost at the trial level).

3. Facts

The facts section of a case brief includes a summary of those facts that describe the history of the events giving rise to the litigation. The facts section should include key facts and just enough background facts to provide the reader with context.

a. Key Facts

The key facts are those facts in the opinion to which the law applies and that are essential to the decision reached by the court. They are those facts upon which the outcome of the case is determined. If the key facts were different, the outcome of the case would probably be different.

b. Background Facts

Background facts are those facts that put the key facts in context. They are facts necessary to make sense of the story and thereby provide the reader with an overall context within which the key facts occur, an overall picture of the events of the case.

For Example

In an automobile collision case, where the impact took place on a country road, the fact that the collision took place on a country road may not be a key fact, but its inclusion in the fact section of the brief helps provide the reader with an overview of the context and scene of the collision.

In some texts, the case-brief format presents the prior proceedings before the facts. Whether the fact section precedes the prior proceedings section or follows it is a matter of preference. As such, be sure to draft your brief to match the preferred format in the workplace, if there is one.

4. Procedural History

Procedural history is the chronology of events that occurred in each court before the case reached the court whose opinion you are briefing. Most opinions are not written by trial courts; they are written by courts of appeals reviewing the decision(s) of a trial court—either:

- An intermediary court of appeals, such as the United States Court of Appeals, or
- The highest court of the jurisdiction, such as the United States Supreme Court

Therefore, there are usually prior proceedings. If you are briefing an opinion of a trial court, there may be no prior proceedings because the trial court was the first court to hear the case.

The procedural history section should include:

1. The party initiating the proceeding and the cause of action
2. The court before which the proceeding was initiated
3. The result of the proceeding
4. The party appealing and what is being appealed
5. The disposition of the case by the court that issued the opinion

The **disposition** includes the relief granted by the court, which is the order entered by the court. This section is usually located at the very end of the opinion. If the opinion was appealed to a higher court, that should be noted in the procedural history section to remind anyone reading the brief later that the opinion needs to be updated to ensure the case was not altered by a subsequent court opinion.

For Example

"The plaintiff sued the defendant claiming medical malpractice. The trial court granted the defendant's motion to dismiss, ruling that the statute of limitations had run. The plaintiff appealed the trial court's ruling that the statute had run. The Court of Appeals affirmed."

5. Issue(s)

The **issue** is the legal question addressed and answered by the court. It is the precise legal question raised by the specific facts of the case. The issue should be stated as narrowly and concisely as possible in the context of the facts of the case. A court opinion may address several issues. Identify each issue separately in the case brief unless you are instructed to brief only one issue.

For Example

In an opinion involving an automobile collision case, the court addresses several issues, some involving insurance, some involving evidence, some involving negligence, and some involving battery. The attorney working on a client's case is interested only in the court's resolution of an evidentiary question raised by the facts in the court case. The client's case involves an evidentiary question and fact situation similar to that addressed in the court opinion. Therefore, a researcher may be instructed to provide a case brief of only the portion of the opinion that addresses the evidentiary question. Although the opinion involves several issues, the case brief will address only one issue.

6. Holding

The **holding** is the court's resolution of the issue. It is the decision of the court, the answer to the issue. There should be a separate holding for each issue identified in the issue section of the case brief. In some brief formats the holding is a simple, one-word, yes-or-no response to the issue. However, the holding should be presented as a complete response to the issue, which means that the presentation of the holding should include all the elements of the issue and should be in the form of a statement.

For Example

The issue in the case is, "Under Indiana's probate code, Ind. Code § 29-1-5-2, is a will valid if the witnesses are brothers of the testator?" If the court ruled that the will was valid, the holding should be presented as follows: "Under Indiana's probate code, Ind. Code § 29-1-5-2, a will is valid if the witnesses are brothers of the testator as long as there is no evidence of undue influence."

7. Reasoning/Rationale

Usually the largest part of an opinion is the court's presentation of the reasons in support of the holding. Just as for each issue there is a holding, for each holding there should be reasons explaining why the holding was reached.

The reasoning portion of an opinion usually consists of two parts:

1. The rule of law that governs the facts of the dispute. It may be constitutional, legislative, or case law, and it may consist of any legal principle, doctrine, or rule of law that applies to the issue in the case.
2. The court's application of the rule to the facts of the case.

For Example

The issue in the case is, "Under state tort law, does a battery occur when law enforcement officers, while making a lawful arrest, encounter resistance, use force to overcome that resistance, and continue to use force after the resistance ceases?"

The reasoning presented in the opinion is as follows:

- Rule of law—"In *Smith v. Jones*, the Supreme Court ruled that a civil battery occurs whenever unauthorized harmful contact occurs."

- Application of this rule to the facts of the case—"The defendants argue that inasmuch as they were making a lawful arrest, they were authorized to use force; therefore, their conduct was not unauthorized within the meaning of *Smith v. Jones*. In this case, however, although the officers were making a lawful arrest, their conduct ceased to be lawful when they continued to use force against plaintiff after plaintiff ceased resisting. Law enforcement officers are authorized to use the amount of force necessary to overcome resistance. After resistance ceases, any continued use of force is unauthorized within the meaning of *Smith v. Jones* and constitutes a civil battery."

In some instances, it is difficult to identify the reasoning in a court opinion because it is scattered throughout the opinion. A helpful approach is to work backward from the holding. Look to the holding first, and keep it in mind while reading the case. It may be easier to see how the court assembled the reasons in support of the holding if you know the holding or outcome while reading the case.

Also, the rule of law or legal principle governing the issue is usually clearly stated by the court and is easy to identify. The reasons for the application of the rule or principle to the facts of the case usually follow the presentation of the governing law. Therefore, identification of the governing law may also help you locate the reasoning.

The reasoning section of the case brief should include the rule of law and a summary of the court's application of the rule of law to the facts—how the rule of law applies to the facts of the case. Lengthy quotes from the case should be avoided. The reasoning should be summarized.

For Example

In the excessive force situation presented in the previous example, the reasoning section of the case brief is as follows: "A civil battery occurs whenever unauthorized harmful contact occurs. *Smith v. Jones.* Law enforcement officers are authorized to overcome resistance. After resistance ceases, any continued use of force is unauthorized and constitutes a civil battery."

Also included in the reasoning section is a summary of the reasoning of any concurring opinion.

8. Comments

Include in this section of the case brief any observations you may have concerning the court opinion. This could include any of the following:

1. Why you agree or disagree with the decision.
2. A summary of any dissenting opinions. Does the dissenting opinion contain information that is useful in understanding the majority opinion? Does the dissenting opinion contain valuable legal arguments that may be useful in arguing against use of the case as precedent? This is especially helpful if the holding of the court goes against your client's position. *Note*: Some case-brief formats have a separate section for dissenting opinions.
3. Why the case may or may not be on point.

For Example

Referring to the excessive force example, assume that in the client's case there is evidence that the client never ceased resisting. You might include the following comment in the comment section of the brief: "It is questionable whether this case can be relied on as precedent due to the differences between the facts of the case and our client's facts. In the court case, force continued after resistance ceased, and the court held that the continued use of force constituted a battery. Inasmuch as in our case there is evidence that resistance never ceased, the court opinion may not be applicable."

4. References to the opinion in subsequent cases or secondary sources, such as a law review article.
5. Any information updating the case, that is, concerning whether the case is still good law (see next section).

E. Case Brief—Updating

Whenever an assignment requires you to brief a case, you should determine if the case is still good law, which means you must check to determine if the opinion has been reversed, modified, or in any way affected by a later court decision. The primary method of accomplishing this is through the use of citators such as *Shepard's*, *Shepard's* Online, and *KeyCite*.

In addition, other computerized services provide online citators. These online services include:

- LexCite—includes a list of the recent cases citing a case (available through LexisNexis)
- Auto-Cite—provides a summary of the prior and subsequent history of a case. It also checks the accuracy of the citation and provides a check on the case's precedential value.
- *KeyCite*—Westlaw's citator service that includes information on whether a case has been reversed, modified, or in any way affected by later court decisions, as well as a list of case that have negative treatment of the citation.

VII. CITING CASE LAW

Any time you report the results of case law research in written form or reference the content of the results of research, you must properly cite to the case(s). Citations to case law provide more than the name of the case and where the case can be located; they also allow a reader to identify the weight of the authority, and whether the case is mandatory or persuasive authority.

Both the *Bluebook* and the *ALWD Guide* contain the same basic rules for proper case law citation format. The citation format for case law can be found in the *Bluebook* at Bluepages B10, Rule 10. Tables T1, T6, T7, and T10 of the *Bluebook* contain necessary abbreviations used in case law citation format. Consult Rule 12 and Appendices 1, 3, and 4 of the *ALWD Guide* for its rules and abbreviations for case law citation format.

The components of a case citation are the following:

1. The case name.
2. Any public domain or vendor neutral citation assigned to the case.
3. The reporter(s) in which the case is published (volume number, abbreviation for the reporter, and page number where case begins). The order of the reporters is dictated by rule. Generally the official reporter must be cited (if there is one) and unofficial reporters follow.
4. Parenthetical information (abbreviation of the court that decided the case and the year the case was decided, if not contained in a public domain citation).
5. Subsequent history of the case, if any.

Some examples are presented first with a ^ symbol, indicating where spaces are placed, followed by the example without the ^ symbol.

For Example

United States Supreme Court:

Without parallel citation:

*Monsanto^Co.^v.^Geerton^Seed^Farms,^561^U.S.^139^* (2010). *Monsanto Co. v. Geerton Seed Farms*, 561 U.S. 139 (2010).

1. *Monsanto v. Geerton Seed Farms*—case name.
2. 561 U.S. 39—official reporter: volume 561 of the United States Reports beginning at page 39.
3. 2010—year of the decision.

With parallel citations:
*Monsanto^Co.^v.^Geerton^Seed^Farms,^561^U.S.^139,^130^S.Ct.^2743^*(2010). *Monsanto Co. v. Geerton Seed Farms*, 561 U.S. 139, 130 S.Ct. 2743 (2010).

1. *Monsanto v. Geerton Seed Farms*—case name.
2. 561 U.S. 39—official reporter: volume 561 of the United States Reports beginning at page 39.
3. 130 S.Ct. 2743—unofficial reporter/parallel citation: volume 30 of the Supreme Court Reporter beginning at page 2743.
4. 2010—year of the decision.

State Court Decisions:

*Spirlong^v.^Browne,^236^Ariz.^146,^336^P.3d^779^* (App.^Div.^1^2014).

Spirlong v. Browne, 236 Ariz. 146, 336 P.3d 779 (App. Div. 1 2014).

1. *Spirlong v. Browne*—case name.
2. 236 Ariz. 146—official reporter: volume 236 of the Arizona Reports beginning at page 146.
3. 336 P.3d 779—unofficial reporter/parallel citation: volume 336 of the Pacific Reporter, Third Series, beginning at page 779.

4. App. Div. 1 2014—the state the case is from is obvious from the abbreviation for the official reporter, so no state abbreviation is necessary in the parenthetical; App. Div. 1 indicates the decision was from the Court of Appeals, Division 1; the year the case was decided was 2014.

New Mexico^v.^Savedra,^2010-NMSC-025,^148^N.M.^301,^236^P.3d^20.
New Mexico v. Savedra, 2010-NMSC-025, 148 N.M. 301, 236 P.3d 20.

1. *New Mexico v. Savedra*—case name.

2. 2010-NMSC-025—public domain citation: 2010, year case decided; NMSC— the case was decided by the New Mexico Supreme Court; 25—the decision was the 25th decision of the year by the Supreme Court.

3. 148 N.M. 301—official reporter/parallel citation: volume 148 of the New Mexico Reports beginning at page 301.

4. 236 P.3d 20—unofficial reporter/parallel citation: volume 236 of the Pacific Reporter, Third Services, beginning at page 20.

5. Note: there is no year or court indicated by a parenthetical because the public domain citation indicates both.

A. Case Names

The particular rules for formatting case names in case law citations can be found at Bluepages B10.1.1 and Rule 10.2, with particular abbreviations at Table 6 (T6) of the *Bluebook*. In the *ALWD Guide* Rules 12.2, 12.4, and Appendix 3 contain the rules regarding case names. Some general considerations to keep in mind in formatting case names for case law citations are as follows:

1. Case names should be italicized or underlined, but never both.
2. Case names vary depending upon whether an individual, business, government, or property is the party. Carefully review the relevant rules in the appropriate citation manual to determine the proper case name for a citation.
3. Often case names can be abbreviated. There are subtle differences in the appropriate form of abbreviations used in the case name component of case law citations between the *Bluebook* and the *ALWD Guide*. As such, be sure to know which, if either, citation manual is the required manual for citation format for the state or courts you are working in. Do not abbreviate words not listed in the citation manuals' list of abbreviations for case names.

B. Public Domain/Vendor Neutral Citations

Many state appellate courts now assign a public domain citation (also known as a vendor-neutral citation) to published opinions. In addition, it is common for court opinions to be available on public domain websites, such as the court's website, even when the courts themselves do not assign public domain or vendor-neutral citations.

When there is a public domain citation assigned by the court itself, that citation should be included in the case citation. The *Bluebook* addresses both types of public domain citation in Rule 10.3.3. Look to Rules 12.17, and 31-33 as well as Appendix 2 of the *ALWD Guide* for public domain citation format.

For Example

Illinois now assigns public domain citations to all appellate court opinions, and these PDF versions of the opinions are the official citation. Beginning in 2011 Illinois discontinued its official state reporters for Court of Appeals and Supreme Court decisions.
O'Toole v. Chicago Zoological Society, 2015 IL 118254.
Smoke N Stuff v. City of Chicago, 2015 IL App (1st) 140936.

For Example

Decision from Maine Supreme Judicial Court (highest appellate court) with public domain citation created based upon availability of decision on public website and including parallel citation to regional reporter:
Beck v. Beck, 1999 ME 110, 733 A.2d 981.

C. Reporter(s)

Following the case name in a citation is the reference to the reporter(s) where the case is printed. The reference includes the volume number of the reporter and the page where the case begins. The volume number precedes the abbreviation for the reporter, which is followed by the page number where the case begins. Local court rules may dictate different requirements as to which reporter(s) are cited and in what order. Therefore, always check both local rules and the appropriate citation manual. The *ALWD Guide*, Appendix 1, contains state local rules related to citation.

1. Abbreviations

Do not assume you know the abbreviation for the various reporters. Consult Table T.1 of the *Bluebook* and Appendix 2 of the *ALWD Guide* for appropriate reporter abbreviations. Also be sure to pay attention to the spacing in abbreviations.

2. Pinpoint Cites

If you are referring to a specific page of a reporter, you will include that specific page in addition to the page where the case begins. Similarly, if the case has a public domain citation, you will include the specific paragraph where the content you are referencing can be located.

For Example

Banfield^v.^Cortes,^110^A.3d^155,^167^(2015).
Banfield v. Cortes, 110 A.3d 155, 167 (2015).
New^Mexico^v.^Savedra,^2010-NMSC-025,^¶^8,^148^N.M.^301,^304,^236^P.3d ^20,^23.
New Mexico v. Savedra, 2010-NMSC-025, ¶ 8, 148 N.M. 301, 304, 236 P.3d 20, 23.

3. Parallel Citations

United States Supreme Court opinions are located in several different reporters. Similarly, many state appellate court opinions are located in several reporters, such as a state reporter and a regional reporter. When a citation includes reference to more than one reporter, the official reporter is listed first, with unofficial reporters listed subsequently. Citations beyond the official citation, whether that is the public domain citation or a citation to the official reporter, are called **parallel citations**.

Rule 10.3.1 of the *Bluebook* and Rules 12 and 30 of the *ALWD Guide* discuss the proper order of parallel citations.

For Example

Nelson v. Rice, 198 Ariz. 563, 12 P.3d 238 (App. Div. 2 2000).
    The official reporter is the *Arizona Reports* (Ariz.) and the parallel citation is to the unofficial reporter, *Pacific Reporter* (P.3d).

D. Parenthetical Information

In parentheses following the reporter information may be the abbreviation for the court deciding the case, if necessary, and the year the case was decided.

1. Court Abbreviation

If the decision is by the United States Supreme Court, no court abbreviation is required. Only the date the case was decided appears in the parentheses. Similarly, if the decision is by the highest appellate court in a state and the state from which the case is from is apparent from the reporter or public domain citation, the court abbreviation does not have to be included in the parenthetical.

For Example

United States v. Matlock, 415 U.S. 164 (1974).
Kline v Angle, 216 Kan. 328, 532 P.2d 1093 (1975).

For other court decisions, include the appropriate abbreviation for the court deciding the case. The abbreviations for courts are in *Bluebook* Tables T.1, T.7, and T.10 and in *ALWD Guide*, Appendix 4.

For Example

United States v. Central R.R., 436 F. Supp. 739 (N.D. Ill. 1990).
Burnon v. State, 55 S.W.3d 752 (Tex. Crim. App. 2001).

2. Date

Generally only the year the case was decided is presented in the parenthetical. If a court abbreviation is included in the parenthetical, the date always follows the court abbreviation.

E. Other Considerations

Case law citation format is the most complex of all the primary authority citation formats. There are different formats for different jurisdictions, different levels of court, and different types of publications of cases (slip opinions, versus opinions in advance sheets, versus cases in reporters). Because more and more jurisdictions allow unpublished cases to be cited, this further expands the complexity of case law citations. It is not feasible to list all the rules and nuances of case law citation format here. It is extremely important that you carefully and thoroughly consult the appropriate citation manual and local rules, if any, to format a case law citation properly.

A few other components of case law citation format to be mindful of include:

- Cases not yet reported—slip opinions or opinions in a loose-leaf service or advance reports.
- Cases available only electronically—and the difference between availability in the public domain and commercial Internet research websites
- Unpublished (unreported) cases
- Additional parenthetical information that may be required, such as notations about concurring or dissenting opinions)

VIII. KEY POINTS CHECKLIST: Locating, Reading, and Briefing Court Opinion

- ✓ If the research question involves a statute, look to the statute and the statutory annotations first to locate case law. If the statutory annotations do not provide help, next look to a digest.

- ✓ Read opinions carefully and slowly. You cannot speed-read case law. Often you may have to take notes as you read a case.

✓   If you have a problem identifying the key facts, refer to Chapter 9.

✓   Watch for the court's statement of the issue. The court may state the issue in a broad or procedural context. If you have a problem identifying or stating the issue, refer to Chapters 10 and 11.

✓   If you have trouble understanding the majority opinion, often the concurring or dissenting opinion will summarize and clarify the arguments and reasoning adopted by the majority. Be aware that the dissenting opinion may mischaracterize the majority opinion in support of its own position.

✓   If you have trouble understanding the opinion, Shepardize or *KeyCite* the case to determine if there are any other cases, law review articles, *ALR* citations, or other secondary sources of information concerning the case. Consult a treatise that discusses the area of law involved in the opinion. Refer to the digest for other cases addressing the same area of law.

✓   Do not be discouraged if you have trouble reading and understanding opinions. It takes time and experience. The more you read opinions, the easier it becomes. Your skill improves only through doing. Therefore, read as many cases as possible.

✓   Read opinions with a critical eye. Court opinions are just that—opinions. On occasion, courts are wrong. Do not read with unquestioning faith. Read critically. Question! Ask yourself, "Does the reasoning support the conclusion?"

IX. APPLICATION

This section first discusses Amelia's assignment to locate a case that could be used to advise the client on whether his son, injured during a shooting after leaving his friend's car, could recover from the friend's uninsured motorist insurance coverage. This is followed by a brief of the case (*Miera v. State Farm Mutual Automobile Ins Co.*). The text and brief of *Sterling Computer Systems of Texas, Inc. v. Texas Pipe Bending Company* follow the brief of *Miera v. State Farm Mutual Automobile Ins Co.* The brief of the *Sterling* case is included to provide another example of a case brief.

A. Locating *Miera v. State Farm Mutual Automobile Ins Co.*

Amelia begins her search for an appropriate case by looking for a statute that states who may recover from uninsured motorist coverage. If there is a statute, Amelia looks to the statutory annotations to see if there is a case on point, that is, a case in which the court addressed the question of whether a passenger who is injured after leaving a driver's vehicle can recover from a driver's uninsured motorist coverage.

If there is no statute or a case on point in the annotations, then Amelia looks to the regional or state reporter digest under the term *insurance*. Assume that Amelia resides in New Mexico. She refers to the index of either the *New Mexico Reports* or the *Pacific Digest* to locate the volume number for insurance. By scanning the topic key numbers she locates Key 217—Insurance. In scanning the subtopics under Key 217 she locates subtopic Coverage—Automobile Insurance. She finds two key numbers that may apply: Key 2668 "Occupancy of Vehicle" and Key 2670 "Uninsured or underinsured motorist coverage." She looks under "Occupancy of Vehicle" first. Looking at the case summaries under Key 2668, Amelia finds *Miera v. State Farm Mutual Automobile Ins Co.*, 2004-NMCA-059, 135 N.M. 574, 92 P.2d 20., a case which is on point (see Exhibit 4-1). She continues her search to locate any other cases that may be on point. She checks to determine if the *Miera* case has been overruled or otherwise modified by subsequent court decisions.

If there is no case under Key 2668, Amelia could then check for cases under Key 2670, and if that did not allow her to locate a case, the digest will refer to a legal encyclopedia cite that addresses the topic and provides reference to cases. At this point, Amelia could also look for an *ALR* annotation that discusses the question.

Amelia could also perform this search electronically using Westlaw or LexisNexis. Had she done so she could have chosen the database for New Mexico Statutes and searched for a statute involving the issue. Had she located a statute online in a commercial database, such as a Westlaw or LexisNexis, she may have been able to hyperlink to any cases listed in the annotation to the statutes.

If Amelia would not have located a statute, she would have switched databases to New Mexico state court opinions. From that database she could have selected the Key Numbers database and searched its topics just as she would have in the print digests. The steps described above for narrowing in on specific key numbers and reviewing the case summaries is identical in the online use of the digest as it is in the print digest. The main difference is that in print digests, Amelia would need to remember to check for pocket parts to ensure she has reviewed all the most recent case and, in a commercial electronic database, new cases are quickly added so that the researcher does not have to look elsewhere to ensure the most recent case summaries have been reviewed.

B. Brief of *Miera v. State Farm Mutual Automobile Ins Co.*

The sample brief is presented first, followed by comments on the brief.

Citation:	***Miera v. State Farm Mutual Auto. Ins. Co.***, 2005-NMCA-059, 135 N.M. 574, 92 P.3d 20.
Parties:	Robert J. Miera, Sr. on behalf of Robert J. Miera, Jr., Plaintiff-Appellant State Farm Mutual Automobile Insurance Company and Safeco National Insurance Company, Defendants-Appellees
Facts:	Miera Jr. was one of four passengers in Tara Hardern's vehicle. As Hardern's vehicle was stopped at a stop sign, a Mustang with its driver and a passenger, approached the intersection opposite of Hardern's vehicle. The Mustang did a U-turn and came behind Hardern's vehicle. Some altercation ensued and Miera Jr. and one other occupant of Hardern's vehicle got out and approached the Mustang. The altercation escalated and the passenger of the Mustang shot Miera Jr. causing his death. Hardern was insured by State Farm and had uninsured motorist coverage. The driver of the Mustang had no insurance. Miera Jr. lived at home and was covered by his father's Safeco uninsured motorist policy. Relevant to this case brief, Miera Sr., as representative for his son's estate, sought to collect damages from Hardern's State Farm uninsured motorist policy. State Farm sought and was granted summary judgment on the basis that Miera Jr. was not occupying Hardern's vehicle when he was shot.
Prior Proceeding:	Robert J. Miera Sr., on behalf of his deceased son, sought to recover damages from Hardern's uninsured motorist coverage. The trial court granted summary judgment to State Farm on the basis that Miera Jr. was not occupying Hardern's vehicle when he was shot. Miera Sr. appealed and the Court of Appeals affirmed.
Issue:	Was Miera Jr. occupying Hardern's vehicle for purposes of being covered by her State Farm uninsured motorist insurance?
Holding:	No. An individual is occupying a vehicle when they are "in, on, entering or alighting from" a vehicle. Although Miera Jr. was in close proximity to Hardern's vehicle, he had severed the necessary connection and was no longer occupying the vehicle at the time he was shot.

Reasoning:	Under the terms of the State Farm policy, uninsured motorist coverage only applies to persons occupying an insured vehicle. The policy specifically defined "occupying" as "in, on, entering or alighting from" a vehicle. The appellate court looked to several prior court opinions where courts applied several factors to determine if a person was "occupying" a vehicle. Specifically the Court of Appeals considered "whether (1) there is a causal relationship between the injury and the vehicle; (s) there is a geographical proximity between the person and the vehicle; (3) the person was oriented to the vehicle; and (4) the person was engaging 'in a transition essential to the use of the vehicle at the time.'" The court found that Miera Jr. was in close proximity to the vehicle and likely would have returned to the vehicle, but he severed the causal connection when he demanded to be let out of Hardern's vehicle to pursue a confrontation with those in the Mustang and that confrontation occurred away from Hardern's vehicle. The trial court, therefore, properly granted summary judgment.

C. Comments on the Case Brief

Note that the brief includes the essential information of the case:

1. The name of the case and where it can be found
2. The names of the parties and their status before the court
3. The facts that gave rise to the dispute
4. What the trial court did and the disposition by the appellate court
5. The issue, or legal question
6. The holding
7. The law governing the issue and the application of that law to the facts of the dispute

No comments were included in this brief. You may include a comments section, although such a section is a matter of your preference and, more importantly, the preference of the lawyer(s) you are working for.

D. Brief of *Sterling Computer Systems of Texas, Inc. v. Texas Pipe Bending Company*

A second example of the application of the principles presented in this chapter is illustrated with the brief of the *Sterling Computer Systems* case. The case is presented in the following text. Comments concerning the case brief follow the brief.

CASE

STERLING COMPUTER SYSTEMS OF TEXAS, INC.,

Appellant,

v. TEXAS PIPE BENDING COMPANY, Appellee.,

No. 965.

OPINION

Court of Civil Appeals of Texas.

Houston (14th Dist.).

March 20, 1974.

Rehearing Denied April 10, 1974.

507 S.W.2d 282 (Tex. Ct. App. 1974) 1974.

Action for breach of contract for data-processing service. The District Court, Harris County, Paul Pressler, J., granted summary judgment for defendant, and plaintiff appealed. The Court of Civil Appeals, Tunks, C. J., held that contract, which contained an express provision that plaintiff would not be liable for an outright refusal to perform data-processing services for defendant, and which contained no requirements that plaintiff make a reasonable effort to perform, failed for want of mutuality and was unenforceable.

Affirmed.

Contracts 10(2)

Contract, which contained an express provision that plaintiff would not be liable for an outright refusal to perform data-processing services for defendant, and which contained no requirement that plaintiff make a reasonable effort to perform, failed for want of mutuality and was unenforceable.

Alvin L. Zimmerman, Houston, for appellant.

Robert H. Singleton, Percy D. Williams, Houston, for appellee.

TUNKS, Chief Justice.

The issue in this case is the propriety of a summary judgment for the defendant in a breach of contract suit, which was granted on the theory that the contract lacked mutuality.

The appellant, Sterling Computer Systems of Texas, Inc., brought suit for breach of contract against the appellee, Texas Pipe Bending Company. In essence, the contract in question provided that Texas Pipe Bending was to provide Sterling with digitized cards and computer programs each month, with which Sterling was to perform data processing services for Texas Pipe Bending. Certain prices were quoted in the agreement, which were "based on a minimum of 20,000 digitized cards per month." The term of the agreement was to have been for one year, but after providing cards and paying in full for eight months, Texas Pipe Bending refused to further provide Sterling with digitized cards. The trial court granted Texas Pipe Bending's motion for summary judgment. Although the judgment does not so recite, it was apparently based on the argument proposed by Texas Pipe Bending that the contract was unenforceable because of the lack of mutuality. Sterling has appealed.

The relevant portion of the contract is found in a clause denominated as "LIMITATION OF LIABILITY." This clause provides in part as follows:

> SCS [Sterling] shall not be liable for its failure to profide [sic] the services herein and shall not be liable for any losses resulting to the client [Texas Pipe Bending] or anyone else by reason of such failure.

The general rule as stated in *Texas Farm Bureau Cotton Ass'n v. Stovall*, 113 Tex. 273, 253 S.W. 1101, 1105 (1923), is:

> [A] contract must be based upon a valid consideration, and . . . a contract in which there is no consideration moving from one party, or no obligation upon him, lacks mutuality, is unilateral, and unenforceable.

Under the express terms of the contract in question Sterling would not be liable for an outright refusal to perform the data processing services. This fact renders its obligation a nullity.

Sterling cites various cases which purportedly support its position that the trial court erred in granting summary judgment for Texas Pipe Bending. The gist of these cases is that although a contract may not expressly obligate a party to perform, such an obligation may be implied by its terms. In *Texas Gas Utilities Company v. Barrett*, 460 S.W.2d 409 (Tex. Sup. 1970), the Texas Supreme Court held, under a similar contention, that there was a mutuality of obligation. In that case the contract provided that the Gas Company would not be liable for failure to deliver when such failure was "caused by conditions beyond its reasonable control," and then enumerated certain situations which exemplified the above phrase (over none of which would the Gas Company have control). The Court noted, "It [Gas Company] was bound, however, to supply available natural gas to respondents . . ." *Texas Gas Utilities Company v. Barrett*, supra 460 S.W.2d at 413. In the present case there existed no requirement that Sterling make a reasonable effort to perform. The exculpatory clause allowed Sterling to refuse to perform with impunity.

Clement v. Producers' Refining Co., 277 S.W. 634 (Tex. Comm'n App. 1925, jdgmt adopted), was another case in which mutuality was found. That case involved a contract for an agent's commission. By the terms of the agreement the principal was to pay the agent a commission on goods which "may be supplied" by the principal. Notwithstanding this provision the Commission of Appeals held that the contract impliedly obligated the principal to supply goods to the agent. However, the Court stated:

> [A]s there is no language used which would clearly indicate that the company was not obligated to furnish goods and products, the courts are not warranted in holding that no such obligation was imposed . . . by its terms. *Clement v. Producers' Refining Co.*, supra at 635.

The case at bar is distinguishable because the contract contained an express provision that Sterling would not be liable if it did not perform. Various other cases cited by appellant are similarly distinguishable because in those cases contracts were involved which did not expressly provide that one of the contracting parties could fail to perform without incurring liability.

As a matter of law the contract in question fails for want of mutuality. The trial court correctly granted summary judgment for the defendant, Texas Pipe Bending Company.

Affirmed.

CITATION:

Sterling Computer Systems of Texas, Inc. v. Texas Pipe Bending Company, 507 S.W.2d 282 (Tex. Ct. App. 1974).

(Continued)

PARTIES:

Sterling Computer Systems of Texas, Inc., Plaintiff-Appellant Texas Pipe Bending Company, Defendant-Appellee

FACTS:

Sterling Computer Systems (Sterling) entered into a contract with Texas Pipe Bending (Texas Pipe) under which Texas Pipe was to provide Sterling with digitized cards and computer programs each month with which Sterling was to perform data-processing services for Texas Pipe. After complying for eight months, Texas Pipe refused to provide Sterling with the cards. The contract contained the following provision, "SCS [Sterling] shall not be liable for its failure to profide [sic] the services herein and shall not be liable for any losses resulting to the client [Texas Pipe] or anyone else by reason of such failure."

PRIOR PROCEEDINGS:

Sterling sued Texas Pipe for breach of contract. Texas Pipe moved for summary judgment, arguing that the contract was unenforceable because it lacked mutuality. The trial court granted the motion. Sterling appealed.

ISSUE:

Under Texas contract law, does a contract lack consideration and is, therefore, unenforceable if it contains a limitation of liability clause that provides that a party "shall not be liable for its failure to provide the services herein and shall not be liable for any losses resulting . . . by reason of such failure"?

HOLDING:

Yes. Under Texas contract law, a contract lacks consideration and is unenforceable if it contains a limitation of liability clause that provides that a party "shall not be liable for its failure to provide the services herein and shall not be liable for any losses resulting . . . by reason of such failure."

REASONING:

The rule of law presented in *Texas Farm Bureau Cotton Association v. Stovall*, 113 Tex. 273, 253 S.W. 1101 (1923), is that where there is no obligation upon a party to a contract, the contract lacks mutuality, is unilateral, and is unenforceable. Under the limitation clause, Sterling is not liable for its refusal to perform. Therefore, as a matter of law, the contract fails for want of mutuality.

DISPOSITION:

The trial court's granting of the motion for summary judgment was affirmed.

COMMENTS:

The court did not address any potential avenues of relief that may be available to Sterling in equity, such as equitable restitution or reliance. Such avenues may be available in our case and should be explored. Also, does Sterling have a claim against the drafters of the contract for legal malpractice?

E. Comments on the Case Brief—Procedural versus Substantive Issues

Note that the court identifies the issue as: "The issue in this case is the propriety of a summary judgment for the defendant in a breach of contract suit. . . ." The actual issue in the case, however, is whether a contract is enforceable when it contains a clause that allows a party to escape liability when it fails to perform. Often a court will state the issue in the procedural context of how the matter came before the court.

For Example

"The issue in this case is whether the motion for summary judgment was properly granted by the trial court." This is how the matter came before the court procedurally: An appeal was taken from the trial court's ruling on the motion for summary judgment. The real issue involves a question of whether, in light of the facts and the applicable law, there was a sufficient basis for the court to rule as it did.

In answering the procedural question, the court actually addresses the substantive question raised by the facts of the case. *The substantive question is what the case is actually about.* In this case, summary judgment was granted because, as a matter of law, the contract failed for want of mutuality (lack of consideration) due to the limitation of liability clause. Therefore, Sterling could not enforce the contract because it was not valid. The substantive issue addressed by the court was whether the clause rendered the contract unenforceable due to the lack of consideration. *Always look for the substantive issue when the court states the issue in a procedural context.*

Summary

A court opinion, often referred to as a case, is the court's resolution of a legal dispute and the reasons in support of its resolution. When resolving disputes, courts often interpret constitutional or statutory provisions or create law when there is no governing law. The body of law that emerges from court opinions is called the common or case law. It constitutes the largest body of law in the United States, far larger than constitutional, legislative, or other sources of law.

Because you must read court opinions to learn the case law, it is necessary to become familiar with and proficient at reading and analyzing case law. There are several additional reasons, however, for reading opinions. A court opinion:

1. Helps you understand and interpret constitutional provisions and statutory law
2. Helps you understand the litigation process
3. Provides insight into the structure of legal analysis and legal argument
4. Provides a guide to proper legal writing

Most court opinions consist of the facts of the case, the procedural history of the case (what happened in the lower court), the legal questions (issues) addressed by the court, the decision or holding of the court, the reasons for the decision reached, and the disposition (the relief granted).

Federal and state court opinions are published in books called reports and reporters and are available through Westlaw and LexisNexis. In addition, court opinions are often available through official court websites and other Internet resources. If the question involves a statute, the search for case law should begin with a review of the annotations following the statute. If the question does not involve a statutory law, the search usually begins with a digest. Internet research is discussed in Chapters 7 and 8.

A case brief is a written summary of a court opinion that presents, in an organized format, all the essential information of the opinion. A researcher may be assigned the task of briefing a case. A case brief is valuable because it:

1. Saves an attorney the time required to read the case
2. Serves as a valuable learning tool
3. Is a reference tool
4. Is a writing tool

The first and possibly most important step in briefing a case is to read it carefully and slowly. Reading case law is often a difficult process, especially for the beginner. It becomes easier as more opinions are read.

Chapter 9 through Chapter 11 provide guidelines that are helpful in identifying many of the elements of a case brief.

The importance of case law cannot be overemphasized. The difficulties you encounter in reading and briefing court opinions can be lessened through the use of the guidelines presented in this chapter.

Quick References

Advance sheets	113	Citation	103
Body of the opinion	109	Common law	100
Caption	103	Court opinion	100
Case brief	121	Disposition	125
Case law	100	Headnotes	108

Internet Resources

http://www.lawschool.cornell.edu
The Legal Information Institute (LII) housed at Cornell Law School, provides free, open access to opinions of the United States Supreme Court.

http://www.oyez.org
You may hear the oral arguments or read the court briefs of United States Supreme Court cases at this site. The oral arguments are available for cases from 1960 to present.

http://www.supremecourt.gov
This official page of the United States Supreme Court features court opinions, orders, rules, calendars and schedules, news releases, and general information.

http://www.uscourts.gov
This site is the home page for all federal courts.

http://www.findlaw.com
Through FindLaw, you can locate court cases in general.

http://www.justice.gov/olc
The Office of Legal Counsel is in charge of publishing select opinions of the United States Attorney General.

http://www.naag.org
This website will link to all state Attorney General's websites. Most state Attorney General's Offices maintain a link on their websites that allows a search of attorney general opinions.

Exercises

ASSIGNMENT 1

Access the case located at 1 N.E.3d 641.

a. Give the name of the case.

b. List all parallel citations.

c. What court decided the case and in what year?

d. Who were the attorneys for the defendants?

ASSIGNMENT 2

Review volume 336 P.3d.

a. Locate the case at 336 P.3d 779.

b. What is the name of the case?

c. Which headnote indicates that the case holds that, contrary to the common law, a statutory dog bite claim does not require proof the owner knew or should have known the dog had dangerous propensities abnormal to its class?

d. What paragraph in the opinion does discussion of the topic in c. above begin?

ASSIGNMENT 3

Consult West's *General Digest*, Tenth Series.

a. Give the name and citation of a 2001 Minnesota case which lists the elements of battery.

b. Referring to the Minnesota case, does battery require the intent to injure?

c. Cite a Kentucky case providing that fourth-degree assault can be proved only if the result of the assault is physical injury, not death.

d. You are researching a question concerning the admissibility of evidence in an arson case. To what key number would you refer?

e. You are looking for the case *Adams v. Noble*. What is the *Federal Supplement* citation? What United States District Court rendered the decision? Under what key numbers may the case be found?

ASSIGNMENT 4

Refer to the regional digest for your state (see Exhibit 4-3) or to your state court digest. Give the name and citation of a decision from your state that discusses who is a passenger for purposes of recovering from under- or uninsured motorist insurance coverage. Refer to the case.

a. What is the definition of passenger?

b. In the alternative, if there is not a definition listed in the case, what are the factors the court will consider in determining if someone is a passenger?

c. If there is no decision from your state, what legal encyclopedia reference is listed?

d. The New Mexico case in Exhibit 4-1 addresses the same issue. How might it be used to locate a case in your state?

ASSIGNMENT 5

The client has been charged with shooting at vehicles on an interstate and the penalty is sought to be enhanced as an act of domestic terrorism pursuant to 18 U.S.C.A. § 2331. Refer to the *United States Code Annotated*, locate 18 U.S.C.A. § 2331 and answer the following questions:

a. Give the *ALR* cite that addresses what constitutes entrapment to commit federal crimes of terrorism.

b. Give the name and citation of the 2015 U.S. Court of Appeals, Second Circuit, decision that held a defendant's act of placing elemental mercury in four hospitals was an act of "domestic terrorism."

ASSIGNMENT 6

Look to your state statute concerning aggravated or armed robbery and the annotations that follow the statute.

a. Give the legal encyclopedia reference(s) that refers to aggravated or armed robbery.

b. Give the *ALR* cite (if any) that addresses the question of how the use of an unloaded gun affects criminal responsibility.

c. Give the name and citation of any case that answers the question of whether a toy or fake gun is a "dangerous weapon."

ASSIGNMENT 7

The client was stopped for failing to maintain lane. The officer learned the client had a warrant and arrested the client. The client's car was searched, a gun was found, and the officer learned the client was a felon. The client was charged with possession of a firearm by a felon. You are asked to search for a published case (opinion) in your state that addresses whether the officer's search of the passenger compartment of the client's car exceeds the permissible scope of such searches. Your attorney refers you to an annotated, unpublished case, *United States v. Guerrero-Heredia*, an unpublished case from the United States District Court of Arizona. How can you use this unpublished case to locate a published case that addresses the right of officers to search the client's car incident to the arrest.

ASSIGNMENT 8

Using Westlaw or LexisNexis (whichever your school provides you access to), locate the *Guerrero-Heredia* decision in Assignment 7.

a. Are there any court opinions of any jurisdiction, state or federal, that cite the decision?

b. What types of secondary sources cite the opinion?

c. What is the *ALR* annotation that could lead you to court opinions that assess the applicability of *Arizona v. Gant*, which limited the right of police to search vehicles incident to arrest.

ASSIGNMENT 9

Access the case located at 798 F.3d 1030.

a. Give the name of the case.

b. What was the disposition of the case?

c. What is the name of the circuit judges that heard the case?

d. What is the name of the judge that authored the opinion?

ASSIGNMENT 10

Access the case located at 536 F. Supp. 2d 883.

a. Where else can the case be found (other citation to decision)?

b. What areas of law does the case involve?

c. What court decided the case and in what year?

ASSIGNMENT 11

Access the U.S. Supreme Court website and locate the Opinions link. Under the Opinions link, go to the link for Sliplists.

a. What information is provided in each Sliplist?

b. What happens to each Sliplist as new bound volumes are produced?

ASSIGNMENT 12

Access the U.S. Supreme Court website and locate the Opinions link, specifically the 2014 Term Opinions of the Court. Specifically locate the case with the docket number 13-1314. In what volume of the *United States Reports* will the opinion be published?

ASSIGNMENT 13

Access the Illinois Supreme Court website and locate the link to Recent Supreme Court Opinions.

a. How many not yet published opinions (NRel) are listed there for the current year?

b. What does the NRel abbreviation mean?

ASSIGNMENT 14

Access your local Supreme Court website. Locate the link for the court's opinions.

a. How are the opinions organized?

b. Are both published and unpublished opinions available?

c. Does the Court's website have any information about citing unpublished opinions? If so, what is your state's rule regarding the citing of unpublished opinions?

ASSIGNMENT 15

Access the Tenth Circuit Court of Appeals website. Locate the link to Opinions. What ways does this website provide for researchers to search for cases?

ASSIGNMENT 16

Brief a case of your instructor's choosing using the format provided in this chapter.

Chapter 5

Secondary Authority and Other Research Sources— Encyclopedias, Treatises, American Law Reports, Digests, Shepard's

Outline

Learning Objectives

After completing this chapter, you should understand:

- The role of secondary authority in general
- The role of encyclopedias, treatises, annotated law reports, digests, and citators in research
- How to locate and conduct research using encyclopedias, treatises, annotated law reports, digests, *Shepard's*, and *KeyCite*

In mid-May, Dan graduated from law school. One night in June, he took a break from the long hours of studying for the bar exam and went to a party with Sam, his best friend from law school. Dan did not drink, but Sam got rather intoxicated. Dan convinced Sam to leave the party, and on the way to drop Sam off, Dan was pulled over by the local college town police.

At first, Dan was not concerned, because he had not been drinking. However, Sam would not be quiet and was rude to the officer. The officer asked Dan to get out of the car and perform field sobriety tests. He did, reasserting to the officer that he had not been drinking and that he was just trying to get his overly intoxicated friend home. The officer told Dan he was going to be arrested and charged with DUI. At that point, Sam had passed out in the car. Dan tried pleading with the officer to believe him and asked the officer to let him call someone to get Sam home safely. The officer replied, "That's his problem, he will have to walk." Frustrated, Dan retorted, "No wonder people think so little of the police." The officer shoved Dan face first into the side of the police car, breaking two of Dan's teeth.

Eventually, the charges against Dan were dismissed by a judge because the lawyer he hired was able to demonstrate doubt as to whether Dan was intoxicated. The dismissal was a relief because the charge was causing Dan to have problems getting past the character and fitness background investigation required to become a lawyer. Dan knew from an externship he had while in law school, that officers could be held civilly liable for using too much force during an arrest.

Since he was so close to becoming an attorney, Dan decided to do the research himself before finding a lawyer to handle his civil case. He knew just enough from his experience as an extern that he should start with reviewing the tort of battery. The research sources Dan would consult to learn about the tort of battery will be discussed in the Application section.

I. INTRODUCTION

Chapters 3 and 4 cover primary authority, the law itself: constitutions, enacted law (statutes), and case law. Courts refer to and rely upon primary authority first when resolving legal problems. In many instances, a court may be bound to follow the primary authority.

For Example

Courts are bound to follow the provisions of the United States Constitution, and lower courts are bound to follow the decisions of the higher courts in the jurisdiction.

Therefore, locating the primary authority that may apply to a problem is *always* the first step of legal research. This chapter and Chapter 6 address **secondary authority** and other sources a court may rely on that are not the law, that is, not primary authority. Secondary authority consists of sources that summarize, compile, explain, comment on, interpret, or in some other way address the law. As mentioned in Chapter 1, secondary authority is used for several purposes:

- To obtain a background or overall understanding of a specific area of the law. If you are unfamiliar with an area of law, legal encyclopedias, treatises, and periodicals are useful for these purposes.

For Example

If the researcher is unfamiliar with a specific area of law, such as defamation, a treatise on tort law or a legal encyclopedia will provide an overview of the area. If the researcher seeks an organized summary of the case law on the topic, the *Restatement (Second) of Torts* would be consulted.

- To locate primary authority (the law) on a question being researched. Secondary authority usually guides the researcher by providing references to statutory and case law. ***American Law Reports (ALR)*** and digests are particularly useful for this purpose. This chapter discusses these sources, *Shepard's Citations*, and Westlaw's *KeyCite*. Cases may also be located through reference to legal encyclopedias, treatises, periodicals, *Restatements of the Law*, and uniform laws.
- To be relied upon by the court when reaching a decision. This usually occurs only when there is no primary authority governing a legal question, or it is unclear how the primary authority applies. Treatises, law reviews, and *Restatements of the Law* are some secondary sources relied on by courts.

There are literally hundreds of secondary sources. This chapter covers the more frequently used secondary sources. It addresses sources that provide the researcher with either an overview or a detailed treatment of specific areas of law: legal encyclopedias, treatises, and *American Law Reports*. The chapter also discusses other research sources that are of great assistance in locating case law: digests, *Shepard's*, and *KeyCite*. Exhibit 5-1 shows the primary use of the secondary and other research sources discussed in this chapter.

Note: As discussed in Chapter 1, secondary authority is not the law. It is persuasive authority, not binding on the courts, but courts may rely on and follow it. Therefore, secondary authority is usually consulted after primary authority. Most legal research focuses on primary authority, with little reference to secondary authority. If there is primary authority that answers a question being researched, such as statutory or case law, then secondary authority is not necessary. If the secondary authority describes and refers to primary authority on a subject, locate and refer to the primary authority when analyzing the law.

AUTHORITY	PRIMARY USE AS A RESEARCH TOOL
Legal Encyclopedias	Use to obtain an overview of a specific area of the law and to locate case law in that area.
Treatises	Use when you are seeking more than the general summary of the law available in a legal encyclopedia. Treatises provide in-depth discussion of legal topics and explain, analyze, and criticize the law.
American Law Reports	Use to obtain a comprehensive analysis of individual legal issues. *ALR* provides a greater in-depth discussion of specific legal issues than available in a treatise. Legal issues are analyzed through synthesis and discussion of cases from every jurisdiction.
Digests	Use to locate case law that addresses specific point(s) of law. Digests are helpful in two situations: ■ You know the name of a case that addresses the point of law being researched and are looking for other cases that address the same point. ■ You do not know of any cases that address the point of law being researched.
Shepard's Citators and Westlaw's KeyCite	Use to determine whether a case or other authority is good law. Both indicate whether a case has been reversed, modified, or overruled. They also refer to any case law or secondary sources that have discussed the primary authority being researched.

© Cengage

Exhibit 5-1 Secondary Authority—Primary Use as a Research Tool.

II. LEGAL ENCYCLOPEDIAS

Legal encyclopedias are designed to provide an overview of all the areas of law. They do not provide the in-depth coverage that is available in a treatise or periodical article.

For Example

In the hypothetical presented at the beginning of the chapter, reference to assault and battery in an encyclopedia would be a good starting point for Dan to begin his research because it would provide him with an overview of the law.

Legal encyclopedias provide a summary of the law; they do not criticize or analyze the law, nor do they provide in-depth coverage. They summarize the law primarily through a summary of case holdings. For that reason, they are valuable for locating cases on a subject. However, due to the large number of cases on any subject, one-half or less of a page of the encyclopedia may be text, with the remainder of the page listing citations in support of the narrative. The problem becomes one of too many cases. Also, in legal encyclopedias, there is less emphasis on statutes and statutory law than on case law. Because of their broad treatment of topics, legal encyclopedias are not frequently cited in court opinions or documents filed in court.

Legal encyclopedias are similar to other encyclopedias in that the subject matter is arranged alphabetically, there is a table of contents for each topic, and a detailed general index.

The two types of legal encyclopedias most often referenced are national and state encyclopedias. However, there are also foreign encyclopedias.

A. National Encyclopedias

The two national encyclopedias are *American Jurisprudence Second*, commonly known as *Am. Jur. 2d*, and *Corpus Juris Secundum*, referred to as *CJS*. Both of these encyclopedias are national in scope; that is, they present a general overview of federal and state law. Both *American Jurisprudence Second* and *Corpus Juris Secundum* are preceded by earlier sets: *American Jurisprudence* and *Corpus Juris*. Many law libraries do not retain the earlier sets due to space constraints. In addition, it is increasingly common for law libraries to carry only one of the two national encyclopedias in print format. *American Jurisprudence Second* and *Corpus Juris Secundum* are available on Westlaw, as West is the publisher of both. *American Jurisprudence Second* is also available on LexisNexis.

Each encyclopedia covers more than 400 legal topics. Inasmuch as they are similar in most respects and share many features, a researcher generally will use one set or the other, not both.

1. Features

The similar and dissimilar features of *American Jurisprudence Second* and *Corpus Juris Secundum* are discussed here.

a. Similarities

Both sets share the following:

- **Topic presentation.** Topics are arranged alphabetically, with each topic beginning with a table of contents (see Exhibit 5-2). The presentation of topics is in the form of a narrative summary, with the narrative and citations presented on each page (see Exhibit 5-3 and Exhibit 5-4). When searching the encyclopedias on Westlaw, the Table of Contents for each topic can be linked from any given section for that topic, thus allowing quick movement within each topic without having to restart from the list of topics.
- **General index.** A comprehensive general index accompanies each set, and each volume has indexes for the topics covered in that volume. The General Index is also available electronically when using Westlaw and LexisNexis.
- **Topic summary.** At the beginning of each topic is a summary of what is covered, what topics are treated elsewhere, and West's key number references. This allows you to use the West digests to locate other cases on the same topic (see Exhibit 5-2). Both sets will refer you to other research sources.
- **Updates.** Pocket parts are used to update each volume in print and replacement volumes are provided as necessary. Westlaw and LexisNexis update topics as new content is available. Each entry specifically indicates when it was last updated by month and year, letting the researcher know how current the content is.
- **Tables.** Each set has a table of statutes, rules, and regulations that lists the title and section where specific statutes, rules, and regulations are cited in the encyclopedia set (see Exhibit 5-5). Neither set has a table of cases.

b. Dissimilarities

The sets are different in the following ways:

- **Size.** *Corpus Juris Secundum* is larger than *American Jurisprudence Second*. This does not mean that *CJS* provides a more comprehensive coverage of topics than *Am. Jur. 2d*. Rather, *CJS* attempts to include every case reported in its discussion of topics, resulting in many pages having one or two sentences of narrative, with the rest of the page consisting of footnotes to cases, which largely accounts for the additional number of volumes.

  Am. Jur. 2d is more selective in its inclusion of cases, presenting a cross-section of leading cases, and includes citations in its footnotes and other research references (see Exhibit 5-4).
- **Emphasis.** *Am. Jur. 2d* emphasizes statutory law somewhat more than *CJS*. Neither set, however, focuses on statutory analysis.

ASSAULT

by Sonja Larsen, J.D. and Thomas Muskus, J.D.

Scope

This title discusses assault and battery, including acts of violence towards the person of another, either with or without any actual touching or striking, which do not constitute an element in or an attempt to commit any other specific injury or offense. Defenses, justification, and excuse for such acts are covered, as well as circumstances of aggravation. Liabilities and remedies therefor, both civil and criminal, are likewise treated.

Treated Elsewhere

Reasonable force in effecting an arrest, see C.J.S., Arrest § 49

Actions for causing death, see C.J.S., Death §§ 17 to 227

Convictions of assault in prosecutions for other offenses, see C.J.S., Indictments and Informations §§ 229, 231 to 235

Assaults by operation of motor vehicles, see C.J.S., Motor Vehicles §§ 1338 to 1353

Municipality's liability for assaults or batteries committed by police officers, see C.J.S., Municipal Corporations § 689

Assaults committed in obstructing process or resisting an officer, see C.J.S., Obstructing Justice or Governmental Administration §§ 21 to 24

Commission of an assault with intent to, or in an attempt to, perpetrate other offenses, see C.J.S., Homicide §§ 98 to 100; C.J.S., Rape §§ 37 to 43; and C.J.S., Robbery §§ 78 to 89

KeyCite®: Cases and other legal materials listed in KeyCite Scope can be researched through West's KeyCite service on Westlaw®. Use KeyCite to check citations for form, parallel references, prior and later history, and comprehensive citator information, including citations to other decisions and secondary materials.

I.   **IN GENERAL (§§ 1 TO 3)**

II. **CIVIL LIABILITY (§§ 4 TO 72)**
    A.   ELEMENTS OF CAUSE OF ACTION AND LIABILITY IN GENERAL (§§ 4 TO 17)
        1.   Assault (§§ 4 to 7)
        2.   Battery (§§ 8 to 17)
    B.   DEFENSES (§§ 18 TO 37)
    C.   ACTIONS (§§ 38 TO 72)
        1.   In General; Pleadings (§§ 38 to 43)
        2.   Proof and Presumptions (§§ 44 to 49)
        3.   Admissibility of Evidence (§§ 50 to 57)
        4.   Weight and Sufficiency of Evidence (§§ 58 to 59)
        5.   Trial (§§ 60 to 64)

Exhibits 5-2   C.J.S. Table of Contents for Assault. Reprinted from West Group, Corpus Juris Secundum, Vol. 6A (2001), pp. 197–198. Reprinted with permission of Thomson Reuters.

6.   Judgment; Costs; Damages (§§ 65 to 72)

III.   **CRIMINAL RESPONSIBILITY (§§ 73 TO 163)**
    A.   OFFENSES AND RESPONSIBILITY THEREFOR (§§ 73 TO 119)
        1.   In General (§§ 73 to 77)
        2.   Elements of Assault (§§ 78 to 83)
        3.   Elements of Battery (§§ 84 to 85)
        4.   Aggravated and Other Heinous Assaults in General (§§ 86 to 98)
           a.   General Considerations (§§ 86 to 88)
           b.   Types of Aggravated Assault (§§ 89 to 98)
              (1)   Cutting, Stabbing, or Wounding (§§ 89 to 90)
              (2)   Use of Dangerous or Deadly Weapon (§§ 91 to 94)
              (3)   Inflicting, or with Means or Intent to Inflict, Great Bodily Harm (§§ 95 to 96)
              (4)   Shooting; Assault on Officer (§§ 97 to 98)
        5.   Defenses and Persons Liable (§§ 99 to 119)
           a.   General Considerations (§§ 99 to 101)
           b.   Consent (§§ 102 to 103)
           c.   Provocation (§§ 104 to 105)
           d.   Self-Defense (§§ 106 to 112)
           e.   Defense of Third Parties or Property (§§ 113 to 116)
           f.   Performance or Exercise of Duty or Authority (§§ 117 to 119)
    B.   PROSECUTION AND PUNISHMENT (§§ 120 TO 163)
        1.   Indictment or Information (§§ 120 to 134)
           a.   General Considerations (§§ 120 to 127)
           b.   Substance of Offense (§§ 128 to 134)
        2.   Evidence (§§ 135 to 152)
           a.   General Considerations (§§ 135 to 137)
           b.   Admissibility of Evidence (§§ 138 to 149)
           c.   Weight and Sufficiency of Evidence (§§ 150 to 152)
        3.   Trial (§§ 153 to 156)
        4.   Instructions (§§ 157 to 160)
        5.   Verdict, Sentence, and Punishment (§§ 161 to 163)

I.   **IN GENERAL**
§ 1   Assault defined
§ 2   Battery defined
§ 3   Distinctions

II.   **CIVIL LIABILITY**

Exhibit 5-2   *(Continued)*

- **New Topic Service.** For *Am. Jur. 2d* in print, a New Topic Service binder that introduces new topics is included and located at the end of the set. New topics are retained in the binder until they are incorporated into revised volumes in the main set. Because of how Westlaw and LexisNexis update their respective content, the New Topic Service is unnecessary for those websites. As new topics are added they are integrated into the databases.
- **Desk Book.** *Am. Jur. 2d* in print includes the *Am. Jur. 2d Desk Book*, which includes general information such as statistical charts, tables, data, and diagrams. It includes, for example, a diagram of various federal agencies, the text of the United States Constitution, and the addresses and telephone numbers of the federal courts.

§ 160   Matters of justification

     5.   Verdict, Sentence, and Punishment

§ 161   Verdict and findings
§ 162   Verdict and findings—Included offenses and degrees of crime
§ 163   Sentence and punishment

I. IN GENERAL

Research References

Annotation References
A.L.R. Digest: Assault and Battery §§ 1, 2, 47, 48
A.L.R. Index: Assault and Battery; Husband and Wife

§ 1   Assault defined

An assault is any unlawful offer or attempt to injure another with apparent present ability to effectuate the attempt under circumstances creating a fear of imminent peril.

Research References

West's Key Number Digest, Assault and Battery ⟐1, 2, 48

An assault may be defined as any intentional, unlawful offer of corporal injury to another by force, or force unlawfully directed toward the person of another, under such circumstances as to create a well founded fear or reasonable apprehension of imminent peril or an immediate battery,[1] coupled with the apparent present ability to effectuate the attempt if not prevented.[2] Also, the term has been defined as an unlawful attempt, coupled with the present ability, to commit a violent injury on the person of another;[3] an attempt or offer, with force or violence, to do a corporal hurt to another, whether from malice or wantonness,[4] under such circumstances as denote, at the time, an intention to do it, coupled with a present ability to effectuate such intention.[5] Additionally, the willful threat or attempt to harm or touch another offensively may be required to be coupled with a definitive act by one who has the apparent ability to do the harm or to commit the offensive touching.[6] No bodily contact is necessary.[7] As also stated, assault occurs where a person: (1) acts intending to cause a harmful or offensive contact with the person of the other or a third person, or an imminent apprehension of such contact,[8] and (2) the other is thereby put in such imminent apprehension.[9] Alternatively, an assault may be defined as an intentional, unlaw-

---

[Section 1]

[1]U.S.—Park v. Shiflett, 250 F.3d 843 (4th Cir. 2001); Lunini v. Grayeb, 305 F. Supp. 2d 893 (C.D. Ill. 2004); Cleveland v. City of Detroit, 275 F. Supp. 2d 832 (E.D. Mich. 2003).

Wash.—State v. Taylor, 140 Wash. 2d 229, 996 P.2d 571 (2000).

[2]U.S.—Woods v. Miamisburg City Schools, 254 F. Supp. 2d 868, 176 Ed. Law Rep. 316 (S.D. Ohio 2003).

Mo.—Phelps v. Bross, 73 S.W.3d 651 (Mo. Ct. App. E.D. 2002), reh'g and/or transfer denied, (Apr. 17, 2002) and transfer denied, (May 28, 2002).

Wash.—State v. Taylor, 140 Wash. 2d 229, 996 P.2d 571 (2000).

[3]D.C.—Mungo v. U.S., 772 A.2d 240 (D.C. 2001).

S.C.—State v. LaCoste, 347 S.C. 153, 553 S.E.2d 464 (Ct. App. 2001), cert. granted, (Feb. 25, 2002) and cert. dismissed as improvidently granted, 353 S.C. 538, 579 S.E.2d 318 (2003).

[4]R.I.—State v. McLaughlin, 621 A.2d 170 (R.I. 1993).

Va.—Zimmerman v. Com., 266 Va. 384, 585 S.E.2d 538 (2003).

[5]Tenn.—Lewis v. Metropolitan General Sessions Court for Nashville, 949 S.W.2d 696 (Tenn. Crim. App. 1996).

Va.—Zimmerman v. Com., 266 Va. 384, 585 S.E.2d 538 (2003).

[6]U.S.—Watkins v. Millennium School, 290 F. Supp. 2d 890, 183 Ed. Law Rep. 454 (S.D. Ohio 2003).

[7]U.S.—Jackson v. Austin, 241 F. Supp. 2d 1313 (D. Kan. 2003).

[8]Miss.—Morgan v. Greenwaldt, 786 So. 2d 1037 (Miss. 2001).

Pa.—Paves v. Corson, 765 A.2d 1128 (Pa. Super. Ct. 2000), decision rev'd in part on other grounds, 569 Pa. 171, 801 A.2d 546 (2002).

Va.—Koffman v. Garnett, 265 Va. 12, 574 S.E.2d 258 (2003).

[9]Miss.—Morgan v. Greenwaldt, 786 So. 2d 1037 (Miss. 2001).

Exhibit 5-3 C.J.S. Main Volume Entry for Assault. Reprinted from West Group, Corpus Juris Secundum, Vol. 6A (2001), p. 204. Reprinted with permission of Thomson Reuters.

ASSAULT AND BATTERY   § 5

§ 4 Assault or battery as intentional act

Research References

West's Key Number Digest, Assault and Battery ⚷3, 49

The intention to do harm, or an unlawful intent, has generally been considered an element of assault and battery.[1] Before drawing the inference of an intent to injure, a court must find that the conduct was intentional and was substantially certain to cause injury.[2] However, the requirement of intent has been relaxed to a certain extent, with some courts holding that battery need not be committed out of malice or an intent to cause harm,[3] to injure,[4] or to inflict actual damage.[5] Some courts hold it is not the actor's hostile intent that determines whether a battery has occurred, but the lack of the plaintiff's consent.[6]

> ♦ **Observation:** Some authorities make a distinction between civil and criminal liability arising from the commission of an assault, holding that although an intent to injure is not essential to civil liability, it is an essential element of the criminal offense.[7]

§ 5 Need for bodily injury

Research References

West's Key Number Digest, Assault and Battery 2, 48

In some jurisdictions, or with regard to certain forms of battery, evidence of bodily injury or physical harm is required to establish bat-

---

678 So. 2d 556 (La. 1996).

[5]In re T.Y.B., 288 Ga. App. 610, 654 S.E.2d 688 (2007).

As to whether this precludes a charge of attempted assault, see §§ 11.

[Section 4]

[1]Gnadt v. Com., 27 Va. App. 148, 497 S.E.2d 887 (1998).

Proof of an intent to cause fear is required in a case of threatened battery. Com. v. Spencer, 40 Mass. App. Ct. 919, 663 N.E.2d 268 (1996).

[2]Macherey v. Home Ins. Co., 184 Wis. 2d 1, 516 N.W.2d 434 (Ct. App. 1994).

[3]In re Gavin T., 66 Cal. App. 4th 238, 77 Cal. Rptr. 2d 701, 128 Ed. Law Rep. 313 (1st Dist. 1998); Paul v. Holbrook, 696 So. 2d 1311 (Fla. Dist. Ct. App. 5th

Dist. 1997).

[4]Price v. Short, 931 S.W.2d 677 (Tex. App. Dallas 1996).

[5]Johnson v. Bergeron, 966 So. 2d 1059 (La. Ct. App. 5th Cir. 2007).

[6]Kling v. Landry, 292 Ill. App. 3d 329, 226 Ill. Dec. 684, 686 N.E.2d 33 (2d Dist. 1997).

The requirement of lack of consent is discussed in § 7.

[7]In re Gavin T., 66 Cal. App. 4th 238, 77 Cal. Rptr. 2d 701, 128 Ed. Law Rep. 313 (1st Dist. 1998).

As to the mens rea required for the crimes of assault and battery, see §§ 15 et seq.

As to the intent required to constitute a civil assault or battery, see §§ 92, 93.

Exhibit 5-4 *Am. Jur. 2d.* Main Volume Entry for Assault and Battery. Reprinted from Thomson West, American Jurisprudence, 2d Ed., Vol. 6 (2001), p. 11 Reprinted with permission of Thomson Reuters.

SECURITIES EXCHANGE ACT OF 1934—Continued

Sec.	Sec.	Sec.	Sec.
21(d)(3)(B)	Securities:1618	25(a)(2)	Securities:1628
21(d)(3)(C)(i)	Securities:1618	25(a)(3)	Securities:1629
21(d)(3)(C)(ii)	Securities:1618	25(a)(5)	Securities:1631
21(d)(3)(C)(iii)	Securities:1618	25(c)(1)	Securities:1630
21(d)(4)	Securities:1616	25(c)(2)	Securities:1627
21A(a)(1)	Securities:1618	27	Securities:1612, 1643
21A(d)(1)	Securities:1618	28(a)	Securities:1028; Secregs:13
21A(d)(2)	Securities:1618	30A(a)	Securities:1657
21A(d)(3)	Securities:1618	32(b)	Securities:1657
22	Securities:1554	781(i)	Securities:561
25(a)(1)	Securities:1621, 1625, 1626		

TRUST INDENTURE ACT

Sec.	Sec.	Sec.	Sec.
312	Securities:822	323	Securities:1392, 1414
315	Securities:1513	323(a)	Securities:921, 994
320	Securities:1554	323(b)	Securities:1005
321(a)	Securities:1538, 1539	323 and 325	Securities:1484
322	Securities:1643	305, 306, or 307	Securities:1484
322(a)	Securities:1524		

UNITED STATES CODE ANNOTATED

U.S.C.A. App.	Sec.	1 U.S.C.A. Sec.	Sec.
2, § 3	Unitedsts:29	201	Statutes:36
		202	Statutes:36
1 U.S.C.A. Sec.	**Sec.**	203	Statutes:36
1 to 7	Statutes:146	204	Evidence:1338
1	Mentalimp:1; Partnershp:3, 501; Statutes:133, 144, 145	204(a)	Bankruptcy:16; Statutes:40
3	Boats:1; Shipping:1	204(b)	Statutes:40
7	Aliens:339, 340; Marriage:2	205 to 212	Statutes:36
78o(k)(2)	Securities:531	209	Evidence:1338
101	Statutes:45	213	Statutes:36
103	Statutes:45	**2 U.S.C.A. Sec.**	**Sec.**
104	Statutes:43, 53	1	Unitedsts:8
105	Publicfund:40; Statutes:46	2a	Census:5; Elections:20
106	Statutes:23, 28, 31	2b	Unitedsts:8
106a	Statutes:37	8	Unitedsts:9
106b	Constlaw:14, 419	21 to 30a	Unitedsts:5
107	Statutes:36	21	Unitedsts:5
108	Statutes:302	25	Unitedsts:5
109	Forfeit:21, 71; Statutes:258, 265, 299	31 to 59h	Unitedsts:5
110	Statutes:264	51	Cemeter:4
112	Evidence:1338; Statutes:40	58	Unitedsts:5
112a(a)	Evidence:1338	59e	Unitedsts:5
113	Evidence:1338; Statutes:40	60-1 to 130	Unitedsts:4
114	Seals:10	601(a)	Jobdiscrim:932

Exhibit 5-5 *Am. Jur. 2d.* Table of Laws and Rules. Reprinted from Thomson West Group, American Jurisprudence, 2d (2006), p. 154. Reprinted with permission of Thomson Reuters.

2. Research Techniques—National Encyclopedias

You use a legal encyclopedia to obtain an overview of a specific area of the law, and to locate case law in that area. The following techniques are helpful for locating legal topics. These techniques can be used for the print encyclopedias as well as searching the encyclopedias on Westlaw and LexisNexis unless noted below.

a. General Index

Usually one begins research by consulting the general index that accompanies each set. Westlaw and Lexis both also have an index that can be searched in a manner similar to the print index.

For Example

If you are interested in aggravated assault with a dangerous or deadly weapon (criminal), you would look in the index under "assault and battery" and be directed to the appropriate topic and section (see page 2 of Exhibit 5-2).

b. Table of Contents

If you know the area of law that covers the subject you are researching, you can refer to the volume that covers the topic and scan the table of contents for the specific topic. When searching electronically, you would select the topic from the list of topics, which opens the table of contents for that topic. Generally, in Westlaw and LexisNexis, if you have linked to a topic from the index, there is a toggle button that will take you to the Table of Contents for that topic. This allows you to easily move around within a topic without returning to the index.

For Example

If you are interested in information regarding admissibility of certain evidence in a civil assault and battery action, you could retrieve the volume that covers the topic and scan the table of contents to locate the applicable sections (see page 1 of Exhibit 5-2).

Note in the print encyclopedias, the spine of each volume identifies the range of subjects covered, such as "Private Franchise Contracts to Process."

c. Statute, Rules, and Regulations

If you are looking for a specific statute, rule, or regulation, the Table of Statutes and Rules Cited will direct you to the sections where it is discussed (see Exhibit 5-5).

When searching in print, *always* consult the pocket part to update your research, to ensure that the narrative summary in the main text has not changed, and to locate the most recent cases. Be sure to check the date the content was updated when searching the encyclopedias in Westlaw or LexisNexis to be sure the content was recently updated. If there appears to be a lengthy lapse in the update date, either consult the print encyclopedia to ensure you have the most updated content, or contact a representative from the website to inquire about issues with content updating.

3. Computer-Aided Research

As noted above, *American Jurisprudence Second* and *Corpus Juris Secundum* are available on Westlaw. *Am. Jur. 2d* is also available on LexisNexis. Neither set is available on non-fee-based websites. Note that copyrighted secondary sources are generally not available for free on the Internet. In many law libraries where only one of the national encyclopedias is available in print, the encyclopedia not available in print may be accessible electronically at a public computer. Check with a research librarian for availability. Internet research will be discussed in more depth in Chapters 7 and 8.

B. State Encyclopedias

Some legal encyclopedias are published for individual states. These encyclopedias are organized like the national encyclopedias and include many of the same features, such as a table of contents for each section, a general index, and pocket part supplements. Some sets have tables of cases, statutes, and regulations. They provide a narrative summary of the laws of the state with citations to state and federal case law that have interpreted state law. Research is conducted in the same manner as when using a national encyclopedia. State encyclopedias are most valuable when conducting research on questions involving state law.

West and Lexis publish many, but not all, of the state encyclopedias that are available. As such, Westlaw and LexisNexis do have secondary source databases that include some of the state encyclopedias. West publishes the "Jurisprudence" series that include sets for California, Georgia, Illinois, Massachusetts, Michigan, New York, Ohio, Pennsylvania, South Carolina and Texas. Lexis publishes *Tennessee Jurisprudence, Jurisprudence of West Virginia,* and *Jurisprudence of Virginia*. These are a few of the state encyclopedias that exist. To determine if there is a state encyclopedia for a given state, you can contact a local law school library reference desk to ask about state encyclopedias, or you can contact the law library for the state's appellate courts, especially the state's highest appellate court.

C. Foreign Encyclopedias

Since encyclopedias contain a summary of areas of law, they provide one of the best ways to gain general information about the law of foreign countries. Even if an encyclopedia for a foreign country is not available in a local library it may be available through an interlibrary loan or through the Internet. Often, obtaining a copy of the table of contents for a foreign encyclopedia will allow you to then seek particular sections through a document delivery service, which is less expensive than trying to obtain the entire encyclopedia set in print or electronically.

One of the easiest ways to determine if there is an encyclopedia for a foreign country is to search WorldCat (http://www.worldcat.org) which is the largest network of library content and services. WorldCat will also lead you to any nearby libraries that have the encyclopedia.

III. TREATISES

Treatises are texts that provide a comprehensive analysis of a single area of law, such as torts or criminal law. Where a legal encyclopedia presents a broad overview of an area of law, a treatise does much more. It provides a more in-depth discussion of the law in which it explains, analyzes, and criticizes the law. Some treatises include guidance for the legal practitioner, such as practice tips, checklists, and legal forms. Legal experts in the field write treatises; therefore, courts rely on and cite treatises more often than legal encyclopedias. Treatises, however, are still secondary authority; they are not the law, and courts do not have to follow a position or adopt an interpretation advocated by the author. However, there are a few treatises that are authored by well-known scholars who are highly regarded by the courts. Those particular treatises are often cited by the courts even though the treatise is secondary authority and the court is not required to follow it.

For Example

Search and Seizure: A Treatise on the Fourth Amendment by Wayne LaFave is a multivolume treatise often cited by the courts when deciding a case involving Fourth Amendment issues because it has comprehensive coverage of federal and state search and seizure laws.

A. Types and Features of Treatises

There are several types of treatises, ranging from single-volume texts to multivolume sets. Single-volume treatises exist on hundreds of legal topics, and the topics covered may be very specific (such as the *First Amendment Law Handbook* by James L. Swanson), or they may cover an entire area of law (such as *The*

Law of Torts by Dan B. Dobbs). The broader the topic covered by the single-volume text, the less detailed the coverage.

There are multivolume treatises for most major areas of law. A multivolume treatise is like an expanded version of a single-text treatise. Due to its size, it provides more extensive and more in-depth treatment of a legal topic than a single-text treatise can.

For Example

Fletcher Cyclopedia Corporations consists of 33 hardbound and loose-leaf volumes. It analyzes corporate law and addresses, in detail, the legal issues corporations may face. Obviously, this publication covers the area of corporate law in much greater detail than a single-volume treatise.

The multivolume sets are more likely to include aids for the practitioner, such as forms, checklists, and practice guides.

Most treatises have the following features:

- **Narrative presentation.** The subject matter is presented in a narrative format similar to that of a legal encyclopedia. Documentation supporting the narrative text, including case citations and references to other sources, is presented in footnotes (see Exhibit 5-6).
- **Index.** An index is included at the end of the single-volume treatise or as a separate volume in multivolume sets.
- **Table of cases.** Most treatises include a table of cases arranged alphabetically and a table of contents for each subject area.
- **Table of statutes.** Many treatises include a table of statutes so you can locate content on a particular statute.
- **Updates.** Most multivolume treatises are updated annually or semiannually through the use of pocket parts for each volume or separate supplements. For multivolume sets that are in loose-leaf binders, supplement packets for new pages are issued at regular intervals. These supplemental packets contain a page that is often in the first volume that indicates the date of the latest supplement. These supplements come with instructions on what pages to remove and insert. Most single-volume treatises are updated through the publication of a new edition with cumulative pocket parts for the years between editions. Some single-volume treatises, such as the softbound *Corporate Communications Handbook* by Walton and Seghetti, are published annually rather than updated. Always check the copyright date of hardbound volumes and the dates on pocket parts or supplements. In loose-leaf services, check the dates on the update sheet often located in the first volume to ensure your research is up to date.

B. Research Using Treatises

Most law libraries have a treatise section where both the single-volume and multivolume treatises are arranged alphabetically by legal topic (e.g., treatises on criminal law will follow treatises on contracts). Some public libraries may have single-volume treatises located in the legal section. Check the catalog or with the librarian to determine which treatises are available.

1. Use as a Research Tool

Use a treatise when you are seeking more than the general summary of the law provided by a legal encyclopedia. The issue you are researching may not be covered in sufficient detail in an encyclopedia. Also, the analysis or criticism of the law provided in a treatise may be necessary when seeking information on how to counter an opponent's interpretation of or reliance upon a law, or when seeking input on how to present an argument contrary to existing precedent.

§ 33   SIMPLE ASSULT   63

attacker would not be liable for a battery if he merely failed to prevent the attacker from hitting the plaintiff.

Duty to protect the plaintiff from others' batteries? On the other hand, the defendant might be under a duty to protect the plaintiff. Employers, for example, are under a duty to protect employees from sexual batteries (and other forms of sexual harassment). If an employer knows that an employee is being sexually battered by another employee, it is not implausible to say that the employer is also guilty of a battery, though he has not committed any "act" and in some instances the battery claim might be advantageous.[5] Similarly, a hospital is under a duty to protect patients from attack, and a knowing failure to do so might be thought of as a battery by inaction. In practice, however, courts are likely to think of both kinds of claims as negligence claims turning on reasonableness rather than battery claims turning upon intent.[6] That is not necessarily the plaintiff's loss, since the defendant's liability insurance may cover negligence but not battery. The upshot is that an affirmative act is at least ordinarily if not invariably required to establish a battery.

Vicarious liability for battery. Liability may, of course, be imposed upon one who instigates a battery or other trespassory tort by another. That is not a case of inaction[7] but a case of liability of one person for the actions of another.[8] It may also be imposed upon employers and persons in analogous roles for the actions of their employees committed within the scope of employment.

TOPIC D. ASSAULT

§ 33. Simple Assault

Nature of the tort. Newspapers and even judges and lawyers sometimes use the term assault to mean a battery. More technically, assault is a quite different tort, although it often precedes a battery. An assault is an act that is intended to and does place the plaintiff in apprehension of an immediate unconsented-to touching that would amount to a battery.[1] The plaintiff's subjective recognition or apprehension that she is about to be touched in an impermissible way is at the core of the assault claim.

Intent and transferred intent. As in other cases, intent may be based either on the defendant's purpose or on his substantial certainty that a

Text ————

5. Because employers are generally protected from negligence claims under workers' compensation laws, but sometimes not for intentional tort claims. See generally, Jean Love, Actions for Non-physical Harm: The Relationship Between the Tort System and No-Fault Compensation (With an Emphasis on Workers' Compensation), 73 CAL. L. REV. 857 (1985).

References to cases ————

6. *Employers liable for negligence:* E.g., Ford v. Revlon, Inc., 153 Ariz. 38, 734 P. 2.d 580 (1987). *Hospital liable for negligence:* Sumblin v. Craven

County Hospital Corp., 86 N.C. App. 358, 357 S.E. 2d 376 (1987) (viewing claim against hospital for failure to protect psychiatric patient from molestation as a negligence case).

7. E.g., West v. LTV Steel Co., 839 F. Supp. 559 (N.D.Ind. 1993).

8. See Chapter 22 on vicarious liability generally.

§ 33

1. Restatement §§ 21 & 32.

Reference to secondary source

Exhibit 5-6 Sample Treatise Page. Reprinted from West Group, Dan B. Dobbs, The Law of Torts (2000), p. 63. Reprinted with permission from Thomson Reuters.

For Example

The research question involves a majority shareholder in a family corporation whose actions harm the minority shareholders. The majority shareholder controls the board of directors and refuses to issue dividends or allow the minority shareholders to benefit from the corporation in any way. The minority shareholders want to know what remedies are available to them. A legal encyclopedia may not address the subject in sufficient detail to be of assistance. *Fletcher Cyclopedia Corporations* will certainly cover the topic in greater detail and likely provide the answer. The two-volume treatise, *O'Neal's Oppression of Minority Shareholders*, will provide an even greater in-depth discussion of the subject, along with citations to cases that discuss various types of oppressive conduct.

Treatises, like legal encyclopedias, are also extremely valuable in locating cases. In the previous example, both *Fletcher Cyclopedia Corporations* and *O'Neal's Oppression of Minority Shareholders* will provide numerous case citations to instances of oppressive conduct, one of which may match the fact situation being researched. A legal encyclopedia usually will not address as many specific fact situations as a treatise.

2. Research Techniques—Treatises

The following techniques are helpful for locating specific topics in treatises. These techniques are the same for searching treatises in print or online, particularly when using Westlaw, LexisNexis, or HeinOnline.

a. General Index

Usually research begins by consulting the index at the end of the text or the set. Westlaw and Lexis also have links to the index for treatises on their respective websites.

For Example

If you are interested in oppressive conduct by majority shareholders, look in the index under "shareholders," "majority shareholders," or "oppressive conduct."

b. Table of Contents/Table of Cases

If you know where the topic you are researching is covered in the treatise, go to the section or volume that covers the subject and scan the table of contents for the specific subtopic. If you are looking for the treatment of a specific case in a treatise, consult the table of cases.

When researching treatises online, generally there is a link to the Table of Contents. Treatises in e-book format also have tables of contents. In both electronic formats, the Table of Contents is directly linked to the content, allowing a particular topic or section to be accessed quickly.

c. Reference from Other Sources

Often another source, such as a citation in a case or legal encyclopedia, will direct you to a specific treatise section. When viewing another source in many commercial Internet research sources, the citation to the specific treatise section is a hyperlink, allowing the researcher to go to the treatise then return to the original source with ease.

For Example

A court opinion may read, "For an exhaustive treatment of derivative actions, see 4 Alan R. Bromberg & Larry E. Ribstein, *Partnership* § 15.059."

As with a legal encyclopedia, *always* consult the pocket part or supplement to update your research, to locate the most recent cases, and to ensure that the narrative summary in the main text has not changed. If searching a treatise through an online source such as Westlaw or LexisNexis, be sure to check the date the treatise was last updated. If the treatise is a single volume that is not updated, check the case citations through *Shepard's* or Westlaw's *KeyCite* to ensure the cases are still good law. *Shepard's Citations* and Westlaw's *KeyCite* will be discussed later in this chapter.

3. Computer-Aided Research

Many treatises are available on Westlaw or LexisNexis, as discussed above. Generally, treatises are not available for free on the Internet.

Many treatises are also available on CD-ROM. Older treatises are often available in full at HeinOnline. HeinOnline is a commercial Internet source that has scans of entire legal texts in PDF format, specializing in older treatises, books, and law journals. Treatises, like other copyrighted secondary sources, usually are not available on non-fee-based websites.

IV. *AMERICAN LAW REPORTS*

One approach to reporting and analyzing the case law is that taken by the *American Law Reports (ALR)*. The *ALR* publishes the text of leading state and federal court opinions addressing specific issues. Following the opinion is an analysis (referred to as *annotations*) of the legal issues raised in the opinion and a summary of the cases from every jurisdiction that have addressed the same or similar issues. The case summaries are arranged by jurisdiction and provide the researcher with a view of the treatment of the legal issue or issues raised in the case.

For Example

Assume the *ALR* annotation analyzes the question: "What constitutes 'occupying' under the owned-vehicle exclusion of uninsured motorist coverage?" The annotation organizes and presents the cases according to how the courts have answered the question. The cases that have held a car was occupied are presented together by state. The cases that have not held a car was occupied are also presented together.

In addition to the case summaries, the annotations provide references to various other research sources. Lawyers with expertise in the area of law select the cases and prepare the annotations. The coverage and analysis of an issue in the *ALR* is so thorough that the *ALR* is one of the most cited secondary sources.

The annotations following the text of the court opinion are thoroughly researched and may range in length from a few pages to more than 100 pages. A single *ALR* volume may run to more than 1,000 pages and provide annotations to fewer than 15 cases. The annotations cover only selected legal issues. If the issue you are researching is addressed by an annotation, the annotation is a research shortcut. It will often provide, in one place, all of your research: a comprehensive analysis of the issue, references to and summaries of the case law on point, and references to other research sources.

ALR began publication in 1919, and for years it was published by Lawyers' Coop. Today, West publishes *ALR*. It is composed of the following multivolume series:

ALR	Federal and state cases from 1919 to 1948; 175 volumes
ALR.2d (Second Series)	Federal and state cases from 1948 to 1965; 100 volumes
ALR.3d (Third Series)	Federal cases from 1965 to 1969 and state cases from 1965 to 1980; 100 volumes
ALR.4th (Fourth Series)	State cases from 1980 to 1991; 100 volumes
ALR.5th (Fifth Series)	State cases from 1991 to June 2005; 125 volumes
ALR.6th (Sixth Series)	State cases from June 2005 to present
ALR Federal	Federal cases from 1969 to 2005; 200 volumes
ALR Federal (Second Series)	Federal cases from 2005 to present

A. *ALR* Components

There were changes in organization and updating when the second series was published, and again with the publication of the third series. The annotations in the third, fourth, fifth, sixth, and federal series are generally similar in format and updating, and share the following components:

- **Prefatory statement.** An annotation begins with a statement that briefly describes the topic of the annotation and cites the case used to illustrate the legal issue discussed in the annotation. At the end of the statement is a reference to the page where the case is printed in the *ALR* volume (see the first page of Exhibit 5-7).
- **Table of contents.** Following the prefatory statement is a detailed table of contents for the annotation (see the second page of Exhibit 5-7).
- **Research references and sources.** A research section follows the table of contents, and lists references related to the annotation. This section includes references to related *ALR* annotations, encyclopedia sections, texts, West key numbers, law review articles, and other publications, practice aids, and Internet research sources (see bottom of second page of Exhibit 5-7).
- **Article index.** Next is an index that lists the subjects and where each subject is covered in the annotation.
- **Jurisdictional tables.** Following the index is a table that lists all the cases cited in the annotation by jurisdiction and the statutes relevant to the annotation (see Exhibit 5-8).
- **Scope.** The body of the annotation begins with a scope section that identifies what is and what is not covered in the annotation (see Exhibit 5-7).
- **Related annotations.** Next is a reference to related *ALR* annotations (see Exhibit 5-7).
- **Summary and comment.** This section presents a summary of the topic that includes background and other information helpful in understanding the topic.
- **Practice pointers.** After the summary and comment section, the next section of the body presents case preparation and other guidelines for practitioners.
- **Substantive provisions.** The bulk of the body of an annotation is composed of the substantive sections which organize, summarize, analyze, and evaluate the case law on the topic of the annotation. For each case discussed in the annotation, there is a presentation of the facts and issue(s) before the court related to the topic of the annotation, the court's conclusions on the issue(s), and the court's reasons for its conclusions (see Exhibit 5-9).

In addition to the components of each annotation, the *ALR* series has the following general features:

- **ALR Index.** The *ALR* General Index lists terms and phrases alphabetically with references to all related annotations. The index is comprehensive with extensive cross-references.

For Example

If you are looking for annotations on uninsured motorists and you first look under "Insurance" the index will direct you to "Automobile Insurance."

The general index is a multivolume set that provides references to annotations in *ALR.2d, ALR.3d, ALR.4th, ALR.5th, ALR.6th,* and *ALR Federal, ALR Federal 2d.*

- **Quick Index.** The one-volume softbound index provides references to *ALR.3d, ALR.4th, ALR.5th, ALR.6th, ALR Federal,* and *ALR Federal.2d.* There is also an *ALR Federal Quick Index* providing references to the *ALR Federal* and *ALR Federal.2d.* The *Quick Indexes* are not as detailed as the *General Index* (see Exhibit 5-10).
- **Table of Laws, Rules, and Regulations.** The index includes a table that indicates where statutes, rules, regulations, are cited in annotations.

- **Annotation History Table.** The last volume of the *ALR General Index* includes a history table that indicates if an annotation has been supplemented in or superseded by a later annotation, and provides the volume number, *ALR* Series, and page number where the later annotation is located.
- *ALR* **Digests.** There are multivolume *ALR* digests similar to the West digests (discussed in the next section of this chapter). In the *ALR* digests, the law is divided into more than 400 topics and arranged alphabetically. Each topic is divided into numerical subsections. The sections include a summary of the annotations and references to other sources, such as encyclopedia references and practice references. There are separate digests for *ALR* and *ALR.2d* and a combined digest for *ALR.3d, ALR.4th, ALR.5th, ALR.6th, ALR Federal,* and *ALR Federal.2d.*

---

59 ALR5th 191

AUTOMOBILE INSURANCE: WHAT CONSTITUTES "OCCUPYING" UNDER OWNED-VEHICLE EXCLUSION OF UNINSURED- OR UNDERINSURED-MOTORIST COVERAGE OF AUTOMOBILE INSURANCE POLICY

by
Jacqueline G. Slifkin, J.D.

The "owned-vehicle" exclusion is a common exclusion found in insurance policies relating to uninsured- and underinsured-motorist coverage. This exclusion precludes UIM coverage for bodily injury sustained while occupying a motor vehicle owned or available for regular use by the insureds which is not covered by liability insurance or by the same policy of insurance. Courts have addressed the issue of what constitutes "occupying" under the owned-vehicle exclusion, and their decisions reveal that the cases are very fact specific. For example, in Mid-Century Ins. Co. v. Henault (1995) 128 Wash 2d 207, 905 P2d 379, 59 ALR5th 789, where the claimant was injured while lying in the road as the result of a previous collision involving her uninsured motorcycle, the court determined that the claimant was not occupying her uninsured motor vehicle at the time she sustained her injuries. This annotation collects and analyzes cases which consider whether, or under what circumstances, a person is deemed to have been "occupying" a motor vehicle under an "owned-vehicle" exclusion pertaining to the uninsured- or underinsured-motorist coverage in an automobile liability insurance policy.

Mid-Century Ins. Co. v. Henault is fully reported at page 789, infra.

Exhibit 5-7 *A.L.R. Annotation and Table of Contents.* Reprinted from West Publishing/West Group, American Law Reports, 5th Ser., Vol. 59 (1998), pp. 191–192. Reprinted with Permission of Thomson Reuters.

UIM—"OCCUPYING" VEHICLE   59 ALR5th
59 ALR5th 191

TABLE OF CONTENTS
Research References
Index
Jurisdictional Table of Cited Statutes and Cases

ARTICLE OUTLINE

Research References

TOTAL CLIENT-SERVICE LIBRARY® REFERENCES

The following references may be of related or collateral interest to a user of this annotation.

Annotations

See the related annotations listed in the body of the annotation.

Encyclopedias and Texts

7 Am Jur 2d, Automobile Insurance § 317

Practice Aids

11 Am Jur Trials 73, Uninsured Motorist Claims

2 Am Jur Trials 1, Investigating Particular Civil Actions

Exhibit 5-7   *(Continued)*

UIM—"OCCUPYING" VEHICLE   59 ALR5th
59 ALR5th 191

Hitting ground, injuries suffered upon, § 5[a]

Introduction to annotation, § 1

Lying in roadway as result of earlier accident, § 5[b]

Motorcycles, § 5

Particular cases, §§ 3-5

Police cruiser, claimant sitting in, § 3[b]

Practice pointers, § 2[b]

Preliminary matters, §§ 1, 2

Related matters, § 1[b]

Removing item from trunk, § 3[a]

Scope of annotation, § 1[a]

Shooting at vehicle, § 4

"Sidewalk oriented" at time of accident, § 3[b]

Standing in front of disabled vehicle, § 3[a]

Striking pavement, injuries suffered upon, § 5[a]

Summary, § 2

Transaction essential to use of vehicle, § 3[b]

Trucks, § 4

Trunk of car, removing item from, § 3[a]

Two vehicles, ability to occupy simultaneously, § 3[b]

"Vehicle oriented" at time of accident, § 3[b]

Jurisdictional Table of Cited Statutes and Cases[*]

MINNESOTA

Minn. Stat. Sec. 65B.49, subd. 3a(5), (7). See § 3[a]

Horace Mann Ins. Co. v. Neuville, 465 N.W.2d 432 (Minn. Ct. App. 1991)—§ 3[a]

OREGON

ORS 743.792(2)(I). See § 3[a]

Mackie v. Unigard Ins. Co. (1988) 90 Or App 500, 752 P2d 1266—§ 3[a]

RHODE ISLAND

General Accident Ins. Co. Of America v. D'Allesandro (1996, Rhode Island) 671 A2d 1233—§ 3[b]

TENNESSEE

Smith v. Hobbs (1993 Tenn App) 848 SW2d 662—§ 5[a]

[*]Statutes, rules, regulations, and constitutional provisions bearing on the subject of the annotation are included in this table only to the extent, and in the form, that they are reflected in the court opinions discussed in this annotation. The reader should consult the appropriate statutory or regulatory compilations to ascertain the current status of relevant statutes, rules, regulations, and constitutional provisions.

For federal cases involving state law, see state headings.

Exhibit 5-8 *A.L.R. Annotation – Jurisdictional Table of Cited Statutes and Cases.* Reprinted from West Publishing/West Group, *American Law Reports,* 5th Ser., Vol. 59 (1998), p. 194. Reprinted with Permission of Thomson Reuters.

ment that there be "physical contact" with unidentified or hit-and-run vehicle. 25 ALR3d 1299.

§ 2. Summary and comment

[a] Generally

The "owned-vehicle" exclusion is a common exclusion found in uninsured-motorist and underinsured-motorist policies and is, in some cases, even mandated by state law. The thrust of the exclusion is that the owner of a vehicle, or a member of the owner's family, who is occupying the vehicle when it is involved in an accident with an uninsured motorist can recover only under an uninsured-motorist endorsement specifically covering that vehicle and may not resort to coverage for a different family vehicle. Accordingly, if the injured party is occupying a vehicle that is not covered by liability insurance, that person may not look to an insurance policy covering a different vehicle owned either by the injured or by a member of the injured's family. This exclusion is designed to encourage motor-vehicle owners to secure insurance on all of their vehicles.

The question then arises, what does "occupying" mean for purposes of the owned-vehicle exclusion? "Occupying" typically is defined in insurance policies or in the state motor vehicle insurance law as "in, upon, getting in, on, out, or off" of the motor vehicle. Of course, if the injured party is physically inside the uninsured vehicle at the time of the accident, there is little question that the injured was occupying the vehicle. The harder question arises in cases where the injured person is injured through a chain of events that somehow involve the uninsured vehicle, but where the injured person is not physically occupying the vehicle at the time the injuries occur.

The courts, when deciding the latter type of cases, are typically confronted with unusual factual situations. In these cases, the courts generally attempt to determine whether a particular injury or accident has some causal connection or relationship to the use of the uninsured vehicle. The courts look at a variety of factors in determining whether that causal connection or relationship exists: the time lapse between the accident involving the uninsured vehicle and the infliction of injuries; whether there were any "intervening causes" between the two events; whether the injuries were of the type normally "flowing" from an accident; whether there was some "continuing relationship" between the injured and his or her vehicle; the geographic proximity of the injured party to the vehicle; whether the injured person was "vehicle oriented" at the time of the accident; whether the injured was engaged in a transaction "essential to the use of the vehicle" at the time of the accident; and, lastly,

Exhibit 5-9 *A.L.R. Annotation–Body of Annotation.* Reprinted from West Publishing/West Group, American Law Reports, 5th Ser., Vol. 59 (1998), p. 197. Reprinted with Permission of Thomson Reuters.

- **Updates.** *ALR* and *ALR.2d* are updated differently than the other *ALR* series.

  - ***ALR.*** The *ALR* is updated by checking the *ALR Bluebook of Supplemental Decisions*. This is a non-cumulative multivolume set, meaning that each volume covers supplemental cases for a set period of years—volume 3, for example, covers supplemental decisions from 1952 to 1958. There is an annual paperback pamphlet for decisions subsequent to the last hardbound volume. This means

ALR QUICK INDEX

UNINSURED MOTORISTS
—Cont'd

Family, relatives, or household—Cont'd
    applicable to different vehicles, **23 ALR4th 12**
    validity under insurance statutes of coverage exclusion for injury to, or death of, insured's family or household members, **52 ALR4th 18**
    who is a "member" or "resident" of same "family" or "household" within no-fault or uninsured motorist provisions of motor vehicle insurance policy, **66 ALR5th 269**

Fellow employees, construction and application of provision of automobile liability policy expressly excluding from coverage liability arising from actions between fellow employees, **45 ALR3d 288**

Fleet policy, combining or stacking uninsured motorist coverages provided in, **25 ALR4th 896**

Good faith, what constitutes bad faith on part of insurer rendering it liable for statutory penalty imposed for bad faith in failure to pay, or delay in paying, insured's claim
    particular conduct of insurer, **115 ALR5th 589**
    risks, causes and extent of loss, injury, disability, or death, particular grounds for denial of claim: risks, causes and extent of loss, injury, disability, or death, **123 ALR5th 259**

Governmental immunity, right of insured, precluded from recovering against owner or operator of uninsured motor vehicle because of governmental immunity, to recover uninsured motorist benefits, **55 ALR4th 806**

Government vehicles, validity, construction, and application of exclusion of government vehicles from uninsured motorist provision, **58 ALR5th 511**

Hit-and-Run (this index)

Husband and wife
    additional insured, who qualifies as spouse within clause of automobile liability, uninsured motorist, or no-fault policy defining additional insured, **36 ALR4th 588**
    owned vehicle, validity of exclusion of injuries sustained by insured while occupying owned vehicle not insured by policy, **30 ALR4th 172**

Impeached witness' prior consistent statement, admissibility of, modern state civil cases, **59 ALR4th 1000**

Indemnity
    prerequisites, necessity and sufficiency of claimant's efforts to recover from other sources as prerequisite of participation in indemnity fund for losses caused by uninsured or

UNINSURED MOTORISTS
—Cont'd

Indemnity—Cont'd
    unknown motorists, **7 ALR3d 851**
    who is within protection of statutes creating indemnity funds for losses caused by uninsured or unknown motorists, **10 ALR3d 1166**

Intended or anticipated damage or injuries, uninsured motorist, coverage under uninsured motorist clause of injury inflicted intentionally, **72 ALR3d 1161**

Intentional injury, coverage under uninsured motorist clause of injury inflicted intentionally, **72 ALR3d 1161**

Intervention, right of insurer issuing uninsured motorist coverage to intervene in action by insured against uninsured motorist, **35 ALR4th 757**

Joint tortfeasors
    recovery efforts, necessity and sufficiency of claimant's efforts to recover from other sources as prerequisite of participation in indemnity fund for losses caused by uninsured or unknown motorists, **7 ALR3d 851**
    right to recover for injuries attributable to joint tortfeasors, one of whom is insured, **24 ALR4th 63**
    subsequent recovery, insured's recovery of uninsured motorist claim against insurer as affecting subsequent recovery against tortfeasors causing injury, **3 ALR5th 746**

Limitation of actions, time limitations as to claims based on uninsured motorist clause, **28 ALR3d 580**

Limitation of liability
    combining or stacking
        multiple insurers, **28 ALR4th 362**
        same insurer, separate policies insured by, **23 ALR4th 108**
        single policy applicable to different vehicles of individual insured, **23 ALR4th 12**
    consent to sue clauses, **24 ALR4th 1024**
    joint tortfeasors, 24 ALR4th 63
    motorcyclist, injuries to as within affirmative or exclusionary terms of automobile insurance policy, **46 ALR4th 771**
    no-fault benefits, exclusion of, **18 ALR4th 632**

Medical expenses
    generally, reduction of coverage by amounts payable under medical expense insurance, **24 ALR3d 1353**
    no-fault insurance, validity and enforceability of policy provision authorizing deduction of no-fault benefit from amounts payable, **20 ALR4th 1104**

UNINSURED MOTORISTS
—Cont'd

Medical expenses—Cont'd
    workmen's compensation, validity and effect of policy provision purporting to reduce coverage by amount paid under workmen's compensation law, **24 ALR3d 1369**

Member or resident, who is a "member" or "resident" of same "family" or "household" within no-fault or uninsured motorist provisions of motor vehicle insurance policy, **66 ALR5th 269**

Motorcycles (this index)

Municipal corporations
    applicability of uninsured motorist statutes to self-insurers, **27 ALR4th 1266**
    right of insured, precluded from recovering against owner or operator of uninsured motor vehicle because of governmental immunity, to recover uninsured motorist benefits, **55 ALR4th 806**

Named driver exclusion, validity, construction, and application of "named driver exclusion" in automobile insurance policy, **33 ALR5th 121**

Named insured within meaning of automobile insurance coverage, **91 ALR3d 1280**

No-consent-to-settlement exclusion clauses in policy, validity, construction, and effect of, **18 ALR4th 249**

No-Fault Insurance (this index)

Notice and knowledge, indemnity fund, necessity and sufficiency of claimant's efforts to recover from other sources as prerequisite of participation in indemnity fund for losses caused by uninsured or unknown motorists, **7 ALR3d 851**

Occupying owned vehicles
    validity of exclusion of injuries sustained by insured while occupying owned vehicle not insured by policy, **30 ALR4th 172**
    what constitutes "occupying" under owned-vehicle exclusion of uninsured or underinsured motorist coverage of automobile insurance policy, **59 ALR5th 191**

Other Insurance (this index)

Payment reduction provision, validity and construction of provision of uninsured or underinsured motorist coverage that damages under the coverage will be reduced by amount of recovery from tortfeasor, **40 ALR5th 603**

Pedestrians
    combining or stacking uninsured motorist coverages provided in policies issued by different insurers to different insureds, **28 ALR4th 362**
    combining or stacking uninsured motorist coverages provided in single policy applicable to different

For assitance using this Index, call 1-800-328-4880

Exhibit 5-10 *A.L.R. Quick Index page.* Reprinted from West Publishing/West Group, American Law Reports, Quick Index June 2015 ed., p. 1710. Reprinted with Permission of Thomson Reuters.

that each volume and supplement must be checked to locate all the supplemental cases. Fortunately, because *ALR* only covers cases through 1948, it is not frequently used. The *Bluebook* lists the *ALR* citation (e.g., 121 A.L.R. 616-627) followed by a list of cases decided after the citation was published. The *Bluebook* also indicates if an annotation has been supplemented or superseded by another annotation.

- **ALR.2d.** The *ALR.2d* is updated by reference to the multivolume *ALR.2d Later Case Service*. Each volume is updated with a pocket part, so you must check the pocket part as well as the main volume. The *Later Case Service* lists the *ALR.2d* citation followed by a summary of the new cases, and lists supplemental or superseding annotations.

- **ALR.3d, ALR.4th, ALR.5th, ALR.6th,** and **ALR Federal**. The *ALR.3d, ALR.4th, ALR.5th, ALR.6th,* and *ALR Federal* are updated through the use of annual cumulative pocket part supplements inserted in the back of each volume. The pocket part lists the *ALR* citation followed by a list of new sections and subsections, a list of new research references, and summary of the new cases. It also indicates if an annotation has been supplemented or superseded by another annotation.

- **Latest Case Service Hotline.** In the front of each pocket part supplement of *ALR.3d, ALR.4th, ALR.5th, ALR.6th,* and *ALR Federal* is a toll-free number for obtaining cites to cases decided since the publication of the pocket part.

- **LexisNexis and Westlaw.** The *ALR Series* are available on LexisNexis (Lexis) and Westlaw. The *ALRs* online are up to date, as supplementation is integrated into the annotation.

B. Research Using *ALR*

1. Use as a Research Tool

The focus of legal research is usually on a specific issue raised by the facts of a client's case. The value of *ALR* as a research tool lies in its comprehensive analysis of specific legal issues. If there is an annotation that addresses the legal issue you are researching, most of your research is done. The issue is analyzed through the discussion and synthesis of cases from every jurisdiction. Secondary sources, such as treatises, West digest key numbers, and practice aids are identified.

For Example

The question being researched involves the admissibility of polygraph evidence by the defendant in a malicious prosecution case. This is a specific question that could require a great deal of research. There is an *ALR* cite that directly addresses this topic: "Steven J. Gaynor, Annotation, *Admissibility of Evidence of Polygraph Test Results or Offer or Refusal to Take Test, in Action for Malicious Prosecution*, 10 ALR.5th 663 (1993)." Reference to this *ALR* annotation saves the researcher an immense amount of time because all the research to the year of the publication is consolidated in one source.

2. Research Techniques

Certain research techniques will help you locate specific *ALR* annotations, as described here.

a. Index to Annotations

Probably the most frequently used approach to locating annotations is to consult the multivolume index. If you know the general area of law, the index will direct you to the appropriate annotation. The *ALR* Quick Index is the second most used approach to locating annotations. The advantage of the multivolume index is that it covers all *ALR* series and it is expansive. This expansiveness allows a researcher to reach the annotation most on point without having the exact wording used by the annotation.

For Example

The question is when does an officer exceed the right to use physical force during an arrest. By looking in the index under "assault and battery," the researcher will be directed to the appropriate annotations.

Use of the index is similar, whether using the print source or accessing the *ALR*s through Westlaw or LexisNexis.

b. *ALR* Digest

As with the index, annotations can be located by looking up the topic in the general area of law in the digest. In addition to references to annotations, the digest summarizes relevant cases printed in the *ALR*. Use of the digest is the same, whether using the print source or accessing the *ALR*s through Westlaw or LexisNexis.

c. Table of Laws, Rules, and Regulations

If you know the statute that governs the issue being researched, you can refer to the table and be directed to the annotations that discuss the statute.

d. Reference from Other Sources

Often, you may be directed to a specific *ALR* annotation from another source, such as a citation in a case, article, *Shepard's Citations*, or Westlaw's *KeyCite*. In such cases, you could go directly to the volume and section cited.

When using *ALR*s in print, always consult the pocket part and supplement to update your research and to locate the most recent cases. In addition, *always* consult the appendix volume to ensure that you have located all the case summaries. Note that the appendix volumes are not cumulative; each must be checked.

Westlaw and LexisNexis update by weekly additions of relevant cases, and as new annotations and topics are added, the database is updated across all indexes, tables, digests, and volumes as necessary.

3. Computer-Aided Research

All *ALR* series are available on Westlaw. All *ALR* series except the first series are available on LexisNexis. E-annotations on particular topics are now available online on both Westlaw and Lexis. Some e-annotations are advance annotations that will eventually be published in the print *ALR*s; others will remain available only electronically. E-annotations are referenced in both the print and electronic indexes.

V. DIGESTS

As discussed in Chapter 4, court opinions are printed in reporters in chronological order; they are not organized by topic. If you are attempting to locate a case that addresses a specific issue, that is, a case on point, it would take you forever to find it by randomly looking through case after case in the reporters. A digest is not secondary authority; that is, it is not a source a court will rely upon to interpret the law. Rather, it is a finding aid—a source designed to allow researchers to locate cases easily.

A **digest** is a set of books that organize the law by topic, such as corporations or torts, and divide each topic into subtopics. The digest provides the citation to and a brief summary, or "digest," of all the court opinions that have addressed the subtopics. The ability to review the case summaries allows the researcher to select the case most similar to the client's case, that is, the case most on point. Thus, a digest serves as a tool for locating cases on specific questions being researched.

A. West's Key Number Digest System

The most comprehensive and frequently used digests are those published by West. As discussed in Chapter 4, the appellate court decisions in the United States are published in the various West reporters. West developed its digest system to facilitate access to those decisions. An understanding of how the system is organized is helpful when learning how to use it.

West organizes the law into the following main categories: Persons, Property, Contracts, Torts, Crimes, Remedies, and Government. These broad categories are divided into subcategories, and the subcategories are subdivided into more than 400 topics. The list of every digest topic is located at the beginning of every West digest volume. Each topic is listed in alphabetical order in the digest. Each topic is subdivided into subtopics and each subtopic is assigned a number called a *key number* (see Exhibit 5-11). Each subtopic is referred to by both its topic and key number.

For Example

Assault and Battery 7 refers to key number 7 of the topic of "assault and battery"; Constitutional Law 7 refers to key number 7 of the topic of "constitutional law."

To determine the subtopic title of a key number, look to the table of contents of the topic in the digest (see Exhibit 5-11).

For Example

If you want to know the title of the subtopic Assault and Battery 7, you would look up "assault and battery" in the digest, then look to key number 7 and find that key number 7 is "excessive force in doing lawful act." (See Exhibit 5-11.)

Following the topic table of contents is the body of the digest that lists the key number followed by a summary (digest) of all the court opinions that have in some way discussed the topic (see Exhibit 5-12).

For Example

Refer to the scenario at the beginning of the chapter. Assume Dan wants to sue the police officer for shoving him into the car and breaking his teeth when he was arrested for a DUI. To find cases that addressed that topic, you would look to the digest under "assault and battery." In the body of the digest under key number 7, "excessive force in doing a lawful act," is a summary of all the cases that have addressed the topic. (See Exhibit 5-12.)

Every court opinion published in the West's reporters is linked to the digests through the use of headnotes. As you will recall from Chapter 4, **headnotes** are summaries of all the points of law discussed in the opinion. The headnotes follow, in sequential order, the relevant paragraphs of the opinion. Each headnote is assigned a topic and subtopic key number from the West classification system according to the area of law discussed in the case.

For Example

Refer back to Exhibit 4-1. In *Miera v. State Farm Mutual Auto. Ins. Co.*, headnote 1 contains a summary of the point of law discussed in the body of the opinion between [1] and [2]. The topic is Insurance, and the subtopics are key numbers 2668 (Occupancy of Vehicle) and 2670 (Uninsured or Underinsured Motorist Coverage). Headnote 2 is a summary of the point of law discussed in the opinion between [2] and [3], also Insurance and the same key numbers. Headnote 3 is a summary of the law discussed in the opinion between [3] and the end of the opinion, Judgment key number 181 (Grounds for Summary Judgment).

The beauty of the classification system is that the same numbering system is used for all the decisions published by West, essentially all the published federal and state appellate court decisions in the United States. All reported decisions are summarized (provided headnotes) using the same key number classification

26 F P D 5th—508

ASSAULT AND BATTERY

SUBJECTS INCLUDED

Acts of violence towards the person of another, with or without actual touching or striking, not constituting an element in, or attempt to commit, any other specific injury or offense

Justification or excuse for such acts, and circumstances of aggravation

Liabilities and remedies therefor, civil or criminal

SUBJECTS EXCLUDED AND COVERED BY OTHER TOPICS

Death, assault resulting in civil liability, see DEATH

Motor vehicles, assaults by operation of, see AUTOMOBILES

Obstructing process or resisting officer, assaults committed in, see OBSTRUCTING JUSTICE

Other offenses—

Commission of assault with intent to, or in attempt to, perpetrate, see HOMICIDE, RAPE, ROBBERY

Convictions of assault in prosecutions for, see INDICTMENT AND INFORMATION

Unlawful arrest, assaults in connection with, see FALSE IMPRISONMENT

For detailed references to other topics, see Descriptive-Word Index

_____

Analysis

I. CIVIL LIABILITY, ⚷1–46.
   (A) ACTS CONSTITUTING ASSAULT OR BATTERY AND LIABILITY THEREFOR, ⚷1–18.
   (B) ACTIONS, ⚷19–46.

II. CRIMINAL RESPONSIBILITY, ⚷47–100.
   (A) OFFENSES, ⚷47–72.
   (B) PROSECUTION, ⚷73–99.
   (C) SENTENCE AND PUNISHMENT, ⚷100.

_____

I. CIVIL LIABILITY.
   (A) ACTS CONSTITUTING ASSAULT OR BATTERY AND LIABILITY THEREFOR.
      ⚷1. Nature and elements of assault and battery.
       2. _____ In general.
       3. _____ Intent and malice.
       4. _____ Ability to execute intent.
       5. _____ Overt act in general.
       6. _____ Unlawful act.
       7. _____ Excessive force in doing lawful act.

Exhibit 5-11 *Assault and Battery Key Number Outline.* Reprinted from Thomson Reuters, Federal Practice Digest 5th Series, vol. 46 (2013), p. 508. Reprinted with permission of Thomson Reuters.

For references to other topics, see Descriptive-Word Index

or unnecessary, thus defeating the resident's Maryland law battery claim.

> Housley v. Holquist, 879 F.Supp.2d 472, reconsideration denied.

E.D.N.Y. 2007. Under New York law, when an arrest is determined to be unlawful, a claim for assault and battery may arise.

> Cunningham v. U.S., 472 F.Supp.2d 366, opinion corrected.

N.D.Okla. 2012. Arrestee stated claim against police officers for assault under Oklahoma law, where arrestee's complaint alleged that officers seized, handcuffed, and placed arrestee in police car based upon arrest warrant that officers knew was unlawful because it lacked both jurisdiction and probable cause. U.S.C.A. Const.Amend. 4.

> Allen v. Town of Colcord, Okla., 874 F.Supp.2d 1276.

E.D.Pa. 2012. Occupants of residence sufficiently stated a claim against government under Pennsylvania law for assault and battery where they alleged that federal law enforcement agents forcibly entered and searched the residence without a search warrant, intentionally seized, threw to the ground and handcuffed occupant, and detained occupants; however, assault and battery claims were not stated as to those residents who were not at home when the incident took place.

> Muhammad v. U.S., 884 F.Supp.2d 306, issued 2012 WL 3194160.

E.D.Tenn. 2010. City police officers who entered homeowner's residence without warrant for purpose of locating homeowner's son, who lived in residence, and who had been observed driving while intoxicated, did not actually touch or inflict physical injury on homeowner in unlawful manner, and thus officers could not be held liable for assault and battery under Tennessee law.

> Arbuckle v. City of Chattanooga, 696 F.Supp.2d 907.

⚷**7. — Excessive force in doing lawful act.**

C.A.D.C. 2007. An officer's unreasonable use of force that violates the Fourth Amendment also constitutes an assault and battery under District of Columbia law. U.S.C.A. Const. Amend. 4.

> Hundley v. District of Columbia, 494 F.3d 1097, 377 U.S.App.D.C. 451, rehearing en banc denied.

†**C.A.8 (Ark.) 2004.** Under Arkansas law, force used by police officer against mentally ill individual was necessary to make arrest, and thus officer did not commit assault by hitting individual twice with his baton, where shop owner did not want individual in shop, individual refused to go with officer, assumed aggressive stance, and made threatening comments, and individual was retreating further into shop, where customers, including children, were present.

> Rollins v. Smith, 106 Fed.Appx. 513, certiorari denied 125 S.Ct. 1710, 544 U.S. 954, 161 L.Ed.2d 534, rehearing denied, rehearing denied 125 S.Ct. 2538, 545 U.S. 1111, 162 L.Ed.2d 288.

C.A.9 (Cal.) 2012. Drug Enforcement Administration (DEA) agents acted reasonably in forcefully pushing homeowner to ground in executing search warrant for home, and therefore, conduct was not assault and battery under California law; homeowner was refusing to follow agents' commands and search was part of a drug trafficking investigation, which was inherently dangerous. U.S.C.A. Const.Amend. 4.

> Avina v. U.S., 681 F.3d 1127.

C.A.9 (Cal.) 2010. Under California law, a plaintiff bringing a battery claim against a law enforcement official has the burden of proving the officer used unreasonable force.

> Bowoto v. Chevron Corp., 621 F.3d 1116, certiorari denied 132 S.Ct. 1968, 182 L.Ed.2d 818.

C.A.9 (Cal.) 2007. Under California law, police officers who arrested plaintiff for trespassing in a mall, and city, were not immune in arrestee's action alleging assault and battery, negligence, and intentional infliction of emotional distress, where claims arose from an alleged use of excessive force and were not based on acts taking place during an investigation, and officers were acting within the scope of their authority. West's Ann.Cal.Gov.Code §§ 815.2, 820.2, 821.6; West's Ann.Cal.Penal Code § 602(j) (2001).

> Blankenhorn v. City of Orange, 485 F.3d 463.

C.A.11 (Fla.) 2006. Pursuant to Florida law, police officers are entitled to a presumption of good faith in regard to the use of force applied during a lawful arrest, and officers are only liable for damage where the force used is clearly excessive; if an officer uses excessive force, the ordinarily protected use of force is transformed into a battery.

> Davis v. Williams, 451 F.3d 759, rehearing and rehearing denied, on remand 2006 WL 3518605.

†**C.A.5 (La.) 2012.** Whether plaintiff was arrested or detained, police officers had probable cause to either arrest or detain plaintiff and amount of force used by police officers was not excessive, precluding his Louisiana state-law claim against officers for assault and battery. U.S.C.A. Const.Amend. 4.

> Francois v. City of New Roads, 459 Fed. Appx. 475.

†**This Case was not selected for publication in the National Reporter System For cited U.S.C.A. sections and legislative history, see United States Code Annotated**

　Exhibit 5-12　*Body of Digest for Key Number 7,* Assault and Battery—Case Summaries. Reprinted from Thomson Reuters Federal Practice Digest 5th Series, vol. 26 (2013), p. 553. Reprinted with permission of Thomson Reuters.

system, and all cases are linked through the same system to digests that identify all other cases that address the same topic.

For Example

If you are interested in any reported case anywhere in the United States, state or federal, that discusses when a police officer's use of force exceeds that allowed during an arrest, permitting an action for assault or battery, you can refer to any West digest under Assault and Battery key number 7 and find the other cases. Assault and Battery key number 7 is the same in all the headnotes and all the digests.

B. Components of West's Digests

West prepares numerous digests, as discussed in detail in the next section. These digests follow the same format and share several components. Each topic presented in a digest begins with the name of the topic title, such as "Assault and Battery." After each topic title is the following:

- **Subjects included and excluded.** This section lists the areas covered in the topic and the areas not covered. For the subjects excluded, there are references to the topics where the subjects are covered (see Exhibit 5-11).
- **Table of contents.** Next is a table of contents listing the title and key number of all the subtopics (see Exhibit 5-11).
- **Case summaries.** Following the table of contents is the body of the digest that presents a summary by key number of every case reported that has addressed a specific subtopic. The digest presents a summary of only that portion of the case that addressed the specific key number (see Exhibit 5-12).

For Example

In the body of the digest under Assault and Battery key number 7, excessive force in doing lawful act, will be a summary of only that portion of each case which discussed the topic of when a person is liable for an assault or battery (see Exhibit 5-12).

This saves you from having to read a summary of the entire case and allows you to focus on the specific question being researched. If there are no cases that address a key number subtopic, the digest will list an encyclopedia reference where the topic is covered. (See Exhibit 5-12.)

In addition to the components previously listed, each digest set includes the following:

- **Outline of the law and list of topics.** At the beginning of each print digest volume is West's outline of the law and a list of digest topics.
- **Topics covered.** Indicated on the spine are the topics covered in the volume, such as "Gas to Habeas Corpus." This allows you to locate the volume you are looking for without having to look in the book. In addition, inside each volume is a list of topics covered in the volume and the page number where the topic begins, such as "Gas . . . 1" or "Gifts . . . 249."
- **Descriptive word index.** A comprehensive descriptive word index accompanies each set. The index is a multivolume set that lists words or phrases in alphabetical order. Following the word or phrase is a reference to the topic and key number where it is discussed (see Exhibit 5-13).
- **Table of cases.** Each digest has a table of cases listing the cases alphabetically by the names of the plaintiffs. Some digests also have a table of cases listing the cases alphabetically by the name of the defendant followed by the plaintiff's name.
- **Words and phrases.** Most federal and state digests include a table that lists, in alphabetical order, words and phrases that have been interpreted or defined in court opinions and the citation to the opinions.

- **Updates.** Digests are updated through use of the following:
  - **Pocket parts**. Each digest volume is updated through the use of an annual pocket part placed at the back of the volume. The pocket part presents by key number the summaries of new cases that address the key number topic. If there are no new cases for a key number, there will be no reference to the key number.
  - **Supplementary pamphlets**. Supplementary pamphlets with further updates are published between annual pocket parts.
  - **Later cases**. Both the pocket parts and supplementary pamphlets include a "Closing" table that lists the names of all the reporters covered in the digest. If there is a reporter volume subsequent to the last one listed, it must be checked to determine if there are cases published after the ones in the supplement. As mentioned in Chapter 4, there is a key number digest in the back of each reporter volume for the cases presented in the volume.

For Example

If the closing table reads, "Closing with cases reported in 243 F.3d 713," then check the key number digest in the back of any *Federal Reporter, 3d Series* volume subsequent to volume 243, page 713 for later cases.

C. Types of Digests

West publishes several different digests, each of which fulfills a specific need. Each of these digests includes the components discussed in the previous section. A brief description of the digests and their function is presented here.

1. American Digest System

The most comprehensive and inclusive digest is the *American Digest System*. This digest presents summaries of all the reported state and federal court decisions. Due to the large number of cases covered, the digest consists of several multivolume sets, with each set covering a specific time period. The *General Digest* covers five-year periods of time and the *Decennial Digest* covers ten-year periods of time. The sets are not cumulative; therefore, if you want to find all cases for a specific key number, you would need to check the most recent *General Digests* and move backward through the *Decennial Digests*.

For Example

If you want to locate the cases addressing Assault and Battery key number 7, you would have to consult the *General Digest* for cases from 2008 to present, the *Twelfth Decennial Digest* for cases from 2008 to present, the *Eleventh Decennial Digest* (first, second, and third parts) for cases from 1996 to 2007, the *Tenth Decennial Digest* for cases from 1986 to 1996, *Ninth Decennial Digest* for cases from 1976 to 1986, and so on.

The weakness of the digest is its strength, that is, it covers all the cases. You may be interested only in federal cases, cases from your region of the United States, or cases from your state. With the *American Digest*, you may have to wade through a lot of case summaries to find the case you want. Fortunately, West also publishes other, more focused digests.

ARTIFICIAL 97 F P D 4th—240

References are to Digest Topics and Key Numbers

ARTIFICIAL INSEMINATION—Cont'd

INSURANCE, coverage of measures to overcome infertility. See heading **INSURANCE**, MEDICAL insurance.

PARENTAL rights as to children conceived by artificial insemination by donor. See heading **CHILDREN OUT-OF-WEDLOCK**, generally.

PATERNITY proceedings, **Child ⚷1**

PRISONER, right to procreate by use of, **Prisons ⚷4(5)**

ARTIFICIAL PONDS

Generally, **Waters ⚷168**

ACTIONS, **Waters ⚷175–179**

DAMAGES, **Waters ⚷178**

ICE, **Waters ⚷295**

INJUNCTION, **Waters ⚷177**

ARTISANS' LIENS

BAILMENT, bailee's lien, **Bailm ⚷18(.5-5)**

REALTY, liens on. See heading **MECHANICS' LIENS**, generally.

ARTISTS

See also heading **ART**, generally.

FREEDOM of expression. See heading **SPEECH, FREEDOM OF**, generally.

ZONING regulations, accessory use of residence, **Zoning ⚷305**

ASBESTOS

PRODUCTS liability. See heading **PRODUCTS LIABILITY**, ASBESTOS.

ASEXUALIZATION

MENTALLY ill persons, sterilization of, **Mental H ⚷57**

ASPERSIONS

LIBEL and slander. See heading **LIBEL AND SLANDER**, generally.

ASPORTATION

KIDNAPPING, element of offense, **Kidnap ⚷1**

LARCENY element of offense. See heading **LARCENY**, ASPORTATION.

ROBBERY, element of offense, **Rob ⚷10**

ASSASSINATION

See heading **HOMICIDE**, generally.

ASSAULT AND BATTERY

See also heading **CRIMINAL LAW**, generally.

ABILITY to execute intent,
Civil cause of action, element of, **Assault ⚷4**
Criminal offense, element of, **Assault ⚷50**

ACCIDENT, defense of,
Civil liability, **Assault ⚷16**
Criminal responsibility, **Assault ⚷70**
Sufficiency of evidence, **Assault ⚷92(6)**

ACCOMPLICES and accessories, liability of,
Civil liability, **Assault ⚷18**
Criminal responsibility, **Assault 71**

ACTION, civil, in general, **Assault 19–46**

AGGRAVATED assault,
Assault with deadly weapon. See subheading WEAPONS under this heading.
Elements, **Assault ⚷54**
Indictment and information, **Assault ⚷78**
Instructions, **Assault ⚷96(7)**
Sufficiency of evidence, **Assault ⚷92**

AGGRAVATION of damages, **Assault ⚷33**

AIDING or abetting,
Civil liability, **Assault ⚷18**
Criminal responsibility, **Assault ⚷71**

AMUSEMENT places, liability of operator. See heading **THEATERS AND SHOWS**, ASSAULT on patrons.

ANOTHER person, defense of,
Civil liability, **Assault 14**
Criminal responsibility, **Assault 68**

ANSWER in civil proceeding, **Assault ⚷24(2)**

ATTEMPTS,
Criminal offense in general, **Assault ⚷61**
Indictment and information, **Assault ⚷79**

AUTHORITY, exercise of, defense,
Civil liability, **Assault ⚷10**
Criminal responsibility, **Assault ⚷64**

AUTOMOBILE, assault with, **Autos 347, 355(14)**

BILL of particulars, **Ind & Inf ⚷121.2(5)**

BODILY harm, assault with intent to inflict,
Indictment and information, **Assault ⚷78**
Instructions, **Assault ⚷96(9)**

Exhibit 5-13 *Descriptive Word Index.* Reprinted from Thomson Reuters Federal Practice Digest 5th Series, vol. 97 (2014), p. 240. Reprinted with permission of Thomson Reuters.

2. Digests of Federal Court Opinions

West publishes separate digests for decisions of the federal courts:

- **United States Supreme Court Digest.** The *United States Supreme Court Digest* provides a summary of all the decisions of the Supreme Court of the United States. Thus, if your research is focused on Supreme Court decisions that have addressed a specific topic, you could consult this digest to find the cases.
- **Federal Court System.** West publishes several digests that cover the decisions of the United States Supreme Court, the United States Courts of Appeals, and the United States District Courts. Each digest covers a specific time period.

Federal Digest	1754 to 1938
Modern Federal Practice Digest	1939 to 1961
West's Federal Practice Digest 2d	1961 to 1975
West's Federal Practice Digest 3d	1975 to 1983
West's Federal Practice Digest 4th	1983 to present*
West's Federal Practice Digest 5th	2003 to present

Note: The *Federal Practice Digest 5th* began to be issued in 2013. The new series is being issued alphabetically over the course of five years. Therefore the *Federal Practice 4th* is updated by pocket parts until the entire *Federal Practice 5th* is available. In addition, there are cumulative softbound updates issued monthly that update the *Federal Practice Digest 4th and 5th*.

The digest summaries of the Supreme Court cases are listed first, then the Court of Appeals cases, followed by the United States District Courts cases and other federal court cases. There are also specialized federal digests that cover the decisions of other specific federal courts, such as *West's Bankruptcy Digest*, *West's Federal Claims Digest*, and *West's Circuit Patent Case Digest*.

3. Regional Digests

West publishes digests for four of the regional reporters:

Atlantic Digest for cases reported in the *Atlantic Reporter*
North Western Digest for cases reported in the *North Western Reporter*
Pacific Digest for cases reported in the *Pacific Reporter*
South Eastern Digest for cases reported in the *South Eastern Reporter*

Each **regional digest** includes summaries of the cases presented in the reporter organized by state. Within the contents for each state, the summaries for the state highest court are listed first, the intermediate appellate courts next, and any other courts of the state last.

For Example

Suppose that you want to locate the cases addressing Assault and Battery key number 7 in the *Pacific Digest*. The digest summaries of the cases from Arizona will be presented together, the digest summaries of the cases from California will be presented together, and so on.

Notice there is not a current digest for the *North Eastern Reporter*, *South Western Reporter*, or the *Southern Reporter*. To locate cases covered by those reporters, consult a state specific reporter or the *American Digests*.

4. State Digests

West publishes 46 state digests and a digest for the District of Columbia. No state digests are published for Delaware, Nevada, and Utah. The Delaware decisions are included in the *Atlantic Digest*, and the Nevada and Utah decisions are included in the *Pacific Digest*. The decisions from Delaware, Nevada, and Utah, along with those from all the other states, are included in the *American Digest System*. The *Dakota Digest* includes both North and South Dakota. The *Virginia and West Virginia Digest* includes both Virginia and West Virginia.

The state digests usually include the reported state court decisions, as well as federal court decisions, arising in the state. Like the federal digest and the regional digests, the state digests list case summaries from federal courts first, then the state courts from highest court to lowest court within the state.

D. Research Using Digests

1. Use as a Research Tool

Digests are used to locate case law that addresses a specific point(s) of law. You can use digests in two situations:

- You know the name of a case that addresses the point of law being researched and are looking for other cases that address the same point.

For Example

The question being researched is the same as that raised in *Miera v. State Farm Mutual Auto. Ins. Co.*, that is, "When is the passenger occupying a vehicle for purposes of uninsured motorist coverage?" (See Exhibit 4-1.) This question is identified in the case headnotes as being covered under the topic Insurance key number 2668. You are familiar with the *Miera* case, but the client's facts are somewhat different from those in *Miera*. Checking Insurance key number 2668 in a digest will lead you to all the other cases that address the question. A scan of the case summaries may lead to a case that is factually closer to your client's facts, a case that is on point.

- You do not know of any cases that address the point of law being researched. In most instances, a researcher has identified the question being researched, but needs to locate court opinions that address the topic.

2. Research Techniques

The starting point for conducting digest research is to locate the correct digest set. Refer to the types of digests discussed previously and select the appropriate digest. If you are looking for federal cases, consult a federal digest. If you are looking for cases from a particular state, use the state court digest for that state. For state cases from a particular region, such as the western part of the United States, check the regional digest such as the *Pacific Digest*. If no state or regional digest is available, refer to the *American Digest*.

After selecting a digest, you may use several techniques to locate specific cases.

a. Case Headnotes

If you already know of a case related to the issue being researched, refer to the topic and key number of the relevant headnote from the case and consult that topic and key number in the digest. By going directly to the key number, you avoid other research steps, such as having to refer to the index.

For Example

You are researching the issue of whether a person was occupying a vehicle for purposes of uninsured motorist coverage. You are familiar with *Miera v. State Farm Mutual Auto. Ins. Co.*, but the client's facts are quite different. Even though *Miera* is not on point, the case headnote, Insurance key number 2668, will lead you directly to the cases that have addressed the topic.

This is by far the quickest way to locate other cases. Therefore, it is helpful if you know of a related case when you begin. This is why it is important when conducting statutory research to consult the case summaries in the annotations to the statute. Although there may not be a case directly on point, there may be a related case summarized in the annotations that will provide the digest key number for the point of law being researched.

b. Descriptive Word Index

If you are unaware of a specific case, think of all the areas of law or words and phrases that may be related to the topic being researched and consult the index. The index will refer you to the digest topic and key number.

For Example

The question involves the firing of a person because of age. You may look under several index topics, such as "age," "discrimination," "civil rights," or "employment" (see Exhibit 5-13). Identification of search terms is discussed in Chapter 2.

c. Topic Outline

If you know the topic that covers the issue, go directly to the topic in the digest and review the topic outline of all the key numbers under the topic. By scanning the outline, you can identify the relevant key numbers and review the relevant cases in the digest.

d. Table of Cases

If you know the name of a case but do not know the citation, consult the table of cases. The table lists the cases alphabetically, provides the citations, and includes the topic and key numbers for the digest entries.

e. Reference from Other Sources

Often, you may be directed to a specific digest topic and key number from another source, such as an *ALR* citation, encyclopedia cite, or an article. In such cases, you could go directly to the volume and section cited. If researching online using a commercial website such as Westlaw, you can hyperlink to the key number.

f. Update

When using print digests, always consult the pocket part and supplement to update your research and to locate the most recent cases.

3. Computer-Aided Research

The digests are not available on non-fee-based Internet sites. Because digests are published by West, Westlaw has a Key Number database that has most of the components of the digests discussed earlier, and that can be searched using most of the techniques discussed thus far. LexisNexis, however, does not have the key number database because the key numbering system belongs to West. Searching Westlaw using the Key Numbers database, and searching for cases in LexisNexis, will be discussed in greater detail in Chapter 8.

Searching online for cases in non-fee-based Internet sources will be discussed in Chapter 7.

VI. UPDATING AND VALIDATING RESEARCH

When you locate primary authority that provides an answer to a question being researched, it is necessary to determine if the authority has been reversed or modified by a subsequent law or court decision. That is, you must determine if the authority is still valid, if it is still "good law." Failure to update and validate research is a serious ethical violation.

The first step to ensuring an authority is "good law" is to use a *citator*. The two most common citators are *Shepard's Citations*, in print or online (Lexis), and Westlaw's *KeyCite*. Traditionally, only *Shepard's Citations* in print was available for validating primary authority. Today, due to cost and the ease of updating and validating law electronically, few law libraries or law offices maintain *Shepard's* in print. Moreover, Westlaw has also developed a citator service called *KeyCite*. The process of consulting a *Shepard's* source to determine the current validity of an authority is called **Shepardizing**. You Shepardize a case or statute when you check it in *Shepard's Citations*. However, today that term is used whether you are using *Shepard's* or Westlaw's *KeyCite*.

A. Using *Shepard's* in Print

Shepard's Citations is a set of books that consist of citations to legal authorities, such as a court opinion, followed by a list of citations to cases and other authorities that discuss, analyze, or in some way affect the legal authority. *Shepard's* will not only tell you whether a case or other authority has been reversed, modified, or overruled, but will also refer you to any other case or authority that has discussed the case. Although it is increasingly common to validate research electronically using *Shepard's* online, understanding the layout and functionality of *Shepard's* in print enhances understanding of online updating. In the front of each volume, you will find instructions on how to use *Shepard's*. Because a researcher more frequently uses *Shepard's* for updating case research, the process of using *Shepard's* in that context is discussed in detail here.

A *Shepard's* citator page is covered with numbers and may look incomprehensible at first glance. After you understand the format and components, however, a citator is easy to use. There are various types of *Shepard's* citators and they all share the same basic format and components. The various types of *Shepard's* citators and their common components are discussed here.

1. Shepard's *Case Law Citators*

Shepard's publishes a set of citators for each case reporter. Usually, the citators are located next to the case reporters in the law library. Some of the citators and the courts they cover are as follows:

- United States Supreme Court cases—*Shepard's United States Citations*
- Lower federal courts, that is, cases from the *Federal Reporter, Federal Supplement, Federal Rules Decisions, Court of Claims Reports*, and *United States Claims Court Reporter*—*Shepard's Federal Citations*
- State court decisions. There is a separate set of *Shepard's* covering the decisions of each state and Puerto Rico. In addition, there is a set of *Shepard's* for each of the regional reporters.

For Example

The cases published in the *Arizona Reports* are covered in *Shepard's Arizona Citations*. The cases published in the *Pacific Reporter* are covered in *Shepard's Pacific Reporter Citations*.

An advantage of a state citator is that it will direct you to more research sources, such as law review articles and Attorney General opinions. A disadvantage of a state citator is that while it includes citations to cases from courts in the particular state—state and federal courts—it does not include citations from courts in other states.

Case law citators share the following features:

- **Abbreviations—analysis and introductory material.** At the front of the citator is a table of abbreviations page that identifies all of the abbreviations used in the citator (see Exhibit 5-14). Following this page are instructions on how to use the citator. These instructions usually include an illustration interpreting a sample citation. If you need guidance on how to use the citator, these pages are invaluable.
- **Case location.** The reporter volume number is printed in the upper right or left corner of each page of the citator (see Exhibit 5-15). The case page number is printed in bold on the page (e.g., —**1055**—). The name of the case and year follow the page number (see Exhibit 5-15).

HISTORY AND TREATMENT ABBREVIATIONS

Abbreviations have been assigned, where applicable, to each citing case to indicate the effect the citing case had on the case you are Shepardizing. The resulting "history" (affirmed, reversed, modified, etc.) or "treatment" (followed, criticized, explained, etc.) of the case you are Shepardizing is indicated by abbreviations preceding the citing case reference. For example, the reference "f434F2d872" means that there is language on page 872 of volume 434 of the *Federal Reporter,* Second Series, that indicates the court is "following" the case you are Shepardizing. Instances in which the citing reference occurs in a dissenting opinion are indicated in the same manner. The abbreviations used to reflect both history and treatment are as follows.

History of Case

a	(affirmed)	The decision in the case you are Shepardizing was affirmed or adhered to on appeal.
cc	(connected case)	Identifies a different case from the case you are Shepardizing, but one rising out of the same subject matter or in some manner intimately connected therewith.
D	(dismissed)	An appeal from the case you are Shepardizing was dismissed.
m	(modified)	The decision in the case you are Shepardizing was changed in some way.
p	(parallel)	The citing case is substantially alike or on all fours, either in law or facts, with the case you are Shepardizing.
r	(reversed)	The decision in the case you are Shepardizing was reversed on appeal.
s	(same case)	The case you are Shepardizing involves the same litigation as the citing case, although at a different stage in the proceedings.
S	(superseded)	The citing case decision has been substituted for the decision in the case you are Shepardizing.
US cert den		Certiorari was denied by the U.S. Supreme Court.
US cert dis		Certiorari was dimissed by the U.S. Supreme Court.
US cert gran		Certiorari was granted by the U.S. Supreme Court.
US reh den		Rehearing was denied by the U.S. Supreme Court.
US reh dis		Rehearing was dismissed by the U.S. Supreme Court.
v	(vacated)	The decision in the case you are Shepardizing has been vacated.

Treatment of Case

c	(criticized)	The citing case disagrees with the reasoning/decision of the case you are Shepardizing.
d	(distinguished)	The citing case is different either in law or fact, for reasons given, from the case you are Shepardizing.
e	(explained)	The case you are Shepardizing is interpreted in some significant way. Not merely a restatement of facts.
Ex	(Examiner's decision)	The case you are Shepardizing was cited in an Administrative Agency Examiner's Decision.
f	(followed)	The citing case refers to the case you are Shepardizing as controlling authority.
h	(harmonized)	An apparent inconsistency between the citing case and the case you are Shepardizing is explained and shown not to exist.
j	(dissenting opinion)	The case is cited in a dissenting opinion.
L	(limited)	The citing case refuses to extend the holding of the case you are Shepardizing beyond the precise issues involved.
o	(overruled)	The ruling in the case you are Shepardizing is expressly overruled.
q	(questioned)	The citing case questions the continuing validity or precedential value of the case you are Shepardizing.

Exhibit 5-14 Abbreviations for Case History and Treatment. LexisNexis, Shepard's Federal Citations, 8th Ed., Vol. 15 (1995), inside cover of text. Reprinted with the permission of LexisNexis.

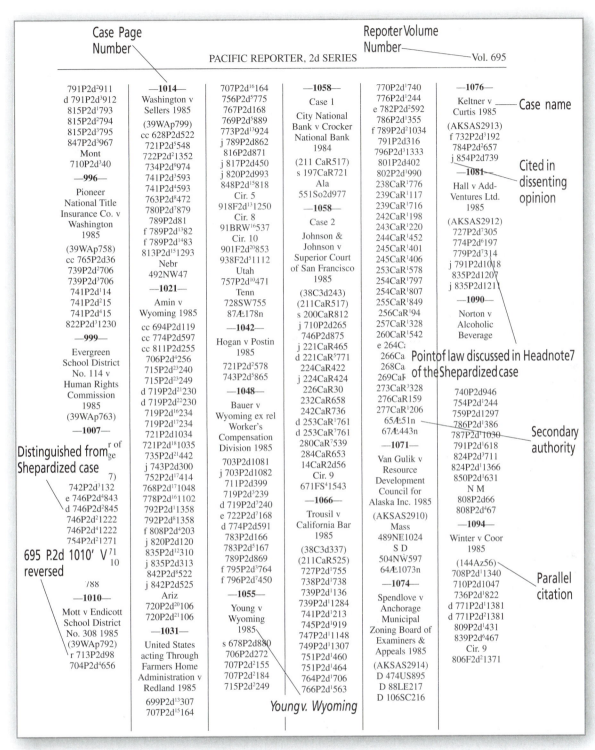

Case Page Number

Reporter Volume Number ——— Vol. 695

PACIFIC REPORTER, 2d SERIES

791P2d²911
d 791P2d³912
815P2d¹793
815P2d²794
815P2d³795
847P2d³967
Mont
710P2d³40
—996—
Pioneer
National Title
Insurance Co. v
Washington
1985
(39WAp758)
cc 765P2d36
739P2d²706
739P2d³706
741P2d¹14
741P2d²15
741P2d¹15
822P2d³1230
—999—
Evergreen
School District
No. 114 v
Human Rights
Commission
1985
(39WAp763)
—1007—

Distinguished from^(r of) Shepardized case ^(7)

742P2d³132
e 746P2d⁴843
d 746P2d⁵845
746P2d²1222
746P2d⁴1222
754P2d²1271

695 P.2d 1010' V ^(71)_(10) reversed

^(788)
—1010—
Mott v Endicott
School District
No. 308 1985
(39WAp792)
r 713P2d98
704P2d⁴656

—1014—
Washington v
Sellers 1985
(39WAp799)
cc 628P2d522
721P2d⁵548
722P2d¹1352
734P2d⁹974
741P2d³593
741P2d⁴593
763P2d⁸472
780P2d⁷879
789P2d81
f 789P2d¹³82
f 789P2d¹⁴83
813P2d¹⁵1293
Nebr
492NW47
—1021—
Amin v
Wyoming 1985
cc 694P2d119
cc 774P2d597
cc 811P2d255
706P2d⁴256
715P2d²³240
715P2d²³249
d 719P2d²¹230
d 719P2d²²230
719P2d¹⁶234
719P2d¹⁷234
721P2d1034
721P2d¹⁸1035
735P2d²¹442
j 743P2d300
752P2d¹⁷414
768P2d¹⁷1048
778P2d¹⁶1102
792P2d¹1358
792P2d⁸1358
f 808P2d⁴203
j 820P2d120
835P2d¹²310
j 835P2d313
842P2d⁸522
j 842P2d525
Ariz
720P2d²⁰106
720P2d²¹106
—1031—
United States
acting Through
Farmers Home
Administration v
Redland 1985
699P2d¹³307
707P2d¹⁵164

707P2d¹⁶164
756P2d⁵775
767P2d168
769P2d⁵889
773P2d¹³924
j 789P2d862
816P2d871
j 817P2d450
j 820P2d993
848P2d¹⁵818
Cir. 5
918F2d¹³1250
Cir. 8
91BRW¹⁶537
Cir. 10
901F2d²⁰853
938F2d⁵1112
Utah
757P2d¹⁰471
Tenn
728SW755
87Æ178n
—1042—
Hogan v Postin
1985
721P2d²578
743P2d⁵865
—1048—
Bauer v
Wyoming ex rel
Worker's
Compensation
Division 1985
703P2d1081
j 703P2d1082
711P2d399
719P2d³239
d 719P2d⁷240
e 722P2d⁷168
d 774P2d591
783P2d166
783P2d⁵167
789P2d869
f 795P2d³764
f 796P2d⁷450
—1055—
Young v
Wyoming
1985
s 678P2d880
706P2d272
707P2d²155
707P2d²184
715P2d²249

Young v. Wyoming

—1058—
Case 1
City National
Bank v Crocker
National Bank
1984
(211 CaR517)
s 197CaR721
Ala
551So2d977
—1058—
Case 2
Johnson &
Johnson v
Superior Court
of San Francisco
1985
(38C3d243)
(211CaR517)
s 200CaR812
j 710P2d265
746P2d875
j 221CaR465
d 221CaR⁵771
224CaR422
j 224CaR424
226CaR30
232CaR658
242CaR736
d 253CaR¹761
d 253CaR⁷761
280CaR⁷539
284CaR653
14CaR2d56
Cir. 9
671FS⁴1543
—1066—
Trousil v
California Bar
1985
(38C3d337)
(211CaR525)
727P2d¹755
738P2d¹738
739P2d¹136
739P2d¹1284
741P2d¹213
745P2d¹919
747P2d¹1148
749P2d¹1307
751P2d¹460
751P2d¹464
764P2d¹706
766P2d¹563

770P2d¹740
776P2d¹244
e 782P2d²592
786P2d¹355
f 789P2d¹1034
791P2d316
796P2d³1333
801P2d402
802P2d¹990
238CaR¹776
239CaR¹117
239CaR¹716
242CaR¹198
243CaR¹220
244CaR¹452
245CaR¹401
245CaR¹406
253CaR¹578
254CaR¹797
254CaR¹807
255CaR¹849
256CaR¹94
257CaR¹328
260CaR¹542
e 264C.
266Ca
268Ca
269CaF
273CaR³328
276CaR159
277CaR¹206
65Æ51n
67Æ443n
—1071—
Van Gulik v
Resource
Development
Council for
Alaska Inc. 1985
(AKSAS2910)
Mass
489NE1024
S D
504NW597
64Æ1073n
—1074—
Spendlove v
Anchorage
Municipal
Zoning Board of
Examiners &
Appeals 1985
(AKSAS2914)
D 474US895
D 88LE217
D 106SC216

—1076—
Keltner v
Curtis 1985
(AKSAS2913)
f 732P2d³192
784P2d²657
j 854P2d739
—1081—
Hall v Add-
Ventures Ltd.
1985
(AKSAS2912)
727P2d⁷305
774P2d⁶197
779P2d⁷314
j 791P2d10l8
835P2d120⁷
j 835P2d12l1
—1090—
Norton v
Alcoholic
Beverage

740P2d946
754P2d¹244
759P2d1297
786P2d¹386
787P2d¹1030
791P2d¹618
824P2d³711
824P2d¹1366
850P2d¹631
N M
808P2d66
808P2d⁴67
—1094—
Winter v Coor
1985
(144Az56)
708P2d¹1340
710P2d1047
736P2d¹822
d 771P2d¹1381
d 771P2d²1381
809P2d¹431
839P2d⁶467
Cir. 9
806F2d²1371

Case name

Cited in dissenting opinion

Point of law discussed in Headnote 7 of the Shepardized case

Secondary authority

Parallel citation

Exhibit 5-15 Case Citation Page from the *Shepard's Pacific Reporter Citations.* LexisNexis, Shepard's Pacific Reporter Citations, 1994 Bound Volume, Vol. 2, p. 13. Reprinted with the permission of LexisNexis.

For Example

You are looking for the citations to *Young v. Wyoming*, 695 P.2d 1055 (Wyo. 1985). You would look to the *Shepard's Pacific Reporter Citations*, locate the page with volume 695 at the top of the page, then look for —1055— (see Exhibit 5-15).

- **Parallel citations.** Immediately following the case name and year are the parallel citations (if any) in parentheses (see bottom right of Exhibit 5-15). When a case is printed in more than one reporter, the citation to each reporter is called a parallel citation, for example: *Winter v. Coor*, 695 P.2d 1094, 144 Ariz, 56 (1985). The parallel citations are included in the first *Shepard's* volume published after the parallel citation is available. They are not included in the supplements. If the state court opinions are only published in the regional reporter, no parallel citation is listed.
- **History of the case.** Following the parallel citation are citations to cases that involve the same case. This is the most important section of the case citations, because any subsequent decision dismissing, modifying, or reversing the Shepardized case will be indicated here. A letter before the citation will indicate the action taken.

For Example

Refer to the citations following 695 P.2d 1010 in Exhibit 5-15 (*Mott v. Endicott School District*). The citation reference "r 713P2d98" means that the case at 695 P.2d 1010 was reversed by the decision found at 713 P.2d 98.

As discussed previously, the list of what the *r* and other abbreviations represent is presented in the abbreviations page at the front of the citator.

- **Later case treatment.** Following the history of the case are citations to every other case that has mentioned the cited case and references to secondary authorities that cite the case. The cases are arranged in chronological order with the earlier cases mentioned first. The case citation is to the page in the case where the Shepardized case is discussed. Thus, if a case citation is to "746 P.2d 875," 875 is the page in the case where the Shepardized case is discussed, rather than the beginning page of the case. The case citations include treatment codes that indicate how the Shepardized case was treated in the cited case. These treatment code abbreviations are presented in the abbreviations page at the front of the citator. (See Exhibit 5-14.)

For Example

There are several citations following 695 P.2d 1048 (see Exhibit 5-15) which show different ways the case was treated by subsequent courts: in "j 703P2d1082," the treatment code *j* means the Shepardized case (695 P.2d 1048) was cited in the dissenting opinion in 703 P.2d at page 1082; in "d 774P2d591," the *d* means that the court distinguished the case from the Shepardized case in 774 P.2d at page 591.

In addition to the treatment codes, the citations include references to specific points of law discussed in the Shepardized case that are also addressed in the cited case. This is accomplished through the use of small, raised-numeral references following the reporter abbreviation in the citation. These numbers correspond to the headnote number of the Shepardized case. These reference numbers are invaluable during research because they allow you to compare the treatment of a specific point of law in both cases. If there is no raised number in a citation, then the case discusses the Shepardized case in general or does not summarize a point of law from the case.

For Example

The case being Shepardized appears at 695 P.2d 1081. One of the case citations is "779P2d⁷314." The raised 7 means that the point of law discussed in headnote 7 of the Shepardized case (695 P.2d 1081) is discussed in 779 P.2d at page 314 (see Exhibit 5-15).

- **Secondary sources.** Following the case citations are references to secondary sources, such as *ALR* annotations, that in some way reference the Shepardized case (see Exhibit 5-15).

2. Shepard's *Statutory, Constitutional, and Other Enacted Law Citators*

Just as you must Shepardize case law to determine if it is "good law," you must also Shepardize statutory and constitutional provisions, administrative regulations, and court rules. This is particularly important if you have located one of these sources of law using a non-fee-based Internet resource, as most non-fee-based Internet research sources do not provide information on currentness of the content. *Shepard's* publishes various citators that allow you to Shepardize these types of laws to determine their history, current status, and how the courts have interpreted them. Some of these citators are:

- **Statutory, constitutional, and court rules.** The *Shepard's* citator for a state's statutes is either included with the *Shepard's* state case citator or published as a separate volume. Citations to state constitutions and state court rules are included with the *Shepard's* citations to the state statutes. *Shepard's Federal Statute Citations* covers the federal statutes and includes the citations to the United States Constitution and federal court rules.
- **Federal and state regulations.** You may Shepardize the regulations of the federal agencies published in the *Code of Federal Regulations* by using *Shepard's Code of Federal Regulations Citations*. Some state administrative agency regulations citations are included in the *Shepard's* state citations. *Shepard's* citators to enacted law are similar to the case law citators in many respects.
- **Abbreviations—analysis and introductory material.** At the front of the citator is a table of abbreviations page that identifies all of the abbreviations used in the citator. Following this page are instructions on how to use the citator.
- **Statute location.** Printed in the upper corner of each page of the citatory is the statute title, volume, or chapter number. As discussed in Chapter 3, statutory or code numbering systems vary from state to state. When more than one title is covered on a page, the title number is usually included in a box. The separate section numbers are printed in bold.
- **History.** The first entries under a section indicate any legislative action taken that affects the statute.

For Example

If the statute you are Shepardizing has been amended, an *A* followed by the citation to the amendment will be presented.

- **Case treatment.** After the history of the statute are citations to cases that have mentioned the statute. Preceding the case citations are treatment codes that indicate how the statute was treated in the cited case. If there is no letter preceding the citation, then the case merely discusses the statute generally.

For Example

A *C* preceding a case citation indicates the statute was held constitutional.

- **Secondary sources.** Following the case citations are references to secondary sources, such as *ALR* annotations, that in some way reference the statute.

3. *Updating* Shepard's Citations *in Print*

Most sets of *Shepard's Citations* consist of one or more hardbound volumes accompanied by one or more supplement pamphlets. For most citators, advance sheets are published approximately every six weeks. The pamphlets and advance sheets update the hardbound volumes. To update between the latest advance sheet and the present date, contact *Shepard's* Daily Update Service (1-800-899-6000). On the cover of each pamphlet is a "what your library should contain" section listing all the hardbound volumes and supplements for the set. Check this list to ensure that your research is complete. If one of the *Shepard's* is missing, check with the librarian.

B. Computerized Updating Using *Shepard's* Online

Traditionally, the only way to update and validate your research was through *Shepard's Citations* in print. Computerized updating is faster and more efficient, and eliminates the need to know what books from each *Shepard's* set are required. Computerized updating and validating is more up-to-date because electronic references are available much more quickly than those in print. In addition, law libraries or law professionals with a subscription to Lexis have *Shepard's* online, obviating the need for the print versions and saving space and money. In addition, often for small price, those with existing subscriptions to Lexis can download a mobile application allowing access to *Shepard's* and the LexisNexis databases on a tablet or smartphone. Significantly, computerized updating with *Shepard's* online eliminates the need to learn or refer to the list of abbreviations for case treatments, case history, and other references. The online service presents treatment of cases, case history, and the like using regular terminology rather than the abbreviations used in the *Shepard's* print versions (see Exhibit 5-16).

As noted earlier in this section, *Shepard's* can be used for updating cases, statutes, constitutional law, rules, and administrative regulations. The techniques below focus on using *Shepard's* to update case law, but the same techniques apply when updating any other source of primary law.

1. *How to Use* Shepard's *Online*

At the time of the writing of this text, Lexis Advance was the latest version of LexisNexis used by most legal professionals. However, in some law libraries and public libraries where print *Shepard's* is not available, public access to *Shepard's Online* is provided through Lexis Academic. These two different web platforms for Lexis provide the same results when Shepardizing the law; however, the look of the screens presenting the results are different. In addition, it is increasingly common that websites often change their user interface, making it highly likely that if this text provided specific and detailed step-by-step instruction and step-by-step screenshots, the content would quickly be outdated.

Regardless of the look of *Shepard's Online* or which platform you use to access it, the results are the same. In addition, the various websites require the same types of steps to Shepardize. As such, the content below will speak in general terms that should allow any new researcher to use *Shepard's Online* with ease.

- If you are using LexisNexis to do case research and you are viewing a case on the screen, there will be a link using terms such as "Shepardize" or "Shepardize this document." There may also be a *Shepard's* signal (discussed shortly) such as a red circle or yellow triangle that is a hyperlink to the full *Shepard's* report. Click either type of link and you will be taken to the full *Shepard's* report.

For Example

You are viewing *State v. Sims*, 2010-NMSC-027, 148 N.M. 330, 236 P.2d 642, in LexisAdvance. Click on either the *Shepard's* signal next to the case caption, or the "Shepardize this document" link in the *Shepard's* preview to the right of the case. A separate screen will open, displaying all of the Shepardized results (see Exhibit 5-16). Here, there is no negative subsequent appellate history, and several other citing references, both other cases and secondary sources (see Exhibit 5-16).

- If you have the citation of a case that you want to Shepardize, log on to Lexis (in whatever platform to which you have access) and type your citation (148 N.M. 330 in Lexis Academic; shep: 148 N.M. 330 in Lexis Advance) in the blank field provided then click the appropriate button to initiate the search. The full *Shepard's* report will be provided (see Exhibits 5-16 and 5-17).

For Example

You want to Shepardize a case to see what other cases have cited it and whether it is still good law. Log in to Lexis Advance and enter shep: 148 N.M. 330 then click "Enter." The full *Shepard's* report will be opened (see Exhibit 5-16).

2. Characteristics of Shepard's *Online*

- The full *Shepard's* report has four components: appellate history, citing decisions, other citing sources, and a table of authorities. The appellate history indicates if there was subsequent appellate history and provides prior history of the case. Citing cases are grouped by positive versus negative treatment. Other citing sources are separated by type of source, such as law reviews, statutes, or treatises. The table of authorities is a list of all the primary law cited within the Shepardized case.
- *Shepard's* Summary—provides an overview of the entire report at a glance. You can quickly see the signal indicator of whether the law is still valid and a listing of the number of references that have positive, negative, and neutral analysis, as well as other citing references. If you click any of the items, you will be taken to the first item in that portion of the report (see the gray areas of Exhibit 5-16 and Exhibit 5-17).
- *Shepard's* Alerts—allows you to set regularly scheduled updates for certain laws. If you set an alert, you will be emailed on the schedule you choose as to whether there has been a change in the validity of the law. This is particularly helpful when you are using a case from an intermediate appellate court that you know still faces review by the highest court.
- Customization—There are numerous ways to customize the report. There are several ways to filter the results of the full *Shepard's* report, such as by depth of treatment, jurisdiction, or headnotes. There is a tutorial link that will guide you through the use of each of the methods of customization.
- Table of Authorities—analyzes the cases cited by a case upon which you are relying. The Table of Authorities feature not only shows the cases your case relied upon, but also the status of those cases. This allows you to discover if the foundation upon which your case rests is weakened in any way, which ultimately may weaken your case.
- Graphical Display—Lexis Advance provides a graphical view of the history of the authority you are Shepardizing. This is particularly helpful if cases have been subject to multiple appeals.

3. Shepard's *Signals*

- **Red Circle.** Warns there is significant negative history or treatment, such as reversal of the case on at least one point of law.
- **Yellow Triangle.** Warns of some negative history or treatment, such as being distinguished from another case (see Exhibit 5-16).
- **Plus symbol (+) in Green Diamond.** Reveals positive history, such as being followed by another case.
- **Letter "Q" in Orange Square.** Warns the validity of the case has been questioned by another jurisdiction.
- **Letter "A" in Blue Circle.** Reveals the case has been analyzed by another case in a neutral manner.
- **Letter "I" in Blue Circle.** Indicates other sources have referred to your case.
- **Red Exclamation Point.** Warns there is a case that negatively interprets a statute.

State v. Sims, 2010 -NMSC- 027, 148 N.M. 330, 236 P.3d 642, 2010 N.M. LEXIS 304, 93 A.L.R.6th 647 (N.M. 2010)

SHEPARD'S Signal(TM): ▲ *Caution: Possible negative treatment*

Restrictions: *Unrestricted*

FOCUS(TM) Terms: *No FOCUS terms*

Print Format: *FULL*

Citing Ref. Signal: *Hidden*

SHEPARD'S SUMMARY

Unrestricted *Shepard's* Summary

No negative subsequent appellate history.

Citing References:

▲ Cautionary Analyses:	**Distinguished (4)**
Positive Analyses:	Followed (8)
Neutral Analyses:	Explained (2)
Other Sources:	Law Reviews (1), Statutes (2), Treatises (6)

LexisNexis Headnotes:	HN1 (18), HN2 (6), HN3 (1), HN4 (19), HN5 (21), HN6 (22), HN7 (15), HN8 (1), HN9 (11)

PRIOR HISTORY (3 citing references)

1. *State v. Sims*, 2008-NMCA-017, 143 N.M. 400, 176 P.3d 1132, 2007 N.M. App. LEXIS 155 (N.M. Ct. App. 2007)

2. **Writ of certiorari granted:**
    State v. Sims, 143 N.M. 399, 176 P.3d 1131, 2008 N.M. LEXIS 39 (N.M. 2008)

3. **Writ of certiorari granted:**
    State v. Sims, 2009 N.M. LEXIS 770 (N.M. Nov. 10, 2009)

    Reversed by (CITATION YOU ENTERED):
    State v. Sims, 2010 -NMSC- 027, 148 N.M. 330, 236 P.3d 642, 2010 N.M. LEXIS 304, 93 A.L.R.6th 647 (N.M. 2010)

SUBSEQUENT APPELLATE HISTORY (1 citing reference)

4. **Later proceeding at:**
    State v. Sims, 2010 N.M. LEXIS 305 (N.M. June 8, 2010)

CITING DECISIONS (27 citing decisions)

NEW MEXICO SUPREME COURT

5. **Cited by:**
    Schuster v. State Dep't of Taxation & Revenue, Motor Vehicle Div., 2012 -NMSC- 025, 283 P.3d 288, 2012 N.M. LEXIS 317 (N.M. 2012) LexisNexis Headnotes HN1, HN4, HN5, HN6

    2012 -NMSC- 025 *p.6*

    283 P.3d 288 *p.292*

Exhibit 5-16 Shepard's Report for *State v. Sims*, 2010 -NMSC- 027, 148 N.M. 330 from Lexis Academic. Reprinted with permission of LexisNexis.

6.   **Followed by, Explained by:**

State v. Mailman, 2010 -NMSC- 036, 148 N.M. 702, 242 P.3d 269, 2010 N.M. LEXIS 369, 95 A.L.R.6th 709 (N.M. 2010)

Followed by:

2010 -NMSC- 036

148 N.M. 702 *p.703*

242 P.3d 269 *p.270*

Explained by:

2010 -NMSC- 036

148 N.M. 702 *p.705*

242 P.3d 269 *p.272*

7.   **Cited by:**

City of Santa Fe v. Martinez, 2010 -NMSC- 033, 148 N.M. 708, 242 P.3d 275, 2010 N.M. LEXIS 368 (N.M. 2010)

2010 -NMSC- 033

148 N.M. 708 *p.711*

242 P.3d 275 *p.278*

Exhibit 5-16   *(Continued)*

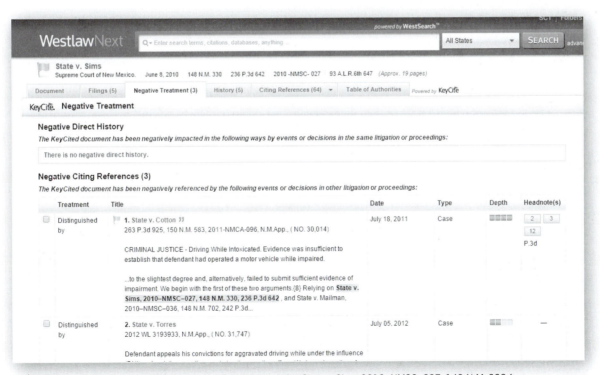

Exhibit 5-17   Screenshot of *KeyCite* Negative Treatment tab for *State v. Sims*, 2010 -NMSC- 027, 148 N.M. 330 from *WestlawNext*. Reprinted with permissions of Thomson Reuters.

C. Other Lexis Validation Products

There are several other tools that complement *Shepard's* service. They include:

- **BriefCheck.** This is a separate software program which will scan your document (memorandum, brief, etc.) and automatically collect citations from it. Each authority in your document is Shepardized, and results can be either displayed on the screen or printed out in a separate document.
- *Shepard's* **Link.** This is another software application which identifies citations in a document. This tool adds *Shepard's* signals so that you can see if there is any weak authority in your document.
- **Best Authority.** Lexis partnered with Levit & James to create a tool that will create a table of authorities for your document. Best Authority replaced Lexis' Full Authority. This is an alternative to manually creating a table of authorities using a word processing program.

D. Using Westlaw's *KeyCite*

1. How to KeyCite Cases

KeyCite is Westlaw's online citator. When using WestlawNext, you will use *KeyCite* to validate and update your research. *KeyCite* is obviously a different citator than *Shepard's*, but you will find they are similar in the ways they are most often used. One major difference between the two is *KeyCite* only reports negative treatment of the law you are validating while *Shepard's* reports both positive and negative treatment. Because a researcher more frequently KeyCites case citations, the process of KeyCiting in that context is discussed here.

- If you are using WestlawNext to do a search and you are viewing a case on the screen, click on any of the *KeyCite* tabs: Negative Treatment, Citing References, or History to see the *KeyCite* results.

For Example

You do a search for cases in New Mexico involving whether a person was in actual physical control of a vehicle for purposes of being convicted of driving while intoxicated. Your results lead you to *State v. Sims*, 2010-NMSC-027, 148 N.M. 330, 236 P.3d 642. The *KeyCite* tabs are visible just above the case. Choose Negative Treatment to see there is no negative subsequent appellate history and several cases that contain negative treatment of the case (see Exhibit 5-17).

- If you have the citation of a case that you want to KeyCite, log on to WestlawNext and type kc: 148 N.M. 330 into the West search box then click "Enter." The case will be opened and you will be able to click on any of the *KeyCite* tabs: Negative Treatment, Citing References, or History, depending on the reason for KeyCiting the case.

For Example

In the West search box, enter kc: 148 N.M. 330 then click "Enter." The Negative Treatment tab is opened and you will see that the first case listed is *distinguished* from *State v. Sims* and thoroughly examines *Sims* because there are four green bars in the depth of treatment column (see Exhibit 5-18).

---

2. How to KeyCite Statutes, Constitutions, and Other Enacted Law

Just as you must validate case law; you must validate any other primary source of law, such as statutes, constitutional provisions, or administrative regulations. The process of KeyCiting these other sources of law is identical to that for KeyCiting case law.

To KeyCite a statute, from the screen displaying the statute click on any of the *KeyCite* tabs. Conversely, if you are not already looking at the statute, using the West Search bar, type in kc: NM Stat. Ann. 66-8-102, then click "Enter."

3. KeyCite Tabs

- **Negative Treatment.** This tab presents direct negative history followed by negative citing references. The section titled Negative Direct History lists events or decisions in the same litigation or proceeding. The Negative Citing References section lists other court decisions that have not followed or in some way distinguished themselves from the case you are KeyCiting. The Negative Treatment tab lists what kind of treatment, such as "not followed by" or "distinguished by" for every entry in the Negative Citing References list. This tab also displays a graphic showing the depth of treatment of the case, and a list of Headnotes representing which point of law the citing document discusses. The next subsection discusses these characteristics in more detail (see Exhibit 5-17).

- **History.** The History tab shows all previous and subsequent history of the case you are KeyCiting. West provides a graphical view which allows the researcher to see the case's history in a visual graph. This makes it easy to see how the case has moved through the courts. There is also a list of the prior and subsequent decisions, and a filter that allows the researcher to narrow the history from all history to principal history or previous history.

- **Citing References.** The Citing References tab is more expansive than the Negative Treatment tab. The Citing References tab lists all types of cases that have referenced the case you are KeyCiting. It provides the same information about the listed sources as in the Negative Treatment tab, such as the depth of treatment, type of treatment, and the point of law the citing document discusses. In addition, the researcher can narrow the list by specifying the type of source, such as other cases, administrative regulations, secondary sources and then apply additional filters to further narrow the results. These narrowing techniques are best for using *KeyCite* to conduct research. The Citing References tab also allows for the researcher to narrow results by searching for specific terms within the list (see Exhibit 5-18).

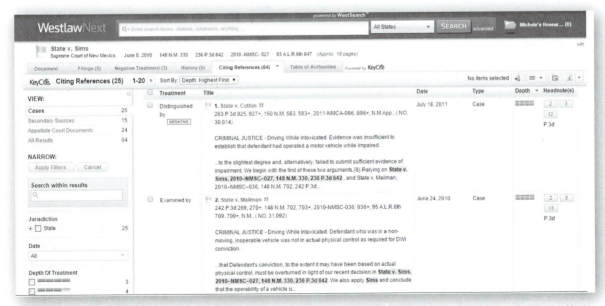

Exhibit 5-18 Screenshot of KeyCite Citing References tab for State v. Sims, 2010 -NMSC- 027, 148 N.M. 330 from *WestlawNext.* Reprinted with permissions of Thomson Reuters.

4. Characteristics of KeyCite

Although discussed here in reference to cases, *KeyCite* for other sources of law has the same characteristics as for KeyCiting cases:

- **Direct history.** Provides a full history of the KeyCited case. This includes both prior and subsequent case history.
- **Filings.** Provides a list of select court filings.
- **Graphical display of direct history.** Shows in a flowchart the progression of the case from trial through the appellate court system.
- **Citing references.** Reveals other sources that have cited the case. This includes levels of treatment such as negative treatment, positive treatment, and secondary sources that have referenced the case (see Exhibit 5-19).
- **Depth of treatment bars.** The list of citing references includes green bars to indicate the level of treatment. The more bars, the more in-depth coverage of the KeyCited case by the citing document.
- **Filters.** Use the filters for the various *KeyCite* tabs to narrow the *KeyCite* results. This feature is particularly helpful when using *KeyCite* as a research tool to find other cases on point, or to find cases that cite, explain, or address a particular statute, constitutional provision, or administrative regulation.
- **Quotation marks.** If quotation marks are included in a listing, the case or other source includes direct quotes from the KeyCited case.

For Example

The entry for *State v. Cotton*, which distinguished itself from *Sims*, has green quotation marks in the listing. *Cotton* will have direct quotations from *Sims* in the opinion (see Exhibit 5-18).

- **Headnote references.** References to specific headnotes in the citing document are provided. This allows the researcher to know exactly which points of law from the KeyCited case are referred to in the citing document.
- **KeyCite Alerts.** KeyCite Alert lets you set regularly scheduled alerts for certain laws. If you set up an alert, you will be emailed on the schedule you choose when there has been any change to the validity of the law, or if there are new citing references.
- **Table of authorities.** This is a list of the cases relied upon by the case you are viewing. This is important when validating case law, as it allows the researcher to check that all of the law relied upon by the case being KeyCited is still good law as well. Essentially, this feature allows you to determine if the case you are validating is weakened by subsequent cases or other laws that do not directly cite the case you are KeyCiting.

5. KeyCite *Signals*

- **Red flag.** Warns there is significant negative history, such as reversal or the case has been overruled on at least one point of law.
- **Yellow flag.** Warns of some negative history or treatment, such as being distinguished from another later case.

VII. RESEARCH USING CITATORS

Shepard's Citations and *KeyCite* are used for two purposes:

1. To determine if the authority you have located is still "good law." This is the most important use of a citator.
2. To locate case law or secondary sources that have discussed primary authority being researched. Even though a court opinion has not been reversed, it is important to determine how other courts have analyzed it.

For Example

If later courts have uniformly criticized the holding and reasoning of a court opinion, or it has been limited in some way, you may not want to rely upon it.

You may also wish to locate additional authority to support and add weight to the case being relied on. It is also possible that the reasoning in the case being researched is not clear, and other cases or secondary authority are necessary to help clarify it.

A. Research Using *Shepard's Citations*

The steps presented here are guidelines for using *Shepard's Citations* to conduct research.

1. *Select the appropriate Shepard's citator (in print) or log in to Lexis Advance (online).*
2. *Locate and review the entry for the authority being Shepardized (in print) or review the Shepard's report of an electronically Shepardized authority (online).* Keep the following in mind:
   a. Carefully review the history for subsequent cases or legislative actions that have reversed, overturned, repealed, amended, modified, or in any way affected the authority being Shepardized. Any such action may mean that the authority is no longer reliable; that is, it is no longer "good law."
   b. Carefully review the treatment of the authority in subsequent court opinions. Even though the authority being Shepardized may not have been reversed, repealed, or the like, reliance on it may be problematic if it has received any negative treatment by the courts.

      You must read the cases that treat the Shepardized case negatively. It is possible that your Shepardized case is being criticized for the treatment of an issue different from the one you are researching. For instance, you may be researching a negligence issue raised in the case being Shepardized, whereas the negative treatment in the subsequent cases involves a different issue, such as an improper jury instruction.
   c. If you are concerned with one issue in the Shepardized case, it may only be necessary to review those cited cases addressing that same issue.
   d. If a case does not appear in a *Shepard's* volume (in print), or the case does not have any *Shepard's* signal next to the citation and the integrated *Shepard's* report summary does not indicate there are any citing sources, it may mean that no court opinion has discussed your case. Always check the citation to be sure it is correct.
3. *Update your research (in print only).* Check the supplementary pamphlets and advance sheets and perform the research steps previously mentioned.

B. Research Using *KeyCite*

The steps presented here are guidelines for using *KeyCite* to conduct research.

1. *Once you have identified a case, statute, or other primary source of law that you will rely upon in your document, log into WestlawNext.*
2. *Enter the citation in the West search box and click "Enter." Choose the Citing References KeyCite tab to review the results.*
   a. Review the results for subsequent cases or legislative actions that have reversed, overturned, repealed, amended, modified, or in any way affected the authority being KeyCited. Any such action may mean that the authority is no longer reliable; that is, it is no longer "good law."
   b. Remember *KeyCite* does not provide references to positive treatment, only negative treatment of the authority in subsequent court opinions. Even though the authority being KeyCited may have not been reversed, repealed, or the like, reliance on it may be problematic if it has received any negative treatment by the courts.

VIII. CITING LEGAL ENCYCLOPEDIAS, TREATISES, AND *AMERICAN LAW REPORTS*

Any time you report the results of research in written form, you must properly cite your sources. This section presents an overview of rules of citation to be used when citing secondary authority, that is, sources upon which a court may rely that are not the law. The examples are to citation forms used in court documents, and legal memoranda rather than scholarly materials.

A detailed discussion of the citation rules for each type of secondary authority is beyond the scope of this text. Therefore, this section presents the citation format for the commonly used secondary sources covered within this chapter. As mentioned in the previous chapters, be sure to review the appropriate citation manual carefully for the detailed rules regarding each citation format.

A. Legal Encyclopedias

Both *Bluebook* and the *ALWD Guide* contain the same basic rules for proper legal encyclopedia citation format. The citation format for legal encyclopedias can be found at Rule 15.8 of the *Bluebook* and Rule 22 of the *ALWD Guide*.

A full citation to a legal encyclopedia should contain the following:

- The volume number of the encyclopedia
- The abbreviated name of the encyclopedia, usually, Am. Jur. 2d or C.J.S. (no underlining or italics)
- The title or topic name (italicized or underlined)
- The section symbol (§) and section number within the article
- The year of publication of the volume in parentheses

For Example

88 C.J.S. *Trial* § 105 (2012).
  59A Am. Jur. 2d *Partnership* § 925 (2001).

1. 88 and 59A—The volume number of the respective encyclopedia

2. C.J.S. and Am. Jur. 2d—The abbreviation for the name of the encyclopedia

3. *Trial* and *Partnership*—The topic name

4. 105 and 925—The section number within the article

5. 2012 and 2001—the date of publication of the volume

B. Treatises and Books

The *Bluebook* and the *ALWD Guide* have some differences in the citation format for treatises and books. Refer to Bluepages B15 and Rule 15 or *ALWD Guide* Rule 20 for citation rules for treatises, books, and other nonperiodic materials.

Generally, treatises and books are cited similarly. A full citation to treatises and books generally contain the following:

- The author's full name (or authors, if more than one)
- The title of the book or treatise
- The page cited
- The editors' names, if any, followed by ed. or eds.
- The edition (if applicable)
- The year of publication

For Example

6A Richard R. Powell, *Powell on Real Property* § 899 (Patrick J. Rohan ed. Matthew Bender 1994).

1. 6A – The volume number (multivolume treatise)

2. Richard R. Powell—The author

3. *Powell on Real Property*—The title of the treatise as it appears on the title page

4. § 899—The number of the section cited (this is often a page number, and occasionally a paragraph number)

5. Patrick J. Rohan ed.—The editor

6. Matthew Bender—The publisher

7. 1994—The year of publication

C. American Law Reports

Both the *Bluebook* and the *ALWD Guide* contain the same basic citation format for citing the *American Law Reports (ALR)*. Refer to Rule 15 of the *Bluebook* and Rule 22 of the *ALWD Guide* for proper citation format.

The components of an *ALR* citation are:

- The full name of the author(s)
- The title of the annotation (italicized or underlined)
- The volume number
- The abbreviated name of the publication, including the series number
- The page number where the annotation begins followed by the specific page(s) cited
- The year of publication

For Example

Michael J. Weber, *Application of Statute of Limitations to Actions for Breach of Duty in Performing Services of Public Accountant*, 7 ALR.5th 852 (1992).

D. Short Form Citation

Once a source is cited by its full citation, subsequent citation to that source often can be in short form. Short-form citation can be as simple as *Id.* or can be a truncated version of the full citation format. Each of the sources referenced above have specific rules related to short form. Generally, if the very next citation is to the exact same citation that was given previously, *Id.* is used to denote the citation is to the exact same resource and exact same pinpoint (specific) location in that resource. If *Id.* is not appropriate, then a truncated version of the full cite is called for. Consult Bluepages B4 and the specific subsection of the rules related to the specific citation form, for how to use *Id.* and other short-form citations in *Bluebook* style. When using the *ALWD Guide*, look to Rule 11 and then to each individual rule controlling citation format for the specific source for rules on use of short-form cites.

IX. KEY POINTS CHECKLIST: Secondary Authority

✓ The first step of legal research is to locate primary authority (the law), because courts look to primary authority first when resolving legal problems. Secondary authority is used when there is no primary authority on a topic in a jurisdiction, in support of the existing primary authority, to help you understand the primary authority, or to locate court opinions and other research sources interpreting the primary authority.

✓ None of the research sources discussed in this chapter are primary authority (the law). A court may refer to and rely upon the secondary authorities mentioned in this chapter, but it is not bound to follow them.

✓ Legal encyclopedias and treatises are primarily used to obtain a familiarity with or understanding of a specific area of the law.

✓ Use an *ALR* if you are looking for a comprehensive analysis and synthesis of cases from every jurisdiction on specific legal issues.

✓ Refer to a digest when you need to locate cases that have addressed a specific legal question or when you already have a case and wish to locate other cases that address the same legal question(s).

✓ Always validate and update the primary authority you are relying on, by using *Shepard's* or *KeyCite*, to ensure that the authority has not been overturned, reversed, repealed, or amended.

✓ With all research sources, you must check the pocket parts, supplements, or whatever is used to update the source to ensure that your research is current.

X. APPLICATION

This section explores the avenues of research Dan may pursue to learn about the tort law of battery. Dan could begin his search by consulting a legal encyclopedia, such as *American Jurisprudence Second* or *Corpus Juris Secundum*, at the local law library. By consulting the General Index, he would be directed to the volume that addresses assault and battery. If Dan knows that the topic he is looking for is "assault and battery," he can go directly to the volumes on the shelf. The spine of each book will indicate the range of coverage of the volume, such as "Assault and Battery to Attachment and Garnishment." Dan would then pull the appropriate volume and read about assault and battery. The encyclopedia will give him a general overview of the topic. He can also access *American Jurisprudence Second* through both Westlaw and LexisNexis. Dan would similarly go to either the Table of Contents or to the General Index and select Assault and Battery. He can then link to the topic and get a general overview of assault and battery.

If Dan wants a more in-depth summary or analysis of the law of civil battery, he could consult a treatise such as *Prosser and Keeton on the Law of Torts* or *The Law of Torts* by Dobbs. He would locate these books by going to the local law library and asking for the treatise section. The treatises are usually arranged alphabetically by topic. Therefore, the tort treatises will be shelved together. Dan is interested in battery in situations such as his, where the attack took place during the course of an arrest. The treatise will provide a discussion of the topic in greater analytical detail than an encyclopedia. If he has access to Westlaw or LexisNexis, he could check to see if a tort treatise is available.

For a more detailed analysis of the subject specifically regarding battery during a lawful act (an arrest), Dan could look for an *ALR* annotation. If he were to locate an annotation that addresses the question in a situation similar to his, it will provide, in one place, a comprehensive analysis of the issue, references to and summaries of the case law on point, and references to other research sources.

If Dan is unable to locate such an annotation, he could refer to a West digest and look under the topic "assault and battery." There he would locate summaries of specific court opinions that discuss assaults and batteries that took place during a lawful act. He would then select the case or cases most factually similar to his situation, and read how the law applies.

Through these sources, Dan could explore the subject in detail and determine if the facts of his case demonstrate the officer exceeded the lawful use of force to arrest allowing him to file a battery claim. He could also determine what remedies are available to him.

Summary

The focus of this chapter is secondary authority, that is, sources regarding law that a court may rely on but that are not themselves the law, that is, not primary authority. Secondary authority consists of legal research sources that summarize, compile, explain, comment on, interpret, or in some other way address the law. Secondary authority is used for several purposes, including:

- To obtain a background or overall understanding of a specific area of the law. Legal encyclopedias, treatises, and periodicals are useful for these purposes.
- To locate primary authority (the law) on a question being researched. *American Law Reports (ALR)* and digests are particularly useful for this purpose.
- To be relied upon by the court when reaching a decision. This usually occurs only when there is no primary authority governing a legal question, or when it is unclear how the primary authority applies to the question at hand.

There are literally hundreds of secondary sources. This chapter covers those secondary sources that provide the researcher with treatment of the law that ranges from the general to the specific. These sources are legal encyclopedias and treatises.

Legal encyclopedias provide an overview of all the areas of law. They do not provide in-depth coverage, and they are similar to other encyclopedias in their general treatment of topics.

Treatises are single-volume or multivolume texts that provide a comprehensive analysis of a single area of law such as torts or criminal law. Whereas a legal encyclopedia presents a broad overview of an area of law, a treatise provides an in-depth discussion and explains, analyzes, and criticizes the law.

This chapter also focuses on sources that help a researcher locate and analyze case law: *American Law Reports (ALR)* and digests. *ALR* exhaustively covers specific legal issues. A digest organizes the law by topic and provides a summary or "digest" of all the court opinions that have addressed the topic. It is an excellent case finder when a researcher needs to locate court opinions on specific topics.

Before relying on any primary authority, the researcher must determine if it is still "good law"; that is, the researcher must determine that it has not been reversed, modified, or otherwise negatively affected by some subsequent opinion or statute. The use of *Shepard's Citations* or Westlaw's *KeyCite* allows a researcher to determine if primary authority is still "good law" and also to locate other cases and secondary authorities that discuss a specific court opinion.

Quick References

Internet Resources

Most of the secondary authority and other research sources discussed in this chapter are available on Westlaw or LexisNexis. Most of the sources are not available on non-fee-based websites.

Exercises

ASSIGNMENT 1

What are the uses of secondary authority?

ASSIGNMENT 2

The client seeks advice concerning the actions of the majority stockholder in a small corporation. The majority stockholder owns 58 percent of the stock, and the client and another shareholder together own 42 percent. The majority stockholder controls the board of directors and is president of the corporation. He refuses to allow the corporation to issue any stock dividends. Until recently, the client and the other minority stockholder worked for the corporation. Last month, the majority stockholder fired the client and the minority stockholder.

What sections of *Am. Jur. 2d* discuss this topic?

ASSIGNMENT 3

Which *Am. Jur. 2d* title and sections address 18 U.S.C.S. § 204?

ASSIGNMENT 4

The client's brother was killed in an automobile collision. Family members disagree about whether viewing of the deceased should be allowed, due to the degree of damage to the body. What section of *Am. Jur. 2d* discusses this topic?

ASSIGNMENT 5

Refer to *Corpus Juris Secundum*. What section defines the term *name*, and what is the definition?

ASSIGNMENT 6

The client, a shareholder in a corporation, believes that the corporation exceeded its authority when it expanded the corporation's business from the repair of automobiles to the sale of automobile parts. What section of *Fletcher Cyclopedia of the Law of Private Corporations* addresses this topic? What is the term for the action of a corporation that exceeds its power?

ASSIGNMENT 7

The clients' son belongs to a religious cult. The clients believe the cult used improper means to indoctrinate their son and keep him in the cult. The son has given all his goods to the cult and refuses to see or talk to his parents. Is there an *ALR* annotation that addresses the liability of a cult for improper activities?

ASSIGNMENT 8

Has 2 A.L.R. Fed. 347 been replaced or superseded? By what annotation has this been done?

ASSIGNMENT 9

Your assignment is to obtain general information on the criminal aspects of causing or procuring the termination of a human pregnancy. Consult the *ALR.3d, ALR.4th, ALR.5th, ALR.6th*, and *ALR Federal* digests. Under the "Practice References," what is the reference to the "Defense of Paternity Charges" in *Am. Jur. Proof of Facts 2d*? What is the citation of a 1999 Nebraska case involving the state's partial-birth abortion statute?

ASSIGNMENT 10

What *ALR* annotation discusses 42 U.S.C.A. § 740?

ASSIGNMENT 11

The client's husband attacked her so severely that she was hospitalized. They are now separated, and the client wants to sue her husband. The husband still lives on the military base where they lived at the time of the incident. Refer to the *Federal Practice Digest* and locate the digest topic and key number that address this topic.

ASSIGNMENT 12

Give the name and citation of a 1994 Nevada case holding that the use of a toy gun to carry out a kidnapping is not a defense to a kidnapping charge. Refer to the *Tenth Decennial Digest*.

ASSIGNMENT 13

Your supervising attorney asks you to locate the digest topic and key numbers for the *Glover v. Lockheed Corp.* case listing. He remembers it is a *Federal Supplement* case, but he cannot remember the citation.

ASSIGNMENT 14

The assignment requires reference to a *Shepard's* citator. Regarding 18 U.S.C. § 1201(a), what is the citation of the *United States Reports* decision that held the provision unconstitutional in part? What Sixth Circuit case found the provision constitutional? What Second Circuit case, in 2001, discussed section 1201(a)(1)?

ASSIGNMENT 15

The assignment requires access to Westlaw online. At the West search box enter kc: 131 S. Ct. 2705 (*Bullcoming v. New Mexico*, 131 S. Ct. 2705 (2011)).

What is the citation for the 2011 Illinois Court of Appeals, First District, case that *Bullcoming* is distinguished by?

ASSIGNMENT 16

This assignment requires access to *Shepard's* online. In Lexis Academic or *Shepard's Online* enter shep: 541 U.S. 36 and click "Enter" (*Crawford v. Washington*, 541 U.S. 36 (2004)).

    a. What is the *Shepard's* signal for *Crawford*?

    b. What types of *cautionary analysis* are there? Provide both the type and the number of references for each.

Chapter 6

Secondary Authority—Periodicals, Restatements, Uniform Laws, Dictionaries, Legislative History, and Other Secondary Authorities

Learning Objectives

After completing this chapter, you should understand:

- The role of periodicals, *Restatements*, uniform laws, dictionaries, legislative history, and miscellaneous secondary sources in legal research
- How to conduct research using periodicals, *Restatements*, uniform laws, dictionaries, legislative history, and other secondary sources
- How to compile legislative histories

Assistant City Attorney Genevieve Gray said to her intern, Luis Sisneros, "Luis, the city council's considering drafting a zoning ordinance restricting the location of adult entertainment businesses. I need some preliminary research on First Amendment and other constitutional limitations on such ordinances. Would you like to take a crack at this?" Luis had just started his internship with the city attorney's office. The city provided three internships for paralegal students. "Yes, I'll start right away," Luis responded, thinking to himself, "This is great. I expected some go-fer type assignments like locating and copying statutes and cases."

The steps Luis follows when performing this assignment, and the results of his search, will be discussed in the Application section of this chapter.

I. INTRODUCTION

Chapter 5 addressed the more frequently used research sources that help a researcher summarize, explain, interpret, locate, or update the law. This chapter presents other frequently used secondary authority sources. The chapter discusses legal periodicals that may be used when seeking an analysis and critique of a specific legal topic that is more in-depth or narrower in focus than that provided by a legal encyclopedia or a treatise. It also covers secondary sources that present definitions or uniform statements of the law, such as dictionaries, *Restatements of the Law*, and uniform laws. In addition, the chapter covers legislative history and practice aids such as form books. Exhibit 6-1 shows the primary use of the secondary sources discussed in this chapter.

AUTHORITY	PRIMARY USE AS A RESEARCH TOOL
Periodicals	Use when you are seeking an analysis and critique of a specific legal topic that is more in-depth or narrower in focus than that provided by a legal encyclopedia or treatise.
Restatements of the Law	Use to locate a standardized definition or statement of the law, reasons in support of the definition or statement of the law, and citations to related cases, treatises, and other secondary authority.
Uniform Laws and Model Acts	Use to locate a model text from which a law may be crafted, arguments in support of the law, and citations to cases, treatises, and articles interpreting the law.
Dictionaries	Use to obtain the spelling, pronunciation, and legal meaning of terms used in the law.
Legislative History	Use to determine the meaning or application of a law. This may be helpful when the meaning of a law that governs a fact situation is unclear, or when the law is written so broadly that its application to a specific fact situation is unclear.

© Cengage

Exhibit 6-1 Secondary Authority–Primary Use as a Research Tool.

II. LEGAL PERIODICALS

Legal periodicals publish articles on legal topics. Through these various publications, articles are available on literally every legal topic. The articles are usually authored by individuals who have expertise in the area, such as law professors and expert practitioners in the field, or by law students who have conducted extensive research on a topic. The articles are valuable for their depth of research, citations to numerous primary and secondary sources, and in-depth analysis of current legal issues, recently emerging areas of the law, and specific topics.

For Example

Nicholas C. Whitley, *An Examination of the United States and European Union Patent Systems with Respect to Genetic Material*, 32 Ariz. J. Int'l & Comp. L. 463 (Summer 2015) is an example of a law review article addressing a very specific topic.

Publications in legal periodicals are secondary authority. They are not primary authority, but courts on occasion cite them when there is no primary authority on a topic or when interpreting primary authority such as a statute.

For Example

"The courts of this state have not addressed the question of the liability of a majority shareholder in a situation such as the one presented in this case. Guidance, however, is provided in [name of law review article] where the question has been thoroughly analyzed."

A. Types of Legal Periodicals

Legal periodicals can be classified into four distinct categories: law reviews, professional publications, commercial publications, and newspapers and newsletters.

1. Law Reviews

Law reviews are scholarly periodicals published by law schools. They contain articles written by law professors, judges, practitioners, and law students, and are usually published two or three times a year. Most accredited law schools in the United States publish at least one law review. Law students edit law reviews under the guidance of the law school faculty and administration. Rigorous standards are employed to ensure high quality. Due to their scholarly nature, law reviews are often cited by courts.

Law reviews are valuable for their detailed analysis of current legal issues, recently emerging areas of the law, and specific topics (see Exhibit 6-2). Law reviews usually include:

- **Articles.** Articles are written by scholars, judges, or practitioners and usually present a comprehensive analysis of specific topics such as the *Patents and Genetic Material* article mentioned previously. The articles are thoroughly researched with footnotes citing numerous cases, studies, and other sources.
- **Notes and comments.** These are shorter pieces written by students. They are similar to the articles in that they are narrow in focus, thoroughly researched, and extensively footnoted. Inasmuch as students and not experts in the field write them, they have less authority and are less frequently cited.
- **Recent developments and cases.** These pieces discuss recent cases and developments in the law such as new statutes. Students also author this section.
- **Book reviews.** Most law reviews include book reviews of recent legal publications.

Many law journals can be accessed using Westlaw or LexisNexis. In addition, some law schools have created online journals, also known as e-journals, which are accessible through the law school's website without a subscription. The online journals often contain materials that have been written for public consumption, making them different than traditional law journals.

For Example

The *Law Journal for Social Justice* was created in 2009 at Arizona State University Sandra Day O'Connor School of Law, and is an all student-created and student-run journal. The students edit, produce, and publish notable works from legal scholars, practitioners, and law students.

2. Bar Association and Other Association Publications

Every state has a bar association whose members are attorneys licensed to practice law in the state. There are national bar associations open to practitioners nationally, the largest and best known being the American Bar Association. Most of these associations publish journals that include articles on specific legal subjects, recent developments in the case and statutory law, and tips and guides for practitioners. They also include book reviews, news about the association, and technology updates. Similar to law reviews, the articles are thoroughly researched, with footnotes citing cases and other sources, but the content of the articles is less scholarly and more practical.

State bar association journals tend to publish articles that are local in nature and of interest primarily to practitioners of that jurisdiction. On occasion, an entire issue will be devoted to a particular topic. The American Bar Association publishes the *American Bar Association Journal*, which includes articles concerning national legal developments.

For Example

The State Bar of Arizona publishes a monthly periodical titled *Arizona Attorney*. In the October 2015 issue, one of the features was titled *Same Sex Marriage Ruling Just First Step in Legal Progress* that included seven separate articles on how the Supreme Court's same sex marriage ruling may affect the rights of same sex couples in seven different areas of law. The magazine is available online to the public at http://www.azbar.org/AZAttorney.

PROTECTING THE GENDER NONCONFORMIST FROM THE GENDER POLICE—WHY THE HARASSMENT OF GAYS AND OTHER GENDER NONCONFORMISTS IS A FORM OF SEX DISCRIMINATION IN LIGHT OF THE SUPREME COURT'S DECISION IN *ONCALE V. SUNDOWNER*

TONI LESTER[*]

INTRODUCTION—THE SILENCE SURROUNDING HARASSMENT BASED ON HOMOPHOBIA

Traditionally, people who are harassed at work because they are gay[1] have found that they have not been granted the same kind of legal protections that their heterosexual counterparts have received.[2] This is true despite the fact that the sexual harassment of gays is motivated by homophobia, which in turn is motivated in large part by misogyny. Since misogyny in all its many manifestations is one of the things that Title VII's prohibition against sex discrimination is supposed to attack,[3] the failure of the courts to recognize that harassment against gays is a kind of sex discrimination is at best misguided and at worst very dangerous.

---

[*] Affiliated Research Scholar Wellesley Centers for Women; former Visiting Law Scholar, Institute for Research on Women and Gender, Stanford University; Associate Professor of Law, and Johnson Research Chair, Babson College; B.S., J.D., Georgetown University.

[1] I use the term "gay" here broadly to mean those who identify themselves as homosexual men, lesbians, bisexuals, and transsexuals. I recognize that the term is the subject of great debate today, however. I will talk about the debate and explain my use of the term in greater detail in Part I.

[2] *See* Ulane v. Eastern Airlines, Inc., 742 F.2d 1081, 1084–86 (7th Cir. 1984) (stating that Title VII does not protect transsexuals, homosexuals or transvestites); Desantis v. Pacific Tel. & Tel. Co., 608 F.2d 327, 329–30 (9th Cir. 1979) (stating that "Title VII's prohibition of "sex" discrimination . . . should not be judicially extended to include sexual preference"); *see also* Regina L. Stone-Harris, *Same-Sex Harassment—The Next Step in the Evolution of Sexual Harassment Law Under Title VII,* 28 ST. MARY'S L.J. 269, 289 (1996) (stating that in dealing with "hostile or abusive work environment claims" brought by a male victim against a male offender "who believed the victim was homosexual," courts have "rule[d] against the plaintiff," with the author finding it "notable . . . how closely the offensive conduct [in these cases] parallels other conduct which courts have found to be discriminatory").

[3] *See, e.g.,* Price Waterhouse v. Hopkins, 490 U.S. 228, 251 (1989) ("An employer who objects to aggressiveness in women but whose positions require this trait places women in an intolerable and impermissible catch 22: out of a job if they behave aggressively and out of a job if they do not. Title VII lifts women out of this bind."); Meritor v. Vinson, 477 U.S. 57, 67 (1986) ("Sexual harassment which creates a hostile or offensive environment for members of one sex is every bit the arbitrary barrier to sexual equality at the workplace that racial harassment is to racial equality." (citing Henson v. Dundee, 682 F.2d 897, 902 (11th Cir. 1982))); Ellison v. Brady, 924 F.2d 872, 881 (9th Cir. 1991) ("Congress designed Title VII to prevent the perpetuation of stereotypes and a sense of degradation which serve to close or discourage employment opportunities for women." (citing Andrews v. Philadelphia, 895 F.2d 1469, 1483 (3d Cir. 1990))); Barnes v. Costle, 561 F.2d 983, 987 (D.C. Cir. 1977) (noting that "[n]umerous studies have shown that women are placed in the less challenging, the less responsible and the less remunerative positions on the basis of their sex alone," and finding "such blatantly disparate treatment . . . particularly objectionable in view of the fact that Title VII has specifically prohibited sex discrimination since its enactment in 1964."); Torres v. Nat'l Precision Blanking, 943 F. Supp. 952, 954 (N.D. Ill. 1996) (stating that "the principal purpose of including the term 'sex' in the Act was to 'do some good for the minority sex.'" (citing 110 CONG. REC. 2577 (1964).

Some have argued that Title VII's prohibition against sex discrimination was the result of a fluke, in which Congressman Howard Smith of Virginia hoped to stymie the bill's passage by adding the word, "sex" to the bill, never expecting it to be approved. *See* CHARLES & BARBARA WHALEN, THE LONGEST DEBATE—A LEGISLATIVE HISTORY OF THE CIVIL RIGHTS ACT 115-118 (1985).

Exhibit 6-2 *Sample Law Review Page. University of New Mexico School of Law, Toni Lester,* Protecting the Gender Nonconformist from the Gender Police—Why the Harassment of Gays and Other Gender Nonconformists Is a Form of Sex Discrimination in Light of the Supreme Court's Decision in *Oncale v. Sundowner.* 29 New Mexico L. Rev. (1999) p. 89. Reprinted with permission from the *New Mexico Law Review.*

In addition to bar associations, there are associations for paralegals and legal assistants. Some of these associations publish newsletters that include articles of interest to paralegals and legal assistants.

Although cited far less often than academic law journals, legal association journals are a good source of information for emerging trends in the law or summaries of change in practice areas that have resulted from recent changes to statutes or court rules, or are the result of a recent court opinion. Because these articles often include citations to statutes, regulations, court rules, and court opinions, they can be both informative and lead to primary sources.

The journal of the American Bar Association and many state bar journals can be accessed through Westlaw or LexisNexis. However, because many of these journals are produced primarily for dues paying members, these are more likely to be found in the law office, local law libraries, or on the association's website. Many associations will provide access to particular articles, or copies of them, for a small fee to nonmembers.

3. Commercial Publications

There are numerous **commercial journals** and periodicals that focus on specific areas of law, such as the *Journal of Taxation*. Individuals interested in a specific area of law may subscribe to such a publication. The articles are similar to bar journal articles in that they are well researched. They often include book reviews, practitioner guides and tips, and technology updates.

4. Legal Newspapers and Newsletters

A number of **legal newspapers** are available by subscription, such as the *National Law Journal* and the *Legal Times*. The *National Law Journal* and *Legal Times* are published weekly, and include articles and features on trends in litigation, developments in the law, information on attorneys and the legal profession, and book reviews. There are many subject-specific newspapers such as the *Corporate Legal Times*. In many cities, there are local newspapers such as the *New York Law Journal* that publish legal notices, court docket information, and articles of local interest.

In addition to newspapers, there are thousands of **newsletters** published by commercial and public interest groups. These newsletters are usually issued weekly or monthly, and focus on current information in specific areas of the law. These newsletters are becoming increasingly available online and can be set up for delivery to an email account.

Many legal newspapers and newsletters may be accessed via Westlaw or LexisNexis. Others can be accessed online through subscription to the specific newspaper or newsletter.

B. Research Using Legal Periodicals

1. Use as a Research Tool

Legal periodicals usually contain extensive footnotes citing relevant primary and secondary sources. The different types of legal periodicals serve various functions. Choosing which type of periodicals to search depends upon the type of information you are seeking.

Refer to a legal periodical when you are seeking an analysis and critique of a specific legal topic that is more in-depth, or narrower in focus, than that provided by a legal encyclopedia or a treatise. In many instances, an article in a legal periodical will go into much greater depth than a treatise and provide more case citations, statistical information, and references to other sources. You may also refer to a periodical when seeking information on a recently emerging legal issue that is not yet addressed in treatises.

2. Research Techniques—Legal Periodicals

As is apparent from the previous section, hundreds of periodicals exist, making it impractical to research each publication for articles on a specific topic. The research tools mentioned here are designed to help you locate specific articles.

a. Index to Legal Periodicals

The **Index to Legal Periodicals and Books (ILP)** provides an index to the contents of most legal periodicals in the United States, the United Kingdom, and most of the British Commonwealth countries. (See Exhibit 6-3 for a sample index page.) The **Current Law Index (CLI)** is a periodical index similar to *ILP*, and provides an index of articles of several hundred periodicals beginning in 1980; it does not reference articles published prior to 1980.

INDEX TO LEGAL PERIODICALS & BOOKS

Ashton, Bruce L.—*cont.*
New safe harbors for employers in the Service's qualified plan correction examples; by C. F. Reish, B. L. Ashton, N. J. White. 91 no6 *J. Tax'n* 349-57 D 1999

Ashton, Roger D.
Consolidation in the financial services sector: tax implications to stakeholders. 49 *Rep. Proc. Ann. Tax Conf. Convened by Can. Tax Found.* 21.1-.58 1997

Ashworth, Andrew
Article 6 and the fairness of trials. 1999 *Crim. L. Rev.* 261-72 Ap 1999
Restorative justice and victims' rights. 2000 *N.Z. L.J.* 84-8 Mr 2000

Asia-Pacific Economic Cooperation (Organization)
The role of APEC in the achievement of regional cooperation in Southeast Asia. L. C. Cardenas, A. Buranakanits. 5 no1 *Ann. Surv. Int'l & Comp. L.* 49-80 Spr 1999

Asia-Pacific legal development; edited by Douglas M. Johnston and Gerry Ferguson. University of B.C. Press 1998 611p ISBN 0-7748-0673-7 LC 99-183418

Asiain, Jorge Hugo
Financing of real estate projects in Argentina. 4 no1 *NAFTA Rev.* 96-104 Wint 1998

Asian Americans
All the themes but one. E. L. Muller. 66 no4 *U. Chi. L. Rev.* 1395-33 Fall 1999
Are Asians black?: The Asian-American civil rights agenda and the contemporary significance of the black/white paradigm. J. Y. Kim, student author. 108 no8 *Yale L.J.* 2385-412 Je 1999
Asian Americans, the law, and illegal immigration in post-civil rights America: a review of three books. H. Gee. 77 no1 *U. Det. Mercy L. Rev.* 71-81 Fall 1999
Beyond black and white: selected writings by Asian Americans within the critical race theory movement. H. Gee. 30 no3 *St. Mary's L.J.* 759-99 1999
Emerging from the margins of historical consciousness: Chinese immigrants and the history of American law. R. P. Cole, G. J. Chin. 17 no2 *Law & Hist. Rev.* 325-64 Summ 1999
Justice held hostage: U.S. disregard for international law in the World War II internment of Japanese Peruvians—a case study. N. T. Saito. 40 no1 *B. C. L. Rev.* 275-348 D 1998
Lexicon dreams and Chinese rock and roll: thoughts on culture, language, and translation as strategies of resistance and reconstruction. S. K. Hom. 53 no4 *U. Miami L. Rev.* 1003-17 H 1999
Lochner [Lochner v. New York, 25 S. Ct. 539 (1905)], parity, and the Chinese laundry cases [Yick Wo v. Hopkins, 6 S. Ct. 1064 (1886)] D. E. Bernstein. 41 no1 *Wm. & Mary L. Rev.* 211-94 D 1999
McCarthyism, the internment and the contradictions of power. M. J. Matsuda. 40 no1 *B.C. L. Rev.* 9-36 D 1998
No right to own?: The early twentieth-century "Alien Land Laws" as a prelude to internment. K. Aoki. 40 no1 *B.C. L. Rev.* 37-72 D 1998
Out of the shadow: marking intersections in and between Asian Pacific American critical legal scholarship and Latina/o critical legal theory. E. M. Iglesias. 40 no1 *B.C. L. Rev.* 349-83 D 1998
Praising with faint damnation—the troubling rehabilitation of Korematsu [Korematsu v. United States, 63 S. Ct. 1124 (1944)] A. C. Yen. 40 no1 *B.C. L. Rev.* 1-7 D 1998
Race, rights, and the Asian American experience: a review essay. H. Gee. 13 no4 *Geo. Immigr. L.J.* 635-51 Summ 1999
Racial reparations: Japanese American redress and African American claims. E. K. Yamamoto. 40 no1 *B.C. L. Rev.* 477-523 D 1998
Reparations and the "model minority" ideology of acquiescence: the necessity to refuse the return to original humiliation. C. K. Iijima. 40 no1 *B.C. L. Rev.* 385-427 D 1998
The stranger who resides with you: ironies of Asian-American and American Indian legal history. J. W. Singer. 40 no1 *B.C. L. Rev.* 171-7 D 1998
Symposium: the long shadow of Korematsu [Korematsu v. United States, 63 S. Ct. 1124 (1944)] 40 no1 *B.C. L. Rev.* 1-535 D 1998
A tale of new precedents: Japanese American internment as foreign affairs law. G. Gott. 40 no1 *B.C. L. Rev.* 179-274 D 1998
Using DSM-IV to diagnose mental illness in Asian Americans. T. B. Tran, student author. 10 *J. Contemp. Legal Issues* 335-57 1999

See/See also the following book(s):
Chang, R. S. Disoriented; Asian Americans, law, and the nation-state. New York University Press 1999 x, 180p

California
The Chinese American challenge to court-mandated quotas in San Francisco's public schools: notes from a (partisan) participant-observer. D. i Levine. 16 *Harv. BlackLetter L.J.* 39-145 Spr 2000
Redeeming whiteness in the shadow of internment: Earl Warren, Brown, [Brown v. Board of Education, 74 S. Ct. 686 (1954)] and a theory of racial redemption. S. Cho. 40 no1 *B.C. L. Rev.* 73-170 D 1998

Asian Pacific Economic Cooperation (Organization) *See* Asia-Pacific Economic Cooperation (Organization)

Asimow, Michael
Bad lawyers in the movies. 24 no2 *Nova L. Rev.* 533-91 Wint 2000
Interim-final rules: making haste slowly. 51 no3 *Admin. L. Rev.* 703-55 Summ 1999
"Justice with an attitude": Judge Judy and the daytime television bunch. 38 no4 *Judges' J.* 24-8+ Fall 1999

Askin, Frank, 1932-
A law school where students don't just learn the law; they help make the law. 51 no4 *Rutgers L. Rev.* 855-74 1999

Askin, Kelly Dawn
Crimes within the jurisdiction of the International Criminal Court. 10 no1 *Crim. L.F.* 33-59 1999
Issues surrounding the creation of a regional human rights system for the Asia-Pacific. 4 no2 *ILSA J. Int'l & Comp. L.* 599-601 Spr 1998
Sexual violence in decisions and indictments of the Yugoslav and Rwandan tribunals: current status. 93 no1 *Am. J. Int'l L.* 92-123 Ja 1999

Åslund, Anders, 1952- ⸻⸻⸻⸻⸻⸻ — *Entry by author*
Law in Russia. 8 no4 *E. Eur. Const. Rev.* 96-101 Fall 1999

Asmus, Daniel G.
Service provider liability: Australian High Court gives the world a first—should the United States follow suit? 17 no1 *Dick. J. Int'l L.* 189-228 Fall 1998

Asouzu, Amazu A.
The adoption of the UNCITRAL model law in Nigeria: implications on the recognition and enforcement of arbitral awards. 1999 *J. Bus. L.* 185-204 Mr 1999

Aspen, Marvin E., 1934-
about
It's how you play the game. L. Leshne. 34 no7 *Trial* 28-32 Jl 1998

Aspin, Larry
Trends in judicial retention elections, 1964-1998. 83 no2 *Judicature* 79-81 S/O 1999

Asplen, Christopher H.
Integrating DNA technology into the criminal justice system. 83 no3 *Judicature* 144-9 N/D 1999

Assafa Endeshaw *See* Endeshaw, Assafa, 1950-

Assault and battery — *Entry by topic* / *Assault and Battery*
See also
   Battered women
   Child abuse
A jurisprudence in disarray: on battery, wrongful living, and the right to bodily integrity. M. P. Strasser. 36 no4 *San Diego L. Rev.* 997-1041 Fall 1999
Score and pierce: crimes of fashion? Body alteration and consent to assault. A. J. Watkins, student author. 28 no2 *Vict. U. Wellington L. Rev.* 371-98 My 1998

Canada
Fraud, HIV and unprotected sex: R. v. Cuerrier [[1998] 2 S.C.R. 371] R. K. Yamada, student author. 6 no1 *Sw. J.L. & Trade Am.* 157-76 Spr 1999
Secrets and lives—the public safety exception to solicitor-client privilege: Smith v. Jones [[1999] 169 D.L.R.4th 385] W. N. Renke. 37 no4 *Alta. L. Rev.* 1045-70 D 1999

Great Britain
Assault, battery and indirect violence. M. Hirst. 1999 *Crim. L. Rev.* 557-60 Jl 1999
Consent, threats and deception in criminal law. J. Horder. 10 no1 *King's C. L.J.* 104-8 1999
Corporal punishment of children: a caning for the United Kingdom. A. Bainham. 58 pt2 *Cambridge L.J.* 291-3 Jl 1999
Theorising the limits of the 'sadomasochistic homosexual' identity in R v Brown [[1994] 1 A.C. 212] S. Chandra-Shekeran, student author. 21 no2 *Melb. U. L. Rev.* 584-600 D 1997

Exhibit 6-3   Page from the *Index to Legal Periodicals and Books.* The H. W. Wilson Company, *Index to Legal Periodicals and Books* (2000), p. 68. Reprinted with permission from The H. W. Wilson Company, a division of EBSCO Publishing.

Hardbound volumes are published annually with monthly soft-cover updates. The volumes and updates are not cumulative. Therefore, if you are looking for an article published in the current year, start with the current soft-cover monthly volume and work your way backwards.

For Example

If you are interested in an article published in the past five years, check the hardbound volume for each year and each update.

b. Common Features of Periodical Indexes

Both the *ILP* and the *CLI* have the following features:

1. *Subject/author index.* Articles are indexed alphabetically by both subject and author. If you know the name of the author or you know the subject, such as "assault and battery," you can use this index to locate articles. The index includes the title of the article, the name of the author, and the name and date of the publication (see Exhibit 6-3).
2. *Table of cases.* Cases that have been noted or discussed in articles are indexed alphabetically by the names of both the plaintiff and the defendant. Following the case name are citations to the articles.
3. *Table of statutes.* If you know the name of a statute, this index will direct you to articles that have discussed the statute.
4. *Book reviews.* The book review index lists by book title and the periodicals that have reviewed the title.

c. Other Periodical Indexes

In addition to the major indexes discussed previously, there are several other indexes. The following are examples of other general periodical indexes and special subject indexes:

- *Index to Foreign Legal Periodicals (IFLP).* Provides an index of periodicals from countries other than the United States and British Commonwealth countries.
- *Current Index to Legal Periodicals (CILP).* Provides access to articles not yet indexed in the *ILP* and *CLI*. This index is published weekly.
- *Index to Periodical Articles Related to Law.* Provides an index of articles found in nonlegal publications.
- *Criminal Justice Periodical Index.* Provides an index to literature on criminal justice, including criminology, law enforcement, correction, and the courts.
- *European Legal Journals Index.* Provides an index to articles relating to the European Community and its member states.

Check with a law library for specific indexes.

d. Reference from Other Sources

Another source, such as a citation in a court opinion, legal encyclopedia, or treatise, may direct you to a legal periodical article. Often, references to law review articles that have analyzed a statute are included in the annotations to the statute. In such instances, you would go directly to the periodical; you would not need to use an index.

3. Computer-Aided Research

Almost all of the legal periodical indexes discussed above, as well as many legal periodicals, are available online in some form. When searching online, there are two methods of searching: index and full-text searching. Searching the indexes online is similar to searching them in print—you can search by article title, author, subject, keyword, and other fields. During a **full-text search**, the researcher looks through the text of the articles themselves for certain words without regard to the specific subject of the articles. Index searching has a distinct advantage over full-text searching in that the articles retrieved will be related to the index term.

For Example

In an index search to locate articles about the right to recover stolen works of art, a researcher might use the subject index of the *ILP* and look at listings under "art thefts—remedies."

In a full-text search the term "stolen art" would lead to all types of articles with the term, regardless of topic of the article.

The *Index to Legal Periodicals* and *Current Law Index* are available in CD-ROM form, on Westlaw and on LexisNexis. Both are the most comprehensive indexes available, and their online versions include all updates. The online *ILP* is called *Index to Legal Periodicals Full Text* and is updated monthly. The *CLI* online, as well as on CD-ROM, is called *LegalTrac* and is available online by subscription. *LegalTrac* includes sources in addition to those listed in the *CLI*.

Many law reviews, periodicals, and legal newspapers are available on both Westlaw and LexisNexis. *Legal Source* is a full-text database of nearly 900 legal journals, yearbooks, bar association publications, and law reviews. *HeinOnline* also is a full-text database of law journals and law reviews. Some law reviews are available through law school websites, and some periodical articles are available through the publisher's website. See Chapters 7 and 8 for further discussion of computers and legal research.

III. *RESTATEMENTS OF THE LAW*

The American Law Institute (ALI) was founded in 1923 to address two major defects in American law: uncertainty and complexity. Uncertainty existed because of a lack of agreement among members of the profession on fundamental principles of the common law. Also, there was a lack of precision in the use of legal terms, and statutes were often poorly drafted. Complexity arose because of numerous differences in the law in the various jurisdictions in the United States.

The primary goal of the ALI is to promote clarification and simplification of the law. The founders decided that this goal could be accomplished through a restatement of the law defining what the law is for basic legal subjects. To accomplish this task, the ALI recruited nationally known scholars to draft the *Restatements*. From 1923 to 1944, **Restatements of the Law** were published for agency, conflict of laws, contracts, judgments, property restitution, security, torts, and trusts. In 1952, the original *Restatements* were republished with updates, expanded comments, and analysis. New Restatements were published in such areas as landlord–tenant and foreign relations law. This second set of publications is called *Restatement Second*. In 1987, the ALI began *Restatement Third* which includes revisions and updates of the *Restatements* as well as new subjects, such as unfair competition, and suretyship and guarantee.

Restatements are the product of highly competent scholars in each area of the law and are a highly respected and valuable research tool. Due to the authoritativeness of the *Restatements*, they are frequently cited by the courts and often accorded a recognition greater than that accorded to treatises.

For Example

Most of the law of torts is not statutory law; that is, it is established in court opinions. Assume a state court has not defined a term such as *superseding cause* in negligence law. An appellate court of the state, when faced with a case that requires the term to be defined, may refer to the *Restatement of the Law of Torts* § 440 and adopt its definition of the term.

Note that the *Restatements of the Law* are secondary authority and used to support primary authority or when there is no primary authority.

Restatement sections currently exist for the following areas of the law:

Agency	Property
Conflicts of law	Restitution and unjust enrichment
Contracts	Security
Employment Law	Suretyship and guaranty
Foreign relations law of the United States	Torts
Judgments	Trusts
Law governing lawyers	Unfair competition

A. Restatement Features

The *Restatements of the Law* have the following features:

- **Organization.** Each *Restatement* is divided into chapters that cover major areas. The chapters are then divided into broader topics, and the topics are divided into individual sections that each present a general principle of law.

For Example

One chapter of the *Restatement of the Law of Torts, Products Liability* is titled, "Liability of Commercial Product Sellers Based on Product Defects at Time of Sale." This chapter is divided into topics. Topic 1 is "Liability Rules Applicable to Products Generally." This topic is divided into four sections. Section 1 presents the general principle of law governing the "Liability of Commercial Seller or Distributor for Harm Caused by Defective Products."

At the beginning of each volume and each chapter is a table of contents listing the topic and sections covered in the respective volume and chapter (see Exhibit 6-4).

- **Restatement of the Law.** Each *Restatement* section begins with a statement of the principle of law or a rule of law, summarizing and defining the American law on the topic (see Exhibit 6-4).
- **Comments and Illustrations.** Following the rule of law is a comment section that includes an analytical discussion of the rule and may present hypothetical illustrations of application of the rule (see Exhibit 6-4). The authority who drafted the *Restatement* prepares the comments and reporters' notes (see "Reporters' Note" next). As the work product of a well-known authority, they add value to the *Restatement*.
- **Reporters' Note.** Following the comments are reporters' notes that include general information concerning the *Restatement* and citations to cases, treatises, articles, and other secondary sources in support of, and opposition to, the *Restatement* (see Exhibit 6-5).
- **Cross-references.** Cross-references to West's digest key numbers and *ALR* annotations accompany each *Restatement*.
- **Appendix volumes.** Beginning with the *Restatement Second*, there are noncumulative appendix volumes that categorize and summarize decisions of courts from different jurisdictions that have cited *Restatements*.
- **Updates.** Each *Restatement* is updated with pocket parts for each hardbound volume and supplements that are placed beside the appropriate hardbound volume. The title page of the pocket part or supplement provides the dates of the cases reported and instructions for locating earlier citations. Interim case citations pamphlets are published semiannually that are used in conjunction with the pocket parts and supplements.
- **Index.** A comprehensive index accompanies each *Restatement* that references sections, comments, and reporters' notes.

B. Research Using *Restatements of the Law*

1. Use as a Research Tool

Restatements of the Law have several uses as a research tool. You may refer to a *Restatement* when a specific legal term, principle, or rule has not been defined in your jurisdiction. In such situations, a court may refer to and adopt the *Restatement* as the law in the jurisdiction. The *Restatement* provides guidance as to how the law should be defined or stated; reasons in support of the definition or statement of the law; and citations to cases, treatises, and other secondary authority.

CHAPTER 1

LIABILITY OF COMMERCIAL PRODUCT SELLERS BASED ON PRODUCT DEFECTS AT TIME OF SALE

TOPIC 1. LIABILITY RULES APPLICABLE TO PRODUCTS GENERALLY

Section

1. Liability of Commercial Seller or Distributor for Harm Caused by Defective Products
2. Categories of Product Defect
3. Circumstantial Evidence Supporting Inference of Product Defect
4. Noncompliance and Compliance with Product Safety Statutes or Regulations

TOPIC 2. LIABILITY RULES APPLICABLE TO SPECIAL PRODUCTS OR PRODUCT MARKETS

5. Liability of Commercial Seller or Distributor of Product Components for Harm Caused by Products Into Which Components Are Integrated
6. Liability of Commercial Seller or Distributor for Harm Caused by Defective Prescription Drugs and Medical Devices
7. Liability of Commercial Seller or Distributor for Harm Caused by Defective Food Products
8. Liability of Commercial Seller or Distributor of Defective Used Products

---

TOPIC 1. LIABILITY RULES APPLICABLE TO PRODUCTS GENERALLY

§ 1. Liability of Commercial Seller or Distributor for Harm Caused by Defective Products

One engaged in the business of selling or otherwise distributing products who sells or distributes a defective product is subject to liability for harm to persons or property caused by the defect.

Comment:

a. History. This Section states a general rule of tort liability applicable to commercial sellers and other distributors of products generally. Rules of liability applicable to special products

Contents —

Rule —

Comment —

Exhibit 6-4 *Restatement (Third) of Torts, Products Liability § 1.* American Law Institute, *Restatement (Third) of Torts, 3d ed., Vol. 1* (1998), p. 5. © 1998 by the American Law Institute. All rights reserved. Reprinted with permission.

Ch. 1   LIABILITY BASED ON TIME-OF-SALE DEFECTS   § 1

nonmanufacturing sellers or distributors do not themselves render the products defective and regardless of whether they are in a position to prevent defects from occurring. See § 2, Comment *o*. Legislation has been enacted in many jurisdictions that, to some extent, immunizes nonmanufacturing sellers or distributors from strict liability. The legislation is premised on the belief that bringing nonmanufacturing sellers or distributors into products liability litigation generates wasteful legal costs. Although liability in most cases is ultimately passed on to the manufacturer who is responsible for creating the product defect, nonmanufacturing sellers or distributors must devote resources to protect their interests. In most situations, therefore, immunizing nonmanufacturers from strict liability saves those resources without jeopardizing the plaintiffs interests. To assure plaintiffs access to a responsible and solvent product seller or distributor, the statutes generally provide that the nonmanufacturing seller or distributor is immunized from strict liability only if: (1) the manufacturer is subject to the jurisdiction of the court of plaintiff's domicile; and (2) the manufacturer is not, nor is likely to become, insolvent.

In connection with these statutes, two problems may need to be resolved to assure fairness to plaintiffs. First, as currently structured, the statutes typically impose upon the plaintiff the risk of insolvency of the manufacturer between the time an action is brought and the time a judgment can be enforced. If a nonmanufacturing seller or distributor is dismissed from an action at the outset when it appears that the manufacturer will be able to pay a judgment, and the manufacturer subsequently becomes insolvent and is unable to pay the judgment, the plaintiff may be left to suffer the loss uncompensated. One possible solution could be to toll the statute of limitations against nonmanufacturers so that they may be brought in if necessary. Second, a nonmanufacturing seller or distributor occasionally will be responsible for the introduction of a defect in a product even though it exercised reasonable care in handling or supervising the product in its control. In such instances, liability for a § 2(a) defect should be imposed on the nonmanufacturing seller or distributor. See § 2, Illustration 2.

REPORTERS' NOTE

Comment a. History.

1. Abundant authority recognizes the division of product defects into manufacturing defects, design defects, and defects based on inadequate instructions or warnings. See, e.g., Caterpillar Tractor Co. v. Beck, 593 P.2d 871, 881–82 (Alaska 1979) (Accord, Shanks v. Upjohn Co., 835 P.2d 1189, 1194 (Alaska 1992)); Dart v. Wiebe Mfg., Inc., 709 P.2d 876, 878–79 (Ariz.1985) (en banc); Barker v. Lull Eng'g Co., 573 P.2d 443, 454 (Cal.1978) (recognizing that different

Exhibit 6-5 *Restatement (Third) of Torts, Products Liability Notes.* American Law Institute, *Restatement (Third) of Torts, 3d ed., Vol. 1* (1998), p. 9. © 1998 by the American Law Institute. All rights reserved. Reprinted with permission.

When a *Restatement* has been adopted, the comments and reporters' notes are invaluable aids in locating cases from other jurisdictions and other secondary sources interpreting the *Restatement*. A *Restatement* may also be used to locate authority to challenge an existing law.

For Example

The client's case requires the challenge of a rule or statement of the law adopted by a state that differs from the one recommended by the *Restatement*. The *Restatement* may provide reasons and persuasive authority that can be used to challenge the existing rule or statement of the law.

2. Research Techniques—Restatements

The following research techniques help you locate specific *Restatement* topics.

a. Index

You may locate *Restatement* topics by consulting the alphabetical index, usually located at the end of each *Restatement*. When searching *Restatements* in Westlaw or LexisNexis, the index is accessible via the table of contents.

For Example

> If you are interested in the definition of *superseding cause* in a negligence case, you would refer to the index to the *Restatement of the Law of Torts, Second*.

b. Table of Contents

If you are familiar with the area and topic, you can scan the table of contents of the *Restatement* volume for the specific section.

For Example

> You are researching strict liability in a torts case involving manufacturing defects. Look in the table of contents to the *Restatement of the Law of Torts, Products Liability* volume.

c. Table of Cases

More recent *Restatements* have a "Table of Cases" in the index volume for the *Restatement*. When searching the *Restatements* online, the Table of Cases may be listed as "General Case Citations." If you look up a case name cited in the *Restatement*, this table will lead you to the relevant section.

d. Appendix Volumes

When researching in print, refer to the noncumulative appendix volumes for summaries of court opinions addressing the *Restatement* section you are researching.

e. Reference from Other Sources

Often you may be directed to a specific *Restatement* section from another source, such as a citation in a case, article, or *Shepard's Restatement of the Law Citations*. You could go directly to the volume and section cited, rather than consult the index.

In print, *always* check the pocket part and supplement to update your research and to locate the most recent cases. In addition, *always* consult the appendix volume to ensure that you have located all the case summaries. Note that the appendix volumes are noncumulative, so each must be checked. When searching the *Restatements* online, there is a date provided at the top of each page noting when the topic and section was last updated.

3. Computer-Aided Research

As noted in the previous section, the *Restatements of the Law* are available on Westlaw and LexisNexis. The *Restatements* are not available on non-fee-based websites.

IV. UNIFORM LAWS AND MODEL ACTS

The National Conference of Commissioners on Uniform State Laws (NCCUSL) was formed to draft and promote uniform laws. The members include judges, attorneys, law professors, and legal scholars. The goal of the NCCUSL is to make available for adoption by states **uniform laws** and **model acts** in areas of the law where uniformity would be beneficial to the states. Uniform laws are drafted by the NCCUSL and presented to all state legislatures with the intent that each state adopt the NCCUSL's version of the law. If a state adopts the uniform law, that law is integrated into the state's legislative scheme.

For Example

For commerce to take place smoothly and efficiently between states, it is beneficial if the laws governing commerce, such as the sale of goods, are uniform among the states. To this end, the National Conference of Commissioners on Uniform State Laws and the American Law Institute drafted the Uniform Commercial Code (UCC). Every state has adopted the code in whole or in part. See Exhibits 3-1 to 3-4.

Model acts are drafted for those situations in which a state does not intend to adopt an entire law, but rather intends to modify a uniform law to meet the state's requirements. The American Law Institute has drafted several model codes. These include the Model Penal Code, the Model Code of Evidence, the Model Land Development Code, and the Model Business Corporations Act.

The uniform laws and model acts are secondary authority. They become primary authority only when they are adopted by a state's legislature. When adopted, they will be assigned statutory numbers that fit within the state's statutory numbering scheme.

For Example

The first two sections of Article 2, Sales, of the Uniform Commercial Code are numbered and titled Section 2-101, Short Title, and Section 2-102, Scope. When the state of Arizona adopted these sections, the numbers were amended to fit within the state's statutory numbering system—Section 2-101 is Section 47-1101, Short Title; Section 2-102 is Section 47-1102, Scope. See Exhibit 3-1.

A. Features of Uniform Laws and Model Acts

The *Uniform Laws Annotated* (*ULA*) have the following features:

- **Organization.** Each law or act is divided into topics and subtopics by articles and sections.
- **Uniform law.** Each section presents a statement of the uniform law (see Exhibit 6-6).
- **Commissioners' notes.** The law may be followed by the commissioners' comments on the law which include, among other things, the purpose of the law, a discussion of the variations adopted by the states, references to law review articles, and a list of the states that have adopted the law.
- **Library references.** Following the law are library references or guides to other research sources, such as digest key numbers and encyclopedia cites (see Exhibit 6-6).
- **Notes to decisions.** Each law includes a summary of court decisions interpreting the law from all adopting states.
- **Tables.** Each volume has tables listing states that have adopted the law.
- **Index.** Each uniform law has an index in the back of the volume.
- **Updates.** For the print source, pocket parts update each volume.

B. Research Using Uniform and Model Laws

1. Use as a Research Tool

If a researcher is proposing or drafting legislation, uniform laws and model acts are invaluable guides. Not only do they provide a model text from which a law may be crafted, but they also provide access to arguments in support of the law and citations to cases, treatises, and articles interpreting the law.

When a jurisdiction has adopted a uniform law, the commissioners' comments and notes to decisions are invaluable aids in locating cases from other jurisdictions and other secondary sources interpreting the law. This is especially helpful when the state courts have not interpreted the law. The commissioners' comments and notes to decisions may also be helpful in locating persuasive authority to challenge an existing law.

MODEL PENAL CODE § 211.1

bodily harm. The third of these circumstances incorporates the civil notion of assault into the criminal law, as had been done in a majority of jurisdictions at the time the Model Code was drafted. Finally, assault is treated as a petty misdemeanor in the case of a fight or a scuffle entered into by mutual consent.

The remaining two offenses in Article 211 generalize principles found in antecedent statutes addressed only to ad hoc situations, such as reckless driving of a motor vehicle or reckless use of firearms. Section 211.2 deals with reckless endangerment by any means, i.e., situations where the actor's conduct recklessly places or may place another person in danger of death or serious bodily injury. Section 211.3 deals with terroristic threats, i.e., situations where the actor threatens to commit a crime of violence with purpose to terrorize another person or a group of persons.

§ 211.0. Definitions.

In this Article, the definitions given in Section 210.0 apply unless a different meaning plainly is required.

WESTLAW Electronic Research

See WESTLAW Electronic Research Guide following the Preface.

§ 211.1. Assault.

1. **Simple Assault**. A person is guilty of assault if he:

    a. attempts to cause or purposely, knowingly or recklessly causes bodily injury to another; or
    b. negligently causes bodily injury to another with a deadly weapon; or
    c. attempts by physical menace to put another in fear of imminent serious bodily injury.

Simple assault is a misdemeanor unless committed in a fight or scuffle entered into by mutual consent, in which case it is a petty misdemeanor.

2. **Aggravated Assault**. A person is guilty of aggravated assault if he:

    a. attempts to cause serious bodily injury to another, or causes such injury purposely, knowingly or recklessly under circumstances manifesting extreme indifference to the value of human life; or
    b. attempts to cause or purposely or knowingly causes bodily injury to another with a deadly weapon.

Aggravated assault under paragraph (a) is a felony of the second degree; aggravated assault under paragraph (b) is a felony of the third degree.

Explanatory Note

Explanatory Note for Sections 211.1-211.3 appears before Section 211.0. For detailed Comment to 211.1, *see* MPC Part II Commentaries, vol. 1, at 174.

Library References

Assault and Battery ⟜ 48–58   WESTLAW Topic No. 37

Exhibit 6-6 Sample U.L.A. Assault Page. West Group, *Uniform Laws Annotated*, Model Penal Code, *Vol. 10A*, 2001, p. 387.

For Example

The client's case requires challenging the applicable state statute, which differs from the uniform law. The annotations to the uniform law may provide reasons and persuasive authority that can be used to challenge the existing statute.

2. Research Techniques—Uniform Laws

The following research techniques will help you locate specific uniform laws and model acts.

a. Uniform Laws Annotated, Master Edition

West's **Uniform Laws Annotated, Master Edition (ULA)** is a multivolume set that includes the uniform laws and annotations to all uniform laws that have been adopted by one or more states. The annotations include the features listed in subsection A and are invaluable research tools. The set includes uniform laws and model acts. The *ULA* lacks a general index or table of contents. The uniform laws and model acts are grouped together by subject area. A pamphlet entitled "Directory of Uniform Acts and Codes: Tables and Codes" is published with the set. This "Directory" lists the uniform laws and model laws by name, subject, and adopting jurisdiction.

b. Reference from Other Sources

Often you may be directed to a specific uniform law section from another source, such as a citation in a case, article, or the *ALR Index to Annotations*. Both the *Am. Jur. 2d* and *CJS* have a "Table of Laws and Rules" that refer to sections in each of the encyclopedias that refer to uniform laws.

3. Computer-Aided Research

Uniform laws and model acts are available on Westlaw and LexisNexis. In addition, the NCCUSL posts all final acts on its website (http://www.uniformlaws.org). The NCCUSL website contains not only the final acts, but a summary of each act and which states have adopted the acts.

V. DICTIONARIES AND WORDS AND PHRASES

A. Legal Dictionaries

Words often have a more complex or different meaning when used in a legal context than in everyday use.

For Example

Most people think the word *publication* means "to make something known to the public in general," such as through publication in a newspaper. When used in conjunction with the law of defamation, *publication* means "communicating information to one or more persons." In this context, telling defamatory information about an individual to one other person is "publication."

Legal dictionaries provide the spelling, pronunciation, and legal meaning assigned to terms used in the law. Legal or "law" dictionaries are similar to other dictionaries in that the terms are arranged alphabetically. They differ from other dictionaries in that they cite the source of the definition, such as a treatise or court opinion.

For Example

Following the definition of a term such as *jurisdiction* will be a citation to the court opinion or a secondary authority source where the term is defined. There will also be a list of related or qualifying terms associated with the term jurisdiction, such as ancillary, appellate, concurrent, and the like.

Legal dictionaries, therefore, are valuable not only for their definitions, but also for the citations that are a research source for both primary and secondary authority.

The two best-known law dictionaries are *Black's Law Dictionary* published by Thomson West, and *Oren's Dictionary of the Law* published by Thomson Delmar Publishing. The dictionaries are similar as each arranges the terms alphabetically, provides citations to the definitions, and consists of a single volume. *Black's* is available on Westlaw.

B. *Words and Phrases*

Words and Phrases is a multivolume set, published by West, a Thomson Reuters company, that provides the judicial definition of words and phrases. It includes only terms that have been defined in federal and state court opinions. If a term has not been defined in an opinion, it will not appear in *Words and Phrases*. This set provides every court definition of a term and a brief summary of the opinion. A term will usually have multiple definitions, sometimes covering several pages. The set is kept up to date with annual pocket parts for each volume. It is available on Westlaw, usually as a separate database. However, court definitions of specific terms are available on both Westlaw and LexisNexis.

Words and Phrases is a valuable case finder, especially in situations when you are looking for a unique definition of a term or phrase (see Exhibit 6-7).

For Example

You are looking for how state courts have defined the phrase "actual physical control" as used in driving while intoxicated or driving under the influence statutes. *Black's Law Dictionary* does not define the phrase, but a search in Westlaw using *Words and Phrases* yields results of cases with a definition of the phrase (see Exhibit 6-7).

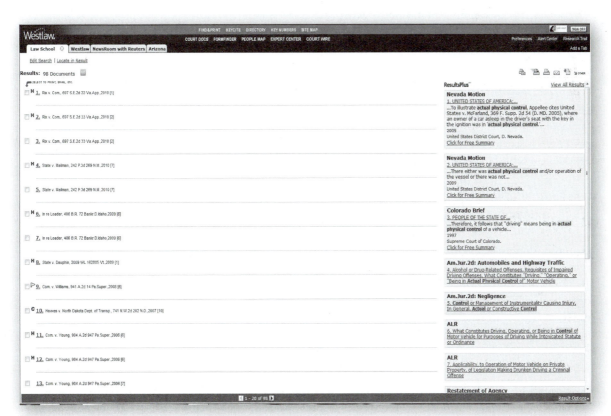

Exhibit 6-7 Screenshot of Results from *Words and Phrases* Search for Cases Providing the Definition of "Actual Physical Control." Reprinted with permission of Thomson Reuters.

VI. LEGISLATIVE HISTORY

Legislative history is the record of the legislation during the enactment process before it became law. It is composed of committee reports, transcripts of hearings, statements of legislators concerning the legislation, and any other materials published for legislative use in regard to the legislation. It is a secondary authority source sometimes relied upon by the courts when interpreting laws.

There are several different sources of legislative history for federal statutes. The research sources for locating the legislative history for state statutes may be similar to some or all of the federal legislative history sources. Therefore, the research sources for locating federal legislative history are discussed here. The state sources vary from state to state, and may be limited or nonexistent, depending on the state. Consult the appropriate state legislative records or service office for the availability of legislative history.

It is important to note that legislative history is considered only if the plain meaning of a statute is not clear or sections of a statute are internally inconsistent. If the meaning is clear, that meaning will be applied by the court even if the legislative history indicates the legislature intended a different meaning.

A. Federal Legislative History Sources

The following are the main sources of legislative history. Usually, information from more than one of these sources is necessary to determine legislative intent.

1. Congressional Bills

Each bill goes through several versions before it is passed. An examination of the terms or provisions deleted or added in the various versions of the bill may reveal the legislative intent.

For Example

An early version of the Housing Discrimination Act may have used the term *citizen* rather than *person*. The substitution of the more expansive term *person* in a later version may support an argument that the legislature intended that the act have an expansive application rather than a limited one.

Information gained through this source concerning legislative intent is based on the *researcher's interpretation* of what the legislature intended when it adopted different versions of a bill. Therefore, other legislative history sources are necessary to obtain additional support for a particular interpretation of legislative intent.

2. Committee Hearings

Congressional committees hold hearings to receive public input and expert testimony concerning proposed legislation. The records of the hearing are composed of transcripts of the legislators' questions and witness testimony along with exhibits and documents submitted. Some of the information may help explain how the legislation applies or the reason certain terms or phrases were used. The hearing records, however, include all arguments and information submitted by individuals and groups, both in support of, and opposition to, some or all of the legislation. It is difficult to determine on which testimony and information the committee relied. Therefore, the information from this source is usually used in support of other legislative history sources.

3. Committee Reports

A committee report on a bill usually includes the text of the bill, the majority's reasons for recommending the bill, an analysis of the contents of the bill, and the minority's reasons for opposing the bill. Because the report clearly states the legislators' intent and is prepared by those who worked with the bill, the report is usually considered by courts as the most authoritative source of legislative history.

4. Congressional Debates

Congress may hold debates on a bill, and the records of the debates are published in the *Congressional Record*. During the debates, members of Congress present arguments for and against a bill and amendments to a bill. The debates often include explanations of provisions of the bill, its purpose, or how it applies. Many different and often contradictory reasons may be presented in support of a bill. For this reason, it may be difficult to determine legislative intent from the debates.

B. Researching Federal Legislative History

1. Use of Legislative History

On some occasions, a law that governs a client's fact situation may be written in such a manner that the meaning of the law is unclear. The lack of clarity may be due to the use of an ambiguous term or phrase, or the law may be written so broadly that it is unclear how it is supposed to apply in a specific factual situation. The courts may resolve the matter by looking to the legislative history of the law to determine the legislature's intended meaning of a term or phrase, or the intention as to when or how the law applies. Legislative history may be of assistance in several ways. The history may identify why an ambiguous term was used and what meaning the legislature intended, what the legislature intended the statute to accomplish, what the general purpose of the legislation is, and so on.

Additionally, it may be necessary to monitor a proposed piece of legislation due to its potential impact on a client or on your employer, particularly if you work for counsel representing business entities. In those situations, you may be asked to monitor the progress of the legislation and report on the actions taken by committees in anticipation of the impact of the legislation if passed and signed into law.

For Example

Section A(9) of the Housing Discrimination Act provides that no person shall deny an individual housing on the basis of gender preference. The court is called upon to interpret the term *person*. Does it include corporations and businesses such as partnerships? In the case before the court, a closely held corporation that owned an apartment complex refused to rent an apartment to a couple because of the couple's gender preference. The corporation argued that a corporation is not a person within the meaning of the statute. Included in the legislative history of the statute is a committee report recommending passage of the legislation. The report contains the following language: "the intent of the legislation is to eliminate any and all forms of gender discrimination in housing. The term 'person' is intended to include all individuals and business entities, including corporations." The legislative history in this example provides the court guidance in interpreting the statute.

2. Sources for Locating and Compiling Federal Legislative History

There are several avenues to pursue when you compile the legislative history of an enacted federal statute. The starting point of your research is to locate the statute in the *United States Code*, *United States Code Annotated*, or the *United States Code Service* and review the history of the statute in the annotations. This will provide you with several pieces of information necessary to locate the legislative history, including the public law number, the date the law was enacted, the Statutes at Large number, and where the law is published in the ***United States Code Congressional and Administrative News (USCCAN)***. Remember there may be multiple public law numbers because a statute may have been enacted but subsequently amended. In order to compile a complete legislative history, a researcher has to know, and therefore locate, documents related to not only the original enactment of the statute, but subsequent amendments to the statute.

For Example

Following the text of 42 U.S.C.A. § 2000aa is the following information: Pub. L. 96-440, Title I § 101, Oct 13, 1980, 94 Stat. 1879, Senate Report No. 96-874, House Conference Report No. 96-1411, 1980 *United States Code Congressional and Administrative News Service*, page 3950; Pub. L. 104-208 Div. A, Title I, § 101(a), Sept. 30, 1996, 110 Stat. 3009-30.

There are both print and electronic sources of legislative history. Researchers can use traditional print sources or electronic sources to locate and compile legislative histories. To locate legislative history sources, you must have the public law number of the statute being researched. The public law number is most important because most of the following sources index laws by the public law number. If you do not know the public law number, some of the sources listed in the following subsections include subject indexes and popular name tables. These indexes and tables will list the public law number of the statute and each amendment to the statute. The following are the main sources for locating and compiling legislative history.

a. Pre-Compiled Legislative Histories

A starting point for researching legislative history is to determine if the legislative history has already been compiled. For many laws, the government agency charged with regulating the legislation, a commercial publisher, or other groups have already compiled the legislative history. If there is a pre-compiled legislative history, then your research may be done and there is no need to investigate further. Several publications list compiled legislative histories; check the catalogue listings at a law library. Some of the sources for locating compiled legislative histories include:

- *Public Laws Legislative Histories on Microfiche*, published by Commerce Clearing House (CCH)
- *Federal Legislative Histories: An Annotated Bibliography and Index to Officially Published Sources*, compiled by Bernard D. Reams, Jr.
- *Sources of Compiled Legislative Histories: A Bibliography of Government Documents, Periodicals, Articles, and Books*, compiled by Nancy P. Johnson

b. Congressional Information Service

The **Congressional Information Service (CIS)**, by ProQuest, is a commercial publication that is considered one of the most comprehensive publications of legislative history documents. Pamphlets, which are published monthly, are assembled into annual bound volumes. The *CIS* includes summaries of the law; committee reports, documents, and hearing testimony; and references to debates published in the *Congressional Record*, but does not contain the *Congressional Record* itself. The *CIS* allows you to locate documents in several ways, such as a bill number, subject, and popular name (see Exhibit 6-8).

The CIS collection has print and electronic indices and a microfiche library. The print indexes include:

- **Monthly CIS Index.** Published twelve times a year, this index catalogs, abstracts, and indexes publications issued by Congress during the previous month.
- **Annual CIS Index.** Each year, this index is published and contains abstracts and index references which have been included in the monthly CIS Index (see Exhibit 6-8). The Annual Index includes legislative histories since 1970 for all public laws enacted during the year. The Annual CIS Index supersedes the Monthly CIS Index and often has additional legislative history.
- **CIS Multiple-year Cumulations.** These multiple-year indexes revise and cumulate all of the indexes for the years covered. They do not include the abstracts from the Annual Indexes.

c. USCCAN *Service*

The *USCCAN* service publishes the texts of federal statutes and committee reports. *USCCAN* is published by West and is available at most law libraries in print and is also available online through Westlaw. West publishes an edition for each session of Congress in monthly pamphlets that are subsequently assembled in bound volumes after each session concludes. In each pamphlet and bound volume is a legislative history table that lists information relating to the law, such as the public law number, date of approval, bill number, the House and Senate report number, and dates on which the House and Senate considered the bill. With the text of each act is a legislative history section that provides references to all reports related to the act. Although *USCCAN* does not publish all committee reports, it is a reliable source for committee and conference report references and an overview of the legislative history of the law. Through this source, you can identify the reports and other sources from which you can assemble the legislative history.

d. Congressional Record

The *Congressional Record* is a record of the debates on the floor of the Senate and House. This record is useful if you are interested in reviewing the floor debates on a bill. It includes an index that references such items as debates, committee reports, and passage information. Information is indexed by subject matter and history. For information in the history section, you must know the House and Senate bill numbers of the legislation.

Index of Bill Numbers

This index lists all Public Bills that were the subjects of hearings, reports, and other publications abstracted in the 2014 CIS Annual. It also lists all bills identified as part of the legislative history of a Public Law enacted during 2014 even if the bill number is not specifically mentioned in the CIS Index Legislative History.

The bills are cross-referenced to CIS Index accession numbers, as well as to Public Law numbers where appropriate.

This index contains bills from various Congresses. Bills are identified by the Congress in which they were introduced. For example, a 105th Congress bill would be listed as (105) H.R. 123.

96th CONGRESS

House Bills

(96) H.R. 2000.................H263-2

96th CONGRESS

Senate Bills

(96) S. Res. 197..............H263-2

97th CONGRESS

Senate Bills

(97) S. 1683....................H263-2
(97) S. 2008....................H263-2
(97) S. 2629....................H263-2
(97) S. 2848....................H263-2

98th CONGRESS

House Bills

(98) H.R. 750..................H263-2
(98) H.R. 2163................H263-2

98th CONGRESS

Senate Bills

(98) S.J. Res. 110.............S523-2

(98) S. 12.........................H263-2
(98) S. 20.........................H263-2
(98) S. 95.........................H263-2
(98) S. 922......................H263-2

99th CONGRESS

House Bills

(99) H.R. 382.................H263-2
(99) H.R. 748.................H263-2
(99) H.R. 2845...............H263-2
(99) H.R. 3461...............H263-2

99th CONGRESS

Senate Bills

(99) S.J. Res. 313..............S523-2

(99) S. Res. 157...............H263-2
(99) S. Res. 159...............H263-2

(99) S. 20.........................H263-2
(99) S. 1556....................H263-2

100th CONGRESS

House Bills

(100) H.R. 22....................H263-2
(100) H.R. 33....................H263-2
(100) H.R. 777.................H263-2
(100) H.R. 805.................H263-2
(100) H.R. 1558...............H263-2
(100) H.R. 2733...............H263-2
(100) H.R. 5205...............H263-2

100th CONGRESS

Senate Bills

(100) S. Con. Res. 49........H263-2

(100) S.J. Res. 21...............S523-2
(100) S.J. Res. 130.............S523-2
(100) S.J. Res. 166.............S523-2
(100) S.J. Res. 282.............S523-2

(100) S. 416.....................H263-2
(100) S. 832.....................H263-2
(100) S. 1362...................H263-2
(100) S. 2478...................H263-2

101st CONGRESS

House Bills

(101) H.R. 1401...............H263-2

(101) H.R. 2142...............H263-2

101st CONGRESS

Senate Bills

(101) S.J. Res. 48............S523-2

(101) S. 29......................H263-2

102d CONGRESS

House Bills

(102) H.R. 1676.............H263-2
(102) H.R. 1889.............H263-2
(102) H.R. 5387.............H263-2
(102) H.R. 6089.............H263-2

102d CONGRESS

Senate Bills

(102) S.J. Res. 35............S523-2

(102) S. 1667.................H263-2

103d CONGRESS

House Bills

(103) H.R. 565...............H263-2
(103) H.R. 1383.............H263-2
(103) H.R. 2221.............H263-2
(103) H.R. 3801.............H263-2

103d CONGRESS

Senate Bills

(103) S.J. Res. 10............S523-2
(103) S.J. Res. 37............S523-2
(103) S. 1287.................H263-2
(103) S. 1477.................H263-2
(103) S. 1824.................H263-2

104th CONGRESS

House Bills

(104) H.R. 252...............H263-2
(104) H.R. 766...............H263-2

Exhibit 6-8 2014 Annual CIS Index, Index to Congressional Publications and Legislative Histories; Legislative Histories of U.S. Public Laws (2014) p. 697–698. Source: ProQuest.

Public Law 113-190   128 Stat. 2028

Albuquerque, New Mexico, Federal Land Conveyance Act of 2013

November 26, 2014

Public Law

1.1   Public Law 113-190, approved Nov. 26, 2014. (S. 898)

(CIS14:PL113-190   2 p.)

"To authorize the Administrator of General Services to convey a parcel of real properly in Albuquerque, New Mexico, to the Amy Biehl High School Foundation."

ELABORATION:

Directs GSA to offer to convey, for fair market value, certain real property in Albuquerque, N.Mex., to the Amy Biehl High School Foundation.

P.L. 113-190 Reports

113th Congress

2.1   H. Rpt. 113-408 on H.R. 3998, "Albuquerque, New Mexico, Federal Land Conveyance Act of 2014," Apr. 9, 2014.

(CIS14:H753-8   6 p.)

(Y1.1/8:113-408.)

Recommends passage, with an amendment in the nature of a substitute, of H.R. 3998, the Albuquerque, New Mexico, Federal Land Conveyance Act of 2014, to authorize GSA to convey, for fair market value, certain real property in Albuquerque. N.Mex., to the Amy Biehl High School Foundation.

H.R. 3998 is similar to S. 898.

P.L. 113-190 Bills

113th Congress

ENACTED BILL

3.1   S. 898 as introduced May 8, 2013; as reported by the Senate Environment and Public Works Committee June 5, 2014; as passed by the Senate Sept. 9, 2014.

COMPANION BILL

3.2   H.R. 3998 as introduced Feb. 5, 2014; as reported by the House Transportation and Infrastructure Committee Apr. 9, 2014; as passed by the House June 17, 2014.

P.L. 113-190 Debate

160 Congressional Record
113th Congress, 2nd Session - 2014

4.1   June 17, House consideration and passage of H.R. 3998, p. H5380.

4.2   Sept. 9, Senate consideration and passage of S. 898, p. S5460.

4.3   Nov. 12, House consideration and passage of S. 898, p. H7914.

Exhibit 6-8 *(Continued)*

e. Congressional Index

The *Congressional Index* is a loose-leaf service published by Commerce Clearing House (CCH). This publication includes various information on bills such as indexes of bills by subject and sponsor, a summary of each bill, tables of actions taken on a bill, companion bills, and voting records on a bill. It does not include the text of the bill, debates, committee reports, and so on, but it is still a valuable aid in locating documents.

f. Other Sources

Copies of legislative history documents, such as bills and committee reports, are usually available through your congressional representatives. You can also Shepardize or KeyCite a statute, and locate law review articles and *ALR* annotations that have analyzed the statute. Often the analysis will include a summary of the legislative history.

g. Computer-Aided Research

There are several online services that may be used to locate and compile legislative history. It is best to have the public law number of the law or the Senate or House bill numbers.

- Westlaw has comprehensive legislative histories and more than 22,000 legislative histories compiled by the Government Printing Office (GPO). Often the compiled histories are part of a Westlaw subscription, but the GPO histories are a premium service, available at an extra charge. Westlaw also has a bill tracking service that can be useful when tracking the progress of proposed legislation.
- LexisNexis has limited compiled legislative histories. However, Lexis has the CIS Index via ProQuest Congressional. ProQuest Congressional provides access to CIS abstracts, indexes, and full text of Congressional reports from 1789 to present. It also contains legislative history information for all U.S. public law numbers from 1970 to present. ProQuest Congressional includes many other features such as biographies of members of congress and voting records.
- ProQuest is available via subscription in addition to through LexisNexis as noted above. ProQuest has an additional service called Legislative Insight that offers legislative histories to thousands of U.S. public laws from 1789 to present.
- HeinOnline is a commercial database containing legislative histories compiled by the Willliam S. Hein Company and the GPO. HeinOnline's database includes legislative histories compiled by two prominent law firms. These legislative histories are a staple of pre-compiled histories. Searching legislative histories on HeinOnline may include costs in addition to a subscription to the database itself. Most of the content on HeinOnline is digitized PDF scans of print sources, and to locate content, researchers must do a full-text search.
- Library of Congress (Congress.gov). The federal government maintains the Congress.gov website, http://www.congress.gov, which is the official website for the U.S. federal legislative information. The website was formerly known as THOMAS. Congress.gov provides access to legislative history documents including committee hearings, committee reports, the *Congressional Record*, legislation, information on nomination and members of Congress, and treaty documents. Congress.gov has bill records dating back to 1973, bill texts dating back to 1993, and the *Congressional Record* dating back to 1995. Congress.gov is usually updated the day after a session of Congress adjourns. (See Exhibit 6-9.)
- GPO FDsys. The Government Printing Office maintains the Federal Digital System (FDsys), discussed previously in Chapter 3. The FDsys website, https://www.gpo.gov/fdsys, provides access to bills, committee reports, committee hearings, the *Congressional Record*, and other legislative documents. FDsys does not contain legislative histories for as far back as other sources, but generally has legislative content going back to 1990.

C. State Legislative History

Just as courts may look to federal legislative history to resolve an ambiguity in a federal law, state courts may look to state legislative history as a guide to interpret state law. The research sources and processes for locating the legislative history for state statutes are similar to those for federal law. State legislative history and its location vary from state to state and may be limited. Consult the appropriate state legislative records or service office for the availability of legislative history. Information on state legislation may be available from the state legislature's website, and Westlaw and LexisNexis both offer state databases. In addition, the local law librarian should be able to guide you to the sources for state legislative history.

If tracking state legislation, state legislature websites increasingly provide the ability to listen to committee hearings and floor debates in a streaming format, or via a digitized recording available shortly after the hearing or debate. State legislature websites also provide access to bills and bill tracking via alerts. Some legislative websites also allow testimony or comments related committee or subcommittee hearings to be submitted electronically.

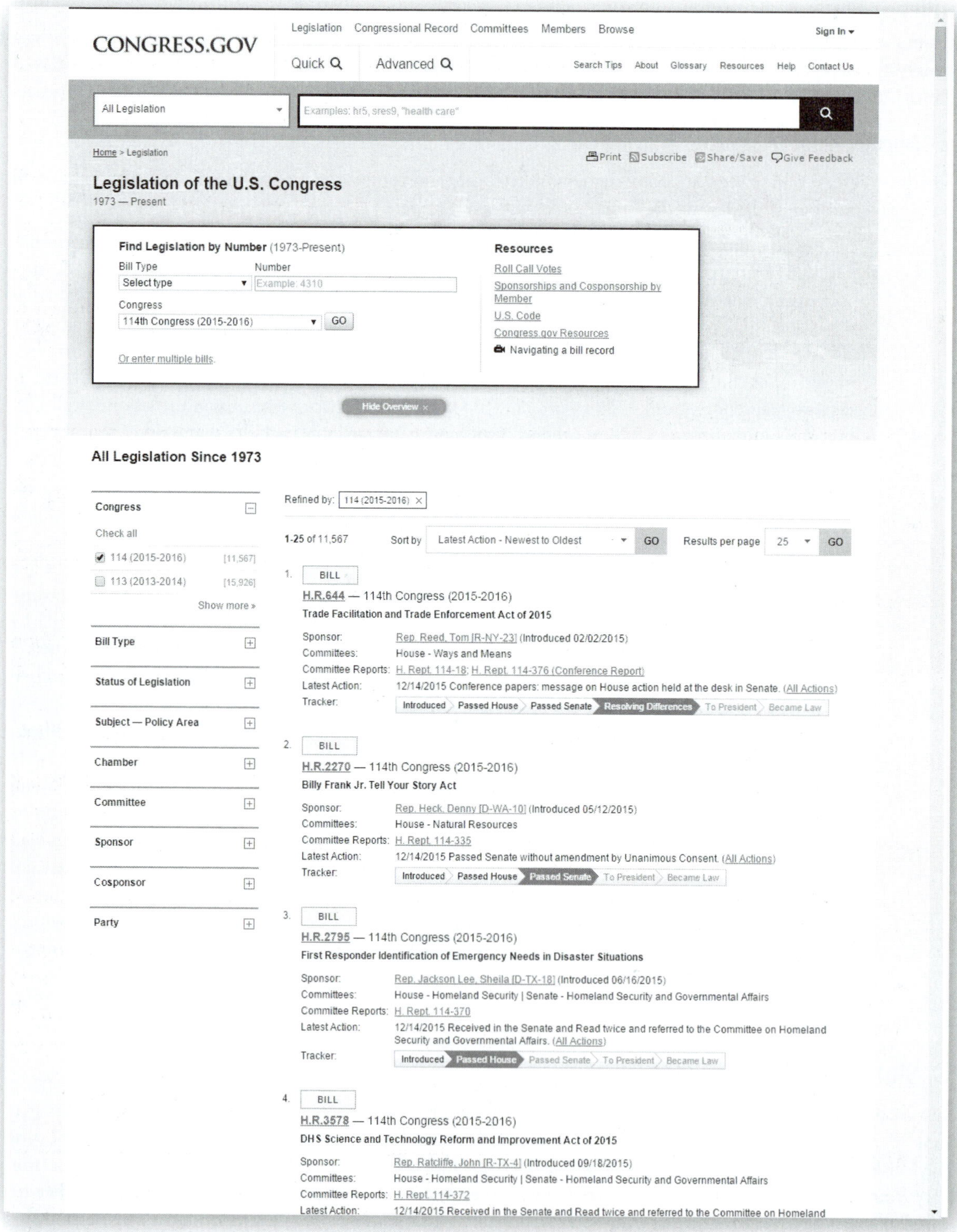

Exhibit 6-9 Screenshot of Legislation search page from Congress.gov. Source: Congress.gov.

VII. JURY INSTRUCTIONS—OTHER RESEARCH SOURCES

In addition to the research authorities mentioned in Chapter 5 and in this chapter, there are other sources, which are briefly discussed in this section.

A. Jury Instructions

Following the presentation of the evidence in a trial, the jury is instructed on the law that applies to the case, such as how terms are defined and what must be proven for a party to prevail (see Exhibit 6-10). Most states adopt uniform or model jury instructions for the courts to follow when instructing the jury. These **jury instructions** are often published with the annotated statutes. If not, check at the local law library or with the court. If there is no approved set of jury instructions, there are several texts that include model jury instructions, such as *Am. Jur. Pleading and Practice Forms*.

It is important to know how to locate jury instructions because you may be called upon to prepare them for a case. In addition, the instructions provide the definitions of terms, the elements of a cause of action that must be proven, and so on, which the state has adopted. The instructions also often provide annotations referencing court opinions that discuss the instruction.

Many states have adopted model jury instructions for the state, and some local jurisdictions have adopted local jury instructions. If a state has model jury instructions, they are often located with the rules of court. There are many form books and loose-leaf services that contain state forms or model jury instructions. These are often available in the law office law library or in a local law library.

For Example

> If you want to determine what your state requires to establish a negligence claim, consult the state's approved jury instructions. The annotations to the instructions reference court opinions that have discussed the topic.

B. Practice and Form Books

There are many types of single-volume and multivolume texts designed to assist practitioners. They range from **form books** to texts that provide detailed litigation guides and strategy. Several of the most popular form books include:

- *American Jurisprudence Legal Forms 2d.* This is a multivolume set arranged alphabetically.
- *American Jurisprudence Pleading and Practice Forms Annotated.* This is a multivolume set that is particularly useful for those in litigation practices.
- *Bender's Federal Practice Forms.* This is a multivolume set that contains litigation forms for both civil and criminal law.
- *Bender's Forms of Discovery.* This multivolume set by Lexis contains forms related specifically to civil discovery, such as sample interrogatories, requests for production, and deposition questions.
- *Fletcher Corporation Forms Annotated.* This set of forms is an example of content specific form books, and contains forms related to corporations.
- *West's Legal Forms, 2d.* This multivolume set by West has a wide variety of forms, including forms for areas such as real estate sales, business organizations, and bankruptcy.

For Example

> If you are called upon to prepare a legal document, such as a contract for the sale of a business, be sure to check a form book to avoid omitting anything.

Check the treatise section of your library or with the librarian. Many law office libraries contain at least one set of form books that are related to the particular areas of law in which the firm practices. Many of the form and practice books are also available on Westlaw and LexisNexis. Increasingly, state bar websites provide attorney members with electronic access to statewide forms and model jury instructions.

INTENTIONAL TORTS 2

Battery

[*Name of plaintiff*] claims that [*name of defendant*] committed a battery against [her/him]]. On this claim, [*name of plaintiff*] must prove:

1. [*Name of defendant*] intended:

    a. To cause a harm or offensive contact with [*name of plaintiff*] [or a third person][1] or

    b. To cause [*name of plaintiff*] [or a third person] apprehension[2] of an immediate harmful or offensive contact; and

2. [*Name of defendant*] caused a harmful or offensive contact with *name of plaintiff*.
3. [*Name of plaintiff*]'s damages.][3]

A contact is offensive if it would offend a reasonable person.

[You may find [*name of defendant*] liable to [*name of plaintiff*] for battery, even though [*name of defendant*] did not intend to bring about the harmful or offensive contact that actually resulted.][4]

SOURCE: RESTAURANT (SECOND) OF TORTS §§ 13-20; A.R.S. § 13-1203(A)(1) and (3); RAJI (CRIMINAL) 12.03 (Assault). *See Garcia v. United States*, 826 F.2d 806 (9th Cir. 1987).

[1] This is commonly known as the doctrine of "transferred intent." *See* RESTATEMENT (SECOND) OF TORTS §§ 23, 32; *Cf.* A.R.S. § 13-203(B)(1).

[2] Apprehension is not the same as fright. For a discussion of the term "apprehension," *see* RESTATEMENT (SECOND) OF TORTS § 24, cmt. b. While the crime of assault requires "reasonable apprehension," the tort of assault has no such requirement. Compare A.R.S. § 13-1203(A)(2) and RESTATEMENT (SECOND) OF TORTS § 27.

[3] Use this bracketed language if appropriate to the facts. A plaintiff is not required to prove damages, since the tort penalizes intentional conduct and damages are presumed. PROSSER, LAW OF TORTS § 7 (4th Ed. 1971). If plaintiff has actual damages, use RAJI (CIVIL) 4th Personal Injury 1 (Measure of Damages) where actual damages are present. It may be appropriate to instruct the jury on punitive damages. *See* RAJI (CIVIL) 4th Personal Injury Damages 4 (Punitive Damages). An award of nominal damages, as opposed to actual damages, will not support an award of punitive damages. *Koepnick v. Sears Roebuck & Co.*, 158 Ariz. 322, 332, 762 P.2d 609, 619 (Ct. App. 1988).

[4] Use this bracketed language if appropriate to the facts.

Exhibit 6-10 Sample Jury Instruction. Revised Arizona Jury Instructions—Civil. Source: Lexis-Nexis.

REVISED ARIZONA JURY INSTRUCTIONS (CIVIL), 5TH

INTENTIONAL TORTS 9

Justification for Non-Deadly Physical Force in Law Enforcement

In arresting or detaining a suspect or escapee, or in preventing escape after arrest or detention, a person is justified in using physical force[1] if:

1. A reasonable person would believe that such force is immediately necessary to arrest or detain the suspect or escapee, or to prevent escape; and

2. The person makes known the purpose of the arrest or detention, if it is reasonable to do so; and

3. A reasonable person would believe the arrest or detention to be lawful.

SOURCE: RAJI (CRIMINAL) 4.09 (Justification for Physical force in Law Enforcement); A.R.S. § 13-409.

[1]"Physical force" is defined in A.R.S. § 13-105(28).

Exhibit 6-10   *(Continued)*

C. Loose-Leaf Services

Loose-leaf services are publications that focus on a specific area of law and include primary authority such as statutes, regulations, and summaries of court and administrative decisions. Also, they usually include an analysis of the law and references to secondary sources. Each publication includes indexes and finding aids that differ according to the subject matter and the publisher. They are not updated by pocket parts; rather, the pages are individually placed in binders and updated by replacement pages. Several different publishers publish loose-leaf services that cover many subjects, such as labor law, environmental law, family law, and tax law. Some of the major publishers include Commerce Clearing House (CCH), Bureau of National Affairs (BNA), and Matthew Bender (MB).

D. Presidential Materials

Presidential materials are directives issued by the President of the United States. The two main types are proclamations and executive orders. Proclamations are announcements that have no legal effect, such as declaring a week, for example, "National Bicyclers Week." Executive orders cover a wide range of topics and are usually directives to agencies. These directives have the force of law. Presidential proclamations and executive orders are published in the *Federal Register*, *CFR*, *USCCAN*, and the *Weekly Compilation of Presidential Documents* (published by the Office of the Federal Register). They are also available on Westlaw and LexisNexis, and on the Government Printing Office website.

E. Martindale-Hubbell Law Directory

The ***Martindale-Hubbell Law Directory***, published by LexisNexis, is a comprehensive directory of attorneys. The multivolume set, arranged alphabetically by state, provides attorneys' names and biographical information, such as date of admission to the bar, law school attended, and publications. There is a multivolume *International Law Directory* listing attorneys from foreign countries. *Martindale-Hubbell* is available on LexisNexis and the directory website (see Internet Resources at the end of this chapter).

Included with the law directory set is a *Martindale-Hubbell Law Digest*, which contains brief summaries of some (but not all) of the laws of the states as well as many foreign countries. The set also includes some uniform laws and model acts, and the American Bar Association's Model Rules of Professional Conduct.

VIII. CITING PERIODICALS, *RESTATEMENTS*, UNIFORM LAWS, DICTIONARIES, AND OTHER SECONDARY AUTHORITY

This section presents an overview of rules of citation to be used when citing secondary authority, that is, sources a court may rely on that are not the law. The examples are specific to citation format used in court documents and legal memoranda, rather than academic articles.

A detailed discussion of the citation rules for each type of secondary authority is beyond the scope of this text. Even a detailed discussion of the citation rules for the types of secondary authority discussed in this chapter are beyond this text. Therefore, this section presents the citation format for the commonly used secondary sources mentioned in this chapter according to *Bluebook* format. As mentioned in each of the previous chapters, be sure to carefully review the appropriate citation manual for the detailed rules regarding each citation format.

A. *Restatements*

Both the *Bluebook* and the *ALWD Guide* contain the same basic citation rules for the proper citation format for *Restatements*. The only difference is that the name of the *Restatement* is underlined or italicized in *ALWD Guide* format, but not *Bluebook* format. Refer to Bluepages B12 and Rule 3.4 in the *Bluebook*, and Rule 23.1 in the *ALWD Guide* for full details of proper citation format.

A citation to a *Restatement* generally should include the following components:

1. The full name and edition of the *Restatement*. In *ALWD Guide* format, the full name of the edition is italicized or underlined, including a subtitle if the reference is to a subtitle. *Bluebook* format does not underline or italicize either.
2. The section symbol (§) and number of the *Restatement*
3. The year of the publication in parentheses

For Example

Bluebook—Reinstatement (Second) of Judgments § 28 (1982).
ALWD Guide—Reinstatement (Second) of Judgments § 28 (1982).
Bluebook—Reinstatement (Second) of Torts: Products Liability § 52 (1989).
ALWD Guide—Reinstatement (Second) of Torts: Products liability § 52 (1989).

B. Legal Dictionaries

Both the *Bluebook* and the *ALWD Guide* contain the same basic citation rules for the proper citation format for dictionaries. Refer to Bluepages B8 and Rule 15.8 in the *Bluebook* and Rule 22.1 and 22.2 in the *ALWD Guide* for full details on proper citation format.

For Example

Black's Law Dictionary 451 (7th ed. West 1999).
    or
Black's Law Dictionary 451 (Bryn A. Garner ed., 7th ed. West 1999).

C. Uniform Laws

The citation format for uniform laws depends upon whether a particular jurisdiction has adopted them. If a state has adopted the uniform laws, the citation format will be the same as for all other types of similar statutes or rules in that jurisdiction. Refer to Rules 15 in the *Bluebook* and Rules 23.3 and 23.8 in the *ALWD Guide* for full details on proper citation format.

Citation format for uniform laws or model acts should include the following:

1. Name of the act
2. Section cited (section symbol and section number, including subsection if a particular subsection is cited)
3. Parenthetical (the citation manuals differ as to content of parenthetical)

For Example

The Uniform Commercial Code, Section 2-315 is cited as: U.C.C. § 2-315. (1997)
    The Model Penal Code is cited as: Model Penal Code § 10 (1974).

D. Loose-Leaf Services

Loose-leaf services contain both primary law and analysis of law. As such, citation may be to the analysis of the law, or to the primary source. There is a format for each type of citation. Both the *Bluebook* and the *ALWD Guide* contain the same basic citation rules for the proper citation format for loose-leaf services. Refer to Bluepages B19 and Rule 19 in the *Bluebook* and Rule 24 in the *ALWD Guide*.

A citation to the loose-leaf service includes the following:

1. Volume of the loose-leaf service
2. Name of the service
3. Publisher
4. Section or paragraph number (including section or paragraph symbol)
5. Date in a parenthetical reference

For Example

4 Lab. L. Rep. (CCH) ¶ 9046 (1996).

A citation to a primary source located in a loose-leaf service includes these components:

1. Basic citation to primary source, such as case name, or statutory code section and code abbreviation
2. Volume number, name/abbreviation of service, and section or paragraph of loose-leaf service
3. Parenthetical reference with the proper jurisdiction and/or date information that would make up the primary source citation

Note: If a primary source is located in an official publication, you should cite the official publication and not the secondary source (loose-leaf).

For Example

Defenders of Wildlife, Inc. v. Watt, 12 Envtl. L. Rep. (Envtl. Law Inst.) 20, 210 (D.D.C. May 28, 1981).

IX. KEY POINTS CHECKLIST: Periodicals, Restatements, Uniform Laws, Dictionaries, Legislative History, and Other Secondary Authorities

✓ Use periodicals primarily to obtain analysis and critique of a specific legal topic that is more in-depth or narrower in focus than that provided by a legal encyclopedia or a treatise.

✓ *Restatements of the Law*, uniform laws, and model acts provide a model text from which a law may be crafted. They provide access to reasons supporting a recommended statement of the law and citations to cases, treatises, and articles interpreting the law.

✓ Consult the legislative history of a law when the meaning or application of that law is unclear. If the meaning or application of a law is clear, a court will not refer to legislative history.

✓ Do not try to draft legal documents or pleadings from scratch. Refer to the forms or samples available in the law office, or consult a form book, such as *Am. Jur. Legal Forms, 2d* or *Am. Jur. Pleading and Practice Forms*.

✓ As with all research sources, you must check the pocket parts, supplements, or whatever is used to update the source to ensure that your research is current.

X. APPLICATION

Luis thinks to himself, "The issue here in the broadest sense is, 'What are the constitutional limitations on the city restrictively zoning adult entertainment businesses?' I remember from my constitutional law class that the First Amendment's freedom of speech guarantees are involved. So I could start by looking at the annotations to the First Amendment in the *United States Code Annotated* and locate the section dealing with adult entertainment. This would lead me to case law on the subject. The problem with this is it would take me a while to find the section, then I would have to wade through all the cases. I could look through a treatise on the First Amendment; but again, I may have to wade through a lot of material before I find what I need. I need a source focused on my specific topic that has addressed the question, such as a law review article."

Luis has performed the important first step in his quest. He has identified the question he needs to research and weighed the research avenues available. He could look for a law review article on the topic by consulting the *Index to Legal Periodicals* or the *Current Law Index*, where he will find several articles that address the topic. Both the *ILP* and *CLI* are available on Westlaw and LexisNexis, on the Internet for a subscription, and may be available in the local law library on CD-ROM. A law review article will thoroughly analyze the topic through a discussion of the constitutional issues and synthesis of the cases that have addressed such ordinances. Law review articles will also include references to other research sources.

Luis could consult the *Uniform Laws Annotated, Master Edition* to determine if there is a uniform law or model zoning ordinance restricting the location of adult entertainment businesses. If there is, Luis will be presented not only with the uniform law, but also with references to states that have adopted the act, discussion of variations adopted by the states, references to law review articles, research references such as digest key numbers and encyclopedia cites, and summaries of court decisions that have interpreted the law.

Summary

This chapter discusses research authority sources that are frequently used to locate, interpret, and analyze statutory and case law: legal periodicals, *Restatements of the Law*, uniform and model laws, legislative history, and other sources.

Legal periodicals publish articles on legal topics in every area of the law. Periodical articles are valuable for their detailed analysis of current legal issues, recently emerging areas of the law, or very specific topics; depth of research; and citation to primary and secondary sources.

Restatements of the Law present a uniform statement of the law for areas of case law such as torts and contracts. Each *Restatement* provides guidance as to how the law should be defined or stated; reasons in support of the definition or statement of the law; and citations to cases, treatises, and other secondary sources.

Uniform laws and model acts provide uniform statements of the law that are available for adoption by states. They are invaluable guides when drafting or interpreting legislation.

The chapter also covers other topics such as legislative history, and other research sources such as form books. The legislative history is the record of the legislation during the enactment process. It often includes guidance as to the meaning or application of the statute.

The chapter briefly covers other research sources that may be valuable to a researcher:

Jury instructions—provide the definition of terms, elements of a cause of action, and so on that a jurisdiction has adopted

Practice and form books—provide guidance when drafting legal documents or pleadings

Loose-leaf services—publications that focus on specific areas of law and compile primary authority such as statutes and summaries of court and administrative decisions

Presidential materials—proclamations and executive orders by the President of the United States

Martindale-Hubbell Law Directory—a comprehensive directory of attorneys

Quick References

Internet Resources

The *Index to Legal Periodicals, Current Law Index, Restatements of the Law,* uniform laws, and model acts are available on Westlaw and LexisNexis. *LegalTrac* is available on the Internet by subscription. Both Westlaw and LexisNexis have databases that allow you to access the full text of bills, selected legislative history documents such as committee reports, and the *Congressional Record. Black's Law Dictionary* is available on Westlaw. *CIS* is available on LexisNexis.

Some law reviews and periodicals are available on the publisher's website. You can check the law school website to determine if a law review is published there.

Using "legal newspaper" or "legal newsletters" as a search topic, you can find thousands of websites that provide access to legal newspapers, law journals, and newsletters.

http://www.washlaw.edu
This website from Washburn University School of Law provides links to legal newspapers, newsletters, magazines, and legislative materials

http://congress.gov
Legislative history is available at this website maintained by the Library of Congress.

http://www.gpo.gov/fdsys
Legislative history is available at this website maintained by the Government Printing Office. Access is available to legislative history, Presidential documents, the United States Code, *the* Code of Regulations, Federal Register, *and numerous other documents.*

http://www.whitehouse.gov/
The White House virtual library website provides access to Presidential material.

http://www.house.gov/
This website is the home page of the United States House of Representatives.

http://www.senate.gov/
This website is the home page of the United States Senate.

http://www.martindale.com
The Martindale-Hubbell *locator website provides links to numerous legal topics.*

http://www.bna.com
Bloomberg Bureau of National Affairs (Bloomberg BNA) is a major publisher of looseleaf services and has an extensive online service for a fee. Bloomberg BNA legal can be tried for free, look for the free trial link.

http://dictionary.law.com
This website offers a legal dictionary.

http://thelawdictionary.org/
Offers Black's Law Dictionary *in an app for both iPhones and Android phones.*

http://www.uniformlaws.org/
The website of the National Conference of Commissioners on Uniform State Laws provides text of final uniform laws, as well as information and legislative status on uniform law.

Exercises

ASSIGNMENT 1

Refer to the *Index to Legal Periodicals*. What 1998 article distinguishes between euthanasia and the withdrawal of life-sustaining treatment?

ASSIGNMENT 2

Your client is a city with a growing urban agriculture movement. The city wants to know about regulation of urban agriculture, particularly microlivestock ordinances. What is a 2015 journal article that addresses how cities are responding to microlivestock?

ASSIGNMENT 3

Refer to the *Legal Resource Index*. What is the title and citation of the article in the *Daily Chicago Law Bulletin* that covered *Arizona State Legislature v. Arizona Independent Redistricting Comm'n.*, 135 S.Ct. 2652 (2015).

ASSIGNMENT 4

Refer to *Restatement (Third) of Torts*.

a. What section sets out the elements of assault?

b. Which comment addresses a key difference between the section identified above and the parallel section in the *Restatement (Second) of Torts*? What is that key difference?

c. Generally, what does the term "imminence" mean?

d. Is there a court opinion listed in the authorities from your state? If so, what is the name of that case, and what principle does it stand for?

ASSIGNMENT 5

Refer to *Restatement (Third) of Unfair Competition*.

a. What section defines a trade secret? What is the definition?

b. What is the reason for providing protection to trade secrets?

c. What Rhode Island law addresses trade secrets?

d. What 1998 case from the U.S. District Court for the Southern District of Indiana discussed trade secrets?

ASSIGNMENT 6

Refer to the *Uniform Laws Annotated*. The client has a spouse who is terminally ill. The terminally ill spouse has a will and a health care power of attorney, but neither address anatomical gifts. The client wants to make an anatomical gift of any organs or tissue that might be deemed by doctors as a benefit for others.

a. What uniform law governs this question?

b. Have there been prior versions of this uniform law? What is the most recent version?

c. In the most recent version, what section(s) address who may make an anatomical gift?

d. In the Library References under each section listed for subpart c. above, what secondary source is listed as having other related information on the subject?

ASSIGNMENT 7

The supervising attorney's son was able to log on to a website that showed children how to torture cats. She seems to remember that some legislation was introduced in the 106th Congress that dealt with the online protection of children. Consult the *United States Code Congressional and Administrative News* and locate what, if any, legislation was introduced.

ASSIGNMENT 8

Refer to the GPO's FDsys website. Using Public Law 114-11, answer the following questions:

a. In what ways can legislative history be gathered from this website?

b. What is the title and date of the House Report on Public Law 114-11?

ASSIGNMENT 9

Determine if your state has uniform or pattern jury instructions.

a. If your state has uniform or pattern jury instructions, retrieve the jury instruction that contains the elements of civil battery.

b. What source(s) did you consult to locate your state's uniform or pattern jury instructions.

c. Retrieve the Arizona pattern jury instruction for battery.

d. What source(s) did you use to locate Arizona's Pattern Jury Instructions—Civil?

ASSIGNMENT 10

While crossing an intersection, the client was struck by a motor vehicle driven by a minor. The minor's parents owned the vehicle, and the minor was driving with their knowledge and consent. The minor has been cited twice for speeding in the past three years. Refer to *Am. Jur. Pleading and Practice Forms* and locate the proper negligence complaint form for suit against the parents.

Chapter 7

Computers and Internet Legal Research

Learning Objectives

After completing this chapter, you should understand:

- The role of computers in legal research
- The role of non-fee-based Internet sources in legal research
- The role and types of non-fee-based legal websites
- How to conduct basic legal research using non-fee-based Internet sources
- Limitations of using non-fee-based law-related websites

Dmitri Rostov works as a paralegal for a small, three-attorney law firm. The firm has a small law library consisting of the state statutes, the state court case reports, and some civil form books and treatises. It does not have a commercial research service such as Westlaw or LexisNexis. Any extensive research must be performed through nonfee-based sources on the Internet or at the nearest law school, a half hour's drive from the office.

A new client of the law firm runs a restaurant and is preparing to jar and sell her favorite sauce recipe. One of the additives that will be in the sauce is malic acid. Dmitri's assignment is to check the federal regulations to determine if malic acid is considered a safe food additive. Dmitri hopes he can find the answer through the Internet; he would prefer to avoid having to drive to the law school to check the federal regulations.

The answer to this question and the research steps Dmitri follows are discussed in the Application section of this chapter.

I. INTRODUCTION
A. In General

The earlier chapters of this text focus on the techniques for conducting research using print resources, such as treatises and bound volume sets. Even as technology develops and research is increasingly conducted using electronic resources, it is still important to know how to research using print resources, for at least five reasons:

1. The organization and elements of the electronic databases are based on the structure of the print material. Therefore, a familiarity with the print source makes it much easier to understand the structure of the electronic database and conduct electronic research.
2. The material you are looking for may not be on an electronic database. This is especially true in the case of treatises and other secondary sources. Experienced researchers recognize that a research project may require knowledge of and reference to print resources. They do not rely exclusively on computer-assisted legal research.
3. On occasion, access to electronic research sources may be unavailable, such as when the local server is down. In such situations you are helpless if you do not know how to conduct research using print materials.

For Example

From October 1 to October 16, 2013, the United States Government entered a shutdown due to failure to secure a budget. All nonessential employees and offices were closed. All nonessential services were stopped. Government websites that contained federal law, such as Congress.gov (then Thomas.gov) and the GPO's FDSys website, ceased to be maintained or updated during those 16 days. Once regular government functions resumed, it took some time for all of the websites to be updated.

4. Cost concerns may limit the amount of time you can spend using commercial electronic services. Some firms use electronic services only to double-check what they have located in print sources or to update their research. This limits the time spent on electronic resources and thus reduces costs.
5. Content on non-fee-based law-related websites may not be up-to-date, reliable, or accurate. In addition these types of websites often have no means of updating your research.

This chapter presents an overview of legal research using the most frequently used non-fee-based (free) Internet research sources. Commercial (fee-based) research sources such as Westlaw and LexisNexis are discussed in Chapter 8.

B. Ethics

There are literally thousands of non-fee-based websites on the Internet. Note that a non-fee-based service does not involve a contractual relationship with the consumer of its information. No laws or regulations govern the accuracy of the content of non-fee-based websites. Such sites do not have a legal duty to provide information that is accurate or up-to-date. However, as noted in Chapter 2, there is an ethical obligation to provide the client with competent representation. *Therefore, you must verify the accuracy of information you obtain from such sites and determine if it is up-to-date.*

When selecting a non-fee-based site, there are no hard and fast rules for determining what makes a "good" site. Sites maintained by government entities, such as legislatures and courts, are usually well maintained, and often more up-to-date than not, but they may not be completely current. Always consider the author/publisher and content of the information, and check the site to determine how frequently the information is updated. There are other non-fee-based websites that are frequently used by legal professionals and are considered among the more reliable websites. These include law school websites or law school hosted websites and bar association websites.

However, there are literally thousands of law-related websites that are either anonymous, are hosted by an advocacy group, or are rooted in special interests. Beware that on these types of websites, information may be limited or slanted in favor of the position advocated by the group or host. Law is always in motion and as such even experts in the field may produce legal resources or information that is less than objective or that has been analyzed through a specific lens.

It is important to understand even the most reputable non-fee-based websites are vulnerable. Increasingly, we hear of sophisticated websites and databases being hacked. Regardless, non-fee-based websites play an important role in legal research. These types of Internet legal resources allow legal research to be started more quickly; allow enacted law, administrative regulations, court rules, and court opinions to be obtained in a moment's notice; and provide a cost-effective alternative to print subscriptions and commercial legal research sources such as Westlaw and LexisNexis. As long as you are aware of risks and limitations (discussed in-depth later in this chapter) involved in using non-fee-based Internet resources, then you will maintain your ethical obligations while being an effective and efficient researcher.

II. CONDUCTING LEGAL RESEARCH USING NON-FEE-BASED INTERNET SOURCES

A. Determine the Scope and Objective of the Research Project

The initial steps for conducting a search discussed in Chapter 2 apply to conducting computer and Internet research: analyze the assignment, do preliminary preparation, identify key facts, and identify the issue. For purposes of this chapter, these steps will be referred to as identifying the scope and objective of your research project. Even though you will be conducting research using non-fee-based (free) websites, you must be efficient in the use of your time. Many law firms require paralegals to accrue a certain number of billable hours, and not every hour worked is billable. Moreover, often clients are either billed for a paralegal's work, or a paralegal's time is tracked for use later in seeking to recover attorneys' fees from the opposing side in a lawsuit. Time spent familiarizing yourself with what Internet resources are available or aimlessly looking at website after website may not be billable, and therefore, that time is lost time. Moreover, unfocused research takes away from other projects and tasks to which you are assigned.

Before beginning any Internet research, take time to determine what areas of law you will be researching and what the types of law are for the area of law you are researching.

For Example

Refer to the scenario at the beginning of the chapter. Dmitri knows he needs to locate federal regulations that address food additives, specifically malic acid. He therefore will search for a website that has federal regulations.

B. Locate a Relevant Website

There are many ways to locate a relevant website containing the legal resources you are seeking. One way to locate a non-fee-based website is to enter the URL (web address) into your Internet browser's address box. This is more common when a researcher has had experience conducting non-fee-based Internet research or has already developed a list of preferred or reliable sources. Subsection III of this chapter provides a number of such sources.

For Example

Dmitri knows the federal Government Printing Office (GPO) has a website that contains federal laws and he knows the URL is http://www.gpo.gov. He types that URL into his browser's web address box and hits enter and he is taken to the home page for the GPO.

More often than not, you will begin your search by conducting a basic Internet search using your preferred web browser's search bar. In order for the results of the search to be relevant it is important to use good search terms. The less specific and broader the terms used, the more likely the results of the search will include websites that are not relevant or do not contain the law or content you are seeking. Conversely, terms that are too narrow will provide results that may exclude the best websites. Use the parameters and terms that resulted from identifying the scope and objective of your research to focus your search.

For Example

As discussed above, Dmitri knows he is searching for federal regulations that discuss food additives—specifically the food additive malic acid. He also knows the federal Food and Drug Administration regulates food additives. Therefore, he can use the following as search terms: *regulation, food additives, malic acid, Food and Drug Administration*.

C. Searching a Specific Website

Once you have identified a website or short list of websites to use to conduct specific research it is important to navigate to the right starting point for conducting your research or locating the content you need. Most websites have multiple pages —meaning the content is divided into distinct categories and each category has a separate page dedicated only to that content. At the same time many websites have global search boxes—meaning a search box that will locate terms across the entire website.

If you are unsure where on a website to locate the content you are seeking, inserting search terms in a global search box to direct the website to search for those terms is the best first step. This often leads the researcher to the particular page(s) of the website containing those terms, or to a list of results that you can navigate through to locate the specific content required by the research project. If the website does not have a global search box, you will need to carefully review the website home page to identify where within the website you can browse content related to your search terms.

For Example

The GPO website home page has a link to the FDsys page where federal regulations can be browsed, and the GPO home page also has a search bar that, when terms are entered, will return results across all pages—all areas of content—for the GPO website.

The key to effective and efficient searches is to understand the organization of the website and navigate to the web page that either has a search box allowing you to enter search terms to conduct your search or navigate to the web page that is content specific to your search.

D. Best Practices for Keeping Research Focused

The Internet offers endless websites and links to an endless amount of content. It is all too common that when conducting Internet research, the researcher becomes distracted and loses focus. Moreover, there is no guarantee that the results of your search will be accurate, authoritative, or credible. In addition, the Internet browser you use will impact the manner that search results will be presented.

For Example

When using Google as your browser, search results will be presented in order of most relevant—based on what Google determines is most relevant. That does not mean the sources presented at the top of the search results list are actually the most relevant. Another browser may present a different list or a different ordering of the same results.

Simple Search Box to search all collections

Exhibit 7-1   United States Government Printing Office Search Query. Source: *http://www.gpo.gov/fdsys/search/home.action*

It is important to know the nuances of how different browsers and individual websites compile and present results. These best practices will help you stay focused and conduct efficient and effective research:

1. Keep the scope and objective of your research in mind. Always refer back to the original research project and your notes on the scope and objective of the research when determining which websites to choose and in navigating content on individual websites.

2. Do not aimlessly click through results of websites. Be sure to take time to look at the overall organization of a website before clicking links or entering search terms in a search box. Having an understanding of the website organization is like understanding how print resources are organized. This will allow you to make effective choices in your navigation of a website.

3. Keep notes. Because of the sheer mass of content available on the Internet, be sure to make notes of results of a search and what website those results were from. Look at each web page you access thoroughly and follow links to other pages within a particular site before moving on to the next website. If a website has a link to another website, make note of that other website and then visit it *after* you thoroughly evaluate the current website.

4. Use the browser history list. If you get distracted and navigate away from a website and want to return to it, you can use the back button in your browser. If you want to locate a previously visited website without starting your search over, locate the dropdown arrow near the browsers web address box to display your browser history.

5. Bookmark. Once you locate reliable websites and resources, bookmark them. Bookmarking makes it easier to go directly to a website to conduct future research.

6. Never rely solely on non-fee-based resources. The Internet is a wonderful tool. It allows us to access information 24/7 and from anywhere we have access to the Internet and across all types of devices. It can be quick and time efficient. However, non-fee-based websites have limitations (discussed below) and should never be a substitute for print sources or commercial legal research websites or computer-based products that are updated regularly, publish their currency, and include analysis of the law.

E. Limitations Inherent in Non-fee-based Internet Sources

A disadvantage of non-fee-based Internet research is the limited amount of information available. On many websites, when you search for statutory law, *only* the statute is available, not the annotations. Therefore, none of the valuable research information, such as *ALR* annotations, law review articles, and case references, is included.

For Example

If you are using https://www.law.cornell.edu/ to search the *United States Code* for the bank robbery statute, you will be able to retrieve the statute but not the annotations.

When you are looking for case law, many non-fee-based sites require that you know the name or citation of the case. If you are trying to find any case that answers the question raised by the issue, you may not be able to conduct the search based on search terms. In many sites that do allow Boolean searching, the search capabilities are not as sophisticated as those of commercial (fee-based) services such as Westlaw and LexisNexis or even sites like Versuslaw and Fastcase. Importantly, most non-fee-based sites do not enable you to update research.

For Example

If you locate a case that is on point, most non-fee-based sites do not allow you to check the history or treatment of the case to determine if it has been overturned or affected by a subsequent case. The sites also have no mechanism such as *Shepard's* or *KeyCite* to identify cases, articles, and other secondary sources that have cited the case.

III. NON-FEE-BASED LAW-RELATED WEBSITES

This section presents an overview of the various non-fee-based (free) Internet legal research sources. The addresses of websites are referred to as **Uniform Resource Locators (URLs)**. The addresses are current as of the date of publication of this text. If a website is not at the address listed, it does not mean that the site no longer exists. The site could be down temporarily due to technical problems, or the address may have changed. To determine if the address has changed, use a search engine to search for a key term in the address.

For Example

If you are looking for Legal-Pad and the site does not come up at http://www.legal-pad.com, then perform a search using the keywords *legal pad*. If you are looking for a school's law library, search under the name of the school and *law library*.

Also, you may have a specific web page address such as <http://www.willamette.edu/wucl/longlib/research_ guides>. This is the address of a specific page from the Willamette College of Law's website. Research guides prepared by library staff are available at this page. Often, specific page addresses change. If you are not able to navigate to a specific page, go to the home page. In this example, the home page is <http://www.willamette.edu/>. The directory of information on the home page will lead you to the law library website and from there you can locate the research guides.

Finally, when determining how to use a particular website, check to see if there is a "help" link or a link to "search tips." (See Exhibit 7-2.)

A. Legal Search Engines

Several sites provide **general access** and links to legal research sites. The links are to websites that have access to statutory law, case law, and other research sources. Some of the most comprehensive sites are the following:

- <http://www.findlaw.com>. FindLaw is considered one of the best and most comprehensive sites providing links to sources for federal and state statutory law, case law, government directories, law firms, legal organizations, law schools, legal practice materials, and numerous other sources.
- <http://web.lawcrawler.com>. LawCrawler uses simple search terms or phrases to search the Internet for legal information sites. FindLaw is the parent site of LawCrawler.
- <https://www.law.cornell.edu/>. Cornell Law School hosts the Legal Information Institute that has an extensive collection of state and federal law and some legal encyclopedia materials. It has a general global search box.

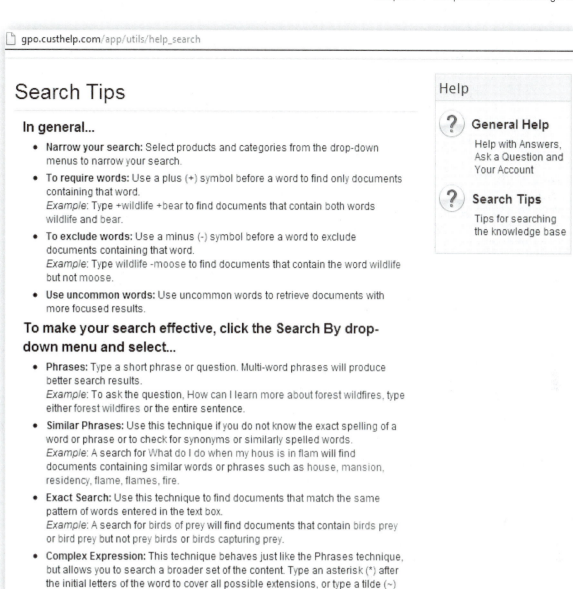

gpo.custhelp.com/app/utils/help_search

Search Tips

In general...

- **Narrow your search:** Select products and categories from the drop-down menus to narrow your search.
- **To require words:** Use a plus (+) symbol before a word to find only documents containing that word.
  Example: Type +wildlife +bear to find documents that contain both words wildlife and bear.
- **To exclude words:** Use a minus (-) symbol before a word to exclude documents containing that word.
  Example: Type wildlife -moose to find documents that contain the word wildlife but not moose.
- **Use uncommon words:** Use uncommon words to retrieve documents with more focused results.

To make your search effective, click the Search By drop-down menu and select...

- **Phrases:** Type a short phrase or question. Multi-word phrases will produce better search results.
  Example: To ask the question, How can I learn more about forest wildfires, type either forest wildfires or the entire sentence.
- **Similar Phrases:** Use this technique if you do not know the exact spelling of a word or phrase or to check for synonyms or similarly spelled words.
  Example: A search for What do I do when my hous is in flam will find documents containing similar words or phrases such as house, mansion, residency, flame, flames, fire.
- **Exact Search:** Use this technique to find documents that match the same pattern of words entered in the text box.
  Example: A search for birds of prey will find documents that contain birds prey or bird prey but not prey birds or birds capturing prey.
- **Complex Expression:** This technique behaves just like the Phrases technique, but allows you to search a broader set of the content. Type an asterisk (*) after the initial letters of the word to cover all possible extensions, or type a tilde (~) before a word to perform a Similar Phrase search on that word only.
  Example: A search for ~forest wild* will find documents that contain forrest or forest or woods or woodland or timberland and wildlife or wildfires.

Help

? General Help
Help with Answers, Ask a Question and Your Account

? Search Tips
Tips for searching the knowledge base

Exhibit 7-2 Sample of Government Printing Office Search Tips. *Source: www.gpo.com.custhelp.com/app/utils/help_search*

- <http://law.gsu.edu/>. This Georgia State University College of Law site provides links to a variety of sources. On the home page, click on "Law Library."
- <http://www.americanbar.org/>. This American Bar Association site includes links to legal research sources, law school libraries, branches of government, courts, and numerous other sources.
- <https://www.loc.gov/>. Through this Library of Congress website you can locate any book that has been published and that has an ISBN.
- <http://www.lawguru.com>. Law Guru includes links to hundreds of legal resource websites.
- <http://www.scholar.google.com>. Google Scholar allows free access to state and federal cases.
- <http://www.lectlaw.com>. Links to numerous research sources may be found at the 'Lectric Law Library.

B. Law Schools

Most law schools have websites, and most sites provide links to the school's law library. The list of all the law school websites—there are about 203 ABA accredited law schools—is too extensive to include here. To locate the website of a school you are interested in, use a search engine and insert the name of the law school, such as "Harvard Law School." Another way to determine which law schools have websites that may allow access to the type of legal source you are searching for is to use a search engine, such as Google or Bing, and conduct a search using key term related to the law you are seeking. Look for law school websites listed in the search results.

Many law school law library websites include a link to research guides. These guides are created by law library staff at the law school and provide step-by-step instruction on conducting research, as well as lists of resources where research for particular sources can be conducted.

The following is a list of law school sites that provide comprehensive legal research links, resources, and information:

a. <http://www.law.indiana.edu>. This Indiana University Law Library site includes links to sites of specialty areas of law, government resources, search engines, and law journals.

b. <http://www.law.cornell.edu/index.html>. This Cornell University Law School site provides extensive resource guides and access to many different legal topics.

c. <http://www.washburnlaw.edu>. In addition to links to numerous law- and legal research–related websites, this Washburn University School of Law site provides links to state and federal court and government sites.

d. <http://www.utexas.edu/>. This University of Texas School of Law site includes a legal resource guide on many different legal topics.

e. <http://www.kentlaw.edu/>. Information on how to find legal materials on the Internet is available at this Chicago-Kent College of Law site. Included are lists governing various areas such as the federal government, computer law, and health law.

f. <http://www.law.emory.edu/>. This Emory University Law School site provides access to links to many federal circuit court decisions and other research material.

g. <http://www.law.villanova.edu/>. At this site, you can use "locators" to find official websites for federal and state courts and federal government information resources.

C. Federal Government Sources

1. General Access Sources

The following sites are helpful in locating federal government online resources.

a. <http://www.usa.gov>. This is the United States government's official public website. This site provides information and access links to various federal government online resources.

b. <http://www.uscourts.gov/>. This site is the home page for the Federal Courts. It contains a wealth of information and links to the various federal courts. It also contains educational material and information about the federal judiciary.

c. <http://www.gpo.gov>. This is the address for the Government Printing Office (see Exhibit 7-1). The site provides information on the executive branch, including the *Code of Federal Regulations*, the *Federal Register*, the *Congressional Record*, and other government reports.

2. Federal Courts Opinions

The following sites provide access to the United States Supreme Court, the United States Circuit Courts of Appeal, and the federal District Courts.

a. United States Supreme Court

Access to United States Supreme Court materials, such as opinions, briefs, links to oral argument audio clips, and court rules can be found at the following sites:

a. <http://www.uscourts.gov/>. This site is the home page for the Federal Courts. It contains links to all federal courts, including by map. The link to "Court Website Links" will take the researcher to a list of every federal court, and each listing is a link to that court's home page.

b. <http://www.supremecourt.gov>. This official page of the United States Supreme Court features court opinions, orders, rules, calendars and schedules, news releases, and general information.

c. <http://www.findlaw.com>. This FindLaw site includes Supreme Court opinions and many other resources.

> d. <http://www.cornell.edu> Cornell's site offers access to all federal and state statutes, court opinions from many state and all federal court opinions.
>
> e. <http://www.oyez.org>. You may hear the oral arguments or read the court briefs of United States Supreme Court cases at this site. The oral arguments are available for cases from 1960 to present. The website is housed through Chicago-Kent School of Law.
>
> f. <http://www.willamette.edu>. Willamette's site offers access to federal and state law.

b. United States Circuit Courts of Appeal

Access to federal circuit court cases is available through several sources. A few are listed here.

> a. <http://www.uscourts.gov>. This is the United States federal courts home page. It provides access to federal court opinions, briefs, and rules. As you may have noted, this website is invaluable when conducting research related to the federal courts, particularly when looking for specific information related to procedural matters within the federal courts.
>
> b. <http://findlaw.com>. Through this FindLaw site, you can locate court cases in general.
>
> c. <http://www.law.villanova.edu>. This Villanova University School of Law site includes Circuit Court opinions and rules.
>
> d. <http://www.law.emory.edu>. Circuit Court opinions may be accessed through this Emory Law School site.

c. United States District Courts

As discussed in Chapter 1, the United States district courts are the primary trial courts in the federal system. Most federal district courts list their opinions on its website. The website for the federal courts, <http://www.uscourts .gov/>, provides information about the courts and links to the district court websites.

d. Attorney General Opinions

United States Attorney General Opinions are available at http://www.justice.gov by linking to the Attorney General. Many state attorney general opinions are available through specific state government websites. To locate a state attorney general office website, use a search engine. Most government websites have a search query box allowing you to enter search terms such as "attorney general opinions."

3. Federal Statutes, Court Rules, and Regulations

The *United States Code*, federal court rules, and the *Code of Federal Regulations* are available at the following sites.

a. United States Code

The Cornell Law School Law Library site, at https://law.library.cornell.edu/, provides access to the *United States Code*. You may search by title and chapter, popular name, title of individual sections, and table of contents. The *United States Code* is also available through Findlaw (http://findlaw.com/) and at the Government Printing Office website (http://www.gpo.gov/fdsys).

b. Federal Court Rules

The federal court rules of procedure are included in the *United States Code*, as discussed in the previous section. Local court rules are usually available through specific federal court's websites, which may be accessed at <http:// www.uscourts.gov/>. The federal court rules are also available at many law school websites.

c. Code of Federal Regulations (CFR) and Federal Register

The *Code of Federal Regulations* and *Federal Register* can be found at the Government Printing Office website (http://www.gpo.gov/fdsys). In addition, many law school websites also allow you to search for federal regulations. Moreover, many federal agencies have the federal regulations for which they have the duty of enforcing. The United States Department of Justice (http://www.justice.gov/) has a web page that provides the list and link to federal executive agencies. Those agency websites can be reached by clicking the logo of a particular agency.

4. Legislation

Information on federal legislation is available at the Congress.gov website. Legislative history is available at this site, which is maintained by the Library of Congress. It includes information on legislation, the full text of the *Congressional Record*, and legislative committee information.

Legislative history is also available at this site maintained by the Government Printing Office: <http://www.gpo.gov/fdsys>. Access to legislative history and presidential documents is also available at this website.

State legislative history is available through many state legislature websites. Using a search engine, put in the name of the state and then the term "legislature" and the state legislatures' website will be in the results. States have more legislative history available today than in the past. Older state legislative history is not likely to be available online.

5. Congress and Federal Agencies

Congress, the White House, and all federal agencies maintain websites. All of those websites provide access to various amounts of information. The websites of government agencies traditionally have contained information on processes, copies of forms, guides on procedures before the agency, and a host of other information that may be useful in your research. Often these government websites also provide links to other public websites where laws, rules, and regulations of the respective agency can be accessed. The addresses for websites of agencies may be accessed through the Library of Congress website: <http://www.congress.gov>. The link to government resources will lead to lists of links to state and federal government websites.

D. State Sources

The amount of legal research material available via the Internet varies from state to state.

Law-related material is usually available through state court, state government, local law school, or state bar association websites. Consider accessing these sites when conducting a search within your state. The legal materials most commonly available are state statutes, court opinions, law reviews, and agency regulations. Rather than a list of all the websites for all the states, a list of the web addresses for those sites that provide links to state sources follows.

   a. <http://www.findlaw.com/>. Through FindLaw, you can access state statutes, case law, administrative law, law schools, professional legal organizations, and some law reviews.
   b. <http://www.lawsonline.com/>. Lawsonline provides links to state sources including state codes.
   c. <http://congress.gov>. The Library of Congress website provides a link to government resources for every state.
   d. <http://www.ncsc.org/>. The National Center for States Courts (NCSC) website includes a list of state courts. Also, law-related Internet sites can be found at this site.
   e. <http://www.statelocalgov.net>. Links to state government sources are available at this Piper Resources site.
   f. <www.naag.org>. Many state attorney general opinions are available at this National Association of Attorneys General website.

E. Secondary Authority and Specialty Areas

Many **secondary authority** and other sources such as *ALR*, *West's Digests*, and treatises are available only at fee-based websites such as Westlaw or LexisNexis. However, many secondary and other materials in specialty areas are available at no charge on the Internet. These specialty area and secondary source materials are discussed here.

1. Specialty Area Sources

The following is a list of legal topics and websites that provide access to information concerning various topics.

   a. Arbitration and Mediation, at <http://www.usa.gov/>. At the usa.gov website, you can locate numerous sources of information on arbitration and mediation. Type in either "arbitration" or "mediation" in the search query box on the home page.
   b. Administrative Law, at <http://www.findlaw.com>. FindLaw provides access to federal administrative codes, regulations, orders, and agency rulings. State and local administrative laws are available

through the Municipal Code Corporation site, <http://www.municode.com>. Administrative law research may be conducted through the American Bar Association's Administrative Procedure Database at <http://www.law.fsu.edu/library/admin>. The Government Printing Office (GPO) site, <http://www.gpo.gov>, provides access to the *United States Code*, the *Code of Regulations*, the *Federal Register*, and numerous other documents. Also, the *LSA: List of CFR Sections Affected* (*LSA*) (a monthly pamphlet accompanying the *CFR*) is available at this site.

c. Bankruptcy, at <http://www.findlaw.com/>. FindLaw provides access information on the various types of bankruptcy, bankruptcy law, and links to bankruptcy courts.

d. Civil Litigation, at <http://amicus.ca/resources/index.html>. This Amicus Attorney site includes links to numerous civil litigation support materials such as deposition techniques and tort law sources. A site that provides links to experts is <http://www.expertpages.com>. A site that includes information on damages is <http://www.lawcatalog.com>. In the search box, type "damages" for a list of sources of information concerning damages.

e. Civil Rights, at <http://www.findlaw.com/>. The civil rights provisions of the *United States Code* may be found through FindLaw. The American Civil Liberties Union (ACLU) website, <http://www.aclu .org/>, provides extensive information on issues concerning civil rights.

f. Consumer Law, at <http://www.consumerlaw.org>. This National Consumer Law Center site includes comprehensive information on consumer law.

g. Corporate Law. General information about corporate law is available through the LawyerExpress website, <http://www.lawyerexpress.com>, and the Amicus Attorney website, <http://amicus.ca /resources/index.html>. State Business and Professional Codes are available through the Cornell University website at <http://www.law.library.cornell.edu/>. The Office of the Secretary of State has information on incorporating in a state. Usually forms and documents are available. Secretary of State offices can be located through each states government website or through <http://www.nass.org>.

h. Criminal Law, at <http://www.criminology.fsu.edu>. This Florida State University School of Criminology site provides extensive information on criminal law. Links to criminal justice sites can be found at the Institute for Law and Justice website at <http://www.ilj.org/>.

i. Elder Law. Information concerning Medicare, Medicaid, and rights of the elderly can be found at <http://www.seniorlaw.com>. Many state court websites also have links to state elder or senior law resources.

j. Environmental Law. The Environmental Protection Agency website is <http://www.epa.gov>. Links to environmental law resources are at the Virtual Library site at <http://vlib.org>.

k. Estate Planning. State probate statutes should be consulted when the question involves estate planning. They are available through FindLaw. Estate planning material may also be located at the Amicus Attorney site, <http://amicus.ca/resources/index.html>.

l. Family Law, at <http://www.divorcenet.com>. This DivorceNet site provides information on state divorce laws. Information on numerous family law matters such as property issues, custody, and tax planning is available at <http://www.nolo.com/>. Many state court websites also have links to family law resources.

m. Immigration. The Citizenship and Immigration Service website is <http://uscis.gov>. Links to all types of material on immigration are available at <http://www.immigrationusa.com/is.html>. Immigration procedures, forms, and other related materials are available at <http://www.us-immigration.com>.

n. International Law. International legal resources are available at the United Nations System of Organizations site at <http://www.unsystem.org/>. See also the American Society of International Law's *ASIL Guide to Electronic Resources for International Law* at <http://www.asil.org/resource/home .htm>.

o. Intellectual Property and Copyright. The United States Copyright Office website is <http://www .lcweb.loc.gov/copyright>. The United States Patent and Trademark Office can be accessed via <http://www.uspto.gov>. Information about copyrights is available at the Copyright Clearance Center, <http://www.copyright.com>.

p. Legal Documents and Forms. Legal documents and forms can be found at several sites. Two popular sites are <http://www.lectlaw.com> (the 'Lectric Law Library) and <http://www.legaldocs.com/> (LegalDocs). Links to form sources are provided in the Internet Legal Resource Guide at <http:// www.ilrg.com/> and FindLaw at <http://www.findlaw.com>.

q. Personal Injury. Links to numerous sites that provide information on personal injury law are available at the Amicus Attorney site at <http://amicus.ca/resources/index.html>. The National Highway Traffic Safety Administration (NHTSA) provides information on traffic safety, and consumer complaints at <http://www.nhtsa.dot.gov>. Data on consumer products are available at the Consumer Product Safety Commission's site at <http://www.cpsc.gov>. Medical information is available at the Virtual Medical Law Center at <http://www.martindalecenter.com>.

r. Real Property and Landlord Tenant Law. Along with many other specialty sites, the Amicus Attorney site at <http://amicus.ca/resources/index.html> includes links to numerous sites that provide information on real property law. The National Association of Realtors site is <http://www.realtor.com>. The site provides links to a wide variety of sources on real estate matters. Nolo Press maintains a landlord/tenant site at <http://www.nolo.com/index.cfm>.

s. Tax Law. The website for the Internal Revenue Service is <http://www.irs.ustreas.gov/>. Links to numerous tax law resources are available through the Tax Prophet website at <http://www.taxprophet.com>.

t. Uniform Commercial Code. Comprehensive information on the Uniform Commercial Code is available at the Cornell University Law School Legal Information site at <http://www.law.library.cornell.edu>. In addition to the Uniform Commercial Code, the site provides links to state commercial code statutes and information about the code. The Amicus Attorney site, <http://amicus.ca/resources/index.html>, also provides numerous links to resources on the commercial code.

2. Secondary Authority and Other Sources

In this section a list of some secondary authority and other source material sites that are available at non-fee-based websites is provided.

a. Law Firms. Information on law firms and locating attorneys is available through FindLaw at <http://www.findlaw.com> and Martindale-Hubbell at <http://www.martindale.com>.

b. Law Reviews, Journals, and Periodicals. Many law reviews, journals, and periodicals are available online. Many law schools publish their law reviews and journals. Some examples are the Harvard Law Review at <http://www.harvardlawreview.org> and the Cornell Law Review at <http://www.lawschool.cornell.edu/clr>.

Directories that provides links to law reviews and law journals include FindLaw at <http://stu.findlaw.com/journals> and the University of Chicago D'Angelo Law Library at <http://www.lib.uchicago.edu/e/law/lawreviews.html>. The University Law Review Project provides information on the availability of law reviews on the Internet at <http://www.lawreview.org/>. See also Anderson's Directory of Law Reviews and Scholarly Legal Publications at <http://www.andersonpublishing.c/>.

Hiros Gamos Journals, at <http://www.hg.org/journals.html> includes a listing of law review articles available on the Internet.

c. Legal Dictionaries. Legal dictionaries are available at the following sites: <http://www.duhaime.org/diction.htm> and <http://www.lectlaw.com/def.htm>.

d. Legal Newspapers and Newsletters. Many legal newspapers and newsletters may be accessed online by using the name as a search term. Many may also be accessed through FindLaw. The Washburn University School of Law website, <http://www.washlaw.edu>, and the Law News Network at <http://www.law.com> provide links to legal newspapers, newsletters, and magazines.

e. Statistical Information. Statistical information on the federal courts may be found online at <http://www.uscourts.gov/publications.html>. The Federal Bureau of Investigations *Uniform Crime Reports* is available at <http://www.fbi.gov>. The Bureau of Justice Statistics provides information at <http://www.usdoj.gov/bjs/>.

f. Treaties. An extensive collection of treaties is available through the *Treaties & International Agreements Researchers' Archive*. It is available through subscription at <http://www.oceanalaw.com>.

g. Uniform State Laws and Model Acts. Uniform state laws and model acts are available at the National Conference of Commissioners on Uniform State Laws (NCCUSL) website at <http://www.nccusl.org/>. Access to information on uniform laws is also available through the Uniform Law Commission website at <uniformlaws.org>.

F. Listservs

A **listserv** is an email discussion group. A listserv links people with common interests and allows them to share information on a topic or area of expertise. To participate, you must subscribe to or join the group. Once you have joined a listserv discussion group, you may send (post) messages and receive messages from group members. When a message is posted, it is available to all members who subscribe to the group. In essence, the information is public; it is not like private email.

There are hundreds of discussion groups on various legal topics. Listservs are valuable because they allow you to receive the input of colleagues who are interested in and are often experts on a certain legal topic. If you have difficulty finding an answer to a legal question, you can post the question on the listserv and obtain an answer or guidance from other members of the group. However, you must always verify the information you receive.

There are two types of listservs:

- *Unmoderated*—All messages by group members are sent to the group.
- *Moderated*—Messages are sent to a moderator, who reviews each message and decides whether to return it to the sender, edit it and post it in on to the group, or post it to the group as submitted.

The rules established by the group usually govern the activities of the moderator.

G. Organizations

The following is a list of law-related organizations and associations:

\<http://www.aallnet.org/\>	American Association of Law Libraries (AALL)
\<http://www.abanet.org/\>	American Bar Association (ABA)
\<http://www.aclu.org/\>	American Civil Liberties Union (ACLU)
\<http://www.alanet.org/\>	Association of Legal Administrators (ALA)
\<http://www.aafpe.org/\>	American Association for Paralegal Education (AAFPE)
\<http://www.nala.org/\>	National Association of Legal Assistants (NALA)
\<http://www.nals.org/\>	National Association of Legal Secretaries (NALS)
\<http://www.nass.org\>	National Association of Secretaries of State (NASS)
\<http://www.paralegals.org\>	National Federation of Paralegal Associations (NFPA)

State Bar Organizations. State Bar organizations may be accessed by using a search engine and typing in the name of the state bar such as "New York State Bar."

International Organizations

\<http://www.europa.eu.int\>	European Union
\<http://www.icj-cij.org\>	International Court of Justice (World Court)
\<http://www.oas.org\>	Organization of American States
\<http://www.un.org/\>	United Nations
\<http://www.wto.org\>	World Trade Organization

IV. CITING INTERNET SOURCES

This section presents an overview of rules of citation to be used when citing content derived from the Internet. A detailed discussion of the citation rules for each type of Internet source is beyond the scope of this text. Therefore, this section, unlike those in Chapters 3 through 6, generally refers the student to the citation rules that govern citation to Internet sources. As mentioned in each of the previous chapters, be sure to carefully review the appropriate citation manual for the detailed rules regarding each citation format.

The latest edition of the *Bluebook* contains more detailed examples of citing Internet sources than previous editions. The *Bluebook* has been slow to embrace use of and therefore citation to Internet sources. *Bluebook* Rule 18 addresses how to cite content from the Internet, electronic media, and other nonprint sources.

Unlike the limited guidance provided by the *Bluebook*, the *ALWD Guide* dedicates an entire part of the manual to citation of electronic sources. Rules 30 and 33 are most relevant for citing non-fee-based websites and other types of electronic media.

V. KEY POINTS CHECKLIST: Computers and Legal Research

✓   It is important to know how to research using print resources because electronic resources may not be available or may be too expensive. Electronic research systems are based on print resources, and a familiarity with print resources makes it easier to understand electronic research.

✓   The most critical step in the research process is framing the issue in the context of the specific facts of the case (see Chapters 10 and 11). A well-framed issue, stated in the context of the facts, provides a researcher with the information necessary to conduct research using natural language or terms and connectors.

✓   As with any research, it is essential to determine if the results of Internet research are still good law.

✓   Non-fee-based online research sources do not have a contractual duty to provide information that is accurate or up-to-date. Verify the accuracy of any information you obtain from such sites and check to determine if the information is current.

VI. APPLICATION

Dmitri knows that a good place to check the Code of Regulations is through the Government Printing Office website at <https://www.gpo.gov/fdsys/search/home.action>. This site includes the code and a search engine for finding code sections. He formulates his search query based on the question of whether malic acid is considered safe as a food substance. After accessing the website, he types in "food substances considered as safe malic acid" in the "Quick Search" query box. One of the search results is 21 C.F.R. § 184, Direct Food Substances Affirmed as Generally Recognized as Safe. Malic acid is included in the list of substances recognized as safe.

Summary

The earlier chapters of the text focus on the techniques for conducting research using print resources such as texts and bound volumes. Experienced researchers do not rely exclusively on non-fee-based Internet research. It is important, however, to know how to research using print resources for at least five reasons:

1. A familiarity with the print source makes it much easier to understand the structure of the electronic database and conduct electronic research.
2. The material you are looking for may not be in an electronic database.
3. On occasion, access to electronic research is unavailable, such as when the local server is down.
4. Cost concerns may limit the amount of time you can spend using commercial electronic services.
5. Content on non-fee-based websites may not be up-to-date or reliable.

There are several best practices to keep in mind when using non-fee-based Internet sources to conduct legal research. They include:

- Keeping the scope and objective of the research project in mind.
- Focus your review of websites and website content.
- Keep notes.
- Use browser history list to revisit websites.
- Bookmark.
- Always use a print source or citatory to update your research.

This chapter presents an overview of various non-fee-based Internet sources.

Thousands of non-fee-based websites provide access to various types of legal information online. There are no laws or regulations governing the accuracy of the content of non-fee-based websites; therefore, they do not have a legal duty to provide information that is accurate or up-to-date. You must verify the accuracy and determine if any information you obtain from such sites is current. When selecting a non-fee-based site, always consider the author and publisher and the content of the information, and check the site to determine how frequently the information is updated.

A limitation of most non-fee-based Internet sources is that they do not have databases as extensive as those offered by the commercial sources. Many sites that provide statutory law do not include the annotations. Many sites that provide access to case law do not allow searches based on search words or terms (Boolean searches).

This chapter discusses and lists the websites (URLs) for many non-fee-based websites that provide access to various types of legal information. Included are federal and state government websites, secondary authority and specialty area sources, and email discussion groups (listservs).

Quick References

Exercises

ASSIGNMENT 1

The client is a shareholder of a corporation in Tennessee. What is required for an action to be taken by shareholders without a meeting?

ASSIGNMENT 2

Perform Assignment 1 using your state law.

ASSIGNMENT 3

Using the Cornell Law School website, locate a 1998 United States Supreme Court Case from the state of Minnesota that involved a warrantless search.

ASSIGNMENT 4

The Hobbes Bridge Act is included in which section of the *United States Code*?

ASSIGNMENT 5

What is the fee charged by the United States district courts for a search of the court records?

ASSIGNMENT 6

Under the *Federal Rules of Civil Procedure*, must leave of the court be obtained to take the deposition of a person detained in prison? Include the rule citation.

ASSIGNMENT 7

How is "claim" defined in National Park Service's regulations dealing with minerals management? Include the CFR citation.

ASSIGNMENT 8

What was the topic of the Federal Reserve notice issued on January 2, 2004 (published in the *Federal Register*)?

ASSIGNMENT 9

The supervising attorney is working on an employee disability benefits claim involving the Employment Retirement Security Act (ERISA). He remembers that there was a 2003 United States Supreme Court Case on the subject. He remembers that one of the parties was Black and Decker. Locate the case.

ASSIGNMENT 10

The client's son is forming a Bible club at the local high school. The club wants to meet during the school's activity period. The school principal refuses to allow them to meet. Using <http://www.findlaw.com /casecode/>, what is the name, case number, and date of a Third Circuit case, involving the Punxsutawney schools, decided after 2000 that addresses this question?

ASSIGNMENT 11

Your supervisory attorney is working on a consumer law case involving a saving and loan company's refusal to grant our client a loan. Our client is female.

The supervisory attorney wants to know the cost of the National Consumer Law Center's Credit Discrimination with CD-ROM Manual.

ASSIGNMENT 12

The client resides in Pennsylvania and has a question concerning child support. Locate information on Pennsylvania child support. Hint: This is a family law matter.

ASSIGNMENT 13

You are working on a simple will. Describe how you can locate a simple will form on the Internet.

ASSIGNMENT 14

Describe how you would obtain, free of charge, a law review article from the Buffalo Criminal Law Review.

ASSIGNMENT 15

What legal research links are provided by the American Bar Association?

Chapter 8

Commercial Internet Research

Outline

Learning Objectives

After completing this chapter, you should understand:

- The role of computers in legal research
- An overview of legal research using the most frequently used commercial services: Westlaw and LexisNexis
- The role and types of other fee-based online legal research sources such as FastCase, Versuslaw, Casemaker, and others
- How to conduct legal research using commercial Internet legal research sources
- What to consider when citing legal sources obtained from commercial Internet legal research websites

James Redhorse was born and raised in Window Rock, Arizona, on the Navajo Reservation. His parents insisted, as many parents do, that all their children graduate from high school, and encouraged them to go to college. After graduating from paralegal school five years ago, James got a job at a law firm in Winslow, Arizona. His dream is to save enough money to go to law school. Over the past five years, James has become skilled at legal research and is routinely assigned research projects. Last month, the firm subscribed to Westlaw. The partners are learning to use the latest version of Westlaw, but because James took a Westlaw course in school, he has become the "Westlaw person."

The senior partner called James into his office and said, "I just had an interview with Mrs. Burgess. She is 80 years old, and since her husband died five years ago, her closest companion is her cat, Alice. Her next-door neighbor hates cats and has repeatedly warned Mrs. Burgess that if Alice continued to use his rose garden as a bathroom, he would 'get rid of her.' Last week, the neighbor set a cat trap for Alice. The cat was caught in the trap and consequently died. The next day, when Mrs. Burgess asked the neighbor if he had seen Alice, he replied, 'I told you I would take care of her, and I did.' The neighbor then showed Mrs. Burgess the trap with her cat Alice still in it. She became so upset over the incident that she went to her doctor. Mrs. Burgess is extremely distraught over the actions of the neighbor and the loss of her cat. She feels that she is now all alone and has lost her best friend. She wants to sue her neighbor. I want you to get on Westlaw and do some research into what type of damages may be recovered for loss of a pet. I'm especially interested if she can recover for the distress this has caused her."

The answer to this question, and the research steps James follows, are discussed in the Application section of this chapter.

I. INTRODUCTION

While Chapters 3 through 6 mention if and where the print resources are available on electronic databases, they do not discuss how to conduct electronic research. This chapter presents an overview of legal research using the two most frequently used commercial (fee-based) services: Westlaw and LexisNexis. It also includes a brief discussion of several smaller and increasingly popular services. Although other electronic research services are available, a familiarity with the major sources will provide you with sufficient information to use other services.

Although the focus of the chapter is on Westlaw and LexisNexis, the discussion is limited to an overview of the information available and how to conduct basic research. There are two reasons for this:

1. Inasmuch as there are entire texts devoted to how to use Westlaw and LexisNexis, a detailed discussion is beyond the scope of this text.
2. Westlaw, LexisNexis, and most other commercial services frequently update and modify their services, rendering a detailed discussion outdated by the time of publication of this text. Because of these frequent modifications, it is unproductive to provide detailed step-by-step instructions and exhibits demonstrating the steps to follow in conducting research on these commercial websites.
3. Westlaw and LexisNexis provide many training and how-to videos and user guides on their websites that are up-to-date with any recent changes to their user interface.

Westlaw and LexisNexis each have thousands of databases that include primary and secondary authority research sources as well as numerous other sources. There are databases for all areas of federal and state law, including statutory and case law. Materials are available on specific practice areas, forms, access to public records of all types, news sources, business materials, periodicals, legal treatises, litigation materials, legal and other statistical information sources, directories of all types, law reviews, and international materials. The databases are not limited to law-related information and are too extensive to list here. For example, the LexisNexis website indicates it has more than 50,000 sources.

II. WESTLAW

Westlaw, by Thomson Reuters, provides access to thousands of primary and secondary research sources. It is available directly on the Internet at http://www.westlawnext.com. Only users with a paid subscription can access Westlaw. In technical terms, the current Westlaw platform is called WestlawNext. This platform was introduced in 2010, and over the course of five years, Thomson Reuters phased out the former Westlaw platform, referred to by many as Westlaw classic. WestlawNext is now the only platform. Regardless of the technicalities of the platform, the legal community still refers to WestlawNext as Westlaw, and therefore throughout this text the author has done the same.

This section discusses locating primary and secondary authority, viewing search results, updating research, and printing results.

A. Overview of WestlawNext

WestlawNext was designed in response to customer feedback seeking a cleaner, less cluttered, and simpler way to search. The result was what Westlaw refers to as WestSearch technology, which eliminates the need for choosing a database and provides a single search query box for all searches. Many compare this universal search box to the search box found on search engines such as Google.

In Westlaw classic, users had to choose specific databases within which to search. In addition, researchers has to choose a specific search box based on whether they were using terms and connectors to search (Boolean search) or were using natural language (akin to the plain English searches we are accustomed to when using Google). WestlawNext removes those multiple layers required in Westlaw classic and streamlines the interface by providing a single search box that allows the researcher to search all Westlaw databases in numerous ways, including by database, citation, search terms (both Boolean and plain English), and key numbers. A researcher using the search box on the homepage will receive results from across all Westlaw databases, and the results will be ranked in order of relevance. At the same time, a researcher seeking a specific source, and who has the citation to that source, can enter the citation in the search box on the homepage and be taken to the specific source. Alternatively, a researcher can search by browsing databases which are organized under content tabs (see Exhibit 8-1).

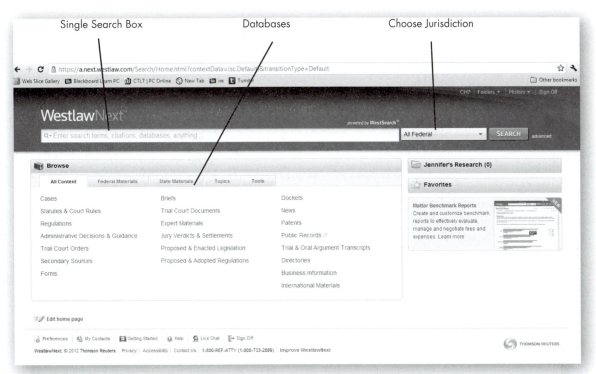

Exhibit 8-1   WestlawNext Search Query Page. Used with Permission of Thomson Reuters.

For Example

You need to locate the federal statute that has the elements of the crime of assaulting a federal officer or employee. You can choose the tab for federal materials and enter search terms in the search box. This will produce results across all federal materials databases—cases, statutes, regulations, and so on. Or, you can click the link under the Federal Materials link for the *USCA* and enter search terms in the search box, and results will be limited to the *USCA*.

B. Finding Primary Authority

As mentioned in Chapter 1, primary authority is the law itself—constitutional law, enacted law (statutes and administrative law), and case law. This section focuses on locating statutory and constitutional law (note that constitutions are usually located with the statutes) and case law.

1. Finding Statutory Laws and Constitutional Provisions

There are four primary ways to locate a statute or constitutional provision, depending on the amount of information you have:

a. Search by Citation

When you know the citation of a statute or constitutional provision, you can locate it by performing the following steps:

1. On the Westlaw homepage, type the citation in the search box then click "Search." The document will open (see Exhibit 8-1).
2. From the Westlaw homepage, select either "Federal Materials" or "State Materials," then click on the specific jurisdiction and statutory code within which to search. Type the citation in the search box and click "Search." The document will open.

For Example

If you wanted to find 18 U.S.C.S.§ 2113, you would type *18 uscs 2113* in the search box on the Westlaw home page or from the Federal Materials/United States Code Annotated (USCA) page.

b. Search by Issue—Plain English

In most instances, you will not know the citation of the statute that governs the issue being researched. Therefore, you must locate the statute by using the information from the issue you have identified. *The most critical step in the research process is framing the issue in the context of the specific facts of the case.* A well-framed issue, stated in the context of the facts, provides a researcher with the information necessary to frame the research query by using the two most common research methods: natural language and terms and connectors. For help identifying and stating issues, see Chapter 10.

Plain English, also sometimes referred to as **natural language**, is a search method that allows you to research by stating the search query (i.e., the issue) using plain English. To conduct a natural language search perform the following steps:

1. *Type the issue you are researching as specifically as possible in the context of the facts* in the Westlaw homepage search box.

For Example

The facts of the case are that an individual robs a bank using a toy gun. The question is whether under federal law a "dangerous weapon" was used in the robbery. The assignment is to locate the federal statute that governs this question. The issue may be stated as follows: Under federal statutory law, does bank robbery with a dangerous weapon occur when the weapon is a toy gun?

2. *Locate the appropriate database.* Using the various content tabs, narrow to a specific database before conducting a search. This will limit the search results to items only within the specific database selected. This often results in more on-point results if your issue is stated well. Just as you would using the homepage search box, *type the issue you are researching as specifically as possible in the context of the facts*, then click "Search."

For Example

When you are looking for federal statutory law, click on "Federal Materials" then click on "United States Code Annotated (USCA)." Type in your issue, then click "Search." A list of results, by relevance, will be given and all of the results will be limited to materials within the *USCA*.

c. Search by Issue—Terms and Connectors

Another way to find the statute that governs the issue is through the use of **terms and connectors**. This type of search (often referred to as a Boolean search) allows you to conduct a search using key words of the issue and symbols, also called "connectors." These connectors specify the relationships between the key terms, and the search then retrieves documents based upon the relationship between the terms.

For Example

In the search box, type *deadly /p weapon /p bank /p robbery.* The connector "/p" locates all of the documents in which the words *deadly, weapon, bank,* and *robbery* appear in the same paragraph of the document.

To perform a terms and connectors search, you must be familiar with the following information:

- *Plurals and possessives.* Westlaw automatically retrieves plurals and possessives of terms. If you type *robber*, Westlaw will search for *robber, robbers, robbers',* and *robber's*. It will not retrieve the singular forms if you type the plural.
- *Root expander* (!). To search for all forms of a word, place the root expander "!" at the end of the root of the word.

For Example

The query *work!* will retrieve the various forms of the term *work: worker, working, works,* and so on.

- *Universal Character* (*). To search for all variations of a word, place an asterisk (*), the universal character, in place of the variable character.

For Example

The query *r*ng* will retrieve all the documents with *ring, rang,* and *rung*.

- *Connectors.* Connectors specify the relationship between the search terms. They govern the scope of the search. Always use a space to separate the connector from the search term. Following is a list of the connectors and an explanation of how they are used.

CONNECTOR	RULES GOVERNING USE OF CONNECTOR
& (and)	The use of an ampersand (&) between the terms retrieves all documents that contain both terms. Thus, the search query *bank & robber* retrieves all documents with both terms: *bank* and *robber*.
space (or)	A space between words retrieves all documents that contain either search term. Thus, the search query *bank robber* retrieves all documents that contain either the word *bank* or *robber*.
/s	The use of /s between the terms retrieves all documents that contain both terms in the same sentence. Thus, the search query *bank /s robber* retrieves all documents in which *bank* and *robber* appear in the same sentence.
/p	The use of /p between the terms retrieves all documents that contain both terms in the same paragraph. Thus, the search query *bank /p robber* retrieves all documents in which *bank* and *robber* appear in the same paragraph.
/n	The use of /n between the terms retrieves all documents in which the terms appear within a certain number of words of each other. The n is the specified number of words. Thus, the search query *bank /5 robber* retrieves all documents in which *bank* and *robber* appear within five words of each other.

(Continues)

CONNECTOR	RULES GOVERNING USE OF CONNECTOR *(Continued)*
" "	Place terms in quotation marks when you want to locate documents in which the terms appear in the exact same order as they appear in the quotation marks. Thus, the search query *"bank robbery"* locates all documents in which the terms *bank* and *robbery* appear together and *bank* precedes *robbery* with no terms between them.
%	To exclude a term from a search query, place the % symbol before the term. Thus, the search query *bank & robber % weapon* retrieves all documents that contain the words *bank* and *robber* and which do not contain the word *weapon*.

To conduct a terms and connectors search, perform the following steps:

1. *Type the issue you are researching as specifically as possible in the context of the facts* using connectors or symbols where appropriate in the search box on the Westlaw homepage, then click "Search."
2. *Locate the appropriate database.* Using the various content tabs, narrow to a specific database before conducting a search. This will limit the results to items within that specific database. This often results in more on-point results if your issue is stated well. *Type the issue you are researching as specifically as possible in the context of the facts* using connectors or symbols where appropriate, then click "Search."

For Example

The search is for a statute that includes the terms *bank, robbery, dangerous,* and *weapon.* The terms *dangerous* and *weapon* probably appear in the same order, so they are placed in quotation marks in the query. The query is *"dangerous weapon" & bank & robbery.* Using the *United States Code Annotated* as a database, your search will retrieve all statutes that include the terms *bank, robbery,* and *dangerous weapon.* The search will retrieve only those statutes in which the terms *dangerous* and *weapon* appear together. To then narrow the search, the query could read *"dangerous weapon" /p bank /p robbery.* The search will retrieve only those statutes in which the terms appear in the same paragraph.

When comparing natural language with terms and connectors searches, you will see certain advantages and disadvantages for both. A terms and connectors search has the disadvantage of requiring a familiarity with the use of the connectors. It has the advantage of allowing the researcher to tailor the search. Although it takes some practice to become familiar with terms and connectors searches, most researchers prefer them because of the ability to limit the search.

d. Search by Table of Contents

In some instances, you may be able to locate a statute or constitutional provision by reviewing the tables of contents of the laws you are searching. Generally, when a table of contents is available for a database Westlaw either defaults to that table of contents when the specific database is selected, or there is a link to the table of contents that appears throughout the particular database.

For Example

You are looking for the federal law that governs bank robbery. Rather than construct a natural language or terms and connectors search, you may be able to locate the statute simply by going to "Federal Materials," selecting "United States Code Annotated (USCA)," then scrolling through the table of contents until you get to the title that covers crimes and criminal procedure.

2. Finding Case Law

There are several ways to locate court opinions. The search methods and steps for locating case law are the same as those used to search for statutory and constitutional law, therefore, this subsection will be an abbreviated form of the prior subsection.

a. Search by Citation

If you know the citation of a case, you can locate the case by using either of the following steps:

1. On the Westlaw homepage, type the citation in the search box then click "Search." The document will open (see Exhibit 8-1).
2. From the Westlaw homepage, select "Federal Materials" or "State Materials," then choose the appropriate jurisdiction and/or database and type the citation in the search box. The document will open.

For Example

If the citation is to volume 713 of the Federal Supplement Reporter at page 1296, type 713 fs 1296 in the homepage search box and click on "Search."

b. Search by Issue—Plain English

In most instances, when you are trying to find the case law that governs the issue being researched, you may not know its name or citation (as is often the case when you are searching for statutes). Therefore, you must locate the case law using the information from the issue and facts available to you. The steps for performing a natural language search for statutory and case law are the same. The most critical step in the research process is framing the issue in the context of the specific facts of the case.

To conduct a plain English search for case law, perform the following steps:

1. *Type the issue you are researching as specifically as possible in the context of the facts* in the homepage search box. As with searching for statutes, the results will include documents from across all databases, not just the court opinions.
2. *Locate the appropriate database.* Locate the appropriate case law database and *type the issue you are researching as specifically as possible in the context of the facts* in the search box. This method will narrow the results only to cases within the database you selected.

For Example

If you are looking for federal case law, specifically opinions from the Ninth Circuit, choose "Federal Materials," then "Federal Cases" and then on "Ninth Circuit." *Type the issue you are researching as specifically as possible in the context of the facts* in the search box and click "Search." Only cases from the Ninth Circuit will be displayed in the results list.

c. Search by Issue—Terms and Connectors

The steps for performing a terms and connectors search for statutory and case law are the same. The same terms and connectors are used for all searches.

Following is a summary of the steps for conducting a terms and connectors search for case law.

1. *Type the issue you are researching as specifically as possible within the context of the facts* using symbols and connectors. This first step is the same as searching for statutes.
2. *Locate the appropriate database. Type the issue you are researching as specifically as possible in the context of the facts* using symbols and connectors.

For Example

The search is for court opinions that include the terms *bank, robbery, dangerous weapon,* and *toy gun.* The terms dangerous and weapon as well as toy and gun probably appear in the same order, so they will be placed in quotation marks in the query. The query would be *"dangerous weapon" & bank & robbery & "toy gun".* If you wanted to narrow the search, then the query could read as follows: *"dangerous weapon" /p bank /p robbery /p "toy gun".* The search would retrieve only those cases in which the terms appear in the same paragraph.

d. Search by Digest—Topic and Key Numbers

If you are searching for case law that addresses an issue, you can perform a Key Number search on Westlaw. As discussed in Chapter 5, West's digests organize the law by topic and subtopics, and each subtopic is assigned a key number. The Westlaw Key Number database is the online version of searching the print digests. To use the key number system, perform the following steps:

1. *Access the Key Number database.* On the Westlaw home page, click "Key Numbers" which is under the "All Content" tab. This tab is the default tab.
2. *Select the jurisdiction.* Select the federal or state jurisdiction(s) you want to search, then add search terms in the search box. You can search multiple jurisdictions at one time.
3. *Select topic and key number.* As an alternative to the first two steps, select the link for the West Key Number database, then review the topics from the topics list and select the key number for the subject you are researching. To see all of the key numbers under a topic, click the plus sign (+) next to the topic number. Check the box next to the key number you want to search; or if you already know the key number, type it in the search box at the top of the page then click "Search." The search results will appear.

One important note about Westlaw: each time you narrow the databases, the universal search box shows the modified search terms as they are created by your selection of databases. As such, any time you enter search terms in the search box, the search will be limited by those parameters and by jurisdiction as you have selected. It is important to always be aware of where you are in Westlaw to know how broad or narrow your search results will be.

For Example

If you are on the Westlaw homepage and enter search terms, the search results will be from all databases within Westlaw. However, if you select "State Materials," "Arizona," "Arizona Tax Court" and enter search terms, the search results will only be from Arizona tax court cases.

3. Updating Research—KeyCite

It is essential to determine whether the statute or case you have found is still "good law." *KeyCite* is Westlaw's online citator. How to use *KeyCite* was discussed in detail in Chapter 5.

C. Finding Secondary Authority

Westlaw provides access to thousands of secondary sources. There are databases for *Am. Jur. 2d, ALR,* and other legal periodicals including law reviews, treatises, legislative history, and legal forms, just to name a few. To view the available databases, click on "Secondary Sources" on the homepage. On the "Secondary Sources" page, you can navigate to secondary sources by type, state, and topic. If you are unsure what secondary source to choose, you can enter search terms in the search box and results from all secondary sources will appear. If you want to search within a specific type of source, click on the link for that source, then enter search terms or navigate through the database by browsing.

The steps for performing a secondary authority search are generally the same as those used for a primary authority search, that is, you may search by citation, terms and connectors, natural language, and so on. Review "Finding Primary Authority" in Subsection B. Recall that in Chapters 5 and 6, there are specific references and guidance on using Westlaw to search secondary sources.

D. Filters

When researching, Westlaw allows you to narrow your search results through the use of **filters**. These filters are located on the left of the search results page. The filters allow you to narrow the search results by searching for terms within the search results.

For Example

You searched for *element* * */p battery*. This led an extremely long list of cases, both civil and criminal. You can narrow the search results by using the "Search within results" filter and adding terms that would narrow the results to cases more specific to the issue you are researching.

Additional filters include: jurisdiction, reported status, topic, date, judge, attorney, law firm, key number, party, and docket number.

E. Search Results

The results of a search are displayed in a list by default. You can change the amount of detail shown for the results. The filters discussed above are visible to the left of the results list (see Exhibit 8-2).

1. Document Text

In the text of each document in a search result list, the search terms are highlighted in yellow. Other sources within the greater Westlaw database are presented in blue and are hyperlinked.

Exhibit 8-2   Results of WestlawNext search. Used with Permission of Thomson Reuters.

For Example

If you searched for *State v. Simms*, and in that opinion read: The Court of Appeals relied primarily on our discussion in *Johnson* concerning the legislative purpose behind Section 66-8-102, which is to "deter persons from placing themselves in a situation in which they can directly commence operating a vehicle while they are intoxicated." You can link directly to the statute because it is a hyperlink. (Note: on the screen, the statute would be in blue and underlined.)

2. Navigating Results

There is a link to return to the search results list when you are viewing a specific document from the search results list. It is also possible to use the arrow toggle buttons to move forward and backward through search results and search terms.

3. Organizing Search Results

Westlaw offers the ability to organize search results and track which items you have viewed. Any item you have previously viewed will have a pair of eyeglasses added to the search results list which can help track what items you have already viewed. In addition, Westlaw allows its subscribers to highlight and add notes to any item whether it is a statute, court opinion, or something from a secondary source. This feature, combined with the ability to create folders and move specific items to those folders, allows the researcher to organize research by topic or by the client's case.

Westlaw also tracks user history. Therefore, if the researcher loses connectivity to the Internet, is interrupted during a research project, or wants to return to a prior search later, the history tab allows quick access by providing a list of prior searches. The researcher merely needs to click on a prior search, and they will be taken to the results for that search.

F. Printing and Saving

Westlaw provides several printing and saving options. You can download documents, have them sent to an email address, or print them. You can control the appearance of the printed document by choosing various print options. There are also various options that allow you to control the appearance of a document when it is downloaded.

III. LEXISNEXIS

LexisNexis (Lexis), as with Westlaw, is a commercial legal research service that provides access to thousands of primary and secondary research sources. The Lexis research service is operated by LexisNexis, a division of Reed Elsevier Inc. It is available directly on the Internet at http://www.LexisNexis.com. Similar to Westlaw's WestlawNext, Lexis has upgraded its user interface with a more streamlined version called Lexis Advance. There are differences between Lexis and Westlaw, but the basic organization and research principles are the same. If you understand how to conduct research on one, with a bit of practice, you can use the other.

Rather than repeating the information that applies to searches on both Lexis and Westlaw, reference is made to the appropriate subsections of the previous section, II. Westlaw. The first subsection addresses finding primary and secondary authority, viewing search results, updating your research, and printing search results in the traditional Lexis interface, which at the time of writing was still available. The second subsection provides similar information tailored to Lexis Advance, which may be the only Lexis platform available at the time of publication of this text.

A. LexisNexis (classic)

1. Finding Primary Authority

This section focuses on locating statutory law, constitutional law, and case law (primary authority).

a. Search by Citation

There are multiple ways to search for primary law for which you already have the citation:

- From the search box on the "My Lexis" tab
- From the "Get a Document" tab
- From the "Quick Tools" box on the Search tab

For Example

If you wanted to find 18 U.S.C.S. § 2113, type 18 uscs 2113 in the "Get by Citation" box and click "Get."

b. Search by Issue—plain English or Terms and Connectors

i. From the My Lexis Tab There are three ways to search under this tab: 1) terms and connectors, 2) plain English (natural language), and 3) easy search. The steps for performing a terms and connectors search for primary authority are the same. The same terms and connectors are used for all searches. You can also search using plain English. As with all plain English searches, the key is framing the issue in the context of the specific facts or terms of the issue. Easy search allows you to enter your search terms with less precision, and is meant to be similar to a Google search. Enter your terms in accord with the search method you have selected.

You will then need to choose a search type. "Recent Sources" provides you a dropdown menu of recent sources you have searched. If you choose "Source Type" you will need to choose a jurisdiction, a practice area, and a source category. Once you have chosen all appropriate boxes, click "Next." Choose which database, then click "Search."

ii. From the Search Tab The Search tab provides several ways to obtain documents.

1. ***Browse Sources.*** To search in this manner choose a source, then choose a specific file and click "Search Selected." This will take researchers to the search query box. As with all searches in Lexis, you may search by terms and connectors, plain English, or easy search.
2. ***Recently Used Sources.*** Choose the recently visited source then click "Go." Researchers will be taken to the search query box where they can search by terms and connectors, natural language, or easy search.

c. Search by Topic or Headnote

Lexis provides a manner of search by Topic and Headnote similar to Westlaw's Key Number search. Because the Key Number system is owned by Westlaw, Lexis does not offer the key number database, but its Topics and Headnotes system is organized on the same topics and principles. Under the Search tab, use the "View More" icon to open the list of topics. As you move through the layers of topic, you will end at a search page allowing you to search by headnote, or search across sources using terms and connectors or plain English. Searching using terms and connectors and natural language is the same as with the other search options.

2. Finding Secondary Authority

Lexis, like Westlaw, provides access to thousands of secondary sources. There are databases for *Am. Jur. 2d, ALR,* and legal periodicals including law reviews, treatises, legislative history, and legal forms, just to name a few. Most of these databases are listed under "Secondary Legal." Recall Chapters 5 and 6 discuss which secondary sources are available in Lexis.

The steps for performing a secondary authority search are generally the same as those used to conduct a primary authority search. That is, you can search by citation, terms and connectors, natural language, or easy search. Following are the basic steps for conducting a secondary authority search when you do not know the citation:

1. *State the issue or research question as specifically as possible in the context of the facts.*
2. *Formulate the issue based on terms and connectors or plain English (natural language).*
3. *Locate the appropriate database and type the issue in the search box.*
4. *Perform the search.*

3. Terms and Connectors

When performing a terms and connectors search on Lexis, note the following information:

- *Plurals and possessives.* Like Westlaw, LexisNexis automatically retrieves plurals and possessives of terms. If you type *robber*, it will search for *robber, robbers, robbers',* and *robber's.* LexisNexis will also search for the singular word when you type a plural. These rules apply to words that form the plural by adding an *s* or *es* or by changing a *y* to an *ies.*
- *Root expander* (!). To search for extensions of a word, place the root expander ! at the end of the root of the word. This is the same in both LexisNexis and Westlaw.

For Example

The search for *work!* retrieves the various forms of the word: *worker, working, works,* and so on.

- *Universal character* (*). Use the asterisk as a placeholder for one character anywhere but at the beginning of a word. This is the same in both LexisNexis and Westlaw.
- *Space between words.* Unlike Westlaw, where a space between words is the same as *or*, a space between words in LexisNexis means that the words will be searched for together. The search will locate documents in which the terms appear in the same order. Thus, the search *bank robbery* locates all documents in which the terms *bank* and *robbery* appear together, and in which *bank* precedes *robbery.*
- *Connectors.* In both LexisNexis and Westlaw, connectors specify the relationship between search terms. Always use a space to separate the connector from the search term with a space.

The connectors are somewhat different in LexisNexis. Following is a list of the LexisNexis connectors and an explanation of how they are used.

CONNECTOR	RULES GOVERNING USE OF CONNECTOR
and	The use of *and* between the terms retrieves all documents that contain both terms. Thus, the search for *bank and robber* retrieves all documents with both terms: *bank* and *robber.*
or	Place *or* between words to retrieve all documents that contain either search term. Thus, the search *bank or robber* would retrieve all documents that contain either the term *bank* or the term *robber.*
/s	The use of */s* between the terms retrieves all documents that contain both terms in the same sentence. Thus, a search for *bank /s robber* would retrieve all documents in which *bank* and *robber* appear in the same sentence.
/p	The use of */p* between the terms retrieves all documents that contain both terms in the same paragraph. Thus, the search for *bank /p robber* would retrieve all documents in which *bank* and *robber* appear in the same paragraph.
/n	The use of */n* between the terms retrieves all documents in which the terms appear within a certain number of words of each other. The *n* is the specified number of words. Thus, the search for *bank /5 robber* would retrieve all documents in which *bank* and *robber* appear within five words of each other.

CONNECTOR	RULES GOVERNING USE OF CONNECTOR
PRE/n	*PRE/n* placed between words locates documents in which the first word precedes the second word by *n* words. Thus, the search for *bank PRE/2 robbery or holdup* would locate all documents that contain the word *bank* within two preceding words of either *robbery* or *holdup*.
and not	To exclude a term from a search, place *and not* before the term. Thus, the search for *bank and robber and not weapon* would retrieve all cases that contain the words *bank* and *robber* but do not contain the word *weapon*. All terms after *and not* are excluded from the search.

4. Search Results

The search results will list all the documents that match your search. The researcher has several options for viewing any document listed.

a. Cite

To view the citations or bibliographic references of a document, click on "Cite."

b. KWIC™

If you want to view only the portions of the document that include the search terms surrounded, click on "KWIC." KWIC (key words in context) displays a window of 15 to 25 words on each side of your search words.

c. Full

To view the complete text of a document the search has retrieved, click on "Full."

d. Term

To move to any of your search terms while viewing a document, click on the arrow next to the number in the bottom right lower navigation bar at the bottom right of the screen.

5. Updating Research

It is essential to determine the currency and validity of primary authority. In other words, whether it is still "good law." *Shepard's* is Lexis' citator. How to use *Shepard's* was discussed in detail in Chapter 5.

6. Printing and Saving

Lexis provides several printing and saving options. You can download documents, have them sent to an email address, or print them. Documents can be printed in single or dual column, with the search terms in bold or italics, among other options.

B. Lexis Advance

Lexis, like Westlaw, has developed a user interface that is more streamlined and does not require the selection of a database source or specific search box to perform a search. This new platform is called Lexis Advance, and it may be the only LexisNexis platform available once this text is in print. At the time of writing, Lexis (classic) was migrating its content to Lexis Advance, and subscribers had access to both platforms with a single subscription. Conducting research in Lexis Advance is very similar to using WestlawNext.

Lexis Advance has all the same databases and resources as LexisNexis, as discussed in the previous section. Lexis Advance has the added feature of searching the Internet at large, not just its own databases.

1. Search by citation

Recall from the Chapter 5 discussion on using *Shepard's*, Lexis Advance has a universal search box at the top of its homepage. If you know the citation of the law or document you are seeking, type the citation into the search box, then click "Search." Lexis Advance will search all of Lexis for that citation, and the document will open.

Exhibit 8-3 Lexis Advance Home Page. Used with Permission of LexisNexis.

2. Search by Issue—Plain English, or Terms and Connectors

Researchers can type the issue being researched in either plain English, or formulate the issue using key terms and connectors into the universal search box on the Lexis Advance homepage. There is no need to choose a database–Lexis Advance will search all Lexis databases and the Internet for those search terms and produce a search results list.

Alternatively, researchers can use a set of dropdown menus below the universal search box to filter the search. To use the filters, after typing the issue in the universal search box, the researcher can choose specific content types, jurisdictions, or practice areas and topics for the search to be conducted in. This will produce a narrower set of search results. (See Exhibit 8-3.)

For Example

You are looking for an Arizona statute that provides the elements of burglary committed with a dangerous weapon. Your search terms are *"dangerous weapon" burglary*. You can use the jurisdiction filter to narrow the search to Arizona, and use the content type dropdown to narrow the search to statutes.

3. Browse Sources

Researchers can browse through the list of available sources in Lexis Advance to locate a particular source. Click "Browse Sources" above the red universal search bar. To locate a source, use the small "Search Sources" search box to the left of the "Sources" tab to enter key words related to the source. Lexis Advance will provide suggestions as you type. Once a source is chosen, the alphabetical list can be used to refine the search. The "Browse Sources" page also allows searches to be narrowed by filters on the left. Once the researcher narrows the search to particular source, search terms—either plain English or terms and connectors—can be entered and the search performed.

4. Browse Topics

Researchers can also browse topics the same way they can browse sources. Click "Browse Topics" above the red universal search bar, enter search terms in the search box, then click "Search." Alternatively, researchers can browse the list of practice areas and chose one before adding it to the search and entering search terms. Once the

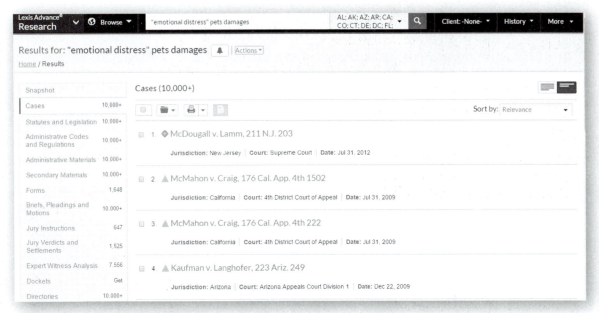

Exhibit 8-4 Lexis Advance Search Results page. Used with Permission of LexisNexis.

researcher narrows the search to a particular topic, search terms—either plain English or terms and connectors—can be entered and the search performed.

5. Search Results

As in LexisNexis, there are a myriad of ways to view search results in Lexis Advance. In general, search results are presented in a list with a portion of the text of the item listed presented. The list of results also has columns providing information about the jurisdiction (federal, state, etc.), level of court, and date of each item in the results list. *Shepard's* signals are also provided for each item in a results list, as applicable. Like WestlawNext, Lexis Advance has several filters in the left margin that the researcher can use to narrow the results list. These filters include jurisdiction, court, practice areas and topics, attorney, law firm, and most cited results. There is also a search box that allows the researcher to search within the results for terms not already part of the search terms. There is also the ability to sort documents by relevance (the default), date, jurisdiction, and court. (See Exhibit 8-4.)

For Example

Referring to the scenario at the beginning of the chapter, James Redhorse has conducted a search using the terms *emotional distress, damages,* and *pets.* The results list contains over a hundred items. James knows he needs Arizona related content, so he chooses to narrow the search results using the filters on the left of the search results list. He chooses the jurisdiction as Arizona and applies the filter. The results are greatly narrowed to just a few items.

Further, Lexis Advance search results can be viewed by content type by way of a series of tabs for each content type that contains the search terms. A unique feature of Lexis Advance is the **Snapshot** tab. This tab presents an overview of the top three results by relevance for each content tab. Each list of top three results is expandable and collapsible. For each of the top three items listed per content type, a few key pieces of information are provided such as: title/citation, *Shepard's* signal for primary sources, the type of sources (article, comment, *ALR* annotation), a brief overview of the item, and so on. The information is tailored to each content type. This allows a researcher to get a big picture idea of the types of resources that are available and the strength of the resources related to the search terms before delving into each content type in depth.

For Example

Referring to the prior example, James' list of results is extensive. After determining there is little Arizona case law and the court opinions in Arizona are not as helpful as he would like, he clicks on the Snapshot tab and can then see the top three relevant results for each type of content. He sees under the Secondary Materials listing there is an *ALR* listed. He knows from an *ALR* he can get a list of other state cases and an overview of the law on the issue. He clicks on the *ALR* and uses it to find on-point cases in other jurisdictions.

Organization of search results can be accomplished through the use of Lexis Advance's Work Folders. Folders can be created and customized, allowing the researcher to save results to various folders for future reference. Similar to WestlawNext's eyeglasses icon, Lexis Advance uses a binocular icon to show what results have previously been viewed. The binocular icon will appear for any document viewed in the last 30 days, therefore, to determine if the item has been previously viewed in a particular research list, hover over the icon, and the date on which that item was last viewed will appear.

6. Print and Download

Like most Internet legal research sources, there are options for the manner in which a document can be printed or downloaded. In addition, a printable list of search results can also be created then printed or downloaded. This customizable print and download option may vary based on the subscription level of the user.

IV. OTHER COMMERCIAL (FEE-BASED) INTERNET RESEARCH SOURCES

There are a number of other commercial, fee-based, Internet search tools. It is becoming more common for state bar associations to provide licensed attorneys with some form of access to these other websites as a part of the attorney's membership services, or for a discounted fee. Be sure to know what Internet research websites your particular office uses and how to access those services.

A. VersusLaw

VersusLaw provides access to state and federal primary sources and the tribal court decisions from 22 different tribes. The resources available is dependent upon the level of subscription. The highest level of subscription includes all state and federal primary law. Access to statutes is provided via links to each state's non-fee-based website containing that state's statutes.

VersusLaw does not have a full citator like *Shepard's* or *KeyCite*, but it does have a tool called V.Cite for court opinions. V.Cite does not update case law, but it does provide a list of cases that have cited the citation you are checking. The list can be narrowed by filters to the jurisdiction of the citing authority and terms within the citing case.

When searching for court opinions, the researcher must first choose a database such as Supreme Court decisions or Federal Circuit decisions. The researcher then chooses the type of search. The search types are: search terms, citation, docket, party name, judge, attorney, or V.Cite. Once the search type is chosen, enter search terms then click "Submit." The only filter provided is one that allows the research to limit results to a set of date ranges. The search results are presented in a list with a column for the case, description, and date of the decision.

A list of VersusLaw services and prices is available at http://versuslaw.com. VersusLaw also has a 24-hour free trial for three of its subscription plans.

B. Fastcase

Fastcase is a fee-based Internet research source that has become increasingly popular. It provides access to state and federal primary law, attorney general opinions, legal forms, newspapers, law reviews through HeinOnline (discussed below), and federal filings (via PACER). Fastcase can be searched by citation, term and connectors, and natural language (plain English). Fastcase uses its own limited set of terms and connectors and provides a list of those in its quick guides.

Fastcase has Authority Check as a validation tool. Authority Check, like VersusLaw's V. Cite, is more limited than *Shepard's* or *KeyCite*, but it does provide a list of other cases citing your case. An Authority Check report provides a citation summary of the total number of times the case has been cited by each jurisdiction: federal appellate courts, federal district courts, state appellate courts, bankruptcy courts, and provides the date of the most recent cite. At the time of this writing, Fastcase was testing a feature called Bad Law Bot, that indicates when a case has been overturned or reversed and provides the citation and link to the case that overturned or reversed the case the researcher is checking. Authority Check also has an interactive timeline that plots the citing cases on a timeline by court level or relevance on one axis, and year on the other axis.

Unlike VersusLaw, Fastcase has each jurisdiction's enacted law as part of its database. To search for statutes, rules, and regulations, the researcher chooses the search database from the "Search Type" dropdown menu, then selects the specific jurisdiction. The search can be conducted by citation, terms and connectors, or natural language (plain English). The search results are presented in a list by relevance.

Search results for case law are presented in a list like most all other fee-based Internet research sources. Fastcase provides the document name/citation and a brief description, the percentage of relevance, the date of the decision, and an Authority Check summary of number of times cited.

Note: In December 2015, Fastcase acquired LoisLawConnect, which was one the most widely used and subscribed to Internet commercial research sources outside of Westlaw and LexisNexis. Not all of LoisLaw's databases, particularly its 125 treatises, were subsumed into Fastcase. At the time of this writing, the acquisition still would have increased Fastcase's resources despite not gaining the treatises. Whether those LoisLaw accessible treatises (owned by Wolters Kluwer) would be available through some other Internet resource was not known.

C. Casemaker

Casemaker is yet another fee-based Internet research source. Many state bar associations provide access for its members. Casemaker has access to state and federal primary sources as well as legal forms, uniform jury instructions (when a jurisdiction has them), court rules, and session laws.

Casemaker has a universal search box like WestlawNext and Lexis Advance. Searches can be conducted by citation, plain English, or terms and connectors. Search results can be narrowed by searching for terms within search results. Casemaker also has the tool Case Check which provides a list of negative authority and uses a red "thumbs down" icon and green "thumbs up" icon to demonstrate whether a citation is still good law. In addition, Casemaker has CiteCheck, which allows a subscriber to upload a brief or memorandum and have each case citation checked to determine if it is still good law.

D. Bloomberg Law

Bloomberg Law is an increasingly popular fee-based Internet search service. Bloomberg is a well-established news company which expanded its news services and business tools to include primary and secondary legal research tools. It provides full text access to a range of legal authorities. The main focus of Bloomberg law is business law–related topics and services. Bloomberg Law's focus is law offices practicing in the areas of antitrust, finance, labor law, corporate law, securities, and intellectual property. In addition, it has a mobile application.

E. HeinOnline

HeinOnline is a searchable, image-based legal search source with access to a wide variety of sources, in particular legal periodicals, law journals and the *Congressional Record*. HeinOnline also provides access to legislative histories, administrative law materials, the *CFR* and *Federal Register* as well as some international materials. The database is unique in that it delivers search results by PDF. HeinOnline's databases go back further than several of the databases listed above and have several subscription options, making it more flexible in cost than other Internet resources.

V. CITING COMMERCIAL INTERNET SOURCES

This section presents an overview of the rules of citation to be used when citing content derived from commercial research databases. A detailed discussion of the citation rules for each type of Internet source is beyond the scope of this text. Therefore, this section, unlike those in Chapters 3 through 6, generally refers the student to the citation rules that govern citation to Internet sources. As mentioned in each of the previous chapters, be sure to carefully review the appropriate citation manual for the detailed rules regarding each citation format.

Rule 18 in the *Bluebook* requires the use and citation of traditional print sources unless an authenticated digital source of the document is available. If a printed source is available, it shall be cited, and a parallel citation to the Internet source may be provided if it will improve access to the relevant content, and the content of the Internet source is identical to the printed source.

Unlike the limited guidance provided by the Bluebook, the *ALWD Guide* dedicates an entire part of the manual to citation of electronic sources. However, the *ALWD Guide* also requires that if a printed source is available, only the print source should be cited *if* it is readily available to most readers. This requires the researcher to know the audience of whom their research results will be produced. If the audience does not have access to Westlaw or Lexis, or whichever commercial database is being cited, the *ALWD Guide* indicats the citation to the electronic source should not be included. Rules 30 and 32 are most relevant for citing non-fee-based websites and other types of electronic media.

Examples of citation from Westlaw or Lexis are not included, as these forms are ever evolving as electronic sources become more accepted and widely used. As such, any example provided here would quickly be out-of-date. For citing both commercial and non-fee-based Internet sources always consult the most recent citation manuals and local rules regarding citing Internet resources.

VI. KEY POINTS CHECKLIST: Commercial Internet Research

- ✓ The most frequently used commercial services are Westlaw and LexisNexis. Familiarity with any of these sources will provide you with sufficient information to use other services.

- ✓ Other commercial services such as Versuslaw and Fastcase are increasingly part of state bar memberships and are increasingly being used in law offices before turning to Westlaw and LexisNexis, particularly for state and local primary law searches.

- ✓ The most critical step in the research process is framing the issue in the context of the specific facts of the case (see Chapter 10). A well-framed issue, stated in the context of the facts, provides a researcher with the information necessary to conduct research using natural language or terms and connectors.

- ✓ A terms and connectors search has the disadvantage of requiring a familiarity with the use of the connectors. It has the advantage of allowing the researcher to tailor the search.

- ✓ As with any research, it is essential to determine if the results of electronic research are still good law. Westlaw and LexisNexis, include services that allow you to update your research.

VII. APPLICATION

A. Chapter Hypothetical

As James Redhorse learned in his legal research course, the first step of any research project is to identify the issue as concretely as possible in the context of the facts. James knows a concise statement of the issue will allow him to focus his search and identify the search terms. After considering the facts of the case and several drafts, his preliminary formulation of the issue is as follows: "Under Arizona law, may damages for emotional distress be recovered when an individual traps and kills a neighbor's pet and shows the dead pet to the owner causing the owner severe distress?" James knows the issue may become more refined as research is conducted.

The next step is to determine where to look. Will he look for statutory law, case law, or secondary authority? Although research normally begins with a search for a governing statute, James knows that recovery for emotional distress is usually governed by tort law and most torts are not statutory. He decides to check Arizona case law for a court opinion that has addressed this question.

Reviewing the issue, James concludes that a terms and connectors search should include *emotional distress, damages*, and *pet*. He chooses "State Materials," "Arizona," "All Arizona State Cases" and formulates his search as: "*emotional distress*" and *damages* and *pet*. The search results reveal no cases on point. This doesn't surprise James, because Arizona doesn't have a large body of case law. This means he will have to look to the law from other jurisdictions.

James can easily expand his search to all state cases by merely changing the jurisdiction to all state cases and clicking search. However, he knows this will result in a list of thousands of cases, and will be quite time consuming to wade through. Rather than search state by state, James decides to look for an *ALR* article that addresses the subject. If there is one, it will provide an analysis of the question and include relevant state statutory law, case law, and secondary authority. He selects "Secondary Sources" and "American Law Reports" then enters the search: "*emotional distress*" and *damages* and *pet*. The results still show more than 4,000 documents.

James doesn't want to wade through that many annotations, so he decides to edit his search by restricting the search to the titles of those *ALR* annotations that include his search terms. He clicks on the "advanced" link next to the search box, then enters his terms into the box for "Title." The search reads: TI ("*emotional distress*" and *damages* and *pet*). The search results in several annotations, but the first listed (most relevant) is: "Recovery of Damages for Emotional Distress Due to Treatment of Pets and Animals" by Jay M. Zitter, 91 *ALR 5th* 545.

This annotation answers the question. It summarizes all the case and statutory law that has addressed this question. It reveals that some states allow damages for emotional distress for the loss of a pet, and some do not. With this information, James can review the cases that are factually close to Mrs. Burgess' case, and prepare a memorandum to the senior partner summarizing the law.

Summary

The earlier chapters of the text focus on the techniques for conducting research using print resources such as texts and bound volumes. Chapter 7 discusses computer and Internet research in general, and the use of non-fee-based Internet resources. This chapter focuses on research using commercial (fee-based) Internet resources. Although commercial (fee-based) Internet resources are reliable, it is important to know how to research using print resources. Experienced researchers do not rely exclusively on Internet legal research.

This chapter presents an overview of legal research using the most frequently used commercial services: Westlaw and LexisNexis. Although many other electronic research services are available, a familiarity with either Westlaw or LexisNexis provides sufficient information to use the other services.

There are differences between Westlaw and LexisNexis, but the basic organization and research principles are the same. The services share the following features:

- Documents can be located by name, title, or citation.
- Documents can be located by plain English (also known as natural language).
- Documents can be located by using terms and connectors (also known as a Boolean search).
- Searches can be conducted through reference to the tables of contents of research sources.
- Documents can be located by focusing research on specific areas of law through Westlaw's Key Number service and LexisNexis's Topic and Headnote search.

Research may be updated through the use of Westlaw's *KeyCite*, LexisNexis's *Shepard's*, services.

In addition to Westlaw and LexisNexis, there are other commercial fee-based legal research services such as VersusLaw, Casemaker, Fastcase, Bloomberg Law, and HeinOnline.

Quick References

Internet Resources

In addition to Westlaw, and LexisNexis, there are other commercial web-based legal research services. The website addresses for Westlaw, LexisNexis, VersusLaw, and HeinOnline are as follows:

http://www.westlawnext.com

http://www.lexisnexis.com

http://www.fastcase.com

http://www.versuslaw.com

http://www.heinonline.org

EXERCISES

For Assignments 1–7, use Westlaw.

ASSIGNMENT 1

The client is the Chairman of the Board of Directors of an Ohio corporation. The Board of Directors has decided to merge the corporation with another Ohio corporation. The client wants to know if shareholder approval is required for the merger. Identify the Ohio statute that governs this question, and what that statute provides concerning shareholder approval.

ASSIGNMENT 2

Perform Assignment 1 using your state law.

ASSIGNMENT 3

Your supervising attorney recalls there was a 1989 Arkansas case where a county court judge was convicted in federal court of vote buying. After the U.S. Court of Appeals denied the appeal, the state circuit court declared the judge ineligible to hold public office. The judge claimed that he had received insufficient notice of the state court hearing because he had less than 24 hours' notice to appear at the hearing. What is the name and citation of the case? Under the holding of the case, when is a person "convicted" for purposes of removal of a public official from office?

ASSIGNMENT 4

What is the citation of a 1993 ALR annotation that discusses the admissibility of polygraph test results in an action for malicious prosecution? What *Am. Jur. 2*, Evidence research references are listed? What "Malicious Prosecution" key numbers are referenced? What 1987 U.S. 6th Circuit Court of Appeals case held that generally the use of polygraph results to prove a party's innocence is prohibited?

ASSIGNMENT 5

Locate a 1998 Alabama criminal case where the defendant, Clark, appealed his criminal conviction claiming that there was not sufficient evidence to support the conviction and his probation was improperly revoked.

  a. What is the citation to the case?

  b. What was the defendant convicted of?

  c. Why was the case remanded?

ASSIGNMENT 6

Access "Key Numbers" from the top of the "Welcome" page.

  a. What is the topic and key number that applies to the arrest and detention of juveniles charged with a crime?

  b. Give the citation of a 1970 Oregon case that held that a reasonable search for weapons may be made when an officer takes temporary custody of a juvenile.

ASSIGNMENT 7

KeyCite this case: *United States v. Martinez-Jimenez*, 864 F.2d 664 (9th Cir. 1989), what are the citations of the 1995 and 1993 cases listed under "Positive History" that have a yellow flag?

For Assignments 8–14, use LexisNexis.

ASSIGNMENT 8

While walking her dog in a city park, Client's dog was attacked by another dog. Before the dogs could be separated, Client's dog was severely injured and died later that day. Client's dog was on a leash and the other dog was not leashed. Client was very close to her pet and wants to sue the owner of the other dog for emotional distress she suffered as a result of witnessing the attack and death of her pet. Your supervisory attorney remembers there was an Arizona case where, under similar facts, recovery was denied. Find the case.

ASSIGNMENT 9

Regarding Assignment 8 above, there is a question in the Client's negligence case of whether there is an intervening force that may cut off Client's right to recover. What *Restatement 2d* sections define intervening force and superseding cause? How are the terms defined?

ASSIGNMENT 10

Client and her husband are residents of the state of Georgia. She wants to sue for divorce claiming adultery. She does not want to file a no-fault divorce. Is adultery a ground for divorce in Georgia? If so, what is the statute, and what does it provide? What law review article presents a survey of Georgia cases dealing with domestic relations?

ASSIGNMENT 11

Answer Assignment 10 using your state law.

ASSIGNMENT 12

Client's son was hitchhiking along a highway where hitchhiking was prohibited. Find an *ALR* annotation that addresses the construction and effect of anti-hitchhiking laws in an action for injury to a hitchhiker. What case mentioned in the annotation addresses an action by a hitchhiker to recover for injuries sustained when a driver went past him on an interstate, stopped, backed up along the shoulder to give him a ride, and hit him?

ASSIGNMENT 13

Select "Shepardize." For the case of *Harris v. Cincinnati*, 79 Ohio App. 3d 163, 607 N.E. 2d 15 (1992), how many citing decisions are listed? Are there any cases showing a negative history? How many law review and periodical references are listed?

ASSIGNMENT 14

Under federal law, what law governs murder? What is the penalty for murder in the first degree? What 1968 case addressed the constitutionality of this statute?

Part 3

The Specifics of Legal Analysis

Overview

Part III covers matters essential to the analysis of a legal problem. It begins with a chapter on a principal component of a legal question (legal issue), the key facts—facts critical to the outcome of the case.

Next are two chapters on identifying and writing legal issues:

1. Identifying the legal issue presented by a fact situation or in a court opinion
2. Stating or presenting the issue

Part III concludes with two chapters on topics fundamental to legal analysis:

1. Case law analysis—the analytical process used to determine if a court opinion applies to a legal question
2. Counteranalysis—the process of discovering and considering the counterargument to a legal position or argument

Chapter 9

Legal Analysis—Key Facts

Learning Objectives

After completing this chapter, you should understand

- What key facts are
- What background and irrelevant facts are
- The role and importance of key facts
- How to identify key facts in a client's case
- How to identify key facts in a court opinion

Alice was recently hired by Kinsey Law Firm and placed under the guidance and supervision of Karen, a 15-year veteran paralegal. Karen did an initial interview with a client, Mr. Aper, and Alice sat in on the interview to observe the process and gain experience. After the interview, Karen told Alice, "I'm going to prepare a summary of the interview, then prepare a list of the potential issues. I want you to identify the key facts that should be included in the statement of the issues."

Alice's notes of the interview indicate that Mr. Aper owns a 1,000-acre farm on the outskirts of town. He has lived on the farm for the past 20 years. About 200 acres of the property are forested, and deer frequent the forest. Mr. Aper refuses to allow hunting on his property and, to discourage hunting, has fenced and posted the property.

One day, two weeks ago, Mr. Aper noticed a new path entering the forested portion of the farm. Someone had removed part of the wood fence surrounding the forest and apparently entered the property several times. He followed the trail and found several small pine trees cut down and a crude lean-to constructed from the trees. In front of the lean-to was a small fire pit where there had been a fire quite recently; the coals were still warm. Some of the wood removed from the fence was still smoldering in the fire. Mr. Aper got up early the next morning, before dawn, and watched the lean-to from a hidden spot in the bushes. Shortly after sunrise, he saw his neighbor, Eric Rascon, an avid bow hunter, come down the trail carrying a hatchet and loaded down with bow-hunting gear.

Eric proceeded to set up camp. He started a fire with wood from the fence and some old tree branches and cut down another small tree and added it to the lean-to. Mr. Aper stepped out from behind the bushes and confronted Eric. "What

are you doing here? You know you can't hunt here. Who told you it's okay to cut down my trees? Get off my property!"
Eric angrily replied, "You stingy old man. These deer should be hunted; it's nature's way. I'll leave, but I'll be back and
start again; you can't watch this forest every hour of every day." Eric then left.

Mr. Aper wants to take whatever legal action he can against Eric. Alice's assignment is to identify the key facts in
the case. The Application section of this chapter addresses how Alice performs her assignment. The chapter discusses facts
in general and emphasizes the critical role of the key facts in a case.

I. INTRODUCTION

Most, if not all, attorney-client relationships begin with the initial interview with the client. During the interview,
the client presents information concerning a situation the client believes requires a legal solution. If a lawsuit is
ultimately filed, the process begins here. The role of the attorney, often performed by the paralegal or law clerk,
is to sift through the facts and determine what relief, if any, the law may provide for the problem raised by the
facts. Any legal solution to a client's problem involves the application of the law to the facts of the client's case.

Usually, some of the factual information the client provides in an interview is not relevant to the outcome
of the case. Sometimes, important factual information is left out. Before a legal solution to the client's problem
can be found or a determination made as to whether a lawsuit should be filed, it is necessary to identify the facts
critical to the outcome of the case—the key facts. To ensure that all the key facts are identified—that is, to make
sure none are missed—all the factual information concerning the problem must be identified at the outset. This
is accomplished by a thorough and comprehensive initial interview.

Often the importance of certain facts may not be determined until the legal issues and the governing law
are identified.

For Example

Regarding the hypothetical at the beginning of the chapter, assume that the researcher,
based on her experience, concludes that the burning of the fence may give rise to a
cause of action for conversion (an improper act that deprives an individual of the rightful
possession of the individual's property). Upon conducting subsequent research, she learns
that conversion requires that the person suing be in possession of the property.

It is an important fact, therefore, that Mr. Aper not only owns the land but also was in
possession of the land when the events took place. If the land were rented out to a tenant, the
tenant would be in possession of the land. The tenant, being the person in possession of the
land, would have the right to sue for conversion. The landlord, Mr. Aper, would not be in possession of the land and, therefore, would not have a right to sue Eric Rascon for conversion. The
importance of the fact that Mr. Aper not only owned the land but was also in possession of it
may not become apparent until the legal question and governing law are identified.

This example illustrates another important point concerning facts. When a lawsuit proceeds to trial, the facts
presented at trial are those facts identified and considered important prior to trial. Identifying and gathering the
facts depend entirely on the thoroughness and quality of the pretrial preparation. If the researcher performs a
sloppy job, that is, fails to gather and examine all the facts, then a poor outcome and a lost case may be the result.

For Example

Referring to the previous example, assume that the land was leased. Mr. Aper did not reveal
this fact during the interview because, being the owner of the land, he did not think it mat-
tered who was in possession. The interview was not thorough because Mr. Aper was not asked
who was in possession of the land. Assume also that the researcher believed that the "possession" requirement of conversion is met if the party suing owns the property. The researcher
did a sloppy job of research and did not thoroughly research what constitutes "possession"
under the law.

> If a lawsuit alleging conversion against Mr. Rascon was initiated, it may not make it to trial because this key fact was not identified. Mr. Rascon's attorney would likely file a motion for summary judgment arguing there is no genuine dispute that there are no key facts to support the element of possession. Mr. Aper's claim of conversion would be dismissed from the lawsuit because there was no material evidence that he was in possession of the land. The key fact of who was in possession of the land was not identified prior to initiating the lawsuit. The poor quality of the interview and subsequent research resulted in a poor outcome.

This may appear to be an extreme example, but it illustrates an important point: The facts presented at trial and the outcome of the trial, or whether a matter is dismissed before even making it to trial, depends entirely on the quality of work done early on in the case. As noted in Chapter 2, Rule 1.1 of the American Bar Association's Model Rules of Professional Conduct requires that a client be provided competent representation. Failure to conduct a proper interview and identify the key facts denies the client competent representation.

The focus of this chapter, and the task assigned to many paralegals and law clerks, is to identify the facts that give rise to the legal dispute in either a client's case or a court opinion. The facts that give rise to the legal dispute are often referred to as *significant, material,* or *key facts*. In this chapter, and throughout the text, these facts are referred to as *key facts*.

As noted in Chapters 10 and 11, key facts and issues are integrally related. The key facts are an essential element of the issue. They are essential in identifying and stating the issue because they give rise to the legal dispute. Disputes arise and take place in the context of facts.

II. FACTS IN GENERAL—DEFINITION

A fact is something that is real, that actually exists, an actual event as opposed to an opinion or someone's interpretation of what took place. In a lawsuit, a **fact** is information present in a case concerning a particular thing, action, event, or circumstance.

For Example

> In the hypothetical at the beginning of the chapter, the presence of the lean-to, Mr. Rascon's actions of entering the property, and Mr. Rascon's statements are all facts.

Facts should not be confused with a **rule of law**. A rule of law is a standard established by a governing authority that prescribes or directs action or forbearance. It may be a constitutional provision, statute, ordinance, regulation, or case law doctrine. Its application determines the outcome of the question raised by the facts of a dispute.

For Example

> Illinois statute, 625 ILCS 5/12-610.2, prohibits a person from operating a motor vehicle on a roadway while using an electronic communication device, which specifically includes mobile/cellular phones. The statute does not apply to a person using an electronic communication device in hands-free or voice-operated mode. When a person physically uses a cell phone to text while driving a car, this statute governs the question of whether they violated the traffic regulations, that is, the outcome of the question raised by the facts.

Before defining and discussing key facts, it is helpful to consider the importance of facts in general, and to identify and distinguish the various types of facts present in a client's case and in a court opinion.

III. IMPORTANCE OF FACTS

The importance of giving due consideration to the facts of a dispute cannot be overemphasized. Often minimal attention is given to the facts. This is surprising, since our legal system revolves around resolving disputes by applying the rules of law to the facts of a case. Notice the two major factors here: *rules of law* and *facts of the case*. Both are equally important. Novice researchers, however, often focus primarily on the rules of law.

The *issue* is the precise question raised by the specific facts of the client's case. Therefore, the facts are an essential element of the issue. Rules of law are general principles designed to apply to multiple fact situations, and a determination of which law governs the issue is controlled primarily by the facts of the client's case. Consequently, facts play a role of primary importance in determining what is in dispute in a case and which law applies. Clients often have little knowledge or concern about general legal principles, but they are very concerned with how the law applies to the facts of their case.

Facts are also important because determining how or if a law applies to the client's case depends on the presence or absence of certain facts.

For Example

Tom is stopped at a light at a four-way intersection in the city, waiting for the light to change. Mary, stopped behind him, is checking her text messages and replying to them. Because she is distracted, she sees some movement of cars around her and without assessing if the light has changed, she lets her foot off the brake. Her vehicle bumps into Tom's vehicle. After exiting their vehicles and examining them, they discover that there is no visible damage to either vehicle. Tom, however, complains of neck pain from whiplash.

Tom sues Mary for negligence. The researcher working for Mary's attorney knows that the elements of negligence are duty, breach of duty, proximate cause, and damages. Based on her research and education, she also knows that to state a claim, Tom must present facts establishing each of the elements of negligence. Although there are facts to support the first three elements, there was no damage to the vehicle; thus, it is questionable whether the impact was severe enough to cause whiplash neck injuries. Also, if the impact did not cause whiplash injuries and there is no damage to Tom's vehicle, there are no facts that establish the element of damages.

This hypothetical is referred to as the "minor impact" example throughout this chapter.

In the minor impact example, as in every case, there are two equally important factors—the law and the facts. The law establishes the conditions that must be met to state a claim for negligence, that is, the elements of negligence. The outcome of the application of the law depends on the existence of facts, and on one fact in particular in the case: Was Tom's injury caused by the impact? Like this example, all legal problems are fact sensitive; that is, the outcome depends on the existence or nonexistence of a particular fact or facts.

Another reason facts are important is that the determination of whether a court opinion is on point is largely governed by the similarity between the facts of the court opinion and the facts of the client's case. There must be a sufficient similarity between the key facts of the court opinion and those of the client's case before the court opinion can be considered on point and apply as precedent in the client's case.

IV. TYPES OF FACTS IN GENERAL

In either a client's case or a court opinion, there may be hundreds of facts, some of which are critically important, and some not. To identify the legal issue, the researcher must sort through the facts and determine which facts give rise to the legal question and are essential to its resolution. Helpful to this process is an understanding of the basic categories of facts present in a case. The facts of a case may be placed within the three broad categories presented in Exhibit 9-1.

A. Irrelevant Facts

Irrelevant facts are facts coincidental to the event that are not of legal significance in the case.

For Example

In the minor impact example, the race or gender of the parties, the day of the week, and whether Mary's car was insured are all irrelevant facts. They are irrelevant because they are facts that are not necessary to establish or satisfy the elements of the cause of action in the case. They are not necessary to prove or disprove the claim. The race or gender of the parties is irrelevant to the question of whether Mary was negligent. Whether it was Sunday or Wednesday when the accident occurred does not affect the outcome of the case. Mary's insurance status will not affect a determination of whether she is liable.

Irrelevant Facts	Facts coincidental to the event but not of significant legal importance in the case
Background Facts	Facts presented in a court opinion, case brief, or legal memorandum that put the key facts in context; facts that give an overview of a factual event and provide the reader with the overall context within which the facts occurred
Key Facts	The legally significant facts of a case that raise the legal question of how or whether the law governing the dispute applies; the facts that establish or satisfy the elements of a cause of action and are necessary to prove or disprove a claim; a fact so essential that, if it were changed, the outcome of the case would be affected or changed

© Cengage

Exhibit 9-1 Types of Facts.

Beware! Certain facts may be relevant in one situation and not relevant in another.

For Example

In the minor impact example, whether it was snowing is probably not a relevant fact. Both vehicles were stopped at a light, and the existence of snow should not affect Mary's duty to keep her foot on the brake pedal and determine if it was safe to move forward before doing so. If the facts, however, were that she was not driving distracted, but when approaching the stoplight, she failed to apply the brakes in a timely fashion, the existence of snow conditions becomes a relevant fact. The nature of her duty to exercise care while operating her car varies with the weather conditions, and the existence of snow conditions requires her to exercise greater care when braking.

B. Background Facts

Background facts are those irrelevant facts that put the key facts in context. They give an overview of the factual event and provide the reader with the overall context within which the key facts occurred. They are not key facts because they are not essential to a determination of the issues in the case, but they are usually necessary and often helpful because they provide information that helps the reader gain an overall picture of the environment within which the key facts occurred.

For Example

In the minor impact example, the location and type of intersection are background facts that provide the reader with an overview of the context and scene of the collision. The reader is aware that the impact took place at an intersection in the city, rather than in the country. This information is not essential, but it may be helpful for many reasons. The reader, for example, may want to visit the scene at a later date to investigate and determine if individuals working in the area witnessed the accident.

C. Key Facts

Key facts are often referred to as *significant, material,* or *ultimate facts*. They are facts that are critical to the outcome of the case. The following section discusses the definition and types of key facts.

V. KEY FACTS—DEFINITION AND TYPES

A. Definition

Key facts are the legally significant facts of a case that raise the legal question of how or whether the law governing the dispute applies. They are those facts upon which the outcome of the case is determined—the facts that establish or satisfy the elements of a cause of action and are necessary to prove or disprove a claim. A key fact is a fact so essential that, if it were changed, the outcome of the case would probably change. In fact, a useful test in determining whether a fact is key is to ask the question, "If this fact is changed, would the outcome of the application of the law be affected or changed?"

For Example

Law enforcement officers are sued for battery based on the following facts: Law enforcement officers pursued a suspect on foot for five blocks after observing him snatch a woman's purse. While making the arrest, the officers encountered resistance, used force to overcome that resistance, and continued to use force for more than a minute after the resistance ceased. The law provides that law enforcement officers may use the amount of force necessary to overcome resistance when making a legal arrest. This hypothetical is referred to in this chapter as the "resisting arrest" example.

What are the key facts in the resisting arrest example? Which of the facts, if changed, would change the outcome in this case? If the suspect had never resisted, the use of force would clearly have been improper. If the suspect never ceased resisting, the officers' continued use of force would have been proper. If the officers stopped using force when the resistance ceased, the use of force probably would have been proper. If the arrest was illegal, the use of force would have been improper. The key facts follow:

- A lawful arrest was being made.
- There was resistance to the arrest.
- Force was used to overcome the resistance.
- The resistance ceased.
- The use of force continued for more than a minute after the resistance ceased.

Each of these facts is a key fact. Each fact, if changed, would affect the outcome of the case.

Other facts, however, are not key facts. How far the officers pursued the suspect or the fact that the pursuit was on foot are not key facts. These facts, if changed, would not change the outcome of the case.

For Example

In the minor impact example, the lack of damage to Tom's automobile is a key fact. It is a fact that, if changed, would affect the outcome of the case. If there had been damage to Tom's vehicle, he clearly would have a claim. Damage is an element of negligence, and the existence of damage is a fact that is essential to establishing a negligence claim.

B. Types of Key Facts

There are two categories of key facts:

- Individual key facts
- Facts considered as a group—groups of facts

1. Individual Key Facts

Often an individual or several **individual facts** are key facts in a case. A key fact is an individual key fact if it meets the following test: If the fact is changed, the outcome of the case will be affected or changed.

For Example

1. In the resisting arrest example, all the facts identified as key facts are individual key facts: A lawful arrest was being made, there was resistance to the arrest, force was used to overcome the resistance, resistance ceased, and the use of force continued after the resistance ceased. Each of these individual facts, if changed, would change or affect the outcome of the case

2. Consider a breach-of-contract case in which the claim of breach is founded on the fact that payment was received nine days late, and the contract specifically provided that late payments constituted a breach of contract. The lateness of the payment is a key fact. This individual fact, if changed, would change the outcome of the case.

2. Groups of Facts

In some fact situations, no individual fact standing alone is a key fact—that is, no single fact is so significant that, if changed, it would change the outcome.

For Example

An inmate is challenging the conditions of his confinement as cruel and unusual punishment. He alleges the following: There are cockroaches in his jail cell, the recreational periods are too short, his mail is improperly censored, his visitation rights are too restricted, and the temperature in his cell is too low in the winter and too high in the summer. It may be that no single fact by itself meets the test of a key fact, that is, no single fact is so critical that, if changed, the outcome of the case would change. The fact that there are cockroaches in his cell may not be sufficient, by itself, to constitute cruel and unusual punishment. The fact that the recreational periods are too short, by itself, may not constitute cruel and unusual punishment; and so on.

All the individual facts, however, when considered as a group, may determine the outcome of the case and, if changed as a group, would change the outcome. This may be identified in a court opinion when the court states, "No single fact of plaintiff's allegations constitutes cruel and unusual punishment. When taken as a whole, however, the individual allegations combine to establish a violation of the Eighth Amendment's prohibition against cruel and unusual punishment."

Recognizing **groups of facts** is important because, when analyzing a case, you must be aware that individual facts that seem to be insignificant may be key facts when considered and weighed as a group. When addressing a problem that involves key facts as a group, first review the facts individually to determine whether any individual fact, standing alone, is a key fact. If there is no individual fact that, if changed, would change the outcome of the case, look to the facts as a group.

There is no magic formula for determining how many or what types of facts are required for facts to be considered as a group, or what is necessary for a group of facts to be considered a key fact. Usually, it is necessary to consult case law and locate a case in which the court addressed a similar legal problem involving a group of facts.

The next step, after defining and categorizing key facts, is to determine how to locate them in both a client's case and a court opinion. Because the key facts are an element of the issue, the steps involved in identifying and stating the issue necessarily include, in part, some of the steps necessary for locating key facts. Therefore, the information from this chapter through Chapter 11 overlaps somewhat regarding the identification of key facts.

VI. KEY FACTS IDENTIFICATION—CLIENT'S CASE

A client's fact situation usually includes a mix of facts—some irrelevant, some background, and some key. A researcher's assignment may be to identify the key facts in the case. The four-step process presented in Exhibit 9-2 is recommended for determining which of the client's facts are key facts.

STEP 1	Identify each cause of action possibly raised by the facts.
STEP 2	Determine the elements of each cause of action identified in step 1.
STEP 3	List all the facts possibly related to the elements of the causes of action identified in step 2.
STEP 4	Determine which of the client's facts apply to establish or satisfy the elements of each cause of action—the key facts.

© Cengage

Exhibit 9-2 Steps in Key Fact Identification—Client's Case.

The following example is referred to in this section's discussion of the operation of this four-step process.

For Example

The researcher is assigned the task of identifying the key facts in a case. A review of the file reveals the following facts: Jerry and Ann are neighbors. They have lived on adjoining half-acre lots in a rural subdivision for the past five years. Their children attend the same school and ride the school bus together. Four years ago, Jerry put in a hedge and planted several fruit trees along his property line with Ann. Every year since then, Jerry sprays the trees with pesticide and hangs bee traps in the trees. The prevailing wind carries the pesticide across Ann's property and into her garden beds, preventing her from working in her garden, and usually causing several vegetable plants to die and killing all of the beneficial insects she releases into her garden. Every year she asks him not to spray the trees, and every year he ignores her request.

Ann wants Jerry to stop spraying the trees and pay her for the plants that have been "ruined" by the pesticide and the loss of crop to harmful insects and pests. This hypothetical is referred to as the "trespass" example in this chapter.

A. Step 1: Identify Each Cause of Action

The first step requires determining the possible cause(s) of action raised by the facts. Depending on the education and legal experience of the researcher, this initial step may not require any research.

In the trespass example, upon reviewing the facts, the researcher may come to a preliminary conclusion that the possible causes of action include trespass to land, private nuisance, and negligence.

B. Step 2: Determine the Elements of Each Cause of Action

The second step, determining the elements of each cause of action, usually requires some research. Such research may be necessary either to determine the elements of the possible cause of action or to ensure that the law has not changed since the last time research was conducted. This step is necessary because, to state a claim and thereby obtain relief, the plaintiff must present facts that establish or prove the existence of each element of the cause of action. These facts are the key facts of the case.

For Example

The paralegal's research reveals that the elements of trespass to land are as follows:

1. An act

2. Intrusion on land

3. In possession of another

4. Intent to intrude

5. Causation of the intrusion

The researcher also would identify the elements of each of the other potential causes of action identified in step 1.

C. Step 3: List All Facts Related to the Elements

The third step is to list all the facts possibly related to the elements of the causes of action identified in step 2. This includes gathering the facts from the client interview and any interviews that have been conducted with witnesses, and reviewing any documents in the case file that may contain factual information. The client files must be checked to ensure that they are complete. At the initial stages of a case, the client interview may be the only available source of information.

When listing the facts, include all facts that may possibly be related to any of the causes of action. Err on the side of listing too many facts. You want to have all possibly related facts at hand when you proceed to step 4, the step in which the irrelevant facts are eliminated and the key facts are identified.

For Example

The fact that the children go to the same school and ride the school bus probably is not related to any of the potential causes of action. The nature of what is being sprayed may be related. The number of years Jerry has sprayed the trees may be related. The weather conditions when the trees are sprayed may be related.

Consider the elements of each cause of action individually when performing this task.

For Example

Using trespass to land as a cause of action, take each element and determine what facts from the client's case possibly establish or are related to that element. Which of the facts relate to intrusion? Which of the facts relate to "in possession of another"? Which of the facts relate to the intent to intrude? Which of the facts relate to causation of the intrusion? After completing this process for the elements of trespass, do the same for each potential cause of action identified in the previous steps.

Note that some facts may establish or relate to more than one cause of action. Some causes of action overlap. Therefore, all the facts must be reviewed when considering the elements of each cause of action.

For Example

The fact that pesticide from the spraying crosses onto Ann's property may establish or relate to both trespass to land and private nuisance. The pesticide crossing to Ann's land may be the act of trespass, and the crossing coupled with the interference to Ann's enjoyment of her gardening and interference to the production of the garden plants may relate to nuisance. The fact that pesticide crosses the property line relates to elements of both of these causes of action.

D. Step 4: Determine Which Facts Apply

The fourth step is to determine which of the client's facts apply to establish or satisfy the elements of each cause of action. The facts identified in this step are the key facts. Be sure to consider each fact listed in step 3 and determine if it is essential to establish or satisfy an element of any potential cause of action. It is important to consider all the facts identified in step 3. Step 4 consists primarily of the process of eliminating those facts listed in step 3 that are not essential or key facts. This is accomplished by taking each element of each cause of action and identifying the facts essential to establish or satisfy that element

For Example

Referring to the trespass to land cause of action, the key facts follow:

1. Act—the spraying of pesticide.
2. Intrusion on land—the pesticide crosses over and onto Ann's land.
3. In possession of another—Ann owns and lives on the land.
4. Intent—Jerry sprays the trees, and he continued to do so after he was notified of the problem.
5. Causation of the intrusion—the spraying caused the pesticide to pass over and onto Ann's property, and there is no evidence that it came from another source.

When determining which facts identified in step 3 establish or satisfy an element, apply the following test:

- "Which of these facts, if changed, would change the outcome of the application of that element?" In other words,
- "Which of these facts, if changed, would affect the determination of whether there is present a fact or facts that establish or satisfy that element?"

For Example

Referring to the trespass to land cause of action, if the pesticide did not pass over and onto Ann's land, there would be no facts to support the element of intrusion. If the pesticide crossing onto her land came from a source other than Jerry's land, Jerry would not be responsible for the causation of the trespass.

Other facts identified in step 3 as related to an element, but that do not establish or satisfy an element, are not key facts.

For Example

In step 3, the facts of what chemical was being sprayed, the weather conditions when the spraying took place, and the number of years Jerry had sprayed the trees were considered as possibly related to the trespass cause of action. If it is determined that these facts, if changed, would not tend to establish or satisfy an element of trespass, they are not key facts and can be eliminated from further consideration.

All the facts identified in step 4 are the key facts. They are essential to the outcome of the case.

E. Multiple Issues

Steps 2 through 4 should be applied to each potential cause of action identified in step 1. Some causes of action may be eliminated because there no facts are present that support the existence of an element.

For Example

If the pesticide passed harmlessly over Ann's land and did not interfere with her use or enjoyment of the land, there may be no cause of action for private nuisance.

Additional causes of action may be identified as research and investigation continue. Be sure to address each element of each possible cause of action and determine if there is any fact in the case that tends to establish or satisfy the element.

Note: These steps are useful tools and helpful guides when identifying key facts. They will usually help you quickly identify the key facts. Nothing, however, is fool-proof. You may not be certain about whether a fact meets the standard required or is necessary to support the existence of an element. In some instances, that determination may not be made until trial.

For Example

The court may rule that the pesticide crossing onto Ann's land is not a sufficient intrusion to constitute trespass.

Just make sure that there is some fact that arguably meets the requirements of each element of the cause of action.

VII. KEY FACTS IDENTIFICATION—CASE LAW

Every court opinion involves the court's application of the law to the facts of the case. The key facts are those facts in the case that the law applies to and that are essential to the decision reached by the court. If the key facts had been different, the outcome of the case probably would have been different.

Situations in which the court clearly points out the key facts are not addressed in this chapter.

For Example

The court states, "The critical facts in the resolution of this dispute are. ..."

The focus here is on those situations in which the key facts are not so easily determined, such as in cases where the court opinion intersperses many irrelevant and background facts with the key facts.

The steps recommended in Chapter 10 for identifying the issue in a court decision are similar, in part, to the steps for identifying the key facts presented here. As with determining the key facts in a client's case, there is no magic formula for identifying key facts in a court opinion. The three-step process presented in Exhibit 9-3 is recommended, however, and may prove helpful.

In this section, the following example is referred to when discussing the application of these steps.

STEP 1	Read the entire case with the following general question in mind: What was decided about which facts?
STEP 2	Look to the holding. What is the court's answer to the legal question? How does the court apply the rule of law to the legal question raised?
STEP 3	Identify the facts necessary to the holding—the key facts. Part 1: List all facts in any way related to the holding. Part 2: Identify which of the listed facts are key facts and determine the key facts.

© Cengage

Exhibit 9-3 Steps in Key Fact Identification—Case Law.

For Example

In the case of *Joins v. Stevens*, the court summarized the facts as follows: Jason Stevens and his nephew Allen Stevens have known Mark Joins for several years. The three occasionally engaged in recreational activities, such as attending baseball games and going on fishing trips. On these outings, they usually drank alcoholic beverages, often to excess. On some occasions, their spouses joined in the activities.

On one of the fishing trips, on a Sunday afternoon in July, they were standing under a tree, drinking beer, and waiting for the rain to stop so they could resume fishing. They had been drinking since morning and were a little drunk. Mark was the only one who had caught any fish earlier in the day. Mark had an annoying habit of bragging, especially when he drank. Jason and Allen became increasingly angry as Mark claimed that he was the only "real fisherman" of the group. He continued bragging for an irritatingly long period. When Mark claimed that he was actually the "only real man" of the three, Allen lost control and beat him up. While the beating was going on, Jason yelled to Allen, "Hit him harder! Kick him! Kick him!"

Mark suffered two broken ribs and was hospitalized. He sued Jason and Allen for the tort of battery. In deciding that Jason had committed a battery, the court stated, "Although liability cannot be based upon one's mere presence at a battery, a person may be held liable for the tort of battery if he encourages or incites by words the act of the direct perpetrator. Because he yelled encouragement to his nephew while the latter was beating Mark Joins, Jason Stevens is jointly liable with his nephew for the battery."

A. Step 1: Read the Entire Case

The first step is to read the entire case with the following general question in mind: "What was decided about which facts?" Because the key facts in a court opinion are those facts necessary to the decision reached by the court, you must have a general overview of the case before you can focus on determining which of the facts are key facts. You must read the entire case to determine the legal question addressed and the decision reached by the court, keeping in mind the question: "What was decided about which facts in this case?"

- "What was decided …" keeps the mind focused on the holding or decision reached.
- "About which facts …" keeps the mind focused on specific facts, those specific facts necessary to the resolution of the legal question—the key facts.

By the time you finish reading the entire case, you usually realize that the decision rests on only some of the facts mentioned in the opinion. If at this point you have not clearly identified which of the facts are the key facts, proceed to step 2.

B. Step 2: Look to the Holding

The *holding* is the court's application of the rule of law to the legal question raised by the facts of the case. It is the court's answer to the legal question. Ask the following questions to help identify the holding:

- "What is the court's answer to the legal question?"
- "How does the court apply the rule of law to the legal question raised?"

In this example, the last two sentences are the court's presentation of the rule of law and the holding—the application of the rule of law to the facts:

- Rule of law—"Although liability cannot be based upon one's mere presence at a battery, a person may be held liable for the tort of battery if he encourages or incites by words the act of the direct perpetrator."
- Holding—"Because he yelled encouragement to his nephew while the latter was beating Mark Joins, Jason Stevens is jointly liable with his nephew for the battery."

C. Step 3: Identify the Key Facts

Identify the facts necessary to the holding. This step is composed of two parts:

    a. List all facts in any way related to the holding.
    b. Identify which of the listed facts are key facts.

1. List All Facts Related to the Holding

List all the facts presented in the case related to the holding. This may require going through the case and listing all the facts presented by the court. The court may present a multitude of background and irrelevant facts that in no way affect the outcome of the case. If that is the situation, identify and list only the facts that are possibly related or necessary to the decision reached.

In the preceding example, it is not necessary to list all the facts presented by the court. Some facts, such as the fact that the spouses sometimes accompanied the men, clearly are not relevant. Other facts—for example, it was a Sunday in July—are merely background facts that provide the reader with the time context of the event. All the facts relating to the argument should be included, such as the location of the argument, the fact the participants had been drinking, and what was said.

2. Determine the Key Facts

From the facts listed, determine the key facts by identifying those facts necessary or essential to the decision reached. Which facts determine the outcome of the case? There are several ways to identify these facts:

1. One test to determine the outcome is to ask yourself whether the decision would have been the same if a fact had not occurred, or if the fact had occurred differently. If Jason had merely stood by and watched, would he be liable for battery? In the previous resisting arrest example, if the individual had never ceased active resistance, would the police be liable for battery? Apply this test to each fact listed.
2. If this test is applied to each fact and no single fact, when changed or omitted, would affect or change the decision, ask whether the decision was governed by the court's consideration of the facts as a group.

For Example

The court may state, "No single act of the defendant is sufficient to constitute breach of contract. The defendant's various acts, however, when taken as a whole, are sufficient to establish breach."

3. If the court lists in its reasoning the elements of a cause of action, ask yourself which of the facts apply to establish the elements. In the battery example, the court stated that an individual may be liable if that individual "incites by words" the acts of the perpetrator. Jason's inciting words are the facts that relate to this element.
4. Ask yourself whether the court indicates that a certain fact is a key fact:
    a. Does the court describe a fact as "essential," "key," or "important"?
    b. Is a fact repeated throughout the opinion, especially in the reasoning supporting the decision?
    c. Does the court agree with a party's description of a fact as critical or key?

For Example

The court may state, "We agree with plaintiff's position that the failure to make timely payment is key to a determination of whether a breach of contract occurred."

5. Does a concurring or dissenting opinion identify the key facts? Be aware, however, that the concurring or dissenting judge may have a different view of which facts are key facts, and may identify as key facts some facts the majority did not consider key.

D. Multiple Issues

The foregoing discussion focuses upon locating the key facts related to a single issue and holding in a case. Often, there are several issues and holdings in a court opinion. Apply the steps presented to determine the key facts related to each issue and holding. Follow each step completely for each issue and holding.

Note: The steps presented in this section are useful tools and guidelines. Following them helps you identify the key facts of a case. In some instances, however, the court may omit key facts. Also, as you read more cases and become more familiar with case law, you may automatically focus on the key facts without using any of the steps presented here.

VIII. KEY POINTS CHECKLIST: Key Facts

✓ Do not overlook the importance of the facts. Facts give rise to the legal dispute and, therefore, are an integral part of it. Disputes have little meaning outside the context of the facts.

✓ Key facts are those facts that establish or satisfy the elements of a cause of action and are necessary to prove or disprove a claim. Therefore, the nature and presence or absence of certain facts determine the outcome of a case.

✓ A useful test for determining whether a fact is a key fact is to ask the question, "If this fact is changed or omitted, would the outcome of the application of the law be changed?"

✓ Follow the steps recommended for the determination of key facts in a client's case. Be aware that the importance of certain facts may not become apparent until legal research is conducted and the elements of a cause of action are determined.

✓ When identifying key facts in a court opinion, keep in mind the question, "What was decided about which facts in this case?"

✓ Do not get discouraged. The process of identifying key facts becomes easier with practice, and parts of the process become intuitive.

IX. APPLICATION

This section presents examples of key fact identification in a client's case and in a court opinion. Each example illustrates the application of the principles discussed in this chapter.

A. Client's Fact Situation

The following example illustrates the application of the principles to the hypothetical presented at the beginning of this chapter.

1. Identify Each Cause of Action

The first step is to identify each cause of action possibly raised by the facts. Based on Alice's recently completed education and limited job experience, she identifies three potential causes of action Mr. Aper may have against

Mr. Rascon: trespass to land, trespass to chattels, and conversion. This preliminary identification may be expanded or reduced upon additional research.

For Example

Case law may reveal that Mr. Rascon's conduct also constitutes a private nuisance.

Step 1 provides a starting point for identification of the key facts in the case.

2. Determine the Elements

The second step is to determine the elements of each cause of action identified in step 1. For each potential cause of action, identify the elements necessary to state a claim. Research is usually required to determine the elements. Facts must be present that establish or satisfy each element of each cause of action. These facts are the key facts of the case. For illustration purposes, we will apply step 2 to the conversion cause of action.

Alice's research reveals that the elements of conversion are as follows:

- Personal property
- Plaintiff is in possession of the property or is entitled to immediate possession
- Intent to exercise dominion or control over the property by the defendant
- Serious interference with plaintiff's possession
- Causation of the serious interference

3. List All Facts Related to the Elements

The third step is to list all the facts possibly related to the elements of the causes of action identified in step 2. List all facts that might relate in some way to each of the elements of each cause of action. In this fact situation, the facts include:

1. Mr. Aper owns a farm with a 200-acre area that is forested and inhabited by deer.
2. The property is fenced and posted.
3. Mr. Aper discovered a newly traveled path through the property.
4. Part of the fence had been removed, several small trees had been cut down, and a lean-to had been constructed from the trees.
5. A fire had been built, and some of the wood from the fence was still smoldering in the fire.
6. Mr. Aper observed Eric Rascon, a neighbor, entering the property with his hunting gear, building a fire, and cutting a tree.
7. Mr. Aper saw Mr. Rascon add a tree to the lean-to.

Note that some of the facts included may not be related to any element, such as the fact that deer inhabit the forest, or that Mr. Rascon is a neighbor. In this step, however, it is better to include all potentially related facts rather than omit them. Later research may demonstrate the importance of a fact initially thought to be insignificant.

4. Determine Which Facts Apply

The fourth step is to determine which of the client's facts apply to establish or satisfy the elements of each cause of action. The facts identified in this step are the key facts. Using the conversion cause of action as an illustration, the key facts are as follows:

- Personal property—the wood from the fence and the trees that were cut are Mr. Aper's personal property. Research may reveal that trees growing on the land are real property and, therefore, are not covered by this tort. It may be though, that once cut down, a tree becomes personal property. This fact should be included until research determines the status of this property.
- Plaintiff is in possession of the property or is entitled to immediate possession— Mr. Aper owns and occupies the land.
- Intent to exercise dominion and control over the property—Mr. Rascon's actions include adding the fence wood and trees to the fire and cutting down the trees for the lean-to.

- Serious interference with plaintiff's possession—the cutting of trees and the burning of wood seriously interfere with Mr. Aper's rights of possession.
- Causation of serious interference—Mr. Rascon's actions of cutting and burning are clearly the cause of the interference. No other factual cause is present.

Note that this step results in the identification of those facts related to the elements of the cause of action and the elimination of all facts that are not necessary to establish a claim. You must apply this step to identify the key facts for each potential cause of action identified in step 1. Once this is done, all the key facts for each claim are identified. Note that the relationship between key facts, issue identification, and stating the issue will be discussed in the next two chapters, Chapter 10 and Chapter 11.

B. Court Opinion

This example illustrates the operation of the principles for identifying the key facts in a court opinion. Read the *Flowers v. Campbell* case presented in the following text and apply the steps discussed in this chapter to determine the key facts of the collateral estoppel issue.

Note that the doctrine of collateral estoppel is discussed in the case. The doctrine of collateral estoppel prevents a party in a lawsuit from relitigating an issue that was decided in a previous lawsuit. In the case, the trial court ruled that the question of whether the defendant, Campbell, used excessive force in resisting the assault of Flowers had already been litigated in an earlier criminal case. Based upon this ruling, the trial court determined that the doctrine of collateral estoppel applied and dismissed Flowers's claim that Campbell used excessive force. The appeal in *Flowers v. Campbell* is from this ruling by the trial court.

CASE

FLOWERS v. CAMPBELL

725 P.2d 01295 (Or. Ct. App. 1986)

ROSSMAN, Judge.

Plaintiff brought this assault and battery action to recover damages for injuries allegedly sustained in a skirmish with defendant Campbell (defendant), who was, at the time, an employee of defendant Montgomery Ward & Company. Plaintiff alleges that defendant used excessive force to repel his own aggressive behavior, for which plaintiff was convicted of assault in the fourth degree and harassment. The trial court dismissed the action after ruling, on defendant's motion for a directed verdict, that all material issues of fact were decided against plaintiff at his criminal trial and that he was precluded from relitigating those issues. We reverse.

The violence erupted after plaintiff accused defendant of charging him $12.99 for a lock that had been advertised for $9.97.[1] Plaintiff admits that he became involved in a verbal exchange with defendant immediately before the fight and that he "threw the first punch." He also concedes both that the jury at his criminal trial necessarily found that his use of force was not justified and that he is collaterally estopped from relitigating that issue. See *Roshak v. Leathers*, 277 Or. 207, 560 P.2d 275 (1977). He contends, however,

that the dispositive issue in this civil action is whether defendant responded to his own admitted aggression with excessive force. He contends that that issue was not litigated at his criminal trial.

Under the doctrine of collateral estoppel, a party to an action may be prevented from relitigating issues that were actually decided and necessary to the judgment in a previous action. *State Farm v. Century Home*, 275 Or. 97, 550 P.2d 1185 (1976); *Bahler v. Fletcher*, 257 Or. 1, 474 P.2d 329 (1970). Plaintiff was convicted in the criminal action of assault and harassment. The victim's use of more force than was justified to repel the attacker's criminal acts is not a defense to either of those crimes. It follows that defendant's response to plaintiff's actions could not have been an issue that was necessarily decided in plaintiff's criminal trial. Accordingly, because an aggressor may recover in an action for battery if he proves that the defendant used more force than was justified in repelling the aggression, *Linkhart v. Savely*, 190 Or. 484, 497, 227 P.2d 187 (1951), the trial court erred in holding that plaintiff was precluded from litigating all issues "essential" to his recovery by reason of the judgment entered in his criminal trial.

Reversed and remanded.

---

[1] Plaintiff was 62 years old at fight time; defendant was 33. Plaintiff allegedly sustained a broken arm and a detached retina. Defendant's jaw was broken.

1. Read the Entire Case

The first step is to read the entire case with the following general question in mind: "What was decided about which facts?" This step helps you keep the facts in mind while obtaining an overview of what legal questions were addressed and answered.

2. Look to the Holding

The *holding* is the court's application of the rule of law to the legal question raised by the facts of the case. "What is the court's answer to the legal question? How did the court apply the rule of law to the legal question(s) raised?" These are questions to ask when looking to the holding.

In this case, the court stated that the doctrine of collateral estoppel prevents a party from relitigating issues that were actually decided in a previous action. The court noted that the victim's use of more force than was justified to repel the attacker's criminal acts is not a defense to assault or harassment. Therefore, the issue of the victim's use of excessive force to repel the plaintiff's attack was not litigated in the plaintiff's criminal trial. The court concluded that the trial court erred in applying the doctrine of collateral estoppel to preclude the plaintiff from litigating the question of the victim's use of excessive force to repel the plaintiff's aggression.

3. Identify the Key Facts

The third step is to identify the facts necessary to the holding—the key facts.

a. Part 1: List All Facts Related to the Holding

What facts are possibly related to the holding? The plaintiff filed an assault and battery civil action against the defendant to recover damages for injuries sustained in a skirmish with the defendant. The plaintiff and the defendant became involved in a fight as a result of a dispute over an amount the plaintiff was charged for an item. The plaintiff threw the first punch. He claims that the defendant responded with excessive force to the plaintiff's aggression. The plaintiff was tried in a separate criminal action and convicted of assaulting and harassing the defendant. The trial court ruled that "all material issues of fact were decided against plaintiff at his criminal trial and he was precluded from relitigating those issues." All of these facts are possibly related to the holding. Some of the facts of the case, such as what they were fighting about, are clearly not related and are eliminated in this part of step 3.

The trial court in this action ruled that the plaintiff was precluded from relitigating his claim in this action because the issues of fact regarding the fight were decided in the criminal action. The trial court, therefore, dismissed his claim.

b. Part 2: Determine the Key Facts

Which of the facts listed in part 1 are necessary or essential to the decision reached? Which of the facts, if changed, would change the outcome of the case?

- The trial court's ruling that the issue of the victim's response was litigated in the criminal case is clearly a key fact. Had the trial court ruled otherwise, the case would not have been dismissed and the appeal filed. Note that a "fact" in this instance is how the trial court ruled.
- The fact that the plaintiff was convicted of assault and harassment in an earlier criminal case is clearly a key fact. Had there been no criminal trial, the civil trial court could not have applied the doctrine of collateral estoppel.
- The fact that the defendant (victim) used force in response to the plaintiff's aggression is a key fact. The plaintiff's lawsuit rests upon the nature of the defendant's response.
- The fact that the victim's alleged use of excessive force to repel an attacker's acts of assault or harassment is not a defense to those acts in a criminal case is also key. Had this been a defense to those acts, the question of the victim's use of excessive force would have been litigated in the criminal case, and the trial court's ruling would have been correct.

Note that in this case, a key fact is a rule of law: The victim's use of force in response to assault and harassment is not a defense to either crime.

- The fact that the plaintiff threw the first punch in his fight with the defendant is probably not a key fact. It is not necessary to establish or satisfy any element of the collateral estoppel issue.

This case is somewhat different from some other cases because the key facts on appeal involve the facts of what occurred between the plaintiff and the defendant, the actions of the trial court, and the law governing defenses to assault and harassment.

Summary

All lawsuits arise as a result of disputes involving facts. Our legal system revolves around resolving disputes through the application of rules of law to the facts of a case. Therefore, the two major components of the dispute resolution process are: 1) the applicable law, and 2) the facts of the dispute. Each component deserves appropriate attention.

Some facts are more important than others, and the most important facts are the key facts—those facts upon which the outcome of the case depends. Key facts are those facts necessary to prove or disprove a claim. A key fact is so essential that if it were changed, the outcome of the case would be different. Key facts are an element of a legal issue, and that role will be discussed in Chapters 10 and 11.

The four recommended steps to follow when determining the key facts of a client's case are:

- Step 1: Identify each cause of action possibly raised by the facts.
- Step 2: Determine the elements of each cause of action identified in step 1.
- Step 3: List all the facts possibly related to the elements of the causes of action identified in step 2.
- Step 4: Determine which of the client's facts apply to establish or satisfy the elements of each cause of action—the key facts.

The three recommended steps for identifying the key facts in a court opinion are:

- Step 1: Read the entire case with the following general question in mind: "What was decided about which facts?"
- Step 2: Look to the holding.
- Step 3: Identify the facts necessary to the holding—the key facts.

These recommended steps are usually helpful in identifying the key facts. You may develop shortcuts or different methods as you become more proficient in analyzing a client's case or a court opinion.

Quick References

Internet Resources

There are no websites dedicated specifically to key facts. However, using a search engine such as http://www.google.com and a topic such as "IRAC key facts" or "legal analysis and key facts", you will find a wide range of websites related to the topic of legal analysis and key facts. Most of these sites provide information without charge. Information you obtain free from other sites may not be closely monitored and may not be as accurate or have the same quality of material as that obtained from fee-based services. Therefore, exercise care when using freely obtained material.

Exercises

ASSIGNMENT 1

Detail the steps for determining the key facts in a client's case.

ASSIGNMENT 2

Detail the steps for determining the key facts in a court opinion.

ASSIGNMENT 3

Identify the background facts in the following cases:

> *Flowers v. Campbell* (presented in this chapter)
> *Lucero v. Sutten* (presented at end of Chapter 10)

ASSIGNMENT 4

Using the hypothetical at the beginning of the chapter, complete the chart below. The cause of action is trespass to land and the elements are: (1) unauthorized intrusion onto land, (2) in possession of another, (3) intent to intrude, (4) causation of intrusion.

Key facts: unauthorized intrusion onto land

Key facts: in possession of another

Key facts: intent to intrude

Key facts: causation of intrusion

Background facts

Irrelevant facts

ASSIGNMENT 5

Using a similar charting system as in Assignment 4, identify the key facts in each of the hypotheticals presented at the beginning of Chapters 10, 11, and 12.

ASSIGNMENT 6

Using the facts in the minor impact hypothetical in this chapter, identify the key facts for each element of the offense of sending, reading, or writing a text message while driving. The elements are: (1) while operating a motor vehicle, (2) sending, reading, or writing a text message, (3) using an electronic wireless communication device.

ASSIGNMENT 7

Facts

Sam was going out with friends to a comedy club and knew he would be drinking. Since he did not have a designated driver, he arranged to get a ride through a rideshare service that does not require minimum insurance coverage for passengers. In the state he lives, it is illegal to operate a rideshare/passenger-for-hire service without a motor carrier license. Because the rideshare service Sam is using believes it is a technology company and not a transportation company, it operates illegally by not having a motor carrier license. On the way to the comedy club, the driver is using his phone to arrange the next passenger, and runs a red light. The car is hit in the passenger side, and Sam suffers significant injuries. His medicals bills were higher than the driver's liability insurance would cover. In addition, the driver's insurance is refusing to pay because the driver was using his car in violation of the state law. Because the driver's insurance will not cover his damages, Sam must bring a civil suit against the driver.

Rule of Law

Sam brings an action for negligence. The elements are duty, breach of duty, proximate cause, and damages.

Assignment

The researcher's assignment is to determine if the actions of the driver constitute negligence. Discuss the assignment from the perspective of individual key facts.

ASSIGNMENT 8

Facts

Terry, a bill collector, has been attempting to collect a bill from Client. Every other evening for the past two weeks, he has called Client at home after 8:30 p.m. and threatened to call her employer and inform him that she refuses to pay her bills. On every Monday, Wednesday, and Friday during the two-week period, he has called Client at work. Client repeatedly requested that Terry stop calling her at work. On the past two Saturdays, he has personally come by her home and threatened to sue her and throw her in jail.

Rule of Law

Infliction of emotional distress—extreme or outrageous conduct that causes severe emotional distress.

Assignment

The researcher's assignment is to determine if the actions of the bill collector constitute "extreme or outrageous conduct." Discuss the assignment from the perspective of individual key facts and from the perspective of a group of facts.

ASSIGNMENT 9

Facts

Bikesmith, a local cycling shop, advertised a model year closeout sale. The advertisement indicated the "early shopper" would "reap the savings" on all of last year's Linder bikes. The advertisement stated bikes that were normally $1,800 would be sold for $800. Jack, an avid cyclist and amateur racer, arrived at Bikesmith an hour after they opened on the day of the sale to find all of the Linder bikes had been sold. He complained to the bike shop owner that it was obligated to sell him a similar bike at a similar discount. The owner declined, and Jack filed an action in small claims court for breach of contract.

Rule of Law

A valid contract requires an offer, acceptance, and consideration. In the state where Jack lives, an advertisement is only an invitation to enter into negotiations, and is not an offer.

Assignment

The researcher's assignment is to determine if the Bikesmith advertisement constitutes a contract.

Discuss the assignment from the perspective of individual key facts.

ASSIGNMENT 10

Facts

Joe, a 14 year old, was at a party. At 12:30 a.m., he was sitting on the steps to the apartment where the party was occurring when he saw two police cars arrive. He yelled to the party-goers, "5-0." Joe remained sitting outside as the police approached. An officer took Joe to a police car and sat him in the back seat. The offer asked Joe his name, date of birth, address, and his parents' names and phone number. The officer cited Joe for the curfew violation.

Rule of Law

A person subject to a custodial interrogation must be given Miranda rights before the questioning begins. "Custody" is defined as a reasonable person's liberty is retrained to the extent they believe they are not free to leave. "Interrogation" is defined as being asked any questions that would likely lead to an answer that would incriminate oneself. The curfew law states a person under the age of 15 who is outside their residence past 11:00 p.m. without the presence of a parent, guardian, or supervising adult, is a delinquent youth.

Assignment

The researcher's assignment is to determine if the officer should have read Joe the Miranda warning before questioning him.

Chapter 10

Legal Analysis:
Issue Identification—Spotting The Issue

Learning Objectives

After completing this chapter, you should understand

- What a legal issue is and the various types of issues
- The elements of an issue
- How to identify (spot) the issue in a client's case
- How to identify the issue in a court case

It was the late afternoon of an already long day when Kevin realized he still had a lot of work to finish before he could go home. Kevin has been Randi McGuire's paralegal for the past five years. He admires her for her tenacity, and he appreciates the responsibility and independence she gives him in the performance of his assignments. Kevin's primary role is to conduct the initial interview with the client, prepare a summary of the interview, then assemble a legal memorandum containing an identification of the legal issues and an analysis of the applicable law.

Identifying the legal issue is often the trickiest part of Kevin's job. It did not seem, however, that it would be too much of a problem in Ida Carry's case. He had just finished his interview with Ms. Carry, whose home is across the street from Roosevelt Elementary School. Ms. Carry's best friend, Karen, lives a block away. Karen's 7-year-old son attends school at Roosevelt.

Last month, on April 14, Ida was in her front yard planting tulips. It was lunchtime, and children were playing on the playground. She heard the crossing guard's whistle blow and tires squealing. She looked up and saw a car approaching a curve in the school zone at a very high rate of speed. It jumped the curb, crashed through the chain-link fence surrounding the playground, and hit the seesaw. The first thing she recognized was the car—it was Bob Barton's hot-rod Camaro. It looked like he was going too fast, lost control on the curve in the school zone, and crashed through the fence.

Bob, a local teen, continually raced in the neighborhood. Several teachers complained to his parents, who did nothing. Bob had received several speeding tickets.

The second thing Ida noticed was that two children playing on the seesaw were injured. One of them was Karen's son, Tim. When Ida realized it was Tim who was injured, she became extremely upset.

Since the wreck, Ida has had severe insomnia and extreme anxiety. When she can sleep, she has nightmares. Her doctor prescribed medication for her nerves and to help her sleep, and he recently referred her to a psychologist. Ida came to Ms. McGuire's office seeking to recover the expenses she has incurred.

After summarizing the interview, Kevin focuses on the next task and asks himself, "What is the legal issue in this case?" The process of identifying the issue is the subject of this chapter. The Application section of this chapter discusses the answer to Kevin's question.

I. INTRODUCTION

The most important task a researcher faces when engaging in legal analysis is to correctly identify the legal issue. Identifying the issue, commonly referred to as "spotting the issue," is the first step of the legal analysis process. Identifying the legal issue(s) presented by the fact situation is the foundation and key to effective legal analysis. It guides the researcher to the specific legal problem raised by the unique facts of the client's case. You must know what the precise legal problem is before you can begin to solve it. Identifying the issue determines which direction the research will take. It is like selecting a road: If you choose the wrong road, you will waste a lot of time before you get to your destination, or you may get lost and never get there. Half the battle of legal research and analysis is knowing what you are looking for; that is, *what is the issue?*

If you misidentify the issue (ask the wrong legal question), you waste time and commit legal error. If you ask the wrong question, you will get the wrong answer to the client's problem.

For Example

If you incorrectly identify the issue as a corporation law issue when it is really a tax law issue, you will waste time researching corporation law, and any law you may find will not apply to the client's case.

The client does not retain counsel to find the answer to the wrong question. The client pays to have a problem solved. If the issue is misidentified, the problem remains unsolved, time is wasted, and you are no better off than when you started. If the error is not caught, you may have committed malpractice because the client is billed for a service that was not requested.

Not only is identifying the issue the most important step in the analytical process, it is often the most difficult. When you ask a lawyer how to spot an issue, the response often is, "I just know" or "After a while it becomes intuitive." Indeed, it does become intuitive after one has read and worked on hundreds of cases. This, however, does not help the beginner. Although no simple rule or magic formula exists, certain techniques and steps are helpful when identifying the issue in a client's fact situation or a court opinion. The starting point is to know what an issue is—how it is defined.

II. DEFINITION AND TYPES

In the broadest sense, the **issue** is a question: the legal question raised by the dispute that must be answered before a case can be resolved. The issue arises whenever there is disagreement or uncertainty about whether or how a rule of law applies to a client's facts. In a narrower sense, it is the precise legal question raised by the specific facts of a dispute.

Issues may fall into one of three broad categories:

1. A question of which law applies

For Example

Do the traffic code provisions of municipal code § 2254 or state statute § 35-6-7-28 apply when an individual is stopped by municipal police for driving under the influence of intoxicants?

2. A question of how a law applies

For Example

Under the provisions of Colorado battery law, does an individual commit a battery when the individual, present at the scene of a battery, encourages others to commit the battery but does not actively participate in the actual battering of the victim?

3. A question of whether a law applies at all

For Example

Does Municipal Code § 2100, Public Sales/Auctions, govern garage sales held on private property?

Regardless of the type of legal question raised by a dispute, the definition is the same as previously stated: The issue is the precise legal question raised by the specific facts of the dispute.

Now that you know what an issue is, the next step is to determine what it is composed of—the elements. Every issue is composed of elements, and these elements must be determined to identify the issue. Identifying the elements is integral to the process of identifying the issue. In fact, once you have determined the elements, you can identify the issue quite easily.

III. ELEMENTS

A client enters the law office with a unique fact situation that may or may not have a legal remedy. The attorney's role is to identify the question raised by the facts and determine if a legal remedy is available and, if so, what legal remedy is available. Because the issue is defined as the precise legal question raised by the specific facts of the client's case, a correctly identified issue is composed of three elements: the applicable law, the legal question, and the key facts (see Exhibit 10-1).

A. Applicable Law

Applicable law is the specific law that governs the dispute. This may be a constitutional provision, statute, ordinance, regulation, or case law doctrine, principle, rule, test, or guide.

For Example

Under Indiana Code § 35-42-3-2, kidnapping...
According to Florida's law governing breach of contract...

B. Legal Question

This portion of the inquiry refers to the **legal question** concerning the law governing the dispute, raised by the facts of the dispute.

Applicable Law	The specific law that governs the dispute. (e.g., a constitutional provision, statute, regulation, ordinance, or case law doctrine, principle, rule, test, or guideline)
Legal Question	The question concerning the law governing the dispute raised by the facts of the dispute
Key Facts	The legally significant facts that raise the legal question of how or whether the law governing the dispute applies; facts that, if changed, would change or affect the outcome of the application of the law

© Cengage

Exhibit 10-1 Elements of an Issue.

For Example

... does kidnapping occur when ...
... is a contract breached when ...

C. Key Facts

Key facts are the key or legally significant facts that raise the legal question of how or whether the law governing the dispute applies.

For Example

...when the individual is held against her will, but is not held for ransom?
...when the product delivered is grade A–, and the contract calls for grade A?

D. Examples

The three elements of the issue—the applicable law, the legal question concerning the law, and the key facts that raise the legal question—are referred to in this text as a comprehensive, **narrow (specific) statement of the issue**. An issue including these elements is *comprehensive* because it includes the specific law and key facts. It is a *narrow* statement of the issue because the more facts you include, the more specific (or narrow) the legal question becomes. Identify each element as precisely and completely as possible. The following are examples of statements of issues containing the three elements:

- Under the Colorado holographic will statute, is a holographic will valid   **(Applicable Law)**
  if it is handwritten by a neighbor at the direction of the testator, but not   **(Legal Question)**
  written in the testator's handwriting?   **(Key Facts)**

- Under Arizona tort law, is it false imprisonment when law enforcement   **(Applicable Law)**
  officers make an arrest, even though video surveillance shows the person   **(Legal Question)**
  robbing the store was much younger and taller than the person arrested?   **(Key Facts)**

- Under the Illinois residential burglary statute, is a detached garage "living   **(Applicable Law)**
  quarters" when the owners converted the garage to a summer retreat for   **(Legal Question)**
  their collegeage son?   **(Key Facts)**

Each of these examples contains the precise law, legal question, and the key facts essential to resolution of the dispute. Note that each issue is narrowly focused upon the law and specific facts of each client's case.

Failure to include these elements results in an abstract question, or a **broad statement of the issue** that is missing the legal (applicable law) and factual context.

For Example

If the three previous examples were stated broadly, and did not include the specific elements discussed in this section, they would appear, respectively, as follows:

- Was the will valid?
- Did the police commit false imprisonment?
- Did the defendant commit a crime?

Each broad statement of the issue in this example could apply to a multitude of cases involving wills, false imprisonment, or residential burglary. Each issue fails to inform the researcher of the specific factual context of the dispute, the precise law involved, and the question that must be resolved to determine if a remedy is available to the client (and if so, what remedy). A broadly stated issue is not appropriate in legal research and writing for several reasons:

1. It is not helpful or useful for the reader who is not familiar with the facts of the case. This may be a judge in the instance of a brief in support of a motion, or an attorney in the office who is referring to an old memorandum from the office files.
2. It does not guide the reader to the specific law in question. In the previous examples, about which specific wills statute are we talking? What actions of the police are involved? What specific criminal statute is involved?
3. It is not useful to the individual drafting and researching the issue.

For Example

The question, "Did Mr. Smith commit a battery?" is such a broad formulation of the issue that it is of little value. Stated this way, the issue applies to all battery cases, both civil and criminal. So stated, it is useless. It fails to focus the researcher's inquiry or guide the researcher to the specific area of battery law in dispute.

In West's digests, which are used to help locate case law, legal topics are identified by key numbers. There are more than 100 key numbers under the topic "assault and battery." A broad statement of the issue forces the researcher to scan all the subtopics looking for the one that applies. If research is conducted electronically, as with Westlaw, the search will locate hundreds (if not thousands) of cases—far too many for the researcher to review. By stating the issue comprehensively, or narrowly, the researcher narrows the inquiry.

For Example

"Under California's tort law, is a battery committed when a bystander encourages and convinces a perpetrator to beat another individual, and that individual is beaten as a result of the encouragement?" This narrow statement of the issue directs the researcher's attention to that specific area of the digest involving individuals liable for battery, that is, Assault and Battery—Key Number 18, Persons Liable. If electronic research is conducted, the search is focused enough so that only cases involving the liability of individuals encouraging a battery will be located.

As the preceding example illustrates, a comprehensive statement focuses the researcher's inquiry on a specific subtopic in the digest, and thereby saves research time. Also, the question is not abstract. The reader does not have to refer to the facts in some other document or file to understand what is in dispute.

In summary, a shorthand or broad statement of the issue fails to inform. It produces an abstract question that forces the reader to engage in further inquiry to determine what specifically is in dispute in the case. It is useless except in casual conversation in which the participants are familiar with the case. In short, an issue broadly identified is an issue not truly identified at all.

A paralegal or an attorney becomes involved in issue identification in two different but related situations:

1. Identifying the issue(s) in a client's case
2. Identifying the issue(s) in a court opinion

In each situation, it is necessary to determine the three elements of the issue to correctly identify the issue. The next two sections recommend steps for identifying the issue in a client's case and in a court opinion.

IV. ISSUE IDENTIFICATION—CLIENT'S CASE

The client's fact situation presents a legal question (issue) or set of questions that must be identified before the case can be resolved. A helpful question to keep in mind from the outset is, "What must be decided about which facts?" or, "What question concerning which law is raised by these facts?" This questioning keeps you focused on the elements of the issue—the law, question, and key facts of the case. It helps you avoid being sidetracked by related or interesting questions raised by the facts that are not necessary to resolve the legal question(s) of the case. The value of keeping these questions in mind will be illustrated throughout this section.

Identifying the legal issue(s) in a client's case is primarily a four-step process (see Exhibit 10-2). Note that steps 1 through 3 are essentially the same as steps 1 through 4 in Chapter 9, section VI. They are summarized here with different examples so you will not have to refer to that chapter.

STEP 1	Identify each type of cause of action and area of law possibly involved.
STEP 2	Determine the elements of each cause of action identified in step 1.
STEP 3	Determine which of the facts of the client's case apply to establish or satisfy the elements of each cause of action—the key facts.
STEP 4	Assemble the issue from the law and key facts identified in steps 2 and 3. Follow the format presented in Chapter 11: relevent law + legal question + key facts.

© Cengage

Exhibit 10-2 Steps in the Identification or Spotting of the Issue in a Client's Case.

A. Step 1: Identify Each Type of Cause of Action

The first step is to identify each type of cause of action and area of law possibly involved. This means to identify the potential cause(s) of action and area(s) of law raised by the client's fact situation, including a broad identification of potential issues, the general areas of law, and the client's facts related to each area of law. This preliminary identification is based upon education and experience and usually does not require research.

For Example

Sally and Susan have been friends for a decade, and Susan has frequently visited Sally's home. A year ago, Sally and Susan argued about Susan doing a major "spring cleaning" at Sally's while Sally was out of town. Susan was regularly checking on Sally's house, as friends often did. After the argument, Sally and Susan did not speak for nine months. Two months ago, Susan arrived unexpectedly at Sally's home. After speaking on the porch for several minutes, the two decided to try to mend their broken friendship, and Sally invited Susan into the house for a glass of wine.

Sally soon determined Susan was already intoxicated and refused to pour her a drink. An argument ensued and Susan grabbed a knife from the counter, shoved Sally into a chair, and tied her to it. In the struggle to force Sally into the chair, Susan stabbed Sally in the arm. Susan fled the house. Luckily, as Susan fled, a neighbor heard Sally's screams and ran into the house. The neighbor untied Sally and took her for medical attention. Sally required five stitches.

Since the incident, Sally has severe insomnia and suffers anxiety any time anyone comes to her door. This hypothetical is referred to as the "false imprisonment" example throughout the chapter.

Based upon experience, the researcher identifies as possible causes of action: false imprisonment, assault, battery, and intentional infliction of emotional distress.

This initial identification of the broad issues and areas of law may be expanded or reduced following subsequent research. The purpose is twofold:

- To identify in general terms the issues involved
- To provide a starting point for the identification and clarification of each specific issue that must be resolved in the case

B. Step 2: Determine the Elements of Each Cause of Action

The second step is to determine the elements of each cause of action identified in step 1. Apply steps 2, 3, and 4 separately to each potential issue or cause of action identified in step 1. In other words:

- Choose one potential issue identified in step 1.
- Apply steps 2, 3, and 4 to that issue.
- Complete the identification of that issue before addressing the next potential issue.

Focusing on one issue at a time avoids the confusion that may occur when dealing with multiple causes of action that often have overlapping elements. In this example, some of Susan's conduct may constitute elements of both assault and intentional infliction of emotional distress. Researching both issues at the same time could cause confusion.

Step 2 requires researching the area of law to determine the elements necessary to establish a cause of action. To know whether the law provides relief for the client, it is necessary to determine what the law requires to be established (the elements) in order to obtain that relief. Locate the elements by researching primary authority, such as the statutory or case law. If there is no primary authority in the jurisdiction, refer to secondary authority governing the topic, such as the *Restatement of the Law*.

For Example

Using the false imprisonment example, suppose the researcher begins with the issue involving intentional infliction of emotional distress. Research reveals that the following elements must be established to prevail:

1. The defendant's conduct must be intentional,

2. The conduct must be extreme and outrageous,

3. There must be a causal connection between the defendant's conduct and the plaintiff's mental distress, and

4. The plaintiff's mental distress must be extreme or severe.

Note: To help you locate the law at this stage of the process, you may roughly identify the issue with the facts you think are important.

After identifying the elements, proceed to step 3.

C. Step 3: Determine the Key Facts

The third step is to determine which of the facts of the client's case apply to establish or satisfy the elements of each cause of action—the key facts. Steps 1 and 2 identify the law that must be included in the issue, and step 3 identifies the key facts that must be included in the issue.

Identify the key facts by determining which facts of the client's case apply to establish or satisfy the requirements of each element of the cause of action. This step is necessary because, in order to state a claim and thereby obtain relief, facts must be presented that establish or satisfy the requirements of each element.

For Example

Using the false imprisonment example, apply the client's facts to the elements:

1. *Defendant's conduct must be intentional.* In this case, the defendant went to the client's home. The defendant grabbed a knife from the counter, forced the client into a chair, and tied her to it. These are the facts showing intentional conduct that satisfy or apply to establish this element.

2. *The conduct must be extreme and outrageous.* The acts identified in number 1 are the facts showing extreme and outrageous conduct that establish this element.

3. *There must be a causal connection between the defendant's conduct and the plaintiff's mental distress.* Since the accident, the client has been unable to sleep and is anxious when anyone comes to her door. These facts satisfy the third element.

4. *Plaintiff's distress must be extreme or severe.* Experiencing anxiety whenever someone comes to the door and severe insomnia are facts showing extreme or severe distress and are the facts that establish the fourth element.

By matching the facts with the required elements, the key facts of the emotional distress issue are identified. Because the question is, "How does the law apply to the facts?" these facts become part of the issue and must be included. After step 3 is completed, all the elements necessary to identify the issue are in place. All that is left is to proceed to step 4 and assemble the issue.

Note: You may not be certain whether a fact meets the standard established for an element. Often that determination is not made until trial. Ensure that some fact arguably meets the requirements of each of the elements of the cause of action.

For Example

A determination of whether Sally's insomnia and anxiety are extreme or severe enough to warrant relief may not be made until trial. Her symptoms, however, are arguably sufficient to meet the requirement of the fourth element. If research reveals that this harm is not sufficiently extreme for the requirements of emotional distress, however, then there is no emotional distress issue.

If there are no facts that satisfy or establish an element, there probably is no cause of action or issue. In this example, if Mary did not suffer anxiety or insomnia, there would be no facts to meet the requirements of the fourth element, and there most likely would be no emotional distress issue.

D. Step 4: Assemble the Issue

The last step is the easiest: gather and assemble the elements of the issue from the law and key facts identified in steps 2 and 3. The law is emotional distress, the legal question is whether emotional distress occurred, and the key facts are the facts identified in step 3. Putting it all together, the issue is as follows:

> Under [name of state] law, does emotional distress occur when the defendant, voluntarily goes to the plaintiff's house and, during an argument, takes a knife from the kitchen, forces the plaintiff into a chair, ties the plaintiff to the chair, and in the process of tying the plaintiff to the chair, stabs the plaintiff, causing the plaintiff to suffer anxiety and insomnia as a result of the conduct?

E. Summary of the Four-Step Process

The four steps presented here simplify the issue identification process by breaking it down into workable steps. It may not be necessary to go through all the steps. The issue may be apparent in step 1 or at some other point. This process, however, takes some of the mystery out of issue identification and provides a useful tool when the issues are not clear or easy to identify. It allows you to answer the question, "What question concerning which law is raised by the client's facts?"

The answer to the emotional distress issue identified in the preceding example may be determined by reference to case law. The important thing to remember is that by concisely identifying the issue in the context of the key facts, the key facts are less likely to be overlooked. By including the key facts in the issue, the researcher's focus is narrowed, and the researcher is less likely to omit a critical fact, and thereby ignore a crucial line of inquiry or misidentify the issue entirely. In the false imprisonment example, it may be that Susan's actions are not sufficiently outrageous to constitute emotional distress—maybe there is not sufficient evidence to connect the anxiety and insomnia to the acts, or maybe the harm is not the type of harm for which relief is granted in emotional distress cases.

Note: At the outset, you may only know the general area of law that applies and not the specific statute. By going through the steps and identifying the key facts or terms and the question components of the issue, you narrow your search. After locating the law, you can make a complete statement of the issue that includes the specific rule of law.

For Example

A high school student is arrested by local police for having a pocketknife in his backpack at school. He is informed that he will be charged with possessing a deadly weapon on school grounds, a felony. By including the known facts, the issue can be stated as, "Under the municipal possession of a deadly weapon on school grounds statute, is there sufficient evidence to support charge when the weapon is an ordinary pocketknife?" By identifying this much of the issue, a researcher is guided to search for the specific weapons statute that addresses possession of deadly weapons on school grounds.

As mentioned, steps 2 through 4 are applied to each of the issues broadly identified in step 1. Certain possible issues may be eliminated as the other steps are followed, such as when research reveals that there are not sufficient facts present to support a cause of action. It may also be that additional issues are identified as research proceeds.

For Example

In the "deadly weapon" example, it may be that misconduct involving weapons was not considered until research on another issue, such as what constitutes a deadly weapon, revealed a case with similar facts that included a discussion of the possession of pocketknives on school grounds being misconduct in involving weapons (a misdemeanor), not possession of a deadly weapons.

F. Multiple Issues

Often there are **multiple issues** in a case. In the false imprisonment example, there were four possible causes of action, each one involving a separate issue. Be sure to list all the facts in the client's case and examine each one to determine if it relates to any identified issue or in any way raises a new issue. In the false imprisonment example, the fact that Sally invited Susan inside for a drink may not be relevant. The fact that Susan had already been drinking may be critical. It is important to ensure that all the facts are considered and nothing is overlooked. All potential issues should be identified, and the four-step process helps ensure that nothing is missed.

Note also that a single issue may have multiple parts or subissues.

For Example

In the false imprisonment example, the intentional infliction of emotional distress issue may have separate subissues:

- Was Susan's conduct sufficiently extreme and outrageous?
- Are anxiety and severe insomnia "extreme or severe distress" within the meaning of the law?
- Did Susan's conduct cause the insomnia?

Each part or subissue should be separately considered and addressed.

Note: The steps presented in this section are useful tools and guides. These steps will usually help you quickly identify the issue. Remember that the process gets easier with experience.

V. ISSUE IDENTIFICATION—CASE LAW

This section focuses on identifying, or spotting, the issue(s) in a court opinion. The issue is the legal question addressed and answered by the court. It is what the case is about. If you do not know what question the court addressed, it is possible to misunderstand the rule of law applied or adopted in the opinion. As a result, it is likely that you will misunderstand how or if the rule of law applies in your client's case.

This section does not address situations in which the issue is easily identified, because somewhere in the opinion, the court clearly states the issue.

For Example

"In this case, we decide whether an juvenile's Fifth Amendment right to be free from self-incrimination is violated when officers question a juvenile about his date of birth at 2 a.m. in a state where there is a 11 p.m. curfew law."

This section covers those situations in which identifying the issue is difficult because the court does not identify the issue, states the issue in such broad terms that it is not helpful, or states the issue in terms of the procedural context in which the case was brought before the court:

- Issue not stated—In some opinions, the court never clearly discusses what the issue is in the case.
- Broad statement of the issue—"The issue in this case is whether the defendant breached the contract." *Comment*: This is a broad statement of the issue, and fails to inform the reader what the case is about. In the ultimate sense, the court decided whether the defendant breached the contract. In reality, however, it reached that conclusion by making a substantive decision concerning the specific facts of the defendant's conduct.

For Example

The court may have concluded that the defendant's timely delivery of the order, 95 percent of the time, was substantial compliance with the contract and, therefore, not a breach.

• Issue stated in the procedural context—"The issue in this case is whether the trial court erred when it granted the motion to suppress the evidence."

Comment: The court stated the issue in the context of how the case came before the court procedurally, namely an appeal of a trial court order granting a motion to suppress. To answer this question, the court actually addressed a substantive question raised by the facts of the case, and the substantive issue is what the case is actually about.

For Example

The substantive issue decided was, "Under the provisions of the exclusionary rule, should evidence be suppressed when law enforcement officers obtained the evidence as a result of requiring the defendant to allow them to inspect the glove box when they were making a routine stop for speeding?"

Beginning students often make the mistake of identifying the issue in the procedural context stated by the court when, in reality, the issue involves a substantive determination of the application of the law to the facts of the case.

The goal when reading a case should be to identify the substantive issue(s) in the case. Ask yourself when reading the case, "What was decided about which facts in this case?" or "What question concerning which law and key facts was decided by the court?" Like a client's case, a court case is about a dispute concerning how the law applies to the facts. Had there been no dispute involving how the law applied to the facts, the case would not have gone to trial. If your identification of the issue in a court opinion fails to include the rule of law applied and the key facts, you have failed to correctly identify the issue.

How, then, is issue identification in a court opinion accomplished? Again, there is no magic formula. The three-step process presented in Exhibit 10-3 is suggested as a useful tool.

Steps 1 and 2 include the requirements of steps 1 through 3 in Chapter 9, Section VII. They are summarized here with a focus on the issue-identification aspect of each step.

STEP 1: General Question	Read the entire opinion before attempting to identify the issue. While reading, keep in mind the question, "What was decided about which facts in this case?"
STEP 2: Look to the Holding	Focus on the holding and ask the following questions: ■ To identify the law applied ask, "What statute, rule of law, or principle did the court apply to reach its decision?" ■ To identify the question addressed by the court ask, "What legal question was addressed and answered by the holding?" ■ To identify the key facts ask, "Which of the facts presented in the case, if changed, would alter or affect the question addressed in the holding?"
STEP 3: Assemble the Issue	Assemble the issue from the answers to the questions in step 2. Structure the issue in the format presented in Chapter 11: Rule of law + legal question + key facts.

© Cengage

Exhibit 10-3 Steps in the Identification or Spotting of the Issue in a Court Opinion.

A. Step 1: General Question

The first part of this step is to read the entire court opinion before attempting to identify the issue. Important information concerning an issue may be scattered throughout the opinion. An initial reading of the entire case provides the researcher with an awareness of where information is located in the opinion and an overview of the case. This is helpful when you begin to analyze specific portions of the opinion. Read the entire opinion at the outset, even if the court clearly identifies the issue.

While reading the case, keep in mind the question, "What was decided about which facts in this case?" This question helps keep your mind focused on what you need to be looking for while reading the case in order to identify the elements of the issue:

- The first part of the question, "What was decided?" keeps your mind focused on searching for the legal issue that was resolved, and the law necessary for its resolution.
- The second part of the question, "About which facts?" keeps your mind focused on looking for the facts essential to the resolution of the legal question.

If you keep this question in mind as you read the case, you remain focused on the essence of the case: the court's application of a rule of law to the legal question raised by the facts. Asking this question forces you to keep the facts in mind as you read because you are aware that you must decide which of the facts relate to the holding. When you get to the end of the opinion, you may realize that the holding relates to only a few of the facts presented.

Do not identify the issue(s) from the syllabus or headnotes of the opinion. As noted in Chapter 4, these are prepared by the publisher of the opinion. They are not part of the court opinion, and are not intended to be used to identify the issue(s) addressed in the opinion. Headnotes, however, may be relied upon to help you locate the issue within the opinion.

If you have not identified the issue by the time you have finished reading the case, proceed to step 2.

B. Step 2: Look to the Holding

As noted in Chapter 4, the *holding* is the court's application of the rule of law to the legal issue raised by the facts of the case. It is the court's answer to the issue. In a court opinion, the key facts, legal question, and holding are all related. Finding one will help you find the others. Therefore, often the fastest way to track down the issue is to focus on the holding and ask the following questions:

1. "What was decided in the holding?" In other words, "What issue was addressed and answered by the holding?" This identifies the second element of the issue—the legal question addressed by the court.
2. "What statute, rule of law, principle, and so on did the court apply to reach this holding?" This question helps identify the relevant rule of law—the first element of the issue.
3. "Which of the facts presented in this case are related and necessary to the determination of the question identified as addressed in the holding?" or "Which of the facts, if changed, would change the outcome of the holding?" These questions help identify the third element of the issue—the key facts.

By answering these questions you identify the elements of the issue: the rule of law, question, and key facts. You can state the issue by adding the rule of law and key facts to the holding and reformulating the holding in question form. This may sound complicated, but it is not.

For Example

In a workers' compensation case, the court presents several facts concerning the plaintiff before and after she joined a monastery, including the following:

1. Her duties as a monastic
2. Her written application for admission as a volunteer to the service of God
3. The written invitation from the monastery, which included an offer of spiritual guidance and room and board in exchange for volunteer service
4. Information concerning her previous career
5. The fact that she did not receive a paycheck

6. Her spiritual motivation

7. Her daily duties

8. The fact that she was injured while mopping the floor

9. Her family relationships

10. The fact that there was no contract of employment

The plaintiff appealed the trial court's decision granting the defendant's motion to dismiss for failure to state a claim. The issue is not stated in the opinion. The holding in the case was: "Plaintiff rendered services out of religious devotion as indicated by her application as a volunteer, lack of employment agreement, and lack of a paycheck; therefore, she was not an employee within the meaning of the law, and the trial court's dismissal of the complaint is affirmed." This example is referred to in this chapter as "the monastery" example.

A quick way to identify the issue in the monastery example is to focus on the holding and keep in mind the question, "What was decided about which facts to reach this holding?" Then, identify the elements of the issue by asking:

1. "What question was decided in this holding?" The question decided is whether the plaintiff was an employee. The answer to this question provides the legal question element of the issue.

2. "What rule of law or principle did the court apply to reach this holding?" The answer to this question provides the rule of law element of the issue. It may be a statute, case law principle, doctrine, and so on. Assume here that it is the Workers' Compensation Act § 36-9-7.

3. "Which facts mentioned in the opinion are related and necessary to the determination of the question of whether the plaintiff is an employee?" The answer to this question provides the key facts element of the issue. In this case, the court focused on the written application as a volunteer, the absence of an employment agreement, and the lack of a paycheck. These facts, if changed, would probably change the outcome. If treated as a group, the changing of all these facts would change the outcome.

C. Step 3: Assemble the Issue

Assemble the identified elements in the relevant law + legal question + key facts format presented in Chapter 11. The rule of law is the Workers' Compensation Act § 36-9-7. The question is whether the plaintiff was an employee. The key facts are the written application for admission to the monastery as a volunteer, the absence of an employment agreement, and the lack of a paycheck. The issue, when assembled, is: "Under the provisions of Workers' Compensation Act § 36-9-7, is an individual an employee when the individual is admitted to a monastery upon a written application as a volunteer, does not receive a paycheck, and does not have an agreement of employment?"

D. Other Aids—Case Law Issue Identification

1. Concurring or Dissenting Opinion

In a concurring or dissenting opinion, the issue may be set out more clearly than in the majority opinion. Therefore, do not overlook these opinions when identifying the issue. Be aware, however, that the concurring or dissenting judge may have a different view of what the issue is, especially in the case of a dissent. Nevertheless, even if the formulation is different, the discussion of the issue by the concurring or dissenting judge may be helpful in determining the issue in the majority opinion.

2. Other Opinions

Reading other opinions cited in the case may provide guidance concerning the issue in the case at hand. Also, reading a later court's discussion of the case may prove helpful, as it may summarize and clarify the issue in the case you are reading. *Shepard's Citations* will guide you to subsequent cases.

E. Multiple Issues

The foregoing discussion focuses on locating a single issue. Often there are multiple issues in a court opinion. Apply the steps presented in Exhibit 10-3 to all the issues in the case, one at a time. Be sure to follow all the steps presented in this section completely when identifying an issue before proceeding to identify the next issue. Remember, for each issue, you must identify the relevant rule of law, specific question, and key facts.

You may read a case to find the answer to a single question relevant to your client's fact situation, or you may be looking for a specific legal principle, doctrine, or rule of law addressed by the court.

For Example

You are researching a court opinion that involves several torts, but you are only interested in the court's discussion of the emotional distress issue. Follow the steps presented in Exhibit 10-3 to identify the emotional distress issue, but ensure that the court's resolution of the other issues does not in some way affect its treatment of the emotional distress issue. You can accomplish this by reading the entire opinion and checking for any overlap of the issues or interconnectedness of the reasoning.

Note: As in Section IV, consider the steps presented in this section as useful tools and helpful guidelines. When followed, they will usually help you to quickly identify the issue in a court opinion. In certain instances, the opinion may be so obscure that you are unable to identify the issue. Also, as you read more and more cases, a sort of intuition develops, and you may immediately spot the issue without going through any of the steps.

VI. KEY POINTS CHECKLIST: Spotting the Issue

✓ When determining the issue(s) in a client's case, it is helpful to keep in mind the question, "What must be decided about which facts in this case?" This question helps keep your mind focused on the rule of law in conjunction with the facts.

✓ When identifying the issue(s) in a court opinion, as you read, keep asking the question, "What was decided about which facts in this opinion?" All cases are about how the law applies to facts. By keeping focused on the law and facts of the case, you are less likely to be sidetracked by issues and questions that need not be addressed.

✓ Address one issue at a time. For each issue under consideration, follow each of the steps presented in this chapter before proceeding to the next issue. In multiple-issue cases, separate the issues and identify one completely before addressing the next one.

✓ When reading a court opinion or working on a client's case, keep in mind the three elements of the issue: rule of law, question, and key facts. This helps you stay focused on what you need to determine to identify the issue.

✓ Do not be concerned if you cannot immediately identify the issue(s) in a client's case. The complete identification of the issue may not take place until you conduct the research, read laws and cases, and identify the required elements of the cause of action. Likewise, the existence of additional issues may not be known until research reveals their presence.

✓ Do not stop when you have identified one issue. Most cases involve more than one legal question. Separate areas of law, such as torts and contracts, may bear on one fact situation. Always look for all possible causes of action that could arise from a fact situation.

✓ Use any technique that works for you. The steps suggested here are designed as guidelines to assist you. Use any or all of them, and anything else that helps.

VII. APPLICATION

This section presents two examples of issue identification. Each example illustrates the principles discussed throughout this chapter and includes a discussion of the application of those principles.

A. Client's Fact Situation

The following example involves the application of the principles to the hypothetical presented at the beginning of the chapter:

1. Identify Each Possible Cause of Action and Area of Law Involved

The first step is to identify each type of cause of action and area of law that may be raised by the client's fact situation. Kevin, based upon his training, realizes that this is a civil, not a criminal, matter. No crime has been committed against Ms. Carry. He also knows that the applicable area of civil law is torts. By a process of elimination, based upon experience, he focuses on infliction of emotional distress. There is no assault or battery claim because there was no act directly or indirectly aimed at the client. Step 1 may require no research. Kevin may arrive at this point based solely on his education and experience, although he may realize, as he conducts research into the emotional distress issue, that other causes of action are present as well. If more than one claim is identified, steps 2 through 4 should be followed separately for each claim.

For Example

If a part from the car flew off and hit Ms. Carry, there are potential battery or negligence issues, and Kevin would follow steps 2 through 4 for each issue.

2. Determine the Elements of Each Cause of Action Identified in Step 1

Kevin's research reveals that emotional distress is a case law doctrine. The legislature has not adopted a statute concerning emotional distress. The state's highest court has recognized the tort of intentional infliction of emotional distress. The court requires that the following elements be established to state a claim:

1. The defendant's conduct must be either intentional or grossly or recklessly negligent.
2. The conduct must be extreme and outrageous.
3. There must be a causal connection between the defendant's conduct and the plaintiff's mental distress.
4. The plaintiff's mental distress must be extreme or severe.

3. Determine Which of the Facts Apply

The third step is to determine which of the facts of the client's case apply to establish or satisfy the elements of each cause of action—the key facts.

1. Defendant's conduct of driving at a very high rate of speed, crashing through the fence, hitting the seesaw, and injuring the son of the plaintiff's friend are the facts that apply to satisfy the first element of intentional or grossly negligent conduct.
2. Driving through a school zone at an extremely high rate of speed is the fact that satisfies the second element of extreme or outrageous conduct.
3. Ms. Carry's insomnia and anxiety immediately after the event are facts that apply to the third element of causation.
4. Ms. Carry's anxiety and insomnia are extreme and apply to establish the fourth element.

If Kevin could not find a fact that would arguably apply to each element, there would be no issue involving that area of law, and that cause of action would have to be abandoned as a potential avenue of redress for Ms. Carry.

For Example

If Ms. Carry did not suffer any anxiety or insomnia, there probably would be no cause of action for emotional distress.

Note: As discussed in Section IV of this chapter, you may not be certain whether a fact meets the established standard for an element. Often that determination cannot be made until trial. Your task is to ensure that some fact arguably meets the requirements of each of the elements of the cause of action.

For Example

A determination of whether Ms. Carry's insomnia and anxiety are extreme enough to warrant relief may not be made until trial; however, her symptoms are arguably sufficient to meet the requirements of the fourth element. If research reveals that this harm is not sufficiently extreme to meet the requirements of emotional distress, then there is no emotional distress issue.

4. Assemble the Issue

Assemble the elements and state the issue. Kevin now has all the elements necessary to identify and state the issue: the area of law, the legal question, and the key facts. He identifies the issue as: "Under [name of state] tort law, does intentional infliction of emotional distress occur when a person suffers severe insomnia and anxiety as a result of witnessing a friend's child being injured by a vehicle that is out of control due to being driven at a high rate of speed through a school zone?"

By following the four steps, moving from a broad identification of the possible causes of action to the specific elements of and facts involved in each cause of action, Kevin has identified an issue. He knows what must be decided about which facts for this cause of action. His research is focused on cases in which the conduct involved accidents in school zones where witnesses suffered harm similar to that experience by Ms. Carry.

If other possible causes of action were identified in step 1, then steps 2 through 4 would be followed for each potential cause.

B. Court Opinion

The following example illustrates the application of the principles to the identification of the issues in a court opinion. The three steps to follow are:

- Step 1: General Question—While reading the case, keep in mind the general question, "What was decided about which facts in the case?"
- Step 2: Look to the Holding—Identify the rule of law and key facts relevant to the holding.
- Step 3: Assemble the Issue

Read the following case of *Lucero v. Sutten.*

CASE

ROLAND LUCERO and R & L STRIGHTLINE TITLE, LLC

a/k/a

R & L STRIGHTLINE TITLE,
Plaintiffs-Appellants,

v.

RICHARD SUTTEN,
Defendant-Appellee.

2015-NMCA-010

OPINION

VANZI, Judge

***

{2}Roland Lucero and his company, R & L Straightline Tile, (collectively, Plaintiff) appeal from a judgment entered in favor of Defendant Richard Sutten following a bench trial on the issue of legal malpractice. The district court found that Defendant negligently failed to apprise Plaintiff of the dangers of providing an unsecured $300,000.00 loan to a Las Vegas development company. However, the district court applied the doctrine of independent intervening cause, a defense that had not been previously raised in Defendant's proposed findings prior to trial, and concluded that the real estate market collapse of the mid-to-late 2000s severed the connection between Defendant's professional negligence and Plaintiff's damages claimed therefrom. On appeal, Plaintiff argues that the district court erred in applying the doctrine of independent intervening cause to these facts. We agree. We reverse and remand for consideration of damages in light of this Opinion.

BACKGROUND

{3} The district court's following findings of fact in this case are not challenged on appeal. Plaintiff was able to amass substantial savings in the course of his business in the tile industry. In February 2008, Plaintiff was approached by Mark Brady, an old friend, about loaning $300,000.00 to a developer for a mixed-use real estate development project in Las Vegas, Nevada. By the terms of the proposed "bridge loan," Plaintiff was to receive a $360,000.00

payment one month after making the loan. Brady, who was also the friend of an officer of the development company, stood to receive a "finder's fee" of up to $30,000.00 for assisting in the transaction. These terms were contained in a document entitled "Secured Promissory Note," (the Note) which was forwarded to Brady by the developer.

{4} Brady suggested to Plaintiff that Defendant, a licensed attorney, review the document on Plaintiff's behalf. Defendant reviewed and made minor changes to the document without notifying Plaintiff that the purported the Note did not, in fact, create any security interest. Nor did Defendant apprise Plaintiff of any of the inherent risks involved in engaging in such a transaction. Instead, Defendant returned the Note with his edits to Brady but did not communicate directly with Plaintiff. Shortly after making the loan, the real estate market in Las Vegas, Nevada, suffered a "cataclysmic decline," and the Las Vegas developer filed for bankruptcy. Plaintiff was never repaid any portion of the loan he had made because the senior lienholder's interests exceeded the value of the secured property after the market collapse.

{5} Plaintiff sued Defendant for professional malpractice, and the district court held a bench trial on the merits. The district court found that the parties had entered into an attorney-client relationship and that Defendant's actions fell below the standard of care and were negligent because he failed to adequately review the Note or advise Plaintiff about the nature and dangers of the proposed transaction. Nevertheless, the district court found that the decline in the Las Vegas real estate market operated as an independent intervening cause, severing the connection between Defendant's professional negligence and Plaintiff's losses. This appeal followed.

DISCUSSION

***

{7} Plaintiff makes two arguments on appeal: (1) that the district court incorrectly applied the doctrine of independent intervening cause, and (2) that the district court's decision creates immunity for a person or entities whose negligence caused harm. Because our reversal is based on the issue of the independent intervening cause, we need not reach Plaintiff's second argument.

***

{8} "The elements of legal malpractice are: (1) the employment of the defendant attorney; (2) the

(continues)

defendant attorney's neglect of a reasonable duty; and (3) the negligence resulted in and was the proximate cause of loss to the client." *Encinias v. Whitener Law Firm,* P.A., 2013-NMSC-045, ¶ 8, 310 P.3d 611 (alteration, internal quotation marks, and citation omitted). At trial, the district court found that the first two elements of representation and negligence were met, but it concluded that the collapse of the real estate market in Las Vegas, Nevada, constituted an independent intervening cause, severing Defendant's negligence from Plaintiff's losses. As a result, the sole issue before this Court is the third element, proximate cause. See *Torres v. El Paso Elec. Co.,* 1999-NMSC-029, ¶ 17, 127 N.M. 729, 987 P.2d 386 ("A finding of an independent intervening cause represents a finding against the plaintiff on proximate cause[.]"), overruled on other grounds by *Herrera v. Quality Pontiac,* 2013-NMSC-018, 134 N.M. 43, 73 P.3d 181.

{9} "An independent intervening cause is a cause which interrupts the natural sequence of events, turns aside their cause, prevents the natural and probable results of the original act or omission, and produces a different result, that could not have been reasonably foreseen." Id. ¶ 12 (internal quotation marks and citation omitted). In *Torres,* our Supreme Court recognized that the doctrine is incompatible with our system of comparative negligence and potentially in conflict with our use of several liability. See Id. ¶¶ 18–19. Thus, our appellate courts have "virtually eliminated" the doctrine's application in cases involving only negligent, as opposed to intentional, conduct. *Silva v. Lovelace Health Sys., Inc.,* 2014- NMCA-086, ¶ 14, 331 P.3d 958, cert. granted, 2014-NMCERT-008, 334 P.3d 425.

***

{10} When the intervening cause does not involve intentional conduct, New Mexico follows the rule that "any harm which is in itself foreseeable, as to which the actor has created or increased the recognizable risk, is always proximate, no matter how it is brought about." *Andrews v. Saylor,* 2003-NMCA-132, ¶ 22, 134 N.M. 545, 80 P.3d 482 (alteration, internal quotation marks, and citation omitted). Thus, the doctrine is inapplicable in New Mexico in cases where a non-intentional intervening force causes the same harm as that risked by the actor's conduct. See *Collins ex rel. Collins v. Perrine,* 1989-NMCA-046, ¶ 19, 108 N.M. 714, 778 P.2d 912 ("An independent intervening cause is a cause that

interrupts the natural sequence of events and produces a different result that could not be reasonably foreseen."). The principle cited in *Andrews, Torres,* and *Collins* is adopted from the *Restatement (Second) of Torts,* which applies equally to forces of nature: If the actor's conduct has created or increased the risk that a particular harm to the plaintiff will occur, . . . it is immaterial to the actor's liability that the harm is brought about in a manner which no one in his position could possibly have been expected to foresee or anticipate. This is true not only where the result is produced by the direct operation of the actor's conduct upon conditions or circumstances existing at the time, but also where it is brought about through the intervention of other forces which the actor could not have expected, whether they be forces of nature, or the actions of animals, or those of third persons which are not intentionally tortious or criminal. Section 442B cmt. b (1965) (emphasis added).

{11}Our application of *Restatement (Second) of Torts* Section 442B to an allegedly intervening force in the legal malpractice context of *Collins* is instructive. In *Collins,* the defendant-attorney negligently settled a complex medical malpractice case without performing a minimum level of discovery (1989-NMCA-046, ¶ 13). After settling with the original defendants, the plaintiffs sued Indian Health Services (IHS) in federal court and obtained a much larger judgment, with damages apportioned between IHS and the original defendants. Id. ¶ 8. Despite the previous settlement with the original defendants, the plaintiffs' attorney planned on collecting all damages from IHS through principles of joint and several liability. Id. ¶ 16. However, while the second suit was pending, New Mexico abolished the concept of joint and several liability. Id. ¶ 17. Thus, as a result of the attorney's negligence in settling the original case, together with the change in state tort law, the plaintiffs were unable to collect a substantial portion of the damages awarded in the federal judgment. Id. ¶ 8.

{12} At trial for legal malpractice and on appeal, the defendant-attorney in *Collins* argued that the unforeseeable change in the law acted as an independent intervening cause. Id. ¶¶ 16–18. This Court rejected that argument, stating: The *Restatement of Torts* addresses this point clearly. In Section 442B, the *Restatement* explains that where the negligent conduct of an actor creates or increases the risk of a particular harm and is a substantial factor in causing that harm, the fact that the harm is brought about through the intervention of

(continues)

another force does not relieve the actor of liability (*Collins*, 1989-NMCA-046, ¶ 20). Applying *Restatement (Second) of Torts* Section 442B, we reasoned that the attorney's negligence created a particular risk—the risk that the plaintiffs would not be able to recover damages caused by the original defendants. We therefore held that the "intervention of the change in law," whether foreseeable or not, brought about a foreseeable harm and could not relieve the attorney of liability (*Collins*, 1989-NMCA-046, ¶¶ 20–21.)

{13} In light of these authorities, the district court should not have considered the doctrine of independent intervening cause in this case. The district court found that Defendant gave the transaction the attorney "seal of approval," negligently creating or increasing the risk of the loss of Plaintiff's investment by failing to warn Plaintiff of the dangers inherent in loaning $300,000.00 to a Las Vegas developer in an unsecured transaction. In the absence of any allegation that the intervening cause was the result of intentional tortious conduct, the six principles articulated in *Restatement (Second) of Torts* Section 442B and adopted in *Collins* apply. As discussed above, these principles apply whether or not the market decline is considered a "force of nature." The district court should not have dismissed this case but, instead, it should have determined whether Defendant's negligence was the proximate cause of Plaintiff's loss and, if applicable, employed a standard comparative fault analysis.

{14} Citing to several out-of-state and federal cases, Defendant asks us to consider whether the collapse of the Las Vegas real estate market was foreseeable. However, Defendant's characterization of the issue relies on the same contention that we specifically rejected in *Collins*: that the manner in which the harm occurs is somehow relevant to the analysis. See *Collins*, 1989-NMCA-046, ¶¶ 17–21. We have made clear that in cases not involving intentional intervening conduct, when the risk of harm is foreseeable, the manner that the foreseeable harm is brought about need not itself be foreseeable. Id. ¶ 21 ("Nor does it matter whether [the attorney] could have foreseen the change in law."). Accordingly, we find Defendant's citations to extra-jurisdictional opinions evaluating the foreseeability of the 2008 real estate market collapse inapposite. We conclude that the district court erred in applying the doctrine of independent intervening cause to its factual determination that the parties had entered into an attorney-client relationship and that Plaintiff made the loan in reliance, at least partially, on Defendant's seal of approval.

CONCLUSION

{15} We reverse the district court's decision dismissing Plaintiff's complaint with prejudice and remand for consideration and apportionment of damages using a comparative fault analysis.

{16} IT IS SO ORDERED.

Courtesy of New Mexico Compilation Commission

---

1. General Question

Read the entire case. While reading the case, ask yourself, "What did the court decide about which facts?" To answer this question, it is necessary to keep in mind the elements of the issue: the rule of law, legal question, and key facts. Keeping this question in mind helps you focus on these elements.

2. Look to the Holding

You probably cannot identify the substantive issue after completing step 1. The court only presented the procedural issue in paragraph 2 ({2}): ". . . the Plaintiff argues that the district court erred in applying the doctrine of independent intervening cause to these facts." Follow step 2 and find the holding. Here, the holding is presented in paragraph 13 ({13}): "The district court should not have dismissed this case but, instead, it should have determined whether Defendant's negligence was the proximate cause of Plaintiff's loss. . . ." Once identified, locate the elements of the issue relevant to this holding. Ask the following questions:

- "What was decided in the holding?" In other words, "What legal question or issue was addressed and answered by the court?" Determine the answer to this question by looking to the holding and deciding what question was answered by the holding.

Here, Lucero, the client, an appellant in the case, argued the district court should not have applied the doctrine of independent intervening cause to the facts because the district court had determined the Defendant's conduct of not advising Plaintiff that the agreement did not create a secured interest was negligent. The appellate court held when the independent intervening cause does not involve intentional conduct, New Mexico follows the *Restatement (Second) of Torts* which states where negligent conduct creates or increases the risk of a particular harm and is a substantial factor in causing that harm, the fact that the harm is brought about through the intervention of another force does not relieve the actor of liability. In other words, if a defendant's conduct is the proximate cause of the plaintiff's injury, the defendant will be held liable. The legal question, then, is whether the Defendant's negligent conduct was the proximate cause of the Plaintiff's loss.

In this case, it is difficult to identify the issue without this step because the opinion includes information that tends to mislead the reader.

- "What statute, rule of law, or principle did the court apply when it reached this holding?" In this case, the court looked to prior court opinions and, most significantly, *Restatement (Second) of Torts* § 442B.
- "Which facts mentioned in the opinion are related and necessary to the determination of the question addressed in the holding?" What are the key facts? In this case, as in many cases, the court presents several facts that have nothing to do with the holding. Usually these facts are presented to give the reader the background and context of the holding. The presentation of too many background facts, however, may mislead the reader and make it difficult to determine what the case is actually about.

This is especially true in this case. The opinion contains several paragraphs discussing how the Plaintiff and Defendant came to interact and the actions of the Defendant in reviewing and commenting on the document. So much is presented concerning these facts that the reader tends to focus on them, and not on the key facts that involve the determination that the Defendant's acts were negligent, the negligence caused or increased the risk, and the independent intervening cause was not the result of intentional conduct.

When the holding, however, is referred to and the question is asked, "Which facts are necessary or related to this holding?" it is clear that the facts relevant to the holding are the facts concerning the negligence of the defendant and that the independent intervening cause was nonintentional.

3. Assemble the Issue

The final step is to assemble the issue. All of the elements have been identified in step 2:

- The rule of law is § 442B of the *Restatement (Second) of Torts*.
- The question is whether the defendant's negligence was the proximate cause of the plaintiff's loss.
- The key facts are that the defendant's actions were negligent and created or increased the risks and the independent intervening cause of the real estate market crash was nonintentional.

The assembled issue is: "Under § 442B of the *Restatement (Second) of Torts* was the defendant's negligence, which created or increased the risk when the independent intervening cause of the real estate market crash occurred, a proximate cause of the plaintiff's loss?"

Summary

The most important task in either analyzing a client's case or reading a court opinion is to correctly identify the issue(s). You must identify the problem before it can be solved. A misidentified issue can result not only in wasted time, but also in malpractice.

The issue is the precise legal question raised by the facts of the dispute. Therefore, each issue is unique because the facts of each case are different, and each issue must be narrowly stated within the context of the facts of that case. The issue is composed of the applicable law, the legal question relevant to the law, and the facts that raise the question. These elements must be precisely identified to determine the issue.

There is no magic formula, but this chapter includes steps that help in issue identification. When working on a client's case, four steps are recommended:

1. Identify each area of law that may possibly be involved.
2. Identify the elements necessary for a cause of action under each law identified in the first step.
3. Apply the elements of the law to the client's facts to determine the key facts.
4. Assemble the issue from the law, elements, and key facts identified in the first three steps.

There are three steps to follow to identify the issue(s) in a court opinion:

1. General question—while reading the case, keep in mind the question, "What was decided about which facts?"
2. Look to the holding to identify the rule of law, legal question, and key facts of the case.
3. Assemble the issue.

These are the recommended steps. They usually work when correctly followed and are always helpful in focusing the practitioner's attention on that which is essential: the rule of law, legal question, and facts.

Quick References

Internet Resources

As of the date of publication of this text, there are no websites dedicated specifically to issue identification. However, using a search engine and "legal analysis spotting issues" as a topic will return a wide range of websites that address some aspect of legal analysis and issue spotting. Some sites discuss identifying legal issues in specific areas of the law, such as labor law, whereas others discuss the topic in relation to taking exams. There are numerous other related sites.

Exercises

ASSIGNMENT 1
Detail the steps for identifying the issue(s) in a client's case.

ASSIGNMENT 2
Detail the steps for identifying the issue(s) in a court opinion.

ASSIGNMENT 3
Statutes: *Criminal Code Section 18-760, Robbery.* A person who knowingly takes anything of value from the person or presence of another by use of force, threats, or intimidation commits robbery.

Criminal Code Section 18-773, Larceny. Any person who wrongfully takes, obtains, or withholds, by any means, from the possession of the owner or of any other person any money, personal property, or article of value of any kind, with intent permanently to deprive another person of the use and benefit of property is guilty of larceny.

Facts: Over the years, Larry borrowed several tools from his next-door neighbor. Usually he returned the items, but on occasion he forgot. One of the tools he did not return is a drill. The neighbor goes to Larry's house and tells him that if he doesn't return the drill, the neighbor will file criminal charges. Larry says, "I'm keeping your drill and if you try to come get it or file charges, I'll beat you up!"

Question

Identify the issue(s) involving criminal law raised by this fact situation.

ASSIGNMENT 4

Perform Assignment 3 using your state's larceny and robbery statutes.

ASSIGNMENT 5

Statute: Arizona Code of Judicial Administration section 3-303, Use of Fee Guidelines, provides in part: Unless otherwise ordered by the court, compensation and reimbursement for professional services shall meet the following requirements. . . . Reasonable costs that are incurred in the best interest of the Estate are reimbursable at actual cost, without increase in price. Reimbursable costs include, but are not limited to . . . electronic database fees charged by an outside vendor (e.g., Westlaw, LexisNexis, PACER) except for charges to research Arizona (or other applicable) statutes, case law, and regulations.

Facts: Predominate area Lisa is an attorney that occasionally is hired to assist in probate matters. Lisa of practice is civil litigation. In her civil litigation practice she charges clients, as detailed in her fee agreement, for charges incurred from searching commercial databases such as WestlawNext. Lisa uses the same fee agreement and has the same practice of charging fees for researching Arizona probate statutes and case law in the probate matters in which she is involved. In some of the probate matters she handles, she is hired by an individual and paid by that individual, usually an heir to an estate. However, in some matters, she does work on behalf of an estate, having been hired by an executor of an estate, in which case the estate is who is charged for her work.

Question: Identify the issue(s) raised by this fact situation.

ASSIGNMENT 6

Identify the issue in the following two fact situations.

Part A.

Beth loaned Allen $5,000. The agreement was oral. Allen commutes to a nearby city to work. Beth needs to go to the city three times in May. Allen told her he would give her three free rides to the city to help repay the loan. On one of the trips, Allen was not paying attention, lost control of the car, and wrecked it. Beth suffered severe injuries and wants to sue Allen to recover damages.

The state automobile guest statute bars suits against drivers by automobile guests. The statute does not apply if the passenger confers a substantial benefit on the driver and that is the reason the driver provided the ride.

Part B.

Tom and Alex are next-door neighbors. While arguing with Tom, Alex breaks Tom's lawn chair, and as Alex begins to break more lawn furniture, Tom makes a citizen's arrest of Alex. Tom's sons help Tom, and after Alex is subdued, they continue to hit and kick him for a few moments. Alex wants to sue Tom.

The state's case law defines battery as unauthorized harmful contact; it also allows a citizen's arrest when the purpose is to prevent the destruction of property.

ASSIGNMENT 7

Elements of Cause of Action: False Imprisonment requires the following elements: (a) the detention or restraint of one against their will, and (b) the detention or restraint is unlawful.

Statute: The state criminal code contains the offense of unlawful imprisonment which states: "A person commits unlawful imprisonment by knowingly restraining another person."

Facts: Refer to the false imprisonment hypothetical.

Question

Identify the issue(s) involving both the civil cause of action and the criminal statute raised by the false imprisonment hypothetical.

ASSIGNMENT 8

Read the following case of *Metropolitan Life Insurance Company v. Syntek Finance Corporation*. The procedural issue is whether the trial court properly denied Syntek's motion for disqualification of counsel. What issue concerning the substantive disqualification of counsel is raised by the facts of the case?

ASSIGNMENT 9

Read the following case of *Morgan v. Greenwaldt*. The procedural issue is whether the trial court properly granted a directed verdict on the false imprisonment claim. What issue regarding the substantive false imprisonment is raised by the facts of the case?

CASE

METROPOLITAN
LIFE INSURANCE COMPANY,

Petitioner

v.

SYNTEK FINANCE CORPORATION,
Respondent.

881 S.W.2d 319 (Tex. 1994) PER CURIAM.

This case turns on the application of the "substantial relationship" test for attorney disqualification based on prior representation of the same or a related client. Following a lengthy hearing, the trial court overruled a motion to disqualify counsel filed by Syntek Finance Corporation. After a jury trial, a judgment for approximately $6.7 million was rendered in favor of Metropolitan Life Insurance Company. The court of appeals reversed that judgment and remanded the case for a new trial, holding that the trial court abused its discretion when it denied Syntek's motion for disqualification of counsel. 880 S.W.2d 26. We reverse the judgment of the court of appeals and remand the case to that court for consideration of points of error not previously addressed.

Gene Phillips owns a controlling interest in Syntek and several other related companies. In 1986, the law firm of Hughes & Luce represented Phillips in a divorce and subsequently drafted a prenuptial agreement. In the course of that representation, Phillips disclosed his personal financial status to Hughes & Luce, including the intricate structure of his various companies. This suit, filed by Syntek in April 1989, arises out of a hotel Syntek purchased from Metropolitan. Hughes & Luce attorney Richard Nelson represented Metropolitan. Nelson made an initial conflicts check and determined to his satisfaction that there was no conflict of interest due to the firm's previous representation of Phillips.

After nearly two years of pretrial activity, Nelson acquired information about Phillips' possible involvement in Syntek's decision to stop loan payments to Metropolitan. Nelson again reviewed the circumstances of his firm's former representation of Phillips and once more satisfied himself that there was no substantial relationship between the two representations. Nelson then amended Metropolitan's pleadings to include new allegations concerning Phillips' involvement. In response, Syntek

and Phillips filed a motion to disqualify Hughes & Luce. The trial court denied the motion.

[1] Rule 1.09 of the Texas Disciplinary Rules of Professional Conduct provides that a lawyer shall not take a representation that is adverse to a former client if the new matter "is the same or a substantially related matter." Tex. Disciplinary R. Prof. Conduct 1.09(a)(3)(1989), reprinted in Tex. Gov't Code Ann., tit. 2, subtit. G. app. (Vernon Supp.1993) (State Bar Rules art. X, § 9). In NCNB Tex. Nat'l Bank v. Coker, 765 S.W.2d 398, 400 (Tex.1989), we stated that to satisfy the substantial relationship test as a basis for disqualification a movant must prove that the facts of the previous representation *321 are so related to the facts in the pending litigation that a genuine threat exists that confidences revealed to former counsel will be divulged to a present adversary. Id.

[2] The disqualification hearing consumed five days. The trial court heard live and deposition testimony from fourteen fact witnesses concerning the previous and pending representations, and from five expert witnesses concerning the Coker standard. There was testimony that the information at issue was both available in the public domain and provided to Metropolitan by Syntek through discovery. There was also testimony that the information used in the amended pleadings was available to the public through an examiners' report from a bankruptcy proceeding against one of the companies controlled by Phillips. The trial court also conducted an in camera review of documents from the former representation.

The test for abuse of discretion is whether the trial court acted without reference to any guiding rules or principles, or acted in an arbitrary or unreasonable manner. See Downer v. Aquamarine Operators, Inc., 701 S.W.2d 238, 241–42 (Tex.1985), cert. denied, 476 U.S. 1159, 106 S.Ct. 2279, 90 L.Ed.2d 721 (1986). We hold that on the evidence presented, based on the Coker standard, it was not an abuse of discretion for the trial court to conclude that no substantial relationship existed between the former and current representations and to deny the motion to disqualify.

We therefore conclude that the court of appeals improperly substituted its judgment for that of the trial court. See Flores v. Fourth Court of Appeals, 777 S.W.2d 38, 41–42 (Tex.1989). Accordingly, a majority of the court grants Metropolitan's application for writ of error, and without hearing oral argument, reverses the judgment of the court of appeals and remands the case to that court for consideration of Syntek's other points of error which it did not previously address. Tex. R. App. P. 170.

CASE

MORGAN v. GREENWALDT

786So. 2d 1037 (Miss. 2001)

SMITH, Justice, for the Court:

1. Genia A. Morgan ("Morgan") sued St. Dominic-Jackson Memorial Hospital ("Hospital"), and two of the Hospital's nurses, Brenda Greenwaldt and Susan Brotherton, and a psychiatric technician, Melinda Leah Lewis, over an incident that occurred in June 1996. Morgan alleged that she had been assaulted and battered, falsely imprisoned, and treated negligently while she was a patient. She also sued for intentional infliction of emotional distress. The trial court granted a directed verdict for all the defendants on the issues of assault and battery, false imprisonment, gross negligence, and intentional infliction of emotional distress, but allowed the jury *1040 to determine if the defendants were negligent in their treatment of Morgan. After four days of trial, the jury returned a verdict in favor of the defendants, and the trial court entered judgment accordingly. Morgan's motion for a new trial was denied January 4, 2000, and thereafter she appealed to this Court. We find no reversible error and affirm the judgment of the trial court.

FACTS

2. Genia Morgan started seeing a psychiatrist in 1990 for depression. In early June 1996, Morgan's psychiatrist, Dr. Barbara Goff, suggested that Morgan voluntarily check into the psychiatric unit of the Hospital due to her severe depression and sleep disorder. Dr. Goff wanted Morgan in a monitored environment while she worked on adjusting Morgan's medication. At the time of her admission, Morgan was having suicidal thoughts, and her depression had advanced to the stage where she had given up her job. Also, Morgan was experiencing hallucinations and trances which required an adjustment in her anti-psychotic medication. During her admission

assessment, Morgan reported having a metaphysical experience. Morgan described this experience to the admitting nurse as one where "[she] was lying in bed when something grabbed [her] neck and then it let go when [she] started to pray." Upon her admittance into the Hospital, Morgan signed a Consent to Treatment Form authorizing the Hospital to treat her for illness. She was placed on the intermediate ward where patients were free to walk around the floor and mingle with other patients.

3. On June 18, 1996, Morgan went to the nurses' station and asked for a bottle of hydrogen peroxide that she said she had brought to the Hospital with her. She claimed that it was her practice to brush her teeth with hydrogen peroxide. Nurse Susan Brotherton looked for the hydrogen peroxide but could not locate it. Melinda Leah Lewis, a psychiatric technician, and Brotherton checked Morgan's personal belongings checklist, which is filled out upon a patient's admittance to the Hospital. The hydrogen peroxide was not listed on the sheet as one of the items brought in by Morgan. Brotherton told Morgan that she would call Dr. Goff to get an order for the hydrogen peroxide. Brotherton called Dr. Goff's office and left a message regarding the peroxide and its intended use by Morgan as a mouth rinse. Dr. Goff stated that Morgan could not have the peroxide but could have Cepacol mouthwash instead. Brotherton informed Morgan of the doctor's orders. Morgan became upset and left the unit. Thereafter, she retreated to her room crying.

4. Brotherton, Lewis, and technician Jeannie Smith walked toward Morgan's room to see what was wrong. Brotherton and Lewis entered Morgan's room. Morgan was lying across the bed crying. In an effort to calm her down, Brotherton told Morgan that even though there was no record of her bringing the hydrogen peroxide into the Hospital, the Hospital could reimburse her if she believed the Hospital was responsible for the loss. According to Brotherton's testimony, Morgan began yelling profanity and ordered the nurses out of her room. The nurses returned to their station.

(continues)

5. Shortly thereafter, Morgan came out of her room and approached the nurses' station. According to Brotherton and Lewis, Morgan yelled, used profanity, and demanded her hydrogen peroxide. She walked to the nurse manager's door and began pounding her fist on the door. At this point, Dr. Goff was again called, and Brotherton left a message with the doctor's secretary that Morgan was out of *1041 control and was acting in a hostile manner. Due to the escalating situation, Brotherton called the nursing supervisor, Brenda Greenwaldt. When Greenwaldt arrived and introduced herself, Morgan started ranting and raving that she demanded an apology. Morgan then proceeded to pound her fist on the nurses' station desk and point her finger in nurse Greenwaldt's face. According to Greenwaldt, Brotherton, and Lewis, the patient appeared totally out of control and became a threat to the safety of herself and others.

6. ... [G]reenwaldt wrote an order that stated "[p]lace in seclusion for threatening staff for four to six hours until calm and nonthreatening."

7. Several witnesses testified that Morgan was escorted, without any physical contact, to the seclusion area. Even Morgan stated in her testimony that she walked to seclusion on her own accord. According to Morgan, she was strip searched and forced to change into a Hospital gown in front of several people. However, various staff members of the Hospital testified that it was standard procedure for someone in seclusion to be searched for dangerous instrumentalities and to change into a Hospital gown. Further, according to Hospital personnel, Leah Lewis stood in front of the window to the seclusion door so there would be privacy. Morgan was left in seclusion for about two hours, from 4:30 P.M. until 6:45 P.M.

§ 8. Morgan raises the following issues on appeal:

I. WHETHER THE TRIAL COURT PROPERLY DIRECTED A VERDICT ON ALL COUNTS OF INTENTIONAL INFLICTION OF EMOTIONAL DISTRESS, FALSE IMPRISONMENT, GROSS NEGLIGENCE, AND ASSAULT AND BATTERY? ***

ANALYSIS

I.§ 9. At the close of the testimony, the defendants moved for a directed verdict on all counts except the medical malpractice negligence claim. The trial court granted the motion, thereby taking from the jury the claims of intentional infliction of emotional distress, false imprisonment, gross negligence, and assault and battery. Morgan argues that there was sufficient evidence to make out a jury question on all of these claims, and thus, the directed verdict for the defendants was reversible error.

[1][2][3] § 10. This Court conducts a de novo review of a motion for directed verdict. _Northern Elec. Co. v. Phillips,_ 660 So.2d 1278, 1281 (Miss.1995). If we find that the evidence favorable to the non-moving party and the reasonable inferences drawn therefrom present a question for the jury, the motion should not be *1042 granted. _Id._ (citing _Pittman v. Home Indem. Co.,_ 411 So.2d 87, 89 (Miss.1982)). This Court has also held that an issue should only be presented to the jury when the evidence creates a question of fact on which reasonable jurors could disagree. _Herrington v. Spell,_ 692 So.2d 93, 97 (Miss.1997).

A. False Imprisonment

[4] § 11. False imprisonment has only two elements: "detention of the plaintiff and the unlawfulness of

such detention." _Lee v. Alexander,_ 607 So.2d 30, 35 (Miss.1992) (citing _Page v. Wiggins,_ 595 So.2d 1291 (Miss.1992); _Thornhill v. Wilson,_ 504 So.2d 1205, 1208 (Miss.1987) (citing _State ex rel. Powell v. Moore,_ 252 Miss. 471, 174 So.2d 352, 354 (1965); _Hart v. Walker,_ 720 F.2d 1436, 1439 (5th Cir.1983)))).

[5] § 12. Morgan contends that the trial court erred in granting a directed verdict because she was locked up against her will, and the determination of whether her detainment was a reasonable one should have been a question of fact for the jury. This Court finds that such an argument lacks merit. Morgan consented to the treatment at the Hospital, and such treatment includes placing patients who are out of control in a secure environment for the protection of both the patient and the others at the Hospital.

§ 13. The evidence indicates that prior to the 1996 incident in question, Morgan had undergone a psychological evaluation that concluded she was suffering from personality disorders. She had a history of mental illness dating back to 1990 and was diagnosed as having been severely depressed upon her admittance to the Hospital in June of 1996. She also suffered from hallucinations and crying episodes. Moreover, on the morning of the alleged incident, Morgan's doctor noted in the medical records that she was experiencing trances that lasted up to fifteen minutes.

§ 14. Morgan argues that the mere fact that she was undergoing treatment in a Hospital does not mean that the Hospital is justified in performing any medical procedures it deems warranted. Although such an argument is a valid one, it is not warranted in the case *sub judice*. The cases Morgan cites as support for such an argument are not applicable to the case at bar. Such cases deal with situations where the appellant did not consent to the treatment or was detained upon a request or attempt of the patient to leave the Hospital. *Felton v. Coyle,* 95 Ill.App.2d 202, 238 N.E.2d 191 (1968); *Fox v. Smith,* 594 So.2d 596 (Miss.1992). Genia Morgan voluntarily signed an Authorization for Treatment form when she was admitted to the Hospital. Moreover, there was substantial testimony to support the fact that Morgan was out of control and was posing a threat to the environment, including herself. Confinement in a secured environment is a common method of treatment in psychiatric wards and Hospitals. The Hospital is charged with the duty of maintaining a safe and secure environment for all patients. The evidence showed that Morgan was acting in a way that clearly conveyed the possibility of violence.

§ 15. Morgan relies on *Fox v. Smith,* 594 So.2d 596 (Miss.1992),* to bolster her argument that the mere fact that she was undergoing treatment in a Hospital does not mean that the Hospital is justified in performing any medical procedure it deems warranted. In *Fox,* the patient was admitted to the Hospital for a laparoscopy and alleged that the removal of an intrauterine device was done without her consent. *Id.* at 596. This case can clearly be distinguished from the case at bar since the patient in *Fox* initially refused to sign the consent form because she objected to a *1043 clause in the form which authorized the Hospital to dispose of severed tissues or specimens. *Id.* at 599. The Court stated that *Fox* turned on the issue of consent, or not, for the removal of the patient's intrauterine device. *Id.* at 597. This Court made clear that a patient's informed consent to treatment is a prerequisite to treatment, and because a material dispute existed on important facts concerning the patient's consent, the question should have been presented to the jury. *Id.* at 604.

§ 16. In comparison, Morgan clearly consented to treatment by the doctors and personnel at the Hospital by signing the consent form. Moreover, Morgan never retracted her consent to receive treatment. She never informed the nurses that she refused their treatment or that she wanted to leave the Hospital. Indeed, she even voluntarily walked to the isolation room.

§ 17. Morgan also relies upon *Felton v. Coyle,* 95 Ill.App.2d 202, 238 N.E.2d 191 (1968), for her argument that she was falsely imprisoned. This case is not only factually distinguishable from the case at bar, but is also from another jurisdiction and, therefore, not controlling on this Court. In *Felton,* the patient suffered a broken clavicle and was taken to a Chicago Hospital for treatment. *Id.* at 192. After an altercation between the patient and Hospital personnel, patient's doctor ordered him out of the Hospital. *Id.* When the patient attempted to leave the Hospital, the doctor grabbed the patient by the shoulders and told him he was going to call the police. *Id.* at 193. The doctor then sent the patient to a psychiatric Hospital. *Id.* The trial court issued a directed verdict in favor of the defendant, and on appeal the patient argued that he was entitled to a directed verdict. *Id.* at 194. The appellate court disagreed, holding that under the facts and circumstances of the case, it was properly presented to the trier of fact to determine whether the patient was improperly detained. *Id.*

§ 18. Unlike *Felton,* here there were no efforts by the Hospital to prevent Morgan from leaving the Hospital at her will. Morgan did not leave the Hospital until two days after the alleged incident. Even after that time, she continued to attend classes at the Hospital.

§ 19. The trial court properly directed a verdict on the issue of false imprisonment. There is simply no proof in the record of the unlawfulness of Morgan's detention. She voluntarily signed an authorization for treatment form. She had a history of psychological problems, and there was substantial testimony to support the fact that she was out of control and was posing a threat to herself and to others.

CONCLUSION

§ 29. In sum, the trial court did not err in granting a directed verdict on the issues of assault and battery, false imprisonment, gross negligence and intentional infliction of emotional distress. Genia A. Morgan simply failed to meet her burden of proof in showing the necessary elements of these causes of action…. For these reasons, we affirm the judgment of the Hinds County Circuit Court.

§ 30. AFFIRMED.

PITTMAN, C.J., BANKS, P.J., MILLS, WALLER, COBB AND DIAZ, JJ., CONCUR. McRAE, P.J., CONCURS IN RESULT ONLY. EASLEY, J., DISSENTS WITHOUT SEPARATE WRITTEN OPINION.

ASSIGNMENT 10

Read *Whitmore v. Union Pacific Railroad Company,* in Appendix A. Identify the issue regarding the grant of summary judgment.

Chapter 11

Legal Analysis: Stating the Issue

Learning Objectives

After completing this chapter, you should understand:

- The elements of a well-crafted issue
- The value and importance of phrasing the issue narrowly and comprehensively
- The best way to assemble the elements to effectively communicate the issue
- The importance of stating the issue objectively

"Mary, I want you to determine if we can get the evidence suppressed in this case. I need a memo on this by the day after tomorrow, if possible." Jan handed Mary the case file as she gave these instructions. Mary Strate is a legal assistant working in an Oregon law firm that specializes in criminal defense. Jan Brite is her supervising attorney, and according to Jan, Mary is her "right hand."

After reviewing the case and conducting some research, Mary's focus turns to the significant facts relevant to the suppression-of-evidence issue. She determines that there are several key facts. The state police seized the evidence during the execution of a search warrant. A state court judge improperly issued the warrant. The warrant was improperly issued, and therefore defective, because the state police did not present the court sufficient probable cause to justify the search. The opposing side, the state, concedes that the warrant was improperly issued. The officers did not know the warrant was defective and executed it in the good-faith belief that it was valid.

Mary's research indicates that the resolution of the issue is governed by Oregon's exclusionary rule, which provides that evidence illegally seized may not be admitted at trial. The rule was adopted by the state supreme court and is not statutory. As Mary begins the assignment, her first question is how to phrase the issue. "What is the proper format? What is the best way to effectively communicate precisely what is in dispute in this case?" The Application section of this chapter presents the answer to the latter question. The material discussed in this chapter prior to the Application section addresses Mary's other questions.

I. INTRODUCTION

Chapter 10 pointed out that the most important step in the case analysis process is correctly identifying the issue. If the issue is misidentified, time is wasted researching and writing about the wrong question. Once the issue is identified, it is equally important to correctly state it. Of what value is it to correctly identify the question, then fail to accurately communicate what you have identified? Therefore, how Mary states the issue is of critical importance, because the issue governs the direction of the research and communicates the nature of the dispute.

A well-crafted issue informs the reader of the scope of the memo by identifying in a sentence the precise legal question raised by the key facts of the case. It informs the reader of the relevant law, the key facts of the case, and the legal question raised by the law. The exactness and the degree of specificity with which the question is posed determine its usefulness to the reader and researcher.

The goal is to inform the reader of what you have identified as the legal question raised by the dispute. This goal is achieved by focusing your attention on drafting the issue clearly, concisely, and completely. Because so much hinges on correct presentation of the issue, several drafts may be required. Do not get discouraged. The final draft may not emerge until well into the process, and often not until after extensive research and writing.

Chapter 10 identified the issue as being composed of the law, the question, and the key facts. The focus of that chapter was on how to identify these elements in a client's situation and a court opinion. Here, the focus is on how to present these elements when framing the issue: how to write the issue to ensure that the reader knows the precise legal question at the core of the dispute; and how to present the law, question, and key facts to effectively communicate that question.

Ultimately, the issue is the legal question raised by the facts of the dispute. Because it is a question, it should be drafted as a question rather than a statement.

Although there are no established rules governing what the issue must contain or how to assemble it, the law, question, and key fact **elements** should be included to achieve the goal of clearly, concisely, and completely communicating the nature of the dispute. A simple test to determine if the statement of the issue is complete (whether it does its job) is the following: If someone reads the issue alone—if the rest of the memorandum or brief is lost or not referred to—would the reader know what specific legal question, concerning what law, and involving what facts is in dispute in this case? Given this test, there are two ways to state the issue, one effective and one not:

- Shorthand, or broad, statement
- Comprehensive, or narrow, statement

II. SHORTHAND OR BROAD STATEMENT OF THE ISSUE

A **shorthand statement** is a broad formulation of the issue that usually does not include the specific facts or law.

For Example

- Did Mr. Jones commit a vehicular homicide?
- Can Mr. Cicero recover damages for medical malpractice?
- Did the court err when it granted the motion for summary judgment?
- Did the fiduciary violate his duty to his ward?

A **broad statement of issue** is often used in conversation or oral communications when the participants are familiar with the facts and know the law that applies to the case. It is appropriate in this informal context. It may also be appropriate initially in the analytical process by helping to focus attention on the general area of the law to be researched; for example, in the preceding list, the first two illustrations focus the researcher's attention on the general areas of vehicular homicide and medical malpractice. A broadly stated issue is not appropriate in legal research and writing.

III. COMPREHENSIVE OR NARROW STATEMENT OF THE ISSUE

The most effective formulation of the issue is a comprehensive, **narrow statement of issue**. In one sentence, the specific law, legal question, and key facts are presented. This form communicates the specific law that may have been violated in a specific fact situation, or whether and how that law applies in a specific situation. It conveys, in the terms and circumstances of the case, the precise law and question in dispute.

For Example

- Under the requirements of Florida tort law, can a claim for negligent infliction of emotional distress be made by a witness, not related to the victim, who witnesses a severe beating of the victim?
- According to New Washington's probate code, N. Wash. Code § 29-1-5, is a will valid if the witnesses are brothers of the testator?

Note that the specific law and question involved in the dispute are presented in the context of the facts of the dispute.

The value and importance of phrasing the issue comprehensively cannot be overemphasized.

1. For a researcher, it directs the research to the specific area of the law that controls the question raised by the facts of the dispute. This narrowing of focus saves research time because the researcher is immediately directed to the specific area of the law, and need only read cases with similar key facts.
2. In an interoffice memorandum or a court brief, a comprehensive, or narrow, formulation of the issue sets the scope of the memo by informing the reader at the outset what precisely is in dispute. It does not force the reader to try to determine what the question is from the analysis section and thereby makes it less likely that the reader will misunderstand what is in dispute.
3. In a law-office setting, a narrowly framed issue saves time. Future researchers, by merely reading the issue, will know precisely what law and facts a memorandum addresses. They are not forced to read the analysis section to determine if the memo is related or may apply to the case at hand.

With this in mind, the issue should include the following elements, as presented in Exhibit 11-1:

1. The specific law or rule that controls the dispute (the *relevant law*)
2. The *legal question* regarding the law raised by the facts
3. The *key facts* that determine whether or how the law or principle applies

The challenge is to include all three elements in one sentence; therefore, focus on:

1. Completeness—include the precise law, question, and key facts.
2. Conciseness—include no more than is absolutely necessary to guarantee completeness.
3. Clarity—craft the complete and concisely assembled material in the most effective manner.

There are several ways to meet this challenge:

1. Present the facts first, followed by the legal question and the law.

For Example

"Can a witness, not related to the victim, who witnesses a severe beating of the victim, establish a claim for negligent infliction of emotional distress under Florida tort law?"

"If the brothers of the testator witness the will, is the will valid under the provisions of the California wills attestation statute?"

2. Present the law first, followed by the facts, then the legal question.

For Example

"Under Florida's tort law, can a witness, not related to the victim, who witnesses a severe beating of the victim, establish a claim for negligent infliction of emotional distress?"

"Under the California wills attestation statute, if the brothers of the testator witness the will, is the will valid?"

3. Present the legal question first, followed by the law and the facts.

For Example

"Can a claim for negligent infliction of emotional distress be established under Florida tort law when a witness, not related to the victim, witnesses a severe beating of the victim?"

"Is a will valid under the California wills attestation statute if the brothers of the testator witness the will?"

4. Present the rule of law first, followed by the legal question and the facts.

For Example

"Under Florida's tort law, can a claim for negligent infliction of emotional distress be established when a witness, not related to the victim, witnesses a severe beating of the victim?"

"Under the California wills attestation statute, is a will valid if the brothers of the testator witness the will?"

Any of these structures may be used. There are no hard-and-fast rules that mandate the selection of one form over another. However, the format presented in number 4 in the preceding list is recommended. The formula for this format is presented in Exhibit 11-1.

In sentence form, the formula in Exhibit 11-1 is, "Under this law, what legal question is raised by these facts?" There are several reasons for recommending this format:

1. It follows the standard legal analysis format, which proceeds from the general to the specific—the general law followed by application of the law to the specific facts.

For Example

In a court brief or an interoffice legal research memorandum, the applicable law is presented first, followed by the application of the law to the specific facts.

Relevant Law	The specific law that governs the dispute (e.g., "Under Ind. Code § 29-1-5-5, legal execution of a will . . .")
Legal Question	The question concerning the application of the law governing the dispute to the facts of the dispute (e.g., "Is a will validly executed . . .")
Key Facts	The legally significant facts that raise the legal question of how or whether the law governing the dispute applies; facts that, if changed, would change or affect the outcome of the application of the law (e.g., "When one of the witnesses is the brother of the deceased.")

© Cengage

Exhibit 11-1 Relevant Law + Legal Question + Key Facts.

The suggested format for formulation of the issue presented in Exhibit 11-1 follows the same format: the general legal context is presented first, followed by the specific facts of the dispute.

2. Present the rule first for readability purposes. A reader understands the importance of the facts in a dispute in the context of the law. If the facts are presented first and the law last, the reader must reread the facts to put them in the proper legal context because the legal context (the law that applies) is not known until the end of the issue.

3. The last and probably most important reason is that it is usually *easier to write the issue following this format*. It is a most effective tool when confronting the complex challenges presented by multiple-fact issues. Multiple facts are generally easier to write and read when placed at the end of a sentence. Try it. Once the specific law and significant or key facts are identified, it is much easier to craft the issue in the sequence of relevant law + legal question + key facts format.

For these reasons, the examples used throughout this chapter and the text follow the relevant law + legal question + key facts format.

IV. ISSUE—LAW COMPONENT

Obviously, you must include the relevant law in the statement of the issue, because every case involves whether or how a law applies in a specific fact situation. If the law is not included, you are asking the reader to either guess or infer what law applies or conduct research to find the applicable law. To avoid possible confusion and save extra work, establish the relevant legal context at the beginning of the issue.

You may present the law in a broad context, such as "corporations," or a narrow one, such as a specific section of a statute. Include the specific jurisdiction and the area of law.

For Example

	(jurisdiction)	*(area)*
• Under	Arizona	probate law
• Under	Ariz. Rev. Stat. § 13-1303	unlawful imprisonment

The law component of the issue consists of either enacted law or case law. As defined in Chapter 1, the term **enacted law** includes any constitutional law or rule or enactment of a legislative body, such as a statute, ordinance, or regulation. **Case law** refers to any court-made doctrine, law, rule, principle, test, or guide.

A. Issue Based on Case Law

When an issue is based on case law, do not cite only a single case, because the case law is usually based on a group or body of cases and generally, no single case encompasses the relevant law. It is sufficient to present the law with a short introductory phrase that includes the jurisdiction and the area of the law. The easiest format follows:

	(jurisdiction)	*(area)*
Under	New Mexico's	corporation law
Applying	Utah's	emotional distress law
According to	Indiana's	doctrine of res ipsa loquitur
In light of	California's	definition of confinement in false imprisonment actions

However you state it, the description should be as focused and specific as possible. The goal is to inform the reader, as precisely as possible, of the area of law involved in the dispute. Therefore, such broad statements as, "According to Colorado case law . . ." or "Under case law . . ." are generally not acceptable. Such statements are so broad as to be meaningless. The reader is given no direction about which area of the law is involved in the dispute.

Along these same lines, a specific description is preferable to a broad one.

For Example

- "Under Wyoming's definition of oppressive conduct by majority shareholders . . ." is preferable to "Under Wyoming corporation law. . . ."

- "Applying Georgia's definition of consideration . . ." is preferable to "Applying Georgia contract law. . . ."

- "Under California's law of trespass to chattels . . ." is preferable to "Under California tort law. . . ."

Again, the key is to be as specific and focused as possible when describing the area of the law. The greater the specificity of the legal description, the better the reader understands what precisely is at issue in the dispute. If you are using a broad description such as "torts," reexamine the issue to determine if a narrower focus such as false imprisonment, battery, and so on can be applied.

B. Issue Based on Enacted Law

You may present an issue based on enacted law, such as a constitutional provision or statute, in several ways. The various ways may include a specific citation, a title, and/or a description.

For Example

      (citation)   *(title)*
- "According to N. Wash. Code § 20-40-1, kidnapping. . . ."

              (title paraphrased)   *(description)*
- "Under the New Washington kidnapping statute, which includes intent to confine as an element of kidnapping. . . ."
                (title paraphrased)
- "In light of the provisions of the involuntary dissolution of corporations statute, N. Wash. Corp. Code § 56-7-14, . . ."
              (citation)

The goal of clearly, completely, and concisely communicating the issue governs the choice or combination of choices selected. This, in turn, is governed by the complexity of the issue and the degree to which the description conveys the necessary information.

1. Enacted Law—Citations

Is it necessary or advisable to include the **citation** in the statement of the issue? Some believe the inclusion of the citation clutters the issue, arguing that it is not necessary because the citation can be determined by referring to the analysis section of the memorandum. Others believe the inclusion of the citation is, if not required, at least advisable. One thing scholars and practitioners agree upon is that a citation alone in a statement of the issue is never appropriate. Whereas a citation in the statement of the issue focuses the reader on the exact section of the law in dispute, allowing the reader to immediately refer to that section if necessary, a citation alone leaves the reader without any way to know what area, type, or even broad topic of law in involved.

When the citation is included in the statement of the issue, a subsequent researcher who is reviewing a memo from the memo files can, by referring to the issue, tell what specific law is discussed in the memo. By merely referring to the issue, the researcher knows if the memo involves the exact same law as the law being researched. Or, when there are multiple memos in a particular client file that deal with interrelated laws, the researcher can retrieve a particular memo involving a particular law by looking at the statement of the issue alone. More commonly, use of the search or find function in computer programs allows researchers to quickly find specific memos or documents involving a specific law, if the citation is included in the statement of the issue.

For Example

A researcher is checking the office memorandum files to determine if any research has been conducted on section 956.05(b) of the state's corporation statutes. If the citation is included in the issue, a mere glance at the issue tells the researcher if the memo involves the same statute. The researcher's time is saved by not having to read the body of the memo to determine if it is on point.

In some instances, the firm may require or prefer the inclusion or exclusion of the citation in the issue. In the case of a court brief, the court rules may determine the answer to that question. If the choice is yours, do what works. If the length or complexity of the issue precludes use of the citation, then leave it out.

Keep in mind the following rules when using a citation:

1. Use the proper citation form. A summary of citation form is presented at the end of Chapters 3 through 8.
2. Do not use a citation alone. In addition to a citation, a title or description is necessary to adequately inform the reader of the legal context of the issue.

For Example

Incorrect: "Under Ariz. Rev. Stat. § 13-3102, is an ordinary pocket knife a deadly weapon?"
Correct: "Under Arizona's misconduct involving weapons statute, Ariz. Rev. Stat. sec. 13-3102, is an ordinary pocket knife a deadly weapon?"

2. Enacted Law—Titles and Descriptions

Whereas citations should not be used without a title or description, you can use a title or description without a citation when describing enacted law. **Titles** and **descriptions** provide the amount of information sufficient to inform the reader of the legal context of the issue. Although the citation is not required, its inclusion may be advisable for the reasons discussed in the previous section.

A title of a constitutional section, statute, and so on, is a heading that provides the name by which an act or section is individually known. A description is a brief summary of the relevant portions of the act and may include part of the title.

For Example

Examples of titles:

- Ariz. Rev. Stat. § 13-3102. Misconduct involving weapons; defenses; classification; definitions
- Cal. Corp. Code § 1800. Verified complaint; plaintiffs; grounds; intervention by shareholder or creditor; exempt corporations

Examples of descriptions:

- "Under the Arizona statute that prohibits possessing a deadly weapon on school grounds, . . ."
- "In light of the provisions of the California corporation statute that applies to lawsuits against corporations and intervention by shareholders, . . ."

When using a title or description of enacted law, the guiding principle is whether it provides the reader with enough information to know the legal context of the issue. The title alone may provide sufficient information. The terms from the titles in the following example are in italic.

For Example

- "Applying the provisions of Maryland's *kidnapping* statute, . . ."
- "Under California's *holographic wills* statute, . . ."

Occasionally, the title may require modification. You may need to add or delete words to enhance clarity and readability. In the following examples, the title is presented followed by the modified statement of the issue containing additional language.

For Example

- Limitation of actions. (Title of N.M. Stat. Ann. § 41-1-2.) "Under the limitation of action provisions of New Mexico's wrongful death statute, . . ."
- Holographic wills; requirements. (Title of Cal. Prob. Code § 6111.) "According to the requirements of the holographic wills section of the California statutes, . . ."

Sometimes it is necessary to delete language from the title because it is not relevant to the issue or needed to enhance clarity. In the following examples, the title is presented first, followed by the modification containing fewer words.

For Example

- Verified complaint; plaintiffs; grounds; intervention by shareholder or creditor; exempt corporations. (Title of Cal. Corp. Code § 1800.) "Under the California corporation statute that allows shareholder intervention in dissolution actions, . . ."
- Writing required—witnesses, competency, interest. (Title of Ind. Code § 29-1-5-2.) "In light of the requirements of the Indiana wills statute that governs witness competency, . . ."

Comment: In these examples, "exempt corporations, interest" and other words were deleted because these terms, although included in the title, are not relevant to the issue in the case.

If the title of a statute or law does not provide the required information, or if it is necessary to emphasize a particular aspect or element of the statute or law, the use of a description may be appropriate. In the following examples, the title is presented first, followed by an example.

For Example

- Nuncupative wills. (Title of Ind. Code § 29-1-5-4.) "Under the Indiana statute providing that an oral will does not revoke an existing written will, . . ."
- Limitations of actions. (Title of N.M. Stat. Ann. § 41-1-2.) "Under New Mexico's wrongful death statute, which requires that an action be brought within three years of the date of death, . . ."
- Ski area sign requirements. (Title of Wash. Rev. Code § 70.117.010.) "Under the Washington statute that requires a resort to post a notice at the top of closed trails, . . ."

As mentioned, there are no rules mandating use of a particular format when composing the legal component of the issue. The unwritten rule, however, is to keep focused on the goal:

- Is the information included sufficient to provide the reader with the specific legal context of the issue?
- Is the legal component of the issue stated narrowly enough that the reader will not have to look elsewhere (in the analysis portion of the memorandum or in the statutes) to determine what precise area of the law is in dispute?

C. Format of the Law Component

There are two basic formats to choose from when presenting the **law component of the issue**:

1. The jurisdiction or citation followed by the title or description
2. The title or description followed by the jurisdiction or citation

For Example

Jurisdiction or citation followed by title or description:

      (jurisdiction)   *(title)*
- "Under the New Mexico wrongful death statutes, . . ."

      (jurisdiction)   *(description)*
- "Under the Washington statute that requires a resort to post a notice at the top of closed trails, . . ."

      (citation)   *(title)*
- "According to Ind. Code § 35-42-3-3, kidnapping, . . ."

      (citation)   *(description)*
- "Under Cal. Civ. Proc. Code § 340, which establishes a one-year statute of limitations in slander cases, . . ."

For Example

Title or description followed by jurisdiction or citation:

      (title)   *(jurisdiction)*
- "According to the wrongful death provisions of the Colorado statutes, . . ."

      (description)
- "In light of the requirement that drivers carry proof of insurance under California law, . . ."

      (jurisdiction)

      (title)   *(citation)*
- "Under the kidnapping statute, Ind. Code § 35-42-3-3, . . ."

      (description)
- "Under the statute that requires skiers to ski within the range of their ability Wash. Rev. Code § 70.117.020, . . ."

      (citation)

V. ISSUE—QUESTION COMPONENT

The question component is really what the issue is about. What legal question is being raised by the facts? In the formula adopted in this chapter, the **question component** follows the law component. It must do the following:

1. Relate to or concern the specific law included in the law component
2. Present the specific legal question raised by the facts
3. Link the law with the facts

In the following examples, the question component is italicized. The linking verbs are boldfaced.

For Example

- Under New York landlord-tenant law, ***does*** *a landlord* **breach** *his duty to provide a habitable residence* when he fails to provide air conditioning?

- Under Cal. Civ. Proc. Code § 340, which establishes a one-year statute of limitations in slander cases, ***did the statute of limitations*** **begin** *to run* when the newsletter was printed, or when the newsletter was distributed to the customers?

- According to the statute governing oppressive conduct, Cal. Corp. Code § 1800, ***does a majority shareholder*** **engage** *in oppressive conduct* when he refuses to issue dividends while providing himself with bonuses equal to twice his salary?

- Under the Colorado law governing ski resorts, *is a resort* **responsible** *for warning* skiers of hazardous areas between ski runs?

Note that in all the preceding examples, the question specifically relates to the law included in the issue. Note, also, that the question links the law to the facts. This connection may be created through the use of **linking verbs**. Linking verbs show a relationship between a subject and the part of the sentence following the verb. In the instance of statements of the issue, they link the law to the facts. There are many possible linking verbs, such as *constitute, establish*, and various forms of *to be* (e.g., *is, was*), *to become* (e.g., *become, became, has become, will become*), and *to seem* (*seemed, seems, has seemed, had seemed*). In drafting this component of the issue, the main focus is to ensure that the legal question raised by the facts is included. In other words, under the law included in the issue, is the precise legal question raised by the facts clearly presented?

VI. ISSUE—SIGNIFICANT OR KEY FACTS COMPONENT

The last section of the formula for writing an issue is the presentation of the significant or key facts. It is especially important to keep in mind the goals of clarity, completeness, and conciseness, because cases with multiple or complex facts often make these goals difficult to achieve. The **facts component of the issue** must do the following:

1. Be readable
2. Include key facts legally relevant to the law component
3. Set the factual scope of the legal question

The facts component should not be so complex that the reader has trouble understanding the issue.

It is always preferable to include all key facts. However, when there are multiple key facts, it may be necessary for the sake of clarity to take other steps, such as categorizing, condensing, or listing the facts. Examples of the key fact component follow.

For Example

All key facts included:

- According to the provisions of Washington's ski safety act, does a resort have a duty to warn skiers of ice hazards on expert runs?

- Under the holographic will statute, Colo. Rev. Stat. § 15-11-503, is a holographic will valid if it is handwritten by a neighbor at the direction of the testator, but not written in the testator's handwriting?

  Comment: Note that the facts are presented clearly and in a logical sequence.

For Example

Key facts condensed—some included and some referred to generally:

- Under Ohio's corporation law governing oppressive conduct, does oppressive conduct occur when a majority shareholder of a closely held corporation engages in several acts that may be harmful to a minority shareholder, such as refusing to issue dividends and firing the minority shareholder from her position in the corporation without a stated cause?

- Under New York's constitutional provision prohibiting cruel and unusual punishment, are conditions of confinement cruel and unusual when the confinement may be unhealthy in several ways, such as the total calories served each inmate daily being less than the recommended minimum, and the jail cells being kept at a temperature under 60 degrees in the winter?

For Example

Key facts presented in general categories:

- Under Indiana corporation law, does oppressive conduct occur when a majority shareholder engages in several actions that are beneficial solely to the majority shareholder and detrimental to the interests of the minority shareholders?

- Under Arizona's constitutional provision prohibiting cruel and unusual punishment, are conditions of confinement cruel and unusual when they are unsanitary, unsafe, and in violation of various health codes?

Comment: Take care to avoid distorting or misstating the issue when condensing or categorizing the key facts. In the previous two examples, assumptions are contained in the categorizations. As stated, the first issue formulation assumes the actions of the majority shareholder are solely beneficial to the majority shareholder, and the second assumes the conditions of confinement are unsanitary. To avoid these problems, present multiple or complex facts in the form of a list.

For Example

Key facts listed:

- According to the provisions of California corporation law, Cal. Corp. Code § 1800, does oppressive conduct occur when a majority shareholder:
  1. fires a minority shareholder from her job without stating a reason;
  2. refuses to issue dividends when the corporation has a cash surplus of more than $1,000,000 and there are no plans for use of the money by the business;
  3. triples his salary three times within one year and his salary already was twice the amount of similarly situated employees when the raises were given; and
  4. gives himself a $100,000 cash bonus without a stated reason for the bonus?

- Under the United States Constitution's prohibitions against cruel and unusual punishment, are conditions of confinement cruel and unusual when:
  1. the food is nutritionally deficient in that the total calories per meal are less than the recommended minimum;
  2. jail cells designed for one inmate currently house three inmates;
  3. jail cell temperatures are routinely kept below 60 degrees in the winter; and
  4. jail cells are roach- and ant-infested?

Remember, it is always best to include all key or significant facts in the fact component of the issue. If doing so would make the issue unreadable or lacking in clarity, however, employ one of the options presented in the preceding examples.

VII. ETHICS—OBJECTIVELY STATING THE ISSUE

The preceding sections discuss the structure of the issue. An additional matter to keep in mind when composing the issue is to state the issue objectively. To state objectively means to construct or write the issue in a manner that fairly and completely presents all the key facts without favoring an outcome.

Rule 3.3(a)(1) of the Model Rules of Professional Conduct provides that a lawyer should not make false statements of law or fact to a tribunal. Broadly interpreted, this means that matters should not be presented in a manner that may mislead the court. Therefore, when writing for the client, for the supervising attorney, and often for the court, state the issue objectively so that a conclusion is not suggested, and the reader is not misled. The purpose of legal analysis, whether in a letter to the client, an office legal memorandum, or a court brief, is to inform the reader how the law applies to a particular legal problem, not to prejudge or distort the law and its application.

There are several additional reasons why you should state the issue objectively:

1. A one-sided presentation of the facts or elimination of some unfavorable key facts can mislead the reader—and may result in disaster. Either the opposing side or the court will discover and point out the misrepresentation or omission.
2. Ultimately, the law will govern the issue, and usually no amount of creative phrasing will change the outcome. Provide the reader with an objective presentation of the facts, and let your legal argument do the persuading.
3. If the issue is presented in a biased or slanted manner, the reader may question the author's ability and credibility and discount the legal argument that follows.

For Example

"Applying Colorado's law of conversion, does conversion occur when an individual, with a known reputation as a thief and a burglary conviction, takes and uses his neighbor's electric saw without permission?"

Comment: The statement is not objective. The facts relating to the individual's reputation and conviction are prejudicial and nonrelevant. Readers will conclude either that you do not know what the relevant facts are, or that you are trying to influence them.

Restated objectively: "Applying Colorado's law of conversion, does conversion occur when an individual takes and uses his neighbor's electric saw without permission?"

For Example

"Under the Colorado ski act, does a resort have a duty to warn of an obviously dangerous ice hazard?"

Comment: In this example, assume these additional facts are left out: The skier was a novice skier using an expert ski run, and the nature and degree of the ice hazard have not been determined. The issue is not stated objectively for two reasons:

1. The ice condition is described in such a way as to lead the reader to a conclusion that it was dangerous.
2. A key fact is omitted: A novice skier was on an expert ski run. This fact could very well govern the outcome of the case. It may be that the ice condition is hazardous only to novice skiers, and since the run is an expert run, the resort does not have a duty to warn. Omission of this fact, which will come to light as the case progresses, only serves to mislead. The reader will conclude either that you are misstating the question with the intent to mislead or that you do not understand the law.

Restated objectively: "Under the Colorado Ski act, does a resort have a duty to warn a novice skier of ice conditions on an expert ski run?"

For Example

> "Under the United States Constitution's prohibitions against cruel and unusual punishment, are conditions of confinement cruel and unusual when the conditions are unsanitary and unhealthy?"
>
> *Comment:* The issue is stated both prejudicially and too broadly. It is prejudicial because it assumes that conditions are unsanitary and unhealthy. Whether the conditions are unsanitary and unhealthy is in dispute and has yet to be decided. The statement is too broad because the facts concerning the conditions are not included; instead, readers are just given conclusions about the facts. What are the factual conditions that are allegedly unsanitary and unhealthy? Are the jail cells unclean? Is the water unsafe to drink?
>
> *Restated objectively:* "Under the United States Constitution's prohibitions against cruel and unusual punishment, are conditions of confinement cruel and unusual when a jail cell is cleaned once a month, its toilet overflows daily, and its tap water is not potable?"

Always state the issue objectively. When in doubt, err on the side of completeness. If condensing or categorizing key facts results in a biased or distorted statement of the question, do not condense or categorize. It is better to have a long or complicated issue statement than a loss of credibility or misleading formulation of the issue.

In many instances, when the question is to be presented to a court in a court brief, it may be desirable to state the issue in a persuasive manner. This may be advantageous when you are trying to persuade the court to adopt a legal position or concept that is favorable to the client. In light of the provisions of Model Rule 3.3(a)(1), great care must be taken when constructing an issue persuasively to avoid misleading the court or misrepresenting the issue. The examples presented in this section point out some of the hazards.

Persuasive issue writing is generally applicable in the courtroom in oral argument or in trial and appellate briefs. It usually is not applicable in research and writing projects such as the preparation of an interoffice legal memorandum. The considerations involved in persuasive issue writing, and persuasive writing in general, will be addressed in Chapter 18.

VIII. GENERAL CONSIDERATIONS

There are several general considerations to keep in mind when drafting an issue.

A. Name

Do not identify people or events specifically by name. Specific names have no meaning to readers unless they are familiar with the case or unless they have read the body of the memorandum. A reader who retrieves a research memo from the office memo files probably will not be familiar with the names of the people or events.

For Example

> *Incorrect:* Under . . ., did oppressive conduct occur when Tom Hardin refused to issue a $3 dividend and gave himself a $20,000 bonus?
>
> *Correct:* Under . . ., does oppressive conduct occur when a majority shareholder refuses to issue dividends and grants himself a $20,000 bonus?

Notice in the example above, the correct construction of the statement of the issue refers to the individual by the descriptive term relevant to their position (majority shareholder) and the law involved. Using descriptive terms related to a person's status in the case (plaintiff, defendant, respondent, petitioner), their position or title (shareholder, police officer, parent) is the best practice. This is particularly true when the person's status or position is relevant to the key facts and the particular area of law or legal topic at issue.

B. Approach

Write the issue several times. Have an issue page in your research outline or material, and keep that page nearby. When you think of a way to state the issue (regardless of how broadly or poorly phrased), write it down on the issue page so your ideas are not lost.

Even your poorly drafted constructions of the issue may contain something valuable. You may ultimately have a page full of various formulations of the issue. The final draft may require a combination of the various initial drafts, and having them all in one place may help you put together that combination. See Chapter 15 for a discussion of the use of an outline when drafting the issue.

The following is a basic approach to drafting an issue:

1. State the question in the context of the general area of law, for example, "Was there false imprisonment?"
2. Identify the specific law that applies.
3. List all the key facts.
4. Put the elements in the sequence recommended in this chapter.

LAW	QUESTION		FACTS
Under	is		when
In light of	did	exist	when
According to	does	constitute	when
Applying	was	required	when
Under	does	establish	when

C. Multiple Issues

Separate the issues. If the research involves several related or complex questions—**multiple issues**—break the questions into individual issues. Address them one at a time, applying the principles presented in this chapter. The law and facts may become confused if you attempt to work on more than one issue at a time.

For Example

The state criminal statute § 13-3102 provides: A person commits misconduct involving weapons by knowingly possessing a deadly weapon on school grounds. The client, a 15 year-old boy, had a small single blade pocketknife in his backpack. He had used the backpack several weeks ago when he went on an overnight fishing trip with his father. He forgot the knife was in his backpack. A separate section of the same statute makes an exception for small pocketknives, stating they are not deadly weapons. Further, the school resource officer's reason for searching the backpack was because another student said he saw a small pocketknife in the client's backpack the day before the search. The single fact pattern involves two separate issues:

1. Under Arizona Revised Statute § 13-3102 did the client "knowingly" possess a "deadly weapon" when he forgot a small pocketknife was in his backpack.

2. Under the Fourth Amendment requirement that school resource officers have specific and articulable facts to believe a student is violating a specific law, was the search unlawful when the item for which the officer searched was not a deadly weapon.

IX. KEY POINTS CHECKLIST: Stating the Issue

✓ Do not expect to accurately state the issue on the first draft or early in the research and analysis process. A broad statement may be all you can develop until you research and study statutory and case law. The key facts may not emerge until you have studied the case in depth.

✓ Always prepare a comprehensive or narrow presentation of the issue. Include in the statement of the issue the specific law, the legal question, and the key facts.

✓ Remember the format recommended in this chapter for presenting the issue: relevant law + legal question + key facts. It is easier to draft the issue in this format.

✓ If you get stuck, *start*. If you cannot seem to get started writing, just write anything about the issue on the issue page—that is, just start.

✓ Sometimes when you are stuck, it may be that you need to *stop*. Often, the brain needs time to assimilate information. Take a break. Sleep on it. The brain will continue to work while you rest, and after you wake, it may all fall into place.

✓ Remember, the issue is the legal question in dispute in the case and should be phrased as a question, not a statement, even though what you are drafting is frequently called an issue statement.

X. APPLICATION

The following are two examples that illustrate the principles discussed in this chapter. Each example includes a discussion of the application of those principles.

A. Chapter Hypothetical

This example is based on the memorandum assignment introduced at the beginning of the chapter. In the assignment, Mary Strate, the legal assistant, has determined that the following are the key facts:

1. The state police were acting in good faith when they relied on the validity of the search warrant.
2. The evidence was seized pursuant to the execution of the warrant.
3. The warrant was improperly issued due to judicial error.

Mary's research reveals that the law governing the issue is the state court's adoption of the exclusionary rule. There are several ways to frame the issue:

a. "Should the evidence be suppressed?"
b. "Does Oregon's exclusionary rule require the suppression of the evidence?"

Comment: Both issues (a) and (b) are too broad. They are examples of a shorthand statement of the issue. Issue (a) is so broadly phrased that it is of little value to the reader. What law is involved? What facts? This statement of the issue could apply to any case involving the suppression of evidence. Issue (b) informs the reader of the applicable law but omits the facts necessary for resolution of the question. Both issues require additional reading and research to determine the law and facts involved in the dispute in the case.

c. "Does Oregon's exclusionary rule require the suppression of evidence seized by officials acting upon a warrant improperly issued due to judicial error?"

Comment: This construction of the issue is neither objective nor complete. It leaves out a key fact: The officers were acting in good faith when they relied on the validity of the warrant. This key fact is critical if the state's exclusionary rule has an exception that allows the admission of evidence when officers execute a warrant in the good-faith belief that it is valid. Failure to include this key fact misleads the reader and slants the question in favor of suppression.

d. "Under Oregon's exclusionary rule, must evidence be suppressed when it is seized by law enforcement officers acting in the good-faith belief that a warrant was valid and not issued without judicial error?"

Comment: This statement of the issue is complete. It identifies the law in question, includes all the significant or key facts necessary for resolution of the issue, and informs the reader of what legal question must be resolved. It meets the test presented at the beginning of the chapter: Does the reader, by reading the issue alone, know what specific factual dispute concerning which law is involved in this case?

B. Battery

The client, Steve, has been an avid fan of the state professional hockey team, the Hawks. Steve's good friend, Bill, is an even more avid fan of another state's professional hockey team, the Maples. Steve and Bill's teams played against each other mid-season, and Steve's team won. It was a physical game and Bill's team had far more penalty time than the Hawks.

After the game, Steve and Bill get into an argument over who should have won the game. Steve says Bill's team, the Maples, are lazy, sloppy, and that if they had any skill, they would not play as dirty and would have had less penalties. Losing control, Bill punches Steve in the mouth. Steve suffers two broken teeth and two chipped teeth. The broken teeth had to be capped. He also suffered a cut lip that requires five stitches.

His dental bill totals $5,000 and he misses 4 full days of work, plus he had to miss 3 half days of work for follow-up dental work to cap the broken teeth. He had to eat soft or liquid foods for a week, and his face remained swollen for two weeks. He also needed pain medication and was uncomfortable for two weeks. Assume this altercation took place in Illinois. Some of the ways the issue can be framed are as follows:

    a. "Can Steve recover his medical expenses?"
    b. "Under Illinois law, did a battery occur?"

Comment: These issues are incomplete and too broadly framed. Issue (a) is of little value, as it provides the reader with no information or guidance as to the facts of the case. Stated this way, the issue could apply to a thousand cases. Issue (b) provides the law but no facts; it too could apply to any battery case—civil or criminal. Neither issue communicates the specific law or facts in dispute in this case.

    c. "Under Illinois law, does a battery occur when an individual maliciously punches another person in the face, intending to cause the person harm?"

Comment: This issue is incomplete, inaccurate, and not objective. It leaves out the critical key facts that Steve was was harmed. It is inaccurate because it does not identify if this is a civil tort law or criminal law matter. It is not objective because it characterizes Bill as malicious and intending to cause harm. It is a prejudicial formulation of the issue that misleads the reader and is slanted against Bill.

    d. "Under Illinois tort law, does a battery occur when an individual punches another person in the face during an argument causing a cut lip, broken and chipped teeth needing dental work, and the injured person misses work and has medical expenses?"

Comment: Issue (d) is complete. The reader is provided with the question, the law, and all the key facts necessary to determine what must be decided under the law. Without any additional reading or research, the reader is informed of the specific legal and factual context of the dispute.

Summary

Writing the issue is one of the most critical tasks in the legal research and writing process. It should communicate what is in dispute. To accomplish this task, it is necessary to completely, concisely, and clearly identify the question to be resolved. A poorly crafted issue either fails to inform because it is too broad, or misleads because it adds improper information or omits critical information.

There are two ways to state an issue:

1. A shorthand or broad statement presents the question in the context of the general area of the law.
2. A comprehensive or narrow statement presents the specific question in the context of the relevant law and specific facts.

A broad statement may be appropriate when the readers are thoroughly familiar with the case. A comprehensive or narrow statement is the appropriate form for use in research and writing. It specifically identifies all the essential information necessary to understand and resolve the dispute.

Several different formats may be followed when crafting the issue, but the recommended format is as follows:

relevant law + legal question + key facts

There are several reasons for this recommendation. First, it follows the standard legal analysis format in which the presentation of the law is followed by the application of the law to the specific facts. Second, it is easier to draft an issue when the facts are inserted at the end.

When drafting the issue, always include the jurisdiction and area of the law in the law component. The question portion must introduce the specific law presented in the law component. The fact section should present all key facts if possible, although it may sometimes be necessary to categorize or condense the key facts.

Present the issue objectively and do not phrase it so as to mislead the reader or misrepresent the nature of the dispute. A well-crafted issue meets the following test: Does the reader, by reading the issue alone, know what specific legal question, concerning what law, involving what facts, is in dispute in the case?

Quick References

Internet Resources

As of the date of publication of this text, there were no websites dedicated specifically to stating the issue. However, because the topic of how to state the issue is often discussed along with issue identification, the websites mentioned in the Internet Resources section of Chapter 10 may prove helpful. Also, law school websites often have resources and guides related to stating the issue.

Exercises

ASSIGNMENT 1

Distinguish between a broad and narrow formulation of an issue. Describe the elements of a narrow statement of an issue. Why is it important to phrase an issue narrowly when engaged in legal writing?

ASSIGNMENT 2

The statute is Cal. Corp. Code § 1800. The title of the statute is, "Verified complaint; plaintiff; grounds; intervention by shareholder or creditor; exempt corporations." The statute applies in dissolution cases and includes the grounds for dissolving a corporation. The dispute involving this corporation statute is whether there are grounds for dissolution of the corporation.

Part A

Draft the law component of the issue, including the relevant portion of the title.

Part B

Draft the law component of the issue and include the relevant portion of the title and the citation.

Part C

Draft the law component of the issue using a description that focuses on an element of the statute. The element in question is the requirement of shareholder deadlock. Assume the statute provides that a court may dissolve a corporation in the event of a dispute among the shareholders only if there is shareholder deadlock.

Part D

To the answer in Part C, add the statutory citation.

ASSIGNMENT 3

The statute is Georgia Code Ann. § 11-2-314. The title of the statute is "Implied warranty: merchantability; usage of trade." The question is whether there is an implied warranty of merchantability. In the following problems, draft a comprehensive or narrow statement of the issue in the relevant law + legal question + key facts format; for the law component, use the Georgia statute. When drafting the law component, include the citation and a relevant portion of the title.

Part A

Alice purchases a new toaster from a booth at the flea market. The market is open year-round, and the same products are always sold at the booth.

Part B

Alice purchases a new toaster at a garage sale.

Part C

Alice becomes ill from a soft drink purchased at a local fast-food restaurant.

Part D

Alice, while shopping at the flea market, purchases a soft drink from a vendor at the market. She becomes sick from the drink.

ASSIGNMENT 4

Perform Assignment 3 using a description of the title when drafting the law component, rather than a relevant portion of the title.

ASSIGNMENT 5

Perform Assignment 3 using your state commercial code statute governing the warranty of merchantability and the sale of goods.

ASSIGNMENT 6

In the following parts:

- Draft a shorthand or broad statement of the issue.
- Draft a comprehensive or narrow statement of the issue in the relevant law + legal question + key facts format. For the law component in Parts A through C, use either the relevant section of your state's probate code or New Wash. Prob. Code § 60, Exception Pertaining to Holographic Wills. Assume this statute applies to all the fact situations presented in Parts A through C. For each part, draft the issue twice. One draft should contain the title or a description of the title. One draft should contain the title or description and the citation.

Part A

Key Facts: A will is handwritten. One-half is in the testator's handwriting, and the other half is in the handwriting of a witness. The will is properly witnessed.
Question: Is the will valid?

Part B

Key Facts: A will is handwritten. One-half is in the testator's handwriting, and the other half is in the

handwriting of a witness. It is witnessed by three witnesses, two of whom will inherit under the will.
Question: Is the will valid?

Part C

Key Facts: A will is handwritten. One-half is in the testator's handwriting, and the other half is in the handwriting of a witness. A witness, at the direction of the testator, signed the testator's name. The will was properly witnessed.
Question: Is the will valid?

ASSIGNMENT 7

In the following parts:

- Draft a shorthand or broad statement of the issue.
- Draft a comprehensive or narrow statement of the issue in the relevant law + legal question + key facts format.

Part A

Key Facts: An individual on a radio talk show states that all the town's psychiatrists are frauds.
Question: Is the statement "concerning" the plaintiff (a local psychiatrist)?
Law: Assume the law of slander in your jurisdiction is case law (court made) and one of the elements is that the statement must concern the plaintiff.

Part B

Key Facts: Use the same facts as in the preceding problem, with the additional fact that the plaintiff is the only psychiatrist in the town.
Question: Same as in Part A.
Law: Same as in Part A.

ASSIGNMENT 8

For the following parts, identify the (a) relevant law, (b) question, and (c) key facts.

Part A

Can a bystander who witnesses the death of a victim from three blocks away recover for negligent infliction of emotional distress under Ohio law?

Part B

Does oppressive conduct occur, according to the provisions of the Texas Corporation Code, when a majority shareholder refuses to issue dividends, triples his salary, and grants himself excessive bonuses?

Part C

Whether a newspaper that publishes an article indicating that Tom Smith has criminal connections has committed libel according to Florida tort law.

Part D

Do law enforcement officers commit a battery when, while making a lawful arrest, they encounter resistance, use force to overcome that resistance, and continue to use force after the resistance ceases?

ASSIGNMENT 9

Using the content in Assignment 8, redraft the issues in the following format: relevant law + question + key facts.

ASSIGNMENT 10

Part A

The issue is: "Under Arizona statute § 13-1302, is a pocket-knife clearly not designed for lethal use, a deadly weapon?" Is the issue stated objectively? If not, explain why?

Part B

The issue is: "Will the court extend time for service?" Is the issue stated completely? If not, explain why.

Part C

The issue is: "Whether Linda Petersen, owner of Petersen Pilates, Inc. fitness center ("PPI") and developer of a unique personalized pilates training method, has a claim against Alexandria Dimitri, a former PPI employee, for misappropriation of a trade secret resulting from Ms. Dimitri's unauthorized use of a similar pilates training method at another fitness center."

Rewrite the issue to be more concise and to exclude information not relevant and necessary.

Chapter 12

Case Law Analysis—Is a Case on Point?

Outline

I. Introduction

II. Definition—On Point

III. On Point—Importance

IV. Determining If a Case Is On Point

V. Key Points Checklist: Is a Case On Point?

VI. Application

Learning Objectives

After completing this chapter, you should understand:

- What *on point* means in relation to case law
- The role and importance of a case being on point in legal analysis
- How to determine if a case is on point

"That bum has cheated us for the last time," David Simms said as he walked out the office door. David Simms and his brother, Don, had just finished their initial interview with Ms. Booth, the attorney who would handle their case. Their tale was one of financial abuse by their older brother, Steve.

Their father, Dilbert Simms, died in December 2007 and left his plumbing business, Simms Plumbing, Inc., to his three sons—Steve, Don, and David. Steve, who had been running the business since 2005, was left 52 percent of the stock. David and Don, who had never worked at Simms Plumbing and were employed in other occupations, were each left 24 percent.

As the majority shareholder, Steve completely controls the business. To date, he refuses to issue stock dividends even though the corporation has an accumulated cash surplus of $750,000.00. He has given himself three very large salary increases and several cash bonuses since his father's death. When questioned by David and Don about stock dividends, he tells them, *"You don't work in the business. You don't deserve any money out of it. If you want any money, you're going to have to work at the store, every day, just like I do."*

After this conversation, David and Don consulted the supervising attorney, Ms. Booth. They seek redress for the wrong they feel their brother has committed in refusing to issue dividends.

Ms. Booth directs the paralegal to find the applicable statute and the leading case on point in the jurisdiction. The statute, § 96-25-16 of the Business Corporation Act, provides that a court may order the liquidation of a corporation when a majority shareholder has engaged in oppressive conduct. The statute, however, does not define what constitutes oppressive conduct.

The hard part of the assignment is locating a case on point in the jurisdiction that defines or provides the elements of oppressive conduct. After an extensive search, the paralegal locates only one case dealing with oppressive conduct, *Karl v. Herald*. In this case, a husband and wife owned a small corporation in which the husband owned 75 percent of the stock and the wife owned 25 percent. When they divorced, he fired her from her salaried position of bookkeeper, took away her company car, and refused to issue stock dividends. The company was very profitable, had a large cash surplus, *and was clearly in a financial position to issue dividends. After the divorce, the husband gave himself a hefty salary increase. The court held that he had engaged in oppressive conduct in freezing his wife out of the corporation. It defined oppressive conduct as "any unfair or fraudulent act by a majority shareholder that inures to the benefit of the majority and to the detriment of the minority."*

Upon finding this case, several questions run through the paralegal's mind. Is this case on point? How does one determine if a case is on point? Why does it matter?

I. INTRODUCTION

Legal research, analysis, and writing are all related and are often part of a single process. Research locates the law, analysis determines how the law applies, and legal writing assembles and integrates the results into a usable form.

The focus of this chapter is on the application of case law to a legal question. It covers **case law analysis**—the analytical process you engage in to determine if and how the decision in a court opinion either governs or affects the outcome of a client's case. A case that governs or affects the outcome of a client's case is commonly referred to as being "on point."

Throughout this chapter, reference is made to single issues and single rules of law or legal principles when discussing court opinions and clients' cases. The focus is on how to determine if a single issue, addressed in a court opinion, is on point and therefore may affect or govern an issue in a client's case. Always be aware that there are often multiple issues and legal rules or principles involved in court opinions, some of which may be on point, and therefore govern the outcome of an issue in the client's case, and some of which may not be on point. When determining if an opinion is on point, follow the steps discussed in this chapter separately for each issue in a client's case.

The chapter opens with a definition of the term *on point*, followed by a discussion of the importance of locating a case on point and the process of determining if a case is on point.

II. DEFINITION—ON POINT

Throughout this chapter, the term *on point* is used to describe a court opinion that applies to the client's case. What do "on point" and "applies to the client's case" mean? A case is **on point** if the similarity between the key facts and the rule of law or legal principle of the court opinion and those of the client's case is sufficient for the court opinion to govern or provide guidance to a later court in deciding the outcome of the client's case. In other words, does the court opinion govern or guide the resolution of an issue in the client's case? Is the court opinion precedent? If a case is on point, it is precedent. The terms *on point* and *precedent* are often used interchangeably.

III. ON POINT—IMPORTANCE

Before discussing the process involved in determining if a case is on point, it is helpful to understand why you must engage in the process of finding past court decisions that affect the client's case. Why is it important?

As discussed in Chapter 1, case law is a major source of law in the legal system. Through case law, courts create law and interpret the language of constitutions, enacted law, and court rules. The determination of whether a case is on point is important because of two doctrines covered in Chapter 1: precedent and stare decisis. The doctrines of precedent and stare decisis govern and guide the application of case law and thereby provide uniformity and consistency in the case law system. They help make the law more predictable. A brief revisiting of these doctrines is helpful in obtaining an understanding of the process involved in determining whether a case is on point.

A. Precedent

Precedent is an earlier court decision on an issue that governs or guides a subsequent court in its determination of an identical or similar issue based on identical or similar key facts. This chapter identifies the steps involved in determining when a case may be either mandatory or persuasive precedent. A case is precedent (on point) if there is a sufficient similarity between the key facts and rule of law or legal principle of the court opinion and the matter before the subsequent court.

For Example

The state collections statute provides that efforts to collect payment for a debt must be made in a reasonable manner. The statute does not define "reasonable." In the case of *Mark v. Collections, Inc.*, the supreme court of the state held that it is not reasonable, within the meaning of the collection statute, for a bill collector to make more than one telephone call a day to a debtor's residence, nor is it reasonable to make calls before sunrise or after sunset.

The facts of the case were that the collector was making seven calls a day, some of which were after sunset.

The facts of the client's case are that a bill collector is calling the client six times a day between the hours of 9:00 a.m. and 5:00 p.m. The ruling in *Mark v. Collections, Inc.* applies as precedent to the issue of whether the frequency of the collector's calls is unreasonable and, therefore, in violation of the act. The *Mark* case is sufficiently similar to the current case to apply as precedent. Both cases involve:

- The same law—the collections statute

- The same question—a determination of when the frequency of the telephone calls constitutes unreasonable conduct within the meaning of the act

- Similar key facts—six telephone calls per day and seven calls per day

The application of *Mark* as precedent guides the court in its resolution of the question, presented in the client's case, of whether six calls a day constitute a violation of the act. The court in *Mark* held that more than one call a day is unreasonable. Therefore, the six calls a day in the client's case are unreasonable in light of the holding in the *Mark* case. This example is referred to as the "collections" example in this chapter.

B. Mandatory Precedent

Mandatory precedent is precedent from a higher court in a jurisdiction. If a court opinion is on point—that is, if it is precedent—the doctrine of stare decisis mandates that the lower courts in the jurisdiction follow that opinion. In the previous example, if the decision in *Mark v. Collections, Inc.* is the ruling of the highest court in the jurisdiction, the lower courts in the jurisdiction must follow it.

C. Persuasive Precedent

Persuasive precedent is precedent that a court may look to for guidance when reaching a decision, but is not bound to follow. Courts in other jurisdictions may, however, choose to refer to and use another court's opinion when deciding a similar case.

For Example

In the collections example, if the *Mark* decision was from an Arizona court, courts in Colorado are not bound to follow the *Mark* decision, but they may choose to do so,

Similarly, if the decision was by a lower court in the jurisdiction, such as a trial court, then a higher court, such as a court of appeals, is not bound to follow the decision. A higher court may, however, choose to refer to and use a lower court decision as guidance when deciding a similar case.

For Example

In the collections example, if the *Mark* decision was from the general jurisdiction trial court, the state Court of Appeals is not bound to follow the decision. However, the Court of Appeals may decide to follow the decision.

D. Stare Decisis

The doctrine of **stare decisis** is a basic principle of the case law system that requires a court to follow a previous decision of that court or a higher court in the jurisdiction when the current decision involves issues and key facts similar to those involved in the previous decision. In other words, the doctrine of stare decisis requires that similar cases be decided in the same way; it mandates that cases that are precedent should be followed. The doctrine applies unless there is good reason not to follow it.

For Example

Regarding the *Mark* case discussed in the collections example, stare decisis is the doctrine holding that once it is determined that the *Mark* case is precedent, the lower courts in the jurisdiction must follow it unless good cause is shown for not doing so. It is mandatory precedent.

E. The Role of Precedent

Without the doctrines of stare decisis and precedent, there would most likely be chaos in the court decision-making process. Judges and attorneys would not have guidance about how matters should be decided. Similar cases could be decided differently based upon the whims and diverse beliefs of judges and juries. These doctrines provide stability, predictability, and guidance for courts and attorneys. An individual can rely on a future court to reach the same decision on an issue as an earlier court when the cases are sufficiently similar.

With this in mind, it becomes clear why determining whether a case is on point is important and why a researcher needs to find a case that is on point:

1. The determination must be made before the case may apply as precedent and be used and relied upon by a court in its determination of how an issue will be decided. Note that if the court is unaware of the case, it may be necessary to bring the case to the court's attention.
2. Inasmuch as the court will consider precedent in reaching its decision, a researcher needs to find cases that are on point to guide the attorney as to how the issue in the client's case may be decided. Cases that are on point must be located and analyzed to determine what impact they may have on the decision in the client's case. Also, they must be analyzed to help the attorney determine what course of action to take. If a case that is on point indicates that the decision will most likely be against the client, it may be appropriate to pursue settlement, plea negotiations, or other options.

IV. DETERMINING IF A CASE IS ON POINT

The process of deciding if a court opinion is on point involves determining how similar the opinion is to the client's case. The more similar the court opinion is to the client's case, the more likely it is to be considered precedent; that is, the more likely it is that the rule or principle applied in the opinion will govern or apply to the client's case.

In Section II of this chapter, a case is defined as being on point if there is a sufficient similarity between the key facts and rule of law or legal principle of the court opinion and those of the client's case. Therefore, for a case to be on point and apply as precedent, there are two requirements:

1. The significant or key facts of the court opinion must be sufficiently similar to the key facts of the client's case; or, if the facts are not similar, the rule of law or legal principle applied in the court opinion must be so broad that it applies to many diverse fact situations.
2. The rule of law or legal principle applied in the court opinion must be the same or sufficiently similar to the rule of law or legal principle that applies in the client's case. *Rule of law* and *legal principle*, as used here, include any constitutional, legislative, or case law provision, act, doctrine, principle, or test relied on by the court in reaching its decision.

If these two criteria are not met, the court opinion is not on point and may not be used as precedent for the client's case. The two-step process presented in Exhibit 12-1 is recommended for determining if the two requirements are met.

	For a court opinion to be on point and apply as precedent, the following requirements must be met:
STEP 1	**Are the key facts sufficiently similar for the case to apply as precedent?** The key facts of the court opinion must be sufficiently similar to the key facts of the client's case. If the facts are not similar, the opinion will serve as precedent only if the rule of law or legal principle is broad enough to apply to other fact situations, including the client's.
STEP 2	**Are the rules or principles of law sufficiently similar for the case to apply as precedent?** The rule of law or legal principle applied in the court opinion must be the same or sufficiently similar to the rule of law or legal principle that applies in the client's case.

© Cengage

Exhibit 12-1   Steps in Determining if a Case Is On Point.

A. Step 1: Are the Key Facts Sufficiently Similar?

The first step in the analysis process is to determine if the significant or key facts in the court opinion are sufficiently similar to the key facts in the client's case for the court opinion to apply as precedent. This is accomplished by comparing the key facts of the court opinion with those of the client's case. A key fact is a fact so essential that it affects the outcome of the case. You must identify the key facts before you can determine if a case is on point. If there is not a sufficient similarity between the key facts of the client's case and the key facts of a court opinion, the opinion usually cannot be used as precedent—that is, it is not on point.

You may encounter two situations when comparing the key facts of a client's case and a court opinion:

1. The key facts are directly on point—that is, they are identical or nearly identical.
2. The key facts are different.

1. Identical or Nearly Identical Key Facts

When the **key facts** in a given court opinion and the client's case are **identical** (or nearly identical), the opinion is on point factually and can be a precedent that applies to the client's case if the requirements of step 2 are met. The phrase **on all fours** is often used to describe such opinions: those in which the facts of the opinion and of the client's case, and the rule of law that applies, are identical or so similar that the court opinion is clearly on point. When such an opinion is the opinion of a higher court in a jurisdiction, it is mandatory precedent that the lower courts in the jurisdiction must follow.

For Example

In the case of *Davis v. Davis*, Ms. Davis had sole custody of her two daughters, ages 8 and 10 years. Ms. Davis had a boyfriend who occasionally stayed overnight at her home. The children were aware of the overnight visits. Mr. Davis, her former husband, filed a motion with the court asking for a change of custody. He based his claim solely upon his ex-wife's alleged "immoral conduct." No evidence was presented indicating how the overnight visits affected the children. The trial court granted a change of custody.

The court of appeals overturned the trial court, ruling that "mere allegations of immoral conduct are not sufficient grounds to award a change of custody." The court required the presentation of evidence showing that the alleged immoral conduct harmed the children.

Assume, for the sake of this example, that the client was divorced one year ago and granted sole custody of his two minor daughters, ages 8 and 12 years. On occasion, his girlfriend stays overnight, and the children are aware of the overnight visits. The client's former spouse has filed a motion for change of custody alleging that his immoral conduct is grounds for a change of custody. She does not have evidence that the children have been harmed or affected negatively.

Clearly, the requirements of step 1 are met. *Davis v. Davis* is factually on point, and is therefore a precedent that applies to the client's case. Note that the requirements of step 2 are also met. The same legal principle is being applied in the court opinion and the client's case: Mere allegations of immorality are not sufficient grounds for granting a change of custody. Step 2 addresses the requirement that the legal principles be sufficiently similar.

Although some of the facts are different—in the client's case, it is the father who has custody and his girlfriend who stays overnight, whereas in *Davis v. Davis* it was the mother who had custody and her boyfriend who stayed overnight—these facts are not key facts. The gender of the custodial parent and the gender of the person staying overnight are not key facts. The key facts are identical: occasional overnight visits, the children are aware of the visits, the children are preteen (the age of the children is always an important consideration), and no evidence was presented that the children are harmed by the visits. This example is referred to as the "custody" example throughout the remainder of this chapter.

It is rare to find instances in which the key facts are identical. Usually there is at least some difference in the key facts. When you find a case with identical facts that you determine is mandatory precedent, the holding may not support your client's position. It is difficult for a lower court not to follow the higher court's decision when it is so clearly on point. When an on point court opinion is in opposition to your client's case, it may be appropriate to pursue settlement, plea negotiations, or other options

2. Different Key Facts

When the key facts of the court opinion and the key facts of the client's case are not identical, the opinion *may* be on point and *may* apply as precedent. It depends on the degree of the difference. When you have **different key facts**, you must determine whether the differences are of such a nature or degree that they render the court opinion unusable as precedent. Use the following three-part process when making this determination (see Exhibit 12-2):

Part 1: Identify the similarities between the key facts.
Part 2: Identify the differences between the key facts.
Part 3: Determine if the differences are of such a significant degree that the opinion cannot apply as precedent.

Throughout this discussion of different key facts, assume that the requirements of step 2 have been met—that is, the rule of law applied in the court opinion is the same or sufficiently similar to the rule of law that applies in the client's case.

For Example

The client's case is the same as the custody example, except that instead of occasional overnight visits by the girlfriend, the girlfriend has moved in with the client. Is the case of *Davis v. Davis* on point?

To answer this question, perform the following steps:

a. Part 1: Identify the similarities between the key facts. In both the client's case and the *Davis* case:
   • The minor children are under the age of 12 years.
   • Someone is staying overnight with the custodial parent.
   • There is no showing that the children have been harmed by the conduct.
b. Part 2: Identify the differences between the key facts. The difference in the key facts is that in *Davis v. Davis*, the overnight visits were occasional. In the client's case, there is cohabitation rather than occasional overnight visits.
c. Part 3: Determine if the differences are of such a significant degree that the opinion cannot apply as precedent. To determine the significance of the differences, substitute the client's key facts for those of

Three-part process for determining if a case is on point when the key facts of the court opinion differ from the key facts of the client's case	
PART 1	Identify the similarities between the key facts.
PART 2	Identify the differences between the key facts.
PART 3	Determine if the differences are of such a significant degree that the opinion cannot apply as precedent.

© Cengage

Exhibit 12-2 Three-Part Process for Addressing Different Key Facts.

the court opinion. If the substitution of the key facts would result in a change in the outcome of the case, the court opinion cannot be used as precedent.

In this example, would the court in *Davis v. Davis* have reached the same conclusion if Ms. Davis's boyfriend had moved in with her? The answer is probably, because the same legal principle applies: Allegations of immoral conduct alone are not sufficient grounds to award a change of custody; there must be a showing that the conduct harmed the children.

As indicated in *Davis v. Davis*, an essential element necessary before a change of custody is granted is a showing of harm to the children. A key fact in the *Davis* decision was the lack of any showing of harm to the children. Both the court opinion and the client's case lack a showing of harm to the children; therefore, the principle applied in *Davis* should apply to the client's case even though the *Davis* opinion involved overnight visits and the client's case involves cohabitation.

You must be careful, however. There may be another statute or case law doctrine providing that cohabitation is *per se* harmful to children; that is, in cohabitation cases such as the client's case, the law presumes that cohabitation is harmful to the children. If this were the situation, the plaintiff would not need to establish harm in cohabitation cases such as the client's, and the *Davis* opinion would not be on point and could not be used as precedent. The difference in the key facts would be so significant that the substitution of the client's cohabitation fact for the *Davis* opinion's occasional overnight visits fact would change the decision reached by the court because a different statute would apply.

Four variations may be encountered when dealing with different key facts. These variations are summarized in Exhibit 12-3.

1. Minor differences in key facts—Some key facts are so insignificantly different that they clearly do not affect the use of a court decision as precedent.

For Example

If, in the custody example, the client's children were ages 9 and 11 years as opposed to 8 and 10 years, *Davis v. Davis* would still clearly apply as precedent. Although the age of the children is a key fact, a minor difference of one year in the ages of the children is not a significant difference in the key facts. If the client's children were several years older than the children in *Davis v. Davis*, such as ages 16 and 17, the age difference could be a major difference in the key facts, because a different standard might apply if the children were in their late teens.

2. Major difference in key facts, and the case is not on point—The following example presents a situation where the key facts of the court opinion and the key facts of the client's case are sufficiently different that the opinion is not on point and does not apply as precedent. The following example is referred to in this chapter as the "arrest" example.

Variations that may be encountered when dealing with different key facts
1. Minor differences in key facts—case on point
2. Major difference in key facts—case not on point
3. Major difference in key facts—case on point
4. Major difference in key facts—case on point, broad legal principle

© Cengage

Exhibit 12-3 Different Key Fact Variations.

For Example

In the court case of *State v. Thomas*, Mr. Thomas was handcuffed and taken to the police station after officers broke up a fistfight. Thomas was not read his rights at the scene of the fight. He was read his rights and formally arrested at the police station 30 minutes later. The court, ruling that he was under arrest when handcuffed at the scene, stated, "An arrest takes place when a reasonable person does not believe he is free to leave."

In the client's case, the client explains that the police handcuffed him and told him to stay in the hallway of the house while they executed a search warrant. He was not allowed to leave. It appears that the key facts regarding whether an arrest has taken place are nearly the same. In both the court opinion and the client's case, the individual was handcuffed and not free to leave. The critical difference in the facts is the context of the seizure of the individual. In *Thomas*, the seizure took place at the scene of a fight. No warrants were involved. In the client's case, the seizure took place during the execution of a search warrant.

Regarding the question of whether the client was under arrest when handcuffed and detained in the hallway, is *State v. Thomas* on point? The answer is no. Although the facts of the detention are similar, the difference in the context of the seizure is a critical key fact difference. There is other case law holding that a seizure during the execution of a search warrant is an exception to the rule stated in *Thomas*, and that such seizures do not constitute an arrest.

The other case law provides that a search warrant implicitly carries with it the authority to detain an individual for the purposes of the officer's safety and to determine if there is cause to make an arrest. Therefore, such detentions do not constitute an arrest within the meaning of the law. Because of this authority, the difference between the key facts of *Thomas* and the client's case is critical, and the case is not on point.

3. Major difference in key facts, but case is on point—A major difference in the key facts does not necessarily result in a determination that the case is not on point. The opinion may still be on point, but the outcome may be different. The legal principle applied by the court may still apply to the client's case, although its application may lead to a different result.

For Example

Suppose that in the custody example, there were an additional key fact in the client's case that the spouse seeking custody had evidence showing that the children were being harmed by exposure to the overnight visits. *Davis v. Davis* could still be on point, even though no evidence of harm to the children was presented in the *Davis* case. Although there is now a major difference between the key facts of the court opinion and the client's case, the court opinion may still apply as precedent and govern the outcome of the change-of-custody question.

The court in the *Davis* case concluded that there were not sufficient grounds to award a change of custody because *no evidence* was presented showing harm to the children. The same principle governing *Davis* governs the facts here: that is, allegations of immorality, *standing alone*, are not sufficient for an award of a change of custody; there must be a showing of harm to the children.

A corollary of the rule, however, is that if there is a *showing of harm* to the children, there may be sufficient grounds for a change of custody. It can be argued that when the key fact of evidence of harm is present, the corollary of the rule applies. Even though the facts of the court opinion and the client's case are different, the corollary applies to support a change of the custody award—a result different from the result reached in the court opinion.

---

4. Major difference in key facts, but case is on point, broad legal principle—Generally, if key facts are significantly different, it is highly probable that a different rule or principle applies and a court case will not apply as precedent. There are, however, instances in which the key facts are different, but the court opinion is on point because the rule of law or legal principle is so broad that it applies to many different fact situations. This situation is addressed in greater detail in the next subsection, IV. B, step 2.

For Example

The client was detained as part of a group of exotic dancers in a bar. The officers who detained the client were not executing a search or arrest warrant. Before informing the dancers they were under arrest, or in any way informing them what was taking place, the officers handcuffed them and moved them to a separate room where they were detained for more than an hour. They were clearly not free to leave. They were formally arrested two hours later, then taken to jail.

For Example

Regarding the question of whether the client was under arrest when detained in the room prior to arrest, *State v. Thomas* (presented in the arrest example) is probably on point. The definition of *arrest* presented in *Thomas* applies to the client's case even though the factual context of the seizure is different (handcuffing at a fist fight versus with a group at a bar). Applying that definition to the client's case results in the conclusion that an arrest occurred when the client was moved to a separate room and detained for more than an hour. A reasonable person in the client's situation would not believe she was free to leave. The definition of *arrest* presented in *Thomas* is so broad that it applies to a wide range of detention situations.

Note: Be careful. It is always preferable to locate an opinion that is as factually similar to the client's case as possible. The more dissimilar the key facts, the easier it is for the other side to argue that the differences are critical, the opinion is not on point, and therefore does not apply as precedent to the case at hand.

A difference in key facts should alert you to be careful and cause you to explore all potential legal avenues that may open due to the fact differences. Focus on the differences. Ask yourself, "Are they important?" Engage in counteranalysis (see Chapter 13). Conduct further research and update the case to determine if there are other cases more on point.

In summary, if the key facts are the same and the same rule of law applies (step 2), the court opinion is usually on point and can be considered precedent that applies to your client's case. If the key facts are different, either in part or totally, you must perform careful analysis to ensure that the factual differences are not so significant that they are detrimental to use of the court opinion as precedent.

B. Step 2: Are the Rules or Principles of Law Sufficiently Similar?

By applying the techniques presented in step 1, you determine whether the key facts of the court opinion are sufficiently similar to the key facts of the client's case for the opinion to apply as precedent factually. Once this is accomplished, half of the task is completed. Note that this is a two-step process, and you must complete both steps before you can determine whether a case is on point and apply it as precedent.

The second step is to determine whether the rule of law or legal principle applied in the court opinion is the same rule of law or legal principle that applies in the client's case. If it is not the same rule of law, is it sufficiently similar to the rule that applies in the client's case for the opinion still to apply as precedent? You may encounter two situations when performing step 2:

1. The rule or principle applied in the court opinion is the same rule or principle that applies in the client's case.
2. The rule or principle applied in the court opinion is different from the rule or principle that applies in the client's case.

1. Same Rule or Principle

If you determine that the key facts are sufficiently similar so that the court opinion can apply as precedent and the same rule of law is involved in both the opinion and the client's case, then the requirements of step 2 are met, and the case is on point. The rule of law comparison is simple. The rule of law applies in the client's case in the same way as it was applied in the court's opinion.

For Example

The client is charged with erecting a sign too close to the street in violation of § 19(b) of the Municipal Code, which prohibits the erection of a sign "unreasonably close" to any property line abutting a street. In your research, you come across the case of *City v. Guess*, which interprets "unreasonably close" as within 10 feet of the property line. If the key facts of the court opinion are sufficiently similar to the client's key facts, then the rule of law analytical process is simple. The same rule of law applied in the opinion applies to the client's case, in the same way: If the client's sign is within 10 feet of the property line abutting the street, it is in violation of the statute.

Note: Even when the same rule of law applies, its application in the client's case may result in an outcome different from the outcome in the court case. As discussed in the previous example on major differences in key facts, the same legal principle applied in both the client's case and the court opinion, but the result was different.

2. Different Rule or Principle

What if there is no court decision in your jurisdiction applying or interpreting the rule or legal principle that applies to your client's case? What if the rule or principle applied in the closest court opinion you can find is different from the rule or principle that applies in the client's case? Can the court opinion apply as precedent? The general rule is no. Usually this is obvious. For example, a child custody opinion can rarely be precedent for a murder case.

Again, there are exceptions. The court's interpretation of a provision of a legislative act or case law rule or principle may be so broad in scope that it applies to the different law or rule that governs the client's case. Keep in mind, though, that because the law or rule applied in the court opinion is different from that which applies to the client's case, the court opinion is at best *persuasive* precedent. The court hearing the client's case does not have to follow it—it is not *mandatory* precedent. The court has discretion and must be persuaded.

There are two areas to explore when considering these exceptions: legislative acts and case law rules or principles. In regard to these two areas, it is important to remember that the discussion involves only those situations in which there is *no court opinion* in the jurisdiction directly interpreting the same legislative act or case law rule that applies to the client's case.

a. Legislative Acts

A court opinion interpreting one legislative act may be used as precedent for a client's case that involves the application of a different legislative act when there is similarity in the following (see Exhibit 12-4):

1. The language used in the legislative acts
2. The function of the legislative acts

Requirements that must be met for a case to be on point when the legislative act applied in the court opinion differs from the legislative act that applies in the client's case
1. There is a similarity in the language used in the legislative acts.
2. There is a similarity in the function of the legislative acts.

© Cengage

Exhibit 12-4 Requirements When Different Legislative Acts Apply.

For Example

Three statutes have been adopted in the jurisdiction:

- Section 56 provides that an individual must be a resident of the county to be eligible to run for the position of county animal control officer.

- Section 3105 provides that an individual must be a resident of the county to be eligible to run for a seat on the county school board.

- Section 4175 provides that an individual must be a resident of the state to be eligible to run for the office of governor.

The term *resident* is not defined in any of the statutes, and none of the statutes establishes a length of residency requirement. The only case in the jurisdiction that defines the term *is Frank v. Teague,* a case involving § 3105. In this case, the court ruled that to be eligible to run for a seat on the school board, the candidate must have been a resident of the county of the school board district for a minimum of three months immediately prior to the election. This example is referred to in this chapter as the "residence" example.

The client, a resident of the county for three and one-half months, wants to run for the office of governor. Does the *Frank* opinion apply as precedent and support the client's claim of eligibility to run for the office of governor? The answer is probably not.

Although there is a similarity in the language of the statutes, in that both use the term *resident,* there is not a similarity in their function. The considerations involved in determining the length of residence required as a prerequisite for eligibility to run for each office are quite different. The court's decision in *Frank,* imposing a three-month residency requirement for the school board position, may be based upon the court's determination that this is the amount of time an individual needs to become sufficiently familiar with the county to perform the duties of a school board member. The position of governor, however, involves different considerations. The office is statewide, and the court could conclude that a longer residency period is necessary for an individual to become sufficiently familiar with the state to adequately perform the duties of governor.

For Example

The client wants to run for the position of animal control officer. He has been a resident of the county for four months. In this situation, it is more likely that *Frank* will apply as precedent—that it is on point and supports the position that the client is eligible to run for animal control officer.

Again, both statutes use the same language, *resident.* They are more closely related in function, however, than the school board and governor statutes. Both involve countywide positions wherein the duties are focused on county concerns. It can be argued that no more time is required to become familiar with the county to perform the duties of animal control officer than is required to perform the duties of a school board member.

The court, following this line of reasoning, could conclude that the residency requirement for the position of animal control officer should not exceed the minimum residency set for a seat on the school board. It could, therefore, adopt the three-month standard established in the *Frank* case as the standard for the animal control officer statute.

Because the statutes are different, you are always open to a counterargument pointing out some critical difference in function between the statutes.

In this example, you could argue that the duties of animal control officer are much different from those of a school board member. The duties of the animal control officer require a great degree of familiarity with the geography of the county; therefore, a longer period of residency should be required to ensure that a candidate has sufficient time to become familiar with the county.

In every situation in which the statutes differ in function, even if they have some similarities, you can argue that the difference, no matter how slight, dictates that a court's interpretation of one statute in one case cannot apply to another statute in a different case.

The preceding examples involve statutes from the same state. All the statutes were passed by the same state legislature, and the court opinion came from a court in that state. What if, in the residency example, there is no case law in the state interpreting the term *resident*, and the *Frank v. Teague* opinion is a decision from another state interpreting a statute of that state that is identical or very similar to § 3105? Can *Frank* apply as precedent?

The answer is the same as the answer discussed in the previous examples. If there is sufficient similarity in language and function of the statutes, the opinion can apply as persuasive precedent. If there is not sufficient similarity, it cannot apply as precedent. As long as the court is convinced that the similarity is sufficient, it can apply.

Bear in mind that a decision from another jurisdiction is only persuasive precedent, and a court is more likely to adopt persuasive precedent from a court within the jurisdiction than from a court without. It is best to locate authority within your jurisdiction. Look out of state only if there is no opinion that could apply as persuasive precedent within your jurisdiction.

Realistically, it is always risky to argue that a court's interpretation of a provision of one statute applies as precedent for the interpretation of a provision of a different statute. You are always open to, and will probably have to fend off, counterarguments that the statutes are functionally different and that reliance on a particular court opinion is misplaced. Your position in such a situation is never solid. Always try to find another opinion or pursue other avenues of research.

b. Case Law Rule or Principle

The same principles discussed in the preceding section apply when attempting to use as precedent a court opinion interpreting a case law rule or principle. Can a court opinion interpreting a case law rule or principle apply as precedent for a client's case that requires the application of a different case law rule or principle? The requirements are similar to those mentioned in the preceding section. Are the case law rules or principles similar in language and function? A court opinion interpreting one case law rule or principle may be used as precedent for a client's case that involves the application of a different case law rule or principle when there is similarity in the following (see Exhibit 12-5):

1. The language used in the case law rules or principles
2. The function of the case law rules or principles

For Example

The jurisdiction recognizes the torts of intrusion and public disclosure of a private fact. Intrusion protects against the act of prying or probing into the private affairs of an individual, and public disclosure of a private fact protects against the act of publishing information concerning the private affairs of an individual. Both of these torts have been established by the highest court in the jurisdiction. There is no statutory law defining or governing the torts. One of the elements of the tort of intrusion is an act of prying or probing into the *private affairs* of the plaintiff. One of the elements of the tort of public disclosure of a private fact is the public disclosure of a fact concerning the *private affairs* of the plaintiff.

In the client's case, the client was having an affair with the wife of a city council member. A campaign rival of the client disclosed the existence of the relationship at a campaign rally. The campaign rival acquired the information from a campaign aide who obtained the information by peeking through the client's bedroom window.

The client wants to sue for public disclosure of a private fact. The question is whether the affair is a private fact.

The only case in the jurisdiction is *Claron v. Clark*, an intrusion case in which a private investigator, by means of a wiretap, discovered that the plaintiff was engaged in an affair. The court ruled that the term *private affairs* includes any sexual activity that takes place within the confines of an individual's residence.

Is the *Clark* opinion an intrusion case on point? Can it be precedent in the client's case, which involves a different tort (public disclosure of a private fact)? May it be used as precedent in the client's case to guide the court in its interpretation of the meaning of the term *private affairs*? There is a similarity in the elements of the torts; both use the term *private affairs*. Both torts are similar in function, in that they are designed to protect the private affairs and lives of individuals.

If the court is convinced that the similarities are sufficient, then the case may apply as precedent. It can always be argued, however, that because the torts are different, there is a difference in function, no matter how slight, that dictates that a court's interpretation of the one tort cannot apply to a different tort. In this case, it can be argued that prying is different from publication; therefore, the difference in the interest being protected in the torts is sufficient to prevent an interpretation of a term in intrusion from being used to interpret the same term in public disclosure of a private fact.

> **Requirements that must be met for a case to be on point when the case law rule or principle applied in the court opinion differs from the case law rule or principle that applies in the client's case**
>
> 1. There is a similarity in the language used in the case law rules or principles, and
>
> 2. There is a similarity in the function used in the case law rules or principles.

© Cengage

Exhibit 12-5 Requirements When Different Common Law Rules/Principles Apply.

Again, be careful. The same pitfalls exist here as when different legislative acts apply. A court opinion within the jurisdiction interpreting a different rule of law is only persuasive precedent. It is not mandatory precedent that must be followed. It is very easy to present a counterargument that the functions of the two doctrines are clearly different, so the court opinion cannot apply as precedent. Also, keep in mind that when the decision is from another jurisdiction, it is still only persuasive precedent, and a court is more likely to adopt persuasive precedent from within the jurisdiction than from without.

Note: It is always preferable to locate an opinion that applies a rule or legal principle that is the same as the rule or principle that applies in the client's case. If different rules or principles are involved, it is easier for the other side to argue that the opinion is not on point and, therefore, does not apply as precedent for the case at hand.

When different rules or principles are involved, you should conduct further research and update the case to determine if there are other cases more on point.

V. KEY POINTS CHECKLIST: Is a Case on Point?

✓ Focus on the key facts and the rule of law or legal principle of both the court opinion and client's case.

✓ When there are differences between the key facts of the court opinion and the client's case, carefully determine whether the differences are significant. Be aware, however, that different key facts may lead to the application of an entirely different law or principle despite other key fact similarities. The rule of law or legal principle, however, may be so broad that it applies to many different fact situations.

✓ Clearly identify the rule of law or legal principle that applies in the court opinion and in the client's case.

✓ When the rule of law applied in the court opinion is different from the rule that applies in the client's case, consider using the court opinion as precedent *only when there is no authority* interpreting or applying the rule or principle that applies in the client's case.

✓ Consider authority from another jurisdiction *only* when there is no authority from the jurisdiction in which the client's case arose.

✓ If in doubt about whether a fact is a key fact, continue your analysis until you are certain. Refer to the steps presented in Chapter 9.

✓ Follow your instincts. If an opinion does not appear to be on point but your intuition tells you it is on point, continue your analysis until you are certain. If you never reach the point of feeling certain, search elsewhere.

VI. APPLICATION

This section presents two examples illustrating the application of the principles presented in this chapter for determining when a case is on point.

A. Chapter Hypothetical

This example is based on the fact pattern presented at the beginning of this chapter. Returning to that problem, is the case of *Karl v. Herald* on point so that it applies as precedent for the client's case?

1. Are the Key Facts Sufficiently Similar?

The first step is to determine whether the key facts of *Karl v. Herald* are sufficiently similar to the client's case for *Karl* to apply as precedent—to be on point. Although the facts in *Karl* are somewhat different, they are sufficiently similar. In both cases, the corporation was in a position to pay dividends. In both cases, while refusing to pay dividends, the majority shareholder allegedly enriched himself through excessive raises and bonuses. In both cases, the minority shareholders were effectively prevented from benefiting by the corporation's success.

A difference in *Karl* is the plaintiff worked in the business. In the client's case, the brothers never worked in the business. This difference in the cases is not a key fact difference. The fact that the plaintiff in *Karl* worked in the business relates to her status as an employee, but does not relate to her status as a shareholder. In *Karl*, the court defined oppressive conduct as conduct against shareholders, not employees. The plaintiff's status as an employee may give rise to employee rights, but it is not related to her rights as a shareholder, and thus is not a key fact.

2. Are the Rules or Principles Sufficiently Similar?

Is there a sufficient similarity between the law that applies in *Karl v. Herald* and that which applies in the client's case for the case to be considered on point and apply as precedent? The same statute, § 96-25-16 of the Business Corporation Act, applies to both the court opinion and the client's case. Both cases involve allegations of oppressive conduct by a majority shareholder against a minority shareholder and are governed by the same section of the statute.

In the *Karl* opinion, *oppressive conduct* was defined as "any unfair or fraudulent act by a majority shareholder that inures to the benefit of the majority and to the detriment of the minority." The client's case also involves questions of oppressive conduct by the majority shareholder and is governed by the same definition. Just as in *Karl*, there is alleged unfair conduct by the majority shareholder that inures to the benefit of the majority and to the detriment of the minority. There are no major differences between *Karl* and the client's case that restrict the application of *Karl* as precedent.

Note: What if you concluded that *Karl* was not on point, but it was the only case in the jurisdiction that discusses oppressive conduct? You would need to be sure to analyze the case in the memorandum to your supervisor and explain why the case is not on point.

B. Libel Case

The following fact situation and court opinion illustrate another example of the use of the steps discussed in this chapter.

For Example

Thomas Abachin is a former attorney who was a lead partner in a well-known local law firm. He has known the current governor for 20 years, having graduated from the same college. The Governor announced she intended to appoint Abachin to a special investigator position in state government. Several days after the announcement, the State Times printed a lengthy article by columnist, Sandra Murphy titled, "Governor backs Abachin despite disbarment." Abachin concedes the article accurately reflects the false charges he levied against a local judge ten years before that led to the loss of his license to practice law. Abachin admitted he had lost his law license for a time, but he was only suspended, not disbarred, and he regained his law license through a reinstatement process.

A week later, a second article was published by Murphy titled, "Abachin's lack of morality makes mockery of Governor's quest for morality in government." The second article further revealed Abachin had a criminal conviction while in college. The article explained "Abachin was convicted of a crime for driving while intoxicated." The article went on to state Abachin failed to disclose the conviction on his application for the investigator position. However, Abachin was charged with driving while intoxicated, but he was convicted of careless driving. He admitted to failing to include the conviction on his application. Ultimately, the Governor denied the appointment of Abachin to the investigator position.

Abachin decides to sue Murphy for defamation. In his complaint, Abachin alleges Murphy's statements were motivated by ill-will, spite, malice, and the intent to injure. Abachin also alleged the articles were politically motivated.

Defamation is a case law tort in the state. It has four elements: (1) false statement, (2) about plaintiff, (3) published without privilege, and (4) caused harm to plaintiff. Because Abachin is a public figure, there is the added element of actual malice by the defendant. A leading case in the state is *Goodman v. White*.

In *Goodman*, White was a columnist for a local weekly publication. Goodman, a former police officer and public figure, was named by the Governor as the next drug czar, a cabinet position. White wrote and published two articles in the week after the appointment was announced. The articles were titled: "Martinez backs White despite arrest record" and "Martinez' handling of White affair may render fraudulent her of title as champion of moral high-mindedness." The articles detailed Goodman's conviction for drug possession 20 years prior to the appointment and his court-martial while in the Army. Goodman acknowledged the conviction and the court-martial. In his complaint, he asserted the articles by White were motivated by ill-will and malice and that the articles were politically motivated. Goodman admitted the conviction and the court-martial.

Goodman's lawsuit was dismissed on a summary judgment motion. The court held that actual malice is not established through evidence of bad motives or personal ill-will. The court further held actual malice requires proof the statements were published with either knowledge they were false or reckless disregard for whether the statements were true of false.

In this example, is *Goodman v. White* on point so that it applies as precedent in Abachin's case?

1. Are the Key Facts Sufficiently Similar?

Both cases involve statements that were published in local newspapers. In both cases, there is the question of whether the statements were made with actual malice. In the *Goodman* case, even though White may have had ill-will, and his writing of the articles may have been politically motivated, ill-will and personal motives were not sufficient to prove actual malice. Moreover, the statements were true.

Are the facts concerning the articles published by Murphy in Abachin's case sufficiently similar? It is questionable. In the *Goodman* case, White's statements in the articles may have been driven by ill-will or a personal bias against Goodman, but there was no evidence of actual malice. Similarly, in Abachin's case, there are only allegations of ill-will and personal bias, but no evidence of more than that—no evidence of actual bias. It could be argued that some key facts are clearly different—those involving the truth or falsity of the statements published—and that the *Goodman* case is therefore not on point. In Abachin's case, Murphy incorrectly stated the offense for which Abachin had been convicted. In addition, she failed to note the disbarment was reduced to a suspension on appeal, with Abachin regaining his license at a later time. Abachin did admit he left the conviction off of his application for the investigator position. In *Goodman*, the statements published were true. But, it could be argued that because there was a conviction, only for a different offense, and there was a loss of Abachin's law license, although not to the same degree published, White was not reckless as to their truth or falsity. Under this argument, the *Goodman* case might apply as precedent. However, the value as precedent rests mostly as to the issue of actual malice.

It is important to note that the difference in the key facts makes it questionable whether the case is on point. To remove doubt, additional research must be conducted to determine what constitutes knowledge or recklessness as to the truth or falsity of the statements.

2. Are the Rules or Principles Sufficiently Similar?

If it is decided that there is a sufficient similarity in the facts, then is there a sufficient similarity between the law that applies in the *Goodman* opinion and that which applies in the client's case for the opinion to be considered on point and apply as precedent? Both cases are defamation cases that apply the same defamation statute. Both cases involve the element of actual malice. Both cases are concerned with an aspect of that element: whether there is "a showing of more than bad motives and ill-will."

Therefore, there is little question that *Goodman* is on point with regard to step 2 as to at least one issue. If it is determined that Murphy's conduct was merely the result of ill-will and bad motives, under the rule of law applied in *Goodman*, Murphy's conduct would not meet one element of the offense.

Summary

Court opinions are important because under the doctrines of precedent and stare decisis, judges reach decisions according to principles laid down in similar cases. Therefore, a researcher should find a case that is precedent (on point) because it guides the attorney as to how the issue in the client's case may be decided. An opinion is on point, and may be considered as precedent, if there is a sufficient similarity between the key facts and the rule of law or legal principle that governs both the court opinion and the client's case.

When considering the key facts, the heart of the process is the identification of the similarities and differences between them. The more pronounced the differences between the facts of the court opinion and those of the client's case, the greater the likelihood that the opinion is not on point. Be very critical in your analysis when there are differences. Always pursue other avenues of research when the key facts are different.

When the key facts are sufficiently similar for the opinion to be considered on point, look to the rule of law that governs the court opinion and the client's case. If the same rule applies in the same way, the opinion is usually on point. If a different rule applies, a court opinion usually cannot apply as precedent. When the language and function of the applicable rules or principles are sufficiently similar, however, it can be argued that an opinion is on point and can be used as precedent.

Reliance on a court opinion that applies a different rule or principle than that which applies in the client's case is risky and should be attempted only when there is no case that interprets the rule or principle governing the client's case.

Quick References

Internet Resources

Various websites discuss the subject of cases on point. Most sites discuss specific cases and topics. These websites may be accessed by using "case law on all fours" or "cases on all fours" as a topic in a search engine. Law school websites are often strong sources for reference. As mentioned in Chapter 9, most websites provide information without charge. Information you obtain for free may not be closely monitored and may not be as accurate or have the same quality of material as that obtained from fee-based services. Therefore, exercise care when using freely obtained material.

Exercises

ASSIGNMENT 1

What does it mean when a case is on point? When is a case on point?

ASSIGNMENT 2

Describe the two-step process for determining when a case is on point.

ASSIGNMENT 3

Describe the three-part process for determining if a case is on point when there are different key facts.

ASSIGNMENT 4

Describe the two steps to follow when the doctrine or rule applied by the court is different from the doctrine that applies in the client's case.

ASSIGNMENT 5

In the following examples, use the statutory and case law presented in the hypothetical at the beginning of the chapter, that is, § 96-25-16 and *Karl v. Herald*. The client seeks redress for the other party's refusal to issue dividends. In each example, determine if *Karl v. Herald* is on point.

Example 1

Client and his sister, Janice, are shareholders in a corporation. Janice is the majority shareholder, the sole member of the board of directors, and the manager of the corporation. For the past five years, she has paid herself a lucrative salary twice that paid to managers of similar corporations. The corporation has a $400,000 cash surplus that Janice claims is necessary for emergencies. No emergency has occurred in the past five years that required an expenditure of more than $50,000.

Example 2

Client and Claire own a fabric store. The business is a corporation, and Claire holds 80 percent of the stock and makes all the business decisions. Client, an employee of the business, owns 20 percent of the stock. The business has a large cash surplus, but Claire has never issued dividends. Claire's salary is three times Client's. When Client asks that dividends be issued, Claire responds, "Your dividend from this corporation is your job."

Example 3

Client and Don are partners in a business. Don owns 70 percent of the partnership and Client owns 30 percent. Client does not work for the business. Don runs the business and pays himself a large salary that always seems to equal the profits. Client thinks this is fishy and believes Don should have a set salary, and the profit above Don's salary should be shared 70/30. There is no partnership case law in the jurisdiction addressing this question.

ASSIGNMENT 6

For each of the three client fact situations presented below, use the following summary court opinion. For each fact situation answer the following:

1. What are the fact similarities and differences between the court opinion and the client's fact situation?

2. Is the court opinion on point? Why or why not?

3. If the court opinion is on point, would it be mandatory or persuasive precedent?

Court Opinion:

Vineyard v. Palo Alto. Mr. Vineyard was injured on December 29, 2009, in a car accident while delivering pizzas for his employer, Palo Alto. Mr. Vineyard began work for Palo Alto on October 1, 2009. He also worked as a horse trainer beginning on September 1, 2009. There is no dispute Mr. Vineyard is entitled to Worker's Compensation benefits reflecting his wages from both jobs. The parties disputed how to compute the aggregate weekly wage to be used to determine the value of those benefits.

For employment less than 26 weeks, § 52-1-20(B)(1) of the New Mexico Workers Compensation Act compels dividing the total wages earned by the worker at that job by the number of weeks "actually worked in that employment." The Court of Appeals held that each employer's average weekly wage is to be individually calculated under subsection (B)(1) and an average weekly wage based on the aggregate of all averages should then be calculated.

Part A

Client's Facts: Samantha was an assembly line worker at a factory that produced plastic bags for use in retail stores. On January 9, 2016, the end of a conveyor line collapsed and crushed Samantha's foot. Samantha started working at the factory on October 1, 2015. Samantha also worked 20 hours a week for a nonprofit agency. She began working for the nonprofit agency on September 15, 2015. She is unable to work at either job for at least three months. The hearing officer assigned to calculate her benefits under New Mexico's Worker's Compensation statute § 52-1-20(B)(1) has calculated her average weekly by averaging her hourly wage for both jobs and averaging the number of weeks she worked at the two jobs. Samantha wants to appeal the manner that the average weekly wage was calculated.

Part B

Client's Facts: Becky, a Wyoming resident, was injured while delivering packages for her employer, D2D (Distributor to Door). She began work for D2D on December 15, 2015. She also works as a dog trainer on weekends and began that job on September 1, 2015. Becky also worked providing closed captioning for a local agency. She had been at that job since August 1, 2015. Wyoming has a Workers Compensation statute that requires "dividing the total wages earned by the worker at that job by the number of weeks actually worked in that employment" for employment less than 30 weeks. There is no applicable Wyoming case. The parties disagree on how to calculate the average wage for purpose of determining benefits.

ASSIGNMENT 7

Each of the following examples presents a brief summary of the court opinion, followed by a client's fact situation. For each client fact situation, Parts A through G, determine the following:

1. What are the fact similarities and differences between the court opinion and the client's situation?

2. Is the court opinion on point? Why or why not?

3. If the opinion is on point, what will the probable decision be in regard to the question raised by the client's facts?

Example 1

Court Opinion: *State v. Jones.* Mr. Jones, a first-time applicant for general relief funds, was denied relief without a hearing. The denial was based on information in Mr. Jones's application indicating that his income was above the threshold maximum set by the agency regulations. The regulation provides that when an applicant's income, or the financial support provided to an applicant plus income, exceeds $12,000 a year, the individual may be denied general relief funds. The regulation is silent about the right to a hearing.

Mr. Jones's application reflected that the gross income from his two part-time jobs exceeded the maximum allowable income for eligibility by $2,000. He believed there were special circumstances that would allow him to be eligible for general relief. His demand for an appeal hearing to explain his special circumstances was denied.

The court held that the due process clause of the state constitution entitles a first-time applicant for general relief funds to a hearing when special circumstances are alleged. The question in the following three fact situations is whether the client is entitled to a hearing.

Part A

Client's Facts: Tom lives at home with his parents. He has a part-time job. He does not pay rent or utilities. He uses the money from his job to attend school, and he has very little left over. His application for general relief was denied. The written denial stated that the combination of the support provided by his parents and his part-time income exceeded the maximum allowable income. His application for an appeal hearing was denied.

Part B

Client's Facts: In the last session of the state legislature, legislation was passed providing that when applicants for general relief are denied relief based on information provided in the application, they are not entitled to an appeal hearing. The purpose of the legislation is to cut costs.

Mr. Taylor, a first-time applicant for general relief funds, was denied benefits based solely on his application. He believes that he has special circumstances that entitle him to benefits. His request for an appeal hearing was denied.

Part C

Client's Facts: Client has been receiving general relief funds for the past year. Last week, he received notice that his relief would be terminated due to information received from his employer indicating that he had received a raise, and his income is now over the statutory maximum. His request for an appeal hearing on the termination of relief was denied.

Example 2

Court Opinion: *Rex v. Ireland.* Mr. Rex, the landlord, filed an eviction suit against his tenant, Mr. Ireland. Mr. Rex served notice of default upon Mr. Ireland by rolling up the notice of default and placing it in Mr. Ireland's mailbox. The mailbox was situated next to the street. Mr. Ireland retrieved the notice the next day. Mr. Ireland, in his defense to the eviction suit, stated that he was not given proper notice of default under the provisions of § 55-67-9 of the Landlord/Tenant Act; therefore, the case should be dismissed. The statute provides that notice of default may be accomplished in one of three ways:

1. Delivery by certified mail

2. Hand delivery to the individual to be evicted

3. Posting at the most public part of the residence

The statute further provides that the court may enter an order of eviction if the notice of default is not responded to within 30 days.

The court, denying the request for dismissal, ruled that the intent of the statute was to ensure that tenants receive notice of default. The court noted that although the method of delivery used by Mr. Rex did not comply with the statute, the intent of the act was accomplished, inasmuch as Mr. Ireland had actual notice of default and was not prejudiced by the improper notice.

The question in the following four fact situations is whether the notice of default is effective.

Part D

Client's Facts: The client is a tenant. The landlord told the client's daughter to inform the tenant that he was in default and, under the terms of the lease, would be evicted if he did not pay or otherwise respond within 30 days. The daughter informed the tenant the next day. Would it make any difference if the daughter informed the tenant after 30 days but before the eviction suit was filed?

Part E

Client's Facts: Client, the tenant, was on vacation when the landlord posted the notice of default on the front door. Client did not return from vacation and learn of the default until after the 30-day default period had passed.

Part F

Client's Facts: Landlord sent the notice of default by regular mail, and the tenant received it.

Part G

Client's Facts: The landlord sent the notice by certified mail, but the client refused to accept it.

Chapter 13

Counteranalysis

Outline

Learning Objectives

After completing this chapter, you should understand:

- What counteranalysis is
- Why counteranalysis is important
- The techniques of counteranalysis
- Where to place counteranalysis in an interoffice research memorandum or a court brief

On a frigid Saturday in December, Mr. Henry "Hot Dog" Thomas, an inexperienced skier, was skiing an expert run at a local resort. As he came over a hill, he encountered a patch of ice, lost control, crashed into a tree, and was severely injured. The ski resort did not post a warning sign indicating the presence of the ice patch. Mr. Thomas consulted with Ms. Booth, a local attorney, and retained her to represent him. Shortly thereafter, Ms. Booth filed a negligence suit against the resort. She sent her paralegal a memo indicating that the resort's attorney had filed a Rule 12(b)(6) motion to dismiss for failure to state a claim. The memo directed the paralegal to prepare a legal research memo assessing the likelihood of the motion being granted.

The Ski Safety Act, which governs the rights and liabilities of skiers and ski resorts, provides that:

- *The resort has a duty to warn of hazardous conditions.*
- *The skier has the duty and the responsibility to be aware of snow and ice conditions.*

The act also provides that skiers have a duty to refrain from skiing beyond the range of their ability. One of the questions to be addressed by the paralegal is which of the duties apply in the client's case.

The memo the paralegal prepared focused on the resort's duty to warn and the skier's duty in regard to snow and ice conditions. Based on this focus and the relevant case law, the paralegal concluded that the resort had the duty to warn of the ice patch that the client encountered. Therefore, the 12(b)(6) motion would probably not be granted.

At the motion hearing, the resort's counsel did not focus on the issue of the resort's duty to warn, but rather argued the issue in the context of probable cause. The resort's counsel contended that the cause of the accident was the skier's admitted violation of his statutory duty to refrain from skiing beyond the range of his ability. As an admitted inexperienced skier, his skiing an expert run violated the statute and, therefore, was the cause of the accident as a matter of law. The skier's attorney, relying on the paralegal's memo, which did not address the proximate cause issue, was unprepared to counter this argument. Consequently, the motion was granted and the case dismissed.

I. INTRODUCTION

What went wrong in the preceding hypothetical? Of course, the supervising attorney should have more carefully reviewed the paralegal's memo, noticed that the assistant had not addressed the proximate cause issue, and engaged in additional research. Often an attorney is too busy and, based on past excellent and reliable performance by a paralegal or law clerk, may rely fully on the individual's work product and not sufficiently review what has been submitted.

What went wrong with the paralegal's research? The paralegal failed to anticipate the legal argument the opposing side was likely to make. He failed to analyze the position from the other side's point of view. In other words, he failed to provide a complete counteranalysis in the memo. A paralegal or law clerk's role in conducting legal research, or in any situation that requires legal analysis, includes determining the potential weaknesses of a legal argument and the counterarguments the other side may present.

The purpose of legal research is not only to discover how the law applies to the client's case but also to determine the strength of that case. To accomplish this, the strength of the opponent's case must be analyzed as well. The case must be looked at in its entirety to determine its strengths and weaknesses.

The focus of this chapter is the process of identifying the strengths and weaknesses of a client's case through an analysis of the case from the perspective of the opposition. That is, the focus is on counteranalysis. Thorough research must be conducted and all applicable law identified prior to beginning the process.

II. COUNTERANALYSIS—DEFINITION

If analysis is the application of the law to the facts of a case, what is **counteranalysis**? At one level, it is an exploration of how and why a specific law does or does not apply to the facts of a case. It is the process of anticipating the argument the opponent is likely to raise in response to your analysis of an issue—the **counterargument**. In essence, it is the process of discovering and considering the counterargument to a legal position or argument. It involves an identification and objective evaluation of the strengths and weaknesses of each legal argument you intend to raise.

III. COUNTERANALYSIS—WHY?

The role of the attorney, paralegal, or law clerk is to represent the client in the best way possible and to pursue a course of action that is in the best interest of the client. This is accomplished by engaging in research and analysis that thoroughly examines all the aspects of the case. One of those aspects, counteranalysis, is important for several reasons:

1. Under Rule 3.3(a)(3) of the American Bar Association's Model Rules of Professional Conduct, an attorney has an **ethical** duty to disclose legal authority adverse to the position of the client that is not disclosed by opposing counsel.

    The goal of the adversary system is that justice be served. The ends of justice require the discovery and presentation of all relevant authority so that a just resolution of the issues may be achieved. Therefore, to properly inform the attorney, a legal researcher must locate and provide the attorney with all relevant authority, including that which is adverse to the client.

2. The attorney, paralegal, and law clerk have an ethical duty to do a complete and competent job. See Model Rule 1.1. Research and analysis are not complete unless all sides of an issue and all legal arguments have been considered. Failure to completely analyze a problem can constitute malpractice.

To represent the client competently, you must be prepared to respond to any legal argument raised by the other side. The identification of opposing arguments allows you to consider what the other side's position is likely to be. It allows you to answer the questions:

- "What will they do?"
- "How can we counter their arguments?"
- "What preparation is necessary to respond?"

In essence, counteranalysis allows you to anticipate opposing arguments and prepare to counter them. The last thing you want is to be responsible for the supervisory attorney being unprepared to respond to an argument.

3. Counteranalysis aids in the proper evaluation of the merits of a case and can assist in selection of the appropriate course of action.

For Example

Counteranalysis may reveal a weakness in the client's case that leads to the conclusion that settlement should be pursued. Without conducting a thorough counteranalysis, an improper course of action could be followed, such as taking the matter to trial rather than pursuing settlement options.

4. It is important to locate and disclose adverse authority to maintain credibility with your supervisor. You may not be considered reliable, and the credibility, accuracy, and thoroughness of your research may be questioned if you ignore or fail to identify and disclose adverse authority. The opposition or the court, if the issue comes before a court, most likely will discover the opposing authority. Your failure to do so indicates lack of ability, sloppiness, or intentional concealment. Your credibility and trustworthiness will be enhanced if you candidly reveal and meet head on unfavorable authority.

5. When a legal brief is submitted to a court, if you identify and address adverse authority in the brief, you have an opportunity to soften its impact by discrediting or distinguishing it. You have an opportunity to provide reasons why the adverse authority does not apply, and your credibility is thereby enhanced. This allows the reader to consider the adverse authority in the context of your response to it. This opportunity is missed if you fail to include the adverse authority.

Weaknesses in your position or analysis will not go away if you ignore them. No matter how strongly you feel you are right, you can count on the other side to raise some counterargument, and if you have not considered and prepared for the counterarguments, you may very well lose in court.

IV. COUNTERANALYSIS—WHEN?

Employ counteranalysis whenever legal research is conducted or the strengths and weaknesses of a case are considered—in other words, *always*. When addressing a legal problem, look for all potential counterarguments to any position taken. Use counteranalysis when preparing an interoffice legal memorandum or conducting any research on an issue in a case. It is certainly necessary when you are assisting in the preparation of a response to a brief filed by the opposing party. Engage in the process even when you are considering the legal issues in the client's case. Counteranalysis may be required even in the initial stages of a case.

For Example

Some paralegals and law clerks conduct the initial interview with a client and provide the supervisory attorney with a summary of the interview and the applicable statutory and case law. The summary of the applicable law should include a counteranalysis section that points out any apparent weaknesses in the client's case.

V. COUNTERANALYSIS—RESEARCH SOURCES

When conducting legal research, counteranalysis means looking for legal authority that supports the argument the opponent is likely to raise in response to your analysis of the issue. There are several things to keep in mind and sources to look to when conducting counteranalysis and legal research.

When researching statutory law, update the statute or check the annotations for cases analyzing or interpreting the statute. The cases may present counterarguments to a position you are taking with regard to the interpretation of the statute.

When researching case law, if you find a case that supports the client's position, then update the case to determine if another case analyzes the law differently. Cases that distinguish, criticize, and limit the case you are researching are identified in *Shepard's* and *KeyCite*. Be sure to check all these cases.

In addition to updating the case that supports the client's position, also check the digest for other cases that may analyze the law differently. *Shepard's* and *KeyCite* will only identify those cases that specifically mention the case you are researching. There may be other cases that analyze the same question, but do not mention the same case. Check the headnote of the case you are researching, identify the key number for the issue in question, and then check the appropriate digest for other cases on the topic.

When reading a case that supports the client's position, always check for a dissent. If there is a dissent, it will present the counterargument to the position taken in the majority opinion and often include references to cases and other sources in support of the counterargument. It is possible that the facts of the client's case are sufficiently different from the court opinion that the dissenter's position may apply.

There are several other sources to check when conducting counteranalysis. A treatise usually presents an analysis of legal issues that includes arguments and counterarguments. If the question being researched has an *ALR* annotation, the annotation will include a thorough analysis of the issue. It will discuss the various ways the courts have decided the issue and the arguments and counterarguments in support of those decisions. The annotation will also include references to numerous cases on the question and other research sources.

Another helpful source when conducting counteranalysis is a law review article. If there is a law review article that discusses the question being researched, it will provide a comprehensive analysis and critique of the legal position(s) the courts have taken. Like an *ALR* annotation, it will include reference to numerous cases that address the question and other research sources.

VI. COUNTERANALYSIS—TECHNIQUES

A. In General

Before counteranalysis can begin, a prerequisite is that you must analyze and thoroughly research the issue or legal position being addressed. You must know the law before you can respond to it. Thorough research should reveal the weaknesses of a legal position and the counterarguments to it.

For Example

Bryce, a door-to-door sales representative for Lumber Beard, sold Beaux Smith a set of beard grooming tools at Mr. Smith's residence. Mr. Smith signed a contract to purchase the grooming tools. The contract provided for three monthly payments. Mr. Smith called two days later and canceled the contract. When Lumber Beard attempted to deliver the goods, Mr. Smith refused to accept the delivery. Lumber Beard sued Mr. Smith for breach of contract.

Tom, a law clerk with the firm representing Lumber Beard, was assigned the task of determining whether Mr. Smith could legally cancel the contract after it was signed. He determined that article II of the state Commercial Code governed the transaction. His research indicated that the code had no provision allowing a cooling-off period for door-to-door sales; therefore, he concluded that Mr. Smith's rejection of the goods was a breach of the contract.

Tom, however, committed a major error. He failed to thoroughly research the question. The state had another statute, called the Consumer Sales Act, which provided that in the event of a credit transaction involving a home solicitation sale, the buyer had a right to cancel the sale within three days of the transaction.

Had Tom's research been thorough, he would have located the weakness in his legal position based upon the Commercial Code and identified the counterargument to the conclusion that the contract was breached.

When embarking on counteranalysis, always assume that there is a counterargument to the position you have taken. Put yourself in the opponent's place and ask yourself:

- "How do I respond to this argument?"
- "What is the argument in response to this position?"

Remember, counteranalysis consists of identifying any possible counterargument the opponent may use to challenge your legal position or argument.

To determine what the counterarguments to an argument or position are likely to be, it is necessary to consider the ways a legal argument is attacked. After you are familiar with the techniques used to challenge an argument, use those techniques to seek out the weaknesses in your own argument and to anticipate the likely counterarguments.

A legal argument or legal position is usually based on enacted law or case law, or both. The various approaches that you may use to attack or challenge an argument based on enacted law or case law are explored separately in the following two sections.

B. Enacted Law

Ways to challenge or attack a legal position or argument based on an enacted law are discussed here. **Enacted law**, for purposes of this section, includes any law passed or adopted by the people through a representative body, such as Congress, a state legislature, city council, and so on. Throughout this section and the remainder of the chapter, the term *statute* is used when discussing legal arguments or positions based on enacted law.

There are several approaches to consider when attacking a legal position based on a statute. Some of these approaches are listed in Exhibit 13-1. Consider all of them when analyzing an argument based on a statute to identify every possible weakness and counterargument.

1. Elements of the Statute Are Not Met

Every statute is composed of elements (see Chapter 3) that must be met before the statute can apply. When a client's case is based on a statute, facts must be present in the case that establish or satisfy each of the elements of the statute.

1. The elements of the statute are not met.
2. The statute is sufficiently broad to permit a construction or application different from that urged by the opposition.
3. The statute has been misconstrued or does not apply.
4. The statute relied upon as a guide to interpret another statute does not apply and, therefore, cannot be used as a guide in interpreting the other statute.
5. The statute relied on has not been adopted in your jurisdiction.
6. The interpretation of the statute urged by the opposition is unconstitutional or violates another legislative act.
7. The statute relied on is unconstitutional.

© Cengage

Exhibit 13-1 Counteranalysis Approaches to a Legal Position Based on a Statute.

For Example

Criminal Code § 13-3102 defines *misconduct involving weapons* as knowingly possessing a deadly weapon on school grounds. The elements are:

1. Knowingly
2. Possessing
3. A deadly weapon
4. On school grounds

Facts must be present that establish each of these elements before an individual can be convicted of misconduct involving weapons.

One way to attack a legal position based on a statute is to argue that the elements of the statute have not been met—that is, facts present in the case fail to establish each element of the statute.

For Example

Mary is charged under Criminal Code § 13-3102 with misconduct involving weapons. On the day in questions, Mary had a pocketknife with her at school.

1. The counterargument to the prosecution's reliance on the statute is that there are no facts present in the case to establish one element of the law: The knife is not a deadly weapon. A different subsection of the statute expressly makes an exception for pocketknives.

When conducting counteranalysis of an argument based on a statute, closely examine the facts relied on to establish *each* of the required elements. Ask yourself, "Have the elements of the statute been met?" Look for any possible argument that the facts do not establish or satisfy an element or elements.

2. Statute Is Sufficiently Broad to Permit Different Construction

In many situations, a statute may be sufficiently broad to allow an interpretation or application different from that relied on by the opposing side.

For Example

Section 54-9-91 of the state domestic relations statute provides that custody shall be determined in the best interest of the children. Gerald contends that he should be granted custody of the children because he lives in a small town, and his former spouse lives in a large city. He argues that a small town is a better environment because it is safer and free from the pressures of gang violence and drug use.

A counterargument can be made that the benefits of the city, such as greater access to the arts, museums, and universities, offset the alleged disadvantages of a large city. The phrase "best interest of the children" can be interpreted in a manner different from that urged by the opposing side.

When the language relied on in a statute is broadly crafted, such as in the previous example, look for the counterargument that a different interpretation is permissible because of the broadness of the language. Ask the question, "Is the statute sufficiently broad to permit a construction or application different from that urged by the opposition?"

3. Statute Misconstrued or Does Not Apply

Explore the possibility of a counterargument that the statute is being misconstrued or misapplied.

For Example

Section 9(A) of the Deceptive Trade Practices Act provides a remedy in tort for "deceptive practices in negotiation or performance" of a contract for the sale of goods. Tom and Larry have a contract for the delivery of goods. Under the contract, Tom is to deliver the goods on the fifth of each month. Every month, Tom comes up with some excuse for not delivering the goods on the fifth, and the goods are always delivered between the seventh and fifteenth of the month. Finally, Larry gets fed up and sues Tom for violation of the Deceptive Trade Practices Act, claiming that Tom is engaging in deceptive practices in violation of § 9(A) of the act.

A review of the legislative history and case law clearly indicates that the Deceptive Trade Practices Act is not designed to apply to simple breach-of-contract cases. The Sale of Goods provisions of the Commercial Code statutes govern breach-of-contract situations. The courts have consistently held that when there is an adequate remedy in contract law, the tort remedy available under the act does not apply. Therefore, a counterargument can be raised that the statute has been misconstrued and does not apply in a simple breach-of-contract case such as that of Tom and Larry.

When a legal position or argument is based on a statute, engage in counteranalysis to ensure that the statute is not being misconstrued or applied in a situation to which it clearly does not apply. Always consult case law to determine if the courts have interpreted or applied the statute in a manner different from that relied on. Ask the following questions: "Has the statute been misconstrued or does not apply?" "Does another statute apply?"

4. Statute Relied on as a Guide Does Not Apply

In some situations, the statute that governs does not have a provision addressing a specific question raised by the facts of a client's case. In such instances, there may be an argument that a different statute, which has a section governing a similar fact situation, can be used as guidance in interpreting the applicable statute. It is usually argued that the different statute can be used as guidance because the language and functions of the statutes are similar.

When this occurs, you can make the counterargument that the statute relied on to interpret another statute is not intended to govern or apply to the type of situation presented by the client's case and, therefore, cannot be used as a guide. The argument usually is that the statute governs or applies only to those limited fact situations covered by the language of the statute, and cannot be used as a guide for the interpretation of another statute.

For Example

The jurisdiction has adopted the following statutes:

- § 59-1 provides that an individual must be a resident of the county to be eligible to run for the position of animal control officer.

- § 200-1 provides that an individual must be a resident of the county for three months to run for a position on the county school board.

Erin, a resident of the county for three months, wants to run for the position of animal control officer. She argues that since § 59-1 is silent on the length of residency necessary to be eligible to run for the position of animal control officer, the three-month residency requirement established in § 200-1 should be used as a guide to determine the length of residency required under § 59-1. She reasons that because both statutes are similar in language (both use the word *resident*) and both involve county elective offices, they are sufficiently similar for the residency requirement of § 200-1 to be used as the standard for § 59-1.

Because the statutes are different, however, a possible counterargument is the duties of an animal control officer are much different from those of a school board member. The duties of the animal control officer require a degree of familiarity with the geography of the county that cannot be acquired in three months. Therefore, the differences in the requirements of the positions represent a factual difference that renders § 200-1 inappropriate for use as a guide to interpret § 59-1.

In every situation in which it is argued that a provision of one statute may apply or be used to interpret a provision of a different statute, a counterargument can always be made that no matter how similar in language and function, the statutes differ functionally in some way. Therefore, the provisions of one statute cannot be relied on or applied to interpret or govern the other statute.

When your legal position or argument is based on the use of one statute as a guide to interpret another statute, consider the counterargument that focuses on the differences in the statutes. Keep in mind the question, "Is it possible that the statute relied on as a guide is so functionally different that it cannot be used as a guide to interpret the statute being analyzed?

5. Statute Relied on Has Not Been Adopted in Jurisdiction

The jurisdiction has no law or statute governing a fact situation, and your legal position is based on an argument that advocates the adoption of the language of, or principles embodied in, a statute from another jurisdiction. In such situations, you are attempting to persuade the court to adopt the law, or the principles embodied in the law, of another jurisdiction.

A counterargument can be made that a statute, or principles that apply to facts in another jurisdiction, should not be adopted to apply to similar facts in your jurisdiction. It is usually possible to point out some difference between the jurisdictions or difference in the public policy of the jurisdictions and argue that the difference precludes the adoption of the language or principles of the statute.

For Example

Ida, a resident of state A, borrows her next-door neighbor's lawn mower. Due to a defect in the mower, Ida is injured. Ida sues the manufacturer, a local company, for breach of warranty. The manufacturer moves for dismissal, claiming that the warranty does not extend to nonpurchasers. The commercial code adopted in state A does not address the question, nor is there any case law on point. Ida argues that the court should adopt the language of the law of state B, a neighboring state. Section 2-389 of state B's commercial code provides that warranties extend to the buyer and any person who may be reasonably expected to use the goods, which includes a neighbor.

The manufacturer's counterargument could be that the law of state B should not be looked to because of policy differences between the states. State A, to encourage and protect the growth of local industry, has traditionally adopted a policy that narrowly limits manufacturer liability. State B's position represents an expansive view that broadly extends manufacturer liability, a position contrary to state A's traditional view.

When conducting counteranalysis, look for the argument that the statute relied on has not been adopted and should not apply. Ask the question, "Where a legal position is based upon an argument that advocates the adoption of the language or principles embodied in a statute of another jurisdiction, are there differences in the jurisdictions that preclude the adoption of the language or principles of the other jurisdiction's statute?" Note that there is always the additional counterargument that such matters are of legislative concern and should be addressed by the legislature, not the courts.

6. Interpretation of Statute Is Unconstitutional or Violates Another Legislative Act

Be alert for an argument that the application or interpretation of the statute advocated is unconstitutional or violates another statute.

For Example

Section 22 of the state's Secured Transaction Code allows a creditor to repossess collateral after providing the debtor with notice of default and allowing the debtor 60 days to cure the default. A car dealer, after providing notice of default and waiting more than 60 days for the customer to cure the default, repossessed the customer's car from the customer's residence while the customer was at work. The car dealer interpreted the statute as not requiring prior court approval, and therefore did not seek a court order authorizing the repossession.

The customer sued the car dealer, claiming that the dealer illegally seized the car because the due process clause of the state constitution requires a court order before property can be seized. The dealer claimed that the seizure was legal because he complied with the statute: he provided notice of default and waited 60 days.

The counterargument is that the interpretation of the statute urged by the dealer is unconstitutional because it allows for prejudgment seizure—that is, it allows the seizure of property without prior court approval.

Always counteranalyze a legal position or argument based on an interpretation of a law for the possibility that the interpretation violates a constitutional or statutory provision. Ask yourself, "Is the interpretation of the statute urged by the opposition unconstitutional, or does it violate another legislative act?"

7. Statute Relied on Is Unconstitutional

Although statutes are not usually unconstitutional and, therefore, are not likely to be vulnerable to constitutional attack, consider the constitutionality of the statute on which a legal position is based. Has the constitutionality of the statute been questioned in scholarly journals, law reviews, and so on? Try to anticipate any argument based on a constitutional challenge.

For Example

Ellen is prosecuted under a local ordinance prohibiting the sale of any material that "shows genitalia or excites a prurient interest." Such a statute may be subject to challenge as being unconstitutional because the term *prurient interest* is too vague.

When working with statutes, consider a counterargument based on a challenge to the constitutionality of the statute. Consider the question, "Is the statute unconstitutional?"

Note: When a legal position or argument is based on a statute, conduct thorough research to ensure that some other law, provision, or court decision does not apply that affects your reliance on the statute.

C. Case Law

To understand how to counteranalyze a legal position or argument based on or relying on **case law**, it is necessary to understand the process involved in determining if a court opinion is on point. Therefore, it is helpful to review Chapter 12 before beginning this section. When used in this section, the terms *rule of law* and *legal principle* include any constitutional, legislative, or case law provision, act, doctrine, principle, or test relied on by the court in reaching its decision.

There are several approaches for challenging a legal position based on a court opinion. Some of these approaches are listed in Exhibit 13-2. Consider each of them when conducting counteranalysis.

1. Reliance on the court opinion is misplaced because the key facts in the opinion and the key facts of the client's case are different to such a nature or degree that they render the court opinion unusable as precedent.

2. Reliance on the court opinion is misplaced because the rule of law or legal principle applied in the court opinion does not apply.

3. The court opinion is subject to an interpretation different from that relied on in support of a legal position.

4. The rule or principle adopted in the opinion relied on is not universally followed.

5. The opinion relied on presents several possible solutions to the problem, and the one urged by the opposition is not mandatory and is not the best choice.

6. The position relied on no longer represents sound public policy and should not be followed.

7. There are other equally relevant cases that do not support the position adopted in the case relied on.

© Cengage

Exhibit 13-2 Counteranalysis Approaches to a Legal Position Based on Case Law.

1. Reliance on Court Opinion Is Misplaced Because Key Facts Differ

Apply the test from Chapter 12, in the section titled Determining if a Case is on Point. Substitute the client's key facts for those of the court opinion. If the substitution of the key facts would result in changing the outcome of the case, the court opinion cannot be used as precedent.

For Example

The plaintiff requests that a psychologist's records be admitted into evidence. The plaintiff bases his argument on the holding in the case of *Smith v. Jones*, which allowed the admission of a psychologist's records into evidence. In that case, the evidence was admitted because no claim was raised that the evidence was privileged. The decision turned on the key fact that privilege was not claimed.

In the plaintiff's case, privilege is vigorously claimed. Therefore, *Jones* cannot be relied on as precedent to support the argument for admission of the records, because *Jones* is not on point. There is such a significant difference in the key facts that the case cannot be relied upon as precedent. In *Jones*, privilege was not claimed, but in the plaintiff's case, it is claimed.

Be cautious when your legal argument relies on a court opinion that has key facts different from those of your case. Conduct counteranalysis to identify a possible counterargument that the court opinion relied on does not apply because of differences in the key facts. Ask the question, "Is the opinion relied on not on point because of key fact differences?"

2. Reliance on Court Opinion Is Misplaced Because Rule of Law or Legal Principle Does Not Apply

When conducting counteranalysis, look for a counterargument that the legal principle applied in the court opinion does not apply in the case at hand. Refer to Chapter 12, Determining if a Case is on Point, when considering this approach.

For Example

In the case of *Davis v. Davis*, Ms. Davis had sole custody of her two daughters. Ms. Davis's boyfriend occasionally stayed overnight at her home, and the daughters were aware of the overnight visits. Mr. Davis, her former husband, filed a motion with the court asking for a change of custody. He based his claim solely on his wife's alleged "immoral conduct." He presented no evidence indicating how the overnight visits affected the children.

The trial court granted a change of custody. In overturning the trial court, the court of appeals ruled that "mere allegations of immoral conduct are not sufficient grounds to award a change of custody." The court stated that evidence must be presented showing that the alleged immoral conduct harmed the children.

In the client's case, the facts are the same as those in *Davis v. Davis* except that instead of occasional overnight visits, the custodial spouse is cohabiting with another person. There is a statute in the jurisdiction providing that cohabitation is per se harmful to children—that is, in cohabitation cases, evidence of harm to the children need not be presented because cohabitation is presumed to be harmful to them.

If the custodial spouse relies on *Davis* for the proposition that the noncustodial spouse's request for change of custody must be denied because he has failed to present evidence of harm to the children, the reliance is misplaced. The reliance is misplaced because the cohabitation statute does not require the presentation of evidence of harm to the children. Therefore, the rule of law presented in *Davis* is not applicable in the client's case, and the case is not on point.

When a court opinion is used to support a legal position, ask the question, "Is reliance on the opinion misplaced because the principle applied does not apply to the case at hand?"

3. Court Opinion Is Subject to a Different Interpretation

The court may have interpreted a term in a manner that is subject to an interpretation different from that relied on in support of a legal position.

For Example

Mr. Johns is charged with violating Municipal Code § 982, which prohibits nude dancing. Mr. Johns was dancing in see-through bikini briefs. In prosecuting Mr. Johns, the city relied on the court opinion of *City v. Dew*. In that case, the court, in interpreting the term *nude dancing*, ruled that a dancer is nude when the breast or genitalia are exposed. In *Dew*, the dancer was completely nude.

In Mr. Johns's case, the city contends that Mr. Johns was dancing nude because his genitalia were exposed by his see-through bikini briefs. A counterargument could be made that the term *exposed*, as used in the opinion, should be interpreted to mean "uncovered." Therefore, a dancer is not nude under the definition adopted in *Dew* when he is covered by any fabric, no matter how sheer. The counterargument is that the language of the opinion is subject to an interpretation different from that relied on by the opposition.

Closely scrutinize the language of the court opinion to determine if it is subject to another interpretation. Be aware that the interpretation you adopt may not be the only possible interpretation. Ask the question, "Is the court opinion subject to a different interpretation from that relied upon?"

4. Rule or Principle Adopted in Opinion Relied on Is Not Universally Followed

This counterargument should be a consideration when the opinion relied on is not mandatory precedent—that is, when there is no court opinion directly on point, and a party is urging the court to follow a rule or principle adopted by another court ruling in a similar case in either the same or a different jurisdiction.

For Example

The counterargument could be, "Although the plaintiff relies on and urges the adoption of the principle presented in *Smith v. Jones*, and that opinion is followed by the Ninth, Fifth, and Seventh Circuits, several other circuits have chosen not to follow it. The better position, presented in the case of *Grape v. Vine*, is followed by the Fourth, Sixth, and Eleventh Circuits. The principle adopted in *Vine* more accurately reflects the policies of this jurisdiction."

Identify other rules or legal principles that may apply by reading the opinions of courts that have adopted other positions in similar cases. Keep in mind the question, "Is the rule or principle of the case relied on universally followed?"

5. Opinion Presents Several Possible Solutions; One Urged by Opposition Is Not Mandatory and Is Not Best Choice

Check the court opinion relied on in support of a legal position to determine if the opinion includes other solutions in addition to the one relied upon. Also, check other court opinions to identify different solutions that may have been adopted in other cases. If it is not mandatory to follow a single solution or position, conduct counteranalysis to identify the other possible solutions and anticipate counterarguments that may be based on one of these other solutions. Ask yourself, "If the opinion relied on is not mandatory precedent, does the opinion or another court opinion allow for other possible positions?"

For Example

A counterargument could be, "In the case of *Smith v. Harris*, the court stated that the plaintiff could pursue several avenues of relief, including injunction and damages. The defendant argues that *Harris* mandates the pursuit of injunctive relief when, in fact, the court allowed the pursuit of several avenues of relief in addition to injunction."

6. Position Relied on No Longer Represents Sound Public Policy and Should Not Be Followed

If the court opinion is mandatory precedent and thus must be followed, explore the possibility that it no longer represents sound public policy and should be overruled. This approach is available only if the court considering the question has the authority to overrule the precedent. A trial court does not have the power to overrule a higher court decision. If an intermediate court of appeal set the precedent, that court has the power to overturn it. If the highest court in the jurisdiction set the precedent, only that court has the power to overturn it.

This approach is always risky because a court will not lightly choose to ignore precedent. A court usually requires a strong argument to support a decision to abandon or not follow precedent. Nevertheless, when a position is based on a court opinion, consider the possibility that the rule or principle adopted in the opinion should no longer be followed due to some change in policy or other change. In such situations, it can be argued that fairness demands that the court reexamine the law.

For Example

The state prosecutor has begun to charge persons with driving while intoxicated for being in possession of car keys and being in their car even though the person was not driving and had not driven. In a particular case, the accused was found by police in his car in the parking lot of a bar shortly after closing. The accused had called for a cab and while the police were arresting the person, the friend who the accused had called for a ride arrived and showed the officer the text messages where the accused asked for a ride because they were intoxicated. The only case on point is the 1995 case of *State v. Johnson*. In that case, the court ruled that a person is in actual physical control of a vehicle, and therefore guilty of driving while intoxicated, when they have the keys to the car and are in the car even if the car is not operable.

A counterargument is that current public policy strongly favors persons making the responsible choice to call for a ride when intoxicated and without evidence of driving, or conduct so near to driving that the risk to the public is the same as actual driving ... *Johnson* should no longer be followed.

Consider the question, "Does the court opinion relied on no longer represent sound public policy and, therefore, should not be followed?"

7. Other Equally Relevant Cases Do Not Support Position Adopted in Case Relied On

In some instances, a matter has not been clearly settled by the highest court in the jurisdiction, or the opinions of the highest court appear to conflict. Look for other opinions that may take a position different from the one taken in the court opinion relied on to support a legal position or argument. Ask yourself, "Are there equally relevant cases that do not support the position adopted in the case relied on?"

For Example

The client is seeking punitive damages in a negligence case. There are three court opinions from the highest court in the jurisdiction. In the case of *Yaws v. Allen*, the court held that punitive damages may be recovered in a negligence case when there is a showing of gross negligence on the part of the tortfeasor. In the case of *X-ray v. Carrie*, the court ruled that before punitive damages can be awarded in a negligence case, there must be some demonstration that the tortfeasor had a culpable state of mind. In the case of *Casy v. Cox*, the court held that the establishment of gross negligence by itself does not indicate the existence of a culpable state of mind; it is also necessary to demonstrate willful and wanton misconduct by the tortfeasor.

Reliance on *Yaws v. Allen*, in support of a legal position that the establishment of gross negligence on the part of the tortfeasor is sufficient to obtain punitive damages, is subject to challenge. A counterargument is that the *Carrie* and *Cox* cases, also from the highest court in the jurisdiction, require more than gross negligence.

Note: When a legal position or argument is based on a court opinion, be sure to conduct thorough research to find any other law, provision, or court decision that may affect your reliance on the opinion. The research should identify all court opinions presenting possible solutions and approaches to the problem being analyzed.

VII. COUNTERANALYSIS TECHNIQUES—COMMENTS

When engaging in legal research or analysis, review all the approaches presented in the preceding sections and determine if the legal position or argument may be challenged through any of them. Be aware, however, that the techniques and considerations presented here do not constitute all of the available ways to attack or challenge a legal position or argument based on a legislative act or court opinion. In addition to using the techniques listed, use any other approach that comes to mind. Also, combinations of methods may be utilized. The particular circumstances of the case will determine which, if any, of the suggested approaches are applicable or helpful. It is most important to remember that when your position or argument is based on a legislative act or court opinion, you must engage in thorough counteranalysis to locate any weaknesses, anticipate any counterarguments, and prepare a responses to each.

VIII. COUNTERANALYSIS—WHERE?

Where does counteranalysis fit in an interoffice research memorandum or court brief? Because counteranalysis involves analysis, it obviously fits in the analysis section. But where in the analysis section does it belong? There are no established guidelines or formal rules for the placement of counteranalysis. The following are recommendations and considerations.

A. Court Brief

In a **court brief**, inasmuch as counteranalysis involves discussing potential counterarguments to or weaknesses in your analysis, it is recommended that counteranalysis be presented in the middle of the analysis, that is, immediately after the analysis but before the conclusion. Present your argument and analysis first. Then present the other side's position after your argument, in the middle of the analysis.

Presenting counteranalysis in the middle of the analysis keeps the focus on your position rather than on your opponent's position. A reader tends to remember the beginning and end of a presentation more than the middle. Because you believe your analysis or legal argument is correct and should prevail, you want the memory of your analysis to be foremost in the reader's mind. Therefore, you do not want to place the counterargument in a location where it is more likely to be remembered or emphasized, such as at the beginning or end. Hence, put it after your own analysis and before the conclusion (i.e., in the middle).

For Example

"It is appropriate for the court to allow the admission of DNA test results based on the IMAK test. In this state, in the case of *State v. Diago*, the supreme court ruled that the results of scientific tests are admissible when the test's reliability and scientific basis are recognized by competent authorities. The IMAK test, developed in 1992, is universally accepted by all competent authorities as scientifically valid.

Defendant's reliance on the state case of *Arc v. Arc* is misplaced. In that case, the court's refusal to allow the admission of DNA evidence was based on the disagreement among experts about the reliability of the test being administered at the time, the ITAK test. The ITAK test was not universally accepted and was not as accurate as the current IMAK test. Indeed, IMAK test results have been admitted into evidence in all cases where they have been submitted. For the reasons of universal scientific acceptance, reliability, and court acceptance, the results of IMAK DNA testing should be admitted in this case."

B. Interoffice Research Memorandum

In an **interoffice research memorandum**, it is recommended that counteranalysis be placed after the analysis of each issue. It logically follows the analysis, and this placement ensures that the supervising attorney will review it before proceeding to the next issue(s). It may be useful, for the purpose of making certain that it is not overlooked, to include a separate counteranalysis subsection for each issue addressed in the memo. One possible outline of the analysis portion of a legal research memorandum is as follows:

Analysis Section—The legal analysis of the issue(s)

Issue I

    A. *Introductory sentence.*
    B. *Rule of law.* State the rule of law that governs the issue. This may be a constitutional provision, statutory provision, court doctrine, principle, and so on.
    C. *Case(s).* Present the case or cases that are on point and illustrate the application of the rule of law to the facts.
    D. *Counteranalysis*
    E. *Conclusion*

Assume the information included in the previous example is presented in an interoffice memorandum. A portion of the analysis and counteranalysis section of the memo might appear as follows:

Analysis

It is likely the court will allow the admission of DNA test results based on the IMAK test. The state supreme court, in the case of *State v. Diago*, ruled that the results of scientific tests are admissible when the test's reliability and scientific basis are recognized by competent authorities. The IMAK test, developed in 1992, is universally accepted by all competent authorities as scientifically valid.

Although the courts of this state have not addressed the question of the admission of DNA evidence based on the IMAK test, the United States Court of Appeals for the Fifth Circuit has considered the matter. In *Eric v. Eric*, the court of appeals stated, "The time has arrived to admit the results of DNA testing into evidence. The IMAK test meets the requirements established by this court for the admission of scientific evidence." IMAK test results have been admitted into evidence in all cases where they have been submitted. For the reasons of universal scientific acceptance, reliability, and court acceptance, the results of IMAK DNA testing should be admitted in this case.

Couneranalysis

Defendant may rely on the state case of *Arc v. Arc* and argue that the results of the test should not be admitted. In *Arc,* the court refused to allow the admission of DNA test results from the ITAK test. The court's refusal was based on the disagreement among experts about the reliability of the test. The ITAK test was not universally accepted and was not as accurate as the current IMAK test. Because the *Arc* opinion involved a different test that was neither as universally accepted nor as accurate as the IMAK test, the opinion is not on point and cannot be relied on as precedent in this case.

For an in-depth discussion of the analysis section of an interoffice legal research memorandum, see Chapter 17.

IX. KEY POINTS CHECKLIST: Counteranalysis

✓ A weakness in an argument will not go away if you ignore it. You can count on either the other side or the court to bring it to light. It is much better for you to raise the counterargument and diffuse it.

✓ For every issue presented in a legal research memorandum, consider how the other side is likely to respond.

✓ Put yourself in your opponent's position. Assume you are the opponent and consider all possible counterarguments, no matter how ridiculous—be ruthless.

✓ The more strongly you believe in the correctness of your analysis, the greater the likelihood that you will miss or overlook the counteranalysis to that analysis. Beware: When you feel extremely confident or sure, take extra precautions. Overconfidence can seriously mislead you.

✓ Do not let your emotions, preconceived notions, or stubbornness interfere with an objective counteranalysis of your position.

✓ When analyzing court opinions, a counteranalysis of the majority opinion may be found in the dissenting opinion or other opinions that criticize or distinguish the majority opinion.

✓ When conducting counteranalysis, always consider each of the approaches listed in this chapter. Remember, more than one approach may apply, and approaches other than those listed may be available.

✓ Even if you find a case on point, always research thoroughly. Look for other laws or court opinions that may also apply.

X. APPLICATION

This section explores the application of the principles discussed in this chapter. Three situations are explored in the following examples.

A. Chapter Hypothetical

Review the example presented at the beginning of the chapter. In the hypothetical, the paralegal failed to conduct a thorough counteranalysis. The assignment was to assess the likelihood that a Rule 12(b)(6) motion to dismiss for failure to state a claim would be granted. In a 12(b)(6) motion, the movant is basically arguing that under the facts of the case, the plaintiff cannot state a claim. To state a claim in a negligence case, facts must be present that establish or satisfy each of the elements of negligence: duty, breach of duty, proximate cause, and damages. In the example, the paralegal focused on duty, that is, on which duty applied. In light of the provisions of the applicable statute, the Ski Safety Act, and the facts of the case, there appeared to be a conflict of duties. The paralegal focused on which duty applied:

- The resort's duty to warn of hazards, or
- The skier's duty to know of and be responsible in snow and ice conditions

The paralegal's mistake was in failing to conduct a complete counteranalysis. A proper counteranalysis would have led the paralegal to consider the opponent's possible challenge involving the other areas of negligence—breach of duty, proximate cause, and damages. Had this been done, the paralegal would have recognized that the opposing side could raise a proximate cause argument: The cause of the accident was the skier's breach of duty by skiing beyond the range of his ability, not the resort's failure to warn. Had the paralegal considered this argument, a response could have been prepared, and the motion might not have been granted.

This example illustrates one of the most important considerations in counteranalysis: When analyzing a legal position, always conduct thorough and complete research that considers every possible attack, no matter how remote.

B. Counteranalysis—Reliance on Legislative Act

Section 35-6-6A of the Construction Industries Licensing Act provides that contractors must be licensed. The section requires all licensed general contractors to take reasonable steps to ensure that the subcontractors they hire are licensed. The section also provides that licensed general contractors who hire unlicensed subcontractors are vicariously liable in breach of contract suits filed against the unlicensed subcontractors.

In the client's case, the client (Plaintiff) is acting as his own general contractor; the subcontractor (SC) is unlicensed. Tom's, Inc. (TI), a licensed general contractor, has used SC on projects in the past and has acted as an agent for SC, often helping SC obtain jobs with other general contractors. Plaintiff, a private individual building his own home, contacted TI seeking assistance in locating a subcontractor. TI arranged the contract between SC and Plaintiff. TI recommended that SC be hired and fully disclosed to Plaintiff that TI was merely an agent for SC. TI was not party to the contract. SC breached its contract with Plaintiff, and Plaintiff sued both SC and TI.

In the lawsuit, Plaintiff argues that § 35-6-6A allows a cause of action for breach of contract against a general contractor who is not a party to the contract. This cause of action exists when the general contractor is acting as an agent for an unlicensed contractor who is a party to the contract. Plaintiff also contends that § 35-6-6A imposes an implied duty on licensed general contractors to protect third parties against all unlicensed contractors, not just unlicensed subcontractors. Plaintiff reasons that the implied duty arises because the intent of the statute is to place a duty on licensed general contractors to assist in the elimination of use of unlicensed contractors on construction projects.

The counterargument is that the statute is being too broadly interpreted. The statute, by its language, applies only to subcontractors hired by general contractors. In the case at hand, TI was merely a disclosed agent. TI did not hire SC, SC was not a subcontractor of TI, and TI was not a party to the contract. Therefore, the statute does not apply.

Further counteranalysis may reveal an additional counterargument: The law of agency governs the case rather than the contractor statute. Agency law provides that disclosed agents who are not parties to a contract are not liable for breach of contract. In this case, TI fully disclosed that it was acting only as an agent for SC and, therefore, under the law of agency, it is not liable.

This example illustrates the application of two counteranalysis approaches:

- The legal position is based on a misinterpretation of the legislative act.
- Another legal principle governs rather than the act relied on.

C. Counteranalysis—Reliance on Court Opinion

Customer is suing Bank, claiming that Bank's debt collection calls to his place of employment constitute intentional infliction of emotional distress. The calls were placed daily for a two-week period between 11:00 a.m. and noon. The issue is whether Bank's conduct is "outrageous conduct"—an essential element of intentional infliction of emotional distress.

There are no cases in the jurisdiction addressing the question of whether contact with a debtor at the debtor's place of employment constitutes outrageous conduct. In the case of *Tyron v. Bell*, a bill collector made daily telephone calls for three weeks to a debtor's residence. In that case, the highest court in the jurisdiction ruled that daily calls to a debtor's residence do not constitute outrageous conduct as long as only one telephone call per day is made and the call is placed at a reasonable time—between 8:00 a.m. and 7:00 p.m.

Bank argues that *Bell* is analogous and on point because both cases involve daily telephone calls to a debtor, made at a reasonable time. Relying on this reasoning, Bank contends that its conduct, like the conduct in *Bell*, cannot be considered outrageous.

The counterargument is that the court opinion is clearly distinguishable and, therefore, cannot apply as precedent. Telephone calls to an individual's place of employment are much more threatening than telephone calls to the individual's residence. Telephone calls to the place of employment disrupt the individual's work, interfere with job performance, and disrupt the work of others who have to answer the calls. Such persistent work interruptions can cause the employer to fire the employee. Calls to the workplace are outrageous because they pose a threat to the individual's livelihood. No such threat exists when the calls are to a residence. Therefore, calls to the workplace are clearly distinguishable, and the court opinion is not analogous, is not on point, and does not apply as precedent.

In this example, the counteranalysis challenges reliance on a court opinion by focusing on differences in the key facts of the opinion and the case. The counterargument is based on a common sense comparison of the facts of *Bell* and the facts of the client's case. This comparison leads to the conclusion that the key facts are so different that *Bell* cannot apply as precedent. Whenever your legal position or argument is based on a court opinion, be sure to conduct a counteranalysis of the position using all the approaches presented in this chapter, as well as any other approach that comes to mind.

Summary

Counteranalysis is the process of discovering and presenting the counterarguments to a legal position or argument. It is important because to adequately address a legal problem, you must consider all aspects of the problem. This includes identifying all the potential weaknesses in a legal position and being prepared to respond to all challenges to the position.

Employ counteranalysis whenever you research a legal issue or address a legal problem. Always be alert and look for counterarguments.

A prerequisite to engaging in counteranalysis is thorough research of the question or legal argument. This may help you identify some counterarguments and give credence to or dismiss those already identified. Once the research is complete, you can choose from many approaches to assist in counteranalysis.

Because most legal arguments are based on either enacted or case law, this chapter focuses on various counterarguments that may be raised when attacking reliance on an enacted law or case law. The list of approaches presented in this chapter is by no means inclusive of all the available ways to challenge a legal argument or position. It is important to make sure that you engage in counteranalysis using *all* the avenues listed (and any other possible approaches) when looking for potential weaknesses in or counterarguments to a legal position. You can count on the opposing side to discover weaknesses in your position and use them against you. Remember, whenever you are reviewing your client's case, you are negligent if you fail to engage in counteranalysis.

Quick References

Internet Resources

As of the date of publication of this text, there are no websites dedicated specifically to counteranalysis. However, using a search engine and "law counteranalysis" or "law counterargument" you will find tens of thousands of items in the search results list. Although some sites briefly mention the role of counteranalysis in the analysis process, no site addresses the topic in depth.

Most of the sites that involve the topic of counterarguments, do so in relation to specific cases or do not discuss the role of counterargument in the legal analysis process.

Exercises

ASSIGNMENT 1

What is counteranalysis? When should counteranalysis be conducted?

ASSIGNMENT 2

Why is counteranalysis important?

ASSIGNMENT 3

Counteranalysis—Legal Position or Argument Based on a Statute

Legislative Acts: Section 359-23A of the state statutes provides that to be eligible to run for the state senate, an individual must have been a resident of the state for three years.

Local ordinance § 2231 provides that an individual must be a resident of the municipality to run for a position on the city council. The ordinance does not define *resident* or *residency*.

Facts: Jerrie wishes to run for the city council. She has been a resident of the state for two years and nine months. The city clerk informs her that she is not eligible to run for city council because she has not been a resident of the state for three years. The clerk says that the city relies on the residency requirement established in § 359-23A.

Assignment: What is the counterargument to the clerk's position?

ASSIGNMENT 4

Counteranalysis—Legal Position or Argument Based on a Court Opinion

Case Law: In the case of *Baldonado v. State*, the plaintiff sued the state for false arrest. In *Baldonado*, a police officer received information from the dispatcher concerning a violent domestic dispute that specifically described the plaintiff and his vehicle.

The dispatcher reported that the plaintiff had been drinking and was leaving the residence with his two minor children. When the officer arrived at the residence, he saw the plaintiff and the two children in the described car. At the scene, the plaintiff's spouse and neighbors corroborated the dispatcher's information that a violent dispute had taken place. When the officer requested the plaintiff to shut off the engine and stay at the scene, the plaintiff attempted to leave. The officer stopped the plaintiff from leaving. The court noted that detention by a police officer is allowable only when there is reasonable suspicion that a crime has been committed. The court concluded that there was reasonable suspicion that a crime had been committed, and that the officer's detention of the defendant was lawful.

Facts: The officer was dispatched to the plaintiff's residence to investigate a domestic dispute. When the officer arrived, he saw a red vehicle driving away from the residence. A neighbor who was standing on the sidewalk informed the officer that he thought a domestic dispute had taken place at his neighbor's house and the plaintiff had just left in the red vehicle. The officer pursued the plaintiff and required him to return to the residence. The plaintiff is suing the officer for illegally detaining him.

Assignment: The state argues that *Baldonado v. State* supports the position that the detention was proper. What is the counterargument?

ASSIGNMENT 5

List seven ways to challenge an argument based on an enacted law.

ASSIGNMENT 6

List seven ways to challenge an argument based on case law.

ASSIGNMENT 7

Counteranalysis—Legal Position or Argument Based on a Statute

Legislative Act: Section 40-3-6-9A of the state criminal code provides that a noncustodial parent may be convicted of custodial interference when the noncustodial parent "maliciously takes, detains, conceals, entices away, or fails to return the child, without good cause, for a protracted period of time."

Assume there is no case law on point in the jurisdiction relevant to the following fact situation.

Facts: Mary has primary custody of her son. The father, Tom, has legal custody for two months in the summer. Tom takes the son for two months in the summer but fails to tell Mary where the son is and does not allow her to communicate with him. Before he leaves with the son, Tom tells Mary, "I'm going to punish you for the way you've treated me."

Assignment: Mary presents the following arguments in support of her claim that Tom is in violation of the statute. What are the counterarguments to each argument?

Part A

Tom's actions constitute concealment within the meaning of the statute.

Part B

Same facts, but when Tom is leaving, he says, "Since you wouldn't allow me to communicate with him when you had custody, I'm going to do the same." Mary argues that Tom's actions constitute concealment.

Part C

Same facts except that Tom says nothing when he picks up the son.

Part D

Tom allows the son to communicate with Mary, but he returns the son one day late. Mary argues that this constitutes failing to return the child without good cause for a protracted period of time.

Part E

Same facts as in part D except that Tom returns the son two weeks late.

Part F

Same facts as in part E except that Tom explains that he was unable to return the son on time because his car engine blew up, and it took two weeks to fix it.

ASSIGNMENT 8

Counteranalysis—Legal Position or Argument Based on Case Law

In the following example, assume that the only court opinion on point is *United States v. Leon* (see Appendix A).

Facts: Officer Jones submits to Judge Bean a request for a search warrant for the search of Steve's apartment. Officer Jones knows that there is not sufficient probable cause for issuance of the warrant, but he also knows that Judge Bean favors law enforcement and will most likely issue the warrant anyway. Judge Bean issues the warrant. Officer Jones gives the warrant to other officers and instructs them to execute it. He does not tell them that he knows it is defective because of the lack of probable cause for its issuance. The other officers execute the warrant in the good-faith belief that it is valid. The officers find drugs, and charge Steve with possession.

Steve moves for suppression of the evidence, claiming that the search was illegal and the evidence must be excluded under the exclusionary rule. What is the counterargument to the prosecution's position in each of the following situations?

Part A

The prosecution argues that because the officers executing the warrant were acting in the good-faith belief that the warrant was valid, *United States v. Leon* governs the case. The good-faith exception to the exclusionary rule applies, and therefore the evidence should not be suppressed.

Part B

Same facts except that Officer Jones delivers the warrant to members of the Citizens Protection Association, a private group of citizens trained by the police to assist in the performance of minor police functions. The group volunteers its services and is not employed by the police. They execute the warrant and make a citizen's arrest of Steve. The prosecution argues that *United States v. Leon* governs, and that case holds that the exclusionary rule is designed only to protect against police misconduct, not misconduct by private citizens.

ASSIGNMENT 9

Legislative Act: Section 41-1-6-9 of the state statutes defines *defamation* as the intentional publication of a false statement about a person. The statute defines *publication* as communication to a third person.

Case Law: *Ender v. Gault* is an opinion of the highest court in the state. In the case, Gault wrote a letter to Ender accusing Ender of defrauding his clients. Gault intended to hand-deliver the letter to Ender at a party at Ender's house. Gault became intoxicated at the party and left the letter on Ender's kitchen table. The letter was in an unsealed envelope with Ender's name on it. A business competitor of Ender, who was at the party, opened and read the letter.

Ender sued Gault for defamation. In its ruling in favor of Ender, the court stated that "*intentional publication* as used in the statute includes publication that occurs as a result of the gross negligence of the defendant." The court held that Gault's act of leaving the envelope unsealed on the kitchen table during a party constituted gross negligence.

Facts: Tom is a business associate of Allen. He believes Allen is stealing from their clients. Tom writes a letter to Allen stating that he knows Allen is stealing and that he intends to file criminal charges.

Tom, intending to hand-deliver the letter to Allen, goes to a restaurant where Allen usually has lunch. After waiting an hour for Allen, one of Allen's friends enters the restaurant. Tom folds the letter and seals it with tape. He gives the letter to the friend and asks him to deliver it to Allen. He does not tell the friend not to open the letter. The friend peels back the tape, reads the letter, reseals it, and delivers it to Allen. Allen finds out that the friend read the letter and sues Tom for defamation under § 41-1-6-9.

Assignment: Take into consideration the statute, the court opinion, and the facts when doing the following.

Part A

Prepare an argument in support of the position that Tom defamed Allen.

Part B

Prepare a counterargument to the argument prepared in part A.

Part 4

Legal Writing

Overview

The focus of Part IV is on legal writing and the legal writing process. It covers the application of the principles presented in the previous chapters to the drafting of legal research memoranda, court briefs, and legal correspondence, with chapters on the following topics:

- Fundamentals of writing
- The legal writing process in general
- Office legal memoranda (two chapters)
- Court briefs
- Correspondence

Chapter 14

Fundamentals of Writing

Learning Objectives

After completing this chapter, you should understand:

- Sentences and paragraphs
- Word selection and usage
- Grammar and punctuation
- Formal writing conventions

Your professional reputation and job performance evaluations are determined by the quality of your work. If the job involves legal writing, your reputation as a paralegal or law clerk is primarily based upon the quality of your writing. The value of the finished product depends not only on the accuracy and thoroughness of legal research and analysis, but also on the manner of its presentation. Excellent research and analysis skills are undermined if you cannot present the results of your research and analysis clearly and free of mechanical errors. Therefore, good writing skills are equally as important as good research and analysis skills.

Writing skills are also important because a poorly written product affects more than the paralegal's or law clerk's reputation. It also affects the reputation of the law firm. A law firm's reputation is affected, either positively or negatively, when a written product is directed to an audience outside the law firm, such as the client. A writing that contains grammatical or other mechanical errors reflects poorly on the firm. The client may wonder if the errors extend to the quality of the research and question the firm's capability to handle the case. Opposing counsel may conclude that the firm is not capable of mounting an effective opposition and be less inclined to settle a case they otherwise would have settled.

The creation of a professionally written product requires knowledge of the fundamentals of writing. This chapter summarizes some of these fundamentals and highlights areas where writing errors commonly occur. In this regard, the chapter presents general information concerning sentences, paragraphs, word selection and usage, grammar, punctuation, and some formal writing conventions. The chapter does not provide a comprehensive, in-depth exploration of these topics. Sources you may refer to for additional guidance are listed at the end of the chapter.

I. PARTS OF SPEECH

There are eight parts of speech: **noun**, **pronoun**, **verb**, **adjective**, **adverb**, **preposition**, **conjunction**, and **interjection**. These parts of speech describe a word's job in a sentence. Sentences are not just words–rather, they are specific parts of speech organized in a particular way with the aid of grammatical marks to convey specific meaning. The organization of the words in a sentence to convey a particular message requires a complete understanding of the parts of speech and what role each word plays.

If you do not know the parts of speech and cannot identify the job a word or group of words does, it is difficult to form strong, clear, concise sentences. This, of course, impacts the formation of paragraphs, which in turn impacts the overall quality of a document. Although it is beyond the scope of this text, diagramming sentences is the best way to learn the parts of speech, the relationship of words to each other, and the role words play in sentences. A comprehensive discussion of the parts of speech would require an entire text. This section provides an overview of the parts of speech, (except interjections, which are rarely used in legal writing), and covers areas which typically cause errors in sentence construction. There are resources for additional information on the parts of speech and for diagramming sentences listed at the end of this chapter.

A. Noun

A **noun** is a word that refers to a person, place, thing, or idea. Nouns take on a variety of jobs in sentences. They can be subjects, direct objects, indirect objects, objects of prepositions, and subject complements.

For Example

The *defendant* testified about the contract terms. (subject)
The jury deliberated through the *night*. (object of preposition)
The juror handled the *gun*. (direct object)

Nouns also have different classes: proper and common, concrete and abstract, count and noncount, and collective. One area a legal professional can run into difficulty is with proper nouns. A proper noun names a specific item. Proper nouns are capitalized.

For Example

Proper nouns are italicized:
The *Court of Appeals* issued its ruling in the client's case today.
The *Committee on Superior Courts* held its meeting at the courthouse and invited the *Chief Justice Smith* a guest speaker.

If you can hear, see, smell, taste, or feel the item, it is a concrete noun. If you cannot detect the noun with your five senses, it is an abstract noun. Collective nouns name groups and can be tricky. Depending upon the way a collective noun is used, it can be singular or plural, which is important in noun/pronoun agreement and subject/verb agreement.

For Example

Despite the danger, the SWAT *team* pursues the shooters into the building. (Singular—team, the collective noun, is acting as one unit)
The SWAT *team* turned in their guns after the exercise was over. (Plural—each member of the team acts individually; note plural pronoun (their) and object (guns).

B. Pronoun

A **pronoun** is a word that replaces a noun. A pronoun must have a clear antecedent. An **antecedent** is the noun which the pronoun replaces. Pronouns come in two forms, both with several characteristics. Although an in-depth discussion of all of the forms and characteristics of pronouns is beyond the scope of this text, the following summarizes some of the most common forms and characteristics of pronouns.

For Example

The *defendant* testified <u>she</u> did not cross the threshold of the exit. The antecedent is in *italics*. The pronoun replacing the antecedent is <u>underlined</u>.

1. Personal Pronouns

Personal pronouns have several characteristics. They can be singular or plural. They can be in one of three points of view: 1st person, 2nd person, or 3rd person. Pronouns can be female, male, or neutral. They also can have three cases: objective, subjective, and possessive.

Personal Pronoun Chart

	Singular			Plural		
	Subjective	Objective	Possessive	Subjective	Objective	Possessive
1st Person	I	Me	My, Mine	We	Us	Our, ours
2nd Person	You	You	You, Yours	You	You	Your, Yours
3rd Person	He She It	Him Her It	His Her, Hers Its	They	Them	Their, Their

2. Demonstrative Pronouns

Demonstrative pronouns point to something specific within the sentence or a nearby sentence. There is a specific list of demonstrative pronouns: *this* (singular), *that* (singular), *these* (plural), *those* (plural).

For Example

Those belong to the plaintiff.
These cases are on point.

3. Reflexive Pronouns

Reflexive pronouns refer to the subject of the sentence, clause, or verbal phrase in which it is located. They are used when you refer back to the subject of the sentence or clause. They end with –self or –selves.

For Example

The plaintiff's lawyers handled media inquiries *themselves*.
The law clerk emailed *himself* a copy of the brief.

4. Indefinite Pronouns

Some pronouns are definite, in that they refer to a specific noun or pronoun. Indefinite pronouns, on the other hand, take the place of a noun, but not a particular noun. There are two categories of indefinite pronouns. The first includes pronouns that refer to a nonspecific noun, for example: *anybody, anyone, anything, everybody, everyone, everything, nobody, none, no one, nothing, somebody, someone,* and *something.* The other includes pronouns that point to a specific noun whose meaning is easily understood because of words used before or shortly thereafter. They include: *all, another, any, both, each, either, few, many, neither, one, some,* and *several.*

For Example

Many from the court are planning to attend the judge's retirement celebration.

5. Relative Pronouns

A relative pronoun is used to connect a clause or phrase to a noun or another pronoun. Often relative pronouns introduce adjectival clauses (adjectives are discussed below). There is a specific list of relative pronouns: *who, whoever, whom, whomever, that, which, when, where,* and *whose.*

For Example

That is the person *whom* I saw running from the scene.
The woman *whose* hand was severed in the accident is my sister.

Note: Use *who, whom,* and *whose* to refer to people. Use *that, which,* and *when* to refer to things.

C. Verb

A **verb** is a word that shows action or a state of being. Verbs are part of the predicate of a complete sentence. Verbs are often described as action verbs or linking verbs. Action verbs are usually easy to identify because they describe action. Some people struggle with linking verbs. Linking verb do not express action, instead they link the subject of the sentence to something else about the subject. The most common linking verb is *be* and all of its forms: *am, is, are, was, were, has been, are being, might have been, become,* and *seem.* Some words can be linking verbs or actions verbs depending on their use. Examples of these linking verbs include: *appear, feel, grow, look, prove, remain, smell, sound, taste* and *turn.*

For Example

Linking verbs are in italics:
The witness *is* dishonest.
The witness lied. (action verb)
The victim *became* sad.

One way to tell if these verbs are linking verbs or action verbs is to substitute *am, is,* or *are* in the sentence for the verb. If the sentence still makes sense, the verb is a linking verb.

For Example

The car smelled like marijuana. (linking verb)
The officer smelled the contents of the bag. (action verb)

Verbs can be singular or plural. If there is a singular subject, then there must be a singular verb. If the subject is plural, then the verb must be plural. Words that come between the subject and verb do not affect whether the verb is singular or plural. Pay attention to the number of the subject (plural or singular) to determine the number of the verb.

For Example

The witnesses (plural subject) read (plural verb) from the letter when asked.
The witness (singular subject) reads (singular verb) from the letter when asked.

D. Adjective

An **adjective** is a word used to modify a noun or pronoun. They are usually placed before the word they modify. Adjectives tell the reader these things about nouns and pronouns: which one, what kind, or how many.

For Example

She wore a *red* dress to the party.
The *race* car had *vinyl* seats.

E. Adverb

An **adverb** is a word used to modify a verb, adjective, or another adverb. An adverb never modifies a noun or pronoun. Adverbs tell the reader these things about the words they modify: where, when, how, how often, or how much.

For Example

John ran *quickly* into the house.

F. Preposition

A preposition is a word that is always used with a noun or a pronoun (the object of the preposition) to create a prepositional phrase. The prepositional phrase shows the relationship between the object of the preposition and another word in the sentence. The list of prepositions is long. Consulting a grammar text or a reliable grammar source on the Internet will provide a more exhaustive list. Examples include: *about, above, after, around, at, before, beneath, by, down, for, from, in, inside, of, off, on, opposite, since, through, throughout, to, underneath, up, with,* and *without*. These words are not always acting as a preposition. They are only prepositions if they are part of a prepositional phrase.

For Example

The book on the dresser is covered with fingerprints.
Which book? The one *on the dresser*.
Before trial, the lawyer reviewed the evidence.
When did the lawyer review evidence? *Before trial*.

G. Conjunction

A **conjunction** is a word that connects words, phrases, clauses, or sentences. Examples of conjunctions include: *and, or, but, yet, for, so, either,* and *because*. A correlative conjunction is a conjunction that pairs up with another word to connect elements of a sentence. Notable examples include: *either / or, neither / nor, both / and,* and *not only / but also*

For Example

We can select the first clause *or* the entire second paragraph.
All of the participants had heard of the agreement, *but* none had seen it.

II. SENTENCES

The **sentence** is the fundamental building block of writing. It is a statement that conveys an idea or ideas. Good writing skills include an understanding of the basics of proper sentence construction.

A. Sentence Structure or Pattern

A sentence is usually a statement in which the actor (the subject) performs some action or describes a state of being (the predicate). The subject is a noun or pronoun. On occasion, the subject is unstated.

For Example

Subject	Predicate
John	wrecked the car.
The pear	is ripe.

The predicate is composed of the verb and object of the verb, such as a direct object (if necessary). An object of the verb may be required to receive the action of the verb.

For Example

Subject	Predicate
John	wrecked the car.

The *car* is a direct object that receives the action of the verb *wrecked*.

At a minimum, a sentence must have a subject and a predicate. In its simplest form, a sentence requires a noun and a verb.

For Example

Judges rule.
The witness lied.

B. Basic Rules in Sentence Writing

The following subsections introduce basic rules involving sentences and sentence structure. Exhibit 14-1 lists the topics covered by these rules. Keep this list in mind when drafting or reviewing sentences.

1. Subject–Verb Distance

Keep the subject and verb as close together as possible. A sentence is easier to understand if the subject and verb are close together. Intervening words, clauses, or phrases disrupt the action and make the sentence difficult to understand.

For Example

Intervening words in italics: John, *apparently upset and in a bad mood*, hit James.

Revision: Apparently upset and in a bad mood, John hit James.

Intervening clause in italics: The argument that the good faith exception applies *because the officers were acting in good faith and the warrant was defective due to magistrate error* is supported by the facts.

Revision: The argument that the good-faith exception applies is supported by the facts. The officers were acting in good faith and the warrant was defective due to magistrate error.

Subject–Verb Distance	Keep the subject and verb as close together as possible.
Sentence Length	A short sentence is easy to understand and concise. A suggested average sentence length is 15 to 25 words.
Active/Passive Voice	The general rule is to draft sentences using active voice. Active voice is easier to understand and more powerful than passive voice. Active: Steve keeps the records. Passive: The records are kept by Steve.
Action Verbs	Select verbs that are active rather than verbs that show a state of being or are passive. Action: Mary keeps the books. State of being: The bookkeeper is Mary. Action: Mary concluded that Tom was guilty. Passive: The conclusion that Mary reached was that Tom was guilty.
Transitions	Use transitional words and phrases to connect sentences and to establish the relationship between the subjects of sentences.

© Cengage

Exhibit 14-1 Topics to Keep in Mind When Drafting Sentences.

2. Sentence Length

Although there is no hard-and-fast rule governing sentence length, shorter sentences are easier to understand. The length of a sentence will vary according to the nature of the information it must convey. A good average for sentence length is 15 to 25 words. If you find that your sentences are too long, eliminate extra words or break the sentence into shorter sentences.

For Example

Sentence too long: The evidence should be suppressed because the warrant did not authorize unannounced entry, and there were no exigent circumstances at the scene that provided justification for the officers' actions of entering the residence unannounced.

Revision: The evidence should be suppressed because the warrant did not authorize unannounced entry. In addition, the circumstances at the scene did not provide justification for unannounced entry.

Watch out for run-on sentences. Each sentence should contain one main idea. It is often tempting to pack more than one idea into a sentence. This usually occurs when the ideas being conveyed are related. If the sentence you are reviewing is very long, it may be that it is a run-on sentence, and you are attempting to convey too many ideas in one sentence.

For Example

Run-on sentence: Thomas does not dispute the fact that the court properly resorted to estimating a plant quantity for the 1991 grow, his dispute concerns the basis for the court's estimation.
   Note that this sentence conveys two related ideas: what he does not dispute and what he does dispute. Each idea should be presented in separate sentences.

Revision: Thomas does not dispute the fact that the court properly resorted to estimating a plant quantity for the 1991 grow. His dispute concerns the basis for the court's estimation.

3. Active and Passive Voice

a. Active Voice

The general rule is that you should draft sentences using **active voice**. When you adopt active voice, the subject of the sentence becomes the actor. In other words, the actor (subject) acts (verb). When you use passive voice, the subject of the sentence is acted upon.

For Example

Active voice: The judge denied the motion.
                     The construction workers built the dam.
Passive voice: The motion was decided by the judge.
                     The dam was built by the construction workers.

Active voice is easier to understand and is more powerful. It is easier to understand because the doer of the action is mentioned at the beginning of the sentence prior to the action. Readers do not have to read the entire sentence before they are informed who is performing the action. Active voice is more powerful because, at the outset, it identifies the actor as the performer of the action. This focuses attention on the actor and emphasizes the actor's actions. When passive voice is used, the actor is removed from the action, or not identified at all.

For Example

Active voice: The defendant breached the contract when he failed to deliver the goods on time.

Passive voice: The contract was breached when the goods were not delivered on time. (The actor is not identified.)

b. Passive Voice

In certain situations, it is appropriate to use **passive voice**. You may use passive voice when the actor is unknown or unimportant or when you do not want to emphasize the actor's conduct. See Chapter 18 for a discussion of the appropriate use of passive voice in court briefs.

For Example

Actor unknown: A portion of the transcript was lost.

Actor unimportant: The bank deposit was found by a passerby.

Actor deemphasized: The vase was broken and the plaintiff injured when the vase slipped from the defendant's hand.

4. Action Verbs

When possible, select **action (active) verbs** rather than passive verbs that show a state of being.

For Example

Passive: Mary reached the conclusion that Tom was guilty.

Revision: Mary concluded Tom was guilty.

Passive Verb/State of being: The record keeper is Steve Jones.

Revision: Steve Jones keeps the records.

5. Transitions

Transitional words and phrases connect sentences and establish the relationship between the subjects of the sentences. **Transitions** are important because they guide the reader and make the writing cohesive.

For Example

No transition: The statute requires that fences exceeding 5 feet in height must be located no closer than 10 feet from the property line. Your fence will be 6 feet high; you must build it at least 10 feet from the property line.

With transition—transition in italics: The statute requires that fences exceeding 5 feet in height must be located no closer than 10 feet from the property line. *Therefore, because* your fence will exceed 5 feet, you must locate it at least 10 feet from the property line.

The following are examples of transitional words and phrases:

however	even so	but	still
furthermore	nevertheless	so	and
although	simply put	for	on the other hand
conversely	moreover	that is	in other words
contrary to	above all	clearly	more importantly
initially	meanwhile	finally	all the same
specifically	therefore	thus	consequently
arguably	in contrast	instead	to illustrate
likewise	allegedly	unlike	subsequently
undoubtedly	in addition	likewise	in conclusion
in summary	nonetheless	since	without question

III. PARAGRAPHS

A **paragraph** is a group of sentences that address the same topic. Paragraphs are important because they organize the writing according to topic. They make it easier for the reader to understand the material by separating it into manageable units. A reader may encounter difficulty understanding the subject matter when it is not divided into paragraphs. Start a new paragraph when addressing a new idea or topic. Use transitional phrases or sentences to link new paragraphs.

A paragraph usually consists of the following elements:

- A topic sentence
- The body
- A closing sentence

Every paragraph does not require each of these elements. A short paragraph, for example, may not have a closing sentence. The following subsections discuss the elements of a paragraph and other considerations to keep in mind when writing paragraphs (see Exhibit 14-2).

A. Topic Sentence of a Paragraph

The **topic sentence** identifies the subject of the paragraph. It introduces the subject and provides the focus of the paragraph for the reader. The topic sentence is usually placed at the beginning of the paragraph.

Topic Sentence	Use a topic sentence to introduce the subject and provide the focus of the paragraph.
Body	The body of the paragraph should support or develop the subject introduced by the topic sentence. Generally, a paragraph should address a single idea or topic rather than several different topics.
Closing Sentence	End with a closing sentence that summarizes or applies the topic addressed in the paragraph.
Transition Sentence	Include transitional words, phrases, or sentences to connect the subjects discussed in the different paragraphs.

© Cengage

Exhibit 14-2 Topics to Keep in Mind When Drafting Paragraphs.

For Example

- Topic sentence of a paragraph that discusses why the exclusionary rule is necessary: "The Supreme Court has identified several reasons why the exclusionary rule is necessary."
- Topic sentence of a paragraph that discusses Mr. Smith's actions: "Mr. Smith's actions do not constitute a breach of contract."
- Topic sentence of a paragraph that addresses required conditions: "A warranty of fitness for a particular purpose is created when the following conditions are present."

B. Paragraph Body

The body of a paragraph consists of sentences that support or develop the subject introduced by the topic sentence. The sentence(s) should develop the subject clearly and logically.

For Example

The topic sentence in this example is printed in italics to separate it from the body:

To support a negligence claim against Mrs. Jones, four elements must be proven. First, we must establish that she had a duty to keep the tree on her property trimmed. Next, we must show that she failed to properly trim the tree. Then it is necessary to prove that, as a result of her failure to trim the tree, a branch fell and struck Mr. Thompson. Finally, we must establish that Mr. Thompson's injuries resulted from the branch striking him.

Notice in this example that the sentences in the body are presented clearly and in logical order. Remember, when preparing the body of a paragraph, the goal is to draft it clearly, concisely, and logically.

C. Closing Sentence of a Paragraph

A paragraph should end with a **closing sentence**. The content of the sentence varies according to the subject matter covered in the paragraph. It should summarize the topic addressed in the body or apply the subject discussed to the facts of the case.

For Example

- **Summary:** Therefore, to establish a claim for negligence, we must show that Mrs. Jones had a duty, the duty was breached, the breach caused the accident, and the accident caused the harm that resulted.
- **Application of subject to the facts of the case:** The rule of law adopted in the *Craig* case clearly applies in this case because Mr. Smith failed to warn Mr. Jones that the brakes were defective.

D. Transition Sentences

Transition sentences (or words, phrases) connect the subjects discussed in different paragraphs. They guide the reader by linking the paragraphs, thereby providing coherence to the overall writing. The topic or closing sentence of a paragraph may include the transitional language. Transitional words, phrases, and sentences are usually placed at either the beginning or the end of the paragraph.

For Example

Transitions at the Beginning of a Paragraph:

The following transitional language is in italics:

- If the *above mentioned* requirements are not met, breach of contract may not be claimed.
- There are, *however*, exceptions to this rule.
- *In addition* to a cause of action for negligence, Mr. Smith may allege ... (Note: Use when the body of the paragraph addresses the other possible causes of action, and the previous paragraph discusses the negligence cause of action.)
- The *second* element of the statute requires ... (Note: Use when separate paragraphs discuss separate elements.)

Transitions at the End of the Paragraph:

The following transitional language is in italics:

- The statute, *however*, does not define "publication"; therefore, case law must be consulted. (Note: Use when the next paragraph introduces the case law.)
- *In addition* to this case, other cases also discuss the requirements of the statute. (Note: Use when the following paragraph discusses the other cases.)

E. Paragraph Length

As with sentences, there is no rule that establishes a standard length for paragraphs. Paragraphs usually are three to six sentences in length. Most paragraph topics can be covered comfortably in six to seven sentences, although a paragraph may be as short as one sentence, or as long as ten. Determine the length by keeping in mind the goal of clearly and completely covering the topic of the paragraph. The reader may have difficulty understanding or become confused by extremely long paragraphs. A series of extremely short paragraphs may lack transition and distract the reader. Therefore, extremely long or short paragraphs should be the exception in legal writing.

IV. WORD SELECTION AND USAGE

Not only is it necessary to be skilled in sentence and paragraph construction, you must also be skilled in selecting and using words. This section presents some guidelines on word selection and usage.

A. Excessive or Redundant Words

Avoid the use of excessive or redundant words. Check each sentence for words that can be eliminated. Simplify the finished product.

For Example

Excessive words: The statute provides individuals protection against the use of evidence obtained by warrantless wiretaps.

Revision: The statute prohibits the use of evidence obtained by warrantless wiretaps.

Redundant words: The sole and exclusive remedy provided by the statute is criminal prosecution.

Revision: The exclusive remedy provided by the statute is criminal prosecution. OR

Revision: The statute establishes criminal prosecution as the exclusive remedy.

The following lists commonly used redundant pairs. Any one of the terms can be used; the use of both terms is not required or appropriate.

full/complete	merged/together	cease/desist
each/every	join/together	null/void
true/correct	due/owing	exact/same
end/result	alter/change	descend/down
and/moreover	sole/exclusive	specific/example

Other unnecessary words occur in phrases such as "few in number," "green in color," "continue on," and "five a.m. in the morning." If omission of a word does not change the intended meaning of the sentence, leave it out.

B. Noun–Verb Strings

A **noun–verb string** is a group of related words used to convey information. It is a form of redundancy that should be avoided when a single descriptive word will accomplish the same end.

For Example

Noun–Verb Strings:
The distributor is not responsible for failures to perform due to *riots, floods, earthquakes, and acts of God.*
A stockholder may not *grant, give, sell, or assign* her interest in the stock without the consent of the other shareholders.

Revisions:
The distributor is not responsible for failure to perform caused by events beyond the distributor's control.
A stockholder may not transfer her interest in the stock without the consent of the other shareholders.

C. Nominalizations

A **nominalization** is a noun created from a verb or adjective.

For Example

Verb	Noun
determine	determination
realize	realization
move	movement
react	reaction
resist	resistance
applicable	applicability

Nominalizations weaken a sentence by taking the action away from the actor. They make the sentence passive and less forceful.

For Example

Nominalizations:
    He came to the realization that the assignment required more work.
    The importance of the opinion is that. . . .
Revisions:
    He realized that the assignment required more work.
    The opinion is important because. . . .

D. Legalese

Legalese, as used here, refers to terms of art used in the legal profession that are not generally known outside the profession. The goal of legal writing is to effectively communicate information. Writing in plain English usually accomplishes this goal, and plain English should be used when possible.

The audience governs the extent to which you incorporate legal terminology in legal writing. Legal terms are appropriate when communicating with others in the field. If the reader is trained in the law, the use of legal terms or phrases, such as *res ipsa loquitur*, is much easier than providing a definition or explanation. When the recipient is a nonlawyer, however, you should avoid using legal terms. Be sure to define legal terms when communicating with nonlawyers if the meaning of the term is not obvious.

For Example

Legalese in italics: The constitution requires *probable cause* before the police can conduct a search of your residence.

Revision: The constitution requires the police to have a valid reason before they can search a house. An example of a valid reason would be if reliable persons informed the police that they saw illegal drugs in the house.

E. Archaic Terms

Archaic terms are words or phrases frequently used in the past that are being phased out of legal writing. Do not include such terms in your writing. Such terms include *undersigned, wherefore, saith, party of the first part, aforesaid, hereinbefore, hereinafter, henceforth,* and *the said party.*

For Example

Archaic and excess verbiage in italics: Upon the signing of the Agreement, *the party of the first part* will *hereinafter cease and desist* from attending hearings where *the party of the second part* acts as chairperson.

Revision: Upon the signing of the Agreement, Mr. Smith will *not* attend hearings where Ms. Carson acts as chairperson. (Assume that names, Mr. Smith and Ms. Carson, are mentioned earlier in the agreement. Rather than use the phrase *party of the first part* and *party of the second part,* simply repeat the names of the parties or use a pronoun such as *he* or *she* when it is clear which party is being referenced.)

F. Sexist Language

In any form of writing, using gender-specific language is prejudicial and inappropriate unless it refers to a specific person whose gender is known. **Sexist language** has no place in legal writing. The following guidelines will help ensure gender-neutral writing.

1. Words

Change gender-specific terms to gender-neutral terms.

For Example

Gender-Specific	Gender-Neutral
chairman	chairperson
wife/husband	spouse
draftsman	drafter
forefathers	forebearers
housewife	homemaker
mankind workman	people, human beings, humanity worker
anchorman	anchor
congressman	congressperson, representative

2. Restructuring Sentences with *He* and *She*

Do not use *he or she* or *he/she* in place of *he* to render a sentence gender-neutral. You may adopt several alternatives to avoid the use of *his or her, he/she,* and so forth.

a. Restate the sentence so the antecedent is plural.

For Example

The rule requires the plaintiff to file his pleadings. . . .

Revision: The rule requires plaintiffs to file their pleadings. . . .

b. Eliminate use of the pronoun; substitute the definite article.

For Example

The officer is responsible for the actions of his troops.

Revision: The officer is responsible for the actions of the troops.

c. Repeat the name

For Example

Before the client may liquidate the assets of the company, he must. . . .

Revision: Before the client may liquidate the assets of the company, the client must. . . .

d. Use *one, you,* or *your* when possible.

For Example

Everyone has a right to his personal preferences.

Revisions: Everyone has a right to personal preferences. You have a right to your personal preferences.

e. Rephrase the sentence.

For Example

A legal assistant should not communicate with the litigants he knows we do not represent.

Revision: A legal assistant should not communicate with litigants we do not represent.

3. Appropriate Reference to Gender

Reference to gender is appropriate only when you intend to refer to a specific sex.

For Example

Each member of the women's basketball team had her name printed on the back of her uniform.

G. Specific Words—Problem Areas

Some words are commonly misused. You can avoid problems of misuse by following some basic rules.

1. Affect/Effect

Affect is a verb meaning "to influence." *Effect* is either a verb or noun. As a verb, it means "to bring about or cause"; as a noun, it means "result."

For Example

"His actions will not *affect* [not *effect*] the outcome of the case." The meaning of *affect* is "to influence."

"He tried to *effect* [not *affect*] an agreement." Here, the meaning of *effect* is "to bring about."

"The test did not bring about the desired *effect* [not *affect*]." The meaning of *effect* (used as a noun) is "result."

2. Among/Between

Use *among* when referring to three or more things, and *between* when referring to two.

For Example

The jury award was divided *among* the six plaintiffs.
The jury award was divided *between* Tom and Grace.

3. And/Or

The use of *and/or* creates an ambiguity and is not proper. When the word *and* is used in regard to a list of words, all the items listed are included and required.

For Example

"The case law requires the plaintiff to prove duty, breach of duty, proximate cause, *and* damages." The use of *and* means that all four elements must be proved. All the listed items are included in the requirement.

When *or* is used, all the items listed are not required to be included. Any one or all of the items are included.

For Example

"The case law requires the corporate president to provide notice orally, by mail, *or* by facsimile." All the listed items are not required. Only one of the items is required. The president has the choice of giving notice by one or all of the means listed.

4. Council/Counsel

A *council* is a deliberative or administrative body. A *councilor* is a member of such a body. *Counsel*, when used as a verb, means to give advice or guidance. *Counsel*, when used as a noun, is advice. A *counselor* (*counsel*) is a person, such as a lawyer, who gives advice or guidance.

For Example

She presented the resolution to the city council.
The city councilor received the petition.
The school guidance officer provided counsel to the new student.
The counselor informed the shareholders of their legal rights.

5. Each Other/One Another

When referring to two nouns, use *each other*. When referring to more than two nouns, use *one another*.

For Example

Bob and Mary supported *each other* during the trial.
The members of the team supported *one another* during the tournament.

6. Good/Well

Good is an adjective (adjectives modify nouns and pronouns). It cannot be used as an adverb (adverbs modify verbs, adjectives, and adverbs). *Well* can act as an adverb or an adjective.

For Example

Incorrect: "She worked good."

Correct: "She worked well." *Well* is an adverb that modifies the verb *worked*. The use of *good* is inappropriate, because *good* is an adjective and should not be used to modify a verb.

Correct: "She did good work." In this sentence, *good* is used as an adjective modifying the noun *work*.

7. Lie/Lay

Lie is an intransitive verb that means "to rest or recline." (An *intransitive verb* is a verb that does not take a direct object.) Its forms are *lie, lay, lain,* and *lying.*

For Example

I think I will *lie* [not *lay*] down.
He was so tired he *lay* [not *laid*] down.
She has been *lying* [not *laying*] around all day.

Lay is a transitive verb that means "to put or place." (A *transitive verb* takes a direct object.) Its forms are *lay, laid, laid,* and *laying.*

For Example

I think I will *lay* [not *lie*] the paper down.
He *laid* [not *lay*] the paper down.
He has been *laying* [not *lying*] brick all day.

8. Like/As

Like should be used as a preposition; it should be followed by a noun or noun phrase. *As* may act as a conjunction or a preposition in a sentence.

For Example

"In this contract he used the same technique as [not like] he did in the other agreement."
    The use of *like* would not be appropriate because here *as* functions as a conjunction, not
    a preposition.
"The legal assistant, *like* all the other participants, was on time." This use of *like* is appropriate
    because *like* functions as a preposition in the sentence.

9. Shall and May

The word *shall* has caused much debate when used in legal context. Although the term permeated statutes and rules of procedure for many years, and many lawyers were taught the word *shall* is used to impose a duty that is mandatory, nearly every jurisdiction has held that *shall* means *may.* In fact, Black's law dictionary lists five meanings for *shall. Shall* became so problematic it has been purged from all but one set of the Federal Rules of Procedure, specifically Rule 56—the summary judgment rule. Many states have also purged the term from procedural rules.

Shall was not a word that was used often in general American English. This may be a reason for the issues surrounding the interpretation of its use in various statutes and procedural rules. Today, it is increasingly common to use words that are more common to America English, such as: *will, may, must, is,* or *is entitled to.* As such, avoid the word shall whenever possible and replace it with one of the words listed in the preceding sentence. Think carefully about what the sentence is to convey before determining which alternative word to use.

10. That/Which

Use *that* to introduce restrictive clauses, and *which* to introduce nonrestrictive clauses. A *restrictive clause* is necessary to the meaning of the sentence.

For Example

"You must perform all the steps *that are listed in the statute*." The italicized clause is a restrictive clause. It informs the reader that the required steps are the steps listed in the statute. It is necessary to an understanding of the steps that must be taken.

A *nonrestrictive clause* is not necessary to the meaning of the sentence. It can be set off from the rest of the sentence with commas without changing the meaning of the sentence.

For Example

"I always buy his products, which *usually are of high quality*." The italicized clause is a nonrestrictive clause. It is not necessary to the main meaning of the sentence.

V. GRAMMAR

The rules of **grammar** govern the construction of sentences. This section introduces basic rules of grammar to keep in mind when performing a writing assignment.

A. Subject–Verb Agreement

The subject and verb should agree in person and number. This means that singular subjects require singular verbs, and plural subjects require plural verbs.

For Example

Incorrect: The decision in the case *require* the defendant to give notice to the plaintiff.
    (This sentence has a singular subject, *decision*, and a plural verb, *require*.)
Correct: The decision in the case *requires* the defendant to give notice to the plaintiff.
    (The singular subject *decision* agrees with the singular verb *requires*.)

The following basic rules concern **subject–verb agreement**:

1. Two or more subjects joined by *and* usually require a plural verb.

For Example

Mary and Joan *were* present.
The president, secretary, and treasurer *are* going to the conference.

2. Two or more subjects joined by *or* or *nor* require a verb that agrees with the subject closest to the verb.

For Example

Tom or his brothers *are* going to attend.
Either the brothers or Tom *is* the responsible party.
Neither Tom nor his brother *is* going to attend.
To accept the contract or to draft a new one *is* your option.

3. Most indefinite pronouns require singular verbs. Indefinite pronouns are pronouns that do not refer to a specific person or thing, such as *anyone, everybody, nobody, someone, each,* and *something*.

For Example

Everybody *is* responsible.
Each of the members *has* a specific task.

4. Some indefinite pronouns require a verb that matches the noun to which they refer. Some of these pronouns are *all, none, most, some,* and *any*.

For Example

All of the property *is* distributed.
All of the items *are* missing.

5. Plural indefinite pronouns such as *both, few, many, several,* and *others* require a plural verb.

For Example

Few *are* selected.
    Although there were multiple presentations, several *were* not in attendance.
    The others *are* not required to be present.

6. Whether a collective noun requires a singular or plural verb depends on the function of the collective noun. Recall from the first section, a *collective noun* is a noun that refers to a group (e.g., *jury, family, crowd, majority*). When a collective noun functions as a unit, a singular verb is necessary. However, when the members of the collective noun act or are acted upon individually, a plural verb is required.

For Example

The jury *was* deadlocked.
The family *is* present.

7. Nouns that are plural in form but have a singular meaning require a singular verb (e.g., *politics, news, mathematics*).

For Example

The news *is* bad.
The politics of the party *is* corrupt.
Mathematics *is* her strength.

8. The title of a work takes a singular verb.

For Example

Legal Research, Analysis, and Writing *is* wonderful reading.

9. A relative pronoun requires a verb that agrees with its antecedent. A *relative pronoun* is one that refers to another noun in the sentence (e.g., *which, who, that*). The *antecedent* is the noun to which the relative pronoun refers. If the antecedent is singular, the verb should be singular. If the antecedent is plural, the verb should be plural.

For Example

Our *client* is one of the persons *who* has been indicted in the case. (*Who* is the relative pronoun, and *client* is the antecedent.)

For Example

Singular: Our *client, who* was present at the scene, *has* been indicted.
The antecedent (*client*) of the relative pronoun (*who*) is singular; therefore, *who* takes a singular verb (*has*).
Plural: The *clients, who* were present at the scene, *have* been indicted.
The antecedent (*clients*) of the relative pronoun (*who*) is plural; therefore, *who* takes a plural verb (*have*).

B. Verb Tense

Verb tense is the time in which a verb's action occurs. Events happening in the present use the present tense. Events that occurred in the past use the past tense. Events that will take place in the future use the future tense. Usually, sentences and paragraphs are written in the same tense. Check to ensure that your writing does not have inappropriate changes in verb tense.

For Example

Inappropriate change in verb tense: The complaint *was* filed on January 1, 2017. The defendants *move* to dismiss the complaint. The motion *was* denied. (Notice that the verb tense in this sentence moves from past, to present, then back to past tense.)
Revision: The complaint *was* filed on January 1, 2017. The defendants *moved* to dismiss the complaint. The motion *was* denied. (Notice that all the verbs are in past tense.)

Guidelines concerning correct verb tense follow:

1. When presenting your position or legal analysis, use present tense.

For Example

Plaintiff *contends* that the rule requires 30 days' notice.

2. When addressing a court opinion that has already been decided, use past tense.

For Example

In *Smith v. Jones*, the court *held* that the rule does not require 30 days' notice.

3. When discussing a law or rule still in effect, use present tense.

For Example

The provisions of § 44-556 *require* a contractor to give 30 days' notice.

C. Parallel Construction

Parallel construction means that items in a list are similar in grammatical structure. The rule requires that in sentences including a list, a group of activities, and so on, each of the items must use the same grammatical form; that is, all the items or members of the group should agree in verb tense, number, and so on.

For Example

Lack parallel construction:

- The defendant is a trained officer with 15 years' experience *who* has won several service medals.
- The goals of the association are the following:
  a. educating the public about crime,
  b. to provide support for the police, and
  c. improvement of local neighborhood watch groups.
- Most states have passed uniform laws for corporations, partnerships, and that allow limited liability companies.
- The client gave consideration not only to the exclusion term but also the waiver clause.

Revisions with parallel construction:

- The defendant is a trained officer *who* has 15 years' experience and *who* has won several service medals.
- The goals of the association are the following:
  a. *to educate* the public about crime,
  b. *to provide* support for the police, and
  c. *to improve* local neighborhood watch groups.
- Most states have passed uniform laws for corporations, partnerships, and limited liability companies.
- The client gave consideration not only to the exclusion term but also to the waiver clause.

D. Superfluous Verbs

Avoid the use of verb constructions that are unnecessarily wordy.

For Example

Superfluous verbs in italics:

- He decided to *perform an investigation* into the matter.
- The arbitrator *decided to give consideration* to the argument.
- The judge *reached a decision* on the question.
- The contractor *made an attempt* to complete the contract on time.

Revisions without superfluous verbs:

- He decided to *investigate* the matter.
- The arbitrator *considered* the argument.
- The judge *decided* the question.
- The contractor *attempted* to complete the contract on time.

E. Modifiers and Infinitives

Modifiers are words or phrases that describe the subject, verb, or object in a sentence. Exhibit 14-3 presents the four types of common problems involving modifiers.

1. Misplaced Modifiers

A *misplaced modifier* is a word or phrase that is placed in the wrong location in a sentence. Because of its placement, it appears to modify one word or phrase when it is intended to modify another. You may create an ambiguity or cause a loss of clarity by misplacing a modifier. The solution is to rephrase the sentence or to move the

Misplaced Modifiers	Words or phrases that are placed in the wrong location in a sentence and may create ambiguity or cause a loss of clarity. "If we contend that the contract applies, it will be attacked by the defense." (What will be attacked, our contention or the contract?)
Dangling Modifiers	Modifiers that do not modify any other part of the sentence. "*To determine whether the contract was breached*, the provisions of the statute must be referred to." (The italicized modifier does not refer to or modify any part of the sentence.)
Squinting Modifiers	A modifier located in a position in the sentence that makes it unclear whether it modifies the word that precedes it or the word that follows it. "The report that was prepared routinely indicates that the structure was unsafe." (Was the report prepared routinely, or did the report routinely indicate the structure was unsafe?)
Split Infinitives	An adverb is placed in an infinitive after *to* and before the verb. "Stephanie began to rapidly climb." (The adverb *rapidly* is placed between the infinitive *to* and the verb *climb*.) Correct: "Stephanie began to climb rapidly."

© Cengage

Exhibit 14-3 Problem Modifiers.

modifier to ensure clarity. Usually this is accomplished by placing the modifier before or after the word or phrase it modifies.

For Example

Misplaced modifiers:
- If we contend that the contract applies, it will be attacked by the defense. (What will be attacked, our contention or the contract?)
- Present the client's counterargument only in the third section of the brief. (Does this mean the counterargument should be presented in the third section and no other section, or does it mean that the third section should consist only of the counterargument?)

Revision—sentence rephrased:
- If we contend that the contract applies, the defense will attack the contention.

Revision—modifier moved:
- In the third section of the brief, present only the client's counterargument.

2. Dangling Modifiers

Modifiers that do not modify any other part of the sentence are *dangling modifiers*.

For Example

Dangling modifier in italics: *To determine whether the contract was breached*, the provisions of the statute must be referred to.

The italicized modifier does not refer to or modify any part of the sentence. It refers to a contract mentioned in another sentence. The problem may be corrected by rewriting the sentence to make sure modifiers refer to a noun or nouns in the sentence.

For Example

Dangling modifier eliminated: To determine whether the terms of the contract violate the statute, the statutory provisions must be referred to.

3. Squinting Modifiers

A *squinting modifier* is a modifier located in a position in the sentence that makes it unclear whether it modifies the word that precedes it or the word that follows it. Eliminate squinting modifiers when you edit your writing.

For Example

Squinting modifier in italics: The report that was prepared *routinely* indicated that the structure was unsafe. (Was the report prepared routinely, or did the report routinely indicate the structure was unsafe?)

Revision: The report that was routinely prepared indicated that the structure was unsafe.

Limiting modifiers such as *only, even, almost, nearly,* and *just* are often misplaced. These modifiers should be placed in front of the word they modify.

For Example

Incorrect: The lawyer only prepared the document.
    As the sentence reads, the lawyer prepared the document and nothing else. If the sentence is intended to mean that the lawyer and no one else prepared the document, *only* is misplaced.

Correction: Only the lawyer prepared the document.

4. Split Infinitives

An *infinitive* is a verb form that functions as a noun or as an auxiliary verb, such as *to argue, to understand,* and *to consider.* The general rule is that infinitives should not be split; that is, an adverb should not be placed after the *to* and before the verb.

For Example

Split infinitives: In each of the following examples, the infinitive is split: "to completely understand," "to rapidly climb," "to thoroughly test." An adverb is placed between the *to* and the verb.

Revisions: "to understand completely," "to climb rapidly," "to test thoroughly."

This general rule is not invariable; technically, split infinitives are not wrong even though they are not preferred. Sometimes an infinitive may be split to emphasize the modification of the verb (e.g., "to better understand") or to avoid an awkward placement of the modifier far from the verb it is modifying (e.g., "to best convey one's actual meaning" rather than "to convey one's actual meaning best").

F. Noun–Pronoun Agreement

Pronouns must agree in number (singular/plural) and gender (feminine/masculine/neuter) with the nouns to which they refer—their antecedents. Refer to the Personal Pronoun Chart in Section I for examples of personal pronouns.

    There are several guidelines to follow to ensure noun–pronoun agreement.

    1. Pronouns must agree with their antecedents (the noun to which the pronoun refers).

For Example

The *workers* put on *their* helmets when *they* entered the building.
    The pronouns *their* and *they* agree in number (plural) with the antecedent *workers* (plural).
    Mary was required to wear *her* helmet.
    The pronoun *her* agrees in number and gender with the antecedent *Mary.*

    2. Pronouns that do not refer to a definite person or thing are *indefinite pronouns.* Some examples of indefinite pronouns are *all, anyone, anybody, each, everyone, someone, somebody, everything, something,* and *none.* Indefinite pronouns are usually singular.

For Example

Everyone has the freedom to select *their* candidate.

3. Antecedents joined by *and* require a plural pronoun.

For Example

Tom and Mary are separating *their* property.
Tom, Jon, and Mary are going *their* separate ways.

4. Antecedents joined by *or* or *nor* require a pronoun that agrees in number and gender with the antecedent closest to the pronoun.

For Example

Mary or the other defendants must conduct *their* investigation.
The defendants or Mary must conduct *her* investigation.

When a construction appears awkward, as the second sentence does, consider rephrasing the sentence.

For Example

Mary or the defendants must conduct an investigation.

5. The number of a pronoun that refers to a collective noun is determined by the function of the collective noun. A *collective noun* is a noun that refers to a group. If the collective noun functions as a unit, the pronoun is singular.

For Example

The *committee*, after reviewing the matter, presented *its* conclusion. (In this sentence, the collective noun, *committee*, functions as a unit; the review is the act of the committee as a whole and therefore the pronoun *its* is singular.)

If the collective noun does not function as a unit, that is, the members of the collective noun are acting separately and not as a unit, then a plural pronoun is required.

For Example

The team have stated *their* various positions on the question of whether *they* should wear the new helmets. (In this example, the collective noun, *team*, does not function as a unit. The reference is to the team as individual members; therefore, the sentence takes the plural pronoun *they*.)

G. Adverbs, Adjectives, and Conjunctions

1. Forming Adverbs and Improper Use of Adjectives

Adverbs modify a verb, adjective, or another adverb. Many, but not all, adverbs are formed by adding *-ly* to a word. A common problem occurs when an adjective is incorrectly used to modify a verb.

For Example

Incorrect: The plant supervisor must see that the factory machinery runs *efficient*.

Correct: The plant supervisor must see that the factory machinery runs *efficiently*.

Incorrect: John behaves *conservative* around his parents.

Correct: "John behaves *conservatively* around his parents." In this sentence, *conservatively* is an adverb; it modifies the verb *behaves*.

"John's *conservative* behavior pleases his parents." In this sentence, *conservative* is an adjective; it modifies the noun *behavior*.

2. Adjectives, Adverbs, and Linking Verbs

In some situations, it is difficult to determine if the correct word to use is an adjective or an adverb. This often occurs with words that follow linking verbs, such as *feel, look, believe, become, grow, smell, taste,* and *appear*. The linking verb does not show physical or emotional action; rather, it suggests a state of being. Use an adjective if the word following the verb describes the subject of the sentence; use an adverb if the word refers to the verb.

For Example

"The inspector felt *careful*." The adjective *careful* is used because it describes the inspector (the subject).

"The inspector felt *carefully* when he searched the table." The adverb *carefully* is used because it modifies the verb *felt* and thus shows action (that is, how the inspector searched the table).

"John looked *sad*." *Looked* describes John. *Looked* is a linking verb because it does not show action. The adjective *sad* is used because it modifies the noun *John*.

"John looked *quickly* around the room." In this sentence, the verb *looked* shows action and is therefore not a linking verb. The adverb *quickly* is used because it modifies (describes) the verb *looked*.

3. Comparatives and Superlatives

Use a comparative to indicate a comparison between two things (e.g., *better, older, easier, faster, worse*). Use a superlative to indicate a comparison of three or more things (e.g., *best, oldest, easiest, fastest, worst*).

For Example

Incorrect: He is the *best* of the two applicants.
Mary is the *fastest* of the two runners.

Correct: He is the *better* of the two applicants.
Mary is the *faster* of the two runners.
The comparatives *better* and *faster* are used because two things are being compared.

Incorrect: He is the *better* of the three applicants.
Mary is the *faster* of all the runners.

Correct: He is the *best* of the three applicants.
Mary is the *fastest* of all the runners.
  The comparatives *best* and *fastest* are used because more than two things are being compared.

To form the comparative and superlative of most one- and two-syllable adjectives, add *-er* or *-est* as in the following examples: *big, bigger, biggest; old, older, oldest; funny, funnier; funniest.*

For some two-syllable adjectives and long adjectives, form the comparative by using *more* and the superlative by using *most: more outrageous, most outrageous; more entertaining, most entertaining.*

To form the comparative and superlative of some one-syllable adverbs, use *-er* and *-est* as in: *faster, fastest; sooner, soonest.* To form the comparative and superlative of longer adverbs and those ending in *-ly,* use *more/less* for the comparative and *most/least* for the superlative such as: *more acutely, most acutely; more likely, most likely.*

Comparatives are not used with concepts that are absolute, such as *perfect, unique, empty, impossible,* and *excellent.*

For Example

Incorrect: It was a most perfect story.

Correct: It was a perfect story.

Incorrect: His viewpoint was very unique.

Correct: His viewpoint was unique.

---

4. Adverbs Used for Emphasis

Place adverbs used for emphasis immediately before the word or phrase they modify. Some examples of words of emphasis are *only, so, very,* and *quite.*

For Example

"John intended only to influence the outcome of the meeting." *Only* modifies the phrase that follows: "to influence the outcome of the meeting."

---

5. Coordinating Conjunctions

Use a coordinating conjunction when joining clauses and words of equal rank. Some coordinating conjunctions are *and, or, but, for, so, yet,* and *nor.*

For Example

"We have three selections available: section a, section b, *or* section c." *Or* joins equal words.
"The landlord had the option to seek restitution, *but* he did not choose this option." *But* joins equal clauses.

---

6. Correlative Conjunctions

Correlative conjunctions are also used to link items of equal rank. Correlative conjunctions are used in pairs. Some correlative conjunctions are *either/or, neither/nor, if/then, both/and, since/therefore,* and *on the one hand/on the other hand.*

For Example

Either they will sign the agreement, *or* we will select another vendor.

If we are forced to pursue that option, *then* we will require additional funds.

Both Thomson *and* Haynes are present.

VI. PUNCTUATION

Punctuation is designed to make writing clear and easy to understand. Poor punctuation may cause the reader to misunderstand the context, or be distracted by the errors and not focus on the context. Poor punctuation usually causes the reader to question the author's competence. A comprehensive discussion of all the rules governing punctuation would require an entire text. This section discusses the major elements of punctuation and summarizes rules that apply to commonly encountered problems.

A. Comma (,)

The function of a comma is to separate the parts of a sentence so the meaning is clear. It is the most frequently used punctuation mark. Basic rules that apply to commas follow:

1. Use a comma before a coordinating conjunction that joins two main or independent clauses. An independent clause can stand alone as a complete sentence.

For Example

The statute provides that the contract must be witnessed, but it does not require that the contract be in writing. (Note that each clause of the sentence could be a complete sentence: The statute provides that the contract must be witnessed. It does not require that the contract be in writing.)

2. Set off introductory phrases or clauses with a comma.

For Example

Introductory phrase in italics: *After the prosecutor concluded his opening statement,* the court declared a recess.

3. Use a comma after each item in a series of three or more items, and place a comma before *and* or *or* at the end of the series. The comma before *and* or *or* is known as the Oxford or serial comma and, although not required, should be used in formal writing such as legal writing.

For Example

The defendant had no identification, money, or other possessions.

Bicycles, tricycles, unicycles, and other nonmotorized vehicles are covered by the statute.

4. Use a comma to avoid a misreading of the subject.

For Example

Instead of rule A, rule B applies in this situation.

5. Separate coordinate adjectives with a comma. Coordinate adjectives independently modify the same noun. To determine if the modifiers are coordinate, reverse their order or insert *and* between them. If the meaning is not changed, they are coordinate.

For Example

Coordinating Adjectives in Italics:
The *correct, concise* interpretation is that. . . .
The *concise, correct* interpretation is that. . . .

6. Set off transitional or interpretive words or phrases with a comma. These are words or phrases that provide qualification or clarification, but are not essential to the meaning of a sentence.

For Example

The plaintiffs, *however,* have failed to comply.
The correct course, *therefore,* is to settle the case.

7. Set off nonrestrictive clauses with a comma. A nonrestrictive clause is one that is not necessary to the meaning of the sentence.

For Example

Nonrestrictive clause in italics: The court of appeals denied the appeal, *finding that the evidence was properly admitted.*

8. Use a comma to set off appositives. An *appositive* is a noun or noun phrase that further identifies another noun or noun phrase.

For Example

Appositives in Italics:
The client, *Ms. Smith,* was elected to the position.
The plaintiffs, *Mr. Evans and Ms. Thompson,* were present at the hearing.

9. Set off contrasting phrases with a comma or commas.

For Example

Contrasting phrase in italics: Mr. Jones, *not Ms. Smith,* was the guilty party.

10. Use commas when required to set off quotations. Place the comma between the quotation and the attribution.

For Example

He said, "I did not do it."

11. Place a comma inside the closing quotation mark, not outside the quotation mark.

For Example

"Witnessing is not required," he said.

12. Place a comma before and after descriptive titles, such as M.D., Ph.D., and Esq.

For Example

The doctor in this case is Mary Place, M.D., who attended medical school at Yale Medical School.

NOTE: Do not use a comma before Jr., II, and so on, following a personal name.

For Example

Mr. Steven Jones Jr. and Arthur Cleaver II delivered the closing address.

13. Do not use a comma before parentheses.

For Example

All employees (executives and assistants) shall arrive at work at 8:00 a.m.

14. In general do not use a comma after short prepositional phrases. A prepositional phrase consists of, at minimum, a preposition and a noun that is the object of the preposition. If the phrase is short (usually three words or less) and the meaning of the sentence is clear, the comma may be omitted.

For Example

Not Necessary—The Prepositional Phrase is in Italics:
In every situation, you should read the contract.
After the test, I'm going to sleep.
Better:
In every situation you should read the contract.
After the test I'm going to sleep.

15. Place a comma between the day and year if the full date is written.

For Example

The hearing will be held on November 16, 2005.

When only the month and year are used, no comma is used.

For Example

The hearing will be held on November 2005.

When the full date is written at the beginning or in the middle of a sentence, generally a comma should also follow the year.

For Example

The court's final order was issued on January 15, 2016, ending the seven-year legal battle.

16. Use a comma when a word or group of words is omitted, but the meaning of the sentence is clear.

For Example

Mary represents the northern and eastern districts; Arthur, the southern district.
Mary prepared the opening and analysis; Jane, the closing.

B. Semicolon (;)

A semicolon is used primarily in two situations:

1. To separate two independent clauses that are closely related
2. To separate items in a series if the items are long or if one of the items has internal commas

Regarding these situations, note the following rules:

1. Use a semicolon to separate two independent clauses in a sentence that are *not* joined by a coordinating conjunction. Both independent clauses have a subject and a verb. Each could be a separate sentence. The subject of both independent clauses is closely related. A *conjunction* is a word that is used to connect words and phrases. A *coordinating conjunction*, such as *and*, *but*, and *or*, is a conjunction that connects like elements.

For Example

Incorrect: The shareholders held their meeting at noon, the board of directors met immediately thereafter. (The use of the comma is incorrect because there is no coordinating conjunction, such as *and*, connecting the two clauses. The coordinating conjunction is in italics in the following sentence.)

Correct—coordinating conjunction used: The shareholders held their meeting at noon, and the board of directors met immediately thereafter.

Correct—semicolon used: The shareholders held their meeting at noon; the board of directors met immediately thereafter.

2. Use a semicolon when independent clauses are joined by a conjunctive adverb. Some examples of conjunctive adverbs are *therefore, however, furthermore, consequently, likewise,* and *nevertheless.*

For Example

The rule requires that the will must be witnessed in writing; *however,* there are three exceptions.

3. When a series of items is long or commas are already used in some of the items in the series, use a semicolon to separate the items.

For Example

Long items: The plaintiffs must prove the following to establish that the will was validly witnessed:

a. there were two witnesses to the will;

b. the witnesses were present in the room when the will was signed; and

c. the witnesses were not related to the testator or were not bequeathed anything in the will.

List of items with internal commas: The stockholders present were Mary Hart, the president; Tom Jones, the secretary; and Monica Murton, the treasurer.

4. At the end of a sentence, use a semicolon to separate an appositive introduced by such terms as *that is, for example,* and *namely.*

For Example

The plaintiff has not shown that the defendant violated all the statutory requirements; for example, the requirements that a firearm be used, that the firearm be in plain sight, and that the firearm be loaded.

C. Colon (:)

Use a colon when you want to introduce or call attention to information that follows it, such as lists, conclusions, explanations, and quotations. The function of a colon is to introduce what follows it.

1. When you use a colon to introduce a list or series, it must be preceded by a main clause that is a complete sentence.

For Example

The statute provides that three steps must be performed before the water right is established: (1) a permit must be obtained from the state engineer; (2) the water must be applied to a beneficial use; and (3) the beneficial use must be continuous for a period of three years.

2. A colon may be used to introduce quotations, or to introduce a short quotation introduced by an independent clause.

For Example

Introduce short quotation: Standing in open court, Smith loudly entered his plea: "I am not guilty."

A colon may be used to emphasize a quotation.

For Example

Emphasize a quotation: The senator concluded his remarks with the following statement: "I do not choose to run for reelection."

A colon is usually used to introduce block quotations, transcripts, statutes, and so on.

For Example

After reviewing the matter at length, the court adopted the following rule:
(Block Quotation)

D. Apostrophe (')

An apostrophe indicates possession or forms a contraction. Some of the basic rules governing the use of apostrophes to indicate possession follow:

1. Make singular nouns possessive by adding an apostrophe and an *s*.

For Example

the officer's car
Mr. Jones's house

Singular nouns ending in *s* take an apostrophe and an *s* ('s) just like any other singular noun. Note the possessive of "Mr. Jones" in the preceding example.

2. Make plural nouns possessive by adding an apostrophe after the s.

For Example

the players' uniforms
the workers' organization

3. Use an apostrophe and an s ('s) after the last word of a compound word or word group.

For Example

attorney general's office
Fred and Tom's car (where Fred and Tom own the same car)
Fred's and Tom's cars (where Fred and Tom own separate cars)

4. The possessives of personal pronouns do not require an apostrophe.

For Example

yours, his, hers, ours, its (possessive of *it*), *whose* (possessive of *who*)

An apostrophe is also used to form contractions. Contractions are generally not used in formal writing. To make a contraction, use an apostrophe in place of the omitted letter or letters. Note the difference between it's and its. "It's" is the contraction for *it is*. "Its" is the possessive pronoun form for it.

E. Quotation Marks (" ")

Use quotation marks to identify and set off quoted material. Note the following guidelines when quoting material:

1. Long quotations are not set off by quotation marks. Instead, they are set off from the rest of the text by a five-space indentation (0.5 inch indentation) from the left and right margins. They are also single-spaced. These quotations are called *block quotations* and, according to *Bluebook* and *ALWD*, should be used for quotations of 50 words or more.

For Example

The court made the following statements regarding the requirement of the presence of the witness:

The statute requires the witnesses to be present when the testator signs the will. The witnesses must be in the same room with the testator, not in a separate room from which they can see the testator. The witnesses also must actually see the testator sign the will. Their presence in the room is not sufficient if they do not actually see the testator sign the will.

Because readers tend to skip over or skim long quotations, use them sparingly and only when the entire language, verbatim, is essential.

2. Place periods and commas inside the quotation marks.

For Example

He was described as "a dangerous individual."

Other punctuation, such as semicolons, colons, question marks, and exclamation marks, are placed outside the quotation marks unless they are a part of the quotation.

For Example

The court defined publication as "communication to a third party"; therefore. . . .
The victim then shouted, "I've been hit!" (The exclamation mark is part of the quotation; therefore, it belongs within the quotation marks.)

3. You may use quotation marks to indicate that a word is used in a special way or is a special term. (Note, though, that a term being defined, or a "word used as a word" is usually indicated by setting in italics.) In legal writing, a proliferation of quotation marks can be confusing and visually irritating; therefore, use such marks sparingly to set off special terms.

For Example

The attorney acted as a "hired gun" in the case.
The term "oppressive conduct" has a special meaning in corporation law.

4. When quoting a quote within a quote, use single quotation marks.

For Example

The court held that "the term 'oppressive conduct' requires that the shareholder engage in some wrongful conduct."

When the quote within a quote is part of a block quotation, use double quotation marks to set off the internal quote.

For Example

The court made the following statements in regard to the requirement of the presence of the witness:

The statute requires the witnesses to be present when the testator signs the will. The witnesses must be in the same room with the testator, not in a separate room from which they can see the testator. The witnesses also must "actually see" the testator sign the will. Their presence in the room is not sufficient if they do not actually see the testator sign the will.

5. Quotation marks may also be used to indicate that a term is informal or questionable.

For Example

William "Wild Bill" James.
The only "injury" sustained in this lawsuit was the cost of the litigation.

F. Ellipses (three spaced dots: ...)

The function of an ellipsis is to indicate the omission of part of a quotation.

For Example

The statute provides that skiers are "responsible for ... snow and ice conditions...."

Note the following rules regarding the use of ellipses:

1. When the omission occurs inside a quotation, use three ellipsis dots (created either by insertion of the three-dot ellipsis symbol on your computer, or by typing three periods in a row). Use hard spaces after the last quoted word, between each ellipsis dot, and the next quoted word.

For Example

When I went on my trip, I first went to the tower ... and saw the mountains on the horizon.

Retain any punctuation that appears before or after the omitted material if it is grammatically necessary for the restructured sentence.

For Example

When we went on the tour of the villa, ... we also visited the famous gardens.

2. When the end of a quoted sentence is omitted, add a period for the punctuation to end the sentence. Follow the last word with a space, the three ellipsis dots, a space, and a period. Place a hard space between the last ellipsis dot and the period.

For Example

The statute requires that "the majority shareholder must refrain from engaging in oppressive conduct...."

3. When the omission is at the beginning of a quote, do not use an ellipsis; merely indicate where the quoted material begins with the opening quotation marks. In legal writing, a bracketed first letter signals that you have changed the case of the initial letter of the quotation.

For Example

Incorrect: The state must establish "... specific intent."

Correct: The state must establish "specific intent."

4. If the quote is a phrase or clause, no ellipsis is required.

For Example

Incorrect: In this case, the court stated that ". . . the act does not require specific intent."

Correct: In this case, the court stated that "the act does not require specific intent."

Incorrect: The court noted that "Ignorance of the law is no excuse."

Correct: The court noted that "[i]gnorance of the law is no excuse."

G. Brackets ([ ])

Brackets are used to perform three separate functions:

1. To show changes in or add information to quotations, usually for the purpose of providing clarification to the quotation
2. To indicate an error in the original quotation
3. To indicate a change of case in the first letter of a quotation.

For Example

To show changes in a quotation: "The privilege [against self-incrimination] allows an individual to remain silent."

To indicate an error in the original quoted material: "The bord [*sic*] of directors voted against the proposal."

To show a change of case: According to this court, "[i]gnorance of the law is no excuse."

In legal writing, do not use brackets to indicate parentheses that fall within parentheses.

For Example

Incorrect: (When the annual meeting was held [June of 2004], the board decided to call for a vote of the members.)

Correct: (When the annual meeting was held (June of 2004), the board decided to call for a vote of the members.)

H. Parentheses ( )

Use parentheses to add supplementary information to the sentence that is outside the main idea of the sentence or of lesser importance.

For Example

The cost of the paper (only $2) was not included in the invoice.

When referring the reader to other cases, attached material, or an appendix, or when providing summary information following a case citation, you may use parentheses.

For Example

Reference to an appendix: (See Appendix A.)

Reference to other cases: See also *Smith v. Jones,* 981 N.E.2d 441 (N. Wash. 1993) (where the court required specific intent in a similar situation).

I. Hyphen (-)

A hyphen is required to form compound modifiers and compound nouns. There are numerous words that may or may not require hyphenation.

For Example

ex-judge
well-known personality
self-defense

Consult a dictionary when you are unsure whether a word must be hyphenated. Be sure to consult a recently published, well-established dictionary. Be wary of using Wikipedia and Dictionary.com or similar user-based sources of information. Hyphenation is an area of the English language that frequently changes.

J. Dash (—)

The true dash is often referred to as the em dash or long dash. Use a dash in the following situations:

- To emphasize something
- To set off lists or briefly summarize materials containing commas
- To show an abrupt change of thought or direction, or an interjection

For Example

To emphasize: The child—only eight years old—was clearly not capable of understanding what he was doing.

To set off a list: The items found at the scene—the knife, the drugs, and the scarf—have disappeared from the evidence room.

To show a sudden break: Basel Corporation—primarily known for its herbs—is involved in the manufacture of glassware.

K. Period (.)

The period is probably the most commonly used punctuation mark. It is used to mark the end of a sentence, in abbreviations, as a decimal point in numbers, and after letters and numbers in an outline or list.

1. Use a period to indicate the end of a sentence that is not a question or exclamation.

For Example

It is clear that the client is not telling the entire story.
Please tell us what you want.

2. Use a period with letters and numbers in an outline or list.

For Example

Outline:

I. Introduction

A. Introduction

B. Body

    1. Introductory sentence

    2. Body

Lists: In a list, the number or letter is placed in parentheses or is followed by a period, but not both parentheses and a period.

Incorrect:	(1.) Creditors		
	(2.) Investors		
	(3.) Debtors		
Correct:	(1) Creditors	**or**	1. Creditors
	(2) Investors	**or**	2. Investors
	(3) Debtors	**or**	3. Debtors

3. Use a period after a heading if the heading is a complete sentence or runs in with the text.

For Example

Complete sentence: I. The position relied on no longer represents sound public policy and should not be relied on.

Heading runs in with text: 1. *The prewriting stage.* The prewriting stage begins with a review of the assignment.

4. Use a period in most abbreviations.

For Example

Mr. (for Mister)
Sept. (for September)
Co. (for Company)

Do not add a second period if an abbreviation falls at the end of a sentence.

For Example

The meeting will begin promptly at 8:00 a.m.

Abbreviations of corporations, government agencies, scientific and technical terms, or those composed of all capital letters do not take periods unless the initials stand for a person's name or a different style is specified.

For Example

NASA, DNA, FBI, CD-ROM
J. R. Smith (in a person's name, periods are used)

L. Question Mark (?)

A question mark is used at the end of a sentence that asks a direct question.

For Example

Has the client made a follow-up appointment?
You filed the deed even when we told you not to, didn't you?

In regard to the use of question marks, note the following guidelines:

1. In a compound sentence, use a question mark if the ending clause is a question.

For Example

Although we discussed this several times, do you still maintain your innocence?

2. If there are multiple endings to a question, use a question mark after each ending word or phrase.

For Example

Is the person responsible for this the president? the secretary? the treasurer?
NOTE: The first word of the ending phrases (*the*) is not capitalized.

3. Place a question mark in parentheses following a term (usually a number or date) to indicate uncertainty.

For Example

Mr. Thompson left his home town in 1988 (?), and moved to New Orleans.
It appears that only one state, Mississippi (?), has adopted this position.

M. Exclamation Point (!)

An exclamation mark is used to indicate the end of a sentence that expresses emotion or deserves special emphasis.

Note: Exclamation points are rarely used in legal writing unless they are part of a quotation. Keep in mind the following when using exclamation points:

1. Use an exclamation point to express a demand, surprise, emotion, and so on.

For Example

> Hurry up, he's coming!
> Come here right now!
> You must pay me immediately!

2. Use an exclamation point to emphasize an interjection or command.

For Example

> No! Don't touch that!
> Oh, my goodness! How could I have done that?

VII. GENERAL CONSIDERATIONS

Three additional matters that require attention when you are performing a writing assignment are spelling, use of numbers, and formal writing conventions. These matters are addressed in the following subsections.

A. Spelling

Obviously, you must correctly spell all the words you use. If you are in doubt about the spelling of a word, use a dictionary. Legal writing requires the use of both a regular dictionary and a legal dictionary; therefore, you must have both of these references.

If you use a computer that checks spelling, you still must carefully check for word usage errors. The computer may catch a spelling error, but it will not catch the use of the wrong word or typographical errors that result in the use of a wrong word.

For Example

> **Use of a wrong word:** You used the word *to* when you intended to use *too*.
> A computer spell-check function will not catch the use of the wrong word.
> **Typographical error that results in the use of a wrong word:** You typed *cast* when you meant to type *case*. *Cast* is a word, and spell-check will not consider this an error.

B. Numbers

The following rules govern the presentation of numbers in legal writing:

1. In text, the general rule is to spell out numbers from one to ninety-nine (that is, numbers that can be spelled out in one or two words). Note that a different style convention, which requires that numbers from one to nine be spelled out, is also very commonly used.

For Example

> one
> twenty-seven
> ninety-nine
> The contract has twenty-seven clauses.

Use numerals for numbers that are more than two words long.

For Example

379
1,300
145,378
The contract has 379 clauses.

There is one exception: if you have a list of numbers and one of the items on the list should be written with numerals, use numerals for all the items listed.

For Example

The numbers in the code are 16, 44, 397, and 1,001. (The numbers sixteen and forty-four are not spelled out.)

As a general rule, do not spell out the following numbers: dates, statute numbers, section numbers, volume numbers, exact times, sums of money, addresses, percentages, scores, identification numbers, ratios, statistics, decimals and fractions, and measurements with symbols or abbreviations.

For Example

Date: May 6, 2005
Statute: Title 18 of the code
Section: Section 3212, § 3212
Percentage: 75 percent, 75%
Score: The final score was 2 to 1.
Exact sum of money: $34.21
Decimal: 9.38
Fraction: 9¼
Measurement with symbol: 9°
Exact time: 5:45 A.M., 7:23 p.m.

Note: Hours are spelled out when the time is accompanied by *o'clock*.

For Example

Incorrect: 11 o'clock
Correct: eleven o'clock

2. Spell out numbers that begin a sentence.

For Example

Incorrect: 506 paralegals were present.
Correct: Five hundred six paralegals were present.

3. Use hyphens for fractions and numbers from twenty-one to ninety-nine.

For Example

Fifty-six of the stockholders were present. The thirty-seven shareholders represented three-fourths of the outstanding shares.

Do not use *and* when writing whole numbers.

For Example

Incorrect: Two hundred *and* seventy-five dollars was needed to pay the debt.
Correct: Two hundred seventy-five dollars was needed to pay the debt.

Hyphenate fractions that are spelled out.

For Example

One-fifth of the student body attended the meeting.

4. To make a number plural, add s (without an apostrophe).

For Example

1990s
There were three 190s in the paragraph.

Possessive numbers are not frequently encountered. If you have to form the possessive of a number, add an apostrophe and *s*.

For Example

The instructor illustrated his point by referring to the 1920's Black Friday.

5. When two numbers appear together that are not of the same kind, spell out the first number.

For Example

Incorrect: There were 190 $50 bills.
Correct: There were one hundred ninety $50 bills.

C. Formal Writing Conventions

Most legal writing is considered formal, and formal **writing conventions** apply, especially to legal briefs and memorandums. Two of these conventions concern the use of contractions and personal pronouns.

As mentioned in the subsection addressing the use of apostrophes, the use of contractions is not considered acceptable in formal writing. Do not use contractions unless instructed to do so.

The general rule is that you should draft legal memoranda or briefs in the third person. Also, unless instructed otherwise, use the third person in correspondence to clients.

For Example

Incorrect: It is my position that the court should grant the motion.
We feel that the contract has been broken.

Correct: The court should grant the motion.
It is Mr. Black's position that the contract has been broken.

When presenting your position or legal analysis, use present tense.

For Example

Plaintiff *contends* that the rule requires 30 days' notice. It *is* the defendant's position that the contract is void.

When addressing a court opinion that has already been decided, use past tense.

For Example

In *Smith v. Jones,* the court *held* that the rule does not require 30 days' notice. The court *listed* three possible solutions to the problem.

When discussing a law or rule still in effect, use present tense.

For Example

The provisions of section 44-556 *require* a contractor to give 30 days' notice. The statute *provides* that the notice must be signed by the owner of the property.

VIII. KEY POINTS CHECKLIST: Fundamentals of Writing

✓ The goal of legal writing is to prepare a professional product—one that is free of substantive and mechanical error. Perform the number of edits and redrafts necessary to attain this goal.

✓ Use short, clear sentences when possible. Fifteen to twenty-five words is a good average length for sentences. Excessively long sentences are difficult to understand.

✓ A paragraph should address one topic and should usually range from three to six sentences.

✓ Keep the reader in mind when drafting. Avoid legalese when possible, especially when the reader is a person not trained in the law.

✓ Make sure the writing is grammatically correct. Check for subject-verb agreement, parallel construction, and so on.

✓ Check the punctuation. Use commas and other punctuation devices correctly.

✓ Check the spelling to ensure that all words are spelled correctly.

IX. APPLICATION

Checklist

The checklist presented in Exhibit 14-4 may be used as a guide to help you proofread and correct your legal writing.

Summary

One requirement of a legal writing assignment is the preparation of a final product that is free from mechanical errors. The value of quality research and analysis is undermined if the written presentation is poorly assembled. This chapter presents an overview of some of the fundamental writing skills essential for good writing. The chapter addresses the eight parts of speech, sentence and paragraph structure, word selection and usage, grammar, punctuation, and other general considerations regarding the mechanics of good writing.

A sentence is the fundamental building block of writing. It is usually a statement; at a minimum, it must have a subject and a predicate.

The second fundamental component of writing is the paragraph. A paragraph is a group of sentences that address the same topic. Paragraphs are usually composed of a topic sentence, a sentence or sentences discussing the topic, and a closing sentence.

Checklist to be used when Proofreading Legal Writing

General Considerations
- Spelling
- Numbers
- Formal writing conventions

Sentence Structure/Pattern
- Subject/verb distance
- Sentence length
- Active/passive voice
- Action verbs
- Transitions

Punctuation
- Commas
- Semicolons
- Colons
- Apostrophes
- Quotations
- Ellipses
- Brackets
- Parentheses
- Hyphens
- Dashes

Grammar
- Subject/verb agreement
- Verb tense
- Parallel construction
- Superfluous verbs
- Modifiers and infinitives
- Noun/pronoun agreement

Paragraphs
- Topic sentence
- Body
- Closing
- Transition sentence
- Paragraph length

Word Selection and Usage
- Excessive/redundant words
- Noun/verb string
- Nominalizations
- Legalese
- Archaic words
- Sexist language
- Specific words—problem areas

© Cengage

Exhibit 14-4 Proofreading Checklist.

The proper selection and use of words are critical elements of good writing. The improper use of words or the use of sexist language or legalese detracts from the quality of the writing.

Rules of grammar guide the drafting of legal writing. Subject–verb agreement, parallel construction, proper verb tense, noun–pronoun agreement, and other rules are necessary to good writing.

Spelling and punctuation are the final subjects addressed in this chapter. Proper spelling is always required. In like manner, proper punctuation is a basic requirement of proper writing. The correct uses of commas, semicolons, apostrophes, and other punctuation devices are summarized in the chapter.

All of the rules and guidelines discussed in the chapter are essential to good writing skills. You must learn and employ them when engaged in legal writing. The chapter only briefly addresses the rules and guidelines that apply to legal writing; you should refer to other resources for detailed coverage of each topic.

Quick References

Internet Resources

Using grammar, punctuation, word selection, sentences, and other topics, you will find various websites (literally thousands) that refer to writing fundamentals. Some websites refer to books; some provide self-help handouts; some present tips, guidelines, and examples; some are materials from various English courses; some are articles on specific writing topics; some are tutorials or workshops; and some advertise writing services and courses.

As with most topics on the Internet, the problem is not the lack of sites, but the abundance of sites. Probably the best strategy is to narrow your search to a specific writing topic such as "parentheses." Look for websites that are related to colleges and law schools. Many schools, particularly those with journalism programs and law schools, provide websites that have detailed information on grammar that include examples.

There are many books and websites devoted to diagramming sentences. One of the best resources is http://www.english-grammar-revolution.com/. Like identifying reliable and strong websites on grammar, look for websites that are associated with colleges, school programming and other academic-related associations when seeking sentencing diagraming resources.

Exercises

ASSIGNMENT 1

Define the following parts of speech: noun, pronoun, verb, adjective, adverb, preposition and conjunction.

ASSIGNMENT 2

Discuss the essential requirements of a well-crafted sentence.

ASSIGNMENT 3

Discuss the elements and requirements of a well-crafted paragraph.

ASSIGNMENT 4

a. Identify the noun(s) in this sentence: The applause coming from the gallery of the courtroom was not what the defendant wanted to hear.

b. Are the underlined words common or proper nouns in this sentence: The <u>judge</u> ordered the <u>plaintiff</u>, <u>Shannon Smith</u>, to pay a fine of $500.

c. Identify any pronouns in this sentence: Anyone in the jury needing a break should raise their hand and signal the bailiff.

d. Identify the adjective(s) in this sentence: The witness testified, "The blue car struck the green car from behind and the tall man on the corner pushed the small child out of the way before the green car struck the child."

e. Identify the adverb(s) in this sentence: The jury swiftly decided the fate of the defendant.

f. Identify the prepositional phrase(s) in this sentence: In the night, the robber stole tools from the shed.

ASSIGNMENT 5

Underline once the subject and underline twice the verb in each sentence.

a. The judge ordered plaintiff's counsel to submit the brief immediately.

b. Witnesses refused to testify.

c. Jurors gasped at the pictures of the injuries.

d. The driver's breath smelled like alcohol.

e. There might have been undue hardship on the jury.

ASSIGNMENT 6

Draft the following sentences in active voice.

a. The defendant was attacked by the plaintiff at the beginning of the argument.

b. It is a requirement of good writing skills that active voice be used.

c. Payment must be made by Mr. Smith no later than May 15, 1997.

d. There were a number of glass fragments on the ground.

e. The reason the judge left the bench was that her health was failing.

ASSIGNMENT 7

Choose the correct answer to create noun/pronoun agreement.

a. When the attorneys are out of town, we forward messages to her.

b. Although the motions were postmarked January 27, 2016, it was not delivered until March 12, 2016.

c. Everybody will share his files with the team members.

d. Everything was out of their place when the homeowner returned from vacation.

e. Even though Joe and Janice called repeatedly, he could not reach his friends.

ASSIGNMENT 8

Rewrite the sentences to omit the underlined wordy phrases.

a. The expert testified <u>he was of the opinion</u> the broken bone required more force than a simple fall.

b. The jury <u>arrived at the conclusion</u> that the damages were $50,000.

c. <u>As a consequence</u> of the fight, the plaintiff's nose was broken.

d. When we <u>ascertain the location of</u> the crime scene, we will send out the evidence technicians.

e. The paralegal <u>came to a realization</u> that the stack of cases on his desk took up too much space.

ASSIGNMENT 9

Rephrase the following sentences using nonsexist language.

a. A paralegal may draft a letter to the client informing him of an upcoming hearing.

b. The lawyer must file his response within 30 days.

c. The chairman of the committee conducted a private hearing.

d. Each person must bring his records to the conference.

e. Everyone must bring his records to the hearing.

ASSIGNMENT 10

Correct the following sentences to remove the nominalization.

a. The sheriff's office conducted an investigation of the matter.

b. Our intention is to audit the records of the business.

c. The paralegal has the intention of finishing the assignment on time.

d. I completed the assignment with much difficulty.

e. Jane has a great collection of Supreme Court memorabilia.

ASSIGNMENT 11

What are the basic rules concerning subject–verb agreement, proper verb tense, and noun–pronoun agreement?

ASSIGNMENT 12

Choose the correct answer to create subject–verb agreement.

a. The list of prohibited items in the court [is/are] posted at the entrance.

b. The witnesses, Joe Friel and Bob Blaze, [arrive/arrives] by plane this afternoon.

c. Neither Judge Mack or Judge Atwood [is/are] available today.

d. Fifty percent of the cases [have/has] settled.

e. If the police [was/were] here, the partygoers would disperse faster.

ASSIGNMENT 13

Correct these sentences by properly using commas, semicolons, and apostrophes.

a. The attorneys fees were disputed.

b. The long complicated statutes were hard to understand.

c. The paralegal said she would do the research yet she has not begun.

d. The police have arrived at the scene everyone has taken cover.

e. The victim's cell phone showed five test messages had come in the detective noted each one.

ASSIGNMENT 14

Correct the following sentences and identify why they are incorrect.

1. The statute requires the witnesses to be present when the testator signs the will, and the witnesses must be in the same room with the testator, not in a separate room, and watch the testator sign the will.

2. Mary reached the conclusion that she had made a mistake.

3. A relative pronoun requires a verb which agrees with its antecedent.

4. Either the cousins or Darryl are going to the party.

5. Sara, after giving careful consideration to the matter, reached the conclusion that she should buy the business.

6. He decided to thoroughly and completely test the theory.

7. Neither the members of the board nor Steve had reached their conclusion.

8. The statute requires stockholder approval for merger but it does not require approval for multiple real estate purchases.

9. The key executives, (president, secretary, and treasurer) are required to attend the board meeting.

10. The corporation statute requires: an annual board of directors meeting, an annual shareholder meeting, and the filing of an annual report.

11. Tom and Pam decided there going to buy stock in the corporation.

12. The law requires a partner to ". . . share partnership profits equally with the other partners. . . ."

13. Joseph and Claire decided they were going too there cabin for two weeks.

14. Fifty five of the partners attended the partnership meeting.

15. The law provides that profits should be shared equally, however, the law allows the partners to provide otherwise in the partnership agreement.

ASSIGNMENT 15

Correct the following sentences by properly using colons and semicolons.

- The court's instructions to the respondent are: to refrain from contacting the plaintiff in person, by telephone, or by mail; to pay monthly child support, and to perform one hundred hours of community service.
- The following statutes govern the issue, section 29-9-516, section 29-9-517, and section 29-9-544.

ASSIGNMENT 16

Correct the paragraphs presented in part A and part B. Use the proofreading checklist presented in Exhibit 14-4.

Part A

The governments' first witness at Bean's sentencing were the DEA Task Force Officer Tony Silva. He testifies that in his debriefing Luiz had told him about four seperate marijuana "grows" in which Luiz had participated. The first was in 1986 In Tress, Texas: this "grow" produced 700 marijuana plants. The second was in 1987 in the Tonto wilderness; and it produced approximatly 1500 marijuana plants. The third "grow" was in 1988 in Sies Colorado and they produced approximately 900 marijuana plants.

The final "grow" was in 1991, also at the Sies site.

Before the plants in this grow had been harveted, a Colorado State Police aircraft was spotted doing a "flyover" of the property. This prompted Luiz to completely destroy the crop, only fifty two plants were seized. As they were seized the officers noted that two or three plants were in a single grow site. Approximately 1,000 "grow holes," with sprinkler heads connected to an extensive irritation system, were found another one thousand uninstalled sprinkler heads, two water tanks and fertilizer also was found on the property.

Part B

The trial court sentenced Smith well within the statutory limits. Therefore the sentence is legal.

The record thoroughly, clearly and positively shows that Smith and his attorney have ample time to thoroughly review Smiths' sentence report prior to sentencing. They did so and had: "no problems with it." It is shown by the record that Smith never appealed his conviction or sentence. His section 2255 Motion were his first and only attempt to challenge his sentence. Any objections to the sentence report as submitted were clearly waived by Smith. The defendant have the responsibility to advise the Court of any claimed errors in the sentence report. His failure to voice any objections waive any issue not properly presented. It has been long held by this court that "Section 2255 is not available to test the legality of matters which should have been raised on appeal." Unless good cause can be shown why a defendant did not appeal or raise a particular issue on appeal; the defendant is barred from raising that issue in a section 2255 Motion.

For Further Reading

O'Conner, Patricia T. *Woe Is I: The Grammarphobe's Guide to Better English* in Plain English, 3rd Ed. New York: Penguin Group, 2009.

Zinsser, William. *On Writing Well*, 7th ed. New York: Harper Collins, 2006.

Garner, Bryan A. *The Redbook: A Manual on Legal Style,* 3rd ed. St. Paul: West Academic, 2013.

Garner, Bryan A. *Legal Writing in Plain English*, 2nd ed. Chicago: University of Chicago Press, 2013.

Wydick, Richard C. *Plain English for Lawyers*, 5th ed. Carolina Academic Press, 2005.

Strunk, William Jr.& E.B. White. *The Elements of Style*, 4th ed. Massachusetts: Allyn & Bacon, 2000.

Longknife, Ann & K.D. Sullivan. *The Art of Styling Sentences*, 5th ed. New York: Barron's 2012.

Williams, Joseph M. & Joseph Bizup. *Style: Lessons in Grace*, 11th ed. Pearson Education, Inc. 2014.

Judith M. Stinson, The Tao of legal Writing. North Carolina: Carolina Academic Press, 2009.

Putman, William H. *Pocket Guide to Legal Writing*. Clifton Park, NY: Thomson/Delmar Learning, 2006.

Chapter 15

The Writing Process for Effective Legal Writing

Outline

I. Introduction
II. Importance of Writing Skills
III. Goal of Legal Writing
IV. Legal Writing Process
V. General Research Suggestions
VI. Key Points Checklist: The Writing Process
VII. Application

Learning Objectives

After completing this chapter, you should understand:

- The importance of writing skills
- What a legal writing process is and its importance in legal writing
- The three stages of the legal writing process
- The importance and use of an expanded outline in the legal writing process

For the past five years, Rick Strong has been the paralegal for Sara Fletcher, a criminal defense attorney. He started law school last year. Rick now works part-time during the school year and full-time in the summer. He performs a wide range of law clerk and paralegal tasks for Sara. He interviews clients and witnesses, conducts legal investigations, arranges and maintains client files, conducts legal research, and occasionally prepares legal memoranda.

Rick enjoys legal research and determining the answers to legal questions. However, he dreads the actual writing process—the assembly of the research and analysis into a written format.

Carol Beck recently retained Sara to represent her in the case of State v. Beck. In the case, police officers obtained a search warrant from a magistrate court judge authorizing a search of Ms. Beck's house for drugs. On the bottom of the warrant, the judge wrote, "Unannounced entry is authorized to ensure officer safety." When the officers obtained the warrant, they told the judge that in other drug search cases, if the officers announced their presence prior to entry, the persons occupying the premises being searched often posed a threat to the officers. Based on this statement, the judge authorized the officers to enter Ms. Beck's house unannounced. When the officers executed the warrant, they did not announce their presence and purpose prior to entry. Their search recovered a plastic bag containing an ounce of cocaine. Carol Beck was charged with possession with intent to distribute.

Sara and Rick have just begun the preliminary stages of preparing Ms. Beck's defense. Rick's assignment is to prepare a legal memorandum addressing the possibility of obtaining suppression of the evidence on the basis that the search was illegal. Sara tells Rick that any suppression motion must be filed in 30 days. What process should Rick follow when preparing the memorandum? The legal writing process is presented in this chapter. The answer to Rick's question is discussed in the Application section of this chapter.

I. INTRODUCTION

This chapter presents a collection of general considerations involved in legal analysis and writing, including an approach to the writing process and guidelines to follow when engaging in the process.

The legal issue raised by the facts of a client's case must be researched and analyzed and the results communicated, usually in written form. Legal research, analysis, and writing are all related. Each is a step in a process designed to answer legal questions and lead to the resolution of disputes. Legal analysis usually takes place when the research is converted into a written product and is part of the writing process. Therefore, legal analysis is included here in the discussion of legal writing. Legal writing is the step where the research and analysis are assembled in a written form designed to concisely record and communicate the answer to a legal question or questions.

For various reasons, many people believe that most legal communication is oral and takes place either in the courtroom or in a law office. This is not the case, however. The bulk of legal communication is written. The vast majority of cases never go to trial. They are settled, and the settlements are reduced to writing. When cases do go to trial, much of the trial work involves writing: written motions, trial briefs, jury instructions, and so on. In many instances, the law firm's practice rarely involves litigation, but instead focuses on the preparation of contracts, wills, corporation instruments, and other legal documents. A great deal of time is spent in research and in communicating the findings of that research in the form of legal memoranda and legal instruments.

II. IMPORTANCE OF WRITING SKILLS

There are several reasons why it is critically important for a paralegal or law clerk to possess good writing skills. This section details some of the major reasons.

In many instances, you may spend most of your time engaged in legal writing in one form or another. If you possess good writing skills, you can produce a finished product in a shorter time than an individual who does not possess such skills. This results in greater productivity, which enhances your value to the law firm.

The quality of a written product depends on writing skill: the greater the skill, the higher the quality of the product. Part of your job evaluation may be based on the quality of your written product. In addition, a written product that leaves the firm, such as correspondence to a client, represents the law firm. A shoddy product reflects poorly on the firm, and may damage its reputation.

Legal research and analysis are meaningless if the results cannot be clearly and concisely communicated. The goal of a legal research memorandum is to inform and record information. An individual who does not possess good writing skills may not be able to fulfill this goal.

Poor writing skills may also lead to miscommunication. One may intend the writing to convey a certain meaning when, in fact, it literally conveys a different meaning. This may lead to disaster if the supervising attorney relies on the literal meaning, and consequently commits an error. Correspondence to a client may be so unclear that the client does not understand the communication.

For Example

The written communication reads, "Individuals who file with the court promptly receive consideration." This is ambiguous. Does it mean that individuals who file promptly with the court receive redress, or does it mean that those who file with the court will receive prompt redress?

III. GOAL OF LEGAL WRITING

Before addressing the considerations involved in the legal writing process, it is important to identify the goal of legal writing. Law offices are busy places, and the reader of a paralegal's or law clerk's work product is usually a busy person who does not have time to wade through flowery prose, extraneous or unclear material, or disorganized material. The primary goal of legal writing, therefore, is to clearly, concisely, and completely convey legal information in a manner that accomplishes both of the following:

- Fully addresses the topic in as few words as possible
- Allows the reader to gain a clear understanding of the information in as little time as possible

You may feel that you do not possess good writing skills, or that you do not have the capability of clearly, concisely, and completely conveying information in a written form. Writing may be a struggle for you. Take heart: Writing skills can be developed and writing made easier through practice and the use of a writing process.

IV. LEGAL WRITING PROCESS

A **legal writing process** is a systematic approach to legal writing. It is an organized approach to legal research, analysis, and writing that helps you develop writing skills. This process makes legal writing easier and is necessary for the following reasons:

1. Legal writing is highly organized and structured. The organized structure helps ensure that complex subject matter is clearly communicated.

For Example

> The IRAC (issue, rule, analysis, conclusion) legal analysis process discussed in Chapter 2 is a structured approach to problem solving. The IRAC format, when followed in the preparation of a legal memorandum, helps ensure the clear communication of the complex subject matter of legal issue analysis.

The use of a legal writing process helps you conduct research and analysis within the structure and format of the type of legal writing assigned. A writing process saves time by providing the means to organize your legal analysis and research material as it is gathered.

2. If you do not have a writing process and merely gather research material and immediately begin to write, you will waste a great deal of time. You are not ready to write. If you begin to write without organizing your research and analysis, or without thinking through what you are going to write, you will flounder. If you gather a mountain of research that requires a great deal of analysis, you will waste time in the struggle to determine what goes where and how. Using a writing process forces you to think before you write, and forces you to follow an organized structure from the beginning. By using a process, when you actually begin to write, you will be ready. Your project, then, will be thorough and organized.

3. When you are researching or analyzing an assignment or engaging in legal writing, a writing process helps you capture ideas as they come to you. A process provides a framework within which to capture ideas and record them in their proper place as they occur. Without a process, ideas may be lost. See the subsection on organization in this chapter for a discussion on creating an outline.

4. A writing process also helps you overcome the difficult areas of legal writing. You may get stuck in a difficult analytical area or encounter writer's block. A writing process helps you avoid these problems by providing a stepped approach. Often, you can become stuck or blocked because you have missed a step or left something out. A process is a guide that includes all the steps and helps ensure that nothing is left out.

This section presents a general overview of the writing process and discusses matters that you should consider at each stage of the process. There are many different processes and combinations of processes that you may adopt when engaging in legal writing. What works for one person may not work for another. You may ultimately adopt a process that includes steps from various approaches to legal writing, including some of those presented in this chapter. It does not matter which process you ultimately adopt, but it is essential that you adopt some writing process.

The legal writing process consists of the three basic stages presented in Exhibit 15-1. The following sections discuss each of these stages. A prerequisite to the first stage—to the beginning of any writing process—is the assembly of all available information concerning the case.

Prewriting Stage	The stage where the assignment is organized, researched, and analyzed.
Writing Stage	The stage where research, analysis, and ideas are assembled into a written product.
Postwriting Stage	The stage where the assignment is revised, edited, and assembled in final form.

© Cengage

Exhibit 15-1 *Stages of the Legal Writing Process.*

For Example

The assignment is to prepare an office legal memorandum addressing the question of when the statute of limitations runs in a client's medical malpractice case. Gather all information concerning the case before you begin. This includes the client's file, depositions, interrogatories, witness interviews, any other discovery information, and so on.

A. Prewriting Stage

The **prewriting stage** is the stage of the legal writing process where an assignment is organized, researched, and analyzed. Novice writers often begin to write without adequate preparation. One of the most important aspects of the writing process is the performance of the steps necessary to become adequately prepared to begin. Drafting becomes much easier if you are fully prepared when you begin to write. This stage of the writing process may be divided into the three sections presented in Exhibit 15-2.

1. Assignment

The writing process begins with an identification of the type and purpose of the **assignment**. Three questions must be considered when reviewing the assignment:

- Is the assignment clearly understood?
- What type of legal writing (document) is required?
- Who is the audience?

a. Is the Assignment Clearly Understood?

You may receive the assignment in the form of a written memorandum or through oral instructions from the supervising attorney. An early and important step in the prewriting stage is to be sure that you understand the task you have been assigned. If you have any questions concerning the general nature or specifics of the assignment, ask.

A misunderstanding of the assignment can result in a great deal of time being wasted in the performance of the wrong task. Most attorneys welcome inquiries and prefer that a paralegal or law clerk ask questions rather than proceed in the wrong direction. In this regard, if the assignment is unclear in any way, summarize the assignment

1. Assignment	An identification of the type and purpose of the writing assignment
2. Constraints	A consideration of any constraints placed on the assignment
3. Organization	The organization of the writing assignment

© Cengage

Exhibit 15-2 *Sections of the Prewriting Stage.*

orally with the attorney. Another approach could be to draft a brief recapitulation of the assignment then submit it for the attorney's review and approval.

b. What Type of Legal Writing (Document) Is Required?

The next step is to determine the type of legal writing that the assignment requires. This is important because each type of legal writing has a different function and different requirements. Before you begin, you must know what form of legal writing is required.

There are various types of legal writing and numerous ways to categorize the types. The focus of this text is on legal research and analysis and the types of writing related to legal research and analysis, such as the following:

1. **Law-office legal research and analysis memoranda.** A researcher may be assigned the task of researching and analyzing the law that applies to a client's case. The law-office legal memorandum is designed to inform the reader of the results of the research and analysis. The assignment may be as simple as identification of the statutory or case law that applies to a legal issue or as complex as identification of the issues in a case and analysis of the law that applies. The preparation of a law-office legal memorandum will be discussed in Chapters 16 and 17.

2. **Correspondence.** There are several types of correspondence that a paralegal or law clerk may be required to draft: demand letters, settlement proposals, notices of events such as hearing dates, and so on. The assignment may require preparation of a draft of a letter to be sent to the client informing the client of the law that applies in the client's case and how the law applies. Neither a paralegal nor a law clerk may give legal advice to the client, but they may prepare a draft of the correspondence that the attorney will send to the client. Legal correspondence will be addressed in Chapter 19.

3. **Court briefs.** A **court brief** is a document filed with a court that contains an attorney's legal argument and the legal authority in support of that argument. There are primarily two categories of court briefs: trial court briefs and appellate court briefs.

   (1) *Trial Court Briefs*—A court may require an attorney to submit a brief in support of a position the attorney has taken in regard to a legal issue in a case. A **trial court brief**, also referred to as a Memorandum in Support or a Memorandum in Opposition, is usually submitted in support of or in opposition to a motion filed with the court.

For Example

An attorney files a motion to dismiss a complaint, claiming that the statute of limitations has run. In support of the motion, the attorney files a legal brief or memorandum in support containing the legal and factual reasons why the court should grant the motion. The opposing side will also file a brief or memorandum in opposition to the granting of the motion.

   (2) *Appellate Court Briefs*—An **appellate brief** is a document filed with an appellate court. It presents the legal arguments and authorities in support of the client's position on appeal, and is designed to persuade the appellate court to rule in the client's favor.

Court briefs will be discussed in detail in Chapter 18.

Each of these types of legal writing is structured in a different manner. The organization and considerations involved in drafting these documents vary. The subsequent stages of the writing process are governed by the type of legal writing the assignment requires. Therefore, an early step in the prewriting stage is the identification of the type of writing required.

Other types of legal writing include the drafting of legal documents such as contracts, wills, and pleadings. Other courses such as contracts and wills cover the specific considerations involved in the drafting of these documents; therefore, they are not covered in this text. You may follow the writing process presented in this chapter, however, when preparing such documents.

c. Who Is the Audience?

An important step when assessing the requirements of an assignment is to identify the intended audience. Inasmuch as the goal of legal writing is to clearly communicate information to the reader, you must ensure that the writing is crafted in a manner suited to meet the needs of that reader.

Legal writing assignments are designed to reach a number of different audiences. The intended reader may be a judge, an attorney, a client, or some other person. The reader's ability to understand the writing will depend on the reader's legal sophistication and how the document is written. A legal writing designed to inform a client or other layperson of the legal analysis of an issue is drafted differently than a writing designed to convey the same information to an attorney. The use of fundamental legal terminology may be appropriate when the writing is to be read by a person trained in the law. In contrast, if the reader has little or no legal training, it may be necessary to use nonlegal terms to clearly convey the same information.

For Example

Communication to the supervising attorney:

The motion to suppress the evidence should be granted. Exigent circumstances that would have justified an unannounced entry were not present at the time the officers executed the warrant, and the judge who issued the search warrant did not authorize unannounced entry.

Communication of the same information to the client:

The court may not allow the prosecution to use at trial the evidence seized when the officers searched your house. The law requires officers to announce their presence before they enter your house to conduct a search. They are required to do this unless a judge gives them permission to enter without first announcing their presence. They may also enter unannounced if, when they arrive at your house, they believe that you are destroying evidence or present a danger to them. In your case, the judge did not authorize the officers to enter unannounced, and nothing occurred when they arrived at your house to indicate that you were destroying drugs or you were a threat to them.

Another factor to consider is whether the writing is intended solely for internal office use. A writing that will be read only by individuals working in the office may contain information, comments, or assessments that would not be included in a writing intended to be read outside the office.

For Example

After analyzing the facts of the client's case and the applicable law, it may be necessary to convince the client to reconsider the amount of damages he believes he is entitled to recover and the possibility of settling this case. He needs to be informed about the amount of damages he can realistically expect to receive. He is adamant in his belief that he is entitled to more than $1 million, and he is not willing to consider settling for less. The range of recovery is more likely between $10,000 and $100,000.

Identify the audience to ensure that the legal communication is crafted in a manner commensurate with the reader's ability to understand the contents.

2. Constraints

The next step in the prewriting process is to consider any possible **constraints** that may affect performance of the assignment. Three major constraints that should be considered are presented in Exhibit 15-3.

Time	If the performance of the assignment is governed by a deadline, allocate a specific amount of time to each stage of the writing process.
Length	If the assignment is limited to a set number of pages, organize the writing to ensure that each section is allotted sufficient space.
Format/Organization	If the assignment is governed by a specific format or style established by office guidelines or court rule, identify the proper format and be sure you follow it.

© Cengage

Exhibit 15-3 Constraints on the Writing Process.

a. Time

A time constraint may govern the performance of an assignment. Most assignments have a deadline. You must determine the deadline, then allocate a specific amount of time to each stage of the writing process to meet that deadline.

For Example

You have 15 days to write a legal research memorandum on an issue in a case. You should allocate your time among the prewriting, writing, and postwriting stages of the writing process. A possible allocation could be six days for prewriting, five days for drafting, and four days for postwriting.

If you fail to allocate your time properly or fail to stick to the allocation, you may become absorbed or stuck in one stage and fail to leave enough time to properly complete the assignment. It does no good to completely research and analyze an issue if you do not have time to translate the research and analysis into a good written form.

For Example

You have 15 days to prepare an office memorandum. You become absorbed in the intricacies of the research and leave only two days to write the memo. This is not sufficient time to prepare a well-crafted product. The memorandum will either not be turned in on time, or be poorly written. Either way, your professional reputation is harmed.

b. Length

The assignment may have a length constraint. The supervising attorney may require that it not exceed a certain number of pages. Courts often have procedural rules limiting length, or there may be a case management order that limits the length of court briefs. If this is so, keep the length limitation in mind from the start. The amount of research material you gather is affected by this limitation. Of course, you must gather all the applicable law. You must, however, screen the research to ensure that you do not gather excessive information. With the space limitation in mind, consider how much of the material you are gathering can be included in the writing. Also, organize the writing to make sure that each section is allotted sufficient space.

For Example

The assignment is to prepare a legal research memorandum that does not exceed 15 pages. The organization must allocate sufficient space for each section of the memorandum. If the analysis ends up consisting of 14 pages, there will not be sufficient space for the statement of the facts, the issue, or the conclusion.

c. Format

Most law offices have rules or guidelines governing the organization and format of most types of legal writing, such as case briefs, office memoranda, and correspondence. Courts have formal rules governing the format and style of briefs and other documents submitted for filing.

For Example

Many courts have rules governing the size of the paper, the size of the margins, the length of briefs, and so on. If you do not conform to these rules, your submission may be rejected.

Inasmuch as you must draft the assignment within the constraints of the required format, you must identify that format at the beginning of the prewriting process.

3. Organization (Format)

Organization in the prewriting stage is the key to successful legal writing. You must be organized when conducting research and analysis in the prewriting stage, and the assignment must be organized when it is written. This may be accomplished through the development and use of an outline. An **outline** is the skeletal structure and organizational framework of the legal writing. Three aspects of outlines follow:

- The value of an outline
- The creation of an outline
- The use of an outline

a. Value of an Outline

An outline is considered useful in the writing stage. It makes writing easier by providing an organized framework for the presentation of research and analysis. An outline, however, is of greatest value when properly used in the prewriting stage. There are several reasons for this:

- The act of creating an outline causes you to organize ideas and prepare an approach to the assignment at the beginning of the process. This helps you to think through all the aspects of the assignment and take a global view, thereby avoiding gaps and weaknesses in your approach. You focus your attention and organize your thinking before you jump into the assignment.
- The use of an outline saves time. When used properly, all the information from a research source is placed in the outline when research is being performed. Time is often wasted having to retrieve a research source for a second or subsequent time to gather information that you either thought was not important or forgot to retrieve. If an outline is used properly, you should not have to retrieve any research source more than once.
- An outline provides an organized framework for the structure of the assignment and for conducting research and analysis. It provides a context within which to place research and ideas.
- An outline breaks complex problems into manageable components. It provides an organized framework from which to approach complex problems.

b. Creation of an Outline

The goal when creating an outline is to prepare the skeletal framework of the document you are going to draft. The outline should provide an overall picture of how all the pieces of the assignment relate to each other and fit together. The form of the outline is not important. Whether you use Roman numerals (I and II), capital letters (A and B), narrative sentences, fragments of sentences, or single words is irrelevant. Use whatever form or style works for you. You should use indentations to separate main topics from subtopics.

For Example

I.   Introduction

II.   Issue

III. Analysis

    a. Rule of law

    b. Case law

       1. Name of case

       2. Facts of case

The outline of the legal writing is governed by the type of writing you are preparing. Locate the standard format used in the office for the type of legal writing you are drafting. In the case of an office legal memorandum or correspondence, the law office may have a special format that must be followed. Use that format as the basis for the outline. If the writing is to be filed in court, such as a court brief, follow the format set out in the court rules. Whatever the basic format might be, it may be necessary to make additions and expand the outline.

For Example

The firm's format for an office legal memorandum is the following:

1. Description of assignment

2. Issue

3. Facts

4. Analysis

5. Conclusion

This is a broad format and requires a lot of filling in to be useful. It may be necessary to fill in details for each section. The outline is a perfect place to do this.

For Example

An expansion of the analysis section may be as follows:

I. Analysis

    1. Introduction

    2. Rule of law

    3. Case interpreting the rule of law

       a. Name of case/citation

       b. Facts of case

       c. Rule of law or legal principle presented in the case that applies to the client's facts

       d. Application of rule/principle from the case to the client's facts

This outline example is referred to in this chapter as the "analysis" outline example.

When developing an outline, keep the following points in mind:

1. Keep the facts and issues of the assignment in mind while developing the outline. It may be necessary to expand the outline to accommodate additional facts and issues.

For Example

The standard office outline may accommodate only one issue, whereas your assignment involves more than one issue. Expand the outline to apply the standard office outline to each issue.

2. Be flexible when creating and working with an outline. Realize that it may be necessary to change the outline as you conduct research.

For Example

The assignment involves the drafting of a simple office legal memorandum that addresses one issue. The outline you decide to follow is the analysis outline example presented previously. When research is conducted, it becomes apparent that two aspects of the rule of law apply to the issue, so two court opinions must be included in the analysis. The memo outline must now be expanded:

I. Analysis
   1. Introduction
   2. Rule of law
   3. Case interpreting the meaning of *publication* as used in the rule of law
      a. Name of case/citation
      b. Facts of case
      c. Interpretation of term
      d. Application of the interpretation of the first case to the client's facts
   4. Case interpreting the meaning of *written* as used in the rule of law
      a. Name of case/citation
      b. Facts of case
      c. Interpretation of term
      d. Application of the interpretation of the second case to the client's facts

3. Do not be surprised if it is necessary to reorganize the outline as a result of your research. Research may provide a clearer picture of the relationship between issues and necessitate a rethinking of the organization of the outline.

For Example

As a result of your research, you realize that the sequence in which you plan to address the issues should be changed. The issue you thought should be discussed first should come second.

4. The basic organizational format for most legal writing that requires legal analysis is the IRAC format. That is, state the question or issue, then identify the rule of law that governs the issue, analyze how and why the rule applies, and finally end with a conclusion summarizing the analysis. You may follow this format when addressing each issue and subissue. If, for some reason, you are at a loss for a format to follow, use the IRAC format.

5. Include in the outline a reference to or some notation for transition sentences. **Transition sentences** connect the major sections of the writing and lead the reader smoothly through the legal analysis. They make the document more readable. It is easy to become so focused on the law, cases, and analysis that you forget the transitions.

For Example

"The rule of law that governs this issue is § 36-6-6, which prohibits oppressive conduct by majority shareholders. In the case of *Jones v. Thomas*, the court held. . . ."

There should be a transition sentence linking the case to the rule of law: "The rule of law that governs this issue is § 36-6-6, which prohibits oppressive conduct by majority shareholders. *Because the statute does not provide a definition of the term oppressive* conduct, *case law must be referred to. A case on point is Jones v. Thomas*, where the court held. . . ."

Outline formats for correspondence, office legal memoranda, and court briefs will be presented in Chapter 16 through Chapter 19.

c. Use of an Outline

The value of an outline is determined by its use. If you prepare an outline then set it aside while you are researching and analyzing the assignment, it is of limited value. Its only value when used in this manner is to help organize your thinking and provide the organizational framework for the writing that follows. An outline is of greatest value when it is actively integrated into the prewriting stage. It can serve as an *invaluable guide* during the research and analysis process.

For Example

Follow the outline format when researching and analyzing: First identify the issue, next locate the rule of law that governs the issue, then identify the case law that interprets the rule of law in a fact situation similar to the client's case, and so on.

When integrated in the research and analysis process, an outline provides an organized context within which to place research and ideas. When so used, it will result in the development of a rough draft while research and analysis are being conducted. The result is a tremendous savings of time and effort. The integrated use of an outline in the prewriting stage simplifies the writing stage and makes it much easier.

How, then, do you integrate an outline into the research and analysis process in the prewriting stage? There are several ways to accomplish this. The practical approach suggested here is to use an **expanded outline**. This approach is composed of the two steps presented in Exhibit 15-4.

For illustration purposes, assume the assignment is to prepare an office legal memorandum addressing a single issue in a client's case. The cause of action is a slander tort claim. The broad issue is whether there was publication within the meaning of the law. Section 20-2-2 of the state statutes provides that civil slander is "the oral publication of a false statement of fact concerning an individual. . . ." The statute does not define *publication*. The facts of the case are that neighbor A, while visiting neighbor B's house, communicated to neighbor B a false statement of fact concerning the client. This example is referred to in this chapter as the "slander" example.

STEP 1	Convert the outline to a usable form— an expanded outline.	Use several sheets of three-holed or binder paper, or create separate pages if you are using a computer. Write the name of each section and subsection of the outline at the top of a separate page (e.g., at the top of one page write "Issue," at the top of another page "Facts," and so on).
STEP 2	Integrate all research, analysis, and ideas into the outline while conducting research and analysis.	As you conduct the research and develop ideas concerning any aspect of the case, enter them on the appropriate page of the expanded outline.

© Cengage

Exhibit 15-4 Two-Step Approach for Use of an Outline in the Prewriting Stage.

The format for the body of an office legal memorandum adopted in the office is as follows:

I. Issue
II. Statement of facts
III. Analysis/application

    1. Rule of law—the rule of law that governs the issue—enacted/case law
    2. Case(s)—court interpretation of rule if necessary

        A. Name and citation
        B. Brief summary of facts showing case is on point
        C. Rule/principle/reasoning applied by the court that applies to client's case
        D. Application—discussion of how the rule of law presented in the court decision applies in the client's case
    3. Counteranalysis
IV. Conclusion—a summary of the analysis

(1) *Convert the Outline to a Usable Form*—The memorandum format used in the office is typed on one page of paper and is not very useful in this form. The first step in the use of the outline is to convert it to a usable form—to expand the outline. This is accomplished by taking several sheets of three-holed or binder paper, or creating separate pages if you are using a computer, and writing the name of each section and subsection of the outline at the top of a separate page.

For Example

At the top of one sheet of paper or computer page, write "Issue." At the top of another page, write "Statement of facts." At the top of another page, write "Analysis—rule of law." Continue with a new page for each of the following: "Analysis—case," "Analysis—application of case to client's facts," "Counteranalysis," and "Conclusion."

Some sections of the outline may require more than one page.

For Example

The "Analysis—case" section may require two pages: one page for "Analysis—case—citation and facts of case" and one page for "Analysis—case—rule/principle/reasoning." Two or more pages may be required for a case because, in many instances, a great deal of information may be taken from a case, such as lengthy quotes from the court's reasoning.

If more than one rule of law applies, there should be a separate page for each rule of law. If several cases apply, there are separate pages for each case. If there are separate issues, research and analyze each issue separately, and prepare a separate expanded outline for each issue.

When completed, there should be a separate page for each section and subsection of the outline. Place the pages in a loose-leaf binder or, when using the computer, separate each page with a page break in the order of the outline. In other words, the first page will be the "Issue" page, followed by the "Statement of facts" page, then the "Analysis—rule of law" page, and so on. If you are using binder paper, insert blank sheets of paper between each section. This allows for the expansion of each section to accommodate additional notes, comments, ideas, and other information. The end result is a greatly expanded outline that is usable in the prewriting stage.

(2) *Integrate Research, Analysis, and Ideas into the Outline*—As you conduct research and develop ideas concerning any aspect of the case, enter them on the appropriate page of the expanded outline.

(i) *Ideas*—When any idea occurs concerning the case, enter it on the page of the expanded outline relating to that idea.

For Example

In the slander example, you may begin with a broad definition of the issue, such as "Was there publication?" As you conduct research and give more thought to the case, more refined formulations of the issue will become apparent, such as: "Under § 20-2-2, does slander occur when one person orally communicates to a third party false statements of fact concerning an individual?" As soon as this formulation of the issue comes to you, write it on the issue page. When it is time to write the memorandum, you will have multiple versions of the issue listed on the issue page. When all the ideas concerning the issue are in one place, it is easier to assemble the final statement of the issue.

The term *ideas* as used here includes all thoughts relating to the writing of the assignment, including how to compose transition sentences.

For Example

While researching a case, an idea may come to you about how the transition sentence linking the case to the rule of law should be written. Write the sentence in the beginning of the case section of the expanded outline or at the end of the rule of law page.

Keep the expanded outline with you. Often, the mind will work on an aspect of a case during sleep. You may wake up in the middle of the night or in the morning with an idea concerning the assignment or the answer to a problem. If the expanded outline is handy, you can immediately enter the idea or answer in the appropriate section. If it is not convenient to keep the outline with you, then carry a notepad. Enter ideas on the notepad as they come to you and place them in the outline later.

The value of the ability to immediately place ideas where they belong in the structure of the writing cannot be overemphasized. Some of the benefits include:

- Ideas are not lost. When researching, you often may have an idea and say to yourself, "I'll remember to include this when I write the _____ section." Five minutes later, the idea is lost. If you can immediately write the idea down where it belongs, it will not be lost.
- You can avoid confusion if you record ideas in the section where they will appear in the writing. If you keep the binder with the expanded outline with you throughout the prewriting stage, and you place all ideas as they come to you where they belong, you will avoid confusion and time lost figuring out which ideas go where.

For Example

While you are reading a case that interprets the rule of law, an idea may occur that relates to another aspect of the assignment, such as, "This gives me an idea about the counteranalysis of this issue." You may jot the idea down on a separate piece of paper or think you will remember it. You say to yourself, "I'll remember to include this when I write the counteranalysis."

By the time you get down to writing, time has passed, and you cannot remember what the idea was or, if you jotted it down, where the idea fits into the assignment. There are several pieces of paper with notes and ideas, and you have forgotten what many of them relate to or why.

- Writing becomes easier. When you sit down to write, all ideas are there, each in its proper place. You do not waste time in performing the additional step of organizing ideas. *Ideas are immediately organized as they come to you.*

For Example

If the "Issue" page of the expanded outline contains all the ideas concerning the ways the issue may be stated, it is easier to craft the final draft of the issue. You have every possible variation at hand. Drafting the issue is just a matter of assembling the issue from the best of the variations.

(ii) *Research* Just as you add ideas in the proper place in the expanded outline as they occur, enter all the relevant data on the appropriate page as you conduct your research.

For Example

Referring to the slander example, when you locate the slander statute, § 20-2-2, place it on the "rule of law" page. Include the proper citation and a copy of the statute. Include on the outline page all the information concerning the statute that you may need when writing. This avoids having to look up the statute more than once.

For Example

When you find a case or cases on point, enter the information concerning the case on the appropriate case page of the outline. This should include information such as the full citation, pertinent quotes concerning the rule of law or legal principle applied by the court, and the legal reasoning.

When researching case law, retrieve everything you may need from the case and include it in the expanded outline as you read the case. Why waste time looking up the same case twice? Place a copy of the case in the outline if necessary.

For Example

First, read through the entire case. Then, on the second reading, as you come upon a statement of the legal principle or legal reasoning that may apply to the client's case, stop reading. Enter the information from the case in the appropriate page of the expanded outline. Indicate the page of the case from which it was taken and, if appropriate, quote the information.

All too often, when reading a case, the tendency is to tell yourself that you will come back later and note the pertinent information. If there is any possibility that you will use information from a case, *retrieve it as you find it* and place on the appropriate case page of the outline. You will save time by not having to reread portions of the case.

Often, the reasoning or rule you want to use is not where you remembered, and then you waste time wading through the case trying to relocate it. If it turns out that information retrieved will not be used in the legal writing, it is simply not used. It is much better to have everything concerning the case in your expanded outline when you begin to write than to have to stop, retrieve, and reread the case.

If you use an expanded outline as suggested here, you are ready to write. All your research and ideas are assembled and organized. In effect, you have prepared a rough draft, so the writing task is made much simpler: The organization is finished, ideas are captured, research is assembled in the proper place, and many transition sentences are already crafted and in place. The writing task is reduced to simply converting the outline to paragraph and sentence form.

B. Writing Stage

The second stage in the writing process is the actual drafting of the legal writing. In the **writing stage** you assemble the research, analysis, and ideas into a written product. Many individuals find it difficult to go from the research stage to the drafting stage, from the prewriting stage to the writing stage. This is often called "writer's block." Some of the obstacles that can make it difficult to begin writing are organizing the research and determining what goes where and how it relates and is connected. If you use an expanded outline in the prewriting stage, it is much easier to begin writing. The research and analysis are already organized, the relationship of the material is already established by the outline, and many introductory and transitional sentences have already been written.

Chapter 16 through Chapter 19 present a detailed discussion of what must be included when writing an office legal memorandum, court brief, or legal correspondence. The rules and guidelines in Exhibit 15-5 will help with the writing process in general.

1. Prepare the writing location.
2. Write during the time of day when you do your best work.
3. Limit interruptions.
4. Begin writing; do not procrastinate.
5. Begin with a part of the assignment you feel most confident about.
6. Do not try to make the first draft the final draft.
7. Do not begin to write until you are prepared.
8. If you become stuck, move to another part of the assignment.
9. Establish a timetable.

© Cengage

Exhibit 15-5 Rules and Guidelines—Writing Stage.

1. Prepare the writing location. Make sure the work environment is pleasant and comfortable. Have all the resources you need at hand, such as paper, computer, and research materials.
2. Write during the time of day when you do your best work.

For Example

If you are a "morning person," write in the morning and save other tasks for later in the day.

3. Limit interruptions. Legal writing requires focus and concentration. Therefore, select a writing time and environment that allow you to be as free from interruptions and distractions as possible. Put your cell phone away, put your office phone on do not disturb, close your email program, and turn off instant messaging or other alerts on your phone or computer that may distract you. Consider marking time on your calendar to show "busy" to dissuade others from stopping by your desk unannounced.
4. Begin writing; do not procrastinate. One of the most difficult steps is beginning. Do not put it off. The longer you put it off, the harder beginning will become. Start writing anything that has to do with the project. Do not expect what you start with to be great, just start. Once you begin writing, it will get easier.
5. Begin with a part of the assignment you feel most confident about. You do not have to write in the sequence of the outline. Write the easiest material first, especially if you are having trouble starting.
6. Set a minimum time to write. It may be 30 minutes or an hour, but setting a time and making yourself write for that period of time, often can lead to significant work on a draft. Use a timer if necessary.
7. Do not try to make the first draft the final draft. The goal of the first draft is to translate the research and analysis into organized paragraphs and sentences, not to produce a finished product. Just write the information in rough form. It is much easier to polish a rough draft than to make the first draft a finished product.
8. Do not begin to write until you are prepared. Do all the research and analysis before beginning. It is much easier to write a rough draft if the prewriting stage is thoroughly completed.
9. If you become stuck, move to another part of the assignment. If you are stuck on a particular section, leave it. The mind continues to work on a problem subconsciously. That is why solutions to problems often seem to appear in the morning. Let the subconscious work on the problem while you move on. The solution to the difficulty may become apparent when you return to the problem.
10. Establish a timetable. Break the project into logical units and allocate your time accordingly. This helps you avoid spending too much time on one section of the writing and running out of time. Do not become fanatical about the time schedule, however. You created the timetable, and you can break it. It is there as a guide to keep you on track and alert you to the overall time constraints.

C. Postwriting Stage

The **postwriting stage** is the stage of the legal writing process where an assignment is revised, edited, and assembled in final form.

1. Revising

The first draft will not be the final draft. Revise all initial drafts with the idea of improving quality and clarity. Do not be surprised if the initial draft requires several **revisions**. Do not set a limit on the number of drafts that may be required. The goal is that the final product clearly, concisely, and completely conveys the information it is designed to convey. The number of drafts should be governed by this goal. Develop a checklist for use when revising a draft (see Exhibit 15-6). Some items that you may wish to include in the checklist follow:

1. Is the writing well organized? Is it organized in a logical manner? Does each section logically follow the previous section?

1. Is the writing well organized?

2. Is it written in a manner the audience will understand?

3. Is the writing clear? Does it make sense?

4. Is the writing concise? Are there extra words that can be eliminated?

5. Is the writing complete? Are all the aspects of the assignment covered?

6. Are the legal authorities correctly cited?

© Cengage

Exhibit 15-6 *Reviewing a Draft Checklist.*

2. Is it written in a manner the audience will understand? If the writing is addressed to a layperson, is the draft written in plain language the reader will understand?

3. Is the writing clear? Does it make sense? Are the sections connected with transition sentences that clearly link the sections and guide the reader from one section to the next?

4. Is the writing concise? Are there extra words that can be eliminated? Is it repetitive? If multiple examples are included to illustrate a single point, are all the examples necessary?

5. Is the writing complete? Are all the aspects of the assignment covered? If there are multiple issues, is each issue and subissue thoroughly analyzed?

6. Are the legal authorities correctly cited? Are all legal citations in the correct form? All legal research sources must be correctly cited. The rules and resources for ensuring your citations are correct are discussed at the end of Chapters 3 through 8.

When reviewing a draft, allow time to elapse between drafting and revising. This allows the mind to clear. You will then be able to approach the revision with a fresh perspective and are more likely to catch errors and inconsistencies.

2. Editing

Editing is actually part of the revision process. The revision process discussed in the previous section addresses the broad intellectual and structural content of the legal writing, such as overall organization, clarity, and conciseness. Editing focuses on technical writing issues, such as punctuation, spelling, grammar, phrasing, typographical errors, and citation errors. Many of these specific areas are discussed in Chapters 14 and 16. A few general editing tips to keep in mind, however, follow:

1. Be prepared to edit a legal writing several times. It may be necessary to edit a revision several times to catch all the errors.

2. Read the document aloud. When you silently read your own draft, the mind may automatically fill in a missing word or correct an error without your knowing it, and you will not catch the error. If possible, have a colleague read it to you.

3. If you have only been working on the document on the computer, print the document and edit a paper copy. The eyes and brain tend to process differently when you change the format in which you are viewing a document.

4. Have a colleague whose writing skills you respect edit the document.

5. Do not rely on spell-check or grammar-check functions.

6. Read the document backwards or read paragraphs in random order. Like printing a document that has only been viewed on a computer screen, reviewing sentences and paragraphs out of context and out of order tend to allow the reader to see things they otherwise miss.

V. GENERAL RESEARCH SUGGESTIONS

Research is a major part of the prewriting stage of the writing process. The steps involved in legal research are discussed in Chapter 2 through Chapter 8; some general suggestions and guidelines concerning legal research as it relates to the prewriting stage are included in Exhibit 15-7.

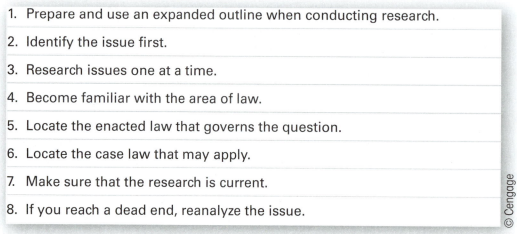

1. Prepare and use an expanded outline when conducting research.

2. Identify the issue first.

3. Research issues one at a time.

4. Become familiar with the area of law.

5. Locate the enacted law that governs the question.

6. Locate the case law that may apply.

7. Make sure that the research is current.

8. If you reach a dead end, reanalyze the issue.

© Cengage

Exhibit 15-7 Suggestions and Guidelines—Legal Research and the Prewriting Stage.

1. Prepare and use an expanded outline when conducting research.

2. Identify the issue first, as you cannot begin to look for an answer until you know the question. The preliminary identification may be very broad, such as "Did negligence occur?" or "Was there a breach of contract when the goods were delivered 10 days late?" This preliminary identification of the issue will usually identify the general area of law to be researched, such as contracts, negligence, and so on.

3. Thoroughly research each issue to its conclusion before proceeding to the next issue. If you find material on another issue, note a reference to it on the page in the expanded outline for that issue. Researching several issues at once only leads to frustration and confusion.

4. Become familiar with the area of law. If you are unfamiliar with the area of law that applies to the issue, obtain a general overview. Legal encyclopedias and treatises are examples of sources to consult to obtain an overview of an area of law.

5. Locate first the enacted law that governs the question, such as a statute or constitutional provision.

6. Locate the relevant case law if there is no enacted law that governs or if the enacted law is so broadly drafted that case law is required to interpret the enacted law. Attempt to locate mandatory precedent first, then persuasive precedent and secondary authority.

7. Make sure that the research is current. Check supplements and Shepardize cases to be sure that the authority located is current.

8. If you reach a dead end, reanalyze the issue. If you cannot find any authority, either primary or secondary, chances are the issue is too broadly or too narrowly stated. Restate the issue. If the issue is too broadly stated, restate it in narrower terms. Return to a basic research source for guidance, such as a legal encyclopedia. If the issue is too narrowly framed, restate it in broader terms.

VI. KEY POINTS CHECKLIST: The Writing Process

✓ Adopt a writing process. An organized approach is essential for legal writing. Develop a process that works for you. Follow the process recommended in this chapter or create your own.

✓ Work from an expanded outline in the prewriting stage. An expanded outline provides a framework for organizing your research and capturing your ideas.

✓ Consider the audience. Always identify the audience early in the process. The type of audience influences the style, depth, and complexity of the finished product.

✓ Consider time, length, and format constraints. Identify any constraints that affect the assignment, and design the approach to the assignment with these constraints in mind.

✓ Do not procrastinate. If you have trouble beginning to write, start with the easiest section. Sit down and begin. Do not worry about quality—just start.

✓ Break large assignments into manageable sections. Do not become overwhelmed by the complexity of an assignment.

✓ Do not try to make the first draft the final draft. Be prepared to compose several drafts. The goal is a quality product. Let the number of drafts be determined by this goal.

✓ Update your research. Check all authority to ensure that it is current.

VII. APPLICATION

This section presents an overview of the writing process by applying the process to the hypothetical presented at the beginning of the chapter. After gathering and reviewing all the information available in the office concerning Ms. Beck's case, Rick follows the process recommended in this chapter. An outline of Rick's application of the process follows.

A. Prewriting Stage

I. *Assignment.* Rick first reviews the assignment.

    A. *Is the assignment clear?* He reviews the assignment to be sure he understands what is required. Rick has no question in this regard. The assignment is to research and analyze the question of whether the evidence seized in the case can be suppressed.

    B. *What type of legal writing is required?* The assignment is to draft an office legal memorandum. Rick retrieves the office memorandum outline form used by the firm. The body of the outline is presented here.

        I. Issue

        II. Statement of facts

        III. Analysis/application

            1. Rule of law—the rule of law that governs the issue—enacted/case law

            2. Case(s)—court interpretation of the rule of law if necessary

                A. Name and citation

                B. Brief summary of facts showing the case is on point

                C. Rule/principle/reasoning applied by the court that applies to client's case

                D. Application—discussion of how the rule of law presented in the court decision applies in the client's case

            3. Counteranalysis

        IV. Conclusion—a summary of the analysis

    C. *Who is the audience?* The memorandum is for office use. Rick knows he does not have to write it in layperson's terms.

II. *Constraints.* What are the constraints on the assignment? Rick has a time constraint. Any motion to suppress the evidence must be filed within 30 days. He must finish the memorandum sufficiently in advance of the 30 days to allow Ms. Fletcher time to review it and prepare the appropriate motion. Based on past experience, he knows Ms. Fletcher prefers to have 10 days to review the memorandum and prepare the motion. This leaves him 20 days to complete the assignment.

      Rick also knows that Ms. Fletcher prefers shorter memos. She has told him that a single-issue memo should not exceed seven pages. He knows he must budget his time and research to meet these constraints.

III. *Organization.* Rick organizes the assignment around the outline.

    A. *Creation of expanded outline.* Rick expands the outline as suggested in section IV.A.3 of this chapter. The initial expanded outline is composed of eight pages of paper or computer pages. He labels the pages as follows: Issue; Facts; Analysis—rule of law; Analysis—case name, facts, and citation; Analysis—case rule/principle and reasoning; Analysis—application of case to facts; Counteranalysis; and Conclusion.

    B. *Use of expanded outline.* Rick begins his research with the expanded outline at hand. He studies the facts and begins to formulate the issue. Every time he thinks of a way to state the issue, he writes it on the "Issue" page.

For Example

The first formulation of the issue is, "Can the evidence be suppressed?" Later formulations are, "Can evidence be suppressed when officers execute a warrant unannounced based on the warrant's authorization of unannounced entry?" and "Under the state's exclusionary rule, can evidence be suppressed when officers conduct a search unannounced, pursuant to a warrant authorizing unannounced entry to ensure officer safety, and the authorization is based upon an affidavit that gives no particularized facts regarding threats to officer safety?"

As he researches, Rick finds article II, section 5, of the state constitution, which prohibits illegal searches and seizures. He copies article II, section 5, and places it on the "Analysis—rule of law" page. He realizes this provision is so broadly formulated that he must locate case law for an interpretation of how it applies in an unannounced entry situation.

For Example

Article II, section 5, does not provide guidance as to what constitutes an illegal search when law enforcement officers enter a residence unannounced; therefore, case law must be consulted.

While looking for a case on point, he thinks of a transition sentence that will connect the rule of law section of the memo to the case law section. Rick immediately writes this sentence at the end of the "Analysis—rule of law" page of the outline.

Rick locates the court opinion of *State v. Brick*. Addressing a fact situation almost identical to Ms. Beck's, the court held that a warrant may authorize unannounced entry. The court went on to state, however, that the authorization must be based on a "particularized showing that the individuals whose residence is being searched have in the past represented a threat to officer safety. Any authorization based upon a generalized statement, such as 'Drug offenders often present a threat to officers' safety during the execution of search warrants,' violates article II, section 5, and the exclusionary rule requires the suppression of any evidence seized."

Rick enters all the relevant information from the case in the appropriate "Analysis—case" pages of the outline. He includes the full citation, any relevant quotations from the case, and the pagenumber references for the quotations. He does not have to reread the case when he writes the memorandum. All the key information is in the expanded outline.

While analyzing the case, Rick thinks of a sentence he will use when discussing how the case applies to the client's facts. He enters this sentence in the "Analysis—application of case to facts" page of the outline.

For Example

"In our case, just as in *State v. Brick*, the officers executed a warrant unannounced, based on the authorization contained in the warrant. In our case, as in *Brick*, the authorization was based upon a generalized statement that drug offenders often pose a threat to officer safety when the officers announce their presence prior to entry. In *Brick*, the court ruled that such searches violate the state constitution and the evidence seized must be suppressed. If the trial court follows the rule of law presented in *State v. Brick*, the evidence should be suppressed."

If there are more cases that should be included in the memo, Rick will insert additional pages in the outline for each case and enter the pertinent information on the appropriate page.

Rick identifies any counterargument, such as that contained in conflicting case law, and enters it in the "Counteranalysis" section of the outline. If Rick has any thoughts concerning the conclusion while conducting the research and analysis, he enters them in the "Conclusion" section of the outline.

While working on the assignment, Rick keeps the outline or a notepad with him. He takes it home after work. He writes any idea concerning the assignment on the appropriate page when the idea occurs. Nothing is lost, and all his ideas and research are organized in the outline. Transition sentences and other parts of the writing, such as how the issue should be written, are already drafted and in the proper place. If more than one issue must be addressed, Rick prepares a separate section of the outline for that issue and the rule of law and case law that apply to it.

B. Writing Stage

After completing the research and analysis, Rick prepares a rough draft. He simplifies the task by using the expanded outline. All the research, analysis, and ideas are already organized, and many of the sentences are written and in place. All Rick has to do is to convert the outline into sentence and paragraph form and fill in the gaps. When drafting, Rick keeps in mind the guidelines presented in writing stage section of this chapter, such as not procrastinating and preparing a comfortable writing location.

C. Postwriting Stage

The final step is to revise and edit the memorandum. Focusing on conciseness, clarity, and completeness, Rick uses a checklist similar to the one presented in the postwriting section of this chapter. Rick may need to create several drafts and spend considerable time revising. Because his work is judged by the finished product, Rick takes care during this stage of the writing process.

Note that this chapter places a great deal of emphasis on the prewriting stage of the writing process. Organization here is the key to simplicity, taking care in this part of the process and using an expanded outline. It may seem like a lot of work to prepare an expanded outline, but its use will actually save time in the long run.

Summary

Contrary to popular belief, the bulk of the practice of law involves writing in one form or another. Legal writing includes the preparation of documents, such as office legal memoranda; legal correspondence to clients and other individuals; litigation documents that will be filed with a court; and transaction documents prepared for clients' use, such as contracts.

Legal writing is often complex, requiring in-depth research and detailed analysis. The complexities of an assignment, time constraints, and heavy workloads dictate the necessity of following a writing process when engaging in legal writing. There is no standard writing process. Each individual should adopt or create a process that works for them. The chapter presents a process that focuses on the three stages of the writing process: prewriting, writing, and postwriting.

The prewriting stage has three sections: the assignment, constraints affecting the assignment, and the organization of the assignment. When approaching an assignment, you should first review the assignment and consider any constraints that affect the assignment, such as time, length, and format.

After you address these matters, prepare an expanded outline and use it when engaging in the research and analysis of the assignment. An expanded outline consists of a separate notebook page or computer-generated page for each topic and subtopic of the outline. Enter research and analysis in the expanded outline throughout the prewriting stage as you gather material and conduct analysis. The end result is a rough draft developed during the prewriting stage.

Adopting a prewriting process simplifies the writing stage. In the writing stage, the rough draft represented by the expanded outline is converted to the finished product (e.g., a legal memorandum).

All drafts must be revised and edited. A revision focuses on ensuring clarity, completeness, and conciseness. Editing focuses on narrower concerns involving accuracy, such as punctuation and grammar.

The chapter concludes with reminders concerning legal research as it relates to the prewriting stage of the writing process. These suggestions include starting with the identification of the issue and making sure to update all research.

Quick References

Internet Resources

Using "legal writing for paralegals" or "legal research memorandum" as a topic, you will find various websites (literally thousands of sites) that concern legal writing. Some sites refer to legal writing textbooks, some focus on legal research and analysis, others focus on legal writing for law school students, some advertise research and writing services, some are websites for specific classes taught at schools, some advertise courses and seminars on legal writing, and some sites discuss legal memoranda in specific areas such as environment law. Several law schools have sample legal memoranda or guides related to writing legal memoranda. From a law school's website, use the search box and enter "legal writing" or "sample memorandum" to find any related materials.

As with most topics on the Internet, the problem is not the lack of websites, but the presence of too many sites. Probably the best strategy is to narrow your search to a specific type of legal writing and topic, such as "legal memorandum, public service contracts." The following sites may provide useful support information when you engage in projects requiring legal research.

http://www.nala.org
This is the site for the National Association of Legal Assistants (NALA). The association site provides a wealth of information ranging from articles on the profession to education and certification programs for paralegals. It includes information on court decisions affecting paralegals and links to other related sites.

http://www.paralegals.org
This is the web page for the National Federation of Paralegal Associations (NFPA), another national paralegal organization. This web page provides links to a wide range of sites of interest to paralegals, such as research sources, publications, and products.

http://www.paralegalttoday.com
Paralegal Today is a magazine geared toward the needs of paralegals. It often includes helpful articles on legal research and writing.

Exercises

The following exercises are helpful in developing an understanding of and familiarity with the use of a writing process.

ASSIGNMENT 1

Describe the stages of the legal writing process.

ASSIGNMENT 2

Describe the steps of the prewriting stage.

ASSIGNMENT 3

Describe the types of legal writing discussed in this chapter.

ASSIGNMENT 4

Why is the type of audience important?

ASSIGNMENT 5

What are some of the constraints that may affect your performance of an assignment? How do they affect your performance of an assignment?

ASSIGNMENT 6

What is an expanded outline? Describe the creation and elements of the body of an expanded outline for an office legal memorandum.

ASSIGNMENT 7

Describe the use of an expanded outline in the preparation of an office legal memorandum.

ASSIGNMENT 8

What are some of the rules to keep in mind during the writing stage?

ASSIGNMENT 9

Prepare a checklist for revising and editing. Include materials related to parts of speech, grammar, and sentence and paragraph structure from Chapter 14.

ASSIGNMENT 10

What are the general factors to keep in mind when engaging in research?

ASSIGNMENT 11

The paralegal is assigned the task of preparing an office legal memorandum. The memorandum is due in 10 days, and there is a five-page limit. The facts and law are as follows:

Facts: Mary was Tom's stockbroker and financial advisor. Tom owned five acres of property. Mary advised Tom to sell the property to Ana at a price slightly below the market value. She recommended that Tom buy stock with the proceeds. Tom sold the property to Ana and now wants to have the transaction set aside because he believes Mary unduly and improperly influenced his decision. Mary and Ana are very close friends.

Law: Statutory law (§ 96-4-4-1 of the state statutes) provides that a contract for the sale of land may be set aside if it is entered into under undue influence.

Case law: *Lorn v. Bell.* In a fact situation similar to Tom's, the court ruled that under § 96-4-4-1, undue influence occurs when:

1. The person influenced is susceptible to undue influence.
2. The person influenced is influenced to enter the contract.
3. The opportunity to influence is present.
4. Undue influence is present.
5. The person exercising the undue influence benefits from the undue influence.

Part A

Detail the application of each step of the prewriting stage to this assignment.

Part B

For the organization step of the prewriting stage, prepare an expanded outline based on the outline presented in Section IV.A.3.c(ii) in this chapter.

Part C

Based only on the preceding information, fill in the expanded outline. Include a statement of the issue, analysis, counteranalysis, conclusion, and recommendations.

ASSIGNMENT 12

The paralegal is assigned the task of preparing an office legal memorandum. The memorandum is due in seven days, and there is a five-page limit. The facts of law are as follows:

Facts: The client, Jim, a 15-year-old boy, had a small single blade pocketknife in his backpack. He had used the backpack several weeks ago when he went on an overnight fishing trip with his dad. The knife was a typical pocketknife. It was 2-½ inches long when folded and the blade was 2 inches in length. The blade locked into place when the knife was opened. The blade was sharp on one edge and had a pointed tip. Jim forgot the knife was in his backpack, it had slipped into the bottom corner and he had not noticed it in the pack since the fishing trip. Another student told a teacher he saw the knife in the client's backpack the day before.

Law: The state criminal statute § 13-3102 provides: A person commits misconduct involving weapons by **knowingly** possessing a **deadly weapon** on school grounds. The criminal code § 13-105 defines "knowingly" as "a person is aware or believes that the person's conducts is of that nature or that the circumstances exist. It does not require any knowledge of the unlawfulness of the act or omission."

Case Law: *In re Vincent V.* In a fact situation similar to Jim's, the court ruled that a deadly weapon is "anything that is defined as lethal use." The court further held that the determination of whether a knife is a deadly weapon under § 13-3102 depends on the "size, shape sharpness, and type of knife."

Part A

Detail the application of each step of the prewriting stage to this assignment.

Part B

For the organization step of the prewriting stage, prepare an extended outline based on the outline presented in Section IV.A.3.c(ii). Note there are two issues in this assignment, one involving the "knowingly" element, the other involving the "deadly weapon" element.

Part C

Based only on the preceding information, fill in the extended outline. Include a statement of the issues, analysis, counteranalysis, conclusion, and recommendation.

ASSIGNMENT 13

The following assignment is based on an assignment of your instructor's choosing in Chapter 17. Use the assignment memo, statutory law, and case law from that assignment. The memo is due in seven days, and there is a five-page limit.

1. Describe in detail the application of each step of the prewriting stage to the assignment.

    For the organization step of the prewriting stage, prepare an expanded outline based on the outline presented in Section IV.A.3.c of this chapter. Using the information presented in the assignment, fill in the expanded outline. Include in the "Issue" section of the outline a broad statement of the issue and at least one narrow statement of the issue.

Chapter 16

Office Legal Memorandum: Issues and Facts

Learning Objectives

After completing this chapter, you should understand:

- The importance of an office legal memorandum
- The purposes and uses of an office legal memorandum
- The sections of a basic office legal memorandum
- How to draft the sections of an office legal memorandum: heading, statement of assignment, issue, brief answer, and facts

Jeff Lyons, a paralegal with Berdwin and Associates, received the following memo:

To: Jeff Lyons, Paralegal

From: Rita Berdwin, Attorney

Date: April 20, 2016

Office File No: CR 16-136

Re: *State of Illinois v. Meril Findo*, CR 16-378, privileged communication

We have been retained to represent Meril Findo in the above-referenced case. He is charged with assault with a deadly weapon. Mr. Findo allegedly assaulted his neighbor Joseph Markham with a hammer. Mr. Findo and Mr. Markham were arguing over the location of a fence Mr. Markham was building. According to Mr. Findo, Mr. Markham became angry and attempted to hit him with a brick. A struggle ensued, and the brick fell and hit Mr. Markham on the head. Mr. Markham claims that Mr. Findo became increasingly angry as the argument progressed; Mr. Findo grabbed a hammer and struck him repeatedly on the head and arms. Mr. Markham claims he never assaulted Mr. Findo with a brick. There were no witnesses to the argument. Mrs. Findo is currently separated from Mr. Findo and has agreed to testify against him. Her testimony is that before the confrontation, Mr. Findo stated, "Markham is out there building that damn fence again. I'll put a stop to this once and for all." He grabbed a hammer and went out the door.

The Findos' children, Tomas, age 16, and Alice, age 10, were present and heard the conversation. Neither Mrs. Findo nor the children saw the confrontation.

Prepare a memorandum addressing the question of whether the conversation between Mr. and Mrs. Findo is a privileged spousal communication and, therefore, not admissible in the trial of Mr. Findo. I need the memo within two weeks. You can probably cover this in three to five pages.

This chapter and Chapter 17 address the process and considerations involved in preparing an office legal memorandum. The office legal memorandum is usually composed of some or all of the sections presented in Exhibit 16-1.

The Application section of this chapter addresses the first half of Jeff's assignment—the heading through the facts sections. The Application section of Chapter 17 covers the remainder of the assignment—the analysis through the recommendations sections.

I. INTRODUCTION

The office legal memorandum is the type of legal writing a paralegal or law clerk engaged in legal research and analysis most frequently prepares. The role of most paralegals and law clerks is to provide assistance and support to an attorney. When this support function involves legal research, it usually focuses on research and analysis of the legal issues in a client's case. The results of this research and analysis are communicated to the attorney in the form of an office legal memorandum. It is one of the most effective and valuable ways paralegals and law clerks can support an attorney.

This chapter and the next are devoted to the preparation of office legal memoranda. Two chapters are devoted to this topic for the following reasons:

- Most law office analytical legal writing involves the preparation of office legal memoranda.
- The considerations involved in the preparation of office legal memoranda also apply to the preparation of legal analysis documents designed for external use, such as court motions and briefs.

This chapter focuses on the basic format for the office legal memorandum and the preparation of the first half of the memorandum: the heading through the statement of facts sections. Chapter 17 will focus on the heart of the memo: the legal analysis through the recommendations sections.

The preparation of an office legal memorandum is a multistep process involving the integration of legal research, analysis, and writing. This chapter and Chapter 17 cannot be read in a vacuum. They require you to integrate the material presented in Chapters 1 through 15. Although it is assumed that you are familiar with those chapters, cross-references to specific chapters are included to help you correlate and integrate the material.

As mentioned previously, the majority of the legal research and writing prepared by paralegals and law clerks is designed for the use of the supervising attorney rather than for use outside the office. The basic format and analytical process that are followed are fundamentally the same for both an office legal memorandum and a legal analysis document designed for external use. Therefore, consider the information presented here and in Chapter 17 when reading Chapters 18 and 19. External-use documents usually involve:

- Correspondence to clients or other individuals informing them of the law or the analysis of a legal problem.
- Briefs submitted to a trial court or court of appeals.

Heading
Statements of Assignment
Issue
Brief Answer
Statement of Facts
Analysis
Conclusion
Recommendations

© Cengage

Exhibit 16-1 Sections of an Office Legal Memorandum.

II. DEFINITION

An **office legal memorandum** provides an objective, critical analysis of a legal problem. It is an informative document that summarizes the research and analysis of the legal issue or issues raised by the facts of a client's case. It contains a summary of the law and how the law applies to the facts of the case. It presents an objective legal analysis and includes the arguments in favor of and in opposition to the client's position

A legal memorandum prepared for office use is referred to by many different names: interoffice legal research memorandum, interoffice memorandum of law, office legal memorandum, office research memorandum, objective memorandum, and legal memo. Here and in Chapter 17, the term *office memo* is used when referring to an office legal memorandum.

III. PURPOSES, USES, AND IMPORTANCE

The major purposes and functions of an office memo are as follows:

1. An office memo identifies and records the law that applies to a specific issue or issues raised by the client's facts.
2. An office memo analyzes and explains how the law applies to the issue.
3. An offices memo assesses the strengths and weaknesses of the client's case.
4. An office memo presents a conclusion and proposed solution based on the analysis.

A well-crafted office memo may be put to a variety of uses in a law office:

- It may be used as a guide to determine whether a claim exists.

For Example

One of the client's potential causes of action involves a breach of the implied warranty of merchantability. In the client's case, the purchase took place at a garage sale. The office memo reveals that under the applicable statute, the warranty applies only if the seller is a merchant. The case on point provides that individuals holding garage sales are not merchants within the meaning of the statute. The office memo reveals that no cause of action exists for a breach of implied warranty of merchantability.

- It may be used as a guide to the course of action to be pursued.

For Example

The case involves a question of whether the client had a duty to discover and disclose information in a real estate transaction. The client was unaware that his house had termites, and consequently, the buyer was not informed of this problem. The office memo reveals that the case law requires the seller to inspect for termites and disclose the results of the inspection to the buyer. This information may lead the attorney to recommend that settlement be pursued.

- It may inform subsequent researchers in the law office, working on other cases with similar issues and facts, how the law applies. Future researchers do not have to spend time reinventing the wheel.
- It may refresh the memory of the attorney assigned to the case on how the law applies to an issue. This is especially true in complex cases. It is also true when the memo is prepared early in the case, and the attorney does not review it until months later when the matter is addressed by the court.
- It may be used as a guide by the attorney preparing a document to be filed with the court or correspondence for the client. The office memo may contain the statutory law, case law, and legal analysis that are the basis for the preparation of the document.

For Example

The office memo addresses the question of whether a search warrant was improperly issued due to the insufficiency of the affidavit in support of the warrant. The standards required for a warrant to be sufficient are spelled out in the office memo. The attorney may use the office memo as a basis for preparing a brief in support of, or opposition to, a motion to suppress the evidence seized when the warrant was executed.

Office memos are of primary importance because they provide the answer to legal questions. Their importance is evidenced by the fact that office memos are required at every stage of the litigation process:

- Early in the case, they identify the required elements of the cause of action and what is required to state a claim.
- They are used to determine whether the client has a defense or a cause of action.
- Throughout the litigation, they help determine what is required to support or oppose a motion.
- In the discovery process, legal memos address discovery issues such as what constitutes an attorney's work product.
- At the trial stage, office memos often analyze evidentiary issues, such as whether evidence is admissible.
- At the post trial stage, office memos may address issues raised on appeal, such as whether the court properly ruled on a matter during the trial.

Ethics. Regardless of the purpose of the memo or at what point in the litigation process it is prepared, the actions of the supervisory attorney and the outcome of the case may largely depend upon the quality of the office memo. Also, as mentioned in Chapter 2, Rule 1.1 of the Model Rules of Professional Conduct requires that a client be provided competent representation. It is critical, therefore, that the performance of research, analysis, and drafting of the memo be thorough, careful, and complete.

As discussed in Chapter 15, legal writing is easier if you use a writing process. In this chapter, you can take that information and use it as the framework for preparing an office memo. Recall the three stages of the writing process: prewriting, writing, and postwriting.

IV. PREWRITING STAGE

The **prewriting stage** consists of three sections:

1. Nature of the assignment—an identification of the type and purpose of the writing assignment
2. Constraints on the assignment—a consideration of any constraints placed on the assignment
3. Organization—the organization of the writing assignment

A prerequisite to beginning the prewriting stage is to assemble all available files and information concerning the client's case. All the relevant files and information must be complete. After this is accomplished, you are able to address the three sections.

A. Nature of the Assignment

The first section of the prewriting stage requires a review of the assignment in which you determine the following:

- Is the assignment clearly understood?
- What type of legal writing is required?
- Who is the audience?

1. Is the Assignment Clearly Understood?

Review the assignment and make a list of all the questions you have concerning the nature or specifics of the assignment. Review the questions with the attorney and take thorough notes when discussing the matter. Most attorneys would prefer that you seek clarification rather than misunderstand the assignment and waste time addressing the wrong question.

For Example

The assignment is to analyze the client's case. You may need to seek clarification on which aspects of the case the supervisory attorney wants you to analyze or the specific questions or areas of law you should address.

The assignment may appear simple and clear at first, but as research and analysis progress, multiple issues or separate causes of action may become apparent. It may be necessary to have a brief follow-up meeting with the supervising attorney to determine if the focus should be narrowed.

For Example

A case that involves what appears to be a car-wreck situation with a simple negligence issue may blossom into a case involving multiple issues, such as negligence, battery, and negligent infliction of emotional distress. It may be necessary to consult with the supervisory attorney to determine if you should pursue each issue or if some of the issues should be assigned to other paralegals or law clerks. If there are time constraints, it may be necessary for others to address the newly identified issues.

An additional concern when you address this question is whether the assignment requires skills you have not yet acquired.

For Example

You have just begun working as a paralegal or law clerk for a solo practitioner, and you are assigned the task of analyzing a complex products liability issue. The research and analysis skills required for the assignment may be beyond your current ability. If this occurs, discuss the matter with the attorney. More harm may occur if you try and fail, than if you communicate your concerns up front. The attorney may divide the task into manageable sections and reassign parts of it to other paralegals or law clerks or assign you to work with others to gain experience.

2. What Type of Legal Writing Is Required?

This question is easy to answer—the assignment usually identifies the type of writing required. In the example at the beginning of the chapter, the assignment calls for the preparation of a law office memorandum. The organization, format, and elements of the office memo are discussed shortly.

3. Who Is the Audience?

An office memo is usually designed for office use only. Therefore, the reader of the memo (the audience) will be familiar with the law, and the use of legal terminology is appropriate. Determine the writing preferences of the person for whom the office memo is being prepared, such as preferences regarding style.

For Example

Some attorneys prefer that the paralegal or law clerk summarize the requirements of the statutory or case law. Some prefer that the law be quoted.

If the memo may be read outside the office, be sure to exclude any comments, recommendations, or other material intended only for office use, such as: "The client's expectations are unreasonable."

B. Constraints on the Assignment

The next section of the prewriting stage requires you to identify any constraint that may affect the preparation of the office memo. Ask yourself if there are any time or page limitations. These matters should be taken into consideration at the beginning. Time constraints govern the allocation of time for research, analysis, and drafting. Length constraints may limit the depth of research and analysis.

For Example

If you are limited to five pages and one week, you may want to focus your research on the lead case or cases. There may not be sufficient time or space to address additional cases or secondary authority.

C. Organization of the Assignment

The most important section of the prewriting stage is the organization of the memo. In this section, the format or outline of the office memo is identified, and an expanded outline is created and used.

Most attorneys have a preferred format for an office memo. This format serves as a basic outline and starting point for the organization of the assignment. The creation and use of an expanded outline from the office format is discussed in Chapter 15. In this chapter, the focus is on the format and outline of an office memo and the requirements and considerations involved in the preparation of each section of the outline. This chapter and Chapter 17 include a discussion of the use of an expanded outline when preparing each section of the office memo.

There is no standard format for an office memo. Formats vary from office to office, and attorneys within the same office may have different preferences. Follow the format preferred by your supervisor. The format presented in Exhibit 16-2 is recommended for a basic office memo. It includes the standard sections of most office memos that you may encounter. Exhibit 16-3 presents the recommended format for a complex office memo. Following presentation of these formats, discussion turns to the requirements and considerations involved in the preparation of each section.

Certain sections, such as statements of assignment and brief answers, are not included in all formats and may not be included in the format preferred by your supervising attorney. They are included here so you will be familiar with them in the event they are part of the format used in your workplace. Other sections, such as issue and analysis, are required in all office memos. In addition, note that the organization of the format may vary among offices.

Heading
Statements of Assignment
Issue
Brief Answer
Statement of Facts
Analysis
   Rule of law
   Case law (if necessary) interpretation of rule of law
   Application of law to facts of case
   Counteranalysis
Conclusion

© Cengage

Exhibit 16-2 Basic Office Legal Memorandum Format.

The recommended format for a complex office legal memorandum

Heading
Statement of Assignment
Issue I
Issue II
Issue III
Brief Answer Issue I
Brief Answer Issue II
Brief Answer Issue III
Statement of Facts
Analysis Issue I
 Rule of Law
 Case law (if necessary)—interpretation of rule of law
 Application of law to facts of case
 Counteranalysis
 Conclusion Issue I
Analysis Issue II
 Rule of Law
 Case law (if necessary)—interpretation of rule of law
 Application of law to facts of case
 Counteranalysis
 Conclusion Issue II
Analysis Issue III
 Rule of Law
 Case law (if necessary)—interpretation of rule of law
 Application of law to facts of case
 Counteranalysis
 Conclusion Issue III
Recommendations (Separate recommendation sections may follow conclusion of each issue.)

© Cengage

Exhibit 16-3 Recommended Format for a Complex Office Legal Memorandum Format.

For Example

Usually, the issue section follows the statement of assignment section and precedes the facts section. Some offices, however, may prefer that the facts section precede the issue section.

There is no definition of what constitutes a complex office legal memorandum. Generally, however, it consists of more than one issue and is relatively long (more than 10 pages). The formal outline of a complex office memo is merely an expansion of the basic office memo format. The components and considerations involved in the preparation of a complex office memo are the same as those for a basic office memo. The sections are the same in basic content, but greater in number.

For Example

A complex memo may cover three issues. The procedures recommended for identifying, stating, and analyzing each issue are the same as those for the preparation of a basic single-issue memo. Each issue is addressed separately, and the process for addressing each issue is the same as that followed when addressing the single issue in a basic office memo.

See Exhibit 16-3 for a complex office legal memorandum format.

V. SECTIONS OF THE OFFICE MEMORANDUM

This section discusses the heading, statement of assignment, issue, brief answer, and facts sections of the office memo. Chapter 17 will address the analysis, conclusion, and recommendations sections.

A. Heading

Most office memos begin with a heading. The **heading** is usually brief, and at a minimum contains:

- A heading in all capitals indicating the type of document (e.g., MEMORANDUM OF LAW).
- The name of the person to whom the memo is addressed.
- The name of the person who prepared the memo.
- The date.
- Information identifying the subject of the memo. This may include the case name, client's name, case number, office file number, and subject matter of the memo. It usually follows "Re:".

There are various styles for the heading, as shown in the following example.

For Example

MEMORANDUM OF LAW

To:	Susan Day, Attorney
From:	Tom Clug, Paralegal
Date:	December 1, 2016
Case:	*Smith v. Garage Doors, Inc.*
Office File No.:	CV. 016-1136
Docket No.:	CV. 16-378
Re:	Whether a contract for the sale and installation of a garage door is a sale of goods covered by the commercial code or is a sale of a service.

OFFICE LEGAL MEMORANDUM—CONTRACTS

Title:	*Smith v. Garage Doors, Inc.*, CV. 016-378
Office File:	CV. 016-1136
Requested by:	Susan Day, Attorney
Submitted by:	Tom Clug, Paralegal
Date Submitted:	December 1, 2016
Re:	Contract law, Commercial Code § 42-2-205 Sale of goods/sale of service

OFFICE LEGAL MEMORANDUM

To:	Susan Day, Attorney
From:	Tom Clug, Paralegal
Date:	December 1, 2016
Re:	Smith v. Garage Doors, Inc., CV. 016-378.
	Whether a contract for the sale and installation of a garage door is a sale of goods or a sale of a service; Commercial Code § 42-2-205.

B. Statement of Assignment

The **statement of assignment** section may also be referred to as a *background* or *purpose section*. Some offices require a section that discusses what the writer has been assigned to do. This section usually follows the heading and may include some background information. The purpose of this section is to provide the reader with a description of the topic covered and the parameters of the assignment.

For Example

STATEMENT OF ASSIGNMENT. You have asked me to prepare a legal memorandum on the question of whether the sale and installation of a garage door by Garage Doors, Inc., is a sale of a service or a sale of goods covered by Commercial Code § 42-2-205.

For Example

STATEMENT OF ASSIGNMENT. You have asked me to research the question of whether the search of our client's automobile was an illegal search when she was stopped for a minor traffic offense and did not consent to the officer's request for permission to search the back seat of her vehicle. Pursuant to your request, this memo includes an analysis of the relevant state and federal law.

C. Issue

In an office legal memo, present the issue(s) at the beginning of the memo following the heading and the statement of assignment. Doing so establishes the focus of the memo. A well-crafted issue informs the reader, at the outset, of:

- the law that applies,
- the precise legal question, and
- the significant facts of the case.

In other words, it identifies the specific question to be addressed and places it in the context of the applicable law and the facts of the case. It sets the scope of the memo, thereby saving the reader from having to determine the issue by reading the analysis section.

Keep in mind the following when preparing the issue section of the memo:

- The issue should be correctly identified.
- The issue should be completely and correctly stated.
- An expanded outline should be used when preparing the section.
- Issues should be addressed separately when preparing complex office memos.

1. Identify the Issue

The **issue** is the precise legal question raised by the facts of the client's case. One of the most important tasks in the legal analysis process is to correctly identify the legal issue. Chapter 10 presents the analytical process that helped you identify the issue when preparing a memo.

2. Correctly State the Issue

Present the issue completely and correctly. When stated correctly, the reader is informed of the focus of the memo at the outset.

For Example

The issue involves a question of whether a will is valid if one of the witnesses does not actually see the testator sign the will. If the issue were stated, "Was the will validly executed?" the reader would have to read the analysis section of the memo to determine why it may not have been validly executed. There could be several reasons why the will may not have been validly executed: It may not have been witnessed correctly, there may not have been enough witnesses, or it may have been signed improperly. If the issue is stated, "Under Probate Code § 29-5-7, is the execution of a will valid if one of the witnesses is present in the room when the testator signs but does not actually see the testator sign?" the issue is correctly and completely stated. The reader knows the precise question being addressed, the key facts, and the applicable law. The reader is not forced to obtain this information from the analysis section of the memo.

3. Use the Expanded Outline

As discussed in Chapter 15, the use of an **expanded outline** can greatly simplify the identification and drafting of the issue. On the issue page of the expanded outline, write every formulation of the issue as it comes to mind. The initial draft may be as simple as, "Was the will valid?" As you conduct research and gain a greater understanding of the applicable law, more complete formulations will become apparent.

For Example

"Under the state probate code, is a will validly executed if a witness is merely present in the room when the testator signs?" "Under the probate code, is the execution of a will valid if one of the witnesses is present in the room when the testator signs, but does not actually see the testator sign?"

When you begin to write the issue section of the memo, all your ideas concerning the issue and drafts of the possible ways it may be stated are before you in one place. The crafting of the final statement of the issue becomes a mere matter of selecting and combining the necessary elements from the various drafts. The Application section of this chapter illustrates the use of an expanded outline in regard to the preparation of an office memo.

4. Address Issues Separately

Office memo assignments, such as a complex memorandum, often involve more than one issue. When performing such assignments, it is preferable to list each issue sequentially in the issue section of the memo. In the analysis section of the format, address each issue separately and completely. (This will be discussed in Chapter 17.) Exhibit 16-4 presents an outline of the format for the analysis section.

When there are multiple issues, list them in the issue section in the order in which they are discussed in the analysis section. The issue listed as "Issue I" in the issue section should be the first issue addressed in the analysis section. "Issue II" in the issue section should be the second issue addressed in the analysis section, and so on. Also, list the issues in logical order. If the analysis of one issue is dependent upon or affected by the analysis of another issue, then present the issue that affects the other issue first. For example, if the analysis of issue B is in some way affected by the analysis of issue A, then address issue A first in the memo.

For Example

The client alleges that she entered into a contract to purchase dresses from a dressmaker, and the dressmaker installed defective zippers in the dresses. The dressmaker claims that the contract between them was not a valid contract, and even if there was a valid contract, the zippers were not defective. There are two separate issues. Present and discuss the issue of whether there is a valid contract first, because if there is no contract, there can be no breach. The issue section would appear as follows:

Issue I: Existence of contract

Issue II: Breach of contract

Analysis Issue I
  Rule of law
  Case law (if necessary) interpretation of rule of law
  Application of law to facts of case
  Counteranalysis
  Conclusion issue I
Analysis Issue II
  Rule of law
  Case law (if necessary) interpretation of rule of law
  Application of law to facts of case
  Counteranalysis
  Conclusion issue II
Analysis Issue III, and so on

© Cengage

Exhibit 16-4 Complex Memorandum—Analysis Section Format.

If the issues are not dependent on or affected by other issues, present them in chronological order.

For Example

The client was involved in an automobile accident. The defendant ran a red light and hit the client's car. After the wreck, the defendant approached the client's car screaming and threatening the client. The defendant then pushed the client. At least four possible causes of action are present. They should be presented in the order in which they occurred:

Issue I: Negligence—the car wreck

Issue II: Assault—approaching client's car threatening and screaming

Issue III: Battery—pushing the client

Issue IV: Infliction of emotional distress—arising from the combined acts of assault and battery

Exhibit 16-5 presents a checklist for the issue section.

- Is the issue correctly identified?
- Is the applicable rule of law included in the issue?
- Is the citation of the rule correct?
- Is the legal question clearly stated in the issue?
- Are the key facts included in the issue?
- If there are multiple issues, are they presented in the proper order, such as logical or chronological?

© Cengage

Exhibit 16-5 Checklist—Issue Section.

D. Brief Answer

The **brief answer** section of the office memo consists of a brief, precise answer to the issue(s). In one or two sentences, this section informs the attorney of the answer to the question and briefly summarizes the reasons in support of the answer. Its purpose is to provide a quick answer to the issue. It should not include information that is not discussed in the analysis section of the memo.

Usually, this section begins with a one- or two-word answer, such as "Yes," "No," "Maybe," or "Probably not." The brief answer is followed by a brief statement of the facts and reasoning in support of the answer.

For Example

Issue:	According to the provisions of the Ski Safety Act § 679-33, does a resort have a duty to warn skiers of ice hazards on expert runs?
Brief Answer:	No. The act provides that resorts have the duty to warn of hazards, and that skiers are responsible for snow and ice conditions. The state supreme court has ruled that resorts have a duty to warn of snow and ice hazards only on intermediate and novice ski runs. The court specifically held that there is no duty to warn of any ice hazard on an expert run.
Issue I:	Under the holographic will statute, Colo. Rev. Stat. § 15-11-503, is a holographic will valid if it is handwritten by a neighbor at the direction of the testator, but not written in the testator's handwriting?
Issue II:	Under the holographic will statute, Colo. Rev. Stat. § 15-11-503, is a holographic will valid if one of the witnesses to the testator's signature is a beneficiary of the will?
Brief Answer Issue I:	Yes. The statute requires a holographic will to be handwritten by the testator. The state court of appeals has held that the statute should be interpreted liberally to effect the intent of the testator. If there is clear and convincing evidence that the writing took place at the direction of the testator, the will is valid even if it is not written in the testator's handwriting.
Brief Answer Issue II:	No. The statute requires that the testator's signature be witnessed by two disinterested witnesses.

Exhibit 16-6 presents a checklist for the brief answer section.

E. Statement of Facts

Following the brief answer section is the presentation of the facts of the case. The purpose of this section is to inform the attorney of the factual context of the issue. There are four considerations to keep in mind when preparing the statement of facts (see Exhibit 16-7).

- ■ Does the brief answer follow the office format (e.g., a one- or two-word answer followed by a short statement of the reasons)?
- ■ Is it brief? Does it summarize the reasons in one or two clear sentences?
- ■ Is there a separate answer for each issue?

© Cengage

Exhibit 16-6 Checklist—Brief Answer Section.

Importance of the facts	Don't underemphasize the importance of the facts. The law is always applied in the context of the facts of the dispute.
Contents of the section	Include the key and background facts.
Organization of the section	Organize the facts chronologically, topically, or a combination of the two.
Manner of the presentation of the facts	Present the facts accurately, objectively, and free of legal conclusions.

© Cengage

Exhibit 16-7   Checklist—Considerations for Statement of Facts Section.

1. Facts Section—Importance

Some writers underemphasize the facts section of an office memorandum because they fail to understand the importance of the facts. The facts, and therefore the facts section of the memo, are important for several reasons:

- Every legal dispute involves a question of how the law applies to the facts of the case. Legal questions are not decided in a vacuum. The law is always applied in the context of a dispute raised by the facts of the case. The rule of law selected is determined by identification of the law that applies to the facts.
- The facts section may refresh the attorney's memory. The attorney may be working on other issues in the case or on several other cases and may not recollect the specific factual context of the issues addressed in the assignment. The facts section saves the supervising attorney from having to review the file to determine the facts.
- In many law offices, office memos are kept in research files, categorized by areas of law. They are available for reference and use in other cases involving similar issues. Subsequent researchers may not be familiar with the facts of the case. A subsequent reader should be able to obtain all the facts necessary to understand the analysis from the facts section. It should not be necessary to review the case file.
- The facts section protects you from possible criticism. If additional facts come to light after preparation of the memo that affect the analysis of the issue and lead to a different conclusion, a well-drafted facts section provides a record of the factual basis of your conclusion. It protects you from the criticism that you misanalyzed or misapplied the law.

2. Facts Section—Content

The **statement of facts** of the office memorandum should not simply repeat the facts included in the memo assignment; it should include only a brief statement of the background and key facts. The preparation of this section requires you to identify those facts necessary to provide the reader with a complete understanding of the factual context of the issues analyzed in the memo. It may require fewer facts than those included in the memo assignment, or it may require additional facts.

Include in the facts section all facts referenced or included in the analysis section of the memo. The goal is to provide, as briefly as possible, enough facts to make the memo a self-contained document; that is, it should be sufficiently complete so that any reader who is not familiar with the facts of the case need not refer to the case file. To accomplish this end, the facts section should include background and key facts.

- *Background facts* are necessary because they put the key facts in context. They provide the reader with the information necessary for an overall understanding of the context within which the key facts occurred.
- *Key facts* are those facts upon which the outcome of the case is determined. The key facts are so essential that if they were changed, the outcome of the case would probably be different.

When preparing the facts section of the office memo, refer to Chapter 9 for assistance in identifying key and background facts.

3. Facts Section—Organization

Organize the statement of facts in a manner that enables the reader to clearly understand the events relating to the issue(s) addressed in the memo. There are basically three organizational formats for presenting the facts:

1. Chronological
2. Topical
3. A combination of chronological and topical

The format selected is usually governed by the nature of the facts.

a. Chronological Order

A **chronological organization** of the facts usually is adopted when the facts are a series of events related by time or date.

For Example

The memo involves the following fact situation: On December 1, the client, Mr. Smith, was driving in the 600 block of First Street when the defendant, Mr. Doe, ran a red light at the intersection of First and Rose Streets. As a result, Mr. Doe's vehicle collided with Mr. Smith's vehicle. Mr. Smith suffered a broken leg, and his wallet was stolen at the scene. On the way to the hospital, the ambulance was involved in a collision when it yielded at a stop sign. Mr. Smith suffered additional injuries, including a separated shoulder, in this collision. At the emergency room, his back was sprained when he was being helped onto the examining table by the hospital staff. Mr. Smith wants to know who he can sue for his various injuries, and whether he can recover from Mr. Doe for the loss of his wallet. This example is referred to as the "auto collision" example in the remainder of this chapter.

The best way to present the facts of the case in the preceding example is chronologically. The facts that give rise to the various causes of action occurred in a linear sequence, and they are most clearly understood when narrated chronologically.

b. Topical Order

Some fact situations do not lend themselves to a chronological presentation. In such situations, the facts are related more by **topical organization** than by time sequence.

For Example

The memo involves the following divorce situation. The client, Mrs. Jones, is the petitioner in a divorce action. Mr. and Mrs. Jones disagree on the property distribution. They own three pieces of real property, parcels A, B, and C. All three parcels are held in both their names as joint tenants.

Parcel A includes the family home. The property is paid for. Forty percent of the mortgage was paid from an inheritance Mrs. Jones received from her father. The remainder was paid by both Mr. and Mrs. Jones from income from their respective employments. The assessed value is $150,000.

Parcel B is a rental property. They purchased the property shortly after the marriage. The mortgage on the property is being paid from the rent payment and contributions from the income of both Mr. and Mrs. Jones. Their current equity is $100,000. Part of the equity ($10,000) was a contribution by Mr. Jones from his separate property.

Parcel C is recreational property. It was purchased five years after the marriage. It includes a small cabin and a storage shed. Their equity in the cabin and shed is $75,000. Mrs. Jones contributed $12,000 of the equity from lottery ticket winnings. The balance of the equity represents equal contributions from Mr. and Mrs. Jones.

In this example, a presentation of the facts by topic is most appropriate. The dates of purchase and the dates payments were made on the various parcels may be available, but presenting these facts by date would not lead to the clearest presentation of the facts. In the statement of facts, all the facts relating to each parcel should be presented separately, by parcel, regardless of the time sequence. All the facts relating to parcel A should be presented together; all the facts relating to parcel B should be presented together; and all the facts relating to parcel C should be presented together. The facts are more clearly understood when all the facts relating to each parcel are presented together; therefore, each parcel should be addressed separately in the facts section of the memo.

c. Combination of Chronological and Topical Order

It may be appropriate to present the facts both chronologically and topically.

For Example

In the previous example, assume that parcel B was purchased by the husband three years prior to the marriage, parcel A immediately after the marriage, and parcel C five years later. Assume also that there is personal property: an automobile purchased two years after the marriage, and a boat purchased three years after the marriage.

In addition to the issues concerning the three parcels, there are other issues in the divorce involving the other property. The appropriate presentation of the facts is a combination of the chronological and topical schemes.

In this situation, the real and personal property should be presented in the facts section in a chronological sequence according to the order of purchase, such as parcel B first, then parcel A, followed by the automobile, the boat, and finally parcel C. Note that all the information concerning each parcel of property is included when the parcel is discussed, even though some factual events concerning the parcel may have occurred after the purchase of another parcel.

For Example

All the information concerning parcel B is included in the discussion of parcel B, even though some of that information concerns occurrences taking place after the purchase of parcel A. Mr. Jones's $10,000 contribution of separate property may have taken place after parcel A, the automobile, and the boat were purchased.

It would be confusing to present all the facts in this example in chronological order only. It is much clearer to present the property in chronological order and, within the discussion of each piece of property, present all the facts relating to that piece of property regardless of when they occurred.

The goal in the organization of the statement of facts is clear presentation of the facts. Select the organizational format that best meets this goal.

4. Facts Section—Presentation and Ethics

As mentioned in Chapter 11, Rule 3.3(a)(1) of the Model Rules of Professional Conduct provides that a lawyer should not make false statements of law or fact to a tribunal. Therefore, when drafting the facts section of the memo, present the facts accurately and objectively, and avoid legal conclusions.

a. Accuracy

Accuracy in presenting the facts means that all the facts are presented, including those unfavorable to the client.

For Example

If, in the auto collision example, Mr. Smith was speeding when the defendant ran the red light, this fact should be included. Although it may not be a key fact that affects the outcome of the negligence claim, it is at minimum a background fact that should be included.

Accuracy also means not adding or changing facts. It is not proper to add a fact even if the existence of the fact seems obvious.

For Example

In the auto collision example, it is not proper to state that the defendant knew she was running a red light if there are no facts indicating her awareness of that fact. It is improper to add such a fact even if it seems obvious.

b. Objectivity

State the facts objectively. This means you should present the facts in a neutral manner that is neither slanted nor biased.

For Example

Slanted presentation: Mr. Banker obviously knew what he was doing when he advised Mrs. Widow to buy a risky stock when the market was at its peak. Mrs. Widow, unfortunately, relied on his bad advice to her detriment.

The use of the words *obviously*, *unfortunately*, *detriment*, *bad*, and *risky* slant the presentation of the facts in favor of Mrs. Widow. The facts should be stated neutrally.

For Example

Neutral presentation: The market was at its peak when Mr. Banker advised Mrs. Widow to buy the stock. Mrs. Widow relied on his advice and purchased the stock. The value of the stock subsequently fell, and Mrs. Widow suffered a loss of $1,000.

c. Legal Conclusions

When composing the facts section, avoid legal conclusions.

For Example

Mrs. Roe was driving negligently through the school zone. (The phrase *driving negligently* is a legal conclusion.)

State the facts without legal conclusions.

For Example

Mrs. Roe was driving 35 miles per hour through the school zone. The posted speed is 15 miles per hour.

- ■ Are sufficient background facts presented to inform the reader of the factual context of the assignment? Will the reader be required to refer to the case file to understand the analysis of the issues?
- ■ Are all the key facts included? Will the reader have to refer to the case file to obtain key facts?
- ■ Are the facts organized chronologically, topically, or chronologically and topically combined?
- ■ Are the facts presented accurately and objectively?
- ■ Are legal conclusions excluded from the fact presentation?
- ■ Is the facts section complete?

© Cengage

Exhibit 16-8 Checklist—Facts Section.

Exhibit 16-8 presents a checklist for the facts section of an office memo.

VI. KEY POINTS CHECKLIST: Office Legal Memorandum— Issues and Facts

✓ An office memo should be a self-contained document. Include in the memo all the information necessary to understand the context of the legal analysis. Subsequent readers should not need to refer to the case file to understand the issue, facts, or analysis.

✓ To achieve the goal of properly presenting the issue, include the rule of law, legal question, and key facts in the issue. Refer to Chapters 10 and 11 when identifying and stating the issue.

✓ Present the fact situation objectively, and include both background and key facts.

✓ Follow the format adopted by your workplace when preparing the office memo. You may be familiar with or prefer a different format; if appropriate, recommend changes to the office format. If your suggestions are not adopted, be sure to follow the approved format used in the office.

✓ Be sure you understand the assignment. If you are unclear about any aspect of the assignment, ask the supervising attorney. Do not waste time pursuing answers to the wrong question or performing the wrong task.

✓ If the complexity of the task requires skills beyond your ability, communicate your concerns.

VII. APPLICATION

This section illustrates the principles and guidelines discussed in the previous sections through their application to the hypothetical assignment presented at the beginning of the chapter. Jeff Lyons's assignment is to research a question involving privileged spousal communications. He performs the assignment by adopting and following the writing process presented in Chapter 15. The brief summary in this section explains the steps Jeff follows when applying the writing process.

The first step of the prewriting stage of the writing process is to review the assignment. After reviewing the assignment, Jeff has no questions concerning the nature of the task ahead and the constraints on performance of the task. The assignment is to prepare an office memo for Rita Berdwin, his supervisory attorney. The memo should not exceed five pages, and he must complete the memo within two weeks.

The next step of the prewriting stage is to organize the approach to the research, analysis, and writing of the assignment. To accomplish this, Jeff retrieves the office memo format preferred by Ms. Berdwin. Assume that the format preferred by Ms. Berdwin is the recommended office memo format presented in Exhibit 16-1. From this format, Jeff prepares an expanded outline. Using three-hole paper or a computer, he creates a separate page for each section of the outline. Jeff titles one page "Statement of Assignment," one page "Issue," one page "Brief Answer," one page "Statement of Facts," and so on. He continues in this manner until he has a separate page for each section and subsection of the outline.

After completing the expanded outline, Jeff begins the prewriting process. As he brainstorms ideas concerning the assignment, Jeff enters each idea on the appropriate page of the outline.

For Example

Assume that, at the outset, Jeff has an idea about how the issue should be stated. "Is the conversation between Mr. and Mrs. Findo a privileged interspousal communication that cannot be admitted at trial?" He immediately enters this possible formulation of the issue on the "Issue" page of the expanded outline.

Jeff locates the statute governing privileged spousal communications, 735 ILCS 5/8-801 (WL current through P.A. 99-93 of 2016 Reg. Sess.). The relevant portion of this statute provides: "In all actions, husband and wife may testify for or against each other, provided that neither may testify as to any communication or admission made by either of them to the other or as to any conversation between them during marriage . . . ." He places a copy of this statute in the "Rule of Law" section of the outline.

Jeff's research locates the lead case on point, *People v. Sanders*, 99 Ill. 2d 262, 457 N.E.2d 1241 (1983). Although there are subsequent cases addressing marital privilege, *Sanders* is the case most on point and most cited by subsequent cases. He places the relevant portions of the case in the "Case Law" section of the expanded outline. These portions follow:

- The defendant's murder conviction was based in part upon the testimony of his wife.
- She was allowed to testify about two conversations she had with the defendant that took place in the presence of their three children, ages 13, 10, and 8 years.
- The conversations implicated the husband in the murder.
- The defendant appealed the conviction, claiming the trial court erred when it allowed the testimony.
- The defendant argued that under the statute the conversations were privileged spousal communications and, therefore, were not admissible.
- The state supreme court, upholding the court of appeals, stated, "The appellate court appears to have exhaustively researched the subject and concluded, as we do, that the great weight of authority is that the presence of children of the spouses destroys confidentiality unless they are too young to understand what is being said (citations omitted). Nothing in the record indicates that Robert, then 13 years old, was not old enough or sufficiently bright to understand the conversation he heard, particularly inasmuch as the wife's testimony indicates that some of it was directed to him. In these circumstances, under the rule followed in this State, his presence rendered the conversation ineligible for the protection of the statutory privilege."

Jeff may place the entire case in the outline or include only the relevant parts. If only the relevant quotations are included in the outline, he notes the page numbers of the quotations.

Upon reviewing the information at hand, Jeff concludes that he has sufficient information to complete the assignment. He continues researching, however, to make sure he has thoroughly explored the question, and he updates his research to ensure that it represents the current law.

While researching and thinking about the case, whenever Jeff has an idea about how something should be written or where something should be placed in the memo, he enters the idea in the expanded outline.

For Example

A reading of the statute reveals that the privilege applies only to conversations between spouses during the marriage; therefore, a key fact is that the conversation took place during the marriage. While reading the case, he discovers that the presence of children of the spouses destroys confidentiality unless the children are too young to understand. Therefore, the fact that the children in the client's case, present during the conversation, were 16 and 10 years old is also a key fact. As he becomes aware of this information, Jeff notes these key facts on the fact and issue pages of the expanded outline.

By the time Jeff completes the prewriting stage of the writing process, the expanded outline contains all the information necessary to write the memo. Each section of the expanded outline contains:

- The research relevant to the section.
- Any draft sentences, sentence fragments, and ideas relevant to the section, such as transition sentences.
- Notes concerning the drafting of each section, such as order of presentation and what must be included.

A brief summary of each section of the expanded outline follows:

- On the statement of assignment page, Jeff has noted all of his thoughts regarding how this section should be written.
- The issue page includes a reference to the statute, key facts, and every formulation of the issue that has occurred to Jeff as he worked on the assignment.
- The brief answer page includes draft sentences on how the brief answer should be phrased. Ideas for this section may have come to him while he was preparing the analysis, conclusion, or other sections of the memo.
- Included on the facts page is a list of all the key and background facts he has identified as he conducted research. Jeff also has noted any drafts of sentences he might use in composing this section.
- On the rule of law page of the analysis section, he has included the applicable statute with the correct citation. He has listed here any ideas he had on drafting this section, such as transition sentences.

For Example

"The statute does not provide guidance concerning what effect the presence of children during the communication has on the privilege. Therefore, case law must be consulted."

- The case law page of the analysis section contains the case citation and a copy of the case or relevant sections of the case. Also included here are any notes Jeff has made concerning the discussion or presentation of the case in the memo.
- On the application page of the analysis section, Jeff has included any information, ideas, or sentences regarding how the rule of law from the case and statute will be applied to the facts.
- The counteranalysis page of the analysis section includes any information concerning the counteranalysis, such as opposing case law.
- On the conclusion and recommendations pages of the outline, just as on the other pages of the expanded outline, Jeff has included notes, ideas, draft sentences, and anything that may be used when drafting these sections.

After Jeff completes the research and analysis, and the expanded outline, he begins the writing process. The use of the expanded outline greatly simplifies his work.

For Example

Included on the issue page of the expanded outline are all the various ways the issue may be stated: "Is the communication between Mr. and Mrs. Findo privileged?" "Is the conversation between Mr. and Mrs. Findo a privileged interspousal communication that cannot be admitted at trial?" "Does the presence of children of the spouses during a conversation render the communication nonprivileged?" "Is the interspousal communication privilege destroyed if the communication takes place in the presence of children of the spouses?" "Under Illinois law, is the inter-spousal communication privilege destroyed when the conversation takes place in the presence of children (ages 16 and 10) of the spouses?"

When Jeff begins to draft the issue section of the memo, his task becomes easier because all the various formulations of the issue are in one place. Jeff has only to compose the issue by selecting and combining the best language from the various formulations on the issue page of the expanded outline.

Using the writing process presented in Chapter 15, the writing tips presented in Chapter 14, and the guidelines presented in the other chapters of this text, Jeff completes the assignment. The completed portions of Jeff's assignment that involve the sections of the office memo discussed in this chapter, the heading through the facts sections, are presented in the following office memo. Because the remaining portions of an office memo—the analysis through recommendations sections—will be discussed in Chapter 17, those sections of Jeff's completed office memo will be presented in the Application section of that chapter.

OFFICE MEMORANDUM OF LAW

To:	Rita Berdwin, Attorney
From:	Jeff Lyons, Paralegal
Date:	January 30, 2017
Case:	*State v. Findo*
Office File No.:	CR 16-136
Docket No.:	CR 16-378
Re:	Privileged spousal communications

STATEMENT OF ASSIGNMENT

You have asked me to prepare a memorandum of law addressing the question of whether the conversation between Mr. Findo (our client) and Mrs. Findo, which took place in the presence of their children, ages 16 and 10 years old, is a privileged spousal communication and, therefore, is not admissible in the criminal trial of Mr. Findo.

ISSUE

Under the Illinois privileged spousal communication statute, 735 ILCS 5/8-801 (WL current through P.A. 99-93 of 2016 Reg. Sess. 1984), is a spousal conversation privileged and not admissible into evidence if it takes place in the presence of the spouses' children, ages 16 and 10 years old?

BRIEF ANSWER

No. The communication is not a privileged communication protected by the provisions of the statute. The state supreme court has ruled that the privilege is destroyed when the conversation takes place in the presence of children of the spouses who are old enough to understand the content of the communication.

STATEMENT OF FACTS

Mr. Findo is charged with assaulting his neighbor, Mr. Markham, with a deadly weapon, a hammer. Mr. Markham claims that Mr. Findo attacked him and struck him several times with a hammer. Mr. Findo claims he did not attack Mr. Markham with a hammer; he claims that Mr. Markham attacked him with a brick, and during the struggle, the brick fell and hit Mr. Markham on the head. Mrs. Findo, currently separated from her husband, has agreed to testify that before the confrontation Mr. Findo stated, "Markham is out there building that damn fence again. I'll put a stop to this once and for all." This conversation took place in the presence of the Findos' children, Tomas, age 16, and Alice, age 10. There were no witnesses to the argument. Neither Mrs. Findo nor the children saw the confrontation.

Summary

The drafting of an office legal memorandum is one of the most important and often most difficult types of legal writing assignments a paralegal or law clerk may perform. It requires integration of the research, analysis, and writing skills discussed throughout this text.

An office memo is designed for office use and is usually drafted for the supervising attorney. It involves the legal analysis of issues raised by the facts of a client's case. The writing process presented in Chapter 15 is recommended when preparing an office memo.

This chapter presents the considerations involved in preparing the heading, statement of assignment, issue, brief answer, and statement of facts sections of the office memo. Chapter 17 will discuss the considerations involved in preparing the analysis through recommendations sections.

The heading section contains information describing who the memo is from and to, the name of the case, and the nature of the issue. The statement of assignment section describes the topic covered and the parameters of the assignment.

The issue section follows the statement of assignment. It is one of the most important parts of the memo, and informs the reader of the precise legal question addressed in the analysis section of the memo. The brief answer section provides a brief and precise answer to the issue, and a brief summary of the reasons in support of the answer.

The statement of facts section provides the facts of the client's case that gave rise to the issue addressed in the memo. It includes the background and key facts of the dispute, and should provide sufficient factual information to allow the reader to understand the analysis without having to refer to the case file or any other source outside the memo.

Many of the procedures and steps involved in preparing an office memo apply to the preparation of legal writing designed for external use, such as correspondence to clients and documents to be filed with a court, including trial court and appellate court briefs.

Quick References

Internet Resources

The Internet resources for this chapter are the same as those listed in Chapter 15. Due to the large number of sites, the best strategy is to narrow your search to a specific type of legal writing and topic, such as "issues, legal memorandum, public service contracts."

The following exercises are helpful in developing an understanding of and familiarity with the use of a writing process.

Exercises

ASSIGNMENT

For the memo or web-based assignment(s) presented at the end of Chapter 17 and as designated or chosen by your instructor, prepare the following sections of an office memo: heading, statement of assignment, issue, brief answer, and statement of facts. Use the format and guidelines presented in this chapter when performing this assignment.

Chapter 17

Office Legal Memorandum: Analysis to Conclusion

Outline

I. Introduction
II. Analysis Section
III. Conclusion
IV. Recommendations
V. General Considerations
VI. Key Points Checklist: Office Legal Memorandum—Analysis to Conclusion
VII. Application

Learning Objectives

After completing this chapter, you should understand:

- The elements and format of the analysis, conclusion, and recommendations sections of an office legal research memorandum
- How to draft the analysis, conclusion, and recommendations sections of an office legal research memorandum
- General considerations to keep in mind when drafting a legal research memorandum

Ellen Taylor is a law clerk working in a district attorney's office in the hypothetical state of New Washington. Ms. Taylor recently received the following assignment.

To:	Ellen Taylor, Intern
From:	Carl Pine, Assistant District Attorney
Re:	*State v. Kent*. Arrest during execution of search warrant and constructive possession
Case:	CR 16-404

On January 7, police officers executed a search warrant authorizing the search of the apartment of David Kent for narcotics. Mr. Kent's apartment is located on the third floor of a four-story apartment complex. Upon entering the apartment, the officers found Mr. Kent lying on the bed in the bedroom. The officers secured the apartment and, after frisking Mr. Kent for weapons, handcuffed him and moved him into the kitchen for the stated purpose of "his and our safety." They did not read him his rights or officially place him under arrest at this time.

The search of the apartment did not reveal any narcotics. The police, however, discovered an "eight-inch hole" in the only window in the bedroom, and the window screen was pushed out. The police went downstairs and searched the area below the window. The bedroom window faces the rear of the apartment complex, and below the window is a parking lot. In the parking lot, three stories below Mr. Kent's bedroom window, the officers found a *plastic bag containing one ounce of rock cocaine. The parking lot is a common area of the complex, accessible to the public and all apartment dwellers. No witnesses have been located who saw the defendant throw the cocaine out the window. There were no fingerprints on the bag or other evidence linking Mr. Kent to the cocaine. After locating the bag, the police read the defendant his rights and placed him under arrest. The charge is possession of a controlled substance.*

Please prepare an office legal memorandum addressing the following questions:

1. *Was the defendant under arrest when he was handcuffed and moved into the kitchen?*
2. *Is the connection between the defendant and the cocaine sufficient to support charges of possession of a controlled substance?*

The office legal memorandum prepared by Ms. Taylor is presented in the Application section of this chapter.

I. INTRODUCTION

Chapter 16 focused on preparing the first half of an office legal memo: the heading, statement of assignment, issue, brief answer, and statement of facts sections. This chapter addresses preparation of the second half of the office legal memo: the analysis, conclusion, and recommendations sections. In this chapter, as in Chapter 16, an office legal research memorandum is referred to as an *office memo*.

The discussion in Chapter 16 addressing the adoption of a writing process and the use of an expanded outline also applies to the preparation of the second half of an office memo. The guidelines presented in that chapter in regard to the writing process and the use of an expanded outline should be followed when preparing the analysis, conclusion, and recommendations sections of the office memo. The examples in this chapter refer to the enacted and case law of the hypothetical state of New Washington.

II. ANALYSIS SECTION

The purpose of an office memo is to provide a legal analysis of the issue(s) in a case. The **analysis section** is the part of the memo where the law is presented, analyzed, and applied to the issue(s). It connects the issue with the conclusion and is the heart of an office memo assignment.

The analysis section is often referred to as the *discussion section*. The conventional analytical format, and the most efficient way to approach a legal question, is the IRAC format (issue, rule, analysis, conclusion). Under the IRAC approach and the office memo format introduced in Chapter 16, the issue is presented at the beginning of the memo; the analysis section covers the rule of law, analysis, and application of the rule of law to the facts; and the conclusion summarizes the analysis. The reasons for following this approach are obvious:

- The reader must know the question to know the context in which the rule is analyzed.
- The rule that applies to the question must be identified before the rule can be analyzed and applied to the facts of the case.
- The rule must be applied to the facts; this must take place before a conclusion can be reached.

Although IRAC is the basic format for addressing legal issues, it is only a broad outline of the format. It is necessary to have a more detailed outline of the analysis section to effectively approach an office memo assignment and prepare an office memo.

A. Analysis Format

Exhibit 17-1 presents the recommended format of the analysis section.

In the prewriting stage of the writing process, assign each subsection of the analysis section at least one page in the expanded outline: a page for the rule of law, a page for each case, at least one page for the application of the law to the facts, and at least one page for the counteranalysis.

If the memo is a complex memo involving multiple issues, follow the same basic format for each issue (see Exhibit 17-2).

If more than one rule of law applies to a specific issue, include a reference to each rule in the outline.

Part A	Rule of law
Part B	Case law (if necessary) interpretation of rule of law 1. Name of case 2. Facts of case sufficient to demonstrate case is on point 3. Rule or legal principle from case that applies to the client's case
Part C	Application of law to facts of case
Part D	Counteranalysis

© Cengage

Exhibit 17-1 Basic Four-Part Format—Analysis Section.

Issue I	Analysis
Part A	Rule of law
Part B	Case law (if necessary) interpretation of rule of law 1. Name of case 2. Facts of case sufficient to demonstrate case is on point 3. Rule or legal principle from case that applies to the client's case
Part C	Application of law to facts of case
Part D	Counteranalysis
Issue II	Analysis
Part A	Rule of law
Part B	Case law (if necessary) interpretation of rule of law 1. Name of case 2. Facts of case sufficient to demonstrate case is on point 3. Rule or legal principle from case that applies to the client's case
Part C	Application of law to facts of case
Part D	Counteranalysis
Issue III	Analysis (same format as issues I and II)

© Cengage

Exhibit 17-2 Complex Memo—Analysis Section Format.

For Example

Issue I Analysis
Part A Rule of law

1. Section 59-703 of the commercial code

2. Section 45-211 of the usury statute

If more than one case is required to interpret the rule of law, such as when more than one element of the rule requires case law interpretation, include a reference to each case in the outline.

For Example

Issue I Analysis
Part A Rule of law—section 59-703 of the commercial code
Part B Case law

1. Case 1: *Smith v. Jones*—interpreting the term *sale* as used in § 59-703

    a. Facts of case—sufficient to demonstrate case is on point

    b. Rule or legal principle from case that applies to the client's case

Part C Application of the law to the facts of the client's case
Part D Counteranalysis

2. Case 2: *Row v. Downs*—interpreting the term *merchant* as used in § 59-703

    a. Facts of case—sufficient to demonstrate case is on point

    b. Rule or legal principle from case that applies to the client's case

Part C Application of the law to the facts of the client's case
Part D Counteranalysis
Part A Rule of law—§ 45-211 of the usury statute
Part B Case law

1. *Doe v. Dean*—interpreting the term *loan* as used in § 45-211

    a. Facts of case—sufficient to demonstrate case is on point

    b. Rule or legal principle from case that applies to the client's case

Part C Application of the law to the facts of the client's case
Part D Counteranalysis

The remainder of this section discusses the elements of the basic format for the analysis section of an office memo. After you master the considerations involved in preparing the analysis of a single issue, you can approach complex memo assignments that address multiple issues or separate subissues by applying the basic process to the analysis of each issue or subissue.

B. Analysis Part A: Rule of Law

Inasmuch as the analysis section of an office memo addresses how the law applies to the issue(s) and facts of the client's case, the starting point is a presentation of the rule of law or legal principle that applies. Simply put, you must present the law before it can be applied.

The governing law may be enacted law, such as a constitutional provision or a legislative act; or case law, such as a court-adopted rule of law. Exhibit 17-3 lists some considerations to keep in mind when preparing the rule of law portion of the analysis section.

Introduction	Use introductory language to introduce the rule of law (e.g., "The law governing the witnessing of wills is . . .").
What to include	Paraphrase or quote only the relevant portions of the law.
Multiple rules of law	Use introductory language and present the relevant portion of each rule.
Citation	Provide the citation for the rule of law. If it is enacted law, cite the statute, ordinance, rule, and so forth; if it is case law, cite the court opinion.

© Cengage

Exhibit 17-3 Part A—Rule of Law—Considerations.

1. Rule of Law—Introduction

The analysis section begins with a presentation of the rule of law. Do not start immediately with the rule itself; use introductory language. The introductory language is italicized in the following examples.

For Example

The rule of law governing the sale of securities is section 59-903 of the New Washington Commercial Code. The section provides. . . .

In New Washington, the doctrine of strict liability was established in the case of Elton v. All Faiths Hospital, 931 N. Wash. 395, 396 (1976), where the court stated. . . .

2. Rule of Law—What to Include

When presenting the rule of law, quote only the relevant portions of the law. In some instances, the rule of law is very lengthy, and only portions of the law apply to the issue being addressed. This is often true when the applicable law is statutory law, the statute is composed of many subsections, and only one subsection applies. If this is so, include only the relevant portion of the law.

For Example

Statutory law:
The rule of law governing oppressive conduct is § 50-14-5, which provides:

A.   The district courts may liquidate the assets and business of a corporation:

    1. in an action by a shareholder when it is established that:. . . .

        (b) the acts of the directors . . . are illegal, oppressive, or fraudulent. . . .

Note: Subsection (a) is omitted because its provisions do not apply to the issue being discussed.

For Example

Case law:
The rule of law governing a ski resort's duty to warn of snow and ice conditions was established in the case of *Jones v. Mountain Ski Resort*, 943 N. Wash. 857, 877 (1988), where the court stated, "Resorts have a duty to warn of snow and ice conditions in the following situations: . . . when the snow or ice condition is a latent hazard. . . ."

Note: Portions of the opinion are omitted because they do not apply to the issue being discussed. The omission is indicated by the three-dot ellipsis.

3. Rule of Law—Multiple Rules

The analysis may require consideration of more than one rule of law. If this is so, use a format similar to that discussed in the preceding text. Use introductory language, and present the relevant portions of each rule.

For Example

The New Washington Commercial Code section 50-101 establishes which contracts must be in writing. In our case, two subsections of that section apply: section 50-101B, which requires that "[a]n agreement which is not to be performed within one year from the making" must be in writing, and section 50-101C, which provides that "[c]ontracts for the sale of goods in the amount of $500 or more" must be in writing.

When the rule of law involves both general and specific sections of a statute, present the relevant general portion of the statute first, followed by the specific portion of the statute.

For Example

Section 50-501 creates an implied warranty of merchantability if the seller is a merchant with respect to goods of that kind. The term *merchant* is defined in section 50-401 as "A person who deals in goods of that kind...."

4. Rule of Law—Citation

Whenever the reference is to a rule of law or legal principle, you must present the authority in support of your statement of the rule. If the source for the rule is enacted law, cite the enacted law; if it is case law, cite the case. Note that in the previous four examples, the reference includes the source for the rule of law, either statutory or case law. Without a reference to the authority, it is merely your word that the rule of law presented in the memo is actually what the law states. Readers need to know the source so they can check for accuracy and answer any questions concerning the law.

C. Analysis Part B: Rule of Law Interpretation—Case Law

Exhibit 17-4 presents three considerations to keep in mind when addressing the interpretation of the rule of law discussed in the memo.

1. Rule of Law Interpretation—No Interpretation Required

In some instances, the rule of law, whether it is statutory or case law, applies directly to the facts of the client's case. Further case law is not required to determine how the rule applies.

For Example

The rule of law establishes a 15 mph speed limit in school zones, and the client was ticketed for driving 30 mph in a school zone. In this situation, case law is not needed to determine how the law applies. The law can be applied directly to the facts: driving 30 mph in the school zone is a violation of the law.

In such instances, proceed to Section II.D of this chapter for guidance. Note, however, that you should always perform at least a cursory check of the case law. This is necessary to ensure that there is not some special interpretation of the rule or a term used in the rule that is not apparent from a plain reading of it.

Is interpretation required?	Does the rule of law require interpretation? Can the law be applied directly to the facts without interpretation?
What is the role of case law?	Is the rule of law so broadly stated that case law must be consulted to determine how it applies?
What is the process for presenting case law?	If case law is required, use a format like the one laid out in Exhibit 17-5 when presenting each case.

© Cengage

Exhibit 17-4 Rule of Law Interpretation—Considerations.

2. Rule of Law Interpretation—Role of Case Law

Usually the rule of law that governs the issue being analyzed has some unexpected quirk or is so broadly stated that you must refer to case law to determine how it applies. Case law, in effect, provides the link between the rule of law and the issue raised by the facts of the client's case. Court opinions determine and explain how the law is interpreted and applied in specific fact situations.

For Example

The First Amendment protects freedom of speech. The amendment does not define what constitutes speech. If the client's case involves the question of whether a symbolic act, such as burning a state flag, is protected under the First Amendment's freedom-of-speech provisions, you must consult case law. The Supreme Court has interpreted how the First Amendment applies in this specific fact situation. Acts such as burning a state flag are considered symbolic speech and are protected under the First Amendment.

For Example

A statute prohibits oppressive conduct by majority shareholders against minority shareholders, but *oppressive conduct* is not defined in the statute. Court decisions may define what constitutes oppressive conduct in specific fact situations, and reference to court decisions is necessary to determine how the law applies.

3. Rule of Law Interpretation—Process for Presenting Case Law

When presenting the case law that interprets how the law applies to a fact situation such as the client's, the recommended format is to present the name and citation of the case first, then the facts of the case, followed by the rule of law or legal principle applied by the court (see Exhibit 17-5).

a. Name and Citation of Court Opinion

When presenting the case, first identify the case name and citation. The reader should know the name of the case at the beginning of the discussion. This eliminates any possible confusion that may arise concerning which case is being discussed.

For Example

The case that defines the term *publication* as used in the statute is *Smith v. Jones*, 956 N. Wash. 441, 881 N.E.2d 897 (1995).

Name and citation of court opinion	First, provide the name and citation of the case.
Facts of the case	Next, provide those facts from the case sufficient to demonstrate that the case is on point.
Rule of law	Then, identify the rule of law or legal principle adopted by the court that applies to the issue addressed in the memo.

© Cengage

Exhibit 17-5 Format for Presenting Case Law.

b. Facts of the Case

The next step is to provide sufficient information concerning the facts and rule of law applied in the case to demonstrate that the case is on point. To accomplish this, you must include enough information about the court opinion to demonstrate that the similarity between the key facts and rule of law of the opinion and those of the client's case is sufficient for the court opinion to govern or provide guidance in deciding how the law applies.

For Example

The client's case involves the question of whether a majority shareholder in a closely held corporation engaged in oppressive conduct when he refused to issue dividends while granting himself, as CEO of the corporation, semiannual bonuses in an amount triple his annual salary. Section 90-9-4 of the state corporation statutes prohibits oppressive conduct by majority shareholders against minority shareholders. The statute does not define *oppressive*. The case on point is *Cedrik v. Ely*, 956 N. Wash. 776, 881 N.E.2d 451 (1995).

The introduction of the case might read as follows:

"The case that defines what constitutes 'oppressive' conduct in a fact situation such as that presented in the client's case is *Cedrik v. Ely*, 956 N. Wash. 776, 881 N.E.2d 451 (1995). In that case, just as in the client's case, a majority shareholder of a closely held corporation granted himself bonuses in excess of triple his salary. In *Cedrik*, the majority shareholder also refused to issue dividends. In defining what constitutes 'oppressive conduct' under 90-9-4, the court stated.... *Id.* at 778, 453."

Chapter 12 presented a comprehensive discussion of the steps and considerations involved in determining if a case is on point. Refer to that chapter for assistance in deciding what must be included in the presentation of a case to demonstrate that the case is on point. Note that the presentation of a case in a case brief is different from the presentation of a case in an office memo. When presenting a case in an office memo, it is not necessary to include all the information that you would include in a case brief. In an office memo, present only the facts sufficient to show the case is on point. A case brief should include more detail, such as background facts and other information.

c. Rule of Law

The last step when discussing a case that is on point is to identify the rule of law or legal principle adopted by the court that applies to the issue being addressed in the office memo.

For Example

The state collections statute provides that efforts to collect payment for a debt must be made in a "reasonable manner." *Reasonable manner* is not defined in the statute. In the client's case, the collector called the client three times a day, often after 9:00 p.m. The case on point is *Cerro v. Collectors*, Inc., 955 N. Wash. 641, 880 N.E.2d 401 (1994). The presentation of the rule of law applied by the court would read as follows:

"In the *Cerro* case, the court stated that 'reasonable contact' as used in the collections statute means no more than one telephone call a day to the debtor's residence. The court went on to state that no calls should be placed before 6:00 a.m. or after 7:00 p.m. *Id.* at 645."

Keep in mind two considerations when presenting the rule of law from the case:

1. Quote the language of the court whenever practical. Quotations are stronger than paraphrases and using quotations avoids issues of misstating the law that can result from paraphrasing. Sometimes, the language does not lend itself to quotation, such as when the rule is composed of several parts or steps that are presented in more than one paragraph of the opinion.

Do not use too many quotations. Use quotations to set forth the law or legal principle presented by the court and key portions of the court's reasoning. They should not be used as a substitute for or in place of your own analysis. You have failed to properly analyze the case law if your analysis consists almost entirely of quotations of a court's presentation of the law and its reasoning.

2. When presenting the law, always cite the page of the court opinion where the rule is discussed, or where quoted material is located within the opinion.

For Example

In defining what constitutes "oppressive conduct" under § 90-9-4, the court stated, "Oppressive conduct occurs when a majority shareholder engages in wrongful conduct which inures to the benefit of the majority and the detriment of the minority." *Cedrik v. Ely,* 956 N. Wash. 776, 881 N.E.2d 451 (1995).

In summary, the sequence when presenting a case is as follows:

- Case name and case citation
- Relevant facts from the case demonstrating the case is on point
- The rule of law or principle adopted by the court that applies to the issue in the client's case

This sequence is recommended because it is logical to discuss a case using this format for the following reasons:

- It is more readable if the reader first knows the name of the case; then what happened, the facts; then the rule of law applied by the court.
- It is logical to discuss the rule of law last because the next step in the memo is application of the rule to the issue(s) and facts of the client's case. The memo flows more smoothly if the *application* of the rule immediately follows the *presentation* of the rule.

This is only a recommended sequence, however, not a hard-and-fast rule. In some instances, it may be better to address the rule of law from the opinion first, then present the case name and facts from the case. Follow a sequence that works best for the memo you are drafting.

D. Analysis Part C: Application of Rule of Law to Client's Case

The purpose of the office memo is to determine how the law applies. Therefore, a critical element of the analysis section is the application of the law to the issue(s) raised by the facts of the client's case. You will encounter two situations when applying the rule of law to the facts of the case:

- The rule does not require interpretation through the use of case law.
- The rule requires interpretation through the use of case law.

1. Application of Rule That Does Not Require Case Law Interpretation

As discussed in Section II.B, in certain instances case law is not required to interpret how the rule of law applies to the issue being analyzed, because it is clear from the face of the rule how it applies. In such instances, simply apply the rule directly to the issue being addressed in the office memo.

For Example

Municipal ordinance 91-1 establishes 25 mph as the maximum speed in residential areas of the municipality. The client was ticketed for driving 55 mph in a residential neighborhood. The application of the ordinance is clear. The client violated the ordinance.

2. Application of Rule That Requires Case Law Interpretation

Most instances involve the question of how the rule of law applies to the issue(s) being analyzed. In such cases, it is necessary to refer to case law for guidance as to how the law applies. After the case on point is discussed, you must apply the rule of law or legal principle adopted by the court to the facts of the client's case. This is the next step of the analysis process. It immediately follows the presentation of the rule of law from the case on point.

For Example

In *Cedrick v. Ely*, the court defined *oppressive conduct* as "wrongful conduct that inures to the benefit of the majority and the detriment of the minority." *Cedrik v. Ely*, 956 N. Wash. 776, 881 N.E.2d 451 (1995). The court ruled that the majority shareholder's act of granting himself a bonus triple his annual salary while refusing to allow dividends was wrongful, inured to his benefit and the detriment of the minority shareholders, and was, therefore, "oppressive conduct" within the meaning of the statute.

In the client's case, just as in the *Cedrik* case, the defendant (the majority shareholder) gave himself bonuses in excess of triple his salary while refusing to allow the issuance of dividends. If the court follows the definition of "oppressive conduct" established in the *Cedrik* case, the defendant engaged in oppressive conduct.

For Example

In the *Cerro* case, the court held that "reasonable contact" as used in the collections statute means no more than one telephone call a day to the debtor's residence, and no call should be placed before 6:00 a.m. or after 7:00 p.m. *Cerro v. Collectors, Inc.*, 955 N. Wash. 641, 880 N.E.2d 401 (1994).

The collection agency contacted our client more than three times a day for seven straight days, and several of the calls were made after 9:00 p.m. If the trial court follows the rule adopted in *Cerro*, the outcome should be in our favor. The collections statute has clearly been violated.

Remember to include in the analysis a discussion of how the law applies to the issue(s) and facts of the client's case. It is useless to introduce the rule of law and discuss how the rule is interpreted through the presentation of a case on point, then fail to apply the law to the facts of the client's case. The purpose of the office memo is to demonstrate how the rule of law and the case law apply to guide or govern the determination of the issue(s) addressed in the memo.

E. Analysis Part D: Counteranalysis

The next part of the analysis section is the counteranalysis. The analysis of a legal issue is not complete unless counterarguments to the analysis are explored. Refer to Chapter 13 when conducting counteranalysis and drafting the counteranalysis portion of the analysis. Note the following when preparing a counteranalysis:

- In the analysis section, the counteranalysis should follow part C, the application of the law to the issue and facts of the client's case. By doing so, you immediately apprise readers of any counterargument so they can easily compare and contrast the arguments and counterarguments and evaluate the merits of each.
- If rebuttal is necessary, it should follow the counteranalysis. Rebuttal may be required if it is necessary to explain why the counterargument does not apply, or if you want to evaluate the merits of the counterargument.

For Example

The opposing side may argue that oppressive conduct did not occur, and the *Cedrik* case does not apply, because the majority shareholder in our case earned the triple bonuses by working long hours and weekends. In *Cedrik*, just as in our client's case, the majority shareholder worked long hours, and the court noted, "Even though the majority shareholder is entitled to receive extra compensation, he is not entitled to receive an amount of compensation that results in the total denial of benefits to the minority shareholders." *Cedrik v. Ely*, 956 N. Wash. 776, 881 N.E.2d 451 (1995).

Exhibit 17-6 presents a checklist for the analysis section.

III. CONCLUSION

Part C of the analysis section, the application of the rule of law to the client's case, is a discussion of how the law applies to the issue. This application of the law to the issue is really a mini-conclusion, because it concludes how the law applies. In effect, the analysis section includes a conclusion. Because the analysis section includes a brief conclusion, some law firms do not require a separate conclusion section. It is recommended, however, that you include a separate conclusion section that summarizes the entire memo.

The conclusion section should not introduce new information or authorities, nor should it merely repeat the brief answer. It should summarize the conclusions reached in the analysis section. It is recommended that the conclusion be crafted to include a reference to and summary of all the law discussed in the analysis section, both the enacted and case law. It requires, however, fewer introductory and transitional sentences. Ideally, the **conclusion** should briefly inform the reader of all the law that applies and how it applies. The reader should be able to obtain from the conclusion a general understanding of the law and its application without having to read the entire memo.

The advantage of this type of conclusion is that researchers working on similar cases can determine from the conclusion whether a memo from the office memo files applies to their case. They should be able to obtain all the essential information merely by reading the conclusion. The researcher saves time by not having to read the entire memo if all that is needed is a summary of the law and analysis.

For Example

Section 30-3-9 of the criminal code prohibits the possession of proscribed drugs. The case of *Smith v. Jones* provides that when an individual does not have actual possession, he may be in constructive possession if there is either direct or circumstantial evidence establishing that the defendant had both knowledge and control of the drugs. In the client's case, there is no evidence, either direct or circumstantial, that the client had either knowledge or control of the drugs he was charged with possessing. If *Smith v. Jones* is followed, there is not sufficient evidence to support charges of possession under § 30-3-9.

- Does the analysis section follow the proper format? The format is rule of law + case interpreting the rule of law (if necessary) + application + counteranalysis.
- If the application of the rule of law is not clear, is case law presented that is on point and interprets how the rule of law applies?
- Is the proper citation presented for each rule of law and authority included in the analysis?
- Is there a separate analysis section for each issue addressed in the memo?
- Is the rule of law, presented in the analysis, applied to the issue raised by the facts of the client's case?
- Is there a counteranalysis and rebuttal to the counteranalysis if necessary?

Exhibit 17-6 Checklist—Analysis Section.

For Example

Article II, Section 7 of the state constitution prohibits illegal searches and seizures. In *State v. Idle*, the court held an individual is seized within the meaning of the law when the actions of the law enforcement officers are such that a reasonable person would not believe that he was free to leave. In the client's case, the client was handcuffed and ordered to sit in the back seat of a police car. He was not placed under arrest. A reasonable person would not believe he was free to leave in this situation; therefore, if in the client's case the court follows the test adopted in *State v. Idle*, the client was under arrest.

Note that in these examples, the reader is able to obtain all the essential information concerning the applicable law by merely reading the conclusion. Note also that introductory sentences are not used to introduce the law, and that transition sentences are not used to connect the statutory and case law. The importance and use of introductory and transition sentences in the other sections of an office memo will be discussed in Section V of this chapter.

When there are multiple issues, a conclusion is usually presented immediately after the analysis of each issue. When there are only two issues and the analysis is not complex, you may present at the end of the memo one conclusion that summarizes the analysis of both issues.

Exhibit 17-7 presents a checklist for the conclusion section.

IV. RECOMMENDATIONS

Not all law firms include a recommendations section as part of the basic format of an office memo. Also, in some formats, recommendations are included in the conclusion section. Generally, a separate section for any comments or recommendations should follow the conclusion section. **Recommendations** are not really part of the analysis or conclusion sections; they frequently address matters to be considered and steps to be taken as a result of the conclusions reached in the analysis section. Include in the recommendations section any comments or suggestions you have concerning the client's case or matters discussed in the memo.

Some areas you may address in the recommendations section include:

1. What the next step should be

For Example

Based on the analysis of the issues, it is apparent that the risk of liability is great. It may be advisable to seek a settlement in this case.

2. The identification of additional information that may be necessary due to questions raised in the analysis of the issue

For Example

It appears from the case file that the neighbors were not asked if they heard any strange noises. Inasmuch as the analysis of this issue reveals that this information is critical, it is recommended the neighbors be reinterviewed.

- ■ Does the conclusion include a brief summary of the analysis of each issue?
- ■ Is all the law discussed in the analysis section, both enacted and case law, summarized in the conclusion?
- ■ Is new information or authority excluded from the conclusion?

© Cengage

Exhibit 17-7 Checklist—Conclusion Section.

3. The identification of additional research that may be necessary on the issue

For Example

Additional research may be required because the necessary research sources are not locally available, the analysis is preliminary due to time constraints, or the factual investigation of the case has not been completed.

4. The identification of related issues or concerns that became apparent as a result of the research and analysis

For Example

The memo addresses a negligence issue concerning an automobile accident. If the analysis of the negligence issue reveals other possible causes of action in the case, such as assault or negligent infliction of emotional distress, the attorney should be advised of the existence of these additional causes of action.

V. GENERAL CONSIDERATIONS

The following are some general considerations when preparing an office research memorandum. A separate section is devoted to these matters because they often apply to more than one section of a memo and you should keep them in mind when approaching any memo assignment.

A. Heading

Although an office memo is written in paragraph form, use headings for each section. **Headings** provide the overall structure of the assignment, guide the reader, and apprise the reader of what is covered in each section. The reader may desire to read a specific section, such as the analysis, in which case a heading allows the reader to quickly locate that section. Headings also guide the preparation of the table of contents if a table is needed. Use the format presented in Chapter 16 as a guide for the appropriate headings (see Exhibit 16-1). Refer to the Application section of this chapter and Chapter 16 for examples.

B. Introductory Sentences

Use **introductory (topic) sentences** to inform the reader of what is to follow. Avoid immediately jumping into a discussion of a topic, such as the presentation of the law.

For Example

No introduction: Section 59-3-2 of the criminal code provides that possession of cocaine is illegal. In *Smith v. Jones*, the defendant. . . .

Provide an introduction when discussing a topic. The introductions are italicized in the following example.

For Example

Includes an introduction: *The rule of law prohibiting the possession of cocaine* is criminal code § 59-3-2, which states that possession of cocaine is illegal. The statute does not define "possession"; therefore, case law must be referred to. *The case that provides guidance as to what constitutes possession in a fact situation such as the client's is Smith v. Jones.* In the *Smith* case, . . .

C. Transition Sentences

Use **transition sentences** to connect sections, subsections, and related topics. The following example lacks a transition.

For Example

The rule of law governing possession of drugs is § 59-3-2. Section 59-3-2c makes it illegal to possess cocaine. *Smith v. Jones* provides that possession occurs when. . . .

A transition should have been used in this example to connect the statutory law with the case law. The reader should be informed why case law is being presented. The following example uses a transition sentence. The transition sentence is italicized in the example.

For Example

The rule of law governing possession of drugs is § 59-3-2. Section 59-3-2c makes it illegal to possess cocaine. *The statute does not define what constitutes possession; therefore, it is necessary to refer to case law for guidance.*

A case that defines what constitutes possession in a fact situation such as the client's is *Smith v. Jones.* In the *Smith* case, . . .

D. Paragraphs

Paragraphs add coherence and make the memo more readable. Address each area or topic in a separate paragraph.

For Example

In the analysis section of the memo, address in a separate paragraph or paragraphs the discussion of the rule of law, the case that serves as a guide to interpretation of the rule of law, the application of the rule to the issue, the counteranalysis, and the rebuttal to the counteranalysis.

E. Persuasive Precedent

When presenting persuasive authority, indicate the reason you are relying on this type of authority and lay a proper foundation for its use.

For Example

Section 90-9-6 prohibits oppressive conduct by a majority shareholder. The statute does not define what constitutes oppressive conduct, and the courts of this state have not addressed the question.

The state of New Washington, however, has a statute identical to our statute, and the New Washington courts have addressed the question of what constitutes oppressive conduct under the statute. In the case of *Darren v. Darren,* . . .

In the preceding example, the reader is informed why the out-of-state law (**persuasive precedent**) is referenced: The statute does not define the term, and the state courts have not addressed the question. A foundation for presentation of the persuasive precedent is thus set: "The statute of the state referred to is identical to our state statute, and the other state's courts have addressed the question." In the following example, a foundation is set for use of a court's interpretation of one statute to interpret another statute.

For Example

Our courts have not defined the term *oppressive conduct* as used in § 90-9-6. Section 45-5-6C of the Small Loan Act prohibits "oppressive conduct" in small loan transactions. The state court of appeals, in the case of *Irons v. Fast Loans, Inc.,* has defined what constitutes oppressive conduct under the Small Loan Act, and that case can be referred to for guidance in interpreting § 90-9-6.

Refer to Chapter 2 and Chapter 18 when relying on persuasive precedent.

F. Conclusions

In many instances, after researching and analyzing a legal problem, you may not be able to provide a definite yes or no answer as to how it may be resolved.

For Example

If there is no mandatory precedent, and persuasive precedent or secondary authority is relied upon, you may not be able to provide an answer as to how the court is likely to resolve the issue. If the case law that applies is very old and policies have changed, it may be questionable if the case law will be followed.

In such instances, present your conclusions and explain your reservations.

For Example

In conclusion, the courts of this state have not addressed this question. The majority of states that have addressed this issue follow the rule adopted by the New Washington Supreme Court in the case of *Tyler v. Tyler.* As stated in the analysis of this issue, the progressive approach of the New Washington court reflects the approach our supreme court has taken in resolving similar issues and will likely be adopted by the court.

G. Revisions and Drafts

When preparing an office memo, it is essential to produce a professional product. This demands thorough research and analysis of all issues assigned and all aspects of each issue. It also requires assembly of the research and analysis into an organized, error-free final product. Be prepared to compose a number of drafts.

H. Additional Authority

If there are several cases on point, it is not necessary to thoroughly discuss each case. Present and discuss thoroughly the most recent case on point, and refer briefly to the other cases.

For Example

The case that defines what constitutes "oppressive" conduct in a fact situation such as that presented in the client's case is *Cedrik v. Ely*, 956 N. Wash. 776, 881 N.E.2d 451 (1995). In this case, the majority shareholder gave himself three bonuses that were triple his salary. At the same time, he refused to allow dividends to be issued. In defining what constitutes "oppressive conduct" under § 90-9-4, the court stated, "Oppressive conduct occurs when a majority shareholder engages in wrongful conduct which inures to the benefit of the majority and the detriment of the minority." *Id.* at 778. See also *Tyre v. Casey*, 953 N. Wash. 431, 878 N.E.2d 49 (1993) (oppressive conduct found when no dividends were issued and majority shareholder received several bonuses and was provided an extravagant expense account); *Ireland v. Ireland*, 952 N. Wash. 288, 873 N.E.2d 553 (1992) (oppressive conduct found when no dividends were issued and majority shareholder was given a house as a bonus).

VI. KEY POINTS CHECKLIST: Office Legal Memorandum—Analysis to Conclusion

✓ Follow the standard format for the analysis section of a memo: rule + case law (interpretation of the rule) + application of rule + counteranalysis. This format is based on the standard IRAC model.

✓ The presentation of a case in a case brief is different from the presentation of a case in an office memo. When introducing a case in the analysis section of a memo, it is not necessary to include all the information you would include in a case brief.

✓ In the analysis section, discuss how the rule of law applies to the issue and facts of the client's case.

✓ Always conduct a counteranalysis. If there is no counterargument, mention the fact that no counterargument or different position is supported by the case law.

✓ Provide enough information in the conclusion to inform the reader of all the applicable enacted and case law.

✓ Use introductory and transition sentences. Do not jump from one topic to another. Provide a smooth transition between subjects.

✓ Before presenting persuasive precedent or secondary authority, indicate why you are not relying on mandatory authority.

✓ Do not be disturbed if you do not reach a definite conclusion as to how the law applies. There are many gray areas and issues that have not been ruled upon. Your job is to inform the reader of the existing law and provide a well-reasoned analysis of its application. Predicting the legal outcome always involves some measure of uncertainty.

✓   As mentioned in Chapter 15, do not try to make the first draft the final draft. Just write the information in rough form. It is easier to polish a rough draft than to try to make the first draft the finished product.

VII. APPLICATION

The first example in this section illustrates the application of the principles to the analysis, conclusion, and recommendations sections of the office memo assignment introduced at the beginning of Chapter 16. Recall that the Application section of that chapter only addressed the first half of the memo assignment presented at the beginning of that chapter, that is, the heading, assignment, issue, brief answer, and facts sections of the memo. The second example in this section illustrates the application of the principles discussed in this chapter and the previous chapter to the office memo assignment presented at the beginning of this chapter.

Both Chapter 15 and Chapter 16 discussed the use of an expanded outline and presented examples that illustrate the use of an expanded outline when drafting an office memo. Inasmuch as the use of an expanded outline was illustrated in those chapters, a detailed discussion of its use is not included in the two examples explored in this section. The examples in this section present the completed office memoranda.

A. Example 1

The first example illustrates the completion of the memorandum assignment introduced at the beginning of Chapter 16. The heading through facts sections of the assignment are included in the Application section of that chapter. The remainder of the memorandum follows.

Analysis

The rule of law governing privileged communications between spouses is 735 ILCS 5/8-801, which provides, "In all actions, husband and wife may testify for or against each other, provided that neither may testify as to any communication or admission made by either of them to the other or as to any conversation between them during marriage. . . ." The statute does not include any sections that address waiver of the privilege. There is, however, Illinois case law that discusses the question of when the privilege is waived.

The Illinois supreme court case that addresses the question of waiver of the privilege when children are present during the spousal communication is *People v. Sanders*, 99 Ill. 2d 262, 457 N.E.2d 1241 (1983). In *Sanders*, the trial court admitted into evidence conversations between the defendant and his spouse. The conversations took place in front of their children, ages eight through thirteen years old; the conversations implicated the defendant in a murder. When addressing the question of whether the communications were privileged, the supreme court stated the rule followed in Illinois is that the presence of children of the spouses destroys confidentiality unless the children are too young to understand what is being said.

In the client's case, just as in *People v. Sanders*, the conversation between the spouses involved incriminating statements made in the presence of children. In the client's case, just as in *Sanders*, the children were old enough to understand the conversation. If the trial court follows the rule of law presented in *Sanders*, the conversation between Mr. Findo and Mrs. Findo is not a privileged communication under the statute and is admissible into evidence in the trial of Mr. Findo.

No case law in this jurisdiction establishes an exception to the rule presented in *Sanders*. The only possible counterargument is that the children, although present, did not hear the conversation. The *Sanders* opinion does not directly state that the children must actually hear the conversation, but this is implied by the requirement that the children must be old enough to understand what is being said. See the Recommendations section in regard to taking steps to determine if the children heard and understood the conversation.

Conclusion

The rule of law governing privileged spousal communications is 735 ILCS 5/8-801. It provides that communications between spouses during the marriage are privileged. In *People v. Sanders*, the court held that the privilege is waived if it takes place in front of children old enough to understand what is being said. In the client's case, because the conversation took place in the presence of children old enough to understand, it appears that the privilege does not apply, and the conversation is admissible into evidence.

Recommendations

1. We should conduct further investigation to determine if the children heard and understood the conversation.
2. Additional research should be conducted to determine if there are any cases addressing the question of whether, in addition to being present, the children must actually hear the conversation.

B. Example 2

The second example illustrates the completion of the office memo assignment presented in the hypothetical at the beginning of this chapter. Assume that Ellen Taylor's expanded outline includes the following law from the state of New Washington that applies to the assignment:

- **Article II, Section 4**, of the state constitution. "The right of the people to be secure in their persons, houses, papers and effects against unreasonable searches and seizures shall not be violated. . . ."
- **Section 95-21-14** of the state criminal code provides that "[i]t is unlawful for any person intentionally to possess a controlled substance . . . ." Cocaine is listed as a controlled substance under the act.
- *State v. Ikard*, 945 N. Wash. 745, 853 N.E.2d 652 (1999). In this case, law enforcement officers were looking for a suspect in an armed robbery. The officers recognized a friend of the suspect walking down a street. They stopped him, handcuffed him, and asked him where the suspect was. When he refused to answer the question, the officers searched him and found marijuana in his shirt pocket. The officers then arrested him for possession of narcotics.
- In regard to the initial stop and handcuffing of the defendant, the court held that a person is seized (arrested) within the meaning of Article II, Section 4, of the state constitution when a reasonable person would believe he was not free to leave. The court held that a reasonable person in the defendant's position would not believe he was free to leave; therefore, the defendant was under arrest when the officers stopped and handcuffed him.
- *State v. Wilson*, 953 N. Wash. 111, 878 N.E.2d 431 (2003). In this case, law enforcement officers were executing a search warrant. Upon entering the premises, an officer held the defendant by the arm and refused to allow him to leave. In addressing the question of whether the defendant was under arrest when the officer held him by the arm and refused to allow him to leave, the court held that "[n]ot all detentions constitute a seizure within the meaning of Article II, Section 4 of the Constitution. A warrant to search for contraband founded on probable cause implicitly carries with it the limited authority to detain the occupants of the premises while a proper search is conducted. Such a detention does not constitute a seizure within the meaning of the Constitution." *Id.* at 121.
- *State v. Bragg*, 955 N. Wash. 221, 880 N.E.2d 998 (2004). In this case, the police searched an apartment where Bragg and several other people resided. Narcotics were found in a drawer in the kitchen. There was no evidence linking Bragg to the drugs. Only Bragg was charged with possession. The court noted that possession may be either actual or constructive.

  In overturning his conviction, the court ruled that in a situation where several individuals have access to the location where the drugs are found, and there is no evidence indicating that the defendant has actual possession of the drugs, a conviction can still take place if there is evidence that the defendant is in constructive possession of the drugs. The court stated that to convict the defendant of constructive possession, either direct or circumstantial evidence must be presented that he had knowledge of the presence of the drugs and control over the drugs. In this case, there was no such evidence.

  The following is the memorandum prepared by Ellen Taylor.

OFFICE RESEARCH MEMORANDUM

To: Carl Pine, Assistant District Attorney

From: Ellen Taylor, Intern

Re: *State v. Kent;* Arrest during the execution of a search warrant and constructive possession of drugs

Case: CR 16-404

STATEMENT OF ASSIGNMENT

You have asked me to prepare a memorandum addressing the following questions: Was Mr. Kent under arrest when he was handcuffed and held in the kitchen while his apartment was searched? Is there sufficient evidence to support charges of possession in this case?

ISSUES

Issue I: Under Article II, section 4, of the state constitution, is an individual seized (under arrest) when police officers handcuff and detain him in the kitchen during the execution of a search warrant?

Issue II: Under § 95-21-14 of the criminal code, is there sufficient evidence to support charges of possession when the defendant is located in the bedroom of a third-story apartment, and the drugs are located below a broken window of the bedroom in a parking lot?

BRIEF ANSWER

Issue I: No. The state supreme court has held detentions during the execution of a search warrant do not constitute seizures within the meaning of Article II, Section 4 of the state constitution.

Issue II: No. When drugs are found in a common area accessible to multiple individuals and there is no evidence the defendant has actual possession, the defendant may constructively possess the drugs. The state supreme court has ruled constructive possession requires evidence the defendant had knowledge and control of the drugs. In Mr. Kent's case, there is no evidence he had knowledge and control of the drugs found in the parking lot.

FACTS

On January 7, police officers executed a search warrant for the apartment of the defendant, David Kent. The apartment is located on the third floor of an apartment complex. When the police entered the apartment, Mr. Kent was lying on the bed in the bedroom. He was frisked for weapons, handcuffed, moved to the kitchen, and detained while the search was conducted. He was not placed under arrest or read his rights. The police found a broken window in the bedroom, and the window screen was pushed out. In the parking lot three stories below the bedroom window, the officers found a bag containing cocaine. There were no witnesses who saw Mr. Kent throw anything out of the apartment window. No fingerprints were found on the bag, nor was there any other evidence linking Mr. Kent to the cocaine. Mr. Kent has been charged with possession of a controlled substance.

ANALYSIS

Issue I

The rule of law governing arrest in New Washington is Article II, Section 4 of the state constitution which provides, in part, "The right of the people to be secure in their person, . . . against unreasonable searches and seizures shall not be violated. . . ." Neither the constitution nor the state statutes define the term *seizure*. There is, however, New Washington case law that defines the term.

The New Washington case establishing the standard for what constitutes a seizure is *State v. Ikard*, 945 N. Wash. 745, 853 N.E.2d 652 (1999). In *Ikard*, law enforcement officers were looking for a suspect in an armed robbery. The officers recognized a friend of the suspect walking down a street. They stopped him, handcuffed him, and asked him where the suspect was. When he refused to answer the question, the officers searched him and found marijuana in his shirt pocket. The officers then arrested him for possession of narcotics. In ruling the defendant was under arrest when he was stopped and handcuffed, the court held a person is seized (arrested) within the meaning of Article II, Section 4 of the state constitution when a reasonable person would believe he was not free to leave. *Id.* at 750, 657.

The rule of law defining seizure adopted in *State v. Ikard* is so broadly stated that it can apply to a number of seizure situations, including the situation presented in Mr. Kent's case. In Mr. Kent's case, a reasonable person would not believe he was free to leave when handcuffed and moved to the kitchen during the execution of a warrant. It appears, therefore, Mr. Kent was seized (under arrest) within the meaning of *Ikard*.

Not all detentions, however, constitute a seizure. There are exceptions. One exception is when the detention takes place while officers are executing a search warrant. This exception was announced by the supreme court in *State v. Wilson*, 953 N. Wash. 111, 878 N.E.2d 431 (2003). In *Wilson*, after entering the premises during the execution of a search warrant, an officer held the defendant by the arm and refused to allow him to leave. In regard to whether the seizure constituted an arrest, the court held, "Not all detentions constitute a seizure within the meaning of Article II, Section 4 of the constitution. A warrant to search for contraband founded on probable cause implicitly carries with it the limited authority to detain the occupants of the premises while a proper search is conducted. Such a detention does not constitute a seizure within the meaning of the constitution." *Id.* at 121,441.

In Mr. Kent's case, just as in *Wilson*, the police were executing a search warrant and the defendant was detained while the search was being conducted. None of our facts indicates the warrant was issued without probable cause. If it was based on probable cause, under *Wilson*, the police had the authority to detain the defendant, and the detention was not a seizure within the meaning of the constitution.

No case or statutory law in New Washington contradicts or limits the *Wilson* ruling in regard to detention during the execution of a warrant. The only possible counterargument is the warrant was issued without probable cause, and therefore, the police did not have authority to detain Mr. Kent. There is no evidence in the case file indicating a problem in this regard. See the Recommendations section below.

Issue II

The rule of law governing the possession of cocaine is section 95-21-14 of the state criminal code, which provides that "[i]t is unlawful for any person intentionally to possess a controlled substance . . . ." Cocaine is listed as a controlled substance under the statute. The statute does not define what constitutes possession; therefore, it is necessary to refer to case law for guidance.

A case in which the supreme court defined possession is *State v. Bragg*, 955 N. Wash. 221, 880 N.E.2d 998 (2004). In this case, the police searched an apartment where Bragg and several other individuals resided. Narcotics were found in a drawer in the kitchen. There was no evidence linking Bragg to the drugs. Only Bragg was charged with possession. The court noted possession may be either actual or constructive. In overturning Bragg's conviction, the court ruled that in a situation where several individuals have access to the location where the drugs are found, and there is no evidence indicating the defendant has actual possession of the drugs, a conviction can still take place if there is evidence the defendant is in constructive possession of the drugs. The court stated that in order to convict for constructive possession, "there must be either direct or circumstantial evidence presented that the defendant had knowledge of the presence of the drugs and control over them." *Id.* at 225, 1002.

In our case, just as in *Bragg*, there is no evidence indicating that the defendant actually possessed the drugs. Also, there is no evidence, either direct or circumstantial, of constructive possession. There is no evidence that the defendant had knowledge of the presence of the drugs in the parking lot. Also, there is no evidence that he had control of the drugs. The drugs were found three stories below his apartment in a parking lot. There is no evidence linking the defendant to the drugs. If the rule of law presented in *Bragg* is followed, it appears that there is not sufficient evidence to support charges of possession.

There is no New Washington case law contradicting *Bragg* or establishing a different definition of *constructive possession*. A possible counterargument is that the fact the drugs were found below the defendant's broken apartment window is sufficient to link him to the drugs. There is no case law to support this position. It may be necessary to look for additional evidence that links the defendant to the drugs. See the Recommendations section below.

CONCLUSION

Article II, Section 4 of the state constitution prohibits the unreasonable seizure (arrest) of individuals. *State v. Ikard* states that an arrest takes place if a reasonable person would not believe he was free to leave. *State v. Wilson* provides that a detention that takes place during the execution of a search warrant does not constitute a seizure within the meaning of the constitution. In Mr. Kent's case, he was detained during the execution of a search warrant. Therefore, under the ruling in *Wilson*, it appears the detention of the defendant was not a seizure (arrest).

Section 95-21-14 of the state criminal code provides that it is illegal to possess cocaine. In *State v. Bragg*, the court held that to establish constructive possession, evidence must be presented showing that the defendant had knowledge of the presence of the drugs and control over them. In the defendant's case,

he did not actually possess the drugs, and there is no evidence indicating he had knowledge of or control over them. Therefore, it appears that there is not sufficient evidence to support charges of possession.

RECOMMENDATIONS

1. The office should determine whether the issuance of the search warrant was supported by probable cause or if there is any other matter that affects the legality of the search. If the issuance of the warrant or the execution of the search was in some way defective, the detention exception established in *State v. Wilson* may not apply.

2. The office needs to conduct further investigation to determine if there is any evidence linking the defendant to the drugs found in the parking lot. For example, was glass from the window embedded in the bag? Were there any individuals in the apartment complex who heard a window being broken?

C. Comments on Examples

Note that the analysis section of both memos follows the same analytical format: rule of law + case law interpreting the rule of law + application of the law to the issue and facts of the client's case + counteranalysis. There are transition sentences linking the presentation of the rule of law to the case law. No extra or superfluous material is presented; the reader is not required to wade through related but unnecessary case law or analysis. The applicable law is introduced, explained, and applied. The reader is clearly and concisely informed of the law and how it applies.

In both examples, there is one conclusion that includes a reference to the applicable law and summarizes the analysis of the issues. The conclusion summarizes all the applicable enacted and case law. If the reader desires a detailed analysis and discussion of the law, the analysis section can be referenced. When the memo is more complex and involves multiple issues, it may be appropriate to provide a conclusion section at the end of the analysis of each issue.

Summary

This chapter addresses considerations involved in preparing the second half of an office memorandum: the analysis, conclusion, and recommendations sections. The focus of the chapter is on the analysis section.

The heart of an office memorandum is the analysis section. The purpose of a memorandum is to inform the reader of the law that governs the issue and how the law applies in the client's case. This information is conveyed in the analysis section of the office memo. In this section, the reader is informed through:

- A presentation of the law that governs the issue.
- An explanation of how the law applies through reference to court opinions that applied the law in similar situations.
- A discussion of how the law applies to the issue(s) in the client's case.

Included in the analysis is a discussion of any counterargument the opposing side may raise.

Following the analysis section is the conclusion. Because the application of the law to the issue is discussed in the analysis section, the conclusion should contain a summary of the law and analysis already presented. It should inform the reader of all the applicable law and how it applies.

The recommendations section is the last section of the office memo. It includes any suggestions or recommendations concerning the next steps to be taken or further research or investigation that should be conducted.

The format discussed in this chapter is a recommended format. There is no standard office memo format. Different law offices have different preferences. Use the format presented in this chapter if appropriate; modify it according to your needs.

Quick References

Internet Resources

The online resources for this chapter are the same as those listed in Chapter 15. Due to the large number of websites, the best strategy is to narrow your search to a specific type of legal writing and topic, such as "analysis, legal memorandum, public service contracts" or "application of law, legal memorandum, highway construction."

Exercises

ASSIGNMENT 1

Detail the process for presenting a case in the analysis section of an office memo.

ASSIGNMENT 2

Detail the format of the analysis section of an office memo.

ASSIGNMENT 3

Describe what should and should not be included in the conclusion section of an office memo.

ASSIGNMENTS 4–13 Instructions

In each of the following exercises, the assignment is to prepare an office memo. Each assignment contains an assignment memo from the supervising attorney that includes all the available facts of the case. Complete the memo based on these facts. If additional facts are needed, note this in the recommendations section of the memo. When preparing the heading of each assignment, use "Supervising Attorney" in the "To" line, and put your name after the "From."

Following each assignment is a reference to the applicable enacted and case law. In some assignments, the case citation includes a reference only to the regional reporter citation; the state reporter citation is not included. Use only the citation presented in the assignment. The cases are presented in Appendix A.

The first time you cite the opinion, use the full citation format for the citation you are given for the opinion in the assignment.

For Example

New Mexico v. Zamora is cited in assignment 4 as 2005-NMCA-039, 137 N.M. 301, 110 P.3d 517

This is how you should cite this opinion the first time it is used in any legal document memorandum. When you need to quote from an opinion in the memo, use a blank line to indicate the page number from which the quotation is taken. Use short-form citation when appropriate. For short-form citations, reference either the *ALWD Guide* or the *Bluebook*, whichever is the citation guide for your course.

For Example

Zamora, 2005-NMCA-039, ¶ _____, 137 N.M. at _____, 301 P.3d at _____:.
or
Id. at ¶ _____, 137 N.M. _____, 301 P.3d _____:.

Do not conduct additional research. Complete the assignment using the facts, enacted law, and case law contained in each assignment. For the purposes of the assignments, assume that the cases have not been overturned or modified by subsequent court decisions.

ASSIGNMENT 4

To:	Paralegal
From:	Supervising Attorney
Re:	*New Mexico v. Deiter*; lawfulness of search of freezer

Our office represents Joseph and Josephine Deiter in *New Mexico v. Deiter*. After meeting with Ms. Deiter and reviewing the police report, I am concerned the search of her home was unlawful.

The Atrisco, police department received a call about a domestic disturbance at 505 Sandia Street. Two officers went to the house and heard several loud voices and the sound of glass breaking when they arrived at the front door. Officers knocked and announced their presence, and a woman opened the door. Officers asked if they could come in and if there was a problem at the house. The woman stood aside and the officers went in.

When officers entered the house they saw broken glass on the living room floor and smelled the odor of burnt marijuana. They also saw a pipe used for smoking marijuana. They did not see any marijuana. Mr. Deiter was sitting on the sofa. The woman volunteered that Mr. Deiter threw a glass at her and officers arrested him for domestic assault. This enraged Ms. Deiter who then spat on one of the officers. She was arrested for assault on a police officer.

Officers then conducted a protective sweep to make sure no one else was in the house. In looking in the kitchen for additional persons, Officer Smith, having been taught people often keep marijuana in the freezer, opened the freezer and found four bags weighing one ounce each of marijuana. Based on the seizure of the marijuana, the Deiters were also charged with possession of a controlled substance.

Review the applicable state search and seizure provision and case law creating the protective sweep exception to the warrant requirement to determine if the search of the freezer was lawful.

Constitutional Law: Article 2, Section 10 of the New Mexico Constitution states: "The people shall be secure in their persons, papers, homes and effects, from unreasonable searches and seizures, and no warrant to search any place, or seize any person or thing, shall issue without describing the place to be searched, or the persons or things to be seized, nor without a written showing of probable cause, supported by oath or affirmation."

Case Law: Case law creates an exception to the warrant requirement of Article 2, Section 10, called a protective sweep. A court opinion that provides the definition of protective sweep and applies the elements of that definition is *New Mexico v. Zamora*, 2005-NMCA-039, 137 N.M. 301, 110 P.3d 517 (see Appendix A).

ASSIGNMENT 5

To:	Paralegal
From:	Supervising Attorney
Re:	*Eldridge v. Eldridge;* modification of child support

We represent Gwen Eldridge in the case of *Eldridge v. Eldridge*. The Eldridges were divorced in 2012. Mrs. Eldridge was awarded custody of their two minor children. Mr. Eldridge was ordered to make child support payments in the amount of $700 per month. He lost his job in January of 2013 and was unemployed from that date through October of 2013. He then obtained employment as an electrician.

Mr. Eldridge did not make child support payments for the months during which he was unemployed. In January of 2014, Mrs. Eldridge filed a motion with the court that entered the divorce decree, seeking an order forcing Mr. Eldridge to pay the child support payments due for the months he did not make payments; the amount totaled $7,000. Mr. Eldridge countered with a petition to modify his child support obligation. The petition requested that he be excused from having to pay the obligations that accrued during the 10 months he was unemployed. The court ordered Mr. Eldridge to pay one-half of the amount due, $3,500, and excused him from paying the remaining $3,500. The court stated that Mr. Eldridge did not have to pay the full amount because he was unemployed during the months the child support accrued. The attorney that represented Mrs. Eldridge in the trial court told her that there is no basis for an appeal of the court order.

Please check the statutory and case law to determine if the trial court acted properly when it excused Mr. Eldridge from paying $3,500 of the back child support.

Statutory Law: Ind. Code § 31-2-11-12, Modification of delinquent support payment, provides:

(a) Except as provided in subsection (b) . . ., a court may not retroactively modify an obligor's duty to pay a delinquent support payment.

(b) A court with jurisdiction over a support order may modify an obligor's duty to pay a support payment that becomes due:

    (1) After notice of a petition to modify the support order has been given . . . to the obligee . . . and

    (2) Before a final order concerning the petition for modification is entered.

Case Law: *Cardwell v. Gwaltney*, 556 N.E.2d 953 (Ind. Ct. App. 1990) (see Appendix A).

ASSIGNMENT 6

> To: Paralegal
> From: Supervising Assistant District Attorney
> Re: *State v. James Young;* burglary charge

On August 7, Mr. Young went to Coronado Mall. He took a coat hanger which he planned to use to break into cars parked at the mall. The mall parking lot was full and Mr. Young went unobserved. As he approached Karl Wilson's vehicle, he noticed that the windows were open about an inch. He also observed Mr. Wilson's wallet on the front seat. Unknown to Mr. Wilson, the wallet fell out of his pocket when he exited the car.

Mr. Young was unable to unlock Mr. Wilson's vehicle. However, after fashioning a hook, he was able to pull the wallet through the open window. The wallet contained $300 and two credit cards, all of which Mr. Young took.

I would like to charge Mr. Young with burglary under our burglary statute. Does Mr. Young's use of the coat hanger to retrieve the wallet constitute entry within the meaning of the statute? Please prepare a memo addressing this question.

Statutory Law: New Mexico Statute § 30-16-3. Burglary

Burglary consists of the unauthorized entry of any vehicle, watercraft, aircraft, dwelling or other structure, movable or immovable, with the intent to commit any felony or theft therein.

Case Law: *NewMexico v. Muqqdin*, 2010-NMCA-069, 148 N.M. 845, 242 P.3d 412 (see Appendix A).

ASSIGNMENT 7

> To: Paralegal
> From: Supervising Attorney
> Re: *United States v. Canter;* armed bank robbery with a dangerous weapon

We have been appointed to represent Eldon Canter in the case of *United States v. Canter*. Mr. Canter is charged with one count of armed bank robbery, in violation of 18 U.S.C. § 2113(a) and (d).

On January 5 of this year, Mr. Canter robbed the First State Bank. After he entered the bank, he approached a teller and pulled from his pocket a crudely carved wooden replica of a 9 mm Beretta handgun. He had carved the replica from a block of pinewood and stained it with dark walnut wood stain to make it look black. He drilled a hole in the barrel end in an attempt to make it look like a real Beretta.

The teller was so frightened that he only glanced at the wooden gun. He believed it was real. The teller at the next window looked at the replica and afterward stated that she was fairly certain at the time that it was fake. No one else noticed whether the wooden replica was real.

Please determine whether, in light of the facts of this case, there is sufficient evidence to support the charge that Mr. Canter committed bank robbery by use of a "dangerous weapon."

Statutory Law: 18 U.S.C. § 2113(a) & (d), Bank robbery and incidental crimes, provides:

(a) Whoever, by force and violence, or by intimidation, takes, or attempts to take, from the person or presence of another . . . any property or money or any other thing of value belonging to, or in the care, custody, control, management, or possession of, a bank. . . .

Shall be fined under this title or imprisoned not more than 20 years, or both.

(d) Whoever, in committing, or in attempting to commit, any offense defined in subsections (a) and (b) of this section, assaults any person, or puts in jeopardy the life of any person by use of a dangerous weapon or device, shall be fined under this title or imprisoned not more than 25 years, or both.

Case Law: *United States v. Martinez-Jimenez*, 864 F.2d 664 (9th Cir. 1989) (see Appendix A).

ASSIGNMENT 8

To:	Paralegal
From:	Supervising Attorney
Re:	*Hatch v. Transcontinental Railroad Company*; prescriptive easement

Our office represents Alejandro Hatch, farm owners, in an action against the Transcontinental Railroad Company. Mr. Hatch acquired the farmland five years ago. Unbeknownst to him, the prior owner had entered into an easement agreement nine years ago with Transcontinental allowing the company to spray herbicides along the edge of the farm bordered by the railroad tracks for purposes of keeping the tracks and area around the tracks clear of weeds and "nuisance" plants. The easement allowed spraying up to 15 feet into the farmland from east of the existing tracks. Although the prior owner and the railroad drafted appropriate easement documents, the easement was never properly recorded. In the lawsuit, we have alleged Transcontinental's activities on the easement land has damaged farmland beyond the easement and caused loss of crops.

Mr. Hatch never saw any activity of chemical spraying by the railroad the first three years he owned the farm. However, he did notice that crops from the railroad track up to 25 feet into the farmland were often stunted and failed to thrive on the edge of the farm where the easement was located (although as noted above he did not know of the easement). Two years ago, Mr. Hatch began to amend the soil in the area of the easement to improve crop growth. His efforts were to no avail. In his efforts to improve growth, he spent more time walking that area of the farm and began to notice a white residue on the crops in April, June, and August. Last year, in June, was the first time Mr. Hatch saw a railroad vehicle going along the track with men walking along side of the vehicle spraying a liquid from a container in the bed of the vehicle. His crops were subsequently covered in white residue.

Transcontinental has asserted is has a prescriptive easement. Based on the above facts please analyze whether there is a prescriptive easement.

Rule of law: There is no applicable statutory law. Case law requires the party asserting a prescriptive easement to show: (1) that it actually and visibly used the land allegedly subject to the easement for a specific purpose for ten years, (2) that the use began and continued under a claim of right, and (3) that the use was hostile to the plaintiff's title. *Paxson v. Glovitz*, 203 Ariz. 63 (App. 2002).

Case law: A court opinion that applies the elements of a prescriptive easement is: *C & G Les Springs Family Home, LLC v. Hinz*, 1-CA-CV-2008-0442 (Ariz. Ct. App., Div. 1 2009) (see Appendix A).

ASSIGNMENT 9

To:	Paralegal
From:	Supervising Attorney
Re:	*Loya v. Department of Child Safety*; termination of parental rights

Our client, Ollie Loya, has sought our firm's representation in a termination of parental right matter. Mr. Loya was released last year from prison after serving a two-year sentence to battery. He was out of custody for six months before being convicted of aggravated battery (with a deadly weapon). His release date would be in six years.

Mr. Loya's son was 18 months old when Mr. Loya was first incarcerated. He was 3-½ years old at the time of Mr. Loya's most recent release. The son would be ten years old when Mr. Loya is released from the most recent conviction.

The mother of the child had custody of Mr. Loya's son while Mr. Loya was first incarcerated. The Department of Child Safety (DCS) recently took the child from the mother because of abuse and neglect charges. DCS initiated termination proceedings against mother and Mr. Loya, and the mother voluntarily surrendered her rights.

Mr. Loya was present in the home with child prior to the first period of incarceration. However, there are multiple police reports indicating violence between Mr. Loya and his son's mother, and Mr. Loya has candidly admitted there was violence in front of the child in that period.

DCS has presented us with documentation that Mr. Loya has not provided financial support for his son since his first incarceration. Mr. Loya has provided us with documentation of sending letters and cards to child while he was incarcerated. DCS has a paternal family relative willing and approved to adopt the child.

Please analyze whether there are sufficient facts to lead a court to find clear and convincing evidence there is a basis to terminate Mr. Loya's parental rights to his son.

Rule of Law: Arizona statutes section 8-533(B) allows a superior court to terminate parental rights upon clear and convincing evidence of at least one of several ground listed in the statute. Section 8-533(B)(4) allows termination on the basis "that the parent is deprived of civil liberties due to the conviction of a felony if the felony of which the parent was convicted is of such a nature as to prove the unfitness of that parent to have future custody and control of the child including . . . the sentence of that parent is of such a length that the child will be deprived of a normal home for a period of years."

Case Law: A court opinion discussing length incarceration as the basis for termination is *Erik T. v. Department of Child Safety,* S.T., 1-CA-JV-2015-0274 (filed Jan. 28, 2016) (see Appendix A).

ASSIGNMENT 10

To:	Paralegal
From:	Supervising Attorney
Re:	*Mad Dog Review v. Jonesville;* First Amendment—freedom of expression

We represent Mad Dog Review, a local rap band. As you know, this is a controversial group. The lyrics of one of their songs, "Mad Dog City Council," describes our city council in explicit terms using "dirty" words and language generally considered obscene. Based upon the language in their songs, and specifically that in "Mad Dog City Council," the city council of Jonesville (a neighboring municipality) has banned the group from performing in their community.

The Jonesville city council based its authority to enact the ban on Municipal Ordinance section 355-20. The ordinance provides: "The City Council, upon majority vote, may prohibit the public performance of any type of entertainment that does not comport with local standards of decency or acceptability." The ordinance does not define "local standards of decency or acceptability" or provide any standards or guidelines that the city council must follow.

Mad Dog Review wants to challenge the authority of the Jonesville city council to ban its performance. Please prepare an office memorandum addressing the question of whether the municipal ordinance violates the group's right to freedom of expression.

Rule of Law: First Amendment to the United States Constitution (U.S. Const. Amend. I).

Case Law: Assume that the only case law governing this question is *Atlantic Beach Casino, Inc. v. Morenzoni,* 749 F. Supp. 38 (D.R.I. 1990). The relevant portions of the case are presented at the end of this chapter.

ASSIGNMENT 11

Note: Assignments 11 and 12 were prepared by Mary Kubichek, JD, director of Paralegal Studies at Casper College in Casper, Wyoming. The initial draft of the model answer to each assignment included in the Instructor's Manual was prepared by Ms. Kubichek's students.

To:	[Your name]
From:	Supervising Attorney
Re:	*Wright v. State;* liability of State University for battery of student

We represent Joe and Ann Wright, parents of Bob Wright, a freshman at State University of Generic who was living 400 miles from home. Bob lived in Smith Hall, a freshman dormitory. Bob wanted to be involved in school activities. The university supported intramural sports activities where dorm students competed against other dorm students. Bob was not very athletic, and his dorm lost games because of his lack of skill and he often got in the way of his team. After a 0–4 record, Bob's teammates threatened him and told him to quit. Bob notified a counselor at the university. Bob did not quit, and after two more losing games, he was beaten by three teammates. Bob, who is a diabetic, suffered a broken arm, had a fifth of alcohol poured down his throat, and required 40 stitches to his torso. Bob withdrew from the university. Bob's parents and Bob want to sue the college under the following sections of the state statute.

You are only to consider the following statutes. Do not bring in any outside facts or law.

Statutes:

(a) Hazing is defined as follows:

    (1) Any willful action taken or situation created, whether on or off any school, college, university, or other educational premises, which recklessly or intentionally endangers the mental or physical health of any student, or

    (2) Any willful act on or off any school, college, university, or other educational premises by any person alone or acting with others in striking, beating, bruising, or maiming; or seriously offering, threatening, or attempting to strike, beat, bruise, or maim, or to do or seriously offer, threaten, or attempt to do physical violence to any student of any such educational institution or any assault upon any such students made for the purpose of committing any

of the acts, or producing any of the results to such student as defined in this section.

(3) The term *hazing* as defined in this section does not include customary athletic events or similar contests or competitions, and is limited to those actions taken and situations created in connection with initiation into or affiliation with any organization.

(4) The academic institution, college, university, etc. is liable for hazing if:

(i) it occurred by members of a campus group;

(ii) it had notice.

Please draft an interoffice memorandum. Include the following:

To:
From:
Re:
Facts: (Remember to include parties and what the clients want.)
Issue(s):   (Remember that the issue or issues must include jurisdiction, key facts, and be in question form.)
Analysis:
Conclusion:

ASSIGNMENT 12

To: Paralegal
From: Supervising Attorney
Re: *Martin v. City Airport;* 42 U.S.C. § 2000e

We represent Jake Martin. Jake is a 25-year-old American citizen. He is olive skinned, 6 feet 3 inches, 220 pounds with thick dark hair and a full beard. Jake applied for an airport security position. He stated that he has filled out all forms. He was informed that he will not be hired. Jake's mother lives on an Indian reservation within five miles of the airport security position. Jake argues that he is being discriminated against under 42 U.S.C. § 2000e-2(a)(1). Jake wants a job with airport security.

You are to consider only the following statutes. Do not bring in any outside facts or law.

Statutes:

42 U.S.C. § 2000e-2

(a) Employer practices
It shall be an unlawful employment practice for an employer

(1) to fail or refuse to hire or to discharge any individual, or otherwise to discriminate

against any individual with respect to his compensation, terms, conditions, or privileges of employment, because of such individual's race, color, religion, sex, or national origin; or . . . .

(g) National security
Notwithstanding any other provision of this subchapter, it shall not be an unlawful employment practice for an employer to fail or refuse to hire and employ any individual for any position, for an employer to discharge an individual from any position, or for an employment agency to fail or refuse to refer any individual for employment in any position, or for a labor organization to fail or refuse to refer any individual for employment in any position, if.

(1) the occupancy of such position, or access to the premises in or upon which any part of the duties of such position is performed or is to be performed, is subject to any requirement imposed in the interest of the national security of the United States under any security program in effect pursuant to or administered under any statute of the United States or any Executive order of the President; and . . . .

(i) Businesses or enterprises extending preferential treatment to Indians.
Nothing contained in this subchapter (regarding national security) shall apply to any business or enterprise on or near an Indian reservation with respect to any publicly announced employment practice of such business or enterprise under which a preferential treatment is given to any individual because he is an Indian living on or near a reservation.

Please draft an interoffice memorandum. Include the following:

To:
From:
Re:
Facts: (Remember to include parties and what the clients want.)
Issue(s):   (Remember that the issue or issues must include jurisdiction, key facts, and be in question form.)
Analysis:
Conclusion:

ASSIGNMENT 13

To: Paralegal
From: Supervising Attorney
Re: *Espinosa v. Capital Insurance;* contract breach

We represent Emilio Espinosa. On May 2 of this year, Mr. Espinosa purchased a home from First City Bank. On that date, he purchased homeowner insurance from Capital Insurance Company. The Bank had foreclosed on the home on March 15, 48 days prior to Mr. Espinosa's purchase. Mr. Espinosa did not plan to move into the home until July 1 On June 5, 34 days after Mr. Espinosa purchased the home and signed the homeowner insurance contract with Capital Insurance, copper thieves broke into the home, tore into the walls and ceiling, and stole the copper water pipes. There was extensive damage to the walls and ceiling and water damage to the carpet. The estimated repair costs were $19,000.

The house was vacant from March 15, the date of the foreclosure until the date of the damage; a period of 82 days. Paragraph 20 of the insurance contract Mr. Espinosa signed with Capital Insurance excludes from coverage loss caused by "theft or attempted theft, damage by burglars, . . . if the described location: is held as a residence and has not been occupied as a residence for more than 60 consecutive days immediately before the loss."

Capital Insurance is denying coverage based upon this section of the contract. Please check the statutory and case law to determine whether Capital Insurance can deny coverage based upon this section.

Statutory Law: For the purposes of this assignment, there is no statutory law that applies.

Case Law: *Pappas Enterprises, Inc. v. Commerce & Industry Insurance Co.*, 422 Mass. 80, 661 N.E.2d 81 (1996) (see Appendix A).

ASSIGNMENT 14

Based on your instructor's direction, perform any of the above assignments using your state's enacted and case law. Your instructor may give you the applicable law or you may be required to conduct independent research to locate the applicable laws.

Use the appropriate citation manual to cite to any legal authority you are provided (unless instructed otherwise).

CASE

ATLANTIC BEACH CASINO, INC.
d/b/a the Windjammer,
et al., Plaintiffs,

v.

Edward T. MARENZONI,
et al., Defendants.
Civ. A. No. 90-0471.
United States District Court,
D. Rhode Island.
Sept. 28, 1990.
749 F. Supp. 38 (D.R.I. 1990)

OPINION AND ORDER

PETTINE, Senior District Judge.

In the last few years, legislators and citizens have paid increasing attention to the lyrical content of popular music. The interest is not entirely new, for "rulers have long known [music's] capacity to appeal to the intellect and to the emotions and have censored musical compositions to serve the needs of the state." *Ward v. Rock Against Racism*, ____ U.S. ____, 109 S.Ct. 2746, 2753, 105 L.Ed.2d 661 (1989). The controversy some groups have ignited is not, in itself, any reason to take such speech outside the First Amendment. Indeed, expression may "best serve its high purpose when it induces a condition of unrest, creates dissatisfaction with conditions as they are, or even stirs people to anger." *Terminiello v. Chicago*, 337 U.S. 1, 4, 69 S.Ct. 894, 96, 893 L.Ed. 1131 (1949). The message and reputation of the rap music group 2 Live Crew evidently came to the attention of the Westerly Town Council, for they have taken steps toward possibly preventing the group from playing a scheduled concert. It is in this way that 2 Live Crew became the subject of, though not a party to, the present litigation.

On September 19, 1990, plaintiffs, who have contracted to present the 2 Live Crew concert, moved for a temporary restraining order prohibiting the defendants, members of the Westerly Town Council, from holding a show cause hearing on September 24, 1990, concerning the revocation of plaintiffs' entertainment license; from revoking the plaintiffs' entertainment license; from prohibiting the 2 Live Crew concert scheduled for October 6, 1990; and from imposing any special requirements on plaintiffs relative to the October 6 presentation. On September 21, 1990, the parties and this Court agreed that the matter would be considered as an application for a preliminary injunction and that the show cause hearing would be continued until October 1, 1990, subject to and dependent upon this Court's ruling. Based on the September 21 conference and my review of the parties' briefs, this Court has determined that the central issue in this case is plaintiffs' facial challenge to the town of Westerly's licensing ordinances on First Amendment grounds. Because I find, for the reasons set out below, that the ordinances as written are unconstitutional under the First and Fourteenth Amendments, defendants are enjoined from conducting a show cause hearing and from revoking plaintiff's entertainment license. I also enjoin the defendants from prohibiting the concert for failing to allege sufficient harm to overcome plaintiffs' First Amendment rights.

III. INJUNCTIVE RELIEF

In order for plaintiffs to prevail in their request for a preliminary injunction, they must meet the following standards: the plaintiff must demonstrate a likelihood of success on the merits, immediate and irreparable harm, that the injury outweighs any harm engendered by the grant of injunctive relief and that the public interest will not be adversely affected by such grant. *LeBeau v. Spirito*, 703 F.2d 639, 642 (1st Cir. 1983). I shall address each of these standards in turn.

A. Likelihood of Success on the Merits

Rather than allow 2 Live Crew to perform and then prosecute for any illegal activity that could occur, the Town Council wishes to review and decide in advance whether to allow the performance to go forward. This is a prior restraint. See *Southeastern Promotions, Ltd. v. Conrad*, 420 U.S. 546, 554–55, 95 S.Ct. 1239, 1244–45, 43 L.Ed.2d 448 (1975). "Any system of prior restraints of expression comes to this Court bearing a heavy presumption against its constitutional validity." *Bantam Books, Inc. v. Sullivan*, 372 U.S. 58, 70, 83 S.Ct. 631, 639, 9 L.Ed.2d 584 (1963). A licensing scheme involving such prior restraint survives constitutional scrutiny only when the law contains "narrow, objective and definite standards to guide the licensing authority." *Shuttlesworth v. Birmingham*, 394 U.S. 147, 150–51, 89 S.Ct. 935, 938–39, 22 L.Ed.2d 162 (1969); see *Lakewood*, 486 U.S. 760, *Southeastern Promotions*, 420 U.S. at 553, 95 S.Ct. at 1243–44, *Cox v. State of Louisiana*, 379 U.S. 536, 557–58, 85 S.Ct. 453,

465–66, 13 L.Ed.2d 471 (1965), *Irish Subcommittee v. R.I. Heritage Commission*, 646 F.Supp. 347, 359 (D.R.I.1986).

The Westerly Ordinance, see *supra* note 3, provides even less guidance than the law struck down in *Shuttlesworth*. Id. 394 U.S. at 149, 89 S.Ct. at 937–38 (permit could be denied if demanded by the "public welfare, peace, safety, health, decency, good order, morals or convenience"). For example, Section 17–87 merely states, "Any license granted under Section 17–84 and 17–88 may be revoked by the Town Council after public hearing for cause shown." As in *Venuti*, the Westerly ordinance is utterly devoid of standards. See 521 F.Supp. at 1030–31 (striking down entertainment license ordinance). It leaves the issuance and revocation of licenses to the unbridled discretion of the Town Council. Our cases have long noted that "the danger of censorship and of abridgement of our precious First Amendment freedoms is too great where officials have unbridled discretion over a forum's use." *Toward a Gayer Bicentennial Committee v. Rhode Island Bicentennial Foundation*, 417 F.Supp. 632, 641 (D.R.I.1976) (quoting Southeastern Promotions, 420 U.S. at 553, 95 S.Ct. at 1242–44).

The defendants assert that they are guided by specific concerns for public safety, as outlined in their notice to plaintiffs, and not by the message of 2 Live Crew's lyrics. When dealing with the First Amendment, however, the law does not allow us to presume good intentions on the part of the reviewing body. *Lakewood*, 486 U.S. at 770, 108 S.Ct. at 1243–44. The standards must be explicitly set out in the ordinance itself, a judicial construction or a well-established practice. *Id*. Without standards there is a grave danger that a licensing scheme "will serve only as a mask behind which the government hides as it excludes speakers from the . . . forum solely because of what they intend to say." *Irish Subcommittee*, 646 F.Supp. at 357. Such exclusion is repugnant to the First Amendment.

This Court recognizes that the Westerly Town Council has a valid interest in regulating entertainment establishments. It is well established that time, place and manner restrictions on expressive activity are permissible, but even then the regulations must be "narrowly and precisely tailored to their legitimate objectives." *Toward a Gayer Bicentennial*, 427 F.Supp. at 638; see Shuttlesworth, 394 U.S. at 153, 89 S.Ct. at 940; Cox, 379 U.S. at 558, 85 S.Ct. at 466. The Westerly licensing ordinances do not even approach the necessary level of specificity constitutionally mandated. Given the complete lack of standards in the ordinances and the long and clear line of precedent, plaintiffs' likelihood of success is overwhelming.

ORDER

Because Westerly Code of Ordinances, Sections 17-84 and 17-87 are facially unconstitutional, because the plaintiffs have met the other requirements for a preliminary injunction, and because defendants have failed to allege sufficient harm. IT IS ORDERED that defendants are enjoined from conducting a show cause hearing, revoking plaintiffs' license pursuant to these ordinances or from otherwise prohibiting the scheduled concert.

Chapter 18

External Memoranda: Court Briefs

Learning Objectives

After completing this chapter, you should understand:

- The similarities and differences between court briefs and office memoranda
- Techniques of persuasive writing
- The elements of trial and appellate court briefs
- How to draft trial and appellate court briefs

Pam Hayes, a paralegal living in the hypothetical state of New Washington, received the following assignment from her supervisor.

To:	Pam Hayes, Paralegal
From:	Alice Black, Attorney
Case:	CV 016-601, *Nick Shine v. Blue Sky Ski Resort*
Re:	Motion to dismiss for failure to state a claim

On December 5, 2015, Nick Shine, an expert skier, was skiing Bright Light, an intermediate ski run, at Blue Sky Ski Resort. At the midway point, the run takes a sharp, slightly uphill turn to the south, then plunges steeply downhill. When Mr. Shine encountered the turn, the sun was shining directly in his eyes; he did not see that the run was completely covered with ice. Due to the sun's glare, he could not see the ice hazard until it was too late to avoid it. He immediately lost control and hit a tree, breaking his left arm. There was no warning sign posted to indicate the presence of the ice hazard.

We filed Mr. Shine's complaint against the resort on April 6, 2016. In the complaint, we allege that the resort was negligent in failing to post a warning indicating the presence of the unavoidable and latent ice hazard.

On April 20, Blue Sky Ski Resort filed a motion to dismiss under Rule 12(b)(6) of the Rules of Civil Procedure for failure to state a claim. In the motion, Resort argues that under the Ski Safety Act, the resort does not have a duty to warn of ice hazards. They argue that ice conditions are the responsibility of the skier under the act; therefore, we cannot, as a matter of law, state a claim in regard to duty.

Please prepare a response to their motion for my review.

Note that this assignment is a variation of the assignment presented at the beginning of Chapter 13. The following sections of this chapter introduce the guidelines that Ms. Hayes will follow when performing her assignment. The completed assignment is presented in the Application section.

I. INTRODUCTION

The focus of this text is on legal analysis and the main type of writing related to legal analysis: the legal research memorandum. Chapters 16 and 17 addressed the type of legal writing most frequently performed by paralegals and law clerks engaged in legal analysis: the office legal memorandum. As discussed in those chapters, the office legal memorandum is designed for use within the law office and is drafted primarily as an objective research and analysis tool. This chapter and Chapter 19 discuss the preparation of documents using legal analysis that are designed for use outside the law office:

- Documents submitted to a court, such as briefs and memoranda in support of motions
- Documents designed for other external use, such as correspondence to clients and opposing attorneys

Paralegals and law clerks are less frequently involved in the preparation of external-use documents than those designed for use within the law office; however, experienced paralegals and law clerks may be called upon to prepare the initial drafts of documents intended for external use—referred to here as *external memoranda.*

The focus of this chapter is on the considerations involved in the preparation of legal analysis documents designed for submission to a court. A trial court brief is often referred to as a *memorandum of law* or a *memorandum of points and authorities.* In this chapter, a legal memorandum or brief submitted to a trial court is referred to as a **trial court brief** or **trial brief**, and a brief submitted to a court of appeals is referred to as an **appellate court brief**. The Application section of this chapter provides an example of a trial court brief; Appendix B includes an example of an appellate court brief.

II. GENERAL CONSIDERATIONS

Both trial and appellate court briefs are similar in many respects to office legal memoranda, and the fundamental principles that apply to the preparation of office memos also apply to the preparation of court briefs. The similarities are outlined here.

A. Similarities—Court Briefs and Office Memoranda

1. Legal Writing Process

Just as it is necessary when preparing an office memo to adopt and use a legal writing process, it is also necessary to do so when preparing a court brief. The basic writing process is the same for both court briefs and office memoranda:

    Prewriting Stage
        Assignment—type of brief, audience, and so on
        Constraints—time, length, format (court rules)
        Organization—creation of an expanded outline
            Use of an expanded outline
    Writing Stage
    Postwriting Stage
        Revising
        Editing

2. Basic Content

Court briefs follow the same basic organization as office memos. Both include a presentation of the issue(s), the relevant facts, a legal analysis, and a conclusion. Refer to Chapters 16 and 17 for information and guidelines concerning the preparation of these components of a brief.

3. Analysis Approach

Court briefs follow the same basic organizational approach to the legal analysis of an issue as office memoranda: the rule of law is presented first, then the interpretation of the rule of law through the case law (if interpretation is necessary), the application of the law to the issues presented by the facts of the case, followed by the conclusion. Exhibit 18-1 presents the basic format of this approach.

B. Dissimilarities—Court Briefs and Office Memoranda

As noted previously, both trial and appellate court briefs are similar in many respects to office legal memos in basic organization and content. The major difference is in the presentation of the format and content. An office memo is designed to present an objective analysis of the law. The goal is to provide a neutral analysis that thoroughly addresses all sides of an issue and provides the attorney with guidance on how the court may resolve the issue.

Whereas an office memo is designed to objectively inform, a court brief is designed to persuade. A court brief is an advocacy document designed to persuade the court to adopt a position or take an action favorable to the client. Therefore, although the elements of an office memo and court brief are basically the same, court briefs are different in that they are drafted to advocate a position and persuade the reader.

Court brief format is generally controlled by procedural rules and local custom of practice. Procedural rules dictate format details such as what type of content must be contained in a trial brief, spacing, margins, font, and length. These and other constraints will be discussed in the section on Trial Court Briefs later in this chapter.

The following subsections address the guidelines, factors, and considerations involved in the preparation of persuasive court briefs. To avoid repetition, this section addresses the factors involved in the persuasive presentation of both trial and appellate court briefs. Therefore, the detailed discussion of court briefs presented in Sections III and IV does not include information on elements and techniques of persuasive writing. The information presented here applies to the preparation of both trial and appellate court briefs, and should be kept in mind when preparing those briefs.

Ethics. As discussed in Chapter 11, Rule 3.3(a)(1) of the Model Rules of Professional Conduct provides that a lawyer should not make false statements of law or fact to a tribunal. Broadly interpreted, this means that matters should not be presented in a manner that may mislead the court. Also, under Rule 3.3(a)(3) of the Model Rules, an attorney has an ethical duty as an officer of the court to disclose legal authority adverse to the client's position that is not disclosed by opposing counsel. Therefore, when preparing a persuasive presentation of a legal position or argument, you must keep in mind the importance of the rules of professional conduct and intellectual honesty as discussed in Chapter 2. Although designed to persuade, a court brief must present the issue(s), facts statement, and analysis accurately, clearly, and concisely. It should not mislead, distort, or hide the truth. The guidelines for how this is accomplished are presented in the following subsections.

1. Issues—Persuasive Presentation

After you identify the issue, introduce each of its elements—the law, the question, and the key facts—in a persuasive manner.

Rule of law—present the rule of law or legal principle that applies.

Case law (if necessary)—follow the rule of law with the presentation of the case law that interprets how the rule of law applies:

1. Name of case
2. Facts of case sufficient to demonstrate case is on point
3. Rule or legal principle from case that applies to the client's case

Application of law to facts of case after the presentation of the case law—apply the law or principle in the case to the facts of the client's case.
　　Include an explanation of why the opposing position does not apply.

Conclusion—provide a summary of the legal analysis.

© Cengage

Exhibit 18-1 Legal Analysis—Court Brief Organizational Approach.

a. Law Component of the Issue

State the law component of the issue persuasively.

For Example

The case involves oppressive conduct by a majority shareholder against the minority shareholders in the hypothetical state of New Washington. The corporation consists of three shareholders. The majority shareholder holds 60 percent of the stock and is employed as president of the corporation. The minority shareholders are not employed by the corporation.

In the case, the defendant, the majority shareholder, controlled the board of directors and has refused to allow the issuance of dividends for a ten-year period. During this period, he gave himself an annual 40 percent raise each year and an annual bonus equal to 50 percent of his salary. The minority shareholders filed a suit claiming that the majority shareholder's actions constitute oppressive conduct.

Section 53-6 of the New Washington statutes authorizes the court to dissolve a corporation when the majority shareholder engages in oppressive conduct. This example is referred to in this chapter as the "corporation" example.

In an office memo, the law component of the issue in this example is stated objectively: "Under the New Washington corporation statute, NWSA § 53-6, did oppressive conduct occur when. . .?" In a court brief, however, the law is presented persuasively. The persuasive language is italicized: "Under the New Washington corporation statute, NWSA § 53-6, *which prohibits oppressive* conduct, did. . .?"

Note that the persuasive presentation of the law component emphasizes the prohibitory nature of the statute.

For Example

If your position is that the statute has limited application, present the law in a manner that focuses on that limitation: "Under NWSA § 51-7, which *limits the requirement of a written contract to. . . .*"

If you want to emphasize the applicability of the statute, present the law in a manner that focuses on applicability: "Under NWSA § 51-7, *which requires that a contract be in writing when. . . .*"

---

b. Question Component of the Issue

Present the question component of the issue in a persuasive manner that suggests a result.

For Example

Objective presentation: "did oppressive conduct occur when . . .?"
Persuasive presentation: "was the majority shareholder's conduct oppressive when . . .?" or "did the majority shareholder engage in oppressive conduct when . . .?"

Note that in the objective presentation, the focus is on the conduct. In the **persuasive presentation**, the statement immediately links the conduct to the majority shareholder.

The language used should focus on the desired result.

For Example

The key language is italicized: "does the statute *allow* oral contracts for . . .?" or "does the statute *require* oral contracts for . . .?" or "does the statute *prohibit* oral contracts for . . .?"

---

c. Fact Component of the Issue

State the key facts of the issue in a manner designed to focus the reader on the facts favorable to the client and persuade the reader to favor the client's position.

For Example

Objective presentation: "did oppressive conduct occur when dividends were not issued for a 10-year period and the majority shareholder received annual salary increases and bonuses?"

Persuasive presentation: "did the majority shareholder engage in oppressive conduct when he refused to issue dividends for a 10-year period while giving himself large annual salary increases and bonuses?"

For Example

Objective presentation: "when the defendant entered the property after being advised not to enter?"

Persuasive presentation: "when the defendant intentionally entered the property even though he was warned not to enter?"

Note that in both examples, the persuasive presentation focuses on the defendant and links the defendant directly to the improper conduct.

Exhibit 18-2 presents a checklist for use in the persuasive presentation of the issues.

2. Statement of Facts—Persuasive Presentation

The **statement of facts** section of a court brief presents the facts of the case. This section is often called the *statement of the case*. In a court brief, just as in an office memo, the statement of facts should include both the background and the key facts. In a court brief, introduce the facts credibly, persuasively, and in a light most favorable to the client's position. This is accomplished by emphasizing favorable facts and deemphasizing or neutralizing unfavorable facts.

There are several techniques you may use to emphasize favorable facts and neutralize unfavorable facts. Some of these are discussed in the following subsections.

a. Placement

Readers tend to remember information presented at the beginning and end of a section, and usually give most attention to opening and closing sentences. Therefore, introduce the facts favorable to the client's position at the beginning and the end of the factual statement. Present the facts unfavorable to the client's position—the ones you wish to deemphasize—in the middle of the section.

- Law component: Is the law correctly presented, stated persuasively, and accurately cited?
- Question component: Are the law, question, and key facts included and stated persuasively?
- Fact component: Are the key and background facts included and stated persuasively?

© Cengage

Exhibit 18-2 Checklist: Issues—Persuasive Presentation.

For Example

Referring to the corporation example, "The defendant is the majority shareholder and controlling member of the board of directors of XYZ Corporation. He has refused to authorize the issuance of dividends for 10 years. During this time, the defendant has been the president of the corporation. As president, he has granted himself a 40 percent raise each year. In addition, he has given himself an annual bonus equal to 50 percent of his salary. It is claimed by the defendant that he is entitled to the salary increases and bonuses because he works long hours, is underpaid, and is the person in charge. The defendant has rebuffed the plaintiff's repeated requests to discuss the defendant's grants to himself of salary increases and bonuses and failure to issue dividends. The defendant has informed the plaintiff that he does not intend to issue dividends."

In this example, the facts least favorable to the defendant—his failure to issue dividends and receipt of salary increases and bonuses—are presented at the beginning. His conduct immediately captures the reader's attention. His conduct is also mentioned again at the end of the presentation. The reader's first and last impressions are focused on the acts least favorable to the defendant. The facts favorable to the defendant—that he is entitled to the salary increases and bonuses—are deemphasized by their placement in the middle of the fact statement.

If the facts statement consists of several paragraphs, place the favorable material at the beginning of the presentation and close with a summary or rephrasing of the favorable key facts. Place the unfavorable facts in the middle of the presentation and mention them only once or as few times as possible.

Note that the goal is a persuasive presentation of the facts. This goal should not be so rigidly pursued as to lose clarity.

For Example

It may not be practical to state the favorable facts at the beginning of a paragraph. To ensure clarity, you may need to present transition or introductory sentences first, then follow them with the presentation of the favorable facts.

b. Sentence Length

Use short sentences to emphasize favorable information and long sentences to deemphasize unfavorable information. Shorter sentences generally draw the reader's attention, and are easier to understand and remember; therefore, they are more powerful.

For Example

The defendant is the majority shareholder and controlling member of the board of directors of XYZ Corporation. He has refused to authorize the issuance of dividends for ten years. During this time, the defendant has been the president of the corporation. As president, he has granted himself a 40 percent raise each year.

The sentences in this example are short and clear, drawing the reader's attention. Longer sentences that string together several facts tend to downplay and reduce the impact of each fact.

For Example

It is claimed by the defendant that he is entitled to the salary increases and bonuses because he works long hours, is underpaid, and is the person in charge.

In this example, if each of the defendant's actions were presented in separate sentences, they would stand out and be clear.

c. Active Voice

Use **active voice** to emphasize favorable information and passive voice to deemphasize unfavorable information. When active voice is used, the subject of the sentence is the actor. When passive voice is used, the subject is acted upon. Active voice draws attention to and emphasizes the actor. It thus lends power to the statement. **Passive voice** draws attention away from and deemphasizes the actor.

For Example

Passive voice: "It is claimed by the defendant that he is entitled to the bonuses ..." draws attention away from the actor, the defendant.
Active voice: "The defendant claims he is entitled ..." is less wordy and focuses the attention on the actor.

d. Word Choice

Ideally, the words you choose should introduce the client's facts in the most favorable light and the opponent's facts in the least favorable light. Present the client's position in the most affirmative manner and the opponent's position in the least favorable manner.

For Example

The plaintiff states that ....
The defendant alleges ....

In this example, notice that the plaintiff's presentation sounds stronger because it is presented as a statement. The defendant's position is presented as a charge—an "allegation" rather than a statement of fact. There are numerous ways to present positions in a strong or weak manner. Be sure to check your word choice.

It is easy, however, to get carried away and state the facts in such a slanted way that your bias is painfully obvious.

For Example

The defendant stubbornly and unreasonably refuses to issue dividends.

In this example, the presentation of the facts is clearly biased and heavy-handed. It is better just to note that the defendant has refused to issue dividends. When in doubt, avoid inflammatory language and exercise restraint.

Refer to the techniques presented in this section when preparing a persuasive presentation of the facts. Exhibit 18-3 presents a checklist for use in conjunction with the guidelines for the persuasive presentation of the statement of facts.

Chapter 9 is helpful when identifying key and background facts. Many of the considerations involved in preparing the statement of facts section of an office legal memo are the same as those involved in preparing the statement of facts section of a court brief. Chapter 16, Section V.E, therefore, will prove helpful when preparing this section.

- Placement of favorable and unfavorable facts: Are the facts favorable to the client's position placed at the beginning and end of the factual statement?
- Sentence length: Are short sentences used to emphasize favorable information and long sentences used to deemphasize unfavorable information?
- Active and passive voice: Is active voice used to emphasize favorable information and passive voice used to deemphasize unfavorable information?
- Word choice: Are words chosen that introduce the client's facts in the most favorable light and the opponent's facts in the least favorable light?

© Cengage

Exhibit 18-3 Checklist: Statement of Facts—Persuasive Presentation.

3. Argument—Persuasive Presentation

The persuasive tone of the court brief is initially established in the issue and facts statements. The persuasive techniques discussed in the previous sections of this text, such as word choice, sentence length, and active and passive voice also apply and should be employed when crafting the argument section of a court brief.

The **argument** section is the heart of the court brief. It is the equivalent of the analysis section of an office legal memorandum. Unlike the analysis section of an office memo, however, the argument section of a court brief is not an objective presentation of the law. Because the goal of the argument section is to persuade the court that your position is valid, be sure to craft it by drafting the following in a persuasive manner:

- The law in support of your position
- The analysis of the law
- The argument that your analysis is valid and the opposition's analysis is invalid

The following text presents a summary of the techniques you may use to ensure that you present the argument component of a court brief in a persuasive manner. Several helpful guidelines apply to both trial and appellate court briefs. Sections III and IV of this chapter introduce additional information concerning the format and content of the argument section. Those sections focus on the differences between trial and appellate court briefs.

Organization. The organization of the argument section is similar to that of the analysis section of the office memo: The rule of law is introduced, followed by an interpretation of the law (usually through case law), then an application of the law to the issue raised by the facts of the case. The opposing position is included in the presentation of the argument rather than in a separate counteranalysis section.

1. Issue presentation. When there is more than one issue or when there are issues and subissues, discuss the issue supported by the strongest argument first. There are several reasons for this:

   - First impressions are lasting. The tone of the argument is set at the beginning. By presenting the strongest argument first, you set a tone of strength and credibility.
   - If you introduce the strongest argument first, the court is more likely to be persuaded that your position is correct and look more favorably on your weaker arguments.
   - Judges are often very busy. On some occasions a judge may not read or give equal attention to all the sections of a brief, especially if the brief is long. In such instances, the judge may not read your strongest argument if you do not present it first or near the beginning of the brief. For this reason, if there are several arguments in support of a position, omit the weak arguments. Weak arguments or positions that have little supporting authority detract and divert attention from the stronger arguments.

2. Rule of law presentation. Present the rule of law, whether it is enacted or case law, in a manner that supports your argument.

For Example

Objective presentation: The statute that *governs oppressive conduct* is....
Persuasive presentation: The statute that *prohibits* oppressive conduct by a majority shareholder is....
The first example merely indicates that the statute governs the area. The second example persuasively emphasizes the prohibitory nature of the statute.

Objective presentation: The courts of other states are split on what constitutes oppressive conduct. Most courts follow *Smith v. Jones*, which provides. . . . A minority of courts follow *Dave v. Roe*. . . . The majority view is based on the premise that the conduct must be either wrongful or improper . . . .

Persuasive presentation: The majority of courts follow the definition of *oppressive conduct* presented in *Smith v. Jones*. In this case, the court defined *oppressive conduct* as. . . . This definition is based on the well-reasoned view that the conduct need only be wrongful or improper. A minority of courts follow. . . .

In this example, the persuasive presentation more forcefully introduces the majority view in a manner indicating that it is preferable. The objective view is passive and treats both the majority and minority views equally. It does not emphasize one view as favorable. Refer to the section in the chapter on the persuasive presentation of issues when drafting the rule of law component of the argument section of a brief.

3. Case presentation. When introducing case law, discuss the favorable case law first, follow with the unfavorable or opposing case law, then include a response or rebuttal that emphasizes why the favorable case law should be followed. This is similar to the format followed in the facts statement: The placement of the unfavorable material in the middle of the presentation following the favorable material tends to minimize its importance.

The discussion of the case law should emphasize the similarities and applicability of the case you rely on and the dissimilarities and inapplicability of the case relied on by the opposition.

For Example

The term *oppressive conduct* is defined in the case of *Tyrone v. Blatt.* In *Tyrone*, the majority shareholder refused to authorize the issuance of dividends. He granted himself four major pay increases, quadrupling his salary during the period dividends were not issued. In the holding, the court noted there was no justification for the salary increases and ruled his conduct was oppressive. The court stated "oppressive conduct" occurs when there is wrongful conduct that inures to the benefit of the majority shareholder and to the detriment of the minority shareholders.

In the matter before this court, just as in *Tyrone*, the *majority* shareholder refused to issue dividends. In the present case, like *Tyrone*, the majority shareholder gave himself large salary increases. In both cases, there was no justification for the increases. Therefore, the court should apply the standard established in *Tyrone* and find that the defendant engaged in oppressive conduct.

It is argued by the defendant that the court should apply the holding reached in *Wise v. Wind* and find the defendant's conduct was not oppressive. The defendant's reliance on *Wise* is misplaced. In *Wise*, there was evidence that the salary increases were justified.

Here, in the matter before this court, the situation is distinguishable. There is no evidence that the salary increases the defendant awarded himself and his refusal to issue dividends were justified. Therefore, the *Wise* opinion is not on point and is not applicable. The *Tyrone* opinion is on point and should be followed.

4. Argument order. When interpreting and applying a rule of law, always introduce your arguments first, address the counterargument, then present your response. In addition, spend more time affirmatively stating your position than responding to the opponent's counterargument. There are several reasons for this:

- As with the presentation of the facts statement and organization of the argument, the reader tends to remember and emphasize information presented at the beginning and end of a section or paragraph. You want to draw attention to and emphasize your argument; therefore, address it first.

- By introducing your argument first, you have the opportunity to soften the impact of the opposing argument through the strong presentation of your position.

- In a busy court, if you discuss your position or argument after the opponent's, you run the risk of it not being read or given equal attention by the court.
- By following the counterargument with a response or rebuttal that sums up your position, you move the counterargument further from the reader's attention. It is buried in the middle of the argument where its significance is downplayed and deemphasized. The defendant's position is italicized in the following example.

For Example

It is appropriate for the court to allow admission of the INDM test results. The court of appeals in *State v. Digo* ruled scientific tests are admissible when the reliability and scientific basis of the test are recognized by competent authorities. The INDM test, developed in 1985, is universally accepted by all competent authorities as scientifically valid. *The defendant argues the test results should not be relied on by the court. Defendant relies on the case of Ard v. State to support this argument. Defendant's reliance on Ard v. State is misplaced. In the 1985 case, the court of appeals did not allow the admission of the INDM test results because the INDM was a new test not universally accepted.* The ruling in *Ard* is no longer applicable. The INDM test is no longer a new test and is universally used and accepted.

5. Word choice. Careful **word choice** is an invaluable aid when crafting a persuasive argument. You can significantly enhance the argument by the use of forceful, positive, and confident language.

For Example

Ineffective: We believe that the defendant engaged in oppressive conduct.
Effective: The defendant engaged in oppressive conduct.
Ineffective: It is the defendant's position that the search was illegal. . . .
Effective: The search was illegal. . . .

Present the opposing position in a manner that deemphasizes its importance or *credibility*.

For Example

Ineffective: The defendant states . . . .
Effective: The defendant alleges . . . .
Ineffective: The defendant's position is . . . .
Effective: The defendant claims . . . .

6. Issue headings. **Issue headings** are a summary of the position advocated in the argument. They are presented at the beginning of each argument. The next section of this chapter will address the details of format, content, and presentation of issue headings. This section discusses the persuasive nature and presentation of issue headings.

The persuasive role of an issue heading is to focus the reader on the position advocated in the argument. Therefore, draft an issue heading in a manner that provides a positive presentation of that position.

For Example

Not persuasive: The court should not grant the motion to suppress. . . . The photos of the victim were inflammatory and should not have been admitted into evidence by the trial court.

Persuasive: The court should deny the motion to suppress. . . . The inflammatory nature of the photographs of the victim outweighs their probative value, and their admission was highly prejudicial to the defendant and was improper.

The difference in the two presentations in this example is that the persuasive presentation more affirmatively and positively characterizes the position argued. The discussions in the previous section concerning word choice and active voice apply to issue headings.

Exhibit 18-4 presents a checklist for use in the persuasive presentation of the argument in a court brief.

III. TRIAL COURT BRIEFS

When a motion is filed in court, procedural rules often require a memorandum in support of the motion, sometimes called a *memorandum of points and authorities*, to be filed with the motion. Recall, these types of documents are referred to as trial briefs in this chapter. In other instances, when the procedural rules have not required a trial brief to be filed, a trial court is in the process of ruling on a motion or an issue in a case, the judge may require the attorneys to submit a memorandum of law. The trial brief presents the legal authority and argument in support of the position advocated by the attorney.

A trial brief is similar to an office memo in many respects. Both are designed to inform the reader how the law applies to the issues raised by the facts of the case. Most of the considerations involved in the preparation of an office memo also apply to the preparation of a trial brief. Therefore, when preparing a trial brief, refer to Chapters 16 and 17, in addition to this chapter, for guidance.

The guidelines for preparing a persuasive trial brief were discussed in the previous section. This section addresses other considerations involved in preparing a trial brief, such as the writing process.

Argument organization:	Follow the standard organizational format: rule of law, followed by the interpretation of the law through case law, followed by the application of the law to the issue.
Issue presentation:	If there is more than one issue, discuss the issue supported by the strongest argument first.
Rule of law presentation:	Present the rule of law in a manner that supports your argument.
Case presentation:	Discuss favorable cases first, followed by unfavorable cases, then a rebuttal emphasizing why the favorable cases should be followed.
Argument order:	When applying the rule of law, introduce your argument first, then the counterarguments, and conclude with your response.
Argument word choice:	Present your argument with forceful, positive, and confident language.
Argument issue heading:	Draft issue headings persuasively.

© Cengage

Exhibit 18-4 Checklist: Argument—Persuasive Presentation.

A. Audience

The audience for the trial brief is the judge assigned to the case. Trial court judges are usually busy people, with heavy caseloads, who may rule on several motions a day. They may not have time to carefully read lengthy briefs. Therefore, a judge usually appreciates a well-organized, concise presentation of the law.

B. Constraints

Court rules are procedural rules that govern the litigation process. Most trial courts have rules that govern various aspects of a trial brief, such as format and style including spacing, length, margins, font, and organization of content. The major constraints on a trial brief are usually imposed by these court rules, so be sure to consult the applicable rules when preparing a trial brief.

For Example

A local rule may establish a maximum length of a trial brief and require the court's permission before that length can be exceeded.

Usually there is a time constraint on the preparation and filing of trial briefs. The court or the local rules often require that the brief be submitted within a certain number of days. Know the time deadline and allocate your time accordingly. If a deadline for submitting a trial brief cannot be met, procedural rules usually require that a motion requesting additional time be filed and be granted before the trial brief can be filed outside the original deadline.

C. Format or Content

The format of a trial brief varies among courts and among jurisdictions. In many instances, the local court rules establish a required format. Generally, a trial court brief includes some or all of the components presented in Exhibit 18-5.

Each of the components in Exhibit 18-5 is briefly discussed in the following subsections. For examples of these components, refer to the Application section of this chapter and Appendix B.

1. Caption

Every brief submitted to a trial court requires a caption. The format varies from court to court, but the caption usually includes:

- The name of the court.
- The names and status of the parties.
- The file number and type of case—civil or criminal.
- The title of the document, such as BRIEF IN SUPPORT OF MOTION TO DISMISS.

Refer to the Application section of this chapter for an example of a caption.

Caption
Table of contents
Table of authorities
Preliminary statements
Question(s) presented/issue(s)
Statement of the case (fact statement)
Argument
Conclusion

© Cengage

Exhibit 18-5 Components of Trial Court Brief.

2. Table of Contents and Table of Authorities

Generally, trial briefs do not require a table of contents or a table of authorities. An exception may be if a judge directs the parties to prepare and file briefs on an issue that arises during a hearing or during trial itself. If a table of contents or table of authorities is required in a trial brief, they take the same format as those filed in appellate briefs. Consult the section on appellate court briefs later in this chapter for guidance on creating a table of contents or table of authorities if you need to prepare one for a trial court brief.

3. Preliminary Statement

The **preliminary statement** introduces the procedural posture of the case. It usually includes:

- An identification of the parties.
- The procedural events in the case relevant to the matter the court is addressing.
- A description of the matter being addressed by the court, such as "This matter is before the court on a motion to dismiss the complaint."
- The relief sought, such as "This memorandum is submitted in support of the motion to suppress the evidence seized during the search."

For Example

PRELIMINARY STATEMENT
Edna and Ida Tule, the plaintiffs, are minority shareholders in Tule, Inc. Their brother, Thomas Tule, is the defendant in this action, the majority shareholder, and president of Tule, Inc. On January 9 of this year, a request for the production of company records relating to salary increases and bonuses granted to Mr. Tule was delivered to him. Mr. Tule refuses to produce the company records. This memorandum is submitted in support of a motion to compel the production of those documents.

4. Question(s) Presented

This section of a brief persuasively presents the legal issue(s) addressed in the brief. The issue should include the rule of law, legal question, and the key facts. When there is more than one issue, list the issues in the order they are discussed in the argument section of the brief. The techniques for persuasively drafting the issue were discussed in the preceding section of this chapter. Chapter 16 addresses the presentation of the issue(s) in an office memo. Refer to that chapter when preparing the issue.

5. Statement of the Case

This section is often referred to as the *statement of facts*. It corresponds to the statement of facts section of an office memo. Its purpose is to introduce the facts of the case in a light that most favors the client's position. The persuasive nature of the facts section was discussed in the preceding section of this chapter. That subsection and the Application section of this chapter introduce examples of persuasive statements of facts. The facts section should be accurate and complete and should include background and key facts. For additional guidance when drafting the facts section, refer to Chapter 16.

6. Argument Section

The argument section of a trial brief, like the analysis section of an office memo, is the heart of the document. It differs from the analysis section of an office memo in that it is not an objective legal analysis. Rather, it is designed to persuade the court to adopt your interpretation of the law. The considerations involved in crafting the argument in a persuasive manner were discussed in the preceding section of this chapter. This section addresses the basic organization of the argument and the components. Exhibit 18-6 presents the organization and components of this section.

1. Summary of argument
2. Issue headings
3. Argument
    Rule of law
    Case law (if necessary) interpretation of rule of law
    Application of law to the issue being addressed
        Discussion of opposing position (similar to counteranalysis in office
        legal memorandum)

© Cengage

Exhibit 18-6   Organization and Components of Argument Section of Trial Brief.

The format in Exhibit 18-6 is recommended; however, it is not necessarily followed in every office, and a different format may be required by local court rule. In some instances, a summary of the argument may not be required, and some local court rules and office formats do not require issue headings. This is often true when the brief is short and involves a single issue. Nevertheless, all of the components of the argument section are presented here so that you will be familiar with them when they are required.

a. Summary of Argument

The argument section of a trial brief should begin with an introductory paragraph that summarizes the argument. It presents the context of the argument, the issues in the order in which they will be discussed, a summary of the conclusions regarding each issue, and the major reasons supporting each conclusion.

For Example

On December 12, 2011, John Jones, the defendant, was arrested for possession of cocaine. On January 1, 2012, he was indicted for possession of 4 ounces of cocaine. The trial commenced on October 25, 2012. On November 11, 2012, he was found guilty by a jury and convicted of possession of 4 ounces of cocaine. This matter is before the court on Mr. Jones's motion for a new trial, filed March 7, 2013. Mr. Jones's motion is based on the claim that new evidence has been uncovered showing that the drugs belonged to a Mr. Tom Smith, a visitor in Mr. Jones's home. For a new trial to be granted on the basis of newly discovered evidence, Mr. Jones must demonstrate that the newly discovered evidence was not available or discoverable at the time of trial. The information concerning Mr. Smith was available at the time of trial. The defense made no effort to interview Mr. Smith or in any way discover whether the drugs belonged to him. The evidence regarding Mr. Smith is not newly discovered evidence, and the motion should be denied.

The use of an argument summary is valuable when you believe the judge may not have time to read the entire brief. It may not be necessary if the brief is short or when a single issue is involved. It should be a complete summary; the reader should not have to refer to the body of the argument to understand the summary.

b. Issue Headings

Issue headings are summaries of the position you are asking the court to adopt. They should be drafted persuasively. The guidelines for drafting persuasive point headings in an argument were discussed in the preceding section of this chapter.

Issue headings are designed to:

- Organize, define, and emphasize the structure of the argument.
- Act as locators that allow the reader to quickly find specific sections of the argument.
- Focus the court's attention on the outcome you advocate and provide an outline of your theory.

Issue headings may not be required in a trial brief, especially when the brief is short or addresses only a single issue. In such instances, they are not needed as an organizational tool, nor are they needed to guide the reader. Check the court rules and office format to determine when they are required.

In regard to issue headings, note the following guidelines:

1. Place the point headings at the beginning of each section of the argument and include them in the table of contents.
2. Divide the issue headings into major and minor point headings. There should be a major issue heading for each issue presented. Use minor headings to introduce significant subissues supporting the major heading.

For Example

ARGUMENT

I. THE TRIAL COURT ERRED WHEN IT RULED THAT MR. SMITH'S CONDUCT DID NOT CONSTITUTE BREACH OF CONTRACT BECAUSE THE GOODS WERE DEFECTIVE AND DELIVERED LATE.

    A. <u>Mr. Smith's delivery of the widgets ten days late constituted a breach of the contract</u>. (text of argument)

    B. <u>The delivery of the widgets with a 5-pound spring instead of a 10-pound spring constituted a breach of the contract</u>. (text of argument)

3. Each heading and subheading should be a complete sentence.
4. Each heading should identify the legal conclusion you want the court to adopt and the basic reasons supporting the conclusion.

For Example

THE TESTIMONY OF DR. SMITH IS PROBATIVE OF THE DEFENDANT'S INTENT AND THEREFORE IS ADMISSIBLE.

    THE DISTRICT COURT'S SUPPRESSION OF THE EVIDENCE WAS IMPROPER BECAUSE THE SEARCH WARRANT WAS SUPPORTED BY PROBABLE CAUSE.

5. Use minor headings only if there are two or more. The rules of outlining require more than one subheading when subheadings are used. Minor headings present aspects of a major issue heading in the context of the specific facts of the case. Note that the minor issue headings in the example in number 2 above present two aspects of the major issue heading. State the minor point headings in the specific context of the facts of the case:

    A. <u>Mr. Smith's delivery of the widgets ten days late constituted a breach of the contract.</u>

    B. <u>The delivery of the widgets with a 5-pound spring instead of a 10-pound spring constituted a breach of the contract.</u>

6. Type major headings in ALL CAPITALS and minor headings in regular upper and lower case. Minor headings may be underlined. Check the court rules for the proper format. The preceding example in number 2 illustrates the format for major and minor point headings.

c. Argument Format

The argument section of the trial brief is similar to the analysis section of an office memo; refer to Chapter 17 when preparing a trial brief. The same basic IRAC format is followed:

    Rule of law

    Case law (if necessary)—interpretation of rule of law

        1. Name of case
        2. Facts of case—sufficient to demonstrate the case is on point
        3. Rule or legal principle from case that applies to the issue being addressed

Application of law to the issue being addressed

Discussion of opposing position (similar to counteranalysis in office legal memorandum)

The major difference between the argument component of an office memo and that of a trial brief is that the trial brief introduces the argument in a persuasive rather than an objective manner.

7. Conclusion

The **conclusion** section of a trial brief requests the specific relief desired. Depending on the complexity of the brief, it may be a single sentence stating the requested relief or a summary of the entire argument.

For Example

Single sentence: For the foregoing reasons, the defendant requests that the motion to dismiss be granted.

A single-sentence conclusion is appropriate when the trial brief is a simple, one- or two-issue brief, and the argument section concludes with a summary of the analysis. When the trial brief is longer and more complicated, the conclusion may include an overall summary of the law presented in the argument section and end with a request for relief. This type of conclusion is similar to the conclusion section of an office memo discussed in Chapter 17. Note the conclusion should summarize the argument section and reflect the persuasive nature of the argument.

IV. APPELLATE COURT BRIEFS

An individual who disagrees with the decision of a trial or lower court may appeal the decision to a court of appeals. The individual who appeals is called the **appellant**, and the individual who opposes the appeal is called the **appellee**. On appeal, the appellant argues that the lower court made an error, the error affected the outcome of the case, and the appellant is entitled to relief. The appellee argues that the lower court did not commit an error that entitles the appellant to relief.

An appellate court brief is an external memorandum of law submitted to a court of appeals. It presents the legal analysis, authority, and argument in support of a position that the lower court's decision or ruling was either correct or incorrect. The format and style of the appellate brief is strictly governed by appellate court rules, and these rules must be consulted when preparing an appellate brief.

The preparation of an appellate brief is a complex undertaking, and a detailed discussion of this subject is beyond the scope of this chapter. Entire texts (available at the local law library) address the detailed considerations involved in preparing an appellate brief. You should refer to those texts when assigned the task of preparing an appellate brief.

Paralegals and law clerks are not usually required to draft appellate briefs. However, they may be called upon to assist in the preparation or finalization of the brief and, therefore, should be familiar with its components. This section summarizes considerations regarding the format and basic components of an appellate brief.

An appellate brief, like a trial brief, is designed to advocate a legal position and to persuade the court to adopt the position argued in the brief. Therefore, you should draft the brief in a persuasive manner. The discussion of the persuasive nature of court briefs, presented earlier in this chapter, applies to the preparation of appellate briefs; that is, an appellate brief should be crafted in a persuasive manner.

An appellate brief, like a trial brief, is similar to an office memo in many respects. For example, a writing process should be used when preparing both briefs. Therefore, in addition to this chapter, refer to Chapters 15 through 17 when performing an appellate brief assignment.

A. Audience

A trial court brief is submitted to a single judge, the trial judge assigned to the case. The audience for the appellate brief is usually a panel of three or more judges. In addition, the judge's law clerk usually reads the brief; on many occasions, the law clerk is the first to read the brief. Although you are writing to a wider audience, the same basic considerations are involved in the preparation of trial court and appellate court briefs. Appellate court judges, like trial court judges, are usually busy persons with substantial caseloads, so they appreciate an appellate brief that is a well-organized and concise presentation of the law.

B. Constraints

The major constraints on appellate briefs are imposed by the court's rules. The appellate court rules differ from trial court rules in that they are usually much more detailed than trial court rules: The appellate court rules may establish the sections that must be included, the format of each of the sections, the type of paper, the citation form, a maximum length for the briefs, and a requirement that permission of the court be obtained before the specified length can be exceeded, and so on. Always consult the appellate court rules when preparing an appellate brief.

C. Format or Content

The format of an appellate brief varies among jurisdictions. Generally, the basic appellate court brief includes some or all of the components presented in Exhibit 18-7.

The following subsections briefly discuss each of the components of the appellate brief. Refer to the appellate brief presented in Appendix B for an example of the components.

1. Cover Page/Title Page

The court rules govern the format of the cover page, often called the *title page*. The cover page usually includes the following:

- Name of the appellate court
- Number assigned to the appeal
- Parties' names and appellate status (appellant and appellee or petitioner and respondent)
- Name of the lower court from which the appeal is taken
- Names and addresses of the attorney(s) submitting the brief

2. Table of Contents/Index

Sometimes referred to as an *index*, the **table of contents** lists the major and minor sections of the brief and the page number on which each section begins. The table of contents provides the reader with a reference tool for locating specific information within the brief. The table includes the issue headings and subheadings. The issue headings, when included in the table of contents, provide the reader with an overview of the legal arguments and allow the reader to easily locate the discussion of the arguments in the brief.

3. Table of Authorities

The **table of authorities** lists all the law cited in the brief. The authorities are listed by category, such as constitutional law, statutory law, regulations, and case law. The table includes the full citation of each authority and the page number or numbers on which it appears.

> Cover page/title page
> Table of contents/index
> Table of authorities
> Opinions below/related appeals
> Jurisdictional statement
> Question/issue(s) presented
> Statement of the case/statement of facts
> Summary of argument
> Argument
> Conclusion
>
> © Cengage

Exhibit 18-7 Components of a Basic Appellate Court Brief.

4. Opinions Below/Related Appeals

The brief *may* include a section that references any prior opinions on the case or related appeals.

For Example

From a Supreme Court brief: The opinion of the Court of Appeals is reported at 580 F.2d 501. The order of the District Court is not reported.

5. Jurisdictional Statement

The brief usually includes a separate section that introduces, in a short statement, the subject matter jurisdiction of the appellate court.

For Example

This court has jurisdiction under 42 U.S.C. § 1983.

Some appellate rules do not require a **jurisdictional statement**. Some appellate rules require, in addition to the jurisdictional statement, a history of the case and how the matter came before the court.

For Example

The judgment of the trial court was entered on October 5, 2012. The notice of appeal was filed on October 26, 2013. The jurisdiction of the court is invoked under 42 U.S.C. § 1983.

6. Question(s) Presented

This section may also be referred to as *legal issues* or *assignment of error*. The section lists the legal issues the party is requesting the court to consider. List the issues in the order they are addressed in the argument section, and write them in a persuasive manner as discussed earlier in this chapter.

7. Statement of the Case/Statement of Facts

The statement of the case section, often referred to as the *statement of facts*, is generally similar to the statement of facts section of the trial brief, and the same considerations apply when preparing both.

The statement of the case in an appellate brief, however, differs from the statement of facts in a trial brief in that the statement of the case should also include a summary of the prior proceedings (what happened in the lower court) and appropriate references to the record. In the following example, "Tr." refers to the pages in the transcript of the trial record, and "Doc." refers to documents included in the record on appeal.

For Example

After the presentation of the key and background facts of the case, the information concerning the prior proceedings might read:

At the hearing on the motion to suppress, held on December 12, 2016, the trial court denied the motion to suppress. (Tr. at 37) At the hearing, Officer Smith, the officer conducting the search, testified . . . (Tr. at 33). The trial court stated that there were sufficient exigent circumstances present at the scene to support the unannounced entry by the officers. (Tr. at 38)

Trial was held on January 15, 2017. (Tr. at 201) On January 18, 2017, the jury found the defendant guilty of possession of an ounce of cocaine. (Tr. at 291) On January 28, 2017, the defendant filed a notice of appeal. (Doc. 44) On March 7, 2017, the defendant was sentenced to a term of imprisonment of five years. (Doc. 49)

---

8. Summary of Argument

This section may be optional under the appellate court rule. Rule 28 of the Federal Rules of Appellate Procedure states that the argument may be preceded by a summary. The content of an argument summary was discussed in the preceding section of this chapter.

9. Argument Section

a. Issue Headings

The considerations involved in preparing point headings are the same for appellate and trial court briefs. Refer to the discussion of issue headings in the preceding section of this chapter when preparing issue headings for appellate briefs.

b. Body

The argument section of an appellate brief is similar to the argument section of a trial brief. The format is the same as in a trial brief. Refer to the section on drafting the argument portion of trial briefs in this chapter when preparing the argument section of an appellate brief. Remember to present the argument section of an appellate brief in a persuasive manner.

10. Conclusion

Prepare the conclusion section of an appellate brief in the same way as the conclusion of a trial brief. The content, structure, and considerations involved are the same for both.

V. KEY POINTS CHECKLIST: External Memoranda–Court Briefs

✓ Trial and appellate briefs are similar to office memoranda in many fundamental respects. Refer to Chapters 15 through 17 when preparing them.

✓ The writing fundamentals presented in Chapter 14 apply to all legal writing and should be kept in mind when preparing court briefs.

✓ Remember to craft the brief persuasively. Court briefs are designed to persuade the reader to adopt the position taken or recommended in the analysis. They are not supposed to present a purely objective analysis.

✓ Deemphasize the position taken by the opposition. Part of the persuasive nature of a court brief is to downplay and discredit the opponent's position. This is accomplished through the use of passive voice, long sentences, placement of the opposing argument in the middle of the analysis, and so on.

✓ Always check the court rules. The format, length, and so on of court briefs are often governed by the rules of the court. The appellate court rules extensively govern most aspects of appellate briefs.

✓ The required components of trial and appellate court briefs may vary among jurisdictions. Some of the components discussed in this chapter may not be required or necessary, such as a table of contents, table of authorities, or argument summary. This is often true when the analysis is brief.

VI. APPLICATION

This section illustrates the guidelines and principles discussed in this chapter by applying them to the hypothetical presented at the beginning of the chapter. The paralegal, Pam Hayes, approaches this assignment through the use of an expanded outline, as discussed in Chapter 15. She also follows the guidelines and principles discussed in Chapters 16 and 17 to the extent they apply to the preparation of a trial brief. What follows is a presentation of the trial brief prepared by Ms. Hayes and comments on the brief.

In regard to the assignment, Ms. Hayes found the following New Washington law on point:

Statutory Law. Chapter 70 of the New Washington Statutes, the Ski Safety Act, governs ski resorts and the sport of skiing. New Washington Statutes Annotated (NWSA) § 70-11-7A provides, "The ski area operator shall have the duty to mark conspicuously with the appropriate symbol or sign those slopes, trails, or areas which are closed or which present an unusual obstacle or hazard." Furthermore, NWSA § 70-11-8B provides, "A person who takes part in the sport of skiing accepts as a matter of law the dangers inherent in that sport, and each skier expressly assumes the risk and legal responsibility for any injury to a person or property which results from . . . surface or subsurface snow or ice conditions. . . ."

Case Law. In *Karen v. High Mountain Pass*, 55 N. Wash. 462, 866 N.E. 995 (Ct. App. 1994), a skier broke his leg after failing to negotiate a series of moguls that were present in the middle of a sharp turn on a ski run. The moguls were unavoidable. The trial court granted the resort's motion to dismiss for failure to state a claim. On appeal, the court of appeals stated that skiers are responsible for snow and ice hazards, and moguls, even though unavoidable, are snow hazards easily observable and routinely present on most ski runs. The court went on to state that under the statute, the skier assumes the risk of snow and ice hazards that are easily observable and routinely encountered on ski runs, and resorts have no duty to warn of such hazards under NWSA § 70-11-7A.

In *Aster v. White Mountain Resort*, 55 N. Wash. 756, 866 N.E. 421 (Ct. App. 1994), a skier was skiing a newly opened intermediate run. Several fairly large rocks had not been removed from the run. Normally, the rocks would have been removed before the run was opened. The rocks were covered by approximately two and one-half feet of new snow and were not visible. The resort did not post a warning that the large rocks were present on the run. Mr. Aster hit a rock with the tip of his ski, lost control, and injured his knee and back. The trial court, in granting the resort's motion to dismiss for failure to state a claim, held that the hazard was a snow hazard for which the skier was responsible under NWSA § 70-11-8B. On appeal, the court of appeals noted that the snow condition was an unavoidable latent hazard. The court ruled that under NWSA § 70-11-7A, a resort has a duty to warn of hazardous snow conditions if they are unavoidable and latent. The court stated, "The statute will not be interpreted to reach an absurd result, and requiring a skier to be responsible for unavoidable latent hazards would lead to an absurd result. Skiers are only responsible for those unavoidable snow or ice conditions which are not latent or unobservable."

Myron v. Cox Inc., 40 N. Wash. 210, 740 N.E. 309 (1989), sets the standard for the granting of a Rule 12(b)(6) motion to dismiss. The court stated, "A Rule 12(b)(6) motion to dismiss is properly granted only if it appears that there is no provable set of facts which entitles the plaintiff to relief."

A. Trial Brief

The following is the trial brief prepared by Ms. Hayes.

LINCOLN COUNTY DISTRICT COURT STATE OF NEW WASHINGTON

NO. CIV. O13-601

NICK SHINE,
    Plaintiff,

vs.

BLUE SKY SKI RESORT,
    Defendant.

BRIEF IN OPPOSITION TO MOTION TO DISMISS
PRELIMINARY STATEMENT

On December 5, 2015, Nick Shine, the plaintiff, was injured while skiing on a ski run at Blue Sky Ski Resort. He was injured skiing on an ice hazard that the resort admits was not marked with any type of warning sign. Mr. Shine filed a complaint against the resort for negligence in failing to warn of the hazard. The resort has filed a Rule 12(b)(6) motion to dismiss for failure to state a claim, alleging that it does not have a duty to warn of ice hazards. This memorandum is submitted in opposition to that motion.

QUESTION PRESENTED

Under the New Washington Ski Safety Act, sections 70-11-1 et seq., can a negligence claim be stated when a skier is injured on an unmarked ice hazard that is unavoidable and unobservable by the skier due to the sun glare?

STATEMENT OF THE CASE

On December 5, 2015, Mr. Shine, an expert skier, was skiing on an intermediate ski run at Blue Sky Ski Resort. Midway through the run there is a slightly uphill turn to the south. When Mr. Shine encountered the turn, the sun was directly in his eyes, and the glare prevented him from seeing that the trail was entirely covered with ice. Due to the glare, he was unable to avoid the dangerous ice hazard. He hit the ice and immediately lost control. As a result, he slid into a tree and broke his left arm and leg. No signs warning of the ice hazard were present.

On April 6, 2016, Mr. Shine filed a negligence complaint against Blue Sky Ski Resort for the resort's negligent failure to warn of the unavoidable ice hazard. On April 20, 2016, the resort filed a motion to dismiss under Rule 12(b)(6), alleging that they do not have a duty to warn of ice hazards, and therefore, as a matter of law, a claim for negligence cannot be stated.

ARGUMENT

MR. SHINE'S ARGUMENT THAT THE ICE HAZARD IS UNAVOIDABLE AND LATENT IS A SET OF FACTS WHICH, IF PROVEN, WOULD ESTABLISH THE DEFENDANT'S DUTY TO WARN AND, THEREFORE, A CLAIM CAN BE STATED AS TO DUTY.

This matter is before the court on a Rule 12(b)(6) motion to dismiss for failure to state a claim. In the case of *Myron v. Cox, Inc.*, 40 N. Wash. 210, 215, 740 N.E. 309, 314 (1989), the New Washington Supreme Court established the standard for the granting of a 12(b)(6) motion. The court stated, "A Rule 12(b)(6) motion to dismiss is properly granted only if it appears that there is no provable set of facts which entitles the plaintiff to relief." Blue Sky Ski Resort's motion specifically alleges that a claim cannot be stated in this case in regard to duty. To survive this motion, Mr. Shine must demonstrate that there is a provable set of facts that would establish the duty of Blue Sky to warn of the ice hazard in this case.

The Ski Safety Act establishes the duties of ski resorts and skiers. Section 70-11-7A sets out the duties of the resort; it provides, "The ski area operator shall have the duty to mark conspicuously with the appropriate symbol or sign those slopes, trails, or areas which are closed or which present an unusual obstacle or hazard."

Section 70-11-8B sets out the duties and responsibilities of the skier:

"A person who takes part in the sport of skiing accepts as a matter of law the dangers inherent in that sport, and each skier expressly assumes the risk and legal responsibility for any injury to a person or property which results from . . . surface or subsurface snow or ice conditions. . . ."

The act does not define the terms "hazard" or "snow and ice conditions." The statute also does not provide guidance as to which duty applies in a fact situation such as the one presented in this case. New Washington case law, however, does provide guidance.

The controlling case is *Aster v. White Mountain Resort*, 55 N. Wash. 756, 866 N.E. 421 (Ct. App. 1994). In the *Aster* case, Mr. Aster was skiing on a newly opened run from which several fairly large rocks had not been removed. Normally, the rocks would have been removed before the run was opened. The rocks were covered by approximately two and one-half feet of new snow and were not visible. The resort did not post a warning that the large rocks were present on the run. Mr. Aster hit a rock with the tip of his ski, lost control, and was injured. The court ruled that under NWSA § 70-11-7A, a resort has a duty to warn of hazardous snow conditions if they are unavoidable and latent. The court stated, "The statute will not be interpreted to reach an absurd result, and requiring a skier to be responsible for unavoidable latent hazards would lead to an absurd result. Skiers are only responsible for those unavoidable snow or ice conditions which are not latent or unobservable." *Id.* at 759.

Mr. Shine's complaint, like the complaint in the *Aster* case, states that the ice condition encountered was an unavoidable latent hazard. Under *Aster*, the resort has the duty under § 70-11-7A to warn of such hazards. Under the rule adopted in *Aster*, Mr. Shine's complaint does present a provable set of facts that establishes a claim as to duty and entitles him to relief. Therefore, the motion to dismiss should be denied.

It is contended by Blue Sky that they do not have a duty to warn of the ice hazard, and in support of this contention, they rely on *Karen v. High Mountain Pass*, 55 N. Wash. 462, 866 N.E. 995 (Ct. App. 1994). In this case, a skier broke his leg after failing to negotiate a series of moguls that were present in the middle of a sharp turn of a ski run. The moguls were obvious to the skier but unavoidable. The trial court granted the resort's motion to dismiss for failure to state a claim. On appeal, the court of appeals, in upholding the trial court, held that under the statute, the skier assumes the risk of snow and ice hazards that are easily observable and routinely present on ski runs.

Blue Sky's reliance on *Karen* is misplaced. The case is clearly distinguishable. The snow condition in *Karen*, though unavoidable, was clearly observable, and moguls are routinely present on ski runs. Skiers are aware that they will encounter moguls and know they must be able to navigate them. Ice conditions also may be encountered on ski runs. The ice condition Mr. Shine encountered, however, was not a routine ice condition. It was unobservable, unavoidable, and extremely dangerous due to the glare of the sun. The *Karen* case involves observable, routine snow hazards. The present case involves unobservable ice hazards that are not routinely encountered. *Karen* is obviously not on point and is not controlling in this case.

The hazard Mr. Shine encountered was identical in nature to the hazard in the *Aster* case: the ice condition was an unavoidable, latent hazard. Under the holding in *Aster*, the resort has a duty under § 70-11-7A to warn of this type of hazard. Mr. Shine's complaint argues that the hazard is an unavoidable and latent hazard. The complaint presents a provable set of facts in regard to duty upon which relief can be granted, and therefore, a claim for duty can be stated and the motion to dismiss should be denied.

CONCLUSION

Blue Sky Ski Resort's motion to dismiss for failure to state a claim should be denied. Mr. Shine's argument that the ice condition constitutes a latent hazard is a provable set of facts that entitles him to relief.

B. Comments

1. Note that the preceding example of a trial brief does not have a table of contents or a table of authorities. When a trial brief is short or involves a single issue and few authorities, these tables may not be required. Be sure to check the local court rule.
2. The preliminary statement presented at the beginning of the brief is often called an *introduction*.
3. A summary of the argument section is not included in this brief. A summary of the argument is usually included in an appellate brief, but not always in a trial brief. It is useful in a trial brief, and may be necessary when there are several issues or the analysis is complex, but it is not necessary when the analysis involves a single issue or is not complex.
4. Note the persuasive tone of the brief:

   - The statement of the case introduces the facts with language that favors the client: "dangerous hazard," "he immediately lost control."
   - The statement of the case and argument sections state the client's position in short, clear sentences using active voice. The opponent's position is presented in a long sentence using the passive voice: "It is contended by Blue Sky that they do not have a duty to warn of the ice hazard. . . ."
   - The argument section downplays the opposition's position. It is placed in the middle of the argument and is immediately discounted after it is presented.
   - The conclusion is very short. In a brief that is short or does not involve a complex analysis, an abbreviated conclusion is appropriate.

Summary

This chapter focuses on the preparation of documents containing legal analysis that are designed to be submitted to a court. Such a document, usually called a court brief, is often formally referred to as a "memorandum of law" or a "memorandum of points and authorities." The chapter presents an overview of the major considerations, key points, and helpful guidelines involved in the preparation of court briefs.

At the trial court level, these documents are trial court briefs submitted in support of a legal position advocated by an attorney. They are usually submitted in conjunction with a motion that requests some action or relief by the trial court. At the appellate court level, the documents submitted to an appellate court that involve legal analysis are appellate court briefs.

Office legal memoranda and court briefs are similar in many respects. When preparing both office memoranda and court briefs, it is helpful to use a writing process such as that suggested in Chapter 15. Office memoranda and court briefs follow a similar format: presentation of the issue, facts, analysis, and conclusion.

The major difference between an office memo and a court brief is the orientation of the presentation. An office memo is designed to inform and is written in an objective manner. A court brief is designed to advocate a position and persuade the court; therefore, the issue(s), facts, and legal argument are crafted in a persuasive manner designed to convince the court to adopt the position advocated.

A trial court brief is a memorandum of law submitted by an attorney to a trial court. In the memorandum, the attorney introduces the legal authority and analysis that supports a position advocated by the attorney. An appellate court brief is the written legal argument submitted to a court of appeals. In the appellate brief, an attorney presents the legal authority and analysis in support of, or in opposition to, an argument that a lower court committed reversible error.

Trial and appellate court briefs are similar in many respects. A major difference is that appellate court briefs are usually more formal: the style and format are more strictly governed by the appellate court rules. Both trial and appellate court briefs, however, are governed to some degree by court rules, and these rules must be carefully reviewed when preparing a court brief.

A legal assistant's role in preparing a court brief usually involves conducting legal research and analysis and preparing a rough draft. The final document requires the attorney's signature and is usually prepared by the attorney assigned to the case.

Quick References

Active voice	503	Passive voice	503
Appellee	512	Persuasive presentation	500
Appellant	512	Preliminary statement	509
Appellate court brief	498	Sentence length	502
Argument	504	Statement of facts	501
Conclusion	512	Table of authorities	513
Court rules	508	Table of contents	513
Ethics	499	Trial court brief	498
Issue headings	506	Word choice	506
Jurisdictional statement	514		

Internet Resources

Using "trial court briefs" or "appellate court briefs" as a topic, you will find a wide range of websites (literally thousands of sites) referring to trial and appellate court briefs. The following is a summary of the categories of websites that may prove helpful when working on court briefs:

Sites of federal and state trial and appellate courts (some of these sites include the court rules and guides and practice tips for preparing briefs)

Sites that provide the trial or appellate court briefs filed in specific cases, such as the O. J. Simpson case or the Florida presidential election cases

Sites advertising businesses that assist in the preparation of trial and appellate court briefs

Sites for schools advertising programs that include as part of the curricula trial and appellate advocacy

Sites that provide links to appellate court websites, court rules, opinions, and resources

As with most topics on the web, the problem is not the lack of sites but too many sites. You are more likely to avoid the frustration of finding too many sites by narrowing your search to a specific type of trial or appellate court brief.

Exercises

ASSIGNMENT 1

Describe how to draft each of the following components of a brief in a persuasive manner. Include the considerations involving organization, word choice, sentence structure, and so on.

a. Issue

b. Fact statement

c. Point heading

d. Argument

ASSIGNMENT 2

Describe in detail the components and format of a trial and appellate court brief.

ASSIGNMENT 3

Restate each of the following question components of the issue in a persuasive manner:

a. "should the evidence be suppressed when . . .?" In the case, the police failed to obtain a search warrant prior to searching a vehicle.

b. "did the court err when . . .?" In the case, the trial court admitted hearsay evidence.

c. "Under the statute of frauds . . ., is an oral contract valid when . . .?" Rewrite this portion of the issue using language that focuses on a desired result.

d. "Under the sale of goods statutes, . . . is a statute enforceable when . . .?" Rewrite this portion of the issue using language that focuses on a desired result.

ASSIGNMENT 4

Restate persuasively each of the following issues. Each issue should be redrafted twice—persuasively from the view of the opposing sides.

a. Under the provisions of the exclusionary rule, should evidence be suppressed when law enforcement officers executed a search warrant by unannounced entry because they saw the defendant run into the apartment upon their arrival at the scene?

b. Did the district court improperly exercise its discretion when it admitted into evidence photographs of the murder victim?

c. In light of the provisions of the hearsay rule, did the trial court improperly admit into evidence the defendant's statements to his neighbor that he would kill his wife?

d. Does the privileged communications statute allow the admission into evidence of the defendant's threats of physical harm to his spouse?

ASSIGNMENT 5

Restate the following point headings in a more persuasive manner:

a. THE EVIDENCE WAS INCORRECTLY SUPPRESSED BY THE TRIAL COURT SINCE THERE WERE SUFFICIENT EXIGENT CIRCUMSTANCES AT THE SCENE.

b. THE DENIAL OF THE DEFENDANT'S MOTION FOR MISTRIAL WAS NOT ERROR BY THE TRIAL COURT BECAUSE THE PROSECUTOR'S COMMENT ON THE DEFENDANT'S PRIOR CONVICTION WAS ADMISSIBLE.

c. THE TRIAL COURT'S ALLOWANCE OF THE PEREMPTORY CHALLENGE WAS PROPER. THE CHALLENGE WAS NOT RACIALLY MOTIVATED.

d. THE COURT SHOULD NOT GRANT THE DEFENDANT'S MOTION TO DISMISS. . . .

ASSIGNMENT 6

Restate the following rule of law presentations in a more persuasive manner:

a. In determining whether an individual has constructive possession, the court decides whether the defendant had knowledge of and control over the drugs.

b. Under the first part of the test, it must be shown that the defendant had knowledge of the presence of the drugs.

c. The court has stated that an arrest has taken place when a reasonable person would not feel free to leave.

ASSIGNMENT 7

In the following exercise, the assignment is to prepare a trial court brief. The assignment contains the memo from the supervising attorney, which includes all the available facts of the case. Complete the brief based on these facts. When preparing the heading of each assignment, use your name for the "To" line, and put "Supervising Attorney" after the "From."

Following the assignment is a reference to the applicable enacted and case law.

The first time you cite the opinion, use the citation format you are given for the opinion in the assignment.

For Example

Melia v. Dillon Cos., Inc., 18 Kan. App. 2d 5, 846 P.2d 257 (1993).

This is how you should cite this opinion the first time it is used in the memorandum. If you are using the opinion provided in Appendix A, when you quote from the opinion in the memo, use a blank line to indicate the page number from which the quotation is taken.

For Example

Melia, 18 Kan. App. 2d 5 at
_____, 846 P.2d at
_____.

Do not conduct additional research. Complete the assignment using the facts, enacted law, and case law contained in the assignment. For the purposes

of the assignment, assume the cases have not been overturned or modified by subsequent court decisions. In most instances, a simple trial court brief such as the one presented in this assignment would not include a table of contents, table of authorities, or preliminary statement. It would be composed of a question presented, statement of the case/facts, and argument sections. For the purposes of this assignment, do not include a table of contents, table of authorities, or preliminary statement section. For the title page, use the format presented in Section VI.A of this chapter. The court is the District Court and the state is New Mexico.

Memo:

To: [Your name]

From: Supervising Attorney

Re: *White v. Calkin,* CV 16-388

Our client, Sage Rent-A-Car Inc., leased a vehicle to Jeffery Calkin. Mr. Calkin failed to stop at a stop sign and collided with Jane White, the plaintiff. Ms. White filed a negligence suit against both Mr. Calkin and Sage Rent-A-Car. In paragraph 36 of the complaint, plaintiff claims that Sage is required to carry insurance under the provisions of the Mandatory Financial Responsibility Act and therefore, under the act, has a duty to assume responsibility for this accident. When Sage incorporated, it filed a surety bond with the superintendent of insurance and is self-insured under the act. I do not read the act to extend liability to lessors for the damages that result from the negligent use of vehicles by lessees. Therefore, I plan to file a Rule 1-012B(6) motion to dismiss for failure to state a claim. Please prepare a rough draft of a brief in support of the motion to dismiss.

Statutory Law:

NMRA 1-012B(6)—The rule provides in part, "the following defenses may at the option of the pleader be made by motion:

. . .

(6) failure to state a claim upon which relief can be granted; . . .."

New Mexico Mandatory Financial Responsibility Act (MFRA), NMSA 1978 § 66-5-201 to 66-5-239.
MFRA, NMSA 1978 § 66-5-205(A) (2013):

a. No owner shall permit the operation of an uninsured motor vehicle, or a motor vehicle for which evidence of financial responsibility as was affirmed to the department is not currently valid, upon the streets or highways of New Mexico unless the vehicle is specifically exempted from the provisions of the Mandatory Financial Responsibility Act. . . .

MFRA, NMSA 1978 § 66-5-218 (1998):

Evidence of financial responsibility, when required under the Mandatory Financial Responsibility Act, may be given by filing:

a. evidence of a motor vehicle insurance policy;

b. a surety bond as provided in Section 66-5-225 NMSA 1978; or

c. a certificate of deposit of money as provided in Section 66-5-226 NMSA 1978.

MFRA, NMSA 1978 § 66-5-207 (1998):

The following motor vehicles are exempt from the Mandatory Financial Responsibility Act:

. . .

e. a motor vehicle approved as self-insured by the superintendent of insurance pursuant to Section 66-5-207.1 NMSA 1978; . . .

Case Law: *Las Lumarias of the N.M. Council v. Isengard*, 92 N.M. 297, 300–301 (Ct. App. 1978). The following quote from the case is all that is needed for the assignment. "A motion to dismiss a complaint is properly granted only when it appears that the plaintiff cannot recover or be entitled to relief under any state of facts provable under the claim. . . ."

Cordova v Wolfel, 120 N.M. 557, 903 P.2d 1390 (1995) (see Appendix A).

ASSIGNMENT 8

Perform Assignment 7 using the law from your state.

ASSIGNMENT 9

The assignment is to prepare a rough draft of the appellee's brief in opposition to the appellant's appeal of the trial court's denial of the motion to suppress evidence seized from appellant's suitcase. The plaintiff/appellee is the United States; the defendant/appellant is Arnold J. Stewart. The trial court ruled that the suitcase had been abandoned and, therefore, the defendant did not have a reasonable expectation of privacy protected by the Fourth Amendment in the suitcase.

Numerous cases deal with the issue of abandonment of personal property, and an appellate brief usually would include references to at least several cases.

This assignment is an exercise in preparing a very simple, single-issue appellate brief and is designed to acquaint students with the basic elements of such a brief. Therefore, when performing this assignment, use only the constitutional and case law presented in the assignment; do not perform additional research. Assume the cases have not been overturned or modified by subsequent court decisions.

Follow the format presented in Section IV of this chapter. The caption is presented in the following text. Prepare a separate statement of the case and statement of the facts. Information necessary for preparing the brief follows. Note that the transcript pages (references to the trial court record) and docketing pages are referenced in parentheses. When drafting the brief, include the references to the record in the brief. References to the case and statutory law also follow. When citing the *United States v. Jones* case, use the citation instructions presented in Assignment 7.

Facts: On October 15, 2012, Arnold Stewart arrived at the airport an hour and fifteen minutes prior to his scheduled flight. (Tr. at 6). He was going to visit a friend in Chicago. (Tr. at 7). He was carrying one suitcase that he intended to carry on the flight. (Tr. at 7). His flight was scheduled to leave from gate 9, but he decided to wait at gate 8 because it wasn't so crowded. (Tr. at 8). After a few minutes, he decided to get something to eat. (Tr. at 8). He approached Larry Holt, who was also waiting at gate 8, and asked if Holt would watch his suitcase. (Tr. at 8). Stewart did not know Mr. Holt. (Tr. at 8). Holt asked him how long he would be gone and Stewart replied, "Just a few minutes." (Tr. at 9). Holt said, "Well, ok." (Tr. at 9). Stewart then walked off. (Tr. at 9). Across from where they were seated were several coin-operated lockers where Stewart could have placed the suitcase. (Tr. 9–10). Stewart went to the food bar. (Tr. at 10). There was a long line, and he wasn't served for 20 minutes. (Tr. at 10). On the way back to his seat, he ran into an acquaintance and talked to him for several minutes. (Tr. at 10). He didn't return to his seat in the gate area for 45 minutes. (Tr. at 13).

Meanwhile, after 20 minutes, Mr. Holt became concerned. (Tr. at 41). He thought, "Where is that guy? I wonder if this suitcase contains a bomb." (Tr. at 41). The more he thought about it, the more concerned he became. (Tr. at 41–42). He contacted airport security and expressed his concerns. (Tr. at 42). Approximately a minute later, Officer Robert Dwyer arrived. (Tr. at 42). There was no nametag on the suitcase, no airline claim ticket attached, and no evidence of ownership on the exterior. (Tr. at 71). In such situations, airport policy is that the suitcase should be immediately inspected, then taken to the security office. (Tr. at

72). Officer Dwyer inspected the suitcase and its contents at the scene. (Tr. at 72). Upon opening the suitcase, he found a large bag that contained 40 smaller bags of a white powdery substance. (Tr. at 73). The substance was later identified as heroin. (Tr. at 122). The suitcase was taken to the security office and federal officers were called. (Tr. at 74).

Approximately 45 minutes after he left, Stewart returned to his seat. (Tr. at 13). Holt informed him that he thought Stewart had abandoned the suitcase so he turned it over to airport security. (Tr. at 44). Stewart left the gate area, went to the ticket counter, and asked for information concerning the next flight. (Tr. at 14). The ticket counter is next to the security office. (Tr. at 75). Stewart never entered the office to inquire about his suitcase. (Tr. at 75). He was arrested when he went to the gate area and attempted to board his flight. (Tr. at 91).

Information for Statement of the Case: On November 21, 2012, Arnold J. Stewart was indicted by a federal grand jury sitting in the District of Utah on charges of possession with intent to distribute more than 100 grams of heroin in violation of 21 U.S.C. §§ 841(a)(1) and 841(b)(1)(B). (Doc. at 5). On January 7, 2013, Stewart filed a motion to suppress the physical evidence. (Doc. at 18). On February 14, 2013, the motion was denied. The trial court found:

> Under the circumstances, for all intents and purposes the suitcase was abandoned. The defendant did not express a possessory interest in the suitcase at any time after he learned its location.
>
> Having been abandoned, the defendant had no expectation of privacy in it or its contents.

(Tr. at 40–41). On March 6, 2013, defendant entered a conditional guilty plea, reserving his right to appeal the suppression ruling. (Doc. at 22). On April 27, 2013, the court sentenced Stewart to imprisonment for 60 months, to be followed by a three-year term of supervised release. (Doc. at 55). Stewart filed his notice of appeal on April 29, 2013.

Constitutional and Case Law: Amendment IV, U.S. Constitution

United States v. Arango, 912 F.2d 441 (10th Cir. 1990). All you need to know for the purposes of this assignment is that the *Arango* case stands for the proposition that one who has the right to possession of personal property has the right to exclude others from searching it.

United States v. Jones, 707 F.2d 1169 (10th Cir. 1983). See Appendix A.

Prior Related Appeals: There are no prior or related appeals in this case.

Caption:

UNITED STATES COURT OF APPEALS

TENTH CIRCUIT

NO. 2009-123

UNITED STATES OF AMERICA

Plaintiff/Appellee,

vs.

ARNOLD J. STEWART,

Defendant/Appellant.

APPEAL FROM THE UNITED STATES DISTRICT COURT FOR THE DISTRICT OF UTAH

ANSWER BRIEF OF APPELLEE

Chapter 19

Correspondence

Outline

I. Introduction
II. Basic Components
III. Types of Correspondence
IV. Key Points Checklist: Correspondence
V. Application

Learning Objectives

After completing this chapter, you should understand:

- The basic components of correspondence
- The types of law office correspondence that communicate the results of legal research and analysis
- The elements of information, opinion, and demand letters
- How to draft information, opinion, and demand letters

In the hypothetical introduced at the beginning of the last chapter, Alice Black, the supervisory attorney, assigned Pam Hayes, the paralegal, the task of preparing a response to a motion to dismiss for failure to state a claim. After Ms. Hayes completed the assignment, she received the following memo.

To:	Pam Hayes, Paralegal
From:	Alice Black, Attorney
Case:	CV 16-601, *Nick Shine v. Blue Sky Ski Resort*
Re:	Correspondence to client

Please prepare a letter to Mr. Shine advising him of the status of the case. Include in the letter the following:

- *Inform Mr. Shine that a motion to dismiss has been filed. Explain to him what a motion is, and tell him how the court will proceed in regard to the motion.*
- *Summarize the analysis of the law contained in the memorandum brief you prepared in response to the motion.*

The Application section of this chapter includes the correspondence prepared by Ms. Hayes and other sample correspondence.

I. INTRODUCTION

This chapter and Chapter 18 focus primarily on the preparation of documents that contain legal research and analysis and are designed for an audience outside the law office. This chapter examines the preparation of documents designed for an external audience other than a court. These documents are usually correspondence addressed to a client. A paralegal or law clerk may, however, be called on to draft correspondence to a variety of external audiences, such as witnesses, court personnel, and opposing counsel.

Correspondence is a major form of written communication between the law firm and the outside world. Other than documents submitted to courts and transaction documents, such as contracts, correspondence is the *primary form* of writing designed for an audience outside the law office.

It is essential, therefore, that correspondence be well crafted, because it helps establish and maintain the image and reputation of the law firm. Correspondence that contains grammatical or substantive errors or is difficult to understand reflects poorly on the law firm:

- A client may question the firm's capability to handle the client's case.
- The court may question the competence of the individual who signed the document.
- Opposing counsel may conclude that if the law firm is incapable of preparing quality correspondence, it is not capable of successfully representing its client.

Because most legal correspondence is in letter rather than memo form, the term *letter* is used in this chapter to refer to legal correspondence. A paralegal or law clerk may prepare letters for a variety of purposes. The three main categories of letters that include legal research and analysis to some degree are:

1. Letters that provide information—*informational letters*
2. Letters that provide answers or legal opinions—*opinion letters*
3. Letters that demand action—*demand letters*

Although the focus in this chapter is on letters that contain legal research and analysis, other types of letters are briefly mentioned. Following a discussion of the components common to all three categories mentioned, separate sections of this chapter address each category.

II. BASIC COMPONENTS

Basic conventions apply to the various types of letters prepared in a law office and basic components are usually present in all types of letters. Each of these components may not be necessary or required in every letter you draft. This section, however, introduces all of the possible components so that you will be familiar with them.

The content and manner of presentation of each of the components discussed in the following text may vary from office to office. Compose your letters according to the guidelines adopted in your office. Refer to the Application section of this chapter for examples of the components discussed in the following subsections.

Exhibit 19-1 presents the basic format and components of letters prepared in a law office.

A. Letterhead

The **letterhead** usually consists of the full name, address, telephone number, facsimile number, and web address of the law firm. It is usually preprinted on the firm's stationery and centered at the top of the page. An example of the information in a letterhead follows:

Thomas, Belter and Ryan

751 Main Street

Friendly, New Washington 00065

(200) 444-7778 • FAX 444-7678 • www.thomaslaw.com

Only the first page of the letter will be on or have letterhead. Subsequent pages contain an identification of the letter, which is usually called a **header**. These pages do not contain the letterhead. The header includes the

- ▪ Letterhead/heading
- ▪ Date
- ▪ Method of delivery
- ▪ Recipient's address block
- ▪ Reference (Re:) line
- ▪ Salutation
- ▪ Body
- ▪ Closing
- ▪ Signature and title
- ▪ Initials of drafter
- ▪ Enclosure notation
- ▪ Others receiving copies

© Cengage

Exhibit 19-1 *Basic Format and Components of Law Office Correspondence.*

name of the addressee, the date, and the page number, and sits at the top left or right margin of the page. An example of a header is as follows:

Jon Jones

May 5, 2016

Page Three

B. Date

The full date is usually below the letterhead at the left margin, or centered below the letterhead. The date includes the full date: the day, month, and year. Because most correspondence is filed chronologically, a date is essential for the chronological file. Note that many offices date-stamp correspondence when it is received in the office and file it according to that date.

C. Method of Delivery

At the left margin, below the date, is the **method of delivery**. This is usually required only if the manner of delivery is other than U.S. mail. Examples are as follows:

Via Federal Express

Via hand delivery

Via facsimile

D. Recipient's Address Block

Below the date and method of delivery is the **address block** of the addressee. Place it at the left margin. The address block is single-spaced and includes:

- • The name of the person to whom the letter is addressed
- • The individual's title (if any)
- • The name of the business (if applicable)
- • The address

The following is an example of an address block:

Elizabeth Counter
President
Friendly Enterprises
139 Main Street
Friendly, NW 00065

E. Reference (Re:) Line

The **reference line** briefly identifies the topic of the letter. A reference line is usually placed at the left margin following the address block. Some firms require that the reference line include the case name and number if the letter concerns a pending lawsuit. The following is an example of a reference line:

Re: Request for production of documents

Smith v. Jones, Civil Action 16-1001

The reference line may also contain the statement *Confidential Attorney Client Communication.*

F. Salutation

Below the reference line is the **salutation** or greeting. Legal correspondence is generally formal in tone, and the greeting is normally formal. An example of a greeting follows:

Dear Ms. Counter:

You may use the first name if you know the addressee well, but this is usually the exception. If in doubt, ask the supervising attorney. If you do not know the name of the addressee, such as may be the case when the letter is addressed to a business, contact the business and ascertain the individual's name. The use of "To whom it may concern:" is impersonal and invites a slow response. A person is likely to respond more quickly when he or she is specifically named. In addition, it indicates the law office is ill-informed as to who it is contacting, which can reflect poorly on the law office.

G. Body

The **body** is the heart of the letter—what the letter is about. The body is usually composed of an introduction, main body, and requests or instructions (see Exhibit 19-2).

1. Introduction

The body of the letter usually begins with an introductory sentence or paragraph (if necessary) that identifies or summarizes the main purpose of the letter. Be sure to use language that sets the appropriate tone. Understanding the type of letter being written and the content of the letter will allow the paralegal to choose words that set an appropriate tone.

For Example

This letter is to advise you of the filing of a motion for summary judgment by the defendant. The hearing on the motion is scheduled to take place on March 4, 2013.

This letter is to confirm our conversation today in which you stated that you would not be able to attend the hearing scheduled to take place on May 16, 2013.

Introduction	Introductory paragraph or sentence summarizing the purpose of the letter
Main body	Detailed explanation of the purpose of the letter
Requests/instructions	Request or instructions for the recipient

© Cengage

Exhibit 19-2 Components of the Body of a Letter.

2. Main Body

The main body of the letter follows the introduction. The main body explains in detail the purpose of the letter. Craft the main body with care to ensure that you communicate the required information clearly and concisely. It may be necessary to use an outline when a letter covers multiple or complex matters. As with an office memorandum or court brief, the body may require several drafts.

You must always consider the audience when drafting the main body. If you are drafting the letter to a layperson, such as the client, avoid the use of legalese; define and clearly explain any legal terms used.

When writing to a layperson, consider the sophistication of the reader. Ask yourself:

- How familiar with legal matters is the reader?
- Does the reader often read material that involves complex subjects?

Although the addressee may not be familiar with the law, the individual may be highly educated or may often deal with complex or technical matters. In such situations, you may be able to craft the letter with greater complexity and present the subject matter with greater legal or technical detail. If the reader does not as a matter of course engage in a lot of complex or technical reading, or is not familiar with such matters, then you should avoid including a detailed, complex discussion in the main body.

The content of the body will differ according to the type of letter you are drafting. The subsections of this chapter that address information, opinion, and demand letters discuss the differences in the format and content of the body of these types of correspondence.

3. Requests/Instructions

Include any **requests** or **instructions** for the recipient in the last section of the body.

For Example

Please bring with you copies of the contract and any other written material related to the contract.

Please keep a daily diary. Include in it a detailed description of all your daily activities, such as how long you sleep, what physical activities you engage in during the day, and so on.

In some instances, a paralegal or law clerk may draft and sign a letter to the client. A paralegal or law clerk may sign a letter that provides general information. Neither may sign a letter that gives a legal opinion or legal advice. Most state laws and rules of ethics prohibit a paralegal or law clerk from practicing law, and providing a legal opinion or legal advice constitutes the practice of law. Therefore, when preparing a letter that you, another paralegal, or law clerk will sign, be sure not to include a legal opinion or provide legal advice.

H. Closing

The **closing** follows the body of the letter. The closing usually consists of some standard statement. The following are examples of closings:

- Thank you for your prompt consideration of this matter.

  Sincerely,

- Please contact me if you have any questions in regard to this matter.

  Very truly yours,

- Thank you for your assistance.

  Best regards,

I. Signature and Title

The signature and title of the person signing the letter follow the closing. An example follows:

———————————————

Sarah Smith

Attorney at Law

When the individual signing the letter is a paralegal, the paralegal status should be clearly indicated below the signature line, as in the following examples:

———————————————

Jon Jones

Paralegal

———————————————

Sarah Smith

Paralegal

J. Initials of Drafter

The final notation on the letter is a reference to the author of the letter and the typist. Note the **initials of the drafter** in all capitals, and note the typist's initials in lowercase letters (e.g., JDR/mwt).

K. Enclosure Notation

If enclosures, such as contracts and documents, are included with the letter, indicate their presence with an **enclosure notation** by typing "Enc." or "Encs." at the left margin following the signature.

———————————————

Sarah Smith

Attorney at Law

Encs.

L. Others Receiving Copies

If other individuals are receiving copies of the letter, indicate this by typing "cc:" and the name of the individual(s) after the signature and title. This follows the enclosure notation if an enclosure notation is used. An example is as follows:

cc: Colin Smith

Mae Carrey

If you are uncertain who should receive copies, check with your supervisor.

M. Format Style

The basic format of a letter varies among firms, and is dictated by personal taste and style. Two fundamental styles are full block and modified block. In full block, everything but the letterhead is flush with the left margin. The information letter in the first example in the Application section is typed in full block format. In modified block, the date is centered, and the signature line may be just to the right of the center of the page or flush left. The first line of each paragraph is indented. The opinion letter in the second example in the Application section is presented in modified block format.

N. General Considerations—All Correspondence

Adopt the highest standards of accuracy, both substantive and stylistic, when drafting legal correspondence. As mentioned in the introduction, correspondence helps determine the image, reputation, and success of the law firm. In many situations, the information provided in the correspondence constitutes the practice of law and subjects the firm to possible liability for claims of legal malpractice. Therefore, the quality of the product is critically important. You should do the following:

- Take the utmost care to ensure that any legal research and analysis are free of error.
- Make sure that the finished product is free from writing errors involving grammar, spelling, and so on.
- Be prepared to perform the number of edits and redrafts necessary to ensure that the final product is professionally prepared.

Draft letters clearly so that they cannot be misinterpreted. A reader may not like the information conveyed in the letter and wish to intentionally misinterpret the contents. The discussion in the following sections is designed to assist in the preparation of letters that clearly convey information and are difficult to misinterpret.

III. TYPES OF CORRESPONDENCE

Although, as discussed in the preceding section, the basic components of legal correspondence are the same, the content of the body of the correspondence varies according to the type of letter being drafted. There are many categories of legal correspondence, and the categorization is based upon the purpose that each category is designed to serve. Inasmuch as this text focuses on legal research and analysis, this section addresses law office correspondence that communicates the results of legal research and analysis. The three basic categories of letters that communicate such information are information letters, opinion letters, and demand letters (see Exhibit 19-3).

This section focuses on the body of these categories of letters and how each differs in the presentation of legal research and analysis. The following subsections address the preparation of letters to nonlawyer recipients, as most of the correspondence a paralegal or law clerk prepares is for that audience.

A. Information Letter

A paralegal or law clerk is often asked to draft a letter that provides information to the client or other layperson. The components of an **information letter** usually include the elements mentioned in Section II of this chapter. The body of the information letter, however, varies according to the type of information being conveyed. There are many types of information letters. Some of the types, and examples of parts of the body of these types, follow:

- Letters that confirm an appointment or inform of the date and time of scheduled events

Information letters	Letters that provide general legal information or background on a legal issue (e.g., the information may be a summary of the law or the requirements of a particular statute)
Opinion letters	Letters that provide information concerning the law, an analysis of that information, and a legal opinion or legal advice
Demand or advocacy letters	Letters designed to persuade someone to take action favorable to the interest of the client or cease acting in a manner that is detrimental to the client (e.g., a summary of the applicable law in support of the requested action)

© Cengage

Exhibit 19-3 Types of Letters That Communicate the Results of Legal Research and Analysis.

For Example

This letter is to advise you that the court hearing on the motion to modify child support will be held on May 6, 2016, in the courtroom of....
This letter is to confirm our appointment at 9:00 a.m., May 22, 2016....

- Letters that inform the client of the current status of the case

For Example

The defendants filed an answer on June 6, 2016. On June 14, 2016, we sent them a request to produce documents concerning the contract and are awaiting their response to that request. We will contact you when we receive their response.

- Letters that present the firm's bill
- Letters that give the results of an investigation

For Example

After performing a thorough investigation, we were unable to locate any witness who actually saw the accident. We interviewed the witnesses at the scene, canvassed the neighborhood, and contacted all the store owners in the area. If you happen to remember the license plate of any vehicle that passed by or have any additional information, please let us know....

- Letters that provide general legal information or background on a legal issue (This is the type of information being provided to Mr. Shine in the assignment at the beginning of the chapter.)

    The information may be a summary of the law involved in the client's case or the requirements of a particular statute. This type of information letter is usually the most complex of the information letters and often involves communicating results of legal research and analysis. The body of this type of information letter is discussed in the remainder of this subsection.

    The body of an information letter that provides the results of legal research and analysis usually consists of an introduction/opening, answer/explanation, and a closing (see Exhibit 19-4).

1. Introduction/Opening

The introduction states the purpose of the letter.

Introduction/opening	A sentence or paragraph explaining the purpose of the letter
Answer/explanation	A detailed presentation of the legal information or background on a legal issue
Closing	A standard closing statement or if the answer/explanation is lengthy, a summary of the answer

© Cengage

Exhibit 19-4 Body of Information Letter—Recommended Format and Components.

For Example

The purpose of this letter is to inform you of a request that has been filed by the defendant and the law the court will consider when addressing the request.

The purpose of this letter is to inform you of a recent law that was passed that affects your business.

2. Answer/Explanation

The answer/explanation section presents the results of legal research and analysis.

For Example

Section 97-355-21 of the corporation statutes was recently amended. Under the provisions of the amendment, you must file your annual report no later than 20 days after the end of the fiscal year. As you know, the statute prior to the amendment allowed 40 days to file the report.

The body of the letter presented in the first example in the Application section provides a detailed illustration of this component of an information letter.

3. Closing

The closing of the letter is similar to the closing of any legal correspondence, as discussed in Section II of this chapter.

For Example

Because you prepare the annual report for your corporation, I feel it is important that you be advised of the change in the law. If you have any questions, please contact me.

In some instances, especially when the answer/explanation is lengthy or complex, it may be necessary to include a summary or a conclusion in the closing. See the closing of the information letter in the first example in the Application section.

This type of information letter merely presents a summary of the law or the legal status of a case. It communicates basic information; it does not give a legal opinion on a question or provide legal advice. That role is performed by an opinion letter.

B. Opinion Letter

An **opinion letter** is similar to an information letter in that it provides information concerning the law. It is different in that it often includes, in addition, an analysis of that information and provides a legal opinion or legal advice. The purpose is to inform the reader how the law applies to the facts. An opinion letter is usually generated in response to a client's question or raised by the facts in a client's case. Therefore, the focus of this section is on opinion letters addressed to the client.

You may be assigned the task of researching, analyzing, and preparing an interoffice memorandum that addresses the question to be answered in an opinion letter. The purpose of the assignment is to provide the attorney with the information necessary to prepare the letter. On occasion, you may be assigned the additional task of preparing a rough draft of the opinion letter. Many of the considerations involved in preparing an opinion letter are the same as those involved in preparing an office memorandum. When you are assigned the task of preparing such a letter, refer to Chapters 16 and 17 as well as this chapter for guidance.

An opinion letter provides the reader with a legal opinion and legal advice; therefore, it constitutes the practice of law and an attorney must sign it. The attorney is subject to legal liability for harm that occurs as a result of the client acting upon erroneous information contained in the letter. If you are preparing the draft of an opinion letter, take great care to ensure that your research and analysis are accurate.

Because the purpose is to inform the client of the law and provide legal advice, the opinion letter is drafted in the same objective tone as the office memorandum. The difference is that the client is usually a layperson unfamiliar with legal terms and legal writing. When this is so, avoid legalese, and keep legal quotations and citations to a minimum. If the reader is familiar with the law and legal writing, you may use more legal terms, quotations, and citations. In some instances, the attorney may direct that the client be provided with the office memorandum rather than an opinion letter.

Although an opinion letter and an office memorandum are similar in many respects, there are differences in format. An opinion letter follows a business format as discussed in Section II of this chapter, whereas an office memorandum follows a memo format as discussed in Chapters 16 and 17. The body of the letter includes the basic elements of the office memorandum, but the elements are presented with less technical detail and fewer legal terms.

As with most legal writing, there is no standard format for the body of an opinion letter. The body of most opinion letters, however, follows the format presented in Exhibit 19-5.

1. Introduction/Opening

The introduction establishes the focus of the letter and identifies the question or questions that will be answered. The opening usually begins with a reference to the question and the context within which the client raised the question.

For Example

On January 2, 2017, you hired me to represent you in your criminal case. When we met in my office on that date, you asked me to determine whether we could obtain a suppression of the evidence (the heroin) seized when the police officers executed a search warrant by entering your residence unannounced.

Notice that the question is stated in broader terms than it would be in an office memorandum. Draft the question in a manner sufficient for the client to understand the question. You do not have to state it as completely

Introduction/opening	A sentence or paragraph identifying the question or questions that will be answered
Facts	A brief presentation of the background and key facts relative to the question(s) being addressed
Answer/conclusion	A brief answer to the question similar to the brief answer section of an office memorandum
Explanation	An explanation of how the law applies to the facts raised by the question, crafted in a manner that the recipient will understand
Closing/conclusion	The last paragraph of the explanation section, containing a standard closing statement (or if the explanation is lengthy, a summary of the explanation); also includes a statement of any action the client should take or what will occur next

© Cengage

Exhibit 19-5 Body of Opinion Letter—Recommended Format and Components.

or as formally as discussed in Chapter 11, nor do you necessarily have to follow the law + question + key facts format. In the preceding example, there is no reference to the rule of law.

Include language in the introduction to indicate that the opinion and advice apply only to the addressee and the specific facts included in the letter. You should also mention that the opinion is based on the law as of the date of the opinion.

For Example

This opinion is provided for your use and solely for your benefit. It applies only to the facts presented in the facts section of this letter and the law as of the date of the letter.

2. Facts

Present the facts in an opinion letter in the same objective manner as in an office memorandum. Include only the key and background facts to keep the section as short as possible.

In letters addressed to a client, you may wonder why the facts need to be included. Inclusion of the facts allows the client to be clear as to which facts are relevant to the content of the letter. Clients can be preoccupied with facts that are important to them, but that do not bear on a particular legal issue. Therefore, including the facts focuses the client on what is relevant to the content.

3. Answer/Conclusion

The answer/conclusion section presents a brief answer to the question. It is similar to the brief answer section of the office memorandum. By placing the answer near the beginning of the letter, the reader immediately knows the result without having to read the explanation. This is helpful if the reader is busy and may not be able to read the explanation until a later time.

The answer should be clear and as short as possible. Because the answer is usually a legal opinion, you should state it as an opinion.

For Example

The court will probably not suppress the evidence based upon the officers' failure to announce their presence prior to entering your residence when they executed the warrant.

Add any needed specifics or limitations after the answer.

For Example

The outcome could be different if Officer Galen changes his testimony and states he did not see you holding a rifle in your front room when they approached the house. Officer Kaler stated that he did not see you in the front room as they approached the house. In light of Officer Kaler's statement, Officer Galen could change his statement.

4. Explanation

The explanation section is similar to the analysis section of an office memorandum. The difference is that the explanation must be crafted in a manner that is not so technical that the client has difficulty understanding it.

Also, the explanation section is usually not as long or as complex as the analysis section of an office memorandum. When preparing this section, note the following guidelines:

- If there is more than one issue, discuss the issues in the order in which they are presented in the introduction.
- If possible, limit the letter to as few issues as possible (i.e., two to three). If there are multiple issues, the letter may become too complex or long, and the reader may have difficulty understanding or keeping track of the subject matter. Separate the issues, and prepare more than one letter if necessary.
- Draft the content with the reader's legal sophistication in mind. The client may not be familiar with the law and technical writing, and an explanation that is as detailed as the analysis section of an office memorandum may not be appropriate. Keep quotations and citations to a minimum. Rather than quoting, rephrase the statutory or case law in a manner that a layperson can understand. If you must use a legal term, make sure its meaning is clear. Define the legal terms that you use.
- Provide a complete explanation. The client must be fully informed. Do not omit important information because the client is unsophisticated in the law. Present all the key information in a manner that fully and clearly informs the client.

The following is an example of an explanation section of an opinion letter.

The Fourth Amendment to the United States Constitution and article II, section 9, of the state constitution prohibit "unreasonable searches and seizures." These amendments do not prohibit all searches and seizures, however, just those that are "unreasonable."

The law provides that anything seized as a result of an unreasonable search may not be admitted into evidence in a trial. The state supreme court has ruled that officers must announce their presence before entering a residence when executing a search warrant. The court stated that an unannounced entry is unreasonable and violates the United States and state constitutions.

There are, however, exceptions to the rule that officers must announce their presence before executing a warrant. One exception is when the officers arrive at the place to be searched and there is evidence that the person or persons present at the scene are a danger to the officers. *Smith v. Jones* is a court case remarkably similar to your case. In this case, when the police arrived at the residence to be searched, they saw the defendant enter the house with a rifle in his hands. The state supreme court ruled that this evidence provided the officers with authority to execute the warrant and enter the residence to be searched without first announcing their presence.

Based upon the ruling in the *Smith v. Jones* case and the similarity between the facts of that case and the facts in your case, the trial court probably will not suppress the evidence seized at your residence and will allow its admission at trial.

5. Closing/Conclusion

The closing is usually not a separate section of an opinion letter. Rather, it is usually the last paragraph of the explanation section. It is similar to the closing of any legal correspondence, as discussed in section II of this chapter. In addition, in an opinion letter, the closing should summarize any action the client should take or what will occur next.

For Example

I hope this letter answers your questions. Please note that, although the officers may have acted properly when they entered your residence unannounced, there is a question as to whether the warrant was properly issued in the first place. When we complete our investigation into this matter, we anticipate that we will file a motion to suppress the evidence because the warrant should not have been issued at all. We will discuss this at our appointment scheduled on Friday the 9th. Please contact me if you have any questions.

An example of an opinion letter is presented in the second example in the Application section of this chapter.

C. Demand or Advocacy Letter

Another basic type of letter you may be called upon to draft is a **demand letter**, sometimes called an *advocacy letter*. This type of letter is designed to persuade someone to take action favorable to the interests of the client or cease acting in a manner that is detrimental to the client. This may be as simple as demanding payment on a debt or as complex as requesting that a course of conduct be taken, such as rehiring an employee. In many instances, a demand letter will include a summary of the applicable law in support of the requested action. This section addresses the considerations involved when preparing a demand letter that includes a reference to the law and an analysis of the law.

You may be given an assignment to prepare an office memorandum summarizing the law that will be used as the basis for the demand letter and to prepare a draft of the letter. Like the opinion letter, the attorney must sign a demand letter.

The basic format and components of a demand letter are similar to those discussed in Section II of this chapter; as with an opinion letter, there is no standard format for the demand letter. A major difference is that a demand letter is not designed to address a legal question, but to encourage action or seek relief. Therefore, it does not contain an answer/conclusion section in the body because it does not address a question that requires a brief answer. The demand letter also differs from an opinion letter in that it is designed to advocate a position and persuade the reader; therefore, it is written in a persuasive manner.

The body of a demand letter follows the same basic format and is composed of elements similar to the body of the opinion letter (see Exhibit 19-6).

This section explores the differences between the body of a demand letter and the body of an opinion letter. The discussion focuses on demand letters sent to nonlawyers. The attorney will usually draft a demand letter that will be sent to another attorney.

1. Introduction/Opening

The introduction of a demand letter is somewhat different from the opening of an opinion letter. It begins with the identification of the writer or the client.

For Example

Our office represents Mr. Jason Hill in the above-referenced case.
  Mr. Jason Hill has retained this office in regard to....

A statement of the purpose of the letter follows the identification. It establishes the focus of the letter and identifies the problem addressed and the relief sought.

Introduction/opening	An identification of the writer or client followed by the statement of the purpose of the letter
Facts	A brief presentation of the background and key facts relative to the question(s) being addressed
Explanation	A presentation of the legal authority in support of the relief requested, crafted in a manner that the recipient will understand
Closing/conclusion	The last paragraph of the explanation section, containing a standard closing statement (or, if the explanation is lengthy, a summary of the explanation); should restate the relief requested and indicate the next course of action

© Cengage

Exhibit 19-6 Body of Demand Letter—Recommended Format and Component.

For Example

Your efforts to collect payment from Mr. Hill on his automobile loan are in violation of the Collections Act, and we demand that they cease immediately.

2. Facts

The content of the facts section is the same as in the opinion letter except that you should present the facts in a persuasive manner similar to the persuasive presentation of the facts in a court brief. See Chapter 18, Section II.B.2, for additional information on persuasive presentation of facts.

For Example

On January 7, 2017, Mr. Hill signed a loan with your company to pay for the purchase of an automobile. From the date of the loan until two months ago, he has paid, on time and in full, every installment on the loan. For the past two months, due to the illness of his oldest child, Mr. Hill has been able to pay only one-half of the required monthly payment. He contacted your office on the fifth day of last month and informed the loan officer that for the next three months he would be making reduced payments. He was informed that he should be making full payments.

For the past three weeks, your collections department has telephoned Mr. Hill after 7:00 p.m. six nights a week demanding full payment. In each instance, Mr. Hill has politely informed the caller that he is paying all he can and requested that the calls cease. The calls have not ceased.

3. Explanation

The explanation section presents the legal authority in support of the relief requested. Because the reader is a nonlawyer, draft the section with this in mind. Refer to the explanation subsection of an opinion letter for guidance. This section of a demand letter differs from the explanation section of an opinion letter in that you should draft the section in a persuasive manner.

For Example

The Collections Act provides that efforts to collect debts shall be made in a reasonable manner. The state supreme court, in the case of *Irons v. Collections, Inc.*, ruled that telephone calls to a debtor's residence after 7:00 p.m. or more frequently than three times a week are unreasonable and violate the act if the debtor objects to the calls. Your office has contacted Mr. Hill after 7:00 p.m. six nights a week for the past three weeks. The calls have continued despite Mr. Hill's objections and requests that they cease.

4. Closing/Conclusion

Like the closing of an opinion letter, the closing of a demand letter is usually not a separate section. It is usually the last paragraph of the explanation section and is similar to the closing of any legal correspondence, as discussed in section II of this chapter. The closing should restate the relief requested and indicate the next course of action.

For Example

Your calls to Mr. Hill are unreasonable, clearly in violation of the Collections Act, and must cease immediately. If the calls do not cease, we will take the appropriate steps necessary to obtain the relief provided in the act.

If you have any questions in regard to this matter, please contact me.

IV. KEY POINTS CHECKLIST: Correspondence

✓ Prepare correspondence accurately and professionally. Letters may affect the reputation of the firm, and poorly drafted letters do not inspire the client's confidence.

✓ Draft the correspondence with the reader's legal sophistication in mind. Avoid legalese; if you must use legal terms, define them clearly.

✓ Keep legal citations and quotations to a minimum. Use quotations only if they are easy to understand and add clarity to the subject matter. Paraphrase the material if it is written in a manner that is difficult to comprehend.

✓ When drafting an opinion letter, be sure to indicate that the letter is limited to the facts of the case, based on the current law, and intended solely for the benefit of the addressee.

✓ If there are multiple issues, divide the subject into separate manageable topics. Prepare and send separate letters covering these topics.

✓ Do not include legal advice or recommend a course of action if the correspondence is to be signed by someone other than an attorney. Such information constitutes the practice of law and must be signed by an attorney.

✓ Keep a file of the letters and other documents you have prepared. Organize the file by topic, such as demand letters and opinion letters. Often, rather than starting a new letter, it is faster and easier to edit an old letter or use it as a guide for the correspondence you are drafting.

V. APPLICATION

This section contains two examples of legal correspondence that illustrate the application of the principles discussed in this chapter. The first example addresses the assignment presented at the beginning of the chapter. This assignment requires the preparation of an information letter by the paralegal, Pam Hayes. The second example illustrates an opinion letter. It is based on the same law used in the first example and on facts that are similar to those of the first example.

A. Example—Information Letter

The assignment introduced at the beginning of the chapter calls for the preparation of an information letter. In this example, the letter is presented in full block style.

Law Offices of Alice Black
2100 Main Street
Friendly, New Washington 00065

(200) 267-7000 • FAX 267-7001 • www.ablacklaw.com

April 29, 2016

Mr. Nick Shine
9100 2nd Street
Friendly, NW 00065
Re: *Shine v. Blue Sky Ski Resort*

Motion to dismiss for failure to state a claim

Dear Mr. Shine:

The purpose of this letter is to inform you of the status of your case and to summarize the law in regard to the motion that will be heard on May 17, 2016.

As you know, on April 6, we filed your complaint against Blue Sky Ski Resort. In the complaint, we claim that the resort was negligent for failing to post a sign warning skiers of the ice hazard you encountered. To prove a claim for negligence, one of the requirements we must establish is that the resort had a duty to warn skiers of the ice hazard.

On April 20, the resort filed a motion with the court asking that the court dismiss the case. A motion is a request submitted to the court asking the court to take some form of action. The court usually holds a hearing on a motion. At the hearing, the parties present their position on whether the request should be granted.

On May 17, 2016, the court will conduct a hearing on the resort's motion to dismiss. At that hearing, we anticipate the resort will claim that under the provisions of the Ski Safety Act, it does not have a duty to warn skiers of ice hazards. The resort will argue that ice hazards are the responsibility of skiers under the act, and therefore, it cannot be sued for negligence, because it had no duty to warn of the ice hazard.

In support of its argument that it does not have a duty to warn of ice hazards, the resort will rely upon section 8B of the act. This section states that skiers are responsible for injuries that result from snow and ice conditions. Our position is that the resort does have a duty to warn of this type of hazard under section 7A of the act. That section provides that resorts have a duty to warn skiers of unusual conditions or hazards on ski runs.

It is unclear from the statute which section of the act applies in a situation such as yours. The state court of appeals, in the case of *Aster v. White Mountain Resort*, interpreted the act in a fact situation similar to yours. In this case, a skier, while skiing on a new ski run, hit a rock covered by snow. The court stated that resorts have a duty to warn of snow conditions if they are unavoidable and present an unobvious or latent hazard.

At the motion hearing, we will argue that the resort's motion to dismiss should be denied because the ice condition you encountered was unavoidable and latent, just as the snow condition was in *Aster v. White Mountain Resort*. We will further argue that the rule of law stated in that case provides that resorts have a duty to warn of hazards such as the one you encountered. Therefore, the resort can be sued for its negligence in failing to post a warning of the ice hazard.

The resort will probably argue that the ruling of the court of appeals in *Karen v. High Mountain Pass* should apply. In that case, a skier broke his leg after failing to negotiate a series of moguls that were present in the middle of a turn on a ski run. The court stated that skiers are responsible for snow and ice hazards, and that moguls, even though unavoidable, are snow hazards easily observable and routinely present on most ski runs. We believe the court will not apply the ruling in the *Karen* case, because that case involved a snow hazard that was observable and routinely encountered by skiers. In your case, the ice hazard was unobservable, unavoidable, and not routinely encountered by skiers.

In conclusion, we are optimistic that the court will rule in our favor and deny the motion. The ice hazard you encountered was unavoidable and latent just like the snow condition in *Aster v. White Mountain Resort*. This being the case, the court should follow the holding in that case and find that Blue Sky Ski Resort had a duty to warn skiers of the hazard. You are not required to attend the hearing, but you may attend if you wish. Please let us know if you plan to attend.

If you have any questions please call.

Sincerely,

_____

Pam Hayes
Paralegal

PAH/wkk

B. Example—Opinion Letter

The example in this section is based on the following fact situation. On January 6, 2017, the client, David Duggan, appeared for an initial interview at the law offices of Alice Black. Pam Hayes, the paralegal, conducted the interview. In the interview, Mr. Duggan stated that he was skiing on December 7, 2016, on an expert ski run at Red Mountain Ski Resort. He encountered a series of moguls near the top of the ski run. The moguls were difficult to ski, and he lost control, fell, and broke his left arm. There was no sign at the top of the run indicating the presence of difficult moguls on the run. He believes the resort should have posted a sign, well in advance of the moguls, warning of their presence. He wants to know if he can sue the resort for its failure to post a warning.

Alice Black assigned Pam Hayes the task of preparing a rough draft of an opinion letter to be sent to Mr. Duggan. The letter should inform him of the likelihood of successfully suing the resort for its failure to post a warning of the presence of the moguls. The governing law is chapter 70 of the New Washington Ski Safety Act. The governing case is *Karen v. High Mountain Pass*, 55 N. Wash. 462, 866 N.E. 995 (Ct. App. 1994). The relevant portions of the statute and case will be introduced at the beginning of the Application section of Chapter 18. The opinion letter is presented in modified block format.

Law Offices of Alice Black

2100 Main Street

Friendly, New Washington 00065

(200) 267-7000 • FAX 267-7001 • www.ablacklaw.com

January 18, 2017

Via Facsimile and U.S. Mail

Mr. David Duggan
5501 Glenview Ave.

Friendly, NW 00065

Re: Possibility of a lawsuit against Red Mountain Ski Resort for failure to warn of moguls

Dear Mr. Duggan:

On January 6, 2017, we met in my office to discuss the possibility of suing Red Mountain Ski Resort for the ski injury you suffered on December 7, 2016. This opinion is based on the facts outlined in the facts section of this letter and the applicable law as of the date of the letter. This letter is solely for your benefit and limited to the facts discussed below. Please contact me if any of the facts are misstated or if you have additional information.

FACTS

On December 7, 2016, you were skiing on an expert run at Red Mountain Ski Resort. Near the top of the run, you encountered a series of moguls. The moguls were difficult to ski, and as a result, you lost control and broke your left arm. There were no signs posted on the run that warned skiers of the upcoming moguls.

ANSWER

Based upon the above facts, you probably cannot successfully sue Red Mountain Ski Resort for its failure to warn of the moguls. The only possible theory under which you could sue is negligence. You would claim that the resort was negligent for failing to warn of the upcoming moguls. Under the applicable state statute and the court opinions interpreting that statute, the resort does not have a duty to warn of the presence of moguls.

EXPLANATION

Chapter 70 of the New Washington statutes, the Ski Safety Act, governs the operation of ski resorts and establishes the duties of skiers and resort operators. Section 7A of the act requires resorts to warn of sections of trails "which present an unusual obstacle or hazard." Section 8B of the act states that a skier "expressly assumes the risk and legal responsibility for any injury to a person or property which results from . . . surface or subsurface snow or ice conditions. . . ."

The act does not discuss whether a mogul is a snow condition for which the skier is responsible. The state court of appeals, however, in the case of *Karen v. High Mountain Pass*, addressed the question of whether a resort has a duty to post a warning of the presence of moguls on a ski run. In this case, a skier broke his leg after failing to negotiate a series of moguls that were present in the middle of a turn on a ski run. The court stated that skiers are responsible for snow and ice hazards. The court noted that moguls, even though unavoidable, are snow hazards easily observable and routinely present on most ski runs. The court ruled that under the act, resorts have no duty to warn of snow hazards such as moguls.

The facts in your case are very similar to the facts in *Karen v. High Mountain Pass*. In your case, just as in that case, the injury occurred as a result of an encounter with moguls. It is apparent from section 8B of the statute, and the court's interpretation of that section in *Karen v. High Mountain Pass*, that skiers are responsible for injuries sustained as a result of encountering moguls on a ski run. Therefore, based on the statute and the court opinion in *Karen v. High Mountain Pass*, it is my opinion that it is highly unlikely that a lawsuit against Red Mountain Ski Resort for the injuries you sustained would be successful.

I hope this information answers your question. I regret that I am not able to provide a more favorable answer. If you have additional information concerning the accident, or if you have any other questions, please contact me.

Sincerely,

_____

Alice Black
Attorney at Law

ALB/wkk

C. Comments on Examples

In regard to the preceding examples, note that both letters:

- Present the subject matter clearly through the use of short sentences rather than complex sentences, which are often more difficult to follow and understand.
- Present the law in an objective and professional manner.
- Avoid legalese and discuss the material in a simple and clear manner. (Although there are references to statutes and case law, a summary of the law is provided rather than a technical discussion. The legal points are simply phrased in lay terms.)

In addition, the opinion letter clearly states at the outset that the opinion is limited to the current law and the facts provided by the client. Reference is made to the fact that the letter is intended solely for the benefit of the recipient.

Summary

This chapter discusses the preparation of legal correspondence, referred to as letters in the chapter. The focus is on letters that communicate the results of legal research and analysis. Letters are one of the primary forms of written communication directed to an audience outside the law office.

There are several fundamental components of all types of legal correspondence. There is no standard format; the content and style of presentation of these components vary according to personal and local preference. Section II of this chapter discusses the fundamental components of all legal correspondence.

Letters that include the results of legal research and analysis fall into three basic categories based upon the purpose of the communication:

1. To provide information—information letters
2. To provide an opinion—opinion letters
3. To demand action—demand letters

These three types of letters differ primarily in the content of the body.

The body of an information letter presents an objective summary of the research and analysis without the inclusion of any legal opinion or advice. The body of an opinion letter, in addition to a summary of the law, usually provides an objective assessment of the application of the law to the facts and often recommends a course of action. Because it includes a legal opinion or legal advice, an opinion letter constitutes the practice of law and must be signed by an attorney.

A demand letter is designed to persuade the reader to act in a manner that benefits the client, for example, to pay a debt. Like an opinion letter, a demand letter is signed by an attorney. The body of a demand letter is similar to the body of an opinion letter. The major difference is that the law and analysis are drafted in a persuasive manner.

Because the recipient of legal correspondence is an individual outside the law office, the correspondence affects the image and reputation of the law firm. For this reason, and because legal liability attaches to some correspondence, it is of paramount importance that you draft an accurate and professional product.

Quick References

Internet Resources

Using "legal correspondence" as a topic, you will find a wide range of websites (thousands) that refer to legal correspondence. The following is a summary of the categories of websites that may prove helpful when working on legal correspondence.

- Sites providing legal correspondence in specific cases, such as correspondence of the Association of Trial Lawyers regarding a specific subject. (Through such sites, you may view the examples of legal correspondence in specific areas.)
- Sites advertising businesses that prepare or assist in the preparation of correspondence
- School sites advertising programs that include preparation of correspondence as part of the curriculum
- Sites advertising legal forms and templates for legal correspondence

Sites containing job announcements for jobs that require the preparation of legal correspondence

Sites advertising texts that cover the preparation of legal correspondence

As with most topics on the Internet, the problem is not the lack of websites, but finding too many sites. You can avoid some of the frustration of finding too many websites by narrowing your search to a topic, such as "preparing legal opinion correspondence" or "legal correspondence, child custody cases."

Exercises

ASSIGNMENT 1

Describe the three types of correspondence discussed in this chapter and the purposes of each type.

ASSIGNMENT 2

Describe how the three types of correspondence are different.

ASSIGNMENT 3

Refer to the assignment introduced at the beginning of Chapter 16 and the law relevant to that assignment presented in the Application section of that chapter. The law firm represents Mrs. Findo. Draft an opinion letter informing her whether she can testify against her husband in light of the applicable Illinois statutory and case law.

ASSIGNMENT 4

Refer to the assignment introduced at the beginning of Chapter 17 and the relevant law included in the Application section of that chapter. You work for a law firm that represents the defendant.

a. Draft an information letter informing the defendant of what constitutes an arrest in the state of New Washington and how the law has been interpreted to apply in search warrant situations.

b. Draft an opinion letter advising the defendant whether there is sufficient evidence to support charges of possession.

ASSIGNMENT 5

The client, Mrs. Tatum, purchased a new microwave oven from Inki Appliances Company. No written or oral warranty was given when the sale was made. The microwave stopped working one week after Mrs. Tatum took it home. She returned the microwave three days after it quit working. The owner of Inki Appliances refused to repair or replace the microwave or give Mrs. Tatum her money back. Prepare a demand letter to be sent to Inki Appliances. The letter is to be signed by your supervising attorney, Alice Black. Use the letterhead presented in the Application section of this chapter. Mr. Terry Spear is the president and owner of Inki Appliances Company, and the address is 1001 Maple Drive, Friendly, NW 00065.

Statutory Law: Section 50-102-314 of the New Washington statutes provides that "a warranty that the goods shall be merchantable is implied . . . if the seller is a merchant with respect to the goods of that kind." Mr. Spear is a merchant. Mrs. Tatum did not misuse the microwave or in any other way cause it to quit working.

Case Law: The case on point is *Smith v. Appliance City*, 56 N. Wash. 162, 868 N.E. 997 (1995). In *Smith*, the New Washington supreme court ruled that the seller has three options when an implied warranty is breached: return the purchase price to the buyer, repair the merchandise, or replace the merchandise.

ASSIGNMENT 6

Refer to Assignment 7 in Chapter 17. Prepare an information letter to Mr. Canter informing him of the results of your research in regard to armed bank robbery.

ASSIGNMENT 7

Refer to Assignment 9 in Chapter 17. Draft an opinion letter to Mr. Loya informing him of the results of your research and the likelihood of a finding that there is clear and convincing evidence his parental rights should be terminated.

ASSIGNMENT 8

The client, Mr. David Keys, would like to know what state law provides concerning the removal of a director from the board of directors of a corporation. Prepare an information letter to Mr. Keys summarizing the requirements of the removal statute. Draft the letter for the signature of your supervisory attorney, Alice Black. Use the letterhead presented in the

Application section of this chapter. Mr. Keys's address is 761 South Vine Street, Sunnydale, NW 00066.

Statute: New Washington Statutes Annotated § 77-11-22. Removal of directors: At a meeting of shareholders called expressly for that purpose, directors may be removed in the manner provided in this section. Any director or the entire board of directors may be removed, with or without cause, by a vote of the holders of a majority of the shares then entitled to vote at an election of directors.

ASSIGNMENT 9

Perform Assignment 9 using your state law. Make up local addresses for the law firm and client.

ASSIGNMENT 10

Draft an information letter to the client, Mr. Daniel Hope, Vice President, National Insurance Company. In the letter, summarize the state law concerning National's duty to defend persons it insures under its automobile insurance policies. Draft the letter for the signature of your supervising attorney, Alice Black. Use the letterhead presented in the Application section of this chapter. National Insurance Company's address is 459 Twenty-Second Street, Friendly, NW, 00065. There is no statutory law governing an insurance company's duty to defend its insured. The relevant case law follows.

Case Law: *Wrickles v. Washington Ins. Co.*, 61 N. Wash. 104 (Ct. App. 2008). Where it is determined that the insurer has unjustifiably failed to defend against claims against its insured, the insurer is liable for any judgment entered against its insured. In addition, the insurer may be liable for any reasonable settlement entered into by the insured.

State Farm Ins. Co. v. Peterson, 56 N. Wash. 38 (1995). The obligation to defend arises out of and must be found in the insuring agreement promising to defend the insured against liability.

Alison v. Lincoln Ins. Co., 60 N. Wash. 677 (Ct. App. 2000). The duty to defend is triggered when an injured party's complaint against the insured states facts that bring the case within the coverage of the policy.

Jamison v. Lincoln Ins. Co., 58 N. Wash. 430 (1998). An insurance company may refuse to defend its insured only when the allegations in the complaint are completely outside the insurance policy coverage.

Wilson v. Washington Ins. Co., 59 N. Wash. 980 (1999). If the allegations in the complaint against the insured may fall within the coverage of the policy but are potentially excluded by any noncoverage provision in the policy, then the insurer is under a duty to defend the insured in the primary action. The duty continues until a court having jurisdiction over the case finds that the insurer is relieved of the liability under the noncoverage provisions of the policy.

ASSIGNMENT 11

In this assignment, draft the letter for the signature of the supervising attorney, Alice Black. Use the letterhead presented in the Application section of this chapter. Mr. Sanders's address is 930 North Hardwood Court, Friendly, NW 00065.

Assignment Memo: We represent Washington Ins. Co. They paid a claim by their insured in the amount of $21,235.00. The claim arose out of an automobile collision between the insured, Deborah Anderson, and Mr. Karl Sanders. Mr. Sanders ran a stop sign, and his vehicle collided with the insured resulting in the damage. Washington Ins. has written to Mr. Sanders requesting that he either provide proof of insurance at the time of the accident or that he pay the claim in full. He has not responded.

Prepare a draft of a demand letter to Mr. Karl Sanders demanding that he pay the $21,235.00 or contact me to see if we can reach an agreement for payment of the debt. Inform him that this is an attempt to collect a debt. Also inform him that if he does not contact us within 30 days of the date of the letter, I will assume that he does not dispute the debt and I will pursue all legal remedies available under the law. Inform him that a lawsuit will be filed in the district court for the full amount of the debt plus interest, and I will request any fees and costs I may incur in pursuit of the litigation.

In addition, inform him that pursuant to New Washington law, once a judgment is obtained I can take action to have his driver's license and vehicle registration suspended under the provisions of the Financial Responsibility Act, NWSA § 45-6-124.

Statutory Law: Section 45-6-124 of the New Washington Financial Responsibility Act allows a judgment creditor to take action to suspend a debtor's driver's license and vehicle registration for nonpayment of any judgment arising from a motor vehicle accident.

ASSIGNMENT 12

Refer to the memorandum you drafted for Chapters 16 and 17. Your instructor will direct you to draft a informational, opinion, or demand letter (whichever is appropriate) based on your memorandum.

Court Opinions Referred to in the Text

Introduction

The court opinions in this appendix are presented in alphabetical order rather than in the order in which they are referred to in the text. To save space, portions of some cases that are not relevant to specific assignments or the discussion presented in the text have been omitted. A series of three asterisks indicates that a portion of the opinion has been omitted.

C&G LES SPRINGS FAMILY HOME, LLC,
an Arizona limited liability company,
Plaintiff/Appellant,

v.

WILLIAM and MARY HINZ, as individuals;

LES SPRINGS HOMEOWNERS ASSOCIATION,
INC., an Arizona corporation,

Defendants/Appellees.

1 CA-CV 08-0442

July 14, 2009

MEORANDUM DECISION

KESSLER, Judge

¶1 Appellant C&G Les Springs Family Home, LLC ("Appellant") appeals from the superior court's summary judgment in favor of Defendants/Appellees William and Mary Hinz ("the Hinzes") and the Les Springs Homeowners Association, Inc. ("HOA") (collectively "Appellees"). Appellant argues the court erred in granting the motion because undisputed facts show that the Hinzes' home encroaches into the subdivision's common area ("common area") and there were fact questions whether the HOA knew of and properly approved the encroachment. ***

FACTUAL AND PROCEDURAL HISTORY

¶2 C&G Les Springs Family Home is a subdivision in Sedona, Arizona comprised of approximately 106 lots. The lots in the subdivision are commonly referred to as building pads because the homes built typically encompass the entire lot leaving no space for a front or backyard area. The homes

built are surrounded by the common area, which is not the homeowners' private property.

***

¶4 Additionally, the HOA was responsible for regulating all construction and improvements within the subdivision. ***

¶5 Due to the homes' limited front and backyard areas, the Declaration includes a section on encroachment easements that states:

> Each Unit and the Common Areas shall be subject to an easement for encroachments created by construction or placement of, settling and overhanging, of Improvements, including, without limitation, construction of any overhanging decks or placement of any air conditioning units, as designed or constructed by the Declarant or as constructed by or on behalf of any Owner as approved by the Board or the Architectural Committee. A valid easement for said encroachments and for the maintenance of the same is hereby created and shall continue, so long as such encroachments continue to exist.

¶6 The Architectural Committee Rules ("Rules") also discuss lot boundaries by providing:

> The residence must be contained within the boundaries of the lot. Plans must indicate perimeter of lot on building plan. The [Architectural Committee] may allow decks to overhang the lot boundaries by up to nine feet on a case-by-case basis . . . The [Architectural Committee] will consider

(continues)

the impact on adjacent lots as well as the suitability of the overhangs in the overall design. If any part of the residence or a deck overhangs the lot, show clearly on plans, in red.

The Rules indicate "[a]ny deviation from approved plans must be submitted to the [Committee] for approval before construction can begin on the deviation." The Rules also provide that "[a] member may place no building, wall, fence, yard ornament or decoration, or other structure of any nature upon common area property except as otherwise permitted herein."

***

¶8 In September 2005, the Hinzes hired Susan Seay at Seay Construction, Inc. ("Seay") to remodel their house. Seay submitted necessary forms and remodeling plans to the Committee for review and approval. In addition to driveway improvements, the Hinzes planned to remodel the home's deck. According to affidavits submitted to the superior court, the Committee considered the topography of the site, the impact the remodeling would have on nearby lots, and the suitability of the proposed project in the overall design of the residence, including the suitability of the overhangs in the overall design. The Committee also consulted its architect and visited the construction site before approving the plans. The Committee determined that the overhang of the proposed decks did not extend more than nine feet into the common areas and did not have a negative effect on neighboring properties. Therefore, once the Committee approved the Hinzes' remodeling project, construction began.

¶9 In October 2006, Miller became aware of the remodeling project and expressed concern that the new decks extended into the common area. On Appellant's behalf, Miller filed a complaint against the Hinzes and HOA alleging breach of contract because Appellees failed to enforce and comply with the Declaration's terms. Appellant also sought injunctive relief against the Hinzes to prevent them from constructing, demolishing, or remodeling their home. In conjunction with the complaint, Miller filed an application for a temporary restraining order ("TRO") to prevent the Hinzes from continuing remodeling work. The superior court vacated Miller's application for a TRO because the parties agreed to temporarily delay the proceedings.

***

¶11 The Hinzes completed the remodeling project in late 2006. On February 20, 2007, the Appellees jointly moved for summary judgment. On March 21, 2007, Appellant filed a motion to enlarge time for filing affidavits pursuant to Arizona Rule 8 of Civil Procedure 56(f) ("Ariz. R Civ. P."). On April 20, 2007, Appellant filed a motion to enlarge the discovery deadline. On April 24, 2007, two days before the stipulated discovery deadline, the superior court denied Appellant's Rule 56(f) motion to enlarge time and its motion to extend the discovery deadline. The court, however,

granted Appellant 30 days to respond to the motion for summary judgment. The following month, Appellant filed a response to Appellees' motion for summary judgment.

¶12 In response to the motion for summary judgment on May 25, 2007, Appellant filed the affidavit of surveyor Dugan McDonald ("McDonald"). McDonald opined that the Hinzes' home was not properly situated upon Lot 31's building pad as recorded. The Appellees moved to strike McDonald's affidavit and accompanying exhibits alleging they violated Ariz. R. Civ. P. 37(c)(1).

¶13 The superior court granted Appellees' motion for summary judgment finding Appellant did not present an issue of material fact to support its assertion that Appellees breached the contract by violating the Declaration. The court also found the Declaration granted the Hinzes an express easement over the encroached-upon common area and that they met the elements establishing a prescriptive easement. ***

¶14 Appellant timely appealed. This court has jurisdiction pursuant to Arizona Revised Statutes ("A.R.S.") sections 12-2101(B) (2003) and -2102(A) (2003).

ANALYSIS

I. Motion for Summary Judgment

¶15 Appellant appeals from the superior court's order granting Appellees' motion for summary judgment. Appellant argues that the court erred in granting the motion because numerous factual issues remained regarding whether Appellees violated the Declaration and restrictions in associated documents.

¶16 Summary judgment may be granted when "[t]here is no genuine issue as to any material fact and . . . the moving party is entitled to a judgment as a matter of law." Ariz. R. Civ. P. 56(c)(1).

***

B. Easement

¶22 Appellant argues the superior court erred in finding that the Hinzes had a right to a prescriptive easement for encroaching upon the common area because the only basis for such an easement was the Declaration and that required proper approval of any encroachment. Appellant claims there was a factual issue about whether such approval was proper. We disagree for several reasons. First, as previously discussed, we agree with the superior court that Appellees complied with the Declaration in approving the remodeling plans. Accordingly, as the court held, the Hinzes had an express easement for encroachment pursuant to Article XII, Section 1 of the Declaration.

¶23 Second, the superior court held the Hinzes had a common law prescriptive easement.[1] Prescriptive easements can arise in at least two ways. Traditionally, a prescriptive easement arises when "[t]he land which is allegedly subject to the easement has been actually and visibly[2] used for a specific purpose for ten years[3] and that the use was commenced and continued under a claim of right inconsistent with and hostile to the claim of another." *Ammer v. Ariz. Water Co.*, 169 Ariz. 205, 208, 818 P.2d 190, 193 (App. 1991) (citation omitted). Once the claimant establishes actual and visible use of the property for the requisite period, the use is presumed to be under a claim of right and not permissive. *Id.*; *Accord Harambasic v. Owens*, 186 Ariz. 159, 160–61, 920 P.2d 39, 40–41 (App. 1996).

¶24 Additionally, when a party attempts to grant an express easement, but that grant fails for a given reason, courts will hold there is a prescriptive easement provided the common law elements have been met. *Paxson*, 203 Ariz. at 69, ¶¶ 32–33, 50 P.3d at 426; Restatement § 2.16(2). As explained by and adopted in *Paxson*, the Restatement provides that a prescriptive easement is either:

(1) [A] use that is adverse to the owner of the land or the interest in land against which the servitude is claimed, or

(2) [A] use that is made pursuant to the terms of an intended but imperfectly created servitude, or the enjoyment of the benefit of an intended but imperfectly created servitude.

Restatement § 2.16; *Paxson*, 203 Ariz. at 69, ¶ 32, 50 P.3d at 426. In contrast to a prescriptive easement under § 2.16(1), which requires adverse use, an easement under § 2.16(2) only requires that there be an intended, but imperfectly created grant and that it be used openly and for the prescriptive period under § 2.17. Restatement § 2.16 cmt. b.:

An "adverse" use as that term is used in subsection (1) is a use made without the consent of the landowner . . . and without other authorization . . . .. Prescriptive uses under subsection (2) must be made pursuant to the terms of an

intended but imperfectly created servitude. "Intended" means that the property owner and user intended to create a servitude . . ..

Restatement § 2.16 cmt. a:

In the second situation, people try to create a servitude but fail, initially because . . . they fail to comply with some other formal requirement imposed in the jurisdiction. If they proceed to act as though they have been successful in creating the servitude and continue to do so for the prescriptive period, the servitude is created by prescription if the other requirements of [Restatement] § 2.17's [open and notorious continuous use for prescriptive period] are met.

¶25 Here, the HOA attempted to grant an express easement pursuant to the Declaration and its approval of the remodeling. Even if that approval was technically defective because of the plans submitted, a prescriptive easement would still arise under the failed express easement theory.

¶26 Additionally, each of the common law elements for such an easement is met here. For example, the original home and the Hinzes' home encroached upon the common area from June 1986 through 2005, and there is no evidence of objections until 2005 or when Miller filed the complaint. Also, the deck's encroachment upon the common area was open because it was outdoors and visible to others. See *Knapp v. Wise*, 122 Ariz. 327, 329, 594 P.2d 1023, 1025 (App. 1979) (reasoning open and notorious includes one figuratively "fl[ying] the flag" over the land putting the true owner on notice that his land is held under an adverse claim of ownership). Further, as Appellees point out, the Shors' plans were on record with the county. In fact, Appellee includes copies of three county building permits from 1986, which show the Shors' home passed final inspection. Additionally, Appellant's own expert admits in his affidavit that the original home plans showed the home encroached onto the common area and the survey was on record with the county. Even if Appellant argues the plans on record did not provide enough notice of the encroachment, Appellant admits that the Declaration and associated documents show that the development's unique nature requires protection from encroachments upon the common area. Thus, Appellant should have known the Hinzes' home encroached upon the common area given the unique nature of these lots. Consequently, the Hinzes meet all of the elements required to establish a prescriptive easement over the common area that their home encroaches upon.

***

CONCLUSION

¶41 For the forgoing reasons, we affirm the superior court's grant of summary judgment in favor of Appellees.***

---

1. Appellant does not address this second theory for a prescriptive easement on appeal, thus waiving the issue. Schabel v. Deer Valley Unified Sch. Dist. No. 97, 186 Ariz. 161, 167, 920 P.2d 41, 47 (App. 1996). The only possible reference to the failed express easement theory is Appellant's statement that the Declaration grants an express easement for encroachment only if approved by the HOA or Committee. This, however, does not preclude a common law easement if the approval was technically defective. It is exactly in that case when a prescriptive easement by a failed express easement arises. In any event, we address this issue on the merits.

2. The Restatement (Third) of Prop.: Servitudes ("Restatement") § 2.17 (2000) provides the use must be open or notorious and continuous for the prescriptive period. "Open or notorious" means the use is sufficient to give the landowner ample opportunity to learn of the use and protect his or her rights. Id. at cmt. h.

3. To meet the ten year requirement, parties using the property can tack their respective periods of use. Paxson v. Glovitz, 203 Ariz. 63, 69 n.5, 50 P.3d 420, 426 n.5 (App. 2002); Restatement § 2.17 ("Periods of prescriptive use may be tacked together to make up the prescriptive period ....").

Dwonna Gayle Gwaltney CARDWELL, Appellant,

v.

Kenneth Wayne GWALTNEY, Appellee.

No. 87A01–9002–CV–80.

Court of Appeals of Indiana, First District.

July 17, 1990.

556 N.E.2d 953 (Ind. Ct. App. 1990)

OBERTSON, Judge.

The sole issue raised in this appeal is whether an individual should be absolved from paying child support because of his incarceration.

The underlying material facts show that the appellant Cardwell and the appellee Gwaltney were divorced with Gwaltney ordered to pay child support. About a year and one-half later, Gwaltney filed a petition to modify the support order based upon the reason that he had spent a year in jail. Gwaltney sought to be absolved from the support which had accrued during that year and to have future support reduced. Cardwell and Gwaltney reached an agreement that, among other things, excused Gwaltney from paying support for the year he was imprisoned. The trial court approved the agreement; however, that agreement was challenged when the county prosecuting attorney appeared in the matter and sought to set aside the agreement because Cardwell had been a recipient of AFDC funds through the State and had assigned her support rights. The trial court refused to set aside the earlier agreements with this appeal resulting.

Even though the trial judge was prompted by equitable concerns when Gwaltney was excused from paying support[,] the law is that any modification of a support order must act prospectively:

In *Biedron v. Biedron* (1958), 128 Ind. App. 299, 148 N.E.2d 209, the Appellate Court of Indiana said, "in this state after support installments have accrued, the court is without power to reduce, annul or vacate such orders retrospectively, and therefore, the court committed error in attempting to do so." (Citations omitted) Therefore, payments must be made in the manner, amount, and at the times required by the support order embodied in the divorce decree until such order is modified or set aside. *Stitle v. Stitle* (1964), 245 Ind. 168, 197 N.E.2d 174,

Indiana does permit cancellation or modification of support orders as to future payments; but, all modifications operate prospectively. *Kniffen v. Courtney* (1971), 148 Ind. App. 358, 266 N.E.2d 72; *Haycraft v. Haycraft* (1978), Ind. App. [176 Ind. App. 211], 375 N.E.2d 252.

Jahn v. Jahn (1979), 179 Ind. App. 368, 385 N.E.2d 488, 490. See also *O'Neil v. O'Neil* (1988), Ind. App., 517 N.E.2d 433 (transfer granted on other grounds).

Additionally, I.C. 31-2-11-12 provides:
Modification of delinquent support payment.

(a) Except as provided in subsection (b), *a court may not retroactively modify* an obligor's duty to pay a delinquent support payment.
(b) A court with jurisdiction over a support order may modify an obligor's duty to pay a support payment that becomes due:

(1) After notice of a petition to modify the support order has been given to each obligee; and
(2) Before a final order concerning the petition for modification is entered. (Emphasis added.)

Although the Indiana Child Support Guidelines, effective October 1, 1989, were not officially in use at the time of the trial court's decision in this appeal, we are of the opinion that a part of the commentary to Ind. Child Support Guideline 2 takes into consideration existing statutes and case law as heretofore cited. That part of the commentary reads:

Even in situations where the non-custodial parent has no income, Courts have routinely established a child support obligation at some minimum level. An obligor cannot be held in contempt for failure to pay support when he does not have the means to pay, but the obligation accrues and serves as a reimbursement to the custodial parent, or, more likely, to the welfare department if he later acquires the ability to meet his obligation.

We conclude that the trial court erred in retroactively excusing Gwaltney's support obligation for the time he was incarcerated.

Cause reversed and remanded for further action not inconsistent with this opinion.

Reversed and remanded.

RATLIFF, C.J., and CONOVER, J., concur.

Michael Anthony CORDOVA, Plaintiff-Appellant,

v.

Frederick WOLFEL, Jr., David Abeyta, James Abeyta, Priscilla Abeyta, and

National Car Rentals Systems, Inc., Defendants-Appellees.

Supreme Court of New Mexico

120 N.M. 557, 903 P.2d 1390 (1995)

MINZNER, Justice.

Cordova appeals from a decision granting summary judgment in favor of National Car Rentals Systems (National). This case raises the issue of whether the Mandatory Financial Responsibility Act (the MFRA), NMSA 1978, §§ 66-5-201 to -239 (Repl. Pamp. 1994), imposes liability upon a self-insured rental car company for the negligence of an unauthorized driver, despite a contrary rental contract provision. We conclude that the MFRA does not impose such liability, and we affirm summary judgment.

I. FACTS

On January 26, 1990, Priscilla Abeyta rented a car from National at the Albuquerque Airport. Her purpose was to drive her son David and his two friends to Reno, Nevada. At the time of renting, she intended to drive the vehicle exclusively herself. There is a factual dispute between the parties about what rental documents Abeyta read and consented to at the time that she entered into the lease. It is clear, however, that Abeyta signed a standard National form wherein she acknowledged that only she had an "additional authorized driver may drive vehicle." A space for the designation of an additional authorized driver appeared next to Abeyta's signature, and that space was blank. Abeyta declined to purchase optional personal accident insurance.

Shortly after picking up the vehicle, Abeyta became ill, and she decided not to make the trip. She gave permission to her son David to drive. There appears to be a factual dispute about whether she also gave David's friends Wolfel and Cordova permission to drive. After the three men started on their trip, they began to drink, and Wolfel took over the driving. There is a factual dispute about whether Wolfel had had anything to drink and whether he was intoxicated at the time of the accident, which occurred on an interstate highway in Arizona.[1] The accident resulted, at least in part,

from Wolfel's negligence, and there were no other vehicles involved.

Cordova claims to have sustained injuries in the amount of $650,000. This figure includes medical expenses exceeding $69,000, lost wages, and permanent loss of the sense of smell. Cordova brought suit against Wolfel, National, Mr. and Mrs. Abeyta, their son David, and Travelers Insurance Company, the Abeytas' personal liability insurer. Cordova has settled his claims against the Abeytas and Wolfel. The trial court granted summary judgment in favor of Travelers after it determined that the insurance contract between Travelers and the Abeytas did not extend coverage to the rental car. National is the sole remaining defendant.

II. DISCUSSION

A. Summary Judgment

Along with its motion for summary judgment, National submitted the car rental agreement wherein Abeyta acknowledged that she was the only authorized driver of the vehicle. National asserted that because the agreement provided liability coverage only to authorized drivers, National had no obligation to indemnify Wolfel for liability resulting from his negligent operation of the vehicle. National maintains that as the self-insured owner of the rental car, it is not an insurer, and there was no insurance contract between it and Abeyta. National further contends that the MFRA specifically exempts self-insurers from its provisions.

Cordova argues that National's "Certificate of Self-Insurance [issued by the State Superintendent of Insurance] provides liability coverage on [the] vehicle driven by Frederick Wolfel." Cordova does not dispute National's contention that Wolfel was not an authorized driver. Rather, Cordova argues that Wolfel was a permissive driver because he operated the vehicle with Abeyta's express or implied permission. *See United Servs. Auto. Ass'n v. National Farmers Union Property & Casualty*, 119 N.M. 397, 891 P.2d 538 (1995). This contention rests upon the premise that National, as a self-insurer, provided insurance coverage under which Abeyta was the "named insured." Cordova asserts that because the MFRA mandates that liability coverage must extend to persons using the vehicle with the express or implied permission of the named insured, coverage extends to Wolfel by operation of law. *See id.;* § 66-5-221(A)(2).

Cordova argues on appeal that the trial court erred when it determined that, as a matter of law, National is not liable for Wolfel's negligence. We agree with the trial court's interpretation of the rental agreement and its resolution of the

---

1. We assume that New Mexico's substantive law applies to this appeal because neither party asserts otherwise.

(continues)

purely legal issues presented by this case. Resolving all disputed facts in favor of Cordova, we conclude that National is entitled to judgment, and we affirm. *See Tapia v. Springer Transfer Co.*, 106 N.M. 461, 462–63, 744 P.2d 1264, 1265–66 (Ct. App.), *cert. quashed*, 106 N.M. 405, 744 P.2d 180 (1987).

B. Self-Insurance

* * *

[3] Most authorities agree that self-insurance is not insurance. Insurance is a contract whereby for consideration one party agrees to indemnify or guarantee another party against specified risks. *See New Mexico Life Ins. Guar. Ass'n v. Moore*, 93 N.M. 47, 50, 596 P.2d 260, 263 (1979); NMSA 1978, § 59A-1-5 (Repl. Pamp. 1992). In contrast, self-insurance is a process of risk retention whereby an entity "set[s] aside assets to meet foreseeable future losses." Robert E. Keeton & Alan I. Widiss, *Insurance Law: A Guide to Fundamental Principles, Legal Doctrines and Commercial Practices* § 1.3, at 14 (1988); *see also Levi Strauss & Co. v. New Mexico Property & Casualty Ins. Guar. Ass'n (In re Mission Ins. Co.)*, 112 N.M. 433, 437, 816 P.2d 502, 506 (1991) (holding that a certificate of self-insurance "cannot be equated with an insurance contract or policy"). A self-insurer protects itself from liability; it does not assume the risk of another. *See Levi Strauss & Co.*, 112 N.M. at 436–37, 816 P.2d at 505–06; *Consolidated Enters., Inc. v. Schwindt*, 172 Ariz. 35, 833 P.2d 706, 709 (1992) (en banc). We note that self-insurance and insurance serve similar purposes and that insurance principles may sometimes apply to self-insurance by way of analogy. Nonetheless, we reject as inaccurate Cordova's theory that self-insurance is a subset of insurance.

[4] The relationship between National and its lessees is one of bailment, and there generally is no common law basis for imposing upon a bailor liability for a bailee's negligent operation of a bailed vehicle. *See Stover v. Critchfield*, 510 N.W.2d 681, 683-84 (S.D. 1994). The legislatures of a few states have altered this common law rule through legislation. *See* Ariz. Rev. Stat. Ann. § 28–324 (1994 Cum. Supp.) (requiring owner of rental vehicles to obtain public liability insurance protecting passengers and third parties against negligence of renter; however, owner not liable for damages beyond limits of insurance policy); Conn. Gen. Stat. § 14–154a (1995) (owner of leased vehicle liable for damage caused by operation of leased vehicle to same extent as operator would be held liable if operator were owner); *cf.* Neb. Rev. Stat. § 25–21,239 (1994 Cum. Supp.) (making owner of leased truck jointly and severally liable with lessee for lessee's negligence). Moreover, the court of at least one state has determined that, as a matter of public policy, a vehicle lessor will be liable for the negligence of a lessee, irrespective of contrary contractual language. *See Motor Vehicle Accident Indem. Corp. v. Continental Nat'l Am. Group Co.*, 35 N.Y.2d 260, 360 N.Y.S.2d 859, 861–63, 319 N.E.2d 182, 184–85 (1974). The New Mexico legislature has not enacted legislation that would make vehicle lessors generally liable for injuries that result when lessees negligently use their vehicles, and we decline to take that step in the absence of legislative action. We conclude that a vehicle lessor is liable for the negligence of a lessee or a lessee's permittee only to the extent that a statute, administrative regulation, or agreement of the parties imposes such liability.

[5] Cordova's arguments on appeal largely proceed from the premise that a self-insured entity such as National is subject to the requirements of the MFRA. However, the MFRA itself belies this contention. In unambiguous language, the MFRA exempts from its provisions "motor vehicle[s] approved as self-insured by the superintendent of insurance." Section 66-5-207(E). We recognize that there may be situations where it is appropriate to apply the provisions of the MFRA to self-insurers by analogy. Nonetheless, we cannot ignore the statute's plain language, *see V.P. Clarence Co. v. Colgate*, 115 N.M. 471, 473 853 P.2d 722, 724, (1993), and a literal interpretation of Section 66-5-207(E) does not lead to an absurd result. *Cf. State v. Gutierrez*, 115 N.M. 551, 552, 854 P.2d 878, 879 (Ct. App.) (holding that where literal language of statute leads to absurd result, court may construe statute to avoid such result), *cert. denied*, 115 N.M. 545, 854 P.2d 872 (1993).

* * *

III. CONCLUSION

We conclude that the trial court correctly determined that National is exempt from the MFRA, and that, in the absence of a contractual agreement, National is not vicariously liable for Wolfel's negligence. Summary judgment in favor of National is affirmed.

IT IS SO ORDERED.
BACA, C.J., and FROST, J., concur.

ERIK T., Appellant,

v.

DEPARTMENT OF CHILD SAFETY, S.T., Appellees.

No. 1 CA-JV 15-0274

Filed January 28, 2016

MEMORANDUM DECISION

JOHNSEN, Judge.

¶ 1 Erik T. ("Father") appeals the superior court's order terminating his parental rights. For the reasons that follow, we affirm.

FACTS AND PROCEDURAL BACKGROUND

¶ 2 Father is the parent of an Indian child ("Child") born in April 2010.[1] Father was incarcerated from November 2010 until October 2012. Shortly after his release, Father was convicted of aggravated assault and sentenced to 10.5 years incarceration beginning in December 2012. The Department of Child Safety ("DCS") took Child and his two half-siblings into custody in September 2013 because of allegations of substance abuse and neglect by their mother ("Mother").[2] The superior court found Child dependent as to Mother and Father in December 2013. In March 2015, DCS moved to terminate parental rights to Child and his two half-siblings. The court terminated Mother's parental rights; she is not a party to this appeal. After a trial, the court terminated Father's parental rights due to his incarceration, pursuant to Arizona Revised Statutes ("A.R.S.") section 8–533(B)(4) (2016).[3]

¶ 3 Father timely appealed. We have jurisdiction pursuant to Article 6, Section 9 of the Arizona Constitution, A.R.S. §§ 8–235(A)(2016), 12–2101 (2016) and Rule 103(A) of the Arizona Rules of Procedure for the Juvenile Court.

DISCUSSION
A. Legal Principles.

¶ 4 The right to custody of one's child is fundamental but not absolute. *Michael J. v. Ariz. Dep't of Econ. Sec.*, 196 Ariz. 246, 248, ¶¶ 11–12 (2000). The superior court may terminate a parent-child relationship upon clear and convincing evidence of at least one of the statutory grounds set out in A.R.S. § 8–533(B). *Michael J.*, 196 Ariz. at 249, ¶ 12. Additionally, the court must find by a preponderance of the evidence that termination is in the child's best interests. *Kent K. v. Bobby M.*, 210 Ariz. 279, 284, ¶ 22 (2005). We review a termination order for an abuse of discretion. *Mary Lou C. v. Ariz. Dep't of Econ. Sec.*, 207 Ariz. 43, 47, ¶ 8 (App.2004). Because the superior court is in the best position to "weigh the evidence, observe the parties, judge the credibility of witnesses, and make appropriate findings," we will accept its findings of fact unless no reasonable evidence supports them. *See Jesus M. v. Ariz. Dep't of Econ. Sec.*, 203 Ariz. 278, 280, ¶ 4 (App.2002).

B. Best-Interests Determination Under § 8–533(B).

¶ 5 On appeal, Father does not contest the superior court's finding by clear and convincing evidence of facts permitting severance under A.R.S. § 8–533(B)(4) (parent "deprived of civil liberties due to the conviction of a felony" that "is of such length that the child will be deprived of a normal home for a period of years"). Father instead takes issue with the court's finding that severance is in Child's best interests. *See* A.R.S. § 8–533(B). A best-interests finding may be supported by evidence of an affirmative benefit or a detriment to the child if the relationship were to continue. *Jennifer B. v. Ariz. Dep't of Econ. Sec.*, 189 Ariz. 553, 557 (App.1997). Being available for adoption is an affirmative benefit that can support a finding that termination is in a child's best interests. *See Maricopa County Juv. Action No. JS-501904*, 180 Ariz. 348, 352 (App.1994). Whether severance is in a child's best interests is a question of fact, and we view the evidence and draw all reasonable inferences from the evidence in favor of supporting the superior court's findings. *Jesus M.*, 203 Ariz. at 282, ¶ 13.

¶ 6 Father argues insufficient evidence supported the court's finding that termination is in Child's best interests. He cites the testimony of an Indian Child Welfare Act ("ICWA") expert, who stated guardianship would be preferable to termination. Notwithstanding Father's contentions, however, the court heard evidence that Child is adoptable and would benefit from being adopted. The DCS case manager testified Child and his two half-siblings currently are placed with paternal relatives of Child's half-sibling and that the current placement is willing to adopt all three children as a group. She testified Child would benefit from severance, as it would provide him with permanence and stability. Accordingly, sufficient evidence supported the court's determination that termination of Father's rights would be in Child's best interests.

***

CONCLUSION

¶ 16 Because sufficient evidence supported the superior court's order terminating Father's parental rights, we affirm.

---

1. Because Child's mother is an enrolled member of the Navajo Nation and Child is eligible for enrollment, he is an Indian child pursuant to the Indian Child Welfare Act. *See* 25 U.S.C. § 1903(4) (2016).

2. Pursuant to S.B. 1001, Section 157, 51st Leg., 2d Spec. Sess. (Ariz. 2014) (enacted), the Department of Child Safety is substituted for the Arizona Department of Economic Security in this matter. *See* ARCAP 27.

3. Absent material revision after the relevant date, we cite a statute's current version.

PAPPAS ENTERPRISES, INC., & others[1]

v.

COMMERCE AND INDUSTRY INSURANCE COMPANY.

661 N.E.2d 81

Supreme Judicial Court of Massachusetts, Suffolk.

Argued Dec. 4, 1995. Decided Feb. 14, 1996.

Insured commenced action in the United States District Court for the District of Massachusetts after insurer declined liability for a fire loss under vacancy exclusion in policy. The District Court certified questions of law to the Supreme Judicial Court. The Supreme Judicial Court, Wilkins, J., held that: (1) 60-day vacancy provision does not apply in case where part of 60 days of vacancy occurred prior to day policy came into force, and (2) however, where policy in force at time of fire was renewal of immediately preceding policy, and portion of vacancy beyond 60 days occurred during immediately preceding policy period, exclusion would operate to preclude coverage for loss.

Certified questions answered.

CERTIFICATION of questions of law to the Supreme Judicial Court by the United States District Court for the District of Massachusetts.

* * *

Before LIACOS, C.J., and WILKINS, O'CONNOR, GREANEY and FRIED, JJ.

OPINION

WILKINS, Justice.

The plaintiffs, whom we shall refer to collectively as the insured, are beneficiaries of an insurance policy issued by the defendant insurer that provided coverage against fire loss to numerous properties in the Boston area. The policy, which became effective on September 1, 1990, was a renewal of property damage policies that had been issued on September 1, 1988, and September 1, 1989. On October 27, 1990, 57 days after the effective date of the policy then in effect, one of the covered properties was damaged by fire. That property had been vacant since May, 1989, a period of well over a year.

When the insurer declined liability for the fire loss, the insured commenced an action in the United States District Court for the District of Massachusetts. In defense

of the claim, the insurer relied in part on policy language, prescribed by G.L. c. 175, § 99 [Twelfth] (1994 ed.), that excluded liability for a loss occurring while the described premises "are vacant or unoccupied beyond a period of sixty consecutive days." The facts presented the question [of] whether the period of 60 consecutive days of vacancy included only days during the policy period in which the loss occurred or could also include consecutive days of vacancy during the prior policy period.

A District Court judge determined that (1) the policy provision was inherently ambiguous; (2) there was no controlling Massachusetts authority; (3) cases elsewhere relied on factors not applicable in the circumstances of this case; and (4) the ambiguity is "contained in every fire insurance policy written in Massachusetts." She invoked S.J.C. Rule 1:03, as appearing in 382 Mass. 700 (1981), and certified the following two questions to this court:

"1. Does the 60-day vacancy provision for fire insurance policies prescribed by M.G.L. ch. 175 § 99—that the insurance company is not liable for losses occurring 'while the described premises, whether intended for occupancy by owner or tenant, are -vacant or unoccupied beyond a period of sixty consecutive days'— apply in the case where part of the 60 days of vacancy occurred prior to the day the policy came into force?"

"2. If the answer to the preceding question is in the negative, would the result be different (that is, would the vacancy provision apply, and thus preclude coverage) where the policy in force at the time of the fire was a renewal of an immediately preceding policy, and a portion of the period of vacancy beyond 60 days occurred during the immediately preceding policy period?"

We conclude that consecutive days of vacancy occurring prior to the policy period may be counted toward the 60 days of vacancy, referred to in the vacancy exclusion provision, only if the current policy is a renewal of substantially the same coverage of the damaged property provided in the previous policy period.

1. Today, and since its insertion in the General Laws (by St.1951, c. 478), § 99 [Twelfth] of G.L. c. 175 has required that a policy state that, unless it otherwise provides, the insurer of premises of the kind involved in this case "shall not be liable for loss occurring . . . (b) while the described premises, whether intended for occupancy by owner or tenant, are vacant or unoccupied beyond a period of sixty consecutive days." Prior to the 1951 amendment, the relevant statute had required that the standard Massachusetts policy provide that the policy was void "if the premises hereby insured shall become vacant by the removal of the owner or occupant, and so remain vacant for more than thirty days." In *Wainer*

---

[1] Pappas Management Corp., The 418 Worcester Wareland Realty Trust, and Capital Site Management Associates.

v. Milford Mut. Fire Ins. Co., 153 Mass. 335, 339, 26 N.E. 877 (1891), the court construed that former language to mean a vacancy of 30 days commencing while the policy was in force. The words "shall become vacant" pointed to a prospective event, a future vacancy. *Id.* The language of the current § 99 concerning premises that "are vacant" for more than 60 days is not as clearly prospective in its focus. The 1951 change in the relevant language tends to suggest that the Legislature may have no longer intended that the focus should be only on a prospective vacancy.

The Legislature may not, however, have had its eye on the *Wainer* case when it placed the relevant language in § 99. That language came from the New York standard fire insurance policy, which was adopted in most States by statute and was adopted in Massachusetts in part. See Annot. of the 1943 Standard Fire Insurance Policy 3 (ed. ABA Tort and Insurance Practice Section, 2d ed. 1994); Vance on Insurance 807-808 (3d ed. 1951). The old standard form policy used nationally (but not here) and replaced generally in this country by the New York standard fire insurance policy, provided that, if premises "be or become vacant or unoccupied and so remain for ten days," the policy was void. See *Old Colony Ins. Co. v. Garvey*, 253 F.2d 299, 301 (4th Cir.1958); *Thomas v. Industrial Fire & Casualty Co.*, 255 So. 2d 486, 488 (La. App. 1971). The abandonment of the old form ("be or become vacant") in favor of the less certain "are vacant" provision was a move away from voiding a policy or coverage based on a vacancy existing at the policy's inception.

We decline to interpret language used in a national standard policy to have a special Massachusetts meaning simply because of an implication that could be derived from an uncertain legislative history. The language "are vacant" (which replaced "be or become vacant") has been consistently regarded as referring only to a vacancy occurring after the commencement of coverage. See *Home Mut. Fire Ins. Co. v. Pierce*, 240 Ark. 865, 402 S.W.2d 672, 674-675 (1966); *Kolivera v. Hartford Fire Ins. Co.*, 8 Ill. App. 3d 356, 360-361, 290 N.E.2d 356 (1972); *Thomas v. Industrial Fire & Casualty Co.*, 255 So. 2d 486, 488 (La. App. 1971); *Hurst v. Donegal & Conoy Mut. Fire Ins. Co.*, 224 S.C. 188, 78 S.E.2d 189, 191 (1953); *Old Colony Ins. Co. v. Garvey*, 253 F.2d 299, 302 (4th Cir.1958) (North Carolina law); *United States Fidelity & Guar. Co. v. Board of Educ. of Fairfield*, 339 F. Supp. 315, 318 (N.D. Ala. 1972) (Alabama law).

2. Some opinions holding that the entire vacancy must occur during the policy period resolve the policy ambiguity by reliance on the principle that ambiguities should be construed against the insurer. See *Home Mut. Ins. Co. v. Pierce, supra*, 402 S.W.2d at 675; *Old Colony Ins. Co. v. Garvey, supra; United States Fidelity & Guar. v. Board of Educ., supra*. That principle has no proper place in construing policy language that is, as in this case, dictated by statute. See *McNeill v. Metropolitan Property & Liab. Ins. Co.*, 420 Mass. 587, 589, 650 N.E.2d 793 (1995); *Bilodeau*

v. Lumbermens Mut. Casualty Co., 392 Mass. 537, 541, 467 N.E.2d 137 (1984).

We conclude that the period of a vacancy existing prior to the date coverage is first effective should not be counted in determining whether a vacancy that excludes liability has occurred. One factor is our interest in giving § 99 the same treatment that is given to identical language in policies issued in other States. Another consideration is the opportunity an insurer has to determine whether a vacancy exists at the inception of a policy and to choose not to underwrite the risk, to amend the policy provisions (where permitted), or explicitly to provide coverage at an additional premium. See *Commerce Ins. Co. v. Koch*, 25 Mass. App. Ct. 383, 388, 522 N.E.2d 979 (1988). Most important is the understanding that the parties should reasonably have concerning the policy language, applying normal reasoning and analysis. See *Save-Mor Supermarkets, Inc. v. Skelly Detective Serv., Inc.*, 359 Mass. 221, 225-226, 268 N.E.2d 666 (1971). See also *Home Indem. Ins. Co. v. Merchants Distrib., Inc.*, 396 Mass. 103, 107, 483 N.E.2d 1099 (1985). If a vacancy exists at the inception of coverage, it is hardly reasonable to believe that the coverage should terminate earlier than 60 days later when, for the premium paid, the insurer has agreed to assume for 60 days the increased risk of loss that vacant premises present.

We answer the first certified question in the negative because the vacancy exclusion does not apply when the loss occurred within 60 days of the effective date of the policy, assuming that there was no prior coverage of the type we shall describe in answer to the next question.

3. We next consider whether the vacancy exclusion applies where, as here, the fire loss occurred during the first 60 days of the policy renewal and the vacancy had existed for more than 60 days before the date of the fire. We conclude that the vacancy exclusion precludes coverage of the fire loss, assuming that the renewal did not involve any change of significance in the coverage provided for the property damaged by fire. See *Thatcher v. Reliance Ins. Co.*, 226 A.2d 919, 924-925 (Del. Super. 1967). We do not have the circumstances of the renewal before us and, therefore, our comments can only be general.

The rule we state would unquestionably apply when a policy by its terms, unlike the case before us, was automatically renewed on the timely payment of premium. See *State Farm Gen. Ins. Co. of Bloomington v. Chambers*, 260 Ark. 637, 640, 543 S.W.2d 470 (1976) (denying coverage because "[t]he old and only insurance contract was simply extended for an additional year by the payment of the premium for the ensuing year"). The result should not turn, however, formalistically on whether a new policy, substantially identical as to the damaged property, was issued or the old policy was continued by its terms.

(continues)

The controlling factor should be what the parties reasonably should have understood the policy language to mean. The property had been vacant since May, 1989. Coverage of the vacant premises undeniably ceased under the first policy sometime in July, 1989, pursuant to the vacancy exclusion clause, 60 days after the vacancy began. That exclusion of coverage continued at least to September 1, 1989, when the second policy period began. An exclusion of coverage unquestionably thereafter existed during the second policy period at least from the end of October, 1989, to September 1, 1990, when the third policy period began. No reasonable insured would believe, in those circumstances, with the uncontestable periods of noncoverage defined above, that the vacant premises would annually be provided coverage during the first 60 days of each renewal period. There is no sensible reason why that result should be reached or expected. The insurer agreed to assume the increased risk during a 60-day period and not during a period of a vacancy lasting more than 60 days.

We answer the second certified question in the affirmative because a period of a vacancy during a prior policy period should be tacked on to the vacancy continuing during the next subsequent policy period, assuming that there was no significant change in the coverage of the premises.

The PEOPLE of the State of Illinois, Appellant,

v.

Robert SANDERS, Appellee.

No. 57801.

Supreme Court of Illinois.

Dec. 16, 1983.

99 Ill. 2d 262, 457 N.E.2d 1241 (1983)

SIMON, Justice

The principal issue raised by this appeal is the construction and application to be given to the Illinois statute which prohibits husband and wife from testifying in criminal trials as to any communication or admission made one to the other or as to any conversation between them (Ill. Rev. Stat. 1981, ch. 38, par. 155-1). More precisely, the question is whether the privilege established by the statute is destroyed when the communication, admission, or conversation in question is in the presence of children of the spouses (including a child of one of the spouses who is not the child of defendant) who are old enough to understand the content of the conversation. A secondary issue is whether the plain error rule (87 Ill. 2d R. 615) should be applied to the admission of testimony about two conversations between spouses which may not have occurred in the presence of children but where no objection was advanced when all that was said in them was repeated in a third conversation which took place a few hours later and concerning which testimony was admissible.

A murder conviction of the defendant, Robert Sanders, in a jury trial in the circuit court of Cook County based in part upon the testimony of his wife was reversed by the appellate court (111 Ill. App. 3d 1, 66 Ill. Dec. 761, 443 N.E.2d 687). We allowed the State's petition for leave to appeal (87 Ill. 2d R. 315(a)).

During pretrial discovery, the defense filed a motion *in limine* to prevent the defendant's wife, Beverly Sanders, from testifying about conversations she had with her husband, the defendant. Shortly after it was filed, the public defender's office, which had been representing the defendant, was replaced by other appointed counsel, who represented the defendant at trial. Defendant's new attorney did not seek a ruling on the motion *in limine*, and that motion was never ruled upon. Neither did defendant's attorney object at trial to the wife's testimony.

She testified to three conversations with her husband which implicated him in the murder of which he was convicted. In the first conversation, which occurred the day before the murder, she testified the defendant told her while one or more of her children was present that he was going to rob the murder victim. The second conversation occurred in their bedroom in the early morning hours of the next day. During this conversation, at which no one else was present, the defendant gave his wife a ring and a watch which the woman who lived with the murder victim identified at trial as the victim's. The third conversation took place later that day. The defendant told her, she testified, that he had robbed the murder victim after striking him with a brick and tying him up. He also told her that he got the watch and ring during the robbery. This conversation, she said, was in the presence of their children.

The State argues that communications between spouses are privileged only when intended to be confidential. In this case the State contends the confidentiality of the first and third conversations was destroyed by the presence of their children. It contends that the second conversation was not confidential because the defendant must have expected that his wife would display the watch and ring he gave her by wearing them in public, and that he did not therefore intend his act to be confidential. The defendant argues that the record does not clearly show that their children were in the immediate presence of his wife and himself in a position to hear their first and third conversations, and that during the second communication he acted in reliance upon the expectation that what transpired would be confidential.

The starting point for our decision is the interpretation given in *People v. Palumbo* (1955), 5 Ill. 2d 409, 125 N.E.2d 518, to the statute relating to the admissibility of interspousal communications (Ill. Rev. Stat. 1981, ch. 38, par. 155-1). This court, in *Palumbo*, rejected the argument advanced by the defendant there that the statute covered all conversations between spouses, holding instead that the statutory privilege, like the similar common law privilege, applied only to conversations which were of a confidential character. The problem is to determine under what circumstances conversations between spouses are to be regarded as confidential in character. This court, in *Palumbo*, adopted the standards announced by the Supreme Court in *Wolfle v. United States* (1934), 291 U.S. 7, 14, 54 S. Ct. 279, 280, 78 L. Ed. 617, 620, a holding which the court 41 years later in *Trammel v. United States* (1980), 445 U.S. 40, 100 S. Ct. 906, 63 L. Ed. 2d 186, said remained undisturbed, by adopting language from *Wolfle* which teaches the following: There is a presumption that interspousal communications are intended to be confidential. But if, because of the circumstances under which the communication took place, it appears that confidentiality was not intended, the communication is not to be regarded as privileged. In this regard, communications made in the presence of third persons are usually not regarded as privileged because they are not made in confidence. In *Palumbo* the communication testified to by the wife was regarded as not privileged because the entire conversation took place in the presence of a third person who, according to the wife, was trying to purchase narcotics from the husband, who was the defendant in the case.

We agree with the appellate court's conclusion that the evidence establishes that the third conversation took place in the presence of her sons, Robert who was 13, and two others who were 10 and 8 at the time. On cross-examination the wife repeated her direct testimony, which is quoted at length in the appellate court opinion, that the three children were present during the third conversation when the following exchange took place:

"Q. Did you know anything about Curtiss Lovelace?
A. Only what my husband had told me.
Q. You say he was bragging when he told you this?
A. Yes.
Q. He wasn't nervous, was he?
A. Not until he found out the man was dead.
Q. When he first told you was he nervous or bragging?
A. Not nervous.
Q. Pacing around the room?

A. No, he wasn't.
Q. Excited?
A. No.
Q. Who was present when this conversation occurred?
A. Robert, Albert and Pee Wee.
Q. They were all there?
A. Yes."

Following this exchange there was another reference during her cross-examination to the presence of the wife's oldest son:

"Q. And that day of the events that you have testified to, October the 14th, that day you had just finished a fight with your husband, right?
A. Yes.
Q. Did he threaten your son, Robert, in any way at that time?
A. No.
Q. But during all of these conversations, Robert, your son, was present, right?
A. Yes, he was."

The question presented in this case is whether the communications fell outside the ambit of the statute's protection because of the presence of the children. We have found no Illinois case holding that the confidentiality of a conversation between a husband and wife is preserved when it takes place in the presence of children. The appellate court appears to have exhaustively researched the subject and concluded, as we do, that the great weight of authority is that the presence of children of the spouses destroys confidentiality unless they are too young to understand what is being said. (See, e.g., *Master v. Master* (1960), 223 Md. 618, 166 A.2d 251; *Freeman v. Freeman* (1921), 238 Mass. 150, 130 N.E. 220; *Fuller v. Fuller* (1925), 100 W. Va. 309, 130 S.E. 270; McCormick, *Evidence* sec. 80, at 166 (2d ed. 1972); 97 C.J.S. *Witnesses* sec. 271, at 777 (1957).) Nothing in the record indicates that Robert, then 13 years old, was not old enough or sufficiently bright to understand the conversation at which he was present, particularly inasmuch as the wife's testimony indicates that some of it was directed to him. In these circumstances, under the rule followed in this State, his presence rendered the conversation ineligible for the protection of the statutory privilege.

The defendant argues that this court should recognize a privilege, which he concedes does not presently exist in Illinois, between parents and children which would include conversations between spouses at which their children are present. Courts in a few other jurisdictions have cloaked communications between parent and child with a privilege. (*In re Agosto* (D. Nev. 1983), 553 F. Supp. 1298; *People v. Fitzgerald* (1979), 101 Misc. 2d 712, 422 N.Y.S.2d 309.) The source of all privileges currently applicable in Illinois,

(continues)

with the exception of the attorney-client privilege which has a long-standing common law existence, is statutory. (See Ill. Rev. Stat. 1981, ch. 51, par. 5.1, Ill. Rev. Stat. 1981, ch. 38, par. 104-14 (physician-patient); Ill. Rev. Stat. 1981, ch. 51, par. 48.1 (clergymen); Ill. Rev. Stat. 1981, ch. 91fi, par. 810 (therapist-client); Ill. Rev. Stat. 1981, ch. 111, par. 5533 (accountants); Ill. Rev. Stat. 1981, ch. 51, par. 5.2 (rape crisis personnel-victims); Ill. Rev. Stat. 1981, ch. 48, par. 640 (public officers, regarding unemployment compensation).) We decline, therefore, to introduce an additional privilege by judicial authority which would be applicable to communications between parents and children. Even if we were to initiate this type of privilege, to assist the defendant here we would have to extend it to children of only one spouse, for Robert, the oldest and presumably the most discerning of the children and who was privy at least to the third conversation, was the son of the wife and not the defendant. The statute by its terms does not contemplate such a stretch. Were we to recognize such a privilege under our judicial authority, it would be impossible to contain it logically from spreading to conversations with other relatives in whom a person might normally confide, or even to close friends.

Moreover, we are constrained not only by the legislature's lack of interest in extending an interspousal communications privilege to communications between parent and child, but also by the fact that evidentiary privileges of this sort exclude relevant evidence and thus work against the truth-seeking function of legal proceedings. In this they are distinct from evidentiary rules, such as the prohibition against hearsay testimony, which promote this function by insuring the quality of the evidence which is presented. The privilege at issue here results not from a policy of safeguarding the quality of evidence at trial but from a policy of promoting family harmony independent of what might occur in a trial at some future date. The Supreme Court in *Trammel v. United States* (1980), 445 U.S. 40, 50, 100 S. Ct. 906, 912, 63 L. Ed. 2d 186, 195, has stated:

"Testimonial exclusionary rules and privileges contravene the fundamental principle that 'the public . . . has a right to every man's evidence.' *United States v. Bryan* [(1950), 339 U.S. 323, 331, 70 S. Ct. 724, 730, 94 L. Ed. 884, 891.] As such, they must be strictly construed and accepted 'only to the very limited extent that permitting a refusal to testify or excluding relevant evidences has a public good transcending the normally predominant principle of utilizing all rational means for ascertaining truth.' *Elkins v. United States* [(1960), 364 U.S. 206, 234, 80 S. Ct. 1437, 1454, 4 L. Ed. 2d 1669, 1695] (Frankfurter, J., dissenting)."

See also 8 J. Wigmore, *Evidence* section 2285, at 527–28 (1961).

The expansion of existing testimonial privileges and acceptance of new ones involves a balancing of public policies which should be left to the legislature. A compelling reason is that while courts, as institutions, find it easy to perceive value in public policies such as those favoring the admission of all relevant and reliable evidence which directly assist the judicial function of ascertaining the truth, it is not their primary function to promote policies aimed at broader social goals more distantly related to the judiciary. This is primarily the responsibility of the legislature. To the extent that such policies conflict with truth seeking or other values central to the judicial task, the balance that courts draw might not reflect the choice the legislature would make.

The defendant argues, however, that inasmuch as the Federal courts have recognized the right of privacy to be of constitutional dimension in the context of certain functions which are intimately associated with the family, we should hold that communications of a confidential nature between a parent and his child enjoy an evidentiary privilege under the Constitution which did not exist under the common law. The defendant points out that in *In re Agosto* (D. Nev. 1983), 553 F. Supp. 1298, and *People v. Fitzgerald* (1979), 101 Misc. 2d 712, 422 N.Y.S.2d 309, courts have recognized the sort of constitutionally based privilege sought to be invoked here.

We need not decide here, and we do not decide, whether the decisions in *In re Agosto* or *People v. Fitzgerald* were sound, for the question in both of these cases was whether a parent or a child could be compelled against his will to testify against the other. (See also *In re A & M* (1978), 61 A.D.2d 426, 403 N.Y.S.2d 375 (same).) The testimony in the instant case, by contrast, was given by the defendant's wife, without protest and apparently of her own free will, after she was approached and requested to give it by an assistant State's Attorney.

We find this difference to be significant. Both *Agosto* and the New York courts, in holding that a constitutional privilege protected the communications there at issue, relied heavily on conjecture that a family member who is forced to testify against her will would face the unpleasant choice of aiding the criminal conviction of a loved one, perjuring herself on the stand, or risking a citation for contempt of court for refusing to testify, and the belief that the harshness of this choice has the effect of sundering the family relationship. (*In re Agosto* (D. Nev. 1983), 553 F. Supp. 1298, 1309–10, 1326; *In re A & M* (1978), 61 A.D.2d 426, 432-33, 403 N.Y.S.2d 375, 380.) Such a fear is without foundation where, as in this case, the witness who is a family member volunteers her testimony; the voluntariness of the act is strong evidence that the choice the witness faced was an easy one for her to make. We conclude that even if the Constitution bestows a privilege on communications between a parent and a child, an issue which we do not decide here, that privilege may be waived by the testifying witness acting alone. Compare *United States v. Penn* (9th Cir. 1980), 647 F.2d 876, 882 (rejecting a challenge to a child's voluntary testimony based on due process, on which the right to privacy depends).

Although they were the subject of the motion *in limine* which was never ruled upon, no objection was advanced at trial when the wife testified about the first and second conversations. Under *Palumbo* the Illinois statute preventing testimony by either spouse concerning confidential communications between them creates only a privilege, and a privilege may be waived by the holder of it, in this case the husband. (See Comment, *Marital Privileges*, 46 Chi.-Kent L. Rev. 71, 82–83 (1969).) Therefore, in order to affirm the appellate court's reversal of the conviction, we would have to conclude that the court properly applied the plain error doctrine (87 Ill. 2d R. 615) in holding that testimony regarding the first two conversations was improperly admitted. We believe the appellate court erred in reaching that conclusion.

The plain error doctrine is properly applied only when the question of guilt is close and the evidence in question might have significantly affected the outcome of the case (*People v. Jackson* (1981), 84 Ill. 2d 350, 359, 49 Ill. Dec. 719, 418 N.E.2d 739; *People v. Pickett* (1973), 54 Ill. 2d 280, 283, 296 N.E.2d 856), or where the error alleged is so substantial as to reflect on the fairness or impartiality of the trial regardless of how closely balanced the evidence is (*People v. Baynes* (1981), 88 Ill. 2d 225, 233-34, 244, 58 Ill. Dec. 819, 430 N.E.2d 1070; *People v. Roberts* (1979), 75 Ill. 2d 1, 14, 25 Ill. Dec. 675, 387 N.E.2d 331). The third conversation which we conclude, as the appellate court did, was properly admitted, incorporated substantially all of what was said in the first two conversations. The defendant, in the third conversation, discussed the robbery of the murder victim, said he hit him over the head with a brick, displayed several items of clothing taken from the victim, and referred to the watch and ring he had given his wife earlier that day. Thus, even conceding that no one overheard the first two conversations and that they were privileged and should have been excluded had timely objections been made, in practical

effect they did no more than duplicate the incriminating content of the third conversation which was properly admitted. For that reason, the testimony which narrated the defendant's conversation and conduct during the first two conversations was not prejudicial. It added nothing to the third conversation that was needed by the prosecutor to implicate the defendant, and after the third conversation was in evidence, the evidence as to the defendant's guilt was no longer closely balanced.

Nor do we regard any errors that might have been made concerning the admissibility of the first and second conversations as depriving the accused of the substantial means of enjoying a fair and impartial trial (*People v. Roberts* (1979), 75 Ill. 2d 1, 14, 25 Ill. Dec. 675, 387 N.E.2d 331; citing *People v. Burson* (1957), 11 Ill. 2d 360, 370-71, 143 N.E.2d 237, see *People v. Whitlow* (1982), 89 Ill. 2d 322, 342, 60 Ill. Dec. 587, 433 N.E.2d 629), as the admission of polygraph evidence does (see *People v. Baynes* (1981), 88 Ill. 2d 225, 244, 58 Ill. Dec. 819, 430 N.E.2d 1070). As we have noted, the husband-wife testimonial privilege operates not to purge a trial of unreliable evidence but to withhold relevant and often highly reliable evidence from the trier of fact. The decision whether to apply the plain error doctrine where the evidence is not close is one of grace. (*People v. Roberts* (1979), 75 Ill. 2d 1, 14, 25 Ill. Dec. 675, 387 N.E.2d 331; *People v. Burson* (1957), 11 Ill. 2d 360, 370-71.) We believe it should not have been applied here, for the fairness and impartiality of the *trial* was not substantially compromised by the errors, if any took place. See *People v. Roberts* (1979), 75 Ill. 2d 1, 14-15, 25 Ill. Dec. 675, 387 N.E.2d 331.

The defendant has raised a number of other issues, none of which were considered by the appellate court because of its erroneous reversal of the conviction on the ground of improper use of privileged communications. The judgment of the appellate court is reversed and the cause is remanded to that court for disposition of the issues raised by the defendant but not reached by its original decision. See *People v. Simpson* (1977), 68 Ill. 2d 276, 284, 12 Ill. Dec. 234, 369 N.E.2d 1248.

Reversed and remanded, with directions.

STATE of New Mexico, Plaintiff-Appellee,

v.

Abdul MUQQDDIN, Defendant-Appellant.

No. 28,474.

May 5, 2010.

Certiorari Granted, Aug. 2, 2010, No. 32,430.

2010 NMCA 69, _____ P.3d _____ (Ct. App. 2010)

* * *

OPINION

KENNEDY, Judge.

{1} Abdul Muqqddin (Defendant) used a nail to penetrate the gas tank of a van parked in a dark alley without the permission of the owner. After piercing the tank, Defendant positioned a container below the hole so as to catch the fuel as it drained from the van. The van was in extremely bad condition and had been parked in the alley for as many as six months, though it had not been abandoned. Defendant appeals his convictions for auto burglary under NMSA 1978, Section 30-16-3 (1971), criminal damage to property under NMSA 1978, Section 30-15-1 (1963), and larceny under NMSA 1978, Section 30-16-1 (1987) (amended 2006). Defendant argues that penetrating a gas tank with a nail is insufficient to constitute an entry under the burglary statute, and because he believed the van to be abandoned, he lacked the requisite intent to commit the crimes of burglary, criminal damage, and larceny. As a result, Defendant claims, his convictions are unsupported by substantial evidence. We hold that entry, under Section 30-16-3, is complete when a defendant penetrates a gas tank with a nail. We also hold that substantial evidence supports Defendant's convictions. We affirm.

FACTS

{2} Neither party disputes what took place in the early morning hours of August 21, 2005. An Albuquerque police officer, responding to an unrelated call, heard loud banging noises coming from an alley. Suspicious of the noise, he stopped his vehicle at the entrance to the alley and cautiously investigated on foot. After proceeding approximately halfway down the alley, the officer saw Defendant lying underneath a van. Next to Defendant was a red plastic container, positioned beneath the van to catch fuel dripping from the tank. The officer detained Defendant, asked him his name, and Defendant falsely identified himself as Edward Edgerton. A routine computer check revealed that Edgerton had an outstanding warrant for his arrest, and at that time, Defendant gave the officer his real name.

{3} When asked what he was doing under the van, Defendant first stated that he was taking gas from the tank with the permission of the owner. Upon further questioning, however, Defendant admitted that he did not have permission to take the gas, but that because the van was abandoned, it was alright [sic] for him to do so. He said he had used a nail to create a hole in the tank so that the gas could escape, and two nails were found in his pocket. At that point, the officer placed Defendant under arrest and called for additional personnel to assist in an investigation of the scene.

{4} Police identified the van's owner as Emil Hanson, the proprietor of a nearby dry cleaning business. Hanson had purchased the van approximately two years prior but stopped driving it when it became too expensive for him to do so. While trying to figure out what to do with it, he purchased a new van and parked the old one in the alley behind his business. He testified that although the van was in bad condition and could have been sitting in the alley for as many as six months, he had neither abandoned it nor given Defendant permission to enter or remove fuel from it.

{5} When the State completed its case in chief, Defendant made a motion for directed verdict on all counts. In pertinent part, Defendant argued that penetration of a gas tank with a nail is insufficient to constitute burglary in New Mexico, and further, that he lacked the requisite intent to commit burglary, criminal damage, and larceny because he thought the van was abandoned. As a result, Defendant contended, substantial evidence did not support the charges against him. These arguments failed to persuade the district court, Defendant's motion was denied, and he was convicted as stated above. Defendant now reasserts the arguments from his motion for directed verdict.

* * *

THE CRIME OF BURGLARY

{7} Section 30-16-3 defines the crime of burglary as "the unauthorized entry of any vehicle, watercraft, aircraft, dwelling or other structure, movable or immovable, with the intent to commit any felony or theft therein." As such, Section 30-16-3 expresses "a radical departure from its common law predecessor," which required "(1) breaking and (2) entering (3) a dwelling house (4) of another (5) in the nighttime (6) with the intent to commit a felony therein." *State v. Rodriguez*, 101 N.M. 192, 193, 679 P.2d 1290, 1291 (Ct. App. 1984); *see State v. Bybee*, 109 N.M. 44, 45, 781 P.2d 316, 317 (Ct. App. 1989). Thus, our Legislature has chosen to keep only the element of entry completely intact. *Rodriguez*, 101 N.M. at 193, 679 P.2d at 1291. As this Court has held, entry contemplates penetration of a space by either a person or an instrument. *State v. Tixier*, 89 N.M. 297,

298-99, 551 P.2d 987, 988-89 (Ct. App. 1976) (holding that a one-half-inch penetration with an instrument is enough to effectuate an entry; "[a]ny penetration, however slight, of the interior space is sufficient").

{8} This Court's opinions in *Rodriguez* and *State v. Reynolds*, 111 N.M. 263, 804 P.2d 1082 (Ct. App. 1990), define the limits of entry in the context of vehicle burglary. In *Rodriguez*, the defendant reached into the uncovered bed of a pickup truck and removed a toolbox with the intent of taking it unlawfully. 101 N.M. at 193, 679 P.2d at 1291. This Court held that such an entry is sufficient to constitute a burglary. "[W]e hold that the bed of a pickup truck, as a part of a vehicle, falls within the statutorily protected area." *Id.* at 194, 679 P.2d at 1292. A similar issue prompted the analysis in *Reynolds*. In that case, like the one before us, police found the defendant on the ground beneath a vehicle. Testimony at trial established that he reached into the engine compartment from underneath in an apparent attempt to remove the vehicle's starter. *Reynolds*, 111 N.M. at 264-65, 804 P.2d at 1083-84. This Court, citing *Tixier*, held that such an act is sufficient to sustain a conviction for burglary. *Reynolds*, 111 N.M. at 270, 804 P.2d at 1089. "In establishing a burglary, [a]ny penetration, however slight, of the interior space is sufficient [to constitute entry]. Since there was no dispute that [the] defendant's hand penetrated the engine compartment of the vehicle, there would have been no rational basis for the jury to find attempted burglary but not burglary itself[.]" *Id.* (second alteration in original) (internal quotation marks and citation omitted). Thus, a jury could reasonably conclude that a burglary had occurred. *Id.*

{9} We are sympathetic to the unique facts of Defendant's case. He was found draining fuel from the tank of a van with no license plate, several broken windows, and four flat tires. The investigating officer testified that the van would have been unsafe to drive, and Hanson, the owner, testified that the van might have been sitting in the alley for as many as six months prior to the incident. In fact, during direct examination, Hanson stated that although the van had not been abandoned, his plan for it was to "just give it to charity or try to sell it for the engine."

{10} Necessary or not, that which might be a prudent measure of justice must bow to that which the State may legally prove. Simply put, Defendant was properly charged. He did not have permission to enter the van, and his actions clearly constitute entry under New Mexico's burglary statute.

{11} By Defendant's own uncontroverted admission to police, he laid down on the ground beneath the van, procured an instrument, and used it to create a hole in the tank. As fuel dripped from the hole, he caught it in a container specifically positioned to do so. He did not own the van or the fuel. Such facts are plainly analogous to this Court's opinions in *Rodriguez* and *Reynolds*. A fuel tank—attached as it is, to a vehicle—is unquestionably *a part of* that vehicle and absolutely necessary for its primary function as a mode of transportation. Any penetration of a vehicle's perimeter is thus a penetration of the vehicle itself. *See Reynolds*, 111 N.M. at 270, 804 P.2d at 1089. Like the defendant's entry of the truck bed in *Rodriguez*, this Defendant reached into the undercarriage of the van and removed fuel from inside the tank located there. *See Rodriguez*, 101 N.M. at 193, 679 P.2d at 1291. In fact, Defendant went even further by puncturing the tank in order to effectuate the theft. But perhaps even more analogous is *Reynolds*. In that case, the defendant reached into the engine compartment from underneath so he could remove the starter. *Reynolds*, 111 N.M. at 265, 270, 804 P.2d at 1084, 1089. Likewise, Defendant in this case reached into the fuel tank, albeit via an instrument, in order to remove fuel, and as this Court has held, "[a]ny penetration, however slight . . . is sufficient." *Id.* at 270, 804 P.2d at 1089.

{12} The facts of the instant case fit cleanly within the conceptual framework established by *Reynolds* and *Rodriguez*, and understandably, Defendant had difficulty distinguishing those opinions. He thus relies heavily upon out-of-state cases to support his argument, but each is readily distinguishable in either law or fact. For instance, in *People v. Davis*, 18 Cal. 4th 712, 76 Cal. Rptr. 2d 770, 958 P.2d 1083, 1090 (1998), the defendant placed a forged check into the deposit window of a check cashing business. The court held that such an act, although technically an entry with the intent to commit a theft, should nevertheless not be considered an entry for purposes of California's burglary statute. *Id.* Likewise, in *R.E.S. v. State*, 396 So. 2d 1219, 1220 (Fla. Dist. Ct. App. 1981), the court analyzed whether, under Florida's burglary statute, siphoning gas from the tank of a vehicle constituted an entry. It held that siphoning did not constitute an entry and based its holding on the notion that Florida's burglary statute contemplates only vehicle compartments "which can be entered either wholly or partially by a person; e.g., engine and passenger compartments, trunks, etc." *Id.* Finally, the Florida Supreme Court reached the same conclusion in *Drew v. State*, 773 So. 2d 46, 47 (Fla. 2000), when it considered whether the removal of tires or hub-caps from a vehicle constituted an entry. In that opinion, the court held that such an act could not constitute a burglary because Florida's common law requires that the theft actually take place "within" the vehicle. Removal of a tire or hubcap, which requires disassembly, thus does not take place within the vehicle as required by the statute. *Id.* at 52.

{13} On the facts and New Mexico law before us, the reasoning of these out-of-state authorities fails to persuade. The facts of *Davis*, for instance, are readily distinguishable. In that case, the California court held that an entry had not occurred because the chute in which the defendant placed the forged check was regularly used by other patrons who also deposited checks. Such an entry does not violate "the

(continues)

occupant's possessory interest in the building." *Davis*, 76 Cal. Rptr. 2d 770, 958 P.2d at 1089. In the case before us, Hanson's possessory interest in the van was clearly violated when Defendant punctured its tank. Nor are we persuaded by *R.E.S.* and *Drew*, the Florida opinions, which both proceed from interpretations of Florida's case law. In those cases, it is apparent that burglary in Florida contemplates the entry of a vehicle compartment large enough to accommodate at least a part of a person and that the theft actually occurred within the vehicle. *See Drew*, 773 So. 2d at 52; *R.E.S.*, 396 So. 2d at 1220. Not so in New Mexico, where a slight entry by use of an instrument is sufficient. *See, e.g., Reynolds*, 111 N.M. at 264-65, 804 P.2d at 1083-84 (providing that removal of a starter from the engine compartment is sufficient to constitute burglary); *Tixier*, 89 N.M. at 298-99, 551 P.2d at 988-89 (including the use of an instrument in the definition of an entry). We turn now to Defendant's other argument on appeal.

* * *

CONCLUSION

{16} For the reasons stated above, we hold that using a nail to penetrate a vehicle's gas tank constitutes an entry under Section 30-16-3. We also hold that substantial evidence supports each of Defendant's convictions. We affirm.

{17} IT IS SO ORDERED.
WE CONCUR: JONATHAN B. SUTIN and TIMOTHY L. GARCIA, Judges.

STATE OF NEW MEXICO, Plaintiff-Appellee,

v.

LEROY ZAMORA, Defendant-Appellant.

Docket No. 23,436

February 11, 2005, Filed

Certiorari Granted, No. 29,117, April 4, 2005

COURT OF APPEALS OF NEW MEXICO

2005-NMCA-039, 137 N.M. 301, 110 P.3d 517

VIGIL, Judge.

{1} Appellee State of New Mexico's motion for rehearing is denied. The opinion filed in this case on January 13, 2005, is withdrawn and this opinion is substituted in its place.

{2} Defendant was convicted of trafficking by possession with intent to distribute cocaine, conspiracy, possession of drug paraphernalia, and concealing identity following the search of a motel room. The dispositive issues are whether Defendant has standing to challenge the search of the motel room and whether a warrantless search of the medicine cabinet in the bathroom of the motel room can be justified as a protective sweep. We hold that Defendant has standing to challenge the search and that the search of the medicine cabinet went beyond the parameters of a protective sweep. We reverse and remand for a new trial.

FACTS

* * *

{4} Sergeant Depies of the Albuquerque Police Department responded to a call from the dispatcher that an individual was trespassing on the premises of the Economy Inn. Sergeant Depies identified the trespasser who admitted he had been smoking crack cocaine. The trespasser subsequently identified Room 244 in the motel as the place where he purchased the crack cocaine. Sergeant Depies then told the motel clerk what he had learned, and the clerk said the room had been rented two days earlier by Thomas Henderson and his mother Erica, according to the registration. Sergeant Depies called other officers for assistance to continue the investigation.

{5} Defendant, his cousin Manuel Hernandez, and Defendant's aunt were in Room 244 at the Economy Inn when police officers knocked on the door. Defendant testified that prior to going to the motel, he had alternated between living on the street and staying at his mother's house. He saw Hernandez at a Walgreen's and Hernandez said that he had a motel room that his mother was also using and he invited Defendant to stay with them in the motel room. Hernandez had rented the room two days earlier, on October 12, 2000, under the aliases of Thomas and Erica Henderson. Defendant testified he called his mother to bring him some clothes when they arrived at the motel. Defendant understood he was invited to spend the night in the motel room. After receiving clean clothes sent by his mother, Defendant said he took a shower, combed his hair, put clean clothes on, and got into the only bed in the room. Defendant testified that he had an expectation of privacy in the room "[b]ecause [his] family was there" and because he was going to spend the night there.

{6} Sergeant Depies went to Room 244, accompanied by Officers Leveling and Melton, wearing his uniform. As

Sergeant Depies approached the room, "a subject peeked out around the drapes" at the officers "and then ran back into the room." Sergeant Depies also heard "running" from inside the room which made him suspicious. Sergeant Depies knocked on the door, announced, "Police," and either ordered or requested the occupant to come to the door. Hernandez opened the door. Sergeant Depies asked whose room it was and Hernandez answered it belonged to him and his mother. Sergeant Depies asked Hernandez if he could "step into his room, talk about an allegation of drug dealing from that room and he nodded yes." Sergeant Depies added, "[he] might have muttered yes or something, opened the door, walked in and left the door open." The officers walked in the room. Present in the room were Hernandez, Defendant, and Defendant's aunt. Sergeant Depies saw pieces of crack cocaine, a long razor blade, and a crack pipe on a table in the corner of the room. Sergeant Depies asked Hernandez if the substance he observed would test positive for cocaine and Hernandez responded, "yeah, because my mom smokes crack." Sergeant Depies then handcuffed Hernandez and instructed the officers to handcuff Defendant and his aunt. Shortly after Officer Melton handcuffed Hernandez, he began a protective sweep of the room, described as follows by Sergeant Depies:

A protective sweep would just encompass going through, looking for bodies, making sure live people, making sure there isn't a person in there that could possibly pose a threat to us while we're doing the investigation. What we would do, anyone hiding in the bathroom, hiding in the tub, hiding in the closet here, there where people can be found and that's what Officer Melton — he was doing. He was looking that these were the only three people inside the motel room.

{7} Officer Melton testified that Hernandez "nodded, [and] walked into the room" when Sergeant Depies asked if the officers could come into the room. Officer Melton testified, "[m]y main responsibility was to come in, make sure for Sergeant Depies' safety as he conducted an investigation." He described how he performed the protective sweep as follows:

I went into the back bathroom, when you walk in I wanted to look inside, make sure no one else was also hiding inside the bathroom. I noticed that the window was open and so I looked outside. I had been on several calls before where people had thrown things out the window where they didn't want us to find. I look outside, I didn't find anything. I look back towards where the bath tub was, shower area was, I notice that the vanity, the medicine cabinet, was opened approximately two or three inches. I looked and I could see . . . inside there. I notice a plastic bag, just a light plastic bag. Several times that I arrested

arrested people I have found narcotics in plastic bags, so I opened the vanity and I found two plastic bags containing a large amount of what I thought at the time was crack cocaine and which was later determined to be by Officer Chavez that came and field tested it for us.

***

B. The Protective Sweep

{15} The search of the bathroom was conducted by Officer Melton without a search warrant.

Once a defendant has established that law enforcement officers have entered the premises of another and conducted a warrantless search and seizure in an area wherein the defendant has a reasonable expectation of privacy, the state has the burden of coming forward with evidence to show that the search and seizure came within a valid exception to the search warrant requirements imposed by the State and United States Constitutions.

Wright, 119 N.M. at 562, 893 P.2d at 458. The State has a heavy burden to justify a warrantless search. Id. A properly justified and conducted protective sweep is a permissible warrantless search under the Fourth Amendment. *State v. Valdez*, 111 N.M. 438, 440, 806 P.2d 578, 580 (Ct. App. 1990).

{16} We assume that the evidence supports a finding that the police officers entered the motel room after securing a valid consent from Hernandez to do so. *See Wright*, 119 N.M. at 562, 893 P.2d at 458 ("Where the state asserts that the search and seizure conducted by law enforcement officers were consensual, the burden is on the state to show by clear and positive evidence that consent was given without duress, coercion, or other factors which would vitiate the voluntary nature of the consent.") (internal quotation marks and citation omitted). We also assume that the protective sweep was performed after Defendant and the others inside the room were arrested. *See Valdez*, 111 N.M. at 440, 806 P.2d at 580 ("A protective sweep is only allowed incident to a lawful arrest."). Finally, we assume that under the circumstances, a protective sweep search was appropriate. *See id.* ("[A] protective sweep may be undertaken if the searching officers possess a reasonable belief based on specific and articulable facts which, taken together with the rational inferences from those facts, reasonably warrant[s] the officer in believing that the area swept harbored an individual posing a danger to the officer or others.") (citations omitted) (quoting *Maryland v. Buie*, 494 U.S. 325, 328 (1990)). What we determine is whether the scope of the search conducted by Officer Melton was within the constitutional parameters of

(continues)

a protective sweep. Defendant argues that the scope of Officer Melton's protective sweep of the bathroom, exceeded "a cursory inspection of those spaces where a person may be found." *Id.* at 335. We agree.

{17} In *Buie*, the Supreme Court recognized a protective sweep as an exception to the warrant requirement of the Fourth Amendment. 494 U.S. at 336. In doing so, it described a protective sweep as, "a quick and limited search of premises, incident to an arrest and conducted to protect the safety of police officers or others. It is narrowly confined to a cursory visual inspection of those places in which a person might be hiding." *Id.* at 327. The Supreme Court emphasized that the police officer must have a "reasonable belief" that "the area swept harbored an individual posing a danger to the officer or others," *id.* and that a protective sweep is "not a full search of the premises, but may extend only to a cursory inspection of those spaces where a person may be found." *Id.* at 335. These limiting parameters on a protective sweep have been recognized and followed by our own Supreme Court. *State v. Jacobs*, 2000-NMSC-026, ¶ 35, 129 N.M. 448, 10 P.3d 127. If the police do not conduct a protective sweep commensurate with the rationale that excludes such a search from the warrant requirement, the search violates the Fourth Amendment, and it is unconstitutional. *See State v. Nemeth*, 2001-NMCA-029, ¶ 38, 130 N.M. 261, 23 P.3d 936 (stating that entry into home to perform community caretaking function must be suitably circumscribed to serve the exigency which prompted the entry); *State v. Ledbetter*, 88 N.M. 344, 346, 540 P.2d 824, 825 (Ct. App. 1975). ("The scope of a warrantless search must be commensurate with the rationale that excepts the search from the warrant requirement.")

{18} Sergeant Depies testified that Officer Melton's role was to determine if any other people were in the motel room that could pose a threat to the officers' safety. However, Officer Melton's testimony shows he was looking for evidence, not people. After entering the bathroom, Officer Melton proceeded to look outside the open window to determine if there was any *evidence* outside the window. Then, seeing "just a light plastic bag" inside the partially opened medicine cabinet, Officer Melton decided to look inside the medicine cabinet. A drawing and photographs of the motel room and bathroom show a traditional medicine cabinet hanging over the sink. It has a mirror on the door which opens to a small storage space for personal toiletries. It is obvious by looking at the medicine cabinet that it is too small for a person to hide inside it. Nevertheless, Officer Melton decided to look inside it because, "[s]everal times that I arrested people I have found narcotics in plastic bags." By his own admission, Officer Melton was looking for *evidence* inside the medicine cabinet, not people who might be threats to the officers. Searching inside the medicine cabinet cannot be justified as a protective sweep exception to the warrant requirement of the Fourth Amendment. *Buie*, 494 U.S. at 327; see *Wilson*,

36 F.3d at 1306 (stating the seizure of a checkbook from a wastebasket in the bathroom of a motel room "was not justified as a protective sweep because it was not within the narrow ambit of a cursory visual inspection of a place where a person could be hiding").

{19} The State argues that the seizure of the plastic bag was proper because it was in plain view while Officer Melton was in the bathroom. We reject this argument. "Under the plain view exception to the warrant requirement, items may be seized without a warrant if the police officer was lawfully positioned when the evidence was observed, and the incriminating nature of the evidence was immediately apparent, such that the officer had probable cause to believe that the article seized was evidence of a crime." *State v. Ochoa*, 2004-NMSC-023, ¶ 9, 135 N.M. 781, 93 P.3d 1286. The context of the incident, coupled with Officer Melton's experience and training are properly considered in determining whether he identified drug paraphernalia or drug packaging within a reasonable degree of probability sufficient for probable cause. *Id.* ¶¶ 13, 15. In *Ochoa*, the police officer saw a vial protruding from the defendant's pocket while he conducted a protective frisk. He testified he was able to identify it as drug paraphernalia based on his experience. *Id.* ¶¶ 3, 13, 17. In *State v. Miles*, 108 N.M. 556, 557, 775 P.2d 758, 759 (Ct. App. 1989), the police officer saw a brown wooden box that was distinctive in appearance lying on the seat in defendant's car after he stopped the defendant for speeding. *Id.* He recognized the box as being drug paraphernalia with a place for a pipe and a compartment for marijuana. *Id.* Again, this was based on his law enforcement experience. *Id.* Here, however, Officer Melton never testified there was anything about the plastic bag when he first saw it which, based upon his law enforcement experience, caused him to believe it was drug paraphernalia or packaging. bags. This was not sufficient to establish probable cause to open the medicine chest. *See State v. Miyasato*, 805 So. 2d 818, 821 (Fla. Dist. Ct. App. 2001) ("Even though the officer claimed he saw the corner of a plastic baggie sticking out of [the defendant's] pocket and knew marijuana was often carried in plastic baggies, these facts would give rise to, at most, a mere suspicion that it contained marijuana, which was not enough to seize it.") (internal quotation marks omitted).

{20} All Officer Melton saw before he opened the medicine cabinet was "a plastic bag, just a light plastic bag." There was no evidence that "a plastic bag, just a light plastic bag" in the medicine cabinet was being used for an illegal purpose. Stated another way, the "incriminating nature" of the plastic bag which Officer Melton saw was not "immediately apparent." *See Commonwealth v. Garcia*, 614 N.E.2d 1031, 1034 (Mass. App. Ct. 1993). ("Here there was no evidence from the trooper that there was some characteristic of this baggie itself, that would have indicated it was being used for an illegal purpose.") Officer Melton opened the medicine cabinet on the mere suspicion the plastic bag he saw might contain drugs. "[A]n officer's mere suspicion about an ordinary object, which has common, non-criminal uses, will not support probable cause for its seizure." *Ochoa*, 2004-NMSC-023, ¶ 14. The reasons for this rule are apparent:

> Benign objects such as [plastic bags], spoons, mirrors, and straws are often used in the narcotic trade. To allow police officers, experienced in narcotics investigations, to conduct a warrantless search whenever they observe one of the above items, and nothing more, would permit random searches, which are condemned by the Fourth Amendment[.]

Garcia, 614 N.E.2d at 1035.

{21} The search of the medicine cabinet cannot be upheld as a protective sweep. Accordingly, Defendant's motion to suppress the contents of the medicine cabinet and all the fruits of the search of the medicine cabinet should have been granted.

***

D. Conclusion

{29} The cause is remanded to the district court for a new trial excluding the unlawfully obtained evidence.

{30} IT IS SO ORDERED.

MICHAEL E. VIGIL, Judge
WE CONCUR: JONATHAN B. SUTIN, Judge; RODERICK T. KENNEDY, Judge

---

UNITED STATES of America, Plaintiff-Appellee,

v.

Carless JONES and Eugene Harvey, Defendants-Appellants.

707 F.2d 1169 (10th Cir. 1983)

SEYMOUR, CIRCUIT JUDGE.

On December 31, 1981, three armed men robbed a Denver area savings and loan branch. Lisa Dalke, a teller, and Marilyn Gates, the branch manager, were bound and forced to lie on the floor. The robbers removed money orders, traveler's checks, and $2,024 in cash, triggering a bank surveillance camera. The robbers were seen leaving the bank and walking toward an automobile by a bank customer, Christine Christensen, who had just driven up to the front of the bank. Because the men appeared suspicious, Christensen wrote down the license number of their car. One of the robbers ordered Christensen into the bank, and the men left.

On January 4, 1982, members of the Denver Police Department responded to a family disturbance call at or near 3434 High Street in Denver. While there, the officers saw a car bearing the license number observed by Christensen at the robbery. Denver Police Officer Andrade saw a man carrying a brown satchel emerge from the back of number 3434. Andrade ordered him to halt, and the man ran. The officers found the man, later identified by Andrade as defendant Jones, hiding in the rear of another building. He no longer had the brown satchel. When questioned about the satchel,

Jones replied, "I don't know what you are talking about." Rec., vol. II, at 27.

The police arrested Jones and took him into the residence from which he had fled. He was questioned several times about the location of the brown satchel. Finally, Jones directed a woman who was present, "Show 'em where I put it," pointing toward a closet. *Id.* at 29. The officers searched the closet, but found nothing. Shortly thereafter, however, other police officers found a satchel lying outside the building where Jones had been found hiding, near the spot where he was apprehended. Officer Andrade identified the satchel as the one Jones had been carrying, and opened it. Inside was a handgun, traffic tickets written out in Jones' name, and a small knapsack. The officers asked Jones if the satchel was his, and he again denied owning it.

Appellants Harvey and Jones were jointly indicted and charged with armed robbery of a savings and loan in violation of 18 U.S.C. § 2113(a), (d) (1976). Both defendants filed motions for severance. Jones also filed a motion to suppress the fruits of the search of the satchel. After a lengthy pretrial hearing, these and other motions were denied. Jones and Harvey were tried and found guilty. Both filed motions for a new trial, alleging that adverse prior contact between the jury forewoman and Jones had denied them a fair trial. The trial court denied the motions.

On appeal, Harvey argues that the trial court erred in denying his motion to sever. Jones argues that the warrantless search of the satchel violated his Fourth

(continues)

Amendment rights. Both defendants argue that their Sixth Amendment rights to a fair trial were violated by juror misconduct. For the reasons discussed below, we affirm defendants' convictions.

* * *

II. Abandonment

Jones argues that the warrantless search of the satchel violated his Fourth Amendment rights. The trial court held that the search was permissible on two grounds: that Jones had abandoned the satchel and therefore had no legitimate expectation of privacy in it entitling him to Fourth Amendment protection; and that the search was permissible as incident to a lawful arrest. Because of our resolution of the first ground, we need not address the court's alternative holding that the search was incident to Jones' arrest, and we offer no opinion as to the correctness of that holding.

In *Abel v. United States*, 362 U.S. 217, 241, 80 S. Ct. 683, 698, 4 L. Ed. 2d 668 (1960), the Supreme Court declared that the Government's warrantless seizure of abandoned property did not violate the Fourth Amendment. *Id.* at 241, 80 S. Ct. at 698. Since *Abel*, the circuit courts have examined the issue, and the following guidelines to the "abandoned property" exception to the Fourth Amendment's warrant requirement have emerged. When individuals voluntarily abandon property, they forfeit any expectation of privacy in it that they might have had. *United States v. Berd*, 634 F.2d 979, 987 (5th Cir. 1981). Therefore, a warrantless search or seizure of abandoned property is not unreasonable under the Fourth Amendment. *For example, United States v. Diggs*, 649 F.2d 731, 735 (9th Cir.), *cert. denied*, 454 U.S. 970, 102 S. Ct. 516, 70 L. Ed. 2d 387 (1981); *Berd*, 634 F.2d at 987; *United States v. D'Avanzo*, 443 F.2d 1224, 1225-26 (2d Cir.), *cert. denied*, 404 U.S. 850, 92 S. Ct. 86, 30 L. Ed. 2d 89 (1971). The existence of police pursuit or investigation at the time of abandonment does not of itself render the abandonment involuntary. *United States v. Colbert*, 474 F.2d 174, 176 (5th Cir. 1973); *see generally, for example, Berd*, 634 F.2d at 987; *United*

States v. Canady, 615 F.2d 694 (5th Cir.), *cert. denied*, 449 U.S. 862, 101 S. Ct. 165, 66 L. Ed. 2d 78 (1980); *United States v. Williams*, 569 F.2d 823 (5th Cir. 1978); *D'Avanzo*, 443 F.2d 1224.

The test for abandonment is whether an individual has retained any reasonable expectation of privacy in the object. *Diggs*, 649 F.2d at 735. This determination is to be made by objective standards. *United States v. Kendall*, 655 F.2d 199, 201 (9th Cir. 1981), *cert. denied*, 455 U.S. 941, 102 S. Ct. 1434, 71 L. Ed. 2d 652 (1982). An expectation of privacy is a question of intent, which "may be inferred from words spoken, acts done, and other objective facts." *Kendall*, 655 F.2d at 202 (quoting *Williams*, 569 F.2d at 826). "A finding of abandonment is reviewed under the clearly erroneous standard." *Diggs*, 649 F.2d at 735.

When Jones discarded the satchel, he may have hoped that the police would not find it and that he could later retrieve it. However, his ability to recover the satchel depended entirely upon fate and the absence of inquisitive (and acquisitive) passersby. When questioned by the police, he repeatedly disavowed any knowledge of the satchel. His comment to the woman in the residence to "[s]how 'em where I put it" appears at most to have been a mere ruse to deceive the police as to the existence of a satchel, rather than "words which acknowledged ownership," Brief of Appellants, at 17. Here, the "words spoken" and, more significantly, the "acts done" objectively manifested Jones' clear intent to relinquish his expectation of privacy and abandon the satchel. This is not a case like *United States v. Burnette*, 698 F.2d 1038 (9th Cir. 1983), where, after an initial disclaimer of ownership, the defendant's subsequent conduct "strongly indicated her intent to retain a 'reasonable expectation of privacy in the purse.'" *Id.* at 1048.

We hold that Jones voluntarily abandoned the satchel. Accordingly, the subsequent warrantless search by the police did not violate his Fourth Amendment rights.

* * *

Affirmed.

UNITED STATES, Petitioner

v.

Alberto Antonio LEON et al.

No. 82–1771.

Argued Jan. 17, 1984.

Decided July 5, 1984.

Rehearing Denied Sept. 18, 1984.

468 U.S. 897 (1984)

Justice WHITE delivered the opinion of the Court.

This case presents the question whether the Fourth Amendment exclusionary rule should be modified so as not to bar the use in the prosecution's case in chief of evidence obtained by officers acting in reasonable reliance on a search warrant issued by a detached and neutral magistrate but ultimately found to be unsupported by probable cause. To resolve this question, we must consider once again the tension between the sometimes competing goals of, on the one hand, deterring official misconduct and removing inducements to unreasonable invasions of privacy and, on the other, establishing procedures under which criminal defendants are "acquitted or convicted on the basis of all the evidence which exposes the truth." *Alderman v. United States*, 394 U.S. 165, 175, 89 S. Ct. 961, 967, 22 L. Ed. 2d 176 (1969).

I

In August 1981, a confidential informant of unproven reliability informed an officer of the Burbank Police Department that two persons known to him as "Armando" and "Patsy" were selling large quantities of cocaine and methaqualone from their residence at 620 Price Drive in Burbank, Cal. The informant also indicated that he had witnessed a sale of methaqualone by "Patsy" at the residence approximately five months earlier and had observed at that time a shoebox containing a large amount of cash that belonged to "Patsy." He further declared that "Armando" and "Patsy" generally kept only small quantities of drugs at their residence and stored the remainder at another location in Burbank.

On the basis of this information, the Burbank police initiated an extensive investigation focusing first on the Price Drive residence and later on two other residences as well. Cars parked at the Price Drive residence were determined to belong to respondents Armando Sanchez, who had previously been arrested for possession of marihuana,

and Patsy Stewart, who had no criminal record. During the course of the investigation, officers observed an automobile belonging to respondent Richardo Del Castillo, who had previously been arrested for possession of fifty pounds of marihuana, arrive at the Price Drive residence. The driver of that car entered the house, exited shortly thereafter carrying a small paper sack, and drove away. A check of Del Castillo's probation records led the officers to respondent Alberto Leon, whose telephone number Del Castillo had listed as his employer's. Leon had been arrested in 1980 on drug charges, and a companion had informed the police at the time that Leon was heavily involved in the importation of drugs into this country. Before the current investigation began, the Burbank officers had learned that an informant had told a Glendale police officer that Leon stored a large quantity of methaqualone at his residence in Glendale. During the course of this investigation, the Burbank officers learned that Leon was living at 716 South Sunset Canyon in Burbank.

Subsequently, the officers observed several persons, at least one of whom had prior drug involvement, arriving at the Price Drive residence and leaving with small packages; observed a variety of other material activity at the two residences as well as at a condominium at 7902 Via Magdalena; and witnessed a variety of relevant activity involving respondents' automobiles. The officers also observed respondents Sanchez and Stewart board separate flights for Miami. The pair later returned to Los Angeles together, consented to a search of their luggage that revealed only a small amount of marihuana, and left the airport. Based on these and other observations summarized in the affidavit, App. 34, Officer Cyril Rombach of the Burbank Police Department, an experienced and well-trained narcotics investigator, prepared an application for a warrant to search 620 Price Drive, 716 South Sunset Canyon, 7902 Via Magdalena, and automobiles registered to each of the respondents for an extensive list of items believed to be related to respondents' drug-trafficking activities. Officer Rombach's extensive application was reviewed by several Deputy District Attorneys.

A facially valid search warrant was issued in September 1981 by a State Superior Court Judge. The ensuing searches produced large quantities of drugs at the Via Magdalena and Sunset Canyon addresses and a small quantity at the Price Drive residence. Other evidence was discovered at each of the residences and in Stewart's and Del Castillo's automobiles. Respondents were indicted by a grand jury in the District Court for the Central District of California and charged with conspiracy to possess and distribute cocaine and a variety of substantive counts.

(continues)

The respondents then filed motions to suppress the evidence seized pursuant to the warrant.[1] The District Court held an evidentiary hearing and, while recognizing that the case was a close one, *see id.*, at 131, granted the motions to suppress in part. It concluded that the affidavit was insufficient to establish probable cause,[2] but did not suppress all of the evidence as to all of the respondents because none of the respondents had standing to challenge all of the searches.[3] In response to a request from the Government, the court made clear that Officer Rombach had acted in good faith, but it rejected the Government's suggestion that the Fourth Amendment exclusionary rule should not apply where evidence is seized in reasonable good-faith reliance on a search warrant.[4]

The District Court denied the Government's motion for reconsideration, *id.*, at 147, and a divided panel of the Court of Appeals for the Ninth Circuit affirmed, judgt. order reported at 701 F.2d 187 (1983). The Court of Appeals first concluded that Officer Rombach's affidavit could not establish probable cause to search the Price Drive residence. To the extent that the affidavit set forth facts demonstrating the basis of the informant's knowledge of criminal activity, the information included was fatally stale. The affidavit, moreover, failed to establish the informant's credibility. Accordingly, the Court of Appeals concluded that the information provided by the informant was inadequate under both prongs of the two-part test established in *Aguilar v. Texas*, 378 U.S. 108, 84 S. Ct. 1509, 12 L. Ed. 2d 723 (1964), and *Spinelli v. United States*, 393 U.S. 410, 89 S. Ct. 584, 21 L. Ed. 2d 637 (1969).[5]

* * *

We have concluded that, in the Fourth Amendment context, the exclusionary rule can be modified somewhat without jeopardizing its ability to perform its intended functions. Accordingly, we reverse the judgment of the Court of Appeals.

II

Language in opinions of this Court and of individual Justices has sometimes implied that the exclusionary rule is a necessary corollary of the Fourth Amendment, *Mapp v. Ohio*, 367 U.S. 643, 651, 655–657, 81 S. Ct. 1684, 1689, 1691–1692, 6 L. Ed. 2d 1081 (1961); *Olmstead v. United States*, 277 U.S. 488, 462–463, 48 S. Ct. 564, 567, 72 L. Ed. 944 (1928), or that the rule is required by the conjunction of the Fourth and Fifth Amendments. *Mapp v. Ohio, supra*, 367 U.S., at 661-662, 81 S. Ct., at 1694-1695 (Black, J., concurring); *Agnello v. United States*, 269 U.S. 20, 33–34, 46 S. Ct. 4, 6–7, 70 L. Ed. 145 (1925). These implications need not detain us long. The Fifth Amendment theory has not withstood critical analysis or the test of time, *see Andresen v. Maryland*, 427 U.S. 463, 96 S. Ct. 2737, 49 L. Ed. 2d 627 (1976), and the Fourth Amendment "has never been interpreted to proscribe the introduction of illegally seized evidence in all proceedings or against all persons." *Stone v. Powell*, 428 U.S. 465, 486, 96 S. Ct. 3037, 3048, 49 L. Ed. 2d 1067 (1976).

A

The Fourth Amendment contains no provisions expressly precluding the use of evidence obtained in violation of its commands, and an examination of its origin and purposes makes clear that the use of fruits of a part[ly] unlawful search or seizure "work[s] no new Fourth Amendment wrong." *United States v. Calandra*, 414 U.S. 338, 354, 94 S. Ct. 613, 623, 38 L. Ed. 2d 561 (1974). The wrong condemned by

---

[1]Respondent Leon moved to suppress the evidence found on his person at the time of his arrest and the evidence seized from his residence at 716 South Sunset Canyon. Respondent Stewart's motion covered the fruits of searches of her residence at 620 Price Drive and the condominium at 7902 Via Magdalena and statements she made during the search of her residence. Respondent Sanchez sought to suppress the evidence discovered during the search of his residence at 620 Price Drive and statements he made shortly thereafter. He also joined Stewart's motion to suppress evidence seized from the condominium.

Respondent Del Castillo apparently sought to suppress all of the evidence seized in the searches. App. 78–80. The respondents also moved to suppress evidence seized in the searches of their automobiles.

[2]"I just cannot find this warrant sufficient for a showing of probable cause."

* * *

"There is no question of the reliability and credibility of the informant as not being established."

"Some details given tended to corroborate, maybe, the reliability of [the informant's] information about the previous transaction, but if it is not a stale transaction, it comes awfully close to it; and all the other material I think is as consistent with innocence as it is with guilt."

"So I just do not think this affidavit can withstand the test. I find, then, that there is no probable cause in this case for the issuance of the search warrant. . . ." *Id.*, at 127.

[3]The District Court concluded that Sanchez and Stewart had standing to challenge the search of 620 Price Drive; that Leon had standing to contest the legality of the search of 716 South Sunset Canyon; that none of the respondents established a legitimate expectation of privacy in the condominium at 7902 Via Magdalena; and that Stewart and Del Castillo each had standing to challenge the searches of their automobiles. The Government indicated that it did not intend to introduce evidence seized from the other respondents' vehicles. *Id.*, at 127–129. Finally, the court suppressed statements given by Sanchez and Stewart. *Id.*, at 129–130.

[4]"On the issue of good faith, obviously that is not the law of the Circuit, and I am not going to apply that law."

"I will say certainly in my view, there is not any question about good faith. [Officer Rombach] went to a Superior Court judge and got a warrant; obviously laid a meticulous trail. Had surveilled for a long period of time, and I believe his testimony—I think he said he consulted with three Deputy District Attorneys before proceeding himself, and I certainly have no doubt about the fact that that is true." *Id.*, at 140.

[5]In *Illinois v. Gates*, 462 U.S. 213, 103 S. Ct. 2317, 76 L. Ed. 2d 527 (1983), decided last Term, the Court abandoned the two-pronged *Aguilar-Spinelli* test for determining whether an informant's tip suffices to establish probable cause for the issuance of a warrant and substituted in its place a "totality of the circumstances" approach.

the Amendment is "fully accomplished" by the unlawful search or seizure itself, *ibid.*, and the exclusionary rule is neither intended nor able to "cure the invasion of the defendant's rights which he has already suffered." *Stone v. Powell, supra,* 428 U.S., at 540, 96 S. Ct., at 3073 (WHITE, J., dissenting). The rule thus operates as "a judicially created remedy designed to safeguard Fourth Amendment rights generally through its deterrent effect, rather than a personal constitutional right of the party aggrieved." *United States v. Calandra, supra,* 414 U.S., at 348, 94 S. Ct., at 620.

* * *

The substantial social costs exacted by the exclusionary rule for the vindication of Fourth Amendment rights have long been a source of concern. "Our cases have consistently recognized that unbending application of the exclusionary sanction to enforce ideals of governmental rectitude would impede unacceptably the truth-finding functions of judge and jury." *United States v. Payner,* 447 U.S. 727, 734, 100 S. Ct. 2439, 2445, 65 L. Ed. 2d 468 (1980). An objectionable collateral consequence of this interference with the criminal justice system's truth-finding function is that some guilty defendants may go free or receive reduced sentences as a result of favorable plea bargains.[6] Particularly when law enforcement officers have acted in objective good faith or their transgressions have been minor, the magnitude of the benefit conferred on such guilty defendants offends basic concepts of the criminal justice system. *Stone v. Powell,* 428 U.S., at 490, 96 S. Ct., at 3050. Indiscriminate application of the exclusionary rule, therefore, may well "generat[e] disrespect for the law and administration of justice." *Id.,* at 491, 96 S. Ct., at 3051. Accordingly, "[a]s with any remedial device, the application of the rule has been restricted to those areas where its remedial objectives are thought most efficaciously served." *United States v. Calandra,* supra, 414 U.S., at 348, 94 S. Ct., at 670; see *Stone v. Powell, supra,* 428 U.S., at 486-487, 97 S. Ct., at 3048-3049; *United States v. Janis,* 428 U.S. 433, 447, 96 S. Ct. 3021, 3028, 49 L. Ed. 2d 1046 (1976).

* * *

II

A

Because a search warrant "provides the detached scrutiny of a neutral magistrate, which is a more reliable safeguard against improper searches than the hurried judgment of a law enforcement officer 'engaged in the often competitive enterprise of ferreting out crime,'" *United States v. Chadwich,* 433 U.S. 1, 9, 97 S. Ct. 2476, 2482, 53 L. Ed. 2d 538 (1977) (quoting *Johnson v. United States,* 333 U.S. 10, 14, 68 S. Ct. 367, 369, 92 L. Ed. 436 (1948)), we have expressed a strong preference for warrants and declared that "in a doubtful or marginal case a search under a warrant may be sustainable where without one it would fall." *United States v. Ventresca,* 380 U.S. 102, 106, 85 S. Ct. 741, 744, 13 L. Ed. 2d 687 (1965). See *Aguilar v. Texas,* 378 U.S., at 111, 84 S. Ct., at 1512. Reasonable minds frequently may differ on the question [of] whether a particular affidavit establishes probable cause, and we have thus concluded that the preference for warrants is most appropriately effectuated by according "great deference" to a magistrate's determination. *Spinelli v. United States,* 393 U.S., at 419, 89 S. Ct., at 590. See *Illinois v. Gates,* 462 U.S., at 236, 103 S. Ct., at 2331; United *States v. Ventresca, supra,* 380 U.S., at 108–109, 85 S. Ct., at 745–746.

Deference to the magistrate, however, is not boundless. It is clear, first, that the deference accorded to a magistrate's finding of probable cause does not preclude inquiry into the knowing or reckless falsity of the affidavit on which that determination was based. *Franks v. Delaware,* 438 U.S. 154, 98 S. Ct. 2674, 57 L. Ed. 2d 667 (1978).[12] Second, the courts must also insist the magistrate purport to "perform his

---

[6]Researchers have only recently begun to study extensively the effects of the exclusionary rule on the disposition of felony arrests. One study suggests that the rule results in the nonprosecution or nonconviction of between 0.6% and 2.35% of individuals arrested for felonies. Davies, A Hard Look at What We Know (and Still Need to Learn) About the "Costs" of the Exclusionary Rule: The NIJ Study and Other Studies of "Lost" Arrests, 1983 A.B.F. Res. J. 611, 621. The estimates are higher for particular crimes the prosecution of which depends heavily on physical evidence. Thus, the cumulative loss due to nonprosecution or nonconviction of individuals arrested on felony drug charges is probably in the range of 2.8% to 7.1%. *Id.,* at 680. Davies' analysis of California data suggests that screening by police and prosecutors results in the release because of illegal searches or seizures of as many as 1.4% of all felony arrestees, *Id.,* at 650, that 0.9% of felony arrestees are released, because of illegal searches or seizures, at the preliminary hearing or after trial, id., at 653, and that roughly 0.5% of all felony arrestees benefit from reversals on appeal because of illegal searches. *id.,* at 654. See also K. Brosi, A Cross-City Comparison of Felony Case Processing 16, 18-19 (1979); U.S. General Accounting Office, Report of the Comptroller General of the United States, Impact of the Exclusionary Rule on Federal Criminal Prosecutions 10-11, 14 (1979); F. Feeney, F. Dill, & A. Weir, Arrests Without Convictions: How Often They Occur and Why 203-206 (National Institute of Justice 1983); National Institute of Justice, The Effects of the Exclusionary Rule: A Study in California 1-2 (1982); Nardulli, The Societal Cost of the Exclusionary Rule: An Empirical Assessment, 1983 A.B.F. Res. J. 585, 600. The exclusionary rule also has been found to affect the plea-bargaining process. S. Schlesinger, Exclusionary Injustice: The Problem of Illegally Obtained Evidence 63 (1977). But see *Davies, supra,* at 668–669; *Nardulli, supra,* at 604–606.

Many of these researchers have concluded that the impact of the exclusionary rule is insubstantial, but the small percentages with which they deal mask a large absolute number of felons who are released because the cases against them were based in part on illegal searches or seizures. "[A]ny rule of evidence that denies the jury access to clearly probative and reliable evidence must bear a heavy burden of justification, and must be carefully limited to the circumstances in which it will pay its way by deterring official unlawfulness." *Illinois v. Gates,* 462 U.S., at 257–258, 103 S. Ct., at 2342 (WHITE, J., concurring in judgment). Because we find that the rule can have no substantial deterrent effect in the sorts of situations under consideration in this case, see *infra,* at 3417–3419, we conclude that it cannot pay its way in those situations.

(continues)

'neutral and detached' function and not serve merely as a rubber stamp for the police." *Aguilar v. Texas, supra*, 378 U.S., at 111, 84 S. Ct., at 1512. See *Illinois v. Gates, supra*, 462 U.S., at 239, 103 S. Ct., at 2332. A magistrate failing to "manifest that neutrality and detachment demanded of a judicial officer when presented with a warrant application" and who acts instead as "an adjunct law enforcement officer" cannot provide valid authorization for an otherwise unconstitutional search. *Lo-Ji Sales, Inc. v. New York*, 442 U.S. 319, 326-327, 99 S. Ct. 2319, 2324-2325, 60 L. Ed. 2d 920 (1979).

Third, reviewing courts will not defer to a warrant based on an affidavit that does not "provide the magistrate with a substantial basis for determining the existence of probable cause." *Illinois v. Gates*, 462 U.S., at 239, 103 S. Ct., at 2332. "Sufficient information must be presented to the magistrate to allow that official to determine probable cause; his action cannot be a mere ratification of the bare conclusions of others." *Ibid.* See *Aguilar v. Texas, supra*, 378 U.S., at 114-115, 84 S. Ct., at 1513-1514; *Giordenello v. United States*, 357 U.S. 480, 78 S. Ct. 1245, 2 L. Ed. 2d 1503 (1958); *Nathanson v. United States*, 290 U.S. 41, 54 S. Ct. 11, 78 L. Ed. 159 (1933).[13] Even if the warrant application was supported by more than a "bare bones" affidavit, a reviewing court may properly conclude that, notwithstanding the deference that magistrates deserve, the warrant was invalid because the magistrate's probable-cause determination reflected an improper analysis of the totality of the circumstances, *Illinois v. Gates, supra*, 462 U.S., at 238–239, 103 S. Ct., at 2332–2333, or because the form of the warrant was improper in some respect.

Only in the first of these three situations, however, has the Court set forth a rationale for suppressing evidence obtained pursuant to a search warrant; in the other areas, it has simply excluded such evidence without considering whether Fourth Amendment interests will be advanced. To the extent that proponents of exclusion rely on its behavioral effects on

judges and magistrates in these areas, their reliance is misplaced. First, the exclusionary rule is designed to deter police misconduct rather than to punish the errors of judges and magistrates. Second, there exists no evidence suggesting that judges and magistrates are inclined to ignore or subvert the Fourth Amendment or that lawlessness among these actors requires application of the extreme sanction of exclusion.[14]

Third, and most important, we discern no basis, and are offered none, for believing that exclusion of evidence seized pursuant to a warrant will have a significant deterrent effect on the issuing judge or magistrate.[15] Many of the factors that indicate that the exclusionary rule cannot provide an effective "special" or "general" deterrent for individual offending law enforcement officers[16] apply as well to judges or magistrates And, to the extent that the rule is thought to operate as a "systemic" deterrent on a wider audience,[17] it clearly can have no such effect on individuals empowered to issue search warrants. Judges and magistrates are not adjuncts to the law enforcement team; as neutral judicial officers, they have no stake in

---

[12]Indeed, "it would be an unthinkable imposition upon [the magistrate's] authority if a warrant affidavit, revealed after the fact to contain a deliberately or recklessly false statement, were to stand beyond impeachment." 438 U.S., at 165, 98 S. Ct., at 2681.

[13]See also *Beck v. Ohio*, 379 U.S. 89, 85 S. Ct. 223, 13 L. Ed. 2d 142 (1964), in which the Court concluded that "the record ... does not contain a single objective fact to support a belief by the officers that the petitioner was engaged in criminal activity at the time they arrested him." *Id.*, at 95, 85 S. Ct., at 227. Although the Court was willing to assume that the arresting officers acted in good faith, it concluded that:

"'[G]ood faith on the part of the arresting officers is not enough,' *Henry v. United States*, 361 U.S. 98, 102, 80 S. Ct. 168, 171, 4 L. Ed. 2d 134. If subjective good faith alone were the test, the protections of the Fourth Amendment would evaporate, and the people would be 'secure in their persons, houses, papers, and effects,' only in the discretion of the police." (*Id.*, at 97, 85 S. Ct., at 228.)

We adhere to this view and emphasize that nothing in this opinion is intended to suggest a lowering of the probable-cause standard. On the contrary, we deal here with the remedy to be applied to a concededly unconstitutional search.

[14]Although there are assertions that some magistrates become rubber stamps for the police and others may be unable effectively to screen police conduct, see, *for example*, 2 W. LaFave, Search and Seizure § 4.1 (1978); Kamisar, Does (Did) (Should) The Exclusionary Rule Rest on a "Principled Basis" Rather than an "Empirical Proposition"? 16 Creighton L. Rev. 565, 569-571 (1983); Schroeder, Deterring Fourth Amendment Violations: Alternatives to the Exclusionary Rule, 69 Geo. L.J. 1361, 1412 (1981), we are not convinced that this is a problem of major proportions. See L. Tiffany, D. McIntyre, & D. Rotenberg, Detection of Crime 119 (1967); Israel, Criminal Procedure, the Burger Court, and the Legacy of the Warren Court, 75 Mich. L. Rev. 1319, 1414, n. 396 (1977); P. Johnson, New Approaches to Enforcing the Fourth Amendment 8-10 (Working Paper, Sept. 1978), quoted in Y. Kamisar, W. LaFave, & J. Israel, Modern Criminal Procedure 229–230 (5th ed. 1980); R. Van Duizend, L. Sutton, & C. Carter, The Search Warrant Process, ch. 7 (Review Draft, National Center for State Courts, 1983).

[15]As the Supreme Judicial Court of Massachusetts recognized in *Commonwealth v. Sheppard*, 387 Mass. 488, 506, 441 N.E.2d 725, 735 (1982):

"The exclusionary rule may not be well tailored to deterring judicial misconduct. If applied to judicial misconduct, the rule would be just as costly as it is when it is applied to police misconduct, but it may be ill-fitted to the job-created motivations of judges. ... [I]deally a judge is impartial as to whether a particular piece of evidence is admitted or a particular defendant convicted. Hence, in the abstract, suppression of a particular piece of evidence may not be as effective a disincentive to a neutral judge as it would be to the police. It may be that a ruling by an appellate court that a search warrant was unconstitutional would be sufficient to deter similar conduct in the future by magistrates."

But see *United States v. Karathanos*, 531 F.2d 26, 33–34 (CA2), cert. denied, 428 U.S. 910, 96 S. Ct. 3221, 49 L. Ed. 2d 1217 (1976).

[16]See, *for example*, *Stone v. Powell*, 428 U.S., at 498, 96 S. Ct., at 3054 (BURGER, C.J., concurring); Oaks, Studying the Exclusionary Rule in Search and Seizure, 37 U. Chi. L. Rev. 665, 709–710 (1970).

[17]See, *e.g.*, *Dunaway v. New York*, 442 U.S. 200, 221, 99 S. Ct. 2248, 2261, 60 L. Ed. 2d 824 (1979) (STEVENS, J., concurring); Mertens & Wasserstrom, The Good Faith Exception to the Exclusionary Rule: Deregulating the Police and Derailing the Law, 70 Geo. L.J. 365, 399-401 (1981).

the outcome of particular criminal prosecutions. The threat of exclusion thus cannot be expected significantly to deter them. Imposition of the exclusionary sanction is not necessary meaningfully to inform judicial officers of their errors, and we cannot conclude that admitting evidence obtained pursuant to a warrant while at the same time declaring that the warrant was somehow defective will in any way reduce judicial officers' professional incentives to comply with the Fourth Amendment, encourage them to repeat their mistakes, or lead to the granting of all colorable warrant requests.[18]

B

If exclusion of evidence obtained pursuant to a subsequently invalidated warrant is to have any deterrent effect, therefore, it must alter the behavior of individual law enforcement officers or the policies of their departments. One could argue that applying the exclusionary rule in cases where the police failed to demonstrate probable cause in the warrant application deters future inadequate presentations or "magistrate shopping" and thus promotes the end of the Fourth Amendment. Suppressing evidence obtained pursuant to a technically defective warrant supported by a probable cause also might encourage officers to scrutinize more closely the form of the warrant and to point out suspected judicial errors. We find such arguments speculative and conclude that suppression of evidence obtained pursuant to a warrant should be ordered only on a case-by-case basis and only in those unusual cases in which exclusion will further the purposes of the exclusionary rule.[19]

We have frequently questioned whether the exclusionary rule can have any deterrent effect when the offending officers acted in the objectively reasonable belief that their conduct did not violate the Fourth Amendment. "No empirical researcher, proponent or opponent of the rule, has yet been able to establish with any assurance whether the rule has a deterrent effect. ..." *United States v. Janis*, 428 U.S., at 452, n. 22, 96 S. Ct., at 3031, n. 22. But even assuming that the rule effectively deters some police misconduct and

provides incentives for the law enforcement profession as a whole to conduct itself in accord with the Fourth Amendment, it cannot be expected, and should not be applied, to deter objectively reasonable law enforcement activity.

As we observed in *Michigan v. Tucker*, 417 U.S. 433, 447, 94 S. Ct. 2357, 2365, 41 L. Ed. 2d 182 (1974), and reiterated in *United States v. Peltier*, 422 U.S., at 539, 95 S. Ct., at 2318:

"The deterrent purpose of the exclusionary rule necessarily assumes that the police have engaged in wilful, or at the very least negligent, conduct which has deprived the defendant of some right. By refusing to admit evidence gained as a result of such conduct, the courts hope to instill in those particular investigating officers, or in their future counterparts, a greater deal of care toward the rights of an accused. Where the official action was pursued in complete good faith, however, the deterrence rationale loses much of its force."

The *Peltier* Court continued, *id.*, at 542, 95 S. Ct., at 2320:

"If the purpose of the exclusionary rule is to deter unlawful police conduct, then evidence obtained from a search should be suppressed only if it can be said that the law enforcement officer had knowledge, or may properly be charged with knowledge, that the search was unconstitutional under the Fourth Amendment."

See also *Illinois v. Gates*, 462 U.S., at 260-261, 103 S. Ct., at 2344 (WHITE, J., concurring in judgment); *United States v. Janis, supra*, 428 U.S., at 459, 96 S. Ct., at 3034; *Brown v. Illinois*, 422 U.S., at 610–611, 95 S. Ct., at 2265–2266 (POWELL, J., concurring in part).[20] In short, where the officer's conduct is objectively reasonable,

---

[18]Limiting the application of the exclusionary sanction may well increase the care with which magistrates scrutinize warrant applications. We doubt that magistrates are more desirous of avoiding the exclusion of evidence obtained pursuant to warrants they have issued than of avoiding invasions of privacy.

Federal magistrates, moreover, are subject to the direct supervision of district courts. They may be removed for "incompetency, misconduct, neglect of duty, or physical or mental disability." 28 U.S.C. § 631(i). If a magistrate serves merely as a "rubber stamp" for the police or is unable to exercise mature judgment, closer supervision or removal provides a more effective remedy than the exclusionary rule.

[19]Our discussion of the deterrent effect of excluding evidence obtained in reasonable reliance on a subsequently invalidated warrant assumes, of course, that the officers properly executed the warrant and searched only those places and for those objects that it was reasonable to believe were covered by the warrant. Cf. *Massachusetts v. Sheppard*, 468 U.S. 981, 989, n. 6, 104 S. Ct. 3424, 3429, n. 6, 82 L. Ed. 2d 737 ("[I]t was not unreasonable for the police in this case to rely on the judge's assurances that the warrant authorized the search they had requested").

[20]We emphasize that the standard of reasonableness we adopt is an objective one. Many objections to a good-faith exception assume that the exception will turn on the subjective good faith of individual officers. "Grounding the modification in objective reasonableness, however, retains the value of the exclusionary rule as an incentive for the law enforcement profession as a whole to conduct themselves in accord with the Fourth Amendment." *Illinois v. Gates*, 462 U.S., at 261, n. 15, 103 S. Ct., at 2344, n. 15 (WHITE, J., concurring in judgment); see *Dunaway v. New York*, 442 U.S., at 221, 99 S. Ct., at 2261 (STEVENS, J., concurring). The objective standard we adopted, moreover, requires officers to have a reasonable knowledge of what the law prohibits. *United States v. Peltier*, 442 U.S. 531, 542, 95 S. Ct. 2313, 2320, 45 L. Ed. 2d 374 (1975). As Professor Jerold Israel has observed:

"The key to the [exclusionary] rule's effectiveness as a deterrent lies, I believe, in the impetus it has provided to police training programs that make officers aware of the limits imposed by the fourth amendment and emphasize the need to operate within those limits. [An objective good-faith exception] is not likely to result in the elimination of such programs, which are now viewed as an important aspect of police professionalism. Neither is it likely to alter the tenor of those programs; the possibility that illegally obtained evidence may be admitted in borderline cases is unlikely to encourage police instructors to pay less attention to fourth amendment limitations. Finally, [it] should not encourage officers to pay less attention to what they are taught, as the requirement that the officer act in 'good faith' is inconsistent with closing one's mind to the possibility of illegality."

Israel, *supra* n. 14, at 1412–1413 (footnotes omitted).

(continues)

"excluding the evidence will not further the ends of the exclusionary rule in any appreciable way; for it is painfully apparent . . . the officer is acting as a reasonable officer would and should act in similar circumstances. Excluding the evidence can in no way affect his future conduct unless it is to make him less willing to do his duty."

Stone v. Powell, 428 U.S., at 539–540, 96 S. Ct., at 3073–3074 (WHITE, J., dissenting).

This is particularly true, we believe, when an officer acting with objective good faith has obtained a search warrant from a judge or magistrate and acted within its scope.[21] In most such cases, there is no police illegality and thus nothing to deter. It is the magistrate's responsibility to determine whether the officer's allegations establish probable cause and, if so, to issue a warrant comporting in form with the requirements of the Fourth Amendment. In the ordinary case, an officer cannot be expected to question the magistrate's probable-cause determination or his judgment that the form of the warrant is technically sufficient. "[O]nce the warrant issues, there is literally nothing more the policeman can do in seeking to comply with the law." *Id.*, 428 U.S., at 498, 96

---

[21]According to the Attorney General's Task Force on Violent Crime, Final Report (1981), the situation in which an officer relies on a duly authorized warrant "is a particularly compelling example of good faith. A warrant is a judicial mandate to an officer to conduct a search or make an arrest, and the officer has a sworn duty to carry out its provisions. Accordingly, we believe that there should be a rule which states that evidence obtained pursuant to and within the scope of a warrant is prima facie the result of good faith on the part of the officer seizing the evidence."

Id., at 55.

[22]To the extent that Justice STEVENS' conclusions concerning the integrity of the courts, *post*, at 3454–3455, rest on a foundation other than his judgment, which we reject, concerning the effects of our decision on the deterrence of police illegality, we find his argument unpersuasive. "Judicial integrity clearly does not mean that the courts must never admit evidence obtained in violation of the Fourth Amendment." *United States v. Janis*, 428 U.S. 433, 458, n. 35, 96 S. Ct. 3021, 3034, n. 35, 49 L. Ed. 2d 1046 (1976). "While courts, of course, must ever be concerned with preserving the integrity of the judicial process, this concern has limited force as a justification for the exclusion of highly probative evidence." *Stone v. Powell*, 428 U.S., at 485, 96 S. Ct., at 3048. Our cases establish that the question whether the use of illegally obtained evidence in judicial proceedings represents judicial participation in a Fourth Amendment violation and offends the integrity of the courts

"is essentially the same as the inquiry into whether exclusion would serve a deterrent purpose.... The analysis showing that exclusion in this case has no demonstrated deterrent effect and is unlikely to have any significant such effect shows, by the same reasoning, that the admission of the evidence is unlikely to encourage violations of the Fourth Amendment."

United States v. Janis, supra, 428 U.S., at 459, n. 35, 96 S. Ct., at 3034, n. 35. Absent unusual circumstances, when a Fourth Amendment violation has occurred because the police have reasonably relied on a warrant issued by a detached and neutral magistrate but ultimately found to be defective, "the integrity of the courts is not implicated." *Illinois v. Gates, supra*, 462 U.S., at 259, n. 14, 103 S. Ct., at 2343, n. 14 (WHITE, J., concurring in judgment). See *Stone v. Powell*, 428 U.S., at 485, n. 23, 96 S. Ct., at 3048, n. 23; *id.*, at 540, 96 S. Ct., at 3073 (WHITE, J., dissenting); *United States v. Peltier*, 442 U.S. 531, 536–539, 95 S. Ct. 2313, 2317–2318, 45 L. Ed. 2d 374 (1975).

S. Ct., at 3054 (BURGER, C.J., concurring). Penalizing the officer for the magistrate's error, rather than his own, cannot logically contribute to the deterrence of Fourth Amendment violations.[22]

We conclude that the marginal or nonexistent benefits produced by suppressing evidence obtained in objectively reasonable reliance on a subsequently invalidated search warrant cannot justify the substantial costs of exclusion. We do not suggest, however, that exclusion is always inappropriate in cases where an officer has obtained a warrant and abided by its terms. "[S]earches pursuant to a warrant will rarely require any deep inquiry into reasonableness," *Illinois v. Gates*, 462 U.S., at 267, 103 S. Ct., at 2347 (WHITE, J., concurring in judgment), for "a warrant issued by a magistrate normally suffices to establish" that a law enforcement officer has "acted in good faith in conducting the search." *United States v. Ross*, 456 U.S. 798, 823, n. 32, 102 S. Ct. 2157, 2172, n. 32, 72 L. Ed. 2d 572 (1982). Nevertheless, the officer's reliance on the magistrate's probable-cause determination and on the technical sufficiency of the warrant he issues must be objectively reasonable, cf. *Harlow v. Fitzgerald*, 457 U.S. 800, 815–819, 102 S. Ct. 2727, 2737–2739, 73 L. Ed. 2d 396 (1982),[23] and it is clear that in some circumstances the officer[24] will have no reasonable grounds for believing that the warrant was properly issued.

Suppression therefore remains an appropriate remedy if the magistrate or judge in issuing a warrant was misled by information in an affidavit that the affiant knew was false or would have known was false except for his reckless disregard

---

[23]In *Harlow*, we eliminated the subjective component of the qualified immunity public officials enjoy in suits seeking damages for alleged deprivations of constitutional rights. The situations are not perfectly analogous, but we also eschew inquiries into the subjective beliefs of law enforcement officers who seize evidence pursuant to a subsequently invalidated warrant. Although we have suggested that, "[o]n occasion, the motive with which the officer conducts an illegal search may have some relevance in determining the propriety of applying the exclusionary rule," *Scott v. United States*, 436 U.S. 128, 139, n. 13, 98 S. Ct. 1717, 1724, n. 13, 56 L. Ed. 2d 168 (1978), we believe that "sending state and federal courts on an expedition into the minds of police officers would produce a grave and fruitless misallocation of judicial resources." *Massachusetts v. Painten*, 389 U.S. 560, 565, 88 S. Ct. 660, 663, 19 L. Ed. 2d 770 (1968) (WHITE, J., dissenting). Accordingly, our good-faith inquiry is confined to the objectively ascertainable question whether a reasonably well-trained officer would have known that the search was illegal despite the magistrate's authorization. In making this determination, all of the circumstances—including whether the warrant application had previously been rejected by a different magistrate—may be considered.

[24]References to "officer" throughout this opinion should not be read too narrowly. It is necessary to consider the objective reasonableness, not only of the officers who eventually executed a warrant, but also of the officers who originally obtained it or who provided information material to the probable-cause determination. Nothing in our opinion suggests, for example, that an officer could obtain a warrant on the basis of a "bare bones" affidavit and then rely on colleagues who are ignorant of the circumstances under which the warrant was obtained to conduct the search. See *Whiteley v. Warden*, 401 U.S. 560, 568, 91 S. Ct. 1031, 1037, 28 L. Ed. 2d 306 (1971).

of the truth. *Franks v. Delaware*, 438 U.S. 154, 98 S. Ct. 2674, 57 L. Ed. 2d 667 (1978). The exception we recognize today will also not apply in cases where the issuing magistrate wholly abandoned his judicial role in the manner condemned in *Lo-Ji Sales, Inc. v. New York*, 442 U.S. 319, 99 S. Ct. 2319, 60 L. Ed. 2d 920 (1979); in such circumstances, no reasonably well-trained officer should rely on the warrant. Nor would an officer manifest objective good faith in relying on a warrant based on an affidavit "so lacking in indicia of probable cause as to render official belief in its existence entirely unreasonable." *Brown v. Illinois*, 422 U.S., at 610–611, 95 S. Ct., at 2265–2266 (POWELL, J., concurring in part); see *Illinois v. Gates, supra*, 462 U.S., at 2345–2346, 103 S. Ct., at 2345–2346 (WHITE, J., concurring in the judgment). Finally, depending on the circumstances of the particular case, a warrant may be so facially deficient—*that is*, in failing to particularize the place to be searched or the things to be seized—that the executing officers cannot reasonably presume it to be valid. Cf. *Massachusetts v. Sheppard*, 468 U.S., at 988–991, 104 S. Ct. at 3428–3430.

In so limiting the suppression remedy, we leave untouched the probable-cause standard and the various requirements for a valid warrant. Other objections to the modification of the Fourth Amendment exclusionary rule we consider to be insubstantial. The good-faith exception for searches conducted pursuant to warrants is not intended to signal our willingness strictly to enforce the requirements of the Fourth Amendment, and we do not believe that it will have this effect. As we have already suggested, the good-faith exception, turning as it does on objective reasonableness, should not be difficult to apply in practice. When officers have acted pursuant to a warrant, the prosecution should ordinarily be able to establish objective good faith without a substantial expenditure of judicial time.

Nor are we persuaded that application of a good-faith exception to searches conducted pursuant to warrants will preclude review of the constitutionality of the search or seizure, deny needed guidance from the courts, or freeze Fourth Amendment law in its present state.[25] There is no need for courts to adopt the inflexible practice of always deciding whether the officers' conduct manifested objective good faith before turning to the question [of] whether the Fourth Amendment has been violated. Defendants seeking suppression of the fruits of allegedly unconstitutional searches or seizures undoubtedly raise live controversies which Art. III empowers federal courts to adjudicate. As cases addressing questions of good-faith immunity under 42 U.S.C. § 1983,

compare *O'Connor v. Donaldson*, 422 U.S. 563, 95 S. Ct. 2486, 45 L. Ed. 2d 396 (1975), with *Procunier v. Navarette*, 434 U.S. 555, 566, n. 14, 98 S. Ct. 855, 862, n. 14, 55 L. Ed. 2d 24 (1978), and cases involving the harmless-error doctrine, compare *Milton v. Wainwright*, 407 U.S. 371, 372, 92 S. Ct. 2174, 2175, 33 L. Ed. 2d 1 (1972), with *Coleman v. Alabama*, 399 U.S. 1, 90 S. Ct. 1999, 26 L. Ed. 2d 387 (1970), make clear, courts have considerable discretion in conforming their decision-making processes to the exigencies of particular cases.

If the resolution of a particular Fourth Amendment question is necessary to guide future action by law enforcement officers and magistrates, nothing will prevent reviewing courts from deciding that question before turning to the good-faith issue.[26] Indeed, it frequently will be difficult to determine whether the officers acted reasonably without resolving the Fourth Amendment issue. Even if the Fourth Amendment question is not one of broad import, reviewing courts could decide in particular cases that magistrates under their supervision need to be informed of their errors and so evaluate the officers' good faith only after finding a violation. In other circumstances, those courts could reject suppression motions posing no important Fourth Amendment questions by turning immediately to a consideration of the officers' good faith. We have no reason to believe that our Fourth Amendment jurisprudence would suffer by allowing reviewing courts to exercise an informed discretion in making this choice.

IV

When the principles we have enunciated today are applied to the facts of this case, it is apparent that the judgment of the Court of Appeals cannot stand. The Court of Appeals applied the prevailing legal standards to Officer Rombach's warrant application and concluded that the application could not support the magistrate's probable-cause determination. In so doing, the court clearly informed the magistrate that he had erred in issuing the challenged warrant. This aspect of the court's judgment is not under attack in this proceeding.

Having determined that the warrant should not have issued, the Court of Appeals understandably declined to adopt a modification of the Fourth Amendment exclusionary rule that this Court had not previously sanctioned. Although the modification finds strong support in our previous cases, the Court of Appeals' commendable self-restraint is not to be criticized. We have now reexamined the purposes

---

[25]The argument that defendants will lose their incentive to litigate meritorious Fourth Amendment claims as a result of the good-faith exception we adopt today is unpersuasive. Although the exception might discourage presentation of insubstantial suppression motions, the magnitude of the benefit conferred on defendants by a successful motion makes it unlikely that litigation of colorable claims will be substantially diminished.

[26]It has been suggested, in fact, that "the recognition of a 'penumbral zone,' within which an inadvertent mistake would not call for exclusion, . . . will make it less tempting for judges to bend fourth amendment standards to avoid releasing a possibly dangerous criminal because of a minor and unintentional miscalculation by the police." Schroeder, *supra* n. 14, at 1420–1421 (footnote omitted); see Ashdown, Good Faith, the Exclusionary Remedy, and Rule-Oriented Adjudication in the Criminal Process, 24 Wm. & Mary L. Rev. 335, 383–384 (1983).

(continues)

of the exclusionary rule and the propriety of its application in cases where officers have relied on a subsequently invalidated search warrant. Our conclusion is that the rule's purposes will only rarely be served by applying it in such circumstances.

In the absence of an allegation that the magistrate abandoned his detached and neutral role, suppression is appropriate only if the officers were dishonest or reckless in preparing their affidavit or could not have harbored an objectively reasonable belief in the existence of probable cause. Only respondent Leon has contended that no reasonably well-trained police officer could have believed that there existed probable cause to search his house; significantly, the other respondents advance no comparable argument. Officer Rombach's application for a warrant clearly was supported by much more than a "bare bones" affidavit. The affidavit related the results of an extensive investigation and, as the opinions of the divided panel of the Court of Appeals make clear, provided evidence sufficient to create disagreement among thoughtful and competent judges as to the existence of probable cause. Under these circumstances, the officers' reliance on the magistrate's determination of probable cause was objectively reasonable, and application of the extreme sanction of exclusion is inappropriate.

Accordingly, the judgment of the Court of Appeals is *Reversed.*

Justice BLACKMUN, concurring.

The Court today holds that evidence obtained in violation of the Fourth Amendment by officers acting in objectively reasonable reliance on a search warrant issued by a neutral and detached magistrate need not be excluded, as a matter of federal law, from the case in chief of federal and state criminal prosecutions. In so doing, the Court writes another chapter in the volume of Fourth Amendment law opened by *Weeks v. United States*, 232 U.S. 383, 34 S. Ct. 341, 58 L. Ed. 652 (1914). I join the Court's opinion in this case and the one in *Massachusetts v. Sheppard*, 468 U.S. 981, 104 S. Ct. 3424, 82 L. Ed. 2d 737 (1984), because I believe that the rule announced today advances the legitimate interests of the criminal justice system without sacrificing the individual rights protected by the Fourth Amendment. I write separately, however, to underscore what I regard as the unavoidably provisional nature of today's decision.

As the Court's opinion in this case makes clear, the Court has narrowed the scope of the exclusionary rule because of an empirical judgment that the rule has little appreciable effect in cases where officers act in objectively reasonable reliance on search warrants. See *ante*, at 3419–3420. Because I share the view that the exclusionary rule is not a constitutionally compelled corollary of the Fourth Amendment itself, see *ante*, at 3412, I see no way to avoid making an empirical judgment of this sort, and I am satisfied that the Court has made the correct one on the information before it. Like all courts, we face institutional limitations on our ability to gather information about "legislative facts," and the exclusionary rule itself has exacerbated the shortage of hard data concerning the behavior of police officers in the absence of such a rule. See *United States v. Janis*, 428 U.S. 433, 448–453, 96 S. Ct. 3021, 3029–3031, 49 L. Ed. 2d 1046 (1976). Nonetheless, we cannot escape the responsibility to decide the question before us, however imperfect our information may be, and I am prepared to join the Court on the information now at hand.

What must be stressed, however, is that any empirical judgment about the effect of the exclusionary rule in a particular class of cases necessarily is a provisional one. By their very nature, the assumptions on which we proceed today cannot be cast in stone. To the contrary, they now will be tested in the real world of state and federal law enforcement, and this Court will attend to the results. If it should emerge from experience that, contrary to our expectations, the good-faith exception to the exclusionary rule results in a material change in police compliance with the Fourth Amendment, we shall have to reconsider what we have undertaken here. The logic of a decision that rests on untested predictions about police conduct demands no less.

If a single principle may be drawn from this Court's exclusionary rule decisions, from *Weeks* through *Mapp v. Ohio*, 367 U.S. 643, 81 S. Ct. 1684, 6 L. Ed. 2d 1081 (1961), to the decisions handed down today, it is that the scope of the exclusionary rule is subject to change in light of changing judicial understanding about the effects of the rule outside the confines of the courtroom. It is incumbent on the Nation's law enforcement officers, who must continue to observe the Fourth Amendment in the wake of today's decisions, to recognize the double-edged nature of that principle.

UNITED STATES of America, Plaintiff-Appellee,

v.

Gilbert MARTINEZ-JIMENEZ, Defendant-Appellant.

No. 87–5305.

United States Court of Appeals, Ninth Circuit.

Submitted Oct. 4, 1988.

Decided Jan.3, 1989

864 F.2d 664 (9th Cir. 1989).

NELSON, Circuit Judge.

Gilbert Martinez-Jimenez appeals his conviction following a bench trial on one count of armed bank robbery in violation of 18 U.S.C. § 2113(a) & (d). He contends that the trial court erred in concluding that the toy gun that he held during the bank robbery was a "dangerous weapon" as defined by 18 U.S.C. § 2113(d). We affirm the judgment of the district court.

PROCEDURAL BACKGROUND

On July 14, 1987, a federal grand jury in the Central District of California returned a three-count indictment that charged the appellant and an accomplice, Joe Anthony De La Torre, with armed bank robbery in violation of 18 U.S.C. § 2113(a) & (d) and with carrying a firearm during a crime of violence in violation of 18 U.S.C. § 924(c). At a bench trial the appellant and his accomplice were found guilty of armed bank robbery as charged in count one and not guilty of carrying a firearm during a crime of violence, as charged in counts two and three.

FACTS

On June 19, 1987, at approximately 12:55 p.m., Martinez-Jimenez and De La Torre entered a bank in Bellflower, California. While De La Torre took cash from a customer and two bank drawers, Martinez-Jimenez remained in the lobby and ordered that the people in the bank lie "face down on the floor." During this time Martinez-Jimenez was holding an object that eyewitnesses thought was a handgun. These persons included two bank employees and a customer who was familiar with guns because he owned handguns, had handled weapons while in military service, and occasionally used weapons at firing ranges. The three witnesses testified that the object was a dark revolver about eight or nine inches long and that it caused them to fear for the safety of themselves and of those around them.

At trial, De La Torre testified that neither he nor Martinez-Jimenez had operable firearms when they entered the bank. He testified that Martinez-Jimenez had a toy gun that he and Martinez-Jimenez had purchased at a department store a few hours prior to the robbery. De La Torre also testified that he hid the toy gun in his closet after the robbery, that neither he nor Martinez-Jimenez wanted the bank employees to believe that they had a real gun, and that they did not want the bank employees to be in fear for their lives. Martinez-Jimenez testified that he had carried the toy gun because he felt secure with it and that during the robbery he held it down toward his leg in order to hide it so that people would not see it. The defense introduced into evidence a toy gun. Martinez-Jimenez testified that the gun used in the robbery was the toy gun introduced into evidence. It was stipulated that De La Torre's attorney had received the toy gun offered as the gun used in the robbery from De La Torre's mother.

Based upon observation of the bank robbery photographs and the toy gun, the court concluded that Martinez-Jimenez possessed a toy gun during the course of the bank robbery and that he had kept the toy gun pointed downwards by his side during the course of the bank robbery. On the basis of his display of the toy gun in the course of the robbery, Martinez-Jimenez was convicted under section 2113(d) which provides an enhanced penalty for use of a "dangerous weapon" during a bank robbery.

STANDARD OF REVIEW

The question presented is whether a toy gun is a "dangerous weapon" within the meaning of the federal bank robbery statute. Interpretation of a statute presents a question of law reviewable de novo. *United States v. Wilson*, 720 F.2d 608, 609 n. 2 (9th Cir. 1983), *cert. denied*, 465 U.S. 1034, 104 S. Ct. 1304, 79 L. Ed. 2d 703 (1984); *United States v. Moreno-Pulido*, 695 F.2d 1141, 1143 (9th Cir. 1983).

DISCUSSION

A robber may be guilty of an armed bank robbery under section 2113(d) if he uses a dangerous weapon or device in the commission of the crime. The instrumentality does not have to be a firearm. The use, or unlawful carrying, of a firearm in a bank robbery is a more serious offense punishable separately under section 924(c). In this case, the appellant carried a toy replica of a firearm that simulated the appearance but not the weight of a genuine firearm. The toy gun did not fit the statutory definition of a firearm under 18 U.S.C. § 921(a)(3). However, it did fall within the meaning of a "dangerous weapon or device" under section 2113(d). Section 2113(d) states that

> Whoever, in committing, or in attempting to commit, any offense defined in subsections (a) and (b) of this section, assaults any person, or puts in jeopardy the life of any person by the use of a dangerous weapon or device, shall be fined not more than $10,000 or imprisoned not more than 25 years, or both.

(continues)

In *McLaughlin v. United States*, 476 U.S. 16, 106 S. Ct. 1677, 90 L. Ed. 2d 15 (1986), the Supreme Court found that a defendant who used an unloaded handgun was convicted properly under section 2113(d) because the unloaded handgun was a dangerous weapon under the statute. *Id.* at 17, 106 S. Ct. at 1677–78. Prior to *McLaughlin* this circuit, and other circuits, had assumed that section 2113(d) was violated only by the use of a loaded operable gun. *United States v. Terry*, 760 F.2d 939, 942 (9th Cir. 1985); see also *Parker v. United States*, 801 F.2d 1382, 1384 n. 2 (D.C. Cir. 1986), *cert. denied*, 479 U.S. 1070, 107 S. Ct. 964, 93 L. Ed. 2d 1011 (1987).

The *McLaughlin* opinion stated:

Three reasons, each independently sufficient, support the conclusion that an unloaded gun is a "dangerous weapon." First, a gun is an article that is typically and characteristically dangerous; the use for which it is manufactured and sold is a dangerous one, and the law reasonably may presume that such an article is always dangerous even though it may not be armed at a particular time or place. *In addition, the display of a gun instills fear in the average citizen; as a consequence, it creates an immediate danger that a violent response will ensue.* Finally, a gun can cause harm when used as a bludgeon.

McLaughlin, 476 U.S. at 17–18, 106 S. Ct. at 1677–78 (footnote omitted) (emphasis added).

The *McLaughlin* opinion recognizes that the dangerousness of a device used in a bank robbery is not simply a function of its potential to injure people directly. Its dangerousness results from the greater burdens that it imposes upon victims and law enforcement officers. Therefore an unloaded gun that only simulates the threat of a loaded gun is a dangerous weapon. The use of a gun that is inoperable and incapable of firing also will support a conviction under section 921(a)(3) and section 2113(d). *United States v. York*, 830 F.2d 885, 891 (8th Cir. 1987), *cert. denied*, _ U.S. _, 108 S. Ct. 1047, 98 L. Ed. 2d 1010 (1988); see also *United States v. Goodheim*, 686 F.2d 776, 778 (9th Cir. 1982).

These cases reflect a policy that the robber's creation of even the appearance of dangerousness is sufficient to subject him to enhanced punishment. Other cases have given effect to this policy by holding that the trier of fact may infer that the instrument carried by a bank robber was a firearm based only on witness testimony that it appeared to be genuine. *Parker*, 801 F.2d at 1283–84; *United States v. Harris*, 792 F.2d 866, 868 (9th Cir. 1986). *McLaughlin* validates this policy but eliminates the inefficiencies associated with the inference process.

A robber who carries a toy gun during the commission of a bank robbery creates some of the same risks as those created by one who carries an unloaded or inoperable genuine gun. First, the robber subjects victims to greater apprehension. Second, the robber requires law enforcement agencies to formulate a more deliberate, and less efficient, response in light of the need to counter the apparent direct and immediate threat to human life. Third, the robber creates a likelihood that the reasonable response of police and guards will include the use of deadly force. The increased chance of an armed response creates a greater risk to the physical security of victims, bystanders, and even the perpetrators. Therefore the greater harm that a robber creates by deciding to carry a toy gun is similar to the harm that he creates by deciding to carry an unloaded gun

The *McLaughlin* opinion examined the floor debate on the provision that became section 2113(d) and concluded that Congress was concerned with the potential of an apparently dangerous article to incite fear. *McLaughlin*, 476 U.S. at 18 n. 3, 106 S. Ct. at 1678 n. 3. The House debate on the provision that became section 2113(d) indicates that an ersatz wooden gun used in a bank robbery would satisfy the statutory meaning of a dangerous weapon or device. *See* 78 Cong. Rec. 8132 (1934). If Congress intended that an ersatz wooden gun would fall within the statute, by analogy an ersatz plastic gun should fall within the statute. Congress' intent focused on the nature of the effect that the robber creates, not the specific nature of the instruments that he utilizes.

Appellant concedes that *McLaughlin* applies to the use of an inherently dangerous weapon such as an unloaded firearm but argues that it does not apply to a harmless instrumentality of a crime, such as a toy gun, unless the defendant used the instrumentality in an assaultive manner. The trial court found that the replica was a "totally plastic and extremely light" toy gun, and that Martinez-Jimenez had held it downward by his side and not toward any of the bank employees or customers. Therefore the defendant urges that his manner of displaying this particular toy gun avoids *McLaughlin's* definition of a dangerous weapon because it would not have instilled fear in an average citizen and would not have created a danger of a violent response.

We disagree. A bank robber's use of a firearm during the commission of the crime is punishable even if he does not make assaultive use of the device. He need not brandish the firearm in a threatening manner. *United States v. Mason*, 658 F.2d 1263, 1270-71 (9th Cir. 1981). His possession of the weapon is an integral part of the crime. *United States v. Moore*, 580 F.2d 360, 362 (9th Cir.), *cert. denied*, 439 U.S. 970, 99 S. Ct. 463, 58 L. Ed. 2d 430 (1978). By analogy, a bank robber's use of a replica or simulated weapon violates section 2113(d) even if he does not make assaultive use of the device. His possession of the instrument during the commission of the crime evidences his apparent ability to commit an assault. The appellant's possession of the toy gun facilitated the crime and increased its likelihood of success. The appellant testified that he carried the toy gun because he "felt secure with it." This suggests that he may not have begun the robbery without it.

Section 2113(d) is not concerned with the way that a robber displays a simulated or replica weapon. The statute focuses on the harms created, not the manner of creating the harm. The record shows substantial evidence that the appellant's possession of the toy gun created fear and apprehension in the victims. Appellant argues that we should put aside this testimony because it was based upon the witnesses' mistaken assessment of the apparent threat. Appellant's argument fails because, during a robbery, people confronted with what they believe is a deadly weapon cannot be expected to maintain a high level of critical perception.[1]

By extension, appellant also argues that the toy gun did not jeopardize the life of any person because it did not increase the police's burden to interdict the crime during its commission or aftermath and could not have provoked the police's use of a deadly response that could have endangered others. This argument fails because the police must formulate a response to an apparently armed robber during the course of the crime, not after it. They must confront the risk that a replica or simulated gun creates before knowing that it presents no actual threat. These confrontations often lead to gunfire and casualties. *See, for example, L.A. Times*, Oct. 18, 1988, § 2, at 3, col. 1 (San Diego County ed.); *id.*, May 13, 1988, § 2, at 2, col. 5 (home ed.).

CONCLUSION

The values of justice, administrability, and deterrence require the rule that a robber's use of a replica or simulated weapon that appears to be a genuine weapon to those present at the scene of the crime, or to those charged with responsibility for responding to the crime, carries the same penalty as the use of a genuine weapon. In this case appellant avoided the harsher penalties associated with use of a firearm in violation of section 924(c) by proving that he only had simulated the use of a firearm. However, the appellant's decision to bluff did not eliminate the harms that Congress intended to address in section 2113(d).

AFFIRMED

---

[1] The recent trend in toy and replica manufacturing to duplicate precisely the outward appearance of genuine weaponry compounds the difficulty and risk of making any distinction. *See N.Y. Times*, Oct. 16, 1988, § 4, at 7, col. 1. This trend has led some state and local governments to enact bans on realistic toy guns. *See N.Y. Times*, Aug. 5, 1988, § A, at col. 1; *L.A. Times*, Apr. 29, 1988, § 1, at 2, col. 6 (home ed.). Congress has held hearings on a federal ban. 134 Cong. Rec. D 1084 (daily ed. Aug. 11, 1988).

EARL LOUIS WHITMORE and
JOHN B. WHITMORE,

Plaintiffs/Appellants,

v.

UNION PACIFIC RAILROAD COMPANY, a Delaware corporation,

Defendant/Appellee.

No. 1 CA-CV 14-0839

FILED DECEMBER 24, 2015

MEMORANDUM DECISION

GOULD, Judge

FACTUAL AND PROCEDURAL BACKGROUND

***

¶2 The Whitmores appeal from a grant of summary judgment; we therefore recite the facts in a light most favorable to them. *Wells Fargo Bank v. Arizona Laborers, Teamsters & Cement Masons Local No. 395 Pension Trust Fund*, 201 Ariz. 474, 482, ¶ 13 (2002). The Whitmores raise farm animals on land they have owned since 1973 and leased from the prior owner from 1960 to 1973. Unbeknownst to them, the prior owner entered into an "Easement Agreement" with Union Pacific's predecessor-in-interest in 1960 establishing an easement to build and operate railroad tracks on part of the land. The Easement Agreement provided that, if the railroad did not build tracks within two years, the easement would expire. According to the Whitmores, the tracks were not completed until 1975.

¶3 The Whitmores filed suit against Union Pacific in 2012, alleging that Union Pacific's use of the tracks had damaged their land in numerous ways. Union Pacific counterclaimed to quiet title, contending that it either held an express easement under the Easement Agreement or that it had established a prescriptive easement through its long-standing use of the tracks. Union Pacific then moved for summary judgment on the Whitmores' breach of contract claim and its counterclaim, which the trial court granted.

¶4 The Whitmores then filed an amended complaint restating the alleged harms they alleged were "a direct result of [Union Pacific] being on their property." Union Pacific moved

(continues)

for a more definite statement under Ariz. R. Civ. P. 12(e), and the trial court granted the motion. The Whitmores then filed a second amended complaint stating approximate dates ranging from the 1970s to 2012 for each alleged harm. Union Pacific responded with a second motion for more definite statement, as well as two partial motions to dismiss.

¶5 The trial court granted both partial motions to dismiss, at which point the Whitmores withdrew the remainder of their second amended complaint. The trial court entered final judgment granting Union Pacific an easement and assessing costs and attorneys' fees against the Whitmores. The Whitmores timely appealed. We have jurisdiction pursuant to A.R.S. § 12-2101(A)(1).

DISCUSSION

I. The Trial Court Properly Granted Summary Judgment on The Whitmores' Breach of Contract Claim and Union Pacific's Quiet Title Claim.

¶6 The Whitmores challenge the grant of summary judgment to Union Pacific on its quiet title claim.[1] We review the grant of summary judgment de novo to determine whether any genuine issue of material fact exists, viewing the evidence and all reasonable inferences in favor of the nonmoving parties. *Russell Piccoli P.L.C. v. O'Donnell*, 237 Ariz. 43, 46-47, ¶ 10 (App. 2015). Summary judgment is appropriate only "if the pleadings, deposition, answers to interrogatories, and admissions on file, together with the affidavits, if any, show that there is no genuine issue as to any material fact and that the moving party is entitled to a judgment as a matter of law." Ariz. R. Civ. P. 56(c)(1) (2012).

¶7 In order to establish a prescriptive easement, Union Pacific had to show that it actually and visibly used the land allegedly subject to the easement for a specific purpose for ten years, that the use began and continued under a claim of right, and that the use was hostile to the Whitmores' title. *Paxson v. Glovitz*, 203 Ariz. 63, 67, ¶ 22 (App. 2002).

A. Union Pacific Actually and Visibly Used the Tracks for More Than Ten Years Before the Whitmores Filed Suit.

¶8 The Whitmores first contend that the trial court improperly granted summary judgment because the parties do not agree as to when the train tracks were built. But the parties agree that the tracks were completed by 1975 at the latest. The Whitmores further concede that Union Pacific has used and maintained the tracks since they were completed. Union Pacific and/or its predecessor thus actually and visibly used the tracks for significantly more than ten years before the Whitmores filed suit in 2012.

---

[1]The Whitmores do not challenge the trial court's ruling on their breach of contract claim, the rulings granting the motions for more definite statement, or the rulings granting the partial motions to dismiss.

B. Union Pacific Used the Tracks Under a Claim of Right.

¶9 Once a claimant shows open, visible, and continuous use of the land for ten years, a presumption arises that the use was under a claim of right. *Gusheroski v. Lewis*, 64 Ariz. 192, 198 (1946); *Inch v. McPherson*, 176 Ariz. 132, 136 (App. 1992). The Whitmores try to rebut this presumption by contending Union Pacific did not "fly the flag" over the disputed land, citing *Knapp v. Wise*, 122 Ariz. 327 (App. 1979).

¶10 Knapp does not support the Whitmores' position. The Knapp court found that the act of fencing in disputed property was sufficient to "fly the flag" and put the owners on notice of an adverse claim. Id. at 329. Again, the Whitmores do not dispute that Union Pacific has operated trains on the tracks since at least 1975. They had ample notice that Union Pacific was using the tracks under a claim of right.

¶11 The Whitmores also contend Union Pacific admitted that genuine issues of material fact existed when it alleged that there was "an actual, justiciable controversy . . . regarding whether Union Pacific has an easement to use the subject property ...." The Whitmores are incorrect; this allegation relates to the trial court's jurisdiction to grant declaratory relief under A.R.S. § 12-1831. See, e.g., *Canyon del Rio Investors, L.L.C. v. City of Flagstaff*, 227 Ariz. 336, 341, ¶ 18 (App. 2011) (declaratory judgments can be sought "[w]hen a justiciable controversy exists"). The Whitmores thus did not establish any genuine issues of material fact as to whether Union Pacific's use of the tracks was under a claim of right.

C. Union Pacific's Use Was "Hostile."

¶12 Because Union Pacific's longstanding use of the tracks was undisputed, the Whitmores also bore the burden to show that the use was not hostile. *Spaulding v. Pouliot*, 218 Ariz. 196, 201, ¶ 14 (App. 2008) (citing *Gusheroski*, 64 Ariz. at 198). The Whitmores first contend Union Pacific's use was not hostile because they "did not interfere with the laying of the tracks; they did not call the police to try to stop the railroad and they never asked the railroad to leave the property." But the Whitmores also acknowledge that they never gave Union Pacific permission to use the tracks. The Whitmores' unwillingness to "call the police" or "interfere with the laying of the tracks," standing alone, does not convert Union Pacific's use into a permissive use. See *Lewis v. Pleasant Country*, Ltd., 173 Ariz. 186, 190 (App. 1992) ("In order for a possession to be permissive, the possessor must acknowledge that he holds the property in subordination to the owner's title"); *see also Inch*, 176 Ariz. at 135-36 (finding that placing gravel on disputed land and using it as a driveway was sufficient to deem use hostile).

¶13 The Whitmores also contend Union Pacific's use was not hostile because it commenced under the Easement Agreement. Even assuming the easement provided for in the Easement Agreement expired as the Whitmores contend,

Union Pacific's continued use of the tracks under the mistaken belief that it held an express easement would satisfy the hostility element. *Inch*, 176 Ariz. at 135.

¶14 For these reasons, we affirm the trial court's order granting summary judgment on the Whitmores' breach of contract claim and Union Pacific's quiet title claim.

***

CONCLUSION

¶18 We affirm the trial court's rulings as set forth above. We grant Union Pacific its costs on appeal upon compliance with ARCAP 21.

Appendix B

Appellate Court Brief

IN THE COURT OF APPEALS OF THE STATE OF NEW MEXICO

STATE OF NEW MEXICO,
    Plaintiff-Appellee,

v.   No. **, ***

D. M.,
    Defendant-Appellant.

APPEAL FROM THE ELEVENTH JUDICIAL DISTRICT COURT
HONORABLE JUDGE THOMAS HYNES, PRESIDING

APPELLANT'S BRIEF IN CHIEF

JENNIFER R. ALBRIGHT
Albright Law & Consulting
1234 Street Address
Albuquerque, New Mexico 87106
Attorney for Appellant

<u>TABLE OF CONTENTS</u>

References to the transcript of proceedings are by type of hearing, date of hearing, and the time stamp associated with the hearing by hour:minute:seconds. Counsel used FTR Gold software on her desktop computer to review the CD's constituting the transcript of recording.

TABLE OF AUTHORITIES
CASES

Nature of the Case

This is an appeal from the conviction and sentencing of Appellant D. M. who was found incompetent at the conclusion of the trial in this matter, and who was sentenced despite the finding of incompetence. This appeal also is from a trial where Appellant's counsel repeatedly tried to raise the issue of Appellant's competence, and was denied that ability by Judge Hynes because he did not "want to hear that crap." CD 8/23/07 at 11:37:10 – 11:37:18.

The entry of verdict and conviction was entered on August 29, 2007. RP 117. A motion and order to stay proceedings pending competency determination was filed September 10 and 17, 2007, respectively. RP 118-19. A hearing on the motion where incompetence was stipulated to by the State was held December 18, 2007. An order sentencing Mr. M. in the underlying matter was entered nine months later on September 4, 2008. RP 143-44. The notice of appeal was timely filed less than two weeks later. RP 145. The Docketing Statement was timely filed and this Court assigned the case to the general calendar.

The Public Defender Department assigned undersigned counsel to this case pursuant to contract in early May 2009, with a due date of June 8, 2009, for the brief in chief. Undersigned counsel requested and was granted a 32-day extension of time making this brief in chief due on or about July 10, 2009.

Summary of Facts

The facts underlying the alleged incident resulting in charges against Mr. M. are not at issue. Facts relating to trial counsel, Ruth Wheeler's diligent efforts to raise the competency of her client before, during and after trial despite repeated rejections of her requests by Judge Hynes are relevant to the issues herein. In addition facts surrounding post-trial, pre-sentencing, and sentencing proceedings and the finding of Mr. M.'s incompetence are relevant. The facts herein will focus only on the proceedings in relation to the narrow issues presented here on appeal.

In this case there was a great deal of time spent in the court's chambers on a pre-trial motion. Chambers 8/23/07 8:06:27 – 8:22:56; 9:12:04 – 9:49:46. On the way between chambers and the courtroom in the presence of the Assistant District Attorney, Ms. Wheeler approached Judge Hynes and requested to return to chambers because she believed there was a problem. Judge Hynes asked what it was and she informed him she thought her client was worse and she had a concern about his competency. The Judge became upset and told Ms. Wheeler she could not play games and she should have raised it earlier. She again requested that they return to chambers to be on the record and Judge Hynes refused her request. This exchange was not captured word for word on the recordings in this matter, but it was preserved for this Court's consideration when Judge Hynes, after the return of verdict, stated that the first time competency was raised in the case by defense counsel was when she came to him earlier in the morning and told him that Mr. M. was "doing all this stuff," referring to the discussion about Mr. M. responding to things not present in court during the trial. Chambers 8/23/2007 at 4:13:50 – 4:14:06. And again this conversation and effort to raise competency before trial in the hallway was discussed during the hearing to declare Mr. M. incompetent and sentence him on the conviction in the underlying case here. Competency 12/18/2007 at 10:18:55-10:19:27.

During trial Mr. M. displayed the same behavior in front of the entire courtroom, including the judge and jury, that had caused Ms. Wheeler concern prior to trial. He was talking under his breath to someone who was clearly not present in the courtroom. He was focused on someone no one in the court could see. It was so distracting that Judge Hynes called a recess and admonished Mr. M. Judge Hynes stated:

> Mr. M. I'm not going to let you disrupt this trial. You have a right to be here, okay. You have a right to be here and you have a right to be present at your trial. If you are going to disrupt the trial I am going to take you out and you are not going to be here. It is in your best interest to not disrupt the trial because the jury is watching everything you are doing and you are making an ass out of yourself, okay. Simple as that and you can choose but next time you do it you are going.

Trial, 8/23/2007 11:36:26 – 11:37:10.

Defense counsel immediately stated "Judge, I need to raise competency." Id. at 11:37:12. Judge Hynes cut defense counsel off and stated "oh I don't want to hear that crap." Id. at 11:37:14. He went on to exclaim to defense counsel:

> He's competent enough to steal two cars in one day but he's not competent to sit here and act like a human being at trial, he's putting on a big show and I'm not going to put up with it. Just not going to, one more time Mr. M. and you are out.

Id. at 11:37:14–11:37:33. Trial then resumed.

A short time later, the state rested and the jury was sent out for their lunch break. Before any other matters could be addressed by the parties, Judge Hynes stated first he was going to address the defendant, Mr. M. Judge Hynes then again admonished Mr. M. regarding his continuing behavior that indicated he was not paying attention and was somehow disengaged in the proceedings by stating:

> Mr. M. I seen a lot of cases and I got to say to you. Listen to what I'm saying to you. This isn't the greatest case in the world I've seen the state present okay, there's a chance the jury could find you not guilty. But you don't help yourself by doing what you are doing. You got to act like you're paying attention to what's going on, sit up in the chair and that's going to help a lot because you are making the job for your attorney really, really hard. Mr. M. do your very best to just try to help her by appearing focused on what is going on and this is of some significance to you because the easiest thing for the jury to say is "well if he doesn't care we don't care, so we'll just find whatever."

Id. at 12:08:45–12:09:40. The trial again resumed and concluded shortly thereafter. The jury was instructed and sent out to deliberate. The jury returned with a verdict of guilty of the single crime charged. Id. at 4:05:30.

As the trial court began to address whether Mr. M. would remain incarcerated pending sentencing defense counsel again attempted to raise the issue of Mr. M.'s competency. Id. at 4:09:02 – 4:09:42. The exchange that followed involved Judge Hynes alternately stating that defense counsel did not raise competency in this matter before trial to acknowledging that she has raised competency at the preliminary hearing, to stating she had not raised it, to stating that she had raised it. Id. at 4:09:42 – 4:18:12. In addition the trial court alternatively agreed after defense counsel read either Section 31-9-1 or Rule 5-602 that competency could be raised at any time during criminal proceedings to stating that he doubted defense counsel could not raise competency before trial and then raise it after trial just because the defense lost. Id. This allegation was repeated numerous times and the court continued to refuse to acknowledge that defense counsel tried to raise competency three times the day of trial. Id. The hearing ended with Judge Hynes indicating he would sign an order to have Mr. M. evaluated, but that he was going to stay the proceedings in another case pending before him involving Mr. M. because he did not want defense counsel to again take a chance at trial and raise competency only after she lost. Id.

The trial court then entered a verdict of conviction. RP 117. Defense counsel then filed a written motion to stay the proceedings, namely sentencing, in this matter, as well as in the other matter pending in front of Judge Hynes, pending a competency determination. RP 118-119. Judge Hynes did stay the proceedings in the case underlying this appeal as requested by the defense motion. RP 122. The evaluations were received and sealed into the record proper. RP 120-121, 126-134. A hearing to determine competency in both the case underlying this appeal and the case still pending before Judge Hynes was then held on December 18, 2007. Competency 12/18/2007.

At that hearing the State immediately stipulated that Mr. M. was not competent. Id. at 10:18:04; 10:33:37. The issue during this hearing was what Judge Hynes could do with Mr. M. It was the defense's position that under both Rule 5-602 and section 31-9-1.2(A) of the New Mexico Mental Illness and Competency Code (hereinafter "NMMIC") the court should dismiss the case. The State and Judge Hynes still held to their position from the end of the trial that neither the Rule nor the statutes could be applied retroactively since the jury had returned a verdict. The defense reiterated that she tried three times; before, during, and after the trial to raise competency but the court would not let her. She also reiterated that both Rule 5-602 and Section 31-9-1 allowed her to raise competency anytime during criminal proceedings. Everyone agreed Mr. M. would not fit the requirements for a dangerousness finding, precluding the court from committing Mr. M. to Las Vegas Medical Center or any other secure facility under section 31-9-105 of the NMMIC.

Much time was spent in the December 18 hearing with the defense arguing that section 31-9-1 and 31-9-1.2 involved substantive law that the court had to follow. Competency 12/18/07, 10:27:04-10:33:30. Defense counsel specifically stated that the NMMIC was not procedural because it involved a defendants substantive due process rights. Id. at 10:33:16–10:33:37. Judge Hynes repeatedly and quite forcefully stated that the NMMIC was procedural and violated separation of powers. Id. at 10:28:06. He stated that the Supreme Court Rule, referring to Rule 5-602, controlled how he proceeded and the NMMIC did not because the Legislature could not control what he did in his courtroom. Id. at 10:32:00–10:33:37.

Judge Hynes then suggested that he would stay the proceedings until Mr. M. became competent. Id. at 10:36:00. Defense counsel pointed out that she did not believe the law allowed such action because that meant Mr. M. could be held in jail indefinitely. Id. at 10:36:14. Judge Hynes agreed that indeed he could order Mr. M. to be held indefinitely since he might not attain competency. Id. at 10:36:17. Ultimately Judge Hynes sentenced Mr. M. for the conviction in this matter despite the finding that he was currently incompetent and was incompetent at the time of the trial. Id. at 10:36:42.

Argument

Questions of constitutional law and constitutional rights such as due process protections are reviewed de novo. *N.M. Board of Veterinary Medicine v. Riegger*, 2007-NMSC-044, ¶ 27, 142 N.M. 248, 164 P.2d 947 (citing *State v. DeGraff*, 2006-NMSC-011, ¶ 6, 139 N.M. 211, 131 P.3d 61). Questions of statutory interpretation are reviewed de novo. *State v. Smith*, 2009-NMCA-028, ¶ 8, 145 N.M. 757, 204 P.3d 1267. Although the denial of a motion for competency evaluation is reviewed for an abuse of discretion, Mr. M. contends that the issues here involve a review of a denial of his request to raise competency not a review of a request for an evaluation. At issue is whether the trial court's refusal to allow Mr. M.'s counsel to raise competency violated his constitutional rights. In this matter a request for an evaluation never occurred because the trial court refused to allow defense counsel to even get to that point. Therefore, Mr. M. argues that none of the issues herein are subject to the abuse of discretion standard. All three of the issues here involve questions of constitutional law, and the meaning of statutory and procedural laws requiring de novo review.

Issue 1: The law of New Mexico allows competency of an accused to be raised at any time during criminal proceedings and it was fundamental constitutional error for Judge Hynes to reject trial counsel's repeated efforts to raise the issue of her client's competency.

"Whenever it appears that there is a question as to a defendant's competency to proceed in a criminal case, any further proceeding in the cause *shall* be suspended until the issue is determined." NMSA 1978, § 31-9-1 (1993). The rules of criminal procedure for the district courts clearly state that an issue of a defendant's competency may be raised at *any* stage of the proceedings. Rule 5-602(B)(1) NMRA. The most basic tenet of competency law in New Mexico is that it is a violation of due process to prosecute a defendant who is incompetent to stand trial. *State v. Rotherham*, 1996-NMSC-048, 122 N.M. 246, 252, 923 P.2d 1131, 1137 (citations omitted). Suspension of the criminal process where the defendant is incompetent is fundamental to assuring the fairness, accuracy, and dignity of the trial. *Id.*

Defense counsel tried to raise competency three times on August 23, 2007—the date of trial. The trial court absolutely refused to entertain the requests all three times. The third time defense counsel moved to raise competency on August 23, 2007 was after the return of the jury's verdict. In order for this Court to fully consider the remaining issues in this matter it needs to address Judge Hynes' repeated refusal to allow competency to be raised and his repeated rulings that competency could not be raised after a jury had returned a verdict. Mr. M. argues here that Judge Hynes erred in refusing to allow defense counsel to raise the issue the first two times because the law requires a stay of proceedings whenever competency is raised. Sec. 31-9-1. Mr. M. also argues that Judge Hynes incorrectly held that competency could not be raised after the return of a verdict by the jury and it was a violation of his Fifth and Fourteenth Amendment due process rights to be sentenced after he was found incompetent. *The first two efforts to raise competency.*

Immediately prior to trial on the way between a pre-trial hearing in chambers on a defense motion regarding undisclosed evidence, defense counsel explained to Judge Hynes that she had concerns about her client because he was not responsive to her and he seemed to be laughing and talking with someone not present. DS at 2-3; Trail 8/23/2007, 4:13:50 – 4:14:06; Competency 12/18/2007, 10:18:55-10:19:27. This effort to raise the issue of Mr. M.'s competency before the start of trial was referred to repeatedly at the end of trial and during the December competency hearing. Id. The record is clear that Judge Hynes refused to allow defense counsel to raise the issue immediately prior to trial.

The very conduct of Mr. M. that led defense counsel to try to raise competency before trial, Mr. M.'s laughing and talking with someone not present, led Judge Hynes to recess the trial early in the State's case in order to admonish Mr. M. to stop "making an ass out of [himself]." Trial 8/23/07, 11:36:26 – 11:37:10. Immediately defense counsel responded to Judge Hynes' outburst by moving to raise competency only to be told by Judge Hynes "oh I don't want to hear that crap." Id. at 11:37:14. He went on to exclaim to defense counsel:

> He's competent enough to steal two cars in one day but he's not competent to sit here and act like a human being at trial, he's putting on a big show and I'm not going to put up with it, just not going to! One more time Mr. M., and you are out.

Id. at 11:37:14–11:37:33.

The above demonstrates two efforts by defense counsel to raise the issue of Mr. M.'s competency during criminal proceedings pursuant to Rule 5-602(B). This Court has adopted the most basic tenet of competency law, that the failure to observe procedures adequate to protect a defendant's right not to be tried or convicted while incompetent to stand trial violates the defendant's due process right to a fair trial. *State v. Flores*, 2005-NMCA-135, ¶

15, 138 N.M. 636, 124 P.3d 1175. Our legislature unambiguously built the due process alert into New Mexico law by stating "[w]henever it appears that there is a question as to the defendant's competency to proceed in a criminal case, any further proceeding in the cause *shall* be suspended until the issue is determined." *Id.* at ¶ 17 (citing NMSA 1978, § 31-9-1 (1993)). The New Mexico Supreme Court also unambiguously built the due process alert into the rules of criminal procedure when it stated "[t]he issue of a defendant's competency may be raised . . . at any stage of the proceedings." Rule 5-602(B)(1) NMRA; *see also* Committee Commentary to Rule 5-602 stating that "[p]aragraph B meets the constitutional requirements of due process in dealing with a defendant who is allegedly not competent to stand trial. Whenever a legitimate concern about the present ability of a defendant to consult and understand is brought to the court's attention, the court is required to consider whatever competency-related evidence is before the court and determine if a reasonable doubt as to the defendant's competency exists." *Flores*, 2005-NMCA-135, ¶ 17 (citing Rule 5-602(B)(2)).

It is clear that when defense counsel brought to Judge Hynes' attention her concern about Mr. M.'s present ability to consult and understand the proceedings Judge Hynes did not act in accordance with the constitutional principles embodied in the NMMIC and rules of criminal procedure to make a determination as to Mr. M.'s competency.

When defense counsel raised the issue prior to trial Judge Hynes refused to take time to address the matter because he was not going to delay trial for any reason. This violated Mr. M.'s fundamental constitutional rights. When defense counsel raised competency before trial, Rule 5-602(B)(2)(a) mandated Judge Hynes to stay further proceedings in the case and order that Mr. M. be evaluated "as provided by law," referring to section 31-9-1.1 requiring a defendant's competency to be evaluated by a qualified professional. NMSA 1978, § 31-9-1.1 (1993). Judge Hynes did not follow the law and in doing so violated Mr. M.'s Fifth and Fourteenth Amendment due process rights. *Rotherham*, 1996-NMSC-048, 122 N.M. at 252, 923 P.2d at 1137.

When defense counsel raised competency the second time, Judge Hynes had knowledge of defense counsel's pre-trial concerns, had the court file in front of him with documentation that competency had been raised at the preliminary hearing, and had his own observations of Mr. M. talking and laughing with someone who was not present in the courtroom. Mr. M. argues that this information was sufficient to raise a reasonable doubt as to his competency to stand trial requiring Judge Hynes to stay any further proceeding of the trial and have Mr. M. evaluated as provided by law. Rule 5-602(B)(2)(a); Sec. 31-9-1.1. Judge Hynes again did not follow the law and as such, violated Mr. M.'s basic constitutional right not to be tried if incompetent when he exclaimed "oh I don't want to hear that crap" in response to trial counsel moving to raise the competency of her client this second time. Trial 8/23/07, 11:37:14.

Compounding the due process violation and Judge Hynes' disregard for the law is his own acknowledgement immediately after the State rested that Mr. M. was behaving in a manner that indicated Mr. M. lacked the ability to consult and understand throughout the trial. Upon the State resting, Judge Hynes told Mr. M.:

> You got to act like you're paying attention to what's going on, sit up in the chair and that's going to help a lot . . . . Mr. M. do your very best to just try to help her by appearing focused on what is going on and this is of some significance to you because the easiest thing for the jury to say is "well if he doesn't care we don't care, so we'll just find whatever."

Id. at 12:08:45–12:09:40. Instead of acknowledging Mr. M.'s behavior as an indication of incompetence, as his trial counsel continually tried to assert, Judge Hynes continued on with the trial further violating the basic tenets of competency law.

Judge Hynes' actions constituted blatant disregard for the law of New Mexico and a blatant violation of Mr. M.'s due process right to a fair trial. *Flores*, 2005-NMCA-135, ¶ 15 (citing *Drope v. Missouri*, 420 U.S. 162, 171-172 (1975)). These violations of Mr. M.'s due process rights alone require this court to overturn his conviction and dismiss the underlying matter. However, the violations continued on through the end of trial and a return of a verdict by the jury.

Defense counsel's final attempt on the date of trial to raise the issue or Mr. M.'s competency.

Despite the ongoing efforts of trial counsel to raise competency and Judge Hynes' own observations of Mr. M.'s inability to consult and understand, the matter was submitted to the jury for deliberation. After a lengthy deliberation, the jury returned a verdict of guilty on the sole charge against Mr. M. Upon releasing the jury, Judge Hynes began to determine when sentencing should occur. Before Judge Hynes got very far, defense counsel again stated to Judge Hynes that, as she had stated earlier in the proceedings, she was "having doubts as to [her] client's competency to proceed through trial today . . . he's been responding to . . ." when Judge Hynes again cut her off indicating his unwillingness to address the issue of Mr. M.'s competency. Trial 8/23/07, 4:09:00–4:09:49. Defense counsel persisted and stated "Judge what I'm asking is for you to set aside the verdict in this case because there is a reasonable doubt as to my client's competency." Id. Judge Hynes responded that he had not seen any evidence that Mr. M. was incompetent. Id. at 4:09:49. Defense counsel reiterated that "while he has been in your court he has been responding to things that are not there," but was again cut off before she could finish articulating what she believed was evidence raising a reasonable doubt as to Mr. M.'s competency. Judge Hynes cut defense counsel off to say "well what can I say, I can do that as well. I can respond to other things and act crazy too." Id. at 4:09:49 – 4:10:14.

The exchange that followed is very hard to present here because Judge Hynes vacillated so widely in his positions, going from one position to the opposite position over and over. Id. at 4:09:00 – 4:18:00. However, in summary, defense counsel steadfastly argued that there was evidence of Mr. M.'s incompetence and that she had now raised the matter four times, including the motion to stay proceedings to determine competency filed at the preliminary hearing. Judge Hynes argued with her that she had not raised competency at all until that very moment, but vacillated between that particular position and acknowledging that counsel had raised the issue of competency repeatedly.

The exchange also involved argument regarding whether defense counsel could raise competency after a jury had returned a verdict. Defense counsel asserted that Rule 5-602(B) clearly allowed her to raise the issue any time during criminal proceedings, including after a verdict and up to and through sentencing. Id. She also reminded the court repeatedly in relation to this portion of the argument that she had tried to raise the issue prior to trial and during trial. However, Judge Hynes was adamant that an issue of competency could not be raised after a verdict was returned and went so far as to accuse defense counsel of raising competency the first time after the verdict (again ignoring all her previous attempts), in bad faith. In the end Judge Hynes resigned himself to the position that the Rule 5-602 allows an issue of competency to be raised at any time, but he required that counsel do so in writing and recessed the matter for the day. Id.

The court entered a verdict of conviction on August 29, 2007 continuing its violation of Mr. M.'s due process right to not be required to stand trial when he was incompetent. RP 117. On September 10, 2007, Defense counsel continued her diligent fight to protect Mr. M.'s rights by filing a motion to stay proceedings pending competency determination and for a hearing to determine competency. RP 118. Judge Hynes signed the order, finally acting in accordance with New Mexico's clear and unambiguous laws requiring that once the issue of a defendant's competency is raised he be professionally evaluated by a qualified professional who submits a report to the court. *Flores*, 2005-NMCA-135, ¶ 17 (citing *State v. Rotherham*, 122 N.M. 246, 253, 923 P.2d 1131, 1138 (1996), NMSA 1978, § 31-9-1.1 (1993), and Rule 5-602(C) NMRA). However, this compliance with the law did not come until well after the court had repeatedly violated Mr. M.'s due process rights.

A hearing was held December 18, 2007 to determine competency, as required by section 31-9-1.1 of the NMMIC. It is undisputed that Mr. M. was found to be incompetent, that the parties stipulated to that finding and Judge Hynes finally held that Mr. M. was incompetent. However, the issues regarding Judge Hynes' compliance with constitutional due process protections as established in New Mexico by Rule 5-602 and the NMMIC continued. Mr. M.'s next issue will address how Judge Hynes continued to violate his constitutional rights by not dismissing the matter once his incompetence was established.

Issue 2: Upon the finding of Mr. M.'s incompetence, Judge Hynes was required to dismiss the matter without prejudice.

The NMMIC provides the constitutional protections required to avoid a violation of an incompetent person's right to due process of law. *State v. Rotherham*, 1996-NMSC-048, 122 N.M. 246, 923 P.2d 1131. The enactment of the NMMIC came as a result of the United States Supreme Court's ruling in *Jackson v. Indiana*, 406 U.S. 715 (1972) in which the U.S. Supreme Court addressed a problem nationally with the "indefinite commitment of a person, for reasons based solely on his incompetence to stand trial." *Rotherham*, 122 N.M. at 252-53, 923 P.2d at 1137-38 (citing *Jackson*, 406 U.S. at 731). The NMMIC's foundation is predecessor provisions of the New Mexico Statutes Annotated and common law governing the basic constitutional tenets of competency law. *State v. Chavez*, 2008-NMSC-001, ¶ 16, 143 N.M. 205, 174 P.3d 988. Due to the U.S. Supreme Court's ruling in *Jackson*, the creation of the NMMIC only changed New Mexico's statutes governing the confinement and treatment of persons incompetent to stand trial. *Id.*, ¶ 15. One of those changes was for the Legislature to state that a defendant must be released if he is not competent, not dangerous, and has not been civilly or criminally committed. NMSA 1978, § 31-9-1.5(D)(4)(c) (1999); *Rotherham*, 1996-NMSC-048, 122 N.M. at 254, 923 P.2d at 1139. Similarly, section 31-9-1.2(A) of the NMMIC allows the trial court to dismiss a criminal case without prejudice when it determines that a defendant is not competent and is not dangerous. NMSA 1978, § 31-9-1.2(A) (1999).

During the December 18, 2007 hearing to determine Mr. M.'s competency the only thing at issue was whether the determination that Mr. M. was incompetent to stand trial could apply retroactively and if so, what did that require Judge Hynes to do. The defense correctly argued that a finding of incompetence to stand trial that was made after trial could invalidate a conviction. There have been past cases involving the same issue. For example, in *State v. Baca*, 95 N.M. 205, 619 P.2d 1249 (Ct. App. 1980), a question of whether the defendant was incompetent when he entered a guilty plea was raised and a hearing was held on the issue three years after the guilty plea. In *Baca*, the court ultimately determined that the defendant had been competent at the time he pled guilty, unlike here in Mr. M.'s case where the evaluation demonstrated that he was incompetent to stand trial at the time of the August 2007 trial. In *Baca*, had the court found that the defendant was incompetent at the time of trial, it would have applied that finding to allow a withdrawal of the defendant's guilty plea. Therefore, precedent dictates that when it was determined that Mr. M. was incompetent at the time of his August trial, Judge Hynes should have dismissed the case.

Judge Hynes did not dismiss the matter. He suggested indefinitely confining Mr. M. until he was competent in violation of *Jackson* and *Rotherham*, but was persuaded not to do so. Instead Judge Hynes sentenced Mr. M. The error in sentencing Mr. M. will be addressed in the next and final issue herein.

Issue 3: It is well established law that it is a violation of due process to sentence an incompetent person and the sentencing of Mr. M. after a finding of incompetence violated his Fifth and Fourteenth Amendment due process rights.

Questions of constitutional law and constitutional rights such as due process protections are reviewed de novo. *N.M. Board of Veterinary Medicine v. Riegger*, 2007-NMSC-044, ¶ 27, 142 N.M. 248, 164 P.2d 947 (citing *State v. DeGraff*, 2006-NMSC-011, ¶ 6, 139 N.M. 211, 131 P.3d 61).

The NMMIC is the statutory framework which presently governs competency and court proceedings in New Mexico. In *State v. Chavez*, 2008-NMSC-001, 143 N.M. 205, 174 P.3d 988, the New Mexico Supreme Court looked at the relationship between the NMMIC and the statutory provisions that were in place prior to the enactment of NMMIC. None of the previous versions of NMSA 1978, § 31-9-1 (1993) are materially different from the current version, which was in force at the time of the trial underlying this appeal. *Chavez*, ¶ 10 (FN1). In fact, the Supreme Court in *Chavez*, acknowledged that Section 31-9-1of NMMIC virtually mirrors the previous provision regarding the long standing legal tenet that anytime a defendant's competency is raised criminal proceedings are suspended until the issue is determined. *Id.* ¶ 17.

The issue here as to whether it was a violation of due process to sentence a defendant who has been found incompetent after trial but before sentencing has not been squarely addressed since the enactment of the NMMIC. However, the case law decided under the predecessor provisions remains good law because the NMMIC is consistent with its predecessor statutes in that both clearly articulated that competency could be raised at any time during criminal proceedings. *Id.*, ¶ 17. Moreover, nothing in the NMMIC impliedly or expressly states that the NMMIC was to alter when competency could be raised. This is supported by the Supreme Court's determination in *Chavez*, that the Legislature revised New Mexico's statutes governing the "confinement and treatment of persons found to be incompetent to stand trial" and did not otherwise affect or abrogate pertinent case law regarding competency proceedings." *Id.*, ¶ 15.

The Legislature's continuing silence on the issue herein is evidence that it was aware of and approved of the existing case law which long ago established that it is a violation of an accused's Fifth and Fourteenth Amendment due process rights to be sentenced if incompetent. *State v. Sena*, 92 N.M. 676, 678-79, 594 P.2d 336, 338-39 (Ct. App. 1979). A basic tenet of statutory interpretation requires this Court to presume that the Legislature was aware of existing case law and acted with knowledge of it. *Chavez*, ¶ 21 (*citing Citation Bingo, Ltd. v. Otten*, 1996-NMSC-003, § 21, 121 N.M. 205, 910 P.2d 281 (for tenet that Court presumes the legislature is aware of existing statutory law and did not intend to enact a law inconsistent with existing law)). To date the Legislature has not amended any part of the NMMIC, including section 31-9-1 to reflect a change to the well-established principles that it is a violation of a defendant's due process rights to be sentenced when incompetent. Had the Legislature intended to modify the rule that an accused may not be sentenced if they are incompetent; it would have done so expressly. Therefore, the rule of law remains that it is a violation of due process to sentence an incompetent person. *Sena*, 92 N.M. at 678-79, 594 P.2d at 338-39.

This rule of law has been well-established in New Mexico for a lengthy period of time. The Supreme Court of this state held in *Sena* that competency to be sentenced involves a question of:

> Whether the prisoner has not at the present time, from the defects of his faculties, sufficient intelligence to understand the nature of the proceedings against him, what he was tried for, the purpose of his punishment, the impending fate which awaits him, a sufficient understanding to know any fact which might exist which would make his punishment unjust or unlawful, and the intelligence requisite to convey such information to his attorneys or the court.

Sena, at 337, 677 (citing *In re Smith*, 25 N.M. 48, 176 P. 819 (1918)).

The rule of law is also well-established in federal jurisprudence. All levels of federal courts have also repeatedly held that the due process clause of the Fifth Amendment, which is applicable to the states through the Fourteenth Amendment, prohibits the government from trying or sentencing a defendant who is legally incompetent. See e.g., *Pate v. Robinson*, 383 U.S. 375, 378 (1966); *United States v. Rahim*, 431 F.3d 753, 759 (11th Cir. 2005); *Allen v. United States*, 563 F. Supp. 2d 1335, 1338 (M.D. Fla. 2008). It has also been recognized that the need for competency survives trial and extends through the sentencing phase of a criminal proceeding. *United States v. Pellerito*, 878 F.2d 1535, 1544 (1st Cir. 1989) (citing *Hall v. United States*, 410 F.2d 653, 658, n. 2 (4th Cir. 1969)); *United States v. Garrett*, 903 F.2d 1105, 1115-1116 (7th Cir. 1990). Indeed the Court in *Pellerito* held similarly to the New Mexico Supreme Court in *Sena* that "the sentencing process necessitates that the defendant possess both a present ability to consult with a lawyer with a reasonable degree of rational understanding and a rational as well as factual understanding of the proceedings." *Pellerito*, 878 F.2d at 1544 (internal quotation omitted) (citing *Dusky v. United States*, 362 U.S. 402 (1960) (defining competence to stand trial)). In Mr. M.'s case it was established that on December 18, 2007 when Judge Hynes sentenced him he was incompetent to stand trial. Incompetency to stand trial and incompetency to be sentenced both involve the same standard, that a defendant be able to understand and consult with his counsel. Therefore, it was a violation of due process to sentence Mr. M. because at the time of sentencing he was incompetent.

In all of the cases cited herein for the tenet that it is a violation of due process to sentence an incompetent person some state or federal legislative framework has been established to protect legally incompetent defendants from due process violations. Similarly, New Mexico has long had some statutory framework that has protected criminal defendants in its criminal courts from due process violations and currently that statutory framework is embodied in the NMMIC. Mr. M. contends that the district court denied him his due process by violating the well-established legal protections against sentencing an incompetent defendant and requests that this Court grant him the relief of ordering that the case against him be dismissed for that violation.

Conclusion

WHEREFORE, based upon the arguments presented here, Mr. M. respectfully requests that this court find that the trial court violated his due process rights, overturn his conviction and sentence and order that the matter be dismissed or any other relief that this Court deems in the interest of justice.

Respectfully submitted,
Jennifer Albright

_____

Albright Law & Consulting
Attorney for Appellee
1234 Street Address
Albuquerque, New Mexico 87106

Certificate of Service

I hereby certify that I have caused to be mailed by U.S. Mail to the Attorney General's office a true and accurate copy of the foregoing Brief, this 10th day of July, 2009.

_____

Jennifer Albright

Interoffice Memorandum Example 1

MEMORANDUM

To: Jennifer Albright

From: Jennifer Van Wiel

Re: Gonzales Case – Posse Comitatus Act

Date: July 5, 2009

QUESTION PRESENTED

Was the Posse Comitatus Act violated when the investigation, arrest and prosecution of Gonzales, a civilian at an off-base location, was initiated and conducted entirely by the Office of Special Investigations of the United States Air Force (AFOSI), when the investigators, confidential source and buy money were provided by the Air Force, when the drugs obtained in the undercover buy were held in custody and transported by the Air Force, when the chemical drug testing was conducted by the U.S. Army, and when the only civilian authority participation was in drafting paperwork to admit the case into the New Mexico court system?

SHORT ANSWER

Yes, the AFOSI was in blatant violation of the Posse Comitatus Act when it independently launched an investigation of a civilian (Gonzales) at an off-base location, when the investigators, confidential source and buy money were all provided solely by the Air Force, when the drugs obtained in the undercover buy were held in custody and transported by the Air Force, when the chemical drug testing was conducted by the U.S. Army, and when the only local civilian authority participation was in drafting paperwork to admit the case into the New Mexico court system.

STATEMENT OF FACTS

For facts, see Docketing Statement.

DISCUSSION

The Gonzales case demonstrates a gross violation of the Posse Comitatus Act (PCA) by the Air Force. Under the PCA, it is a criminal offense to "willfully" use "any part of the Army or Air Force as a posse comitatus or otherwise to execute the laws" "except in cases and under circumstances expressly authorized by the Constitution or Act of Congress." Whoever violates this act "shall be fined under this title or imprisoned not more than two years, or both." 18 USC § 1385. The PCA, passed shortly after the end of the Reconstruction Era, "was designed to limit 'the direct active use of federal troops by civil law enforcement officers' to enforce the laws of this nation." *United States v. Hartley*, 796 F2d 112, 114 (5th Cir. 1986) (*quoting United States v. Red Feather*, 392 F. Supp. 916, 922 (D.S.D.1975)). "Underlying the PCA is the continuing recognition of the threat to civil liberties caused by the use of military personnel to execute civilian laws." *State v. Cooper*, 1998-NMCA-180, ¶ 13, 126 NM 500, 972 P.2d 1. Later, as a response to the "war on drugs," in 1981 Congress created exceptions to the PCA and passed the Military Cooperation with Law Enforcement Officials Act, 10 USCA §§ 371-382. Sean J. Kealy, *Reexamining the Posse Comitatus Act: Toward a Right To Civil Law Enforcement*, 21 Yale L. & Pol'y Rev. 383, 384 (2003). Through this act, the military is authorized to share information with civilian law enforcement, §371, make available equipment to aid civilian law enforcement, §372, train civilian law enforcement in the operation and maintenance of equipment, §373, and provide personnel to assist in the maintenance and operation of equipment for the benefit of civilian law enforcement under specific prescribed circumstances, §374(a) and (b). Section 375 incorporates the Navy and Marines and mandates:

> The Secretary of Defense shall prescribe such regulations as may be necessary to ensure that any activity (including the provision of any equipment or facility or the assignment or detail of any personnel) under this chapter does not include or permit direct participation by a member of the Army, Navy, Air Force, or Marine Corps in a search, seizure, arrest, or other similar activity unless participation in such activity by such member is otherwise authorized by law.

While courts have constructed a variety of tests to determine if the PCA has been violated,

most courts recognize that where military involvement is limited *and does not invade the traditional functions of civilian law enforcement officers, such as in making arrests, conducting searches or seizing evidence,* the coordination of military efforts with those of civilian law enforcement does not violate the PCA. (emphasis added)

Cooper, 1998-NMCA-180, ¶ 14. This memorandum addresses the violations of the PCA in our case.

In the present case, the Air Force was in violation of the PCA during every step of the investigation and undercover drug purchases leading to Gonzales' arrest and prosecution. In determining if the PCA has been violated in cases of suspected drug trafficking activity off-base, the courts look at factors such as the purpose of the investigation, the controlling party in the investigation, the nature of the individuals targeted in the investigation, and to what degree each party of the investigation participated. In cases where the military participates in investigations of suspected drug trafficking in off-base locations, the PCA is not violated when a primary military purpose is established, *Cooper*, 1998-NMCA-180, ¶ 19; *Applewhite v. U.S. Air Force*, 392 F. Supp. 916, 1001 (10th Cir. 1993); and *State of Hawaii v. Pattioay*, 896 P.2d 911, 922 (Haw. 1995), the investigation targets the illegal behavior of active military personnel instead of civilians, *Cooper*, 1998-NMCA-180, ¶19; *Applewhite*, 995 F.2d at 1001, and *Hawaii* 896 P.2d at 921, the civilian law enforcement authorities have strict control over undercover drug purchases and any undercover military agents used for drug purchases, *Cooper*, 1998-NMCA-180, ¶17, and when civilian law enforcement authorities are solely responsible for the arrest of civilians, *Cooper*, 1998-NMCA-180, ¶16; *Applewhite*, 995 F.2d at 1000, and the seizure, transportation, and testing of the drugs. *Cooper*, 1998-NMCA-180, ¶ 17. In the present case, the Air Force investigation only targeted a civilian (Gonzales), local law enforcement authorities were not part of the investigation, the buy money was provided by the military, the undercover military agent was at all times under the supervision and control of the military, and the transportation of the drugs and testing of the drugs was done entirely by the military. The record fails to demonstrate a verifiable primary military purpose to the investigation, and the only person prosecuted as a result of the investigation was a civilian. The military only involved local civilian law enforcement at the completion of the investigation for assistance in writing the Criminal Complaint and the Arrest Warrant and in conducting the arrest. With the sole exception being the actual arrest, the Air Force in the case against Gonzales blatantly violated the PCA in every step of the investigation.

The PCA is not violated when the military participates in a joint investigation of suspected drug trafficking at an off-base location where the investigation stems from evidence of illegal drug activity by active duty military personnel, when the military involvement in the investigation is limited to providing an undercover agent, when the civilian law enforcement authorities oversee the activities of the military undercover agent, provide the buy money, and when the drugs obtained in the undercover buy are immediately relinquished to the civilian law enforcement authorities. *Cooper*, 1998-NMCA-180, ¶ 15. In this case, the United States Air Force Office of Special Investigations (OSI) obtained information that Air Force personnel were involved in the purchasing and trafficking of crack cocaine at an off-base location. *Cooper*, 1998-NMCA-180, ¶ 2. The OSI approached the local police about Air Force personnel trafficking cocaine in the area, and a joint investigation was launched between the OSI and the local police. The OSI provided a trained undercover agent to aid in the investigation by making drug purchases and observing the activities of suspects. The subject of the investigation was a known crack house located off of the Air Force base. *Cooper*, 1998-NMCA-180, ¶ 4. During the investigation, the local police controlled the actions of the undercover military agent, including searching his vehicle, placing a transmitter on him, providing him with buy money, and instructing him on how to make the drug purchase. The local police kept the agent under surveillance while driving to and from the drug purchase. *Cooper*, 1998-NMCA-180, ¶ 7. After making the purchase, the drugs were handed over to the local police, who took the drugs to be tested by a lab operated by civilian law enforcement authorities. The court held that these facts did not create a "sufficiently pervasive" involvement by the military to constitute a violation of the PCA. The court reasoned that since the OSI had information about active Air Force personnel engaged in the purchase and trafficking of illegal drugs, there was a sufficient military purpose for the OSI to participate in the investigation. *Cooper*, 1998-NMCA-180, ¶ 19. The court also determined that since the military agent was under the supervision and surveillance of the local police, was not involved in arrest activities, and relinquished the purchased drugs to the local police, the military agent's involvement was no more direct than that of a civilian undercover informant. In sum, the court concluded that the military involvement did not rise to the level of enforcing civilian laws, and therefore did not meet the requirements for a violation of the PCA. *Cooper*, 1998-NMCA-180, ¶ 17.

Unlike the military involvement in *Cooper*, which was limited to providing an undercover agent to make drug purchases, the military acted alone in the Gonzales case up until the point of the warrant and arrest. The mild involvement by the military in *Cooper* is in direct opposition to our case, in which there was no civilian law enforcement involvement or supervision of the drug purchases. In *Cooper*, the fact that the local police controlled the drug purchases, maintained custody and testing of drug evidence, and the supervision of the undercover agent were key elements in determining that the military involvement did not amount to enforcing civil laws. *Cooper*, 1998-NMCA-180, ¶ 17. In our case, the military was at all times in control of the drug purchases, the custody and testing of drug evidence, and the supervision of the undercover agent. While the limited involvement of the military throughout the investigation in *Cooper* prevented a violation of the PCA, *Cooper*, 1998-NMCA-180, ¶ 16, the total control of the military in the Gonzales case amounts to the enforcement of civilian laws and therefore a violation of the PCA.

The PCA is not violated when the military independently conducts an off-base investigation singularly targeting active military personnel. *Applewhite*, 995 F.2d at 1001. In this case, the United States Air Force Office of Special Investigations (OSI) set up a short-term "sting operation " at an off-base apartment for the purpose of arresting military personnel caught purchasing illegal drugs. This was a "bust-buy" operation in which "any military personnel purchasing drugs was to be immediately arrested." If any civilians were inadvertently caught in the sting, the OSI agents were advised they could detain the civilians and turn them over to the local police. *Applewhite*, 995 F.2d at 998. One Airman brought his wife with him for a drug buy and both were caught in the sting. The Airman was immediately arrested and his wife was searched and found to be in possession of drugs. She was removed to the military base while local police were notified and given the opportunity to take over her case. *Applewhite*, 995 F.2d at 1000. The court held that under these circumstances, the Air Force was not in violation of the PCA. The court reasoned that the Air Force had a justifiable military interest in attempting to stem illegal drug activity by its enlisted personnel. In agreeing with the OSI's off-site investigation, the court stated the PCA "is not intended to limit the military in preventing illicit drug transactions by active duty military personnel, whether such conduct occurs on or off a military installation." *Applewhite*, 995 F.2d at 1001, citing *Hayes v. Hawes*, 921 F.2d 100 (7th Cir.1990). The court deemed the military's search and detention of the Airman's wife by the military reasonable since she was a participant in the drug buy, was found with drugs on her person, and was being held only until the local police could be contacted and given the opportunity to follow up with her case. The court additionally noted that the wife was only involved in the OSI's investigation because her husband brought her to the drug buy, thereby ruling out the "willful use of any part of the Air Force as a posse to execute civilian laws". *Applewhite*, 995 F.2d at 1001. The court relied on the fact that the OSI's investigation was solely focused on the arrest of military personnel engaged in illegal drug activity as the key element in justifying the off-base investigation and in ultimately determining that the PCA was not violated. *Id.*

Like the military in *Applewhite*, the Air Force in our case conducted an independent investigation at an off-base location. While the investigation in *Applewhite* was a short-term sting operation solely focused on catching and arresting military personnel engaged in illegal drug purchases, *Applewhite*, 995 F.2d at 998, and therefore reflected "an independent military purpose" for the investigation, *Applewhite*, 995 F.2d at 1001, the investigation in our case targeted a single civilian selling drugs to an undercover military agent and only involved the arrest and prosecution of the civilian. Since the Applewhite investigation's focus on military personnel and independent military purpose determined that the PCA was not violated, *Id.*, it follows that the investigation in our case targeting only a civilian does not reflect the independent military purpose required to avoid a violation of the PCA.

The PCA is violated when the military participates in an investigation solely targeting civilians engaged in off-base drug transactions and where there is no evidence of a primary military purpose. *Hawaii*, 896 P.2d at 922. In this case, the U.S. Army Criminal Investigation Department (Army CID) initiated a joint investigation of civilians who were reported to have sold drugs to a military dependent. The Army CID turned the military dependent into an undercover informant who then worked alongside an undercover Army CID agent to make drug purchases from the civilian targets. After several undercover drug purchases, the civilian targets were eventually arrested and prosecuted by the local police. *Hawaii*, 896 P.2d at 913. The court held that the PCA was violated due to an absence of a primary military purpose. *Hawaii*, 896 P.2d at 922. The court, in reviewing the record, did not find an attempt by the Army CID or local police to connect the sale of drugs by the targeted civilians to military personnel other than the Army CID agent. The court also found the record lacked indications of drug trafficking between the civilians and the Army base. *Hawaii*, 896 P.2d at 919. Although in this case the Army CID did not participate in the investigation beyond sharing surveillance and providing an undercover agent, the court stated,

> where an investigation targeting civilians does not have the primary purpose of furthering a military function, even military involvement that falls short of participation in the search, seizure, or arrest of civilians may constitute a violation of the PCA.

Hawaii, 896 P.2d at 922.

As with the investigation in Hawaii, the military investigation in our case was targeting a civilian in off-base drug transactions. Just as the court in *Hawaii* found no evidence of a primary military purpose, *Hawaii*, 896 P.2d at 922, the record in our case does not demonstrate a primary military purpose. Like the *Hawaii* court's admonishment that there was no indication of a connection between the sale of drugs by the civilian targets and the military base or military personnel beyond the undercover agent, the only indication of a military purpose in our case is a vague allegation that Gonzales sold drugs to military personnel without necessarily knowing they were military. In the *Hawaii* case, the military in all other ways followed the tenets of the PCA by not participating in the investigation beyond providing an undercover agent. *Hawaii*, 896 P.2d at 921. In the Gonzales case, however, the military in all other ways acted in opposition to the PCA by controlling all aspects of the investigation. Since the *Hawaii* case was deemed violation of the PCA, the facts of our case should make a stronger case for violation of the PCA.

The State will likely argue that the Air Force in our case actually had a primary military purpose justifying the investigation against Gonzales, based on information that Gonzales was selling drugs to Air Force personnel. The State will also point to the "Memorandum 5" issued by the Air Force as proof of a valid and primary military purpose. According to the testimony of Special Investigator McMackin, the Memorandum 5 is the means by which an investigation of civilians is authorized by the Air Force. (RP 88 1:53:40 PM, see also Docketing Statement page 5.) This should be a fairly weak argument. Notably,

> before the military may directly participate in an undercover investigation of these civilians and their off-base activities, the state carries the burden of demonstrating that there exists a nexus between drug sales off base by civilians to military personnel and the military base at which the purchasers are stationed.

Hawaii, 896 P.2d at 921 (citing *Moon v. State*, 785 P.2d 45, 46-47 (Alaska Ct. App. 1990)). According to the record, the investigation against Gonzales was launched after the Confidential Source heard about a civilian who sold drugs to both civilians and military personnel. (Docketing Statement page 6.) The record does not reflect any proof of any active military personnel purchasing drugs from Gonzales prior to the start of the investigation. The Air Force also did not connect any drugs purchased by Gonzales with drug trafficking on the base. Additionally, the Memorandum 5 that was reportedly issued prior to the start of the Gonzales investigation was not entered into evidence. Even if a Memorandum 5 had been produced, the mere existence of military documentation authorizing an investigation against civilians is not proof of PCA compliance. *Hawaii*, 896 P.2d at 921. In the Hawaii case, the Army received authorization documentation from its military command for the investigation of civilians. *Id.* The authorization documents, however, did not prove the existence of a primary military purpose. In our case, the Air Force did not verify a connection between any drugs sold by Gonzales and the active military personnel on the base before launching its investigation, and any documentation of Air Force authorization that might have indicated a sufficient military purpose was absent from the presented evidence.

CONCLUSION

In the present case, the Air Force completely violated the PCA during its investigation of Gonzales. The Air Force only targeted the off-base activities of Gonzales, a private citizen, and failed to demonstrate a primary military purpose in launching the investigation. Additionally, the Air Force in this case was the only entity involved in the undercover drug buys and in the seizure and testing of the evidence. The Air Force was fully and solely in control of an investigation targeting a civilian, and therefore violated the PCA entirely.

Interoffice Memorandum Example 2

INTEROFFICE MEMORANDUM

To: Supervising Attorney

From: Paralegal

Re: Matter of Trucker Smith; analysis if knife is a "deadly weapon"

Date: November 13, 2015

QUESTION PRESENTED

Is there sufficient evidence for a jury to determine Trucker's knife meets the definition of a deadly weapon?

SHORT ANSWER

Yes, there is sufficient evidence for a jury to determine whether Trucker's knife meets the definition of a deadly weapon.

STATEMENT OF FACTS

Defendant, Trucker Smith, was charged with one count of misconduct involving weapons for possessing a knife on school grounds. Trucker's belongings were searched based on information he was in possession of a knife, which was reported to the school resource officer by a fellow student. During the search, the officer discovered a knife in Trucker's backpack. The officer described the knife as being "like a pocketknife, but larger." Like a pocketknife, Trucker's knife must be unfolded in order to access the blade. When unfolded, the knife was described by the officer as being approximately 6–8 inches long. Trucker's knife was also described as having a sharp edge on one side and a pointed tip.

DISCUSSION

In the state of Arizona, a person commits misconduct involving weapons by "knowingly possessing a deadly weapon on school grounds." The legislature defined "deadly weapon" as "anything that is designed for lethal use." In addition, school grounds is defined as meaning "in, or on the grounds of, a school." There is no dispute here as to whether or not Trucker was in possession of the knife on school grounds. A search was conducted during his third period class and a knife was found in Trucker's backpack. Whether Trucker was knowingly in possession of the knife is also not at issue. The question presented here is whether the jury will have sufficient evidence to determine if the knife found in Trucker's possession meets the definition of a deadly weapon.

If a jury is shown sufficient evidence regarding the characteristics of a knife, the jury is able to determine whether or not that knife is a deadly weapon. *In re Vincent V.*, 1-CA-JV-07-0039 (Ct. App. Div. 1, 2007). In *Vincent V.*, the court held that the determination of whether a knife is a deadly weapon is a question for the jury to decide. Ample evidence was made available to the jury in that case, including officer testimony, photographic evidence of the knife, and descriptions of the knife's size, sharpness, shape, and type. The court found that this evidence was sufficient for the jury to determine that Vincent V.'s knife met the definition of a deadly weapon.

Our client Trucker's case is similar to *Vincent V.* in that both cases center around a juvenile charged with misconduct involving weapons for being in possession of a knife on school grounds. Additionally, both cases involve the specific question of whether the particular knives meet the definition of a deadly weapon. The court in *Vincent V.* found the knife to be a deadly weapon based on its characteristics. Trucker's knife is similar to Vincent V.'s in size and sharpness. Vincent V.'s knife was approximately 6 inches long when opened, and Trucker's measures approximately 6–8 inches long when unfolded. Both knives have a sharp edge on one side, with Trucker's knife also having a pointed tip.

Where the two knives differ is in the type and mechanism. Vincent V.'s knife was labeled in officer testimony as a "switchblade" knife, as it opened instantaneously at the press of a button and the blade then locked into place. The officer testimony in *Vincent V.* focused on this label precisely because of his opinion that "any switchblade [is] a deadly weapon." In contrast, Trucker's knife was described as being "like a pocketknife" by the officer who conducted the search.

CONCLUSION

Trucker's knife has similar qualities relating to the size and sharpness of a knife which previously met the definition of a deadly weapon. However, the distinction between a switchblade knife and a pocketknife is an important one. A pocketknife, like the one found in Trucker's possession, is substantially less dangerous than a switchblade due to the functionality of the knife. Based on the evidence presented, it is unlikely that a jury will find Trucker's knife meets the definition of a deadly weapon.

Client Letter Example

December 4, 2015

Chester Tate
123 Cerro Grande Boulevard
Folsum, Illinois 62702

Dear Mr. Tate:

Thank you for the opportunity to work on your case. After reviewing your case, and in particular, the charge of aggravated kidnapping, I have identified a court of action. The State will need to prove that you "knowingly… and secretly confined another against his will…while armed with a dangerous weapon" in order to convict you of aggravated kidnapping. Fortunately, your case does not appear to justify an aggravated kidnapping offense.

While you did knowingly confine Mr. Campbell, this was done in a location "close to a public area" and "was visible to potential witnesses." You did not make any efforts to try to conceal Mr. Campbell. Illinois courts have relied on these factors in the past to determine that the aggravated form of this crime would not apply in your case.

The State may try to claim that because no one actually witnessed the kidnapping, it was done in secret. However, the courts are clear and have declared that "it is the possibility of a witness viewing the confinement that is important rather than the happenstance of an actual witness." You confined Mr. Campbell in front of a large picture window and anyone could walk by and see him.

Your lack of criminal history bodes well for you and will also aid in your defense. Given the facts of your case, it is likely that you will be convicted of the less severe crime of kidnapping.

Please contact my office once you have reviewed this letter. I would like to go over your options and come up with a plan for how to proceed with your case.

I can be reached at (602) 321-4321, extension 5882.

Sincerely,

Sid Yancy
Attorney at Law
Bw/JRA

Glossary

A

active voice   *See* voice.

adjective   A word that modifies a noun or pronoun. An adjective usually describes a noun or pronoun (a *red* car).

administrative law   Rules, regulations, orders, and decisions adopted by administrative agencies that have the authority of law.

advance sheets   Temporary pamphlets (often soft cover books) that contain the full text of several recent court opinions.

adverb   A word used to modify a verb, adjective, or other adverbs.

advocacy   To support or urge the adoption of a position through the use of an argument.

advocacy letter   *See* demand/advocacy letter.

affirm   A decision of an appellate court that upholds the decision of the trial court.

agreement   Words that are related must agree in number (singular/plural) and gender (feminine/masculine/neuter) (e.g., *Workers* must wear *their* helmets. *Mary* must wear *her* helmet.).

antecedent   A word, clause, or phrase referred to by a pronoun. In the following sentence, the word *workers* is the antecedent for the pronoun *their*: The *workers* put on *their* helmets.

apostrophe (')   A mark that indicates possession (Mary's hat) or forms a contraction (can't).

appellant   The party who files an appeal. On appeal, the appellant argues that the lower court made an error that entitles the appellant to relief.

appellate brief   An external memorandum of law submitted to a court of appeals. It presents the legal analysis, authority, and argument in support of a position that the lower court's decision or ruling was either correct or incorrect. It is often referred to as an appellate brief.

appellee   The party who opposes the appeal. On appeal, the appellee usually argues that the lower court did not make an error that entitles the appellant to relief.

authority   Anything a court may rely on when deciding an issue. It includes the law, such as constitutions and statutes, and nonlaw sources, such as legal encyclopedias and treatises.

B

brackets ([ ])   Marks used to show changes in or additions to quotations, usually for the purpose of providing clarification to the quotation or indicating an error in the original quotations. (The privilege [against self-incrimination] allows an individual to remain silent.)

brief   *See* appellate court brief, case brief, and trial court brief.

brief answer   A section of a memorandum of law that presents a brief, precise answer to the issue(s) addressed in the memo.

C

canons of construction   The rules and guidelines courts use when interpreting statutes.

caption   In an opinion, the caption consists of the names of the parties to a lawsuit and their court status (e.g., Eddie RAEL, Plaintiff-Appellee v. Emillio CADENA and Manuel Cadena, Defendants-Appellants).

case brief   A written summary identifying the essential components of a court opinion.

case law   *See* common law/case law.

case law analysis   The analytical process engaged in to determine if and how a decision in a court opinion either governs or affects the outcome of a client's case.

certiorari   *See* writ of certiorari.

citation   Information that allows the reader to locate where a reference can be found. In case law, the term refers to the volume number, page number, and name of the reporter where a case may be found.

cite   *See* citation.

colon (:)   A punctuation mark used to introduce or call attention to information that follows. (The statutory requirements are the following: the will must be witnessed by two witnesses . . .)

comma (,)   The most frequently used punctuation mark. It is used to separate parts of a sentence.

common law/case law   The body of law created by courts. It is composed of the general legal rules, doctrines, and principles adopted by courts when interpreting existing law or when creating law in the absence of controlling enacted law.

concurrent jurisdiction   When more than one court has the authority to preside over the same subject matter.

constitution   A governing document adopted by the people that establishes the framework for the operation of the government, defines the powers of the government, and guarantees the fundamental rights of the people.

contraction   A word formed by combining two words: *can't* (cannot), *isn't* (is not).

counteranalysis   The process of discovering and considering the counterargument to a legal position or argument; the process of anticipating the argument the opponent is likely to raise in response to the analysis of an issue. It is the identification and objective evaluation of the strengths and weaknesses of a legal argument.

counterargument   The argument in opposition to a legal argument or position. The argument the opponent is likely to raise in response to the analysis of an issue.

court opinion   The statement of a court of its decision reached in a case, the rule that applies, and the reasons for the court's decision.

court rules   Procedural rules adopted by a court that govern the litigation process. Court rules often govern the format and style of documents submitted to the court.

D

dangling modifier   A modifier that does not modify any other part of a sentence.

dash (—)   A mark used in a sentence to emphasize something, set off lists, briefly summarize materials containing commas, or show an abrupt change of thought or direction. (The items located at the scene—the knife, the drugs, and the scarf—have disappeared from the evidence room.)

defendant   The party against whom a lawsuit is brought.

demand/advocacy letter   Correspondence designed to persuade someone to take action favorable to the interests of the client or cease acting in a manner that is detrimental to the client.

dissenting opinion   A judicial opinion in a case that disagrees with the majority opinion.

district court   In many states, the district court is the trial court of general jurisdiction. *See also* United States District Court.

E

ellipsis (...)   The use of three dots to indicate the omission of part of a quotation (e.g., The statute provides that contractors are responsible for . . . the preparation of work orders . . .).

enacted law   The body of law adopted by the people or legislative bodies, including constitutions, statutes, ordinances, and administrative rules and regulations.

expanded outline   *See* outline, expanded.

F

fact   Information concerning some thing, action, event, or circumstance.

federalism   The separation of power between the federal government and the several states.

G

general jurisdiction   A court of general jurisdiction has the power, with few exceptions, to hear and decide any matter brought before it.

H

headnotes   Summaries of the points of law discussed in a court opinion prepared by the publisher of the opinion.

holding   The court's application of the rule of law to the legal question raised by the facts of a case; the court's answer to the legal issue in a case.

hyphen (–)   A mark used to form compound modifiers and compound nouns (e.g., *well-known, ex-judge*).

I

infinitive   A verb form that functions as a noun or as an auxiliary verb (e.g., to argue, to leave). A *split infinitive* refers to the placement of an adverb between *to* and the verb in an infinitive (e.g., to *completely* understand).

information letter   Correspondence that provides general legal information or background on a legal issue. It usually involves the communication of the results of legal research and analysis to a client or a third party.

in personam jurisdiction   *See* personal jurisdiction.

intellectual honesty   In the context of legal analysis, to research and analyze a problem objectively. This includes analyzing all aspects of a problem free of preconceived notions, personal views, and emotions.

interoffice memorandum of law   *See* office legal memorandum.

IRAC   An acronym commonly used in reference to the legal analysis process. It is composed of the first letter of the descriptive term for each step of the process—*i*ssue, *r*ule, *a*nalysis/application, *c*onclusion. The standard legal analysis process is the identification of the issue, followed by the presentation of the governing rule of law, the analysis/application of the rule of law, and the conclusion.

issue   The precise legal question raised by the specific facts of a dispute.

issue heading   A summary of the position advocated in the argument section of a trial or appellate brief.

issue comprehensive/narrow statement   A complete statement of the issue that includes the specific law, legal question, and key facts.

issue short/broad statement   A broad formulation of the issue that usually does not include reference to the specific facts of the case or the applicable law.

J

jurisdiction   The court's authority to hear and resolve specific disputes. Jurisdiction is usually composed of *personal jurisdiction* (authority over persons) and *subject matter jurisdiction* (authority over the types of cases a court may hear and decide).

K

key fact(s)   The legally significant facts of a case that raise the legal question of how or whether the law governing the dispute applies; the facts upon which the outcome of the case is determined. They are the facts that establish or satisfy the elements of a cause of action and are necessary to prove or disprove a claim. A key fact is so essential that, if it were changed, the outcome of the case would probably change.

key facts groups   Individual facts that, when considered as a group, are key facts. Individual facts, when treated as a group, may determine the outcome of a case.

key facts individual   A key fact that, if it were changed, the outcome of the case would be affected or changed.

key numbers   West Group has divided all areas of American law into various topics and subtopics. Each area is identified by a topic name, and each specific topic or subtopic is assigned a number called a key number.

L

law   The enforceable rules that govern individual and group conduct in a society. The law establishes standards of conduct, the procedures governing standards of conduct, and the remedies available when the standards are not followed.

legal analysis   The process of identifying the issue or issues presented by a client's facts and determining what law applies and how it applies; the process of applying the law to the facts of a case. It is an exploration of how and why a specific law does or does not apply.

legal analysis process   The systematic approach to legal research and analysis.

legal issue   *See* issue.

legal research   The process of identifying the law or legal authority that applies to the issue.

legal writing process   A systematic approach to legal writing; an organized approach to legal research, analysis, and writing. It is composed of three stages: prewriting, writing, and postwriting.

legislative history   The record of legislation during the enactment process. It is composed of committee reports, transcripts of hearings, statements of legislators concerning the legislation, and any other material published for legislative use in regard to the legislation.

M

majority opinion   The opinion in a court decision of the majority of judges.

mandatory authority   Any authority or source of law that a court must rely on or follow when reaching a decision (e.g., a decision of a higher court in the jurisdiction on the same or a similar issue).

memorandum of law   A written analysis of a legal problem. It is an informative document that summarizes the research and analysis of the legal issue or issues raised by the facts of a case. It contains a summary of the law and how the law applies in the case.

N

nominalization   A noun created from a verb (e.g., *realization* from the verb *realize*).

nouns   Words that refer to persons, places, things, or qualities.

O

office legal memorandum   A legal memorandum prepared for office use. It presents an objective legal analysis of the issue(s) raised by the facts of the client's case and usually includes the arguments in favor of and in opposition to the client's position. It is often referred to by other names, such as interoffice legal research memorandum, office research memorandum, and interoffice memorandum of law.

on all fours   A prior court opinion in which the key facts and applicable rule of law are identical or nearly identical with those of the client's case or the case before a court.

on point   A term used to refer to a prior court opinion in which the facts are sufficiently similar to the facts of the client's case or the case before the court for the prior court opinion to apply as precedent. A case is on point if the similarity between the key facts and rule of law or legal principle of the court opinion and those of the client's case is sufficient for the court opinion to govern or provide guidance to a later court in deciding the outcome of the client's case.

opinion   The written statement by the court expressing how it ruled in a case and the reasons for its ruling.

opinion letter   Correspondence, usually written to a client, that in addition to informing the reader of how the law applies to a specific question, provides legal advice. It informs the reader how the law applies and advises which steps should be taken.

ordinance   Enacted law; generally used to refer to laws enacted by local (city) government.

outline   The skeletal structure and organizational framework of a writing.

outline, expanded   An outline that has been expanded so that it may be used in the prewriting stage. The use of an expanded outline allows the integration of all research, analysis, and ideas into an organized outline structure while research and analysis are being conducted. It facilitates the preparation of a rough draft.

P

paragraph   A group of sentences that address the same topic.

parallel citation   When a court opinion is printed in more than one reporter, each citation is a parallel citation to the other citation or citations, for example, "*Britton v. Britton*, **100 N.M. 424, 671 P.2d 1135** (1983)." The parallel citations are in bold.

parentheses ( )   Marks used to add to a sentence information that is outside the main idea of the sentence or of lesser importance.

party   A plaintiff or defendant in a lawsuit.

passive voice   *See* voice.

personal jurisdiction   The authority of the court over the parties to resolve a legal dispute involving the parties.

persuasive authority   Any authority a court is not bound to consider or follow but may consider or follow when reaching a decision (e.g., a decision of a court in another state on the same or a similar issue, secondary authority, and so on).

plain meaning rule   A canon of construction that provides that if the meaning of a statute is clear on its face, it will be interpreted according to its plain meaning and the other canons of construction will not be applied by the court.

plaintiff   The party who starts (files) a lawsuit.

postwriting stage   The stage in the legal writing process where an assignment is revised, edited, and assembled in final form.

precedent   An earlier court decision on an issue that applies to govern or guide a subsequent court in its determination of an identical or similar issue based upon identical or similar facts. A court opinion is precedent if there is a sufficient similarity between the key facts and rule of law or legal principle of the court's opinion and the matter before the subsequent court.

predicate   A verb, its modifiers, and the object of the verb, such as a direct object (if necessary). The predicate of a sentence provides information concerning the subject of a sentence (e.g., Tom *ran to the store*.). The predicate of the sentence is in italic.

preposition   A word that is used with a noun or pronoun to create a prepositional phrase.

prewriting stage   The stage in the legal writing process where the assignment is organized, researched, and analyzed.

primary authority   Authority that is composed of the law (e.g., constitutions, statutes, and court opinions).

pronoun   A word that replaces a noun.

punctuation   Marks or characters used in writing to make the meaning clear and easy to understand, such as period (.), comma (,), semicolon (;), and colon (:).

purpose clause   A statutory section that includes the purpose the legislative body intended to accomplish when drafting the statute.

Q

quotation   Marks used to identify and set off quoted material. (Mary said, "I do not believe it is true.")

R

Re   A term that means, "in the matter of, about, or concerning." It is usually placed at the beginning of the reference line in a memo or correspondence.

S

salutation   The part of a letter that presents the greeting (Dear Ms. Jones).

scope   A statutory section that states what is specifically covered and not covered by the statute.

secondary authority   Any source of law a court may rely on that is not the law (e.g., legal treatises, restatements of the law, and legal encyclopedias).

semicolon (;)   A punctuation mark used to separate major elements of complex sentences, or to separate items in a series if the items are long or if one of the items has internal commas. (The shareholders held their meeting at noon; the board of directors met immediately thereafter.)

sentence   The fundamental building block of writing. It is composed of a group of words that convey a single thought. It is usually a statement in which the actor (subject) performs some action or describes a state of being (the predicate).

short title   The name by which a statute is known (e.g., Uniform Commercial Code Sales).

slip law   The first publication of the full text of a statute.

slip opinion   The first publication of a court opinion as issued directly from a court.

split infinitive   *See* infinitive.

stare decisis   A basic principle of the common law system that requires a court to follow a previous decision of that court or a higher court when the current decision involves issues and facts similar to those involved in the previous decision; the doctrine that provides that precedent should be followed.

statement of facts   The section of a memorandum of law that presents the factual context of the issue(s) addressed in the memorandum.

statutes   Laws passed by legislative bodies that declare rights and duties, or command or prohibit certain conduct.

statutory analysis   The interpretation and application of statutory law; the process of determining if a statute applies to a specific fact situation, how it applies, and the effect of that application.

statutory elements   The specific conditions or components of a statute that must be met for the statute to apply.

statutory law   The body of law composed of laws passed by legislative bodies. The term includes laws or ordinances passed by any legislative body.

subject   A noun or pronoun that is the actor in a sentence (e.g., *Tom* ran to the store.). The subject of the sentence is in italic.

subject matter jurisdiction   The types or kinds of cases the court has the authority to hear and decide.

T

topic sentence   The sentence that identifies the subject of a paragraph. It introduces the subject and provides the focus of a paragraph.

trial court   The court where the matter is heard and decided. In the trial court testimony is heard, evidence is taken, and a decision is reached.

trial court brief   An external memorandum of law submitted to a trial court. It presents the legal authority and argument in support of a position advocated by an attorney, usually in regard to a motion or issue being addressed by the court. It is often referred to as a trial brief.

U

United States District Court   The trial court of general jurisdiction in the federal judicial system.

United States Supreme Court   The final court of appeals in the federal system and the highest court in the United States.

V

verbs   Words that express action, a state of being or feeling, or a relation between two things (e.g., Tom *ran* to the store.). The verb in this sentence is in italic.

voice   The relationship of the subject to the action of the sentence.

Active voice: the subject of the sentence is performing the action in the sentence. (The automobile hit the child.)
Passive voice: the subject of the sentence is acted upon. (The child was hit by the automobile.)

W

writing stage   The stage in the legal writing process where research, analysis, and ideas are assembled into a written product.

writ of certiorari   A writ from a higher court asking a lower court for the record of a case. A petition for a writ of certiorari is a request filed by a party in a lawsuit that a higher court is to review the decision of a lower court.

Index

NOTES

NOTES

NOTES

NOTES

NOTES